NELSON

For more information contact Nelson Education Ltd., 1120 Birchmount Road, Toronto, Ontario M1K 5G4. Or you can visit our website at nelson.com.

Social Science: An Introduction

Copyright © 2011, McGraw-Hill Ryerson Limited. All rights reserved. Excerpts from this publication may be reproduced under licence from Access Copyright, or with the express written permission of Nelson Education Ltd., or as permitted by law. Requests which fall outside of Access Copyright guidelines must be submitted online to cengage.com/permissions. Further questions about permissions can be emailed to permissionrequest@cengage.com.

ALL RIGHTS ARE OTHERWISE RESERVED. No part of this publication may be reproduced, stored in a retrieval system, or transmitted in any form or by any means, electronic, mechanic, photocopying, scanning, recording or otherwise, except as specifically authorized.

Every effort has been made to trace ownership of all copyrighted material and to secure permission from copyright holders. In the event of any question arising as to the use of any material, we will be pleased to make the necessary corrections in future printings.

ISBN-10: 0-07-105818-4
ISBN-13: 978-0-07-105818-6

2 3 4 5   20 19 18 17

Printed and bound in Canada.

Care has been taken to trace ownership of copyright material contained in this text; however, the publisher will welcome any information that enables them to rectify any reference or credit for subsequent editions.

PUBLISHER: Ian Nussbaum
PROJECT MANAGER: Kimberly Murphy
DEVELOPMENTAL EDITORS: Kimberly Murphy, Caroline Winter, Alisa Yampolsky
MANAGER, EDITORIAL SERVICES: Crystal Shortt
SUPERVISING EDITOR: Jaime Smith
COPY EDITORS: Karen Kligman/Karen Rolfe
REVIEW COORDINATOR: Jennifer Keay
PRODUCTION COORDINATOR: Tammy Mavroudi
PERMISSIONS EDITOR: Monika Shurmann
EDITORIAL ASSISTANT: Michelle Malda
INTERIOR DESIGN: Liz Harasymczuk
ELECTRONIC PAGE MAKE-UP: Miriam Brant/ArtPlus Ltd.
COVER DESIGN: Liz Harasymczuk

SOCIAL SCIENCE
An Introduction

Senior Author
Jan Haskings-Winner
Instructional Leader
Toronto District School Board

Authors
Rachel Collishaw
Glebe Collegiate Institute
Ottawa-Carleton District School Board

Sandra Kritzer
Centre Wellington District High School
Upper Grand District School Board

Patricia Warecki
Sacred Heart Catholic High School
York Region Catholic District School Board

NELSON

ADVISORS

Trisha De Coeur
St. Thomas Aquinas Catholic High School
Catholic District School Board of Eastern Ontario

Marc Keirstead
retired York Catholic District School Board

Andrew Street
Albert Campbell Collegiate Institute
Toronto District School Board

Jill Goodreau
Ontario Institute for Studies in Education of
  the University of Toronto
Upper Grand District School Board

Christopher Rawes
Stratford Central Secondary School
Avon Maitland District School Board

Stacy Tomioka
Agincourt Collegiate Institute
Toronto District School Board

Tracy Williams-Shreve
Parkdale Collegiate Institute
Toronto District School Board

PEDAGOGICAL REVIEWERS

James Delodder
Department Head, Canadian and World Studies,
  Social Sciences and Humanities
St. Mary's Catholic High School
London District Catholic School Board,
  Woodstock, ON

Christopher Dueck
Educator
Grimsby Secondary School
District School Board of Niagara, Grimsby, ON

Matthew Flynn
Department Head, History
Delta Secondary School
Hamilton-Wentworth District School Board,
  Hamilton, ON

Mary-Leigh Gray
Department Head, Social Sciences and Humanities
Dunbarton High School
Durham District School Board, Pickering, ON

Crissa Hill
Vice Principal
Rick Hansen Secondary School
Peel District School Board, Mississauga, ON

R. Darlene Tapp
Social Sciences and Humanities Teacher
Westminster Secondary School
Thames Valley District School Board, London, ON

Lori Stryker
Curriculum Consultant

ACCURACY REVIEWERS

Dr. Mike Atkinson
Associate Professor of Psychology
University of Western Ontario
London, ON

Dr. Kathryn Denning
Associate Professor
Department of Anthropology
York University, Toronto, ON

Dr. Bonnie Haaland
Professor
Kwantlen Polytechnic University
Surrey, BC

STUDENT CONTRIBUTORS

McGraw-Hill Ryerson and the authors thank the students from Centre Wellington District High School in Fergus and Glebe Collegiate Institute in Ottawa for their contributions to this resource.

DEDICATIONS

Jan Haskings-Winner
For Ray Winner, who provides encouragement and unconditional love. For my family and friends—who believe all things are possible with perseverance!

Rachel Collishaw
To my parents for the gift of travel, the space, meals, and conversations. To Craig for your faith, love, and support, and to my children, Beatrix and Cole. May the gift of culture inspire you to seek your own adventures.

Sandra Kritzer
Thank you to Gayle and Ken Kritzer for their encouragement and culinary support throughout this project, and to Linda Mowatt for her years of mentorship.

Patricia Warecki
To Marc, my pedagogical godfather. For Emma, Jacob, and Evelyn, my darling children who inspire me to try new things everyday and for my husband John whose love, patience, and encouragement continue to see me through all of life's adventures.

CONTENTS

A Tour of Your Textbook	xii
Introduction	2

UNIT 1 What is Social Science? — 12

Chapter 1 What is Anthropology? — 14

Spotlight on Anthropology: Yanomamö and the Anthropologists — 16
Research and Inquiry Skills — 17
Creating a Central Research Question — 17
Recording Data and Analyzing Information — 17

Section 1.1 Cultural Anthropology and Understanding Human Culture and Behaviour — 18

Cultural Anthropology — 18
The Language of Social Science: Introducing Social Sciences — 19
Research Tools of Cultural Anthropologists — 20
Finding Informants — 20
Interviews — 20
Ethnology — 22
How Do Ethnologists Study Culture? — 22
Youth Perspectives: What is Canadian Culture? — 23
The Problems of Participant Observation — 24
Landmark Case Study: Richard Lee and the Dobe Ju/'hoansi — 26
Schools of Thought in Cultural Anthropology — 28
Cultural Relativism — 28
Functional Theory — 28
Cultural Materialism — 29
Feminist Anthropology — 30
Postmodernism — 31
Linguistic Anthropology — 32
Historical Linguistics — 32
Structural Linguistics — 32
Sociolinguistics — 33
Archaeology — 34
In the Field: Archaeological Services Inc. — 34
Prehistoric Archaeology — 35
Archaeology and History — 35
In Focus: Kwaday Dän Ts'inchi — 36

Section 1.2 Human Evolution and Defining Humans — 37

Physical Anthropology — 37
Paleoanthropology — 38
What Can Anthropologists Learn from Ancient Bones? — 38
Where Do Humans Come From? — 39
When Did Humans Walk Upright? — 40
In Focus: Ardipithecus Ramidus — 41
Human Evolution—A Timeline — 41
In Focus: Who Were the Neanderthals? — 42
What Can Anthropologists Learn from Ancient Stones? — 43
Social Science in Popular Culture: Forensic Anthropology — 44
Primatology — 46
How Do Primatologists Study Primates? — 46
How Are Humans Similar to Other Primates? — 47
How Are Humans Different from Other Primates? — 48
Can Nonhuman Primates Use Language? — 48
Human Variation — 49
Why Are Humans Different from One Another? — 49
Do Human Subgroups Exist? — 49
Can We Study Human Variation in a Legitimate Way? — 50
Point/Counterpoint: Skin Variations — 51
Chapter 1 Review — 52

Chapter 2 What is Psychology? — 54

Spotlight on Psychology: Flash Mobs — 56
Research and Inquiry Skills — 57
Variables and Control Groups in Social Science — 57
Sources in Social Science — 57
Quantitative and Qualitative Research — 57

Section 2.1 Schools of Thought — 58

Psychodynamic Theorists — 59
Sigmund Freud (1856–1939) — 59
Karen Horney (1885–1952) — 60
Carl Jung (1875–1961) — 61
The Psychology of Dreams — 63
Behavioural Psychologists — 64
Ivan Pavlov (1849–1936) — 64
B. F. Skinner (1904–1990) — 65
Impact of Behaviourism — 66
In Focus: Is It Ethical to Experiment on Animals? — 67
Humanist Psychologists — 68
Abraham Maslow (1908–1970) — 69
Viktor Frankl (1905–1997) — 69
Carl Rogers (1902–1987) — 70
Impact of Humanistic Psychology on Society — 70
Cognitive Psychology — 72
Albert Bandura (1925–) — 72
Elizabeth Loftus (1944–) — 72

False Memories in the Visual Age	73
Section 2.2 Psychological Approaches to Understanding Behaviour	**74**
Developmental Psychologists	74
Sigmund Freud (1856–1939)	74
In Focus: Core Knowledge	75
Jean Piaget (1896–1980)	75
Erik Erikson (1902–1994)	76
Leta Stetter Hollingworth (1886–1939)	78
Harry Harlow (1905–1981)	79
Landmark Case Study: Mary Ainsworth (1913–1999): Infant–Mother Attachment	80
Understanding the Brain	82
New Technology: Windows into the Brain	82
How the Brain Works	82
In Focus: Phineas Gage	83
Perception	84
Controlling the Ever-Changing Brain	85
Is Meditation the Answer?	85
Focusing Therapies	86
Point/Counterpoint: How Does Internet Use Affect the Brain?	87
How Do We Learn Language?	88
The "Teen Brain"?	89
Chapter 2 Review	**90**
Chapter 3 What is Sociology?	**92**
Spotlight on Sociology: Energy Drinks and Risky Behaviour	94
Research and Inquiry Skills	95
Surveys	95
Assessing and Recording Sources	95
Section 3.1 Schools of Thought	**96**
Sociology: Past and Present	96
The Roots of Sociology	96
Defining Sociology	97
What Do Sociologists Do?	97
In Focus: Sociologists and the Fall of the Berlin Wall	99
Sociological Schools of Thought	100
Macrosociology	100
Microsociology	100
Structural Functionalism	101
Emile Durkheim (1858–1917)	101
Talcott Parsons (1902–1978)	103
In Focus: Herbert Spencer (1820–1920) and Social Darwinism	104
Conflict Theory	105
Karl Marx (1818–1883)	105
Landmark Case Study: William Foote Whyte and the Street Corner Society	106
Feminist Sociology	107
Dorothy Smith (1926–)	107
Current Research	107
In Focus: M. N. Srinivas (1916–1999)	108
Symbolic Interactionism	109
Max Weber (1864–1920)	109
The Chicago School	110
Charles Cooley, George Herbert Mead, and the Looking-Glass Self	111
C. Wright Mills and Sociological Imagination	112
Section 3.2 Socialization and Social Development	**113**
What is Social Behaviour?	113
What Influences Behaviour?	113
The Language of Social Sciences: Sex and Gender	114
Different Cultures, Different Greetings	116
In the Field: Social Worker Egerton Blackwood	117
Measuring Social Behaviour	118
Socialization	119
The Categories of Socialization	119
In Focus: Female Violence and the Murder of Reena Virk	120
Abnormal Socialization	121
Agents of Socialization	124
The Primary Agent of Socialization: The Family	124
Secondary Agents of Socialization	125
Chapter 3 Review	**128**

UNIT 2 Social Science and Me 130

Chapter 4 Anthropology and Me	**132**
Spotlight on Anthropology: Cyborg Anthropology	134
Research and Inquiry Skills	135
Creating a Research Plan	135
Section 4.1 Culture and Identity	**136**
How Does Culture Shape Identity?	137
Canadian Culture and Identity	137
Rites of Passage	138
Three-Stage Process	139
Male Rites of Passage	140
Female Rites of Passage	141
Body Modification and Body Art	142

Coming of Age in Contemporary Canadian Culture	144
Gender and Culture	**146**
Female Identity and Culture	146
Male Identity and Culture	148
Alternate-Gender Identity	150
In Focus: Pink Shirt Day	151
Section 4.2 Anthropology and Behaviour	**152**
Physical Environment and Culture	**152**
Cold Climate Adaptation	152
Hot Climate Adaptation	153
Technology and Culture	**154**
Air Conditioning and the End of the Front Porch in North America	154
Digital Technology	154
Landmark Case Study: Steel Axes Among the Yir Yoront	155
Language and Culture	**156**
Sapir-Whorf Hypothesis	156
The English Language	157
Body Language	158
Economic Systems and Culture	**159**
Foraging Societies	159
Horticultural Societies	159
Agricultural Societies	160
Industrial Societies	160
Postindustrial Societies	160
Distribution Types in Canada	161
The Impact of Globalization on Cultural Systems	**162**
Sex Workers in Sosua, Dominican Republic	162
The Kayapó: Resisting and Harnessing the Power of Globalization	163
Globalization: Connecting the World	164
Culture as an Agent of Socialization: Kinship Systems	**165**
Patrilineal Case Study: The Bhil in India	167
Bilineal Case Study: The Dobe Ju/'hoansi Three Systems of Kinship	168
Marriage: A Cultural Universal	**169**
No Marriage in the Na Society	169
Arranged Marriage	170
In Focus: Indo-Canadian Arranged Marriage	171
Types of Marriage	172
In Focus: Canada's Polygamous Community: Bountiful British Columbia	173
Family Roles in Culture	**175**
Self-concept in Western and Eastern Asian Families	175
Landmark Case Study: Death Without Weeping: Poverty and Family Roles	176
Section 4.3 Ethical Issues in Anthropology	**178**
Attitudes of Anthropology	**178**
How Fieldwork Transforms	178
Ethical Guidelines of Anthropology	179
Landmark Case Study: Shakespeare in the Bush	180
Anthropology's Ethical Transformations	**181**
Anthropology and the Military	181
Point/Counterpoint: Should Anthropologists Work with the Military?	182
Fieldwork in Contemporary Culture and Subcultures	**183**
Baseball Magic	183
Cultural Diffusions: Japanese Hip-Hop Culture	184
Research Dilemmas	**185**
Personal Belief Dilemmas	185
Moral Dilemmas in Cultural Anthropology	185
Moral Dilemmas in Physical Anthropology	188
Applied Anthropology	**190**
Medical Anthropology: Goats in Malawi	190
Ecological Anthropology: The Domestication of Wood in Haiti	192
Applied Policy: Improving Immigrant Services in Saskatoon	193
Chapter 4 Review	**194**
Chapter 5 Psychology and Me	**196**
Spotlight on Psychology: Obedience	198
Research and Inquiry Skills	199
Creating a Research Plan in Psychology	199
Analyzing and Interpreting Research Information	199
Section 5.1 Development of Self	**200**
The Influence of Heredity and Environment	**200**
Heredity	200
Environment	200
Twin Studies	201
The Roots of Intelligence Testing	202
Environmental Influences on IQ	203
The Link Between Heredity and Environment	204
Applying Our Understanding: Behavioural Genetics	205
Landmark Case Study: Genie: The Story of an Isolate Child	206

Personality	207	Section 5.3 Ethical Issues in Psychology	234
Categorizing Personality	207	**Introduction to Ethics in Psychology**	234
Predicting Personality	208	**Issues in Ethical Experimentation**	235
Using Facial Patterns to Determine Personality	208	Why Experiment?	235
Introversion	209	The Benefits of Empirical Research	235
Perfectionism	210	Unethical Experiments	236
Birth Order	212	*Landmark Case Study: Philip Zimbardo (1933–): Stanford Prison Experiment*	238
Sex and Gender Differences	213	Ethics in Research	240
The Influence of Biology	213	Creating an Ethical Experiment	241
Experiment: Gender Roles or Obedience?	213	Ethical Experiments on the Internet	242
Neurosexism	214	**Issues in Ethical Testing**	243
Gender Identity	214	Tests of Intelligence	243
In Focus: A Question of Circumstance?	215	Multiple Intelligences	244
Section 5.2 Psychology and Behaviour	216	Studying the Unstudiable	245
Psychological Influences on Behaviour	216	Surveys at School	246
How Does Motivation Affect Behaviour?	216	*Point/Counterpoint: Gender and the Classroom*	247
Biological Explanations for Motivation	217	**Should We Change People Based on Psychological Beliefs?**	248
Cognitive Explanations: Rewards and Punishments	217	Left Is Not Right	248
Intrinsic Versus Extrinsic Motivators	217	Homosexuality	248
Achievement Motivation	218	Advertisements for Children	249
How Does Attitude Affect Behaviour?	220	Memory Alteration	250
How Are Attitudes Formed?	220	**Ethics and Mental Illness: Helping Those in Need**	252
Types of Attitudes	220	Mental Illness in Prison	252
Can Attitude Predict Behaviour?	221	*In Focus: Ashley Smith*	252
Can Attitudes Be Changed?	222	Moving Forward: Veterans Get Help	253
The Psychology of Marketing: How It Can Change Our Minds	223	**Chapter 5 Review**	254
Social Science in Popular Culture: Behavioural Profiling	224	**Chapter 6 Sociology and Me**	256
Social Thinking	224	Spotlight on Sociology: Group Conflict: Sherif's Robbers Cave Experiment	258
How Do We Explain Behaviour?	224	Research and Inquiry Skills	259
Examining Stereotypes	225	Gathering and Processing Information	259
Positive Attraction	226	Section 6.1 Sociology and Identity	260
The Truth Behind Facial Expressions	226	**Social Identity**	260
How Do We Change Our Behaviour?	227	Social Identity and the Life Cycle	260
How Does Mental Health Affect Behaviour?	228	*Landmark Case Study: Henri Tajfel: The Social Identity Theory*	262
Psychotic Disorders	228	**Role Theory**	264
Neurotic Disorders	228	Social Roles	264
Post-traumatic Stress Disorder	229	Dating and Courtship in the Digital Age	265
Treatment for PTSD	229	*In Focus: David Reimer: The Boy Who Lived as a Girl*	267
Attention/Deficit Hyperactivity Disorder (ADHD)	230	**Identity and Discrimination**	268
Point/Counterpoint: Addiction	231	Stereotypes, Prejudice, and Discrimination	268
New Research in Mental Health	232		
Nature-Deficit Disorder	232		
Hoarding	233		

Defining New Ways to Discriminate in a Post-9/11 World	270
The Discrimination Against Obese People by Doctors	270
What Causes Prejudice and Discrimination?	**271**
Learned Theory	271
Competition Theory	271
Social Science in Popular Culture: Little Mosque on the Prairie	272
Frustration-Aggression Theory	274
Ignorance Theory	274
Point/Counterpoint: Do Parents Have the Right to Teach Their Children Antisocial Beliefs?	275
Section 6.2 Sociology and Behaviour	**276**
Social Belonging and Groups	**276**
In Focus: The Social Network	278
The Power and Influence of Groups	279
Collective Behaviour	**280**
Convergence Theory	280
The Rational Decision Theory	281
Prosocial Behaviour	281
Crowds	**283**
Mobs	283
In Focus: The Expressive Crowd: SARS-Stock	284
Fear and Collective Behaviour	285
Smart Mobs	285
Conformity	**286**
Conformity in Individualistic Cultures	287
Conformity in Collectivistic Cultures	287
Breaking Social Norms: The Breaching Experiments	288
Landmark Case Study: Stanley Milgram: Subway Experiments	289
Groupthink	290
Obedience	290
Charles Hofling's Obedience Study	291
Aggression	**292**
Bullying	292
In Focus: Cyberbullying	294
Section 6.3 Ethical Issues in Sociology	**295**
Ethical Guidelines in Sociology	**295**
Ethical Guidelines in Research	295
Ethical Guidelines for Research Subjects	296
Sociology Is Inclusive	297
What Is Old Is New Again	297
Landmark Case Study: The Clark Doll Experiment (1939)/CNN Doll Experiment (2010)	298

The Challenges of Class in Sociology	**300**
The Invasion-Succession Model	301
Demographic Studies and Sociology	301
Census	302
The Danger of Value Judgments	**304**
Health and Sociology	304
The Sick Neighbourhood	305
The Ethics of Racial Profiling	**306**
Point/Counterpoint: Racial Profiling	307
Racial Profiling: An Issue of Human Rights	308
Communication Technology and Sociology	**309**
Video Surveillance	309
Social Networking	310
Visual Sociology and YouTube	311
Chapter 6 Review	**312**

UNIT 3 Social Science and Us 314

Chapter 7 Anthropology and Us 316

Spotlight on Anthropology: Canada's Residential Schools	318
Research and Inquiry Skills	319
Evaluating Sources	319
Section 7.1 Understanding Cultures	**320**
Social Customs, Manners, and Values	**320**
Social Customs in Conflict: Teeth	321
Technology and Canadian Culture	322
Point/Counterpoint: Digital Technology and Culture	324
Legal Systems and Cultural Values	**325**
Restorative Justice Systems	326
Landmark Case Study: James Gibbs: The Kpelle Moot	326
Religion and Ritual	**330**
Purposes of Religion	330
Stanley and Ruth Freed: Taraka's Ghost	330
The Language of Social Sciences: Anthropological Religious Concepts	332
In Focus: The Hijab	333
Cargo Beliefs in New Guinea	334
Witchcraft Among the Azande	335
The Toronto Jewish Film Festival	336
Section 7.2 Canadian Cultures, Past and Present	**337**
Race: Myths and Reality	**337**
Cultural Anthropology Perspective	338
Physical Anthropology Perspective	341

Theoretical Perspectives of Ethnicity	342
Stage-Model Theories	342
Acculturation Theory	343

Canadian Multiculturalism — 344

Urban Youth and Multiculturalism in Toronto	344
English Canada: Diverse, Imperial, or Invisible?	346
French-Canadian Culture	346
First Nations Communities in Canada: Kitchenuhmaykoosib Inninuwug	349

Constructing Identity in Multicultural Society — 351

Indo-Canadian Youth Create Bicultural Identities	352
Perceptions of Physical Discipline	352
In Focus: Corporal Punishment Laws in Canada	353
Greek and Jewish Youth in Halifax	354
Second-Generation Finnish Canadians: A Disappearing Ethnicity?	355
Migration Revisited: Canadians in the Interconnected Age	357
Chapter 7 Review	**358**

Chapter 8 Psychology and Us — 360

Spotlight on Psychology: Conformity	362
Research and Inquiry Skills	363
Presenting Research in Psychology	363

Section 8.1 Influence of Others on Self — 364

Psychology and Socialization — 364

Socialization and Emotional Development	364
The Importance of Play in Childhood Development	365
Social Isolation and Emotional Development	365
The Effect of Media on Socialization	366
In the Field: Sport Psychologist Shaunna Taylor	367
Socialization and Immigration	368

Conformity — 370

Factors that Affect Conformity	370
The Effects of Conformity	371
In Focus: The Bystander Effect	372
Issues in Youth Conformity	373
Nonconformity	373

Prejudice: A Psychological Perspective — 374

Prejudice	374
Landmark Case Study: Jane Elliot: Brown Eyes/Blue Eyes	376
Scapegoating	377
Promoting Heroism	377

Issues in Mental Illness — 378

The Stigma of Mental Illness	378
Diagnoses and Medication	379

Section 8.2 Personality and Environment — 380

Influence of Family Environment — 380

Parental Influence	380
How Can Parenting Styles Influence Personality?	381
Issues Related to Family Environment	382
Understanding Family Influence	383

Influence of Friends and Group Environments — 384

Friends	384
Conforming to Expectations	384
False Consensus	385
Crowds	386

Influence of Media on Personality — 387

The Power of Music	387
What is the Link Between Music, Personality, and Behaviour?	387
Internet Communication	388
Point/Counterpoint: Adolescents' Online Identities	389
Psychology of Cyberbullying	390
Influence of Social Media	391
The Psychology of Rumours and Gossip	392
Consumer Psychology: The Psychology of Persuasion	393

Influence of Workplace Environments — 395

Industrial/Organizational Psychology	395
Engineering Psychology	395
The Right Person for the Job	396
Social Media in the Workplace	396
Workplace Motivation	397
Mental Health in the Workplace	397
In Focus: Chilean Miners	398
Youth Perspectives: Ginny Elliot	399
Chapter 8 Review	**400**

Chapter 9 Sociology and Us — 402

Spotlight on Sociology: Joshua Bell Plays the Metro	404
Research and Inquiry Skills	405
Writing Reports	405

Section 9.1 Identity in Different Contexts — 406

What Determines Social Identity? — 406

Norms and Social Identity	407

Social Attitudes and Identity — 409

Testing Social Attitudes: Sexual Orientation	409
What is Culture?	**411**
Deviance	411
In Focus: Richard Nesbitt: The Geography of Thought	412
Alienation	414
In Focus: Alienation and Mental Health	415
Subcultures	415
Countercultures and Cults	417
Social Networks	**419**
Landmark Case Study: Food for Thought: The Influence of Social Networks in Health	420
The Global Identity	421
In Focus: Think Globally, Act Locally: Fair Trade	422
Section 9.2 Canadian Social Structures and Institutions	**423**
Social Structures and Organization	**423**
Collectivist and Individualistic Societies	424
Multiculturalism	**425**
Postmulticulturalism	426
Social Stratification	**428**
Social Status	429
Social Inequality	**431**
The "isms" in Sociology	432
The Language of Social Sciences: The Gini Coefficient	433
In Focus: Feminist Theory	433
Social Institutions	**434**
Sociologists Take Sides: Theoretical Perspectives of Social Institutions	434
Social Institutions and Their Primary Goals	**435**
Family	436
Religion	437
Education	439
Government	440
Point/Counterpoint: Use of Tanning Salons by Minors	441
Economy	442
In Focus: Googleplex	444
Social Change	445
Chapter 9 Review	**446**

Appendices	**448**
Appendix 1: Research and Inquiry Skills	**448**
Appendix 2: Landmark Case Studies	**450**
Appendix 3: Key Theorists	**453**
Glossary of Key Terms	**454**
References	**462**
Index	**467**
Credits	**478**

A TOUR OF YOUR TEXTBOOK

Welcome to *Social Science: An Introduction*. The following pages provide a brief guided tour of this textbook—and will help you understand how *Social Science: An Introduction* is set up to help you complete the course successfully. Unit 1 provides an overview of each of the three social sciences—anthropology, psychology, and sociology. Unit 2 helps you find connections between social science and everyday life, and Unit 3 connects social science to the world and society around you.

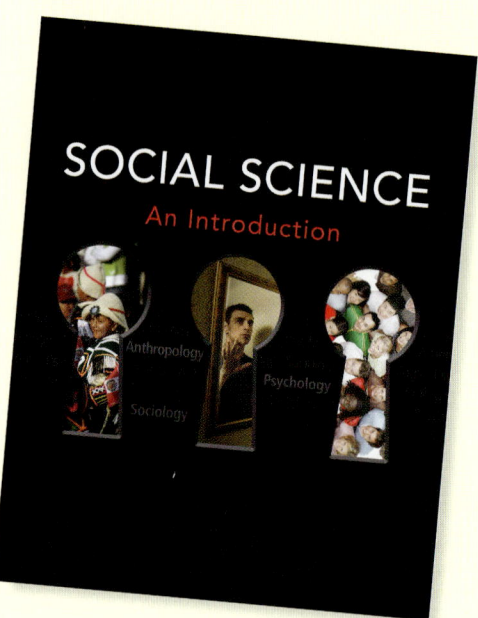

Cover
- The cover illustrates that by studying each discipline, you are opening a keyhole—or window—into how each discipline views our world.

Unit Opener
- Mini **Table of Contents** lists the chapters in the unit.
- **Photographs** capture the essence of the unit.
- A list of the **research and inquiry skills** taught in each chapter in the unit.
- An **Overview** summarizes the unit content that will be covered and highlights key information.

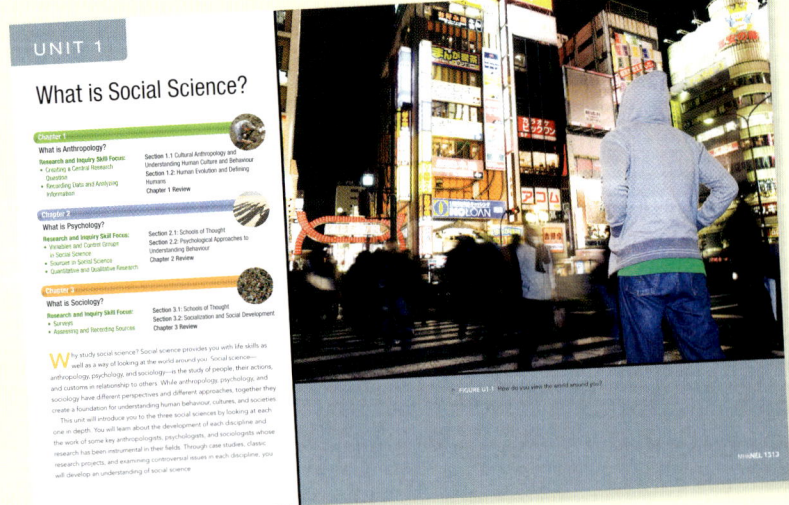

Chapter Opener

- **Chapter Expectations** are your learning goals and include the curriculum expectations covered by the chapter content.
- **Key Terms** list the words used in the chapter that will become part of your social sciences vocabulary. These terms, which are often used with specific meaning within the social sciences, are also defined in the margins and in the Glossary.
- **Landmark Case Studies** identifies the major case studies contained in the chapter; each case study is called "landmark" because of its importance to the discipline.
- **Key Theorists** lists the important contributors to each discipline; in chapters 1–3, the key theorists are displayed in a graphic organizer that shows the relationships between the schools of thought within each discipline.
- A photograph captures the main theme of the chapter.
- The Chapter Introduction onlines the content that is explored within the chapter.

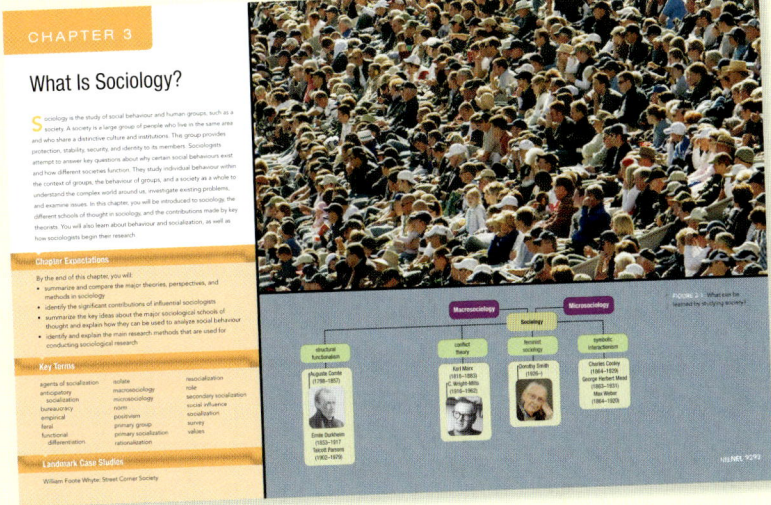

Chapter Review

- End-of-chapter questions that help you to review chapter content.

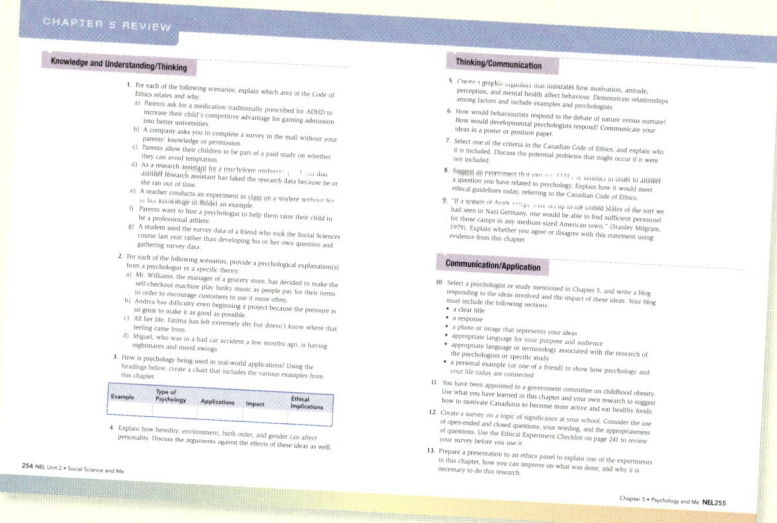

A Tour of Your Textbook   NEL   xiii

Social Science: An Introduction has a number of features that will highlight the content, make the social sciences relevant to you, and provide interesting and sometimes challenging viewpoints on topics under study.

Spotlight on …

- A high-interest topic related to the chapter content that is based on a current event, idea, or issue to engage and prepare you for the chapter content.

Research and Inquiry Skills

- introduces you to an important social science skill
- outlines the skill focus for the chapter
- provides a model of how the skill is used in the field

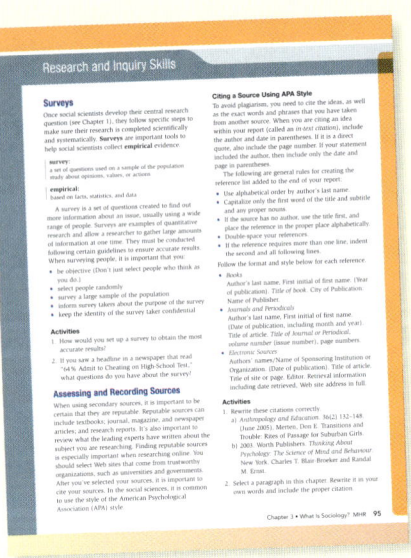

Landmark Case Study

- An in-depth examination of an important work in a particular discipline. Each case study describes the key people and issues related to the study and the lasting effect the case study has had on our understanding of the discipline and of how we see the world around us.

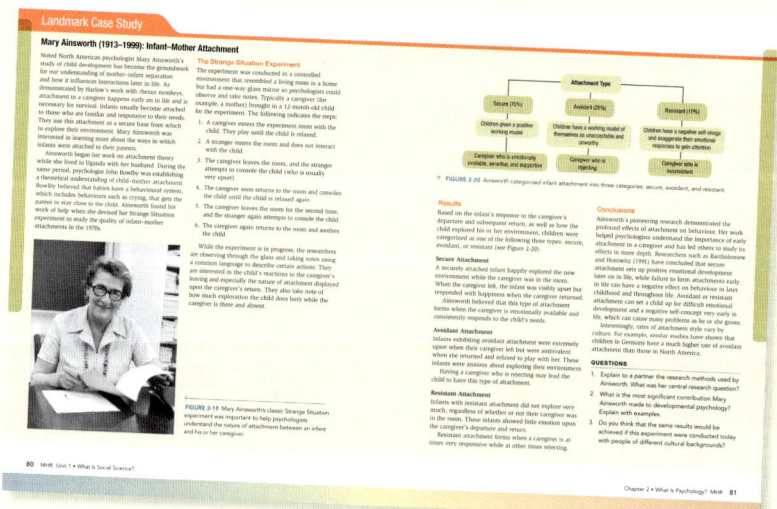

In Focus

- A general interest feature that highlights an important person or topic within a discipline. In Focus is related to the content that surrounds it and provides a more in-depth examination of the person or topic discussed.

In the Field

- Features a Canadian social scientist at work to meaningfully demonstrate careers in social science and what you can do with social science skills.

The Language of Social Sciences

- Social scientists often use terms and phrases that may be unfamiliar to us, or may be used differently than we are used to. This feature explores the language that social scientists use in the context in which it is used in the field.

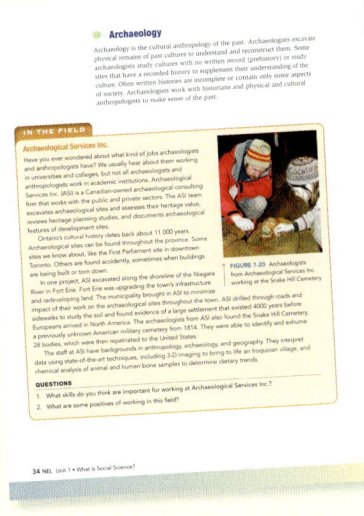
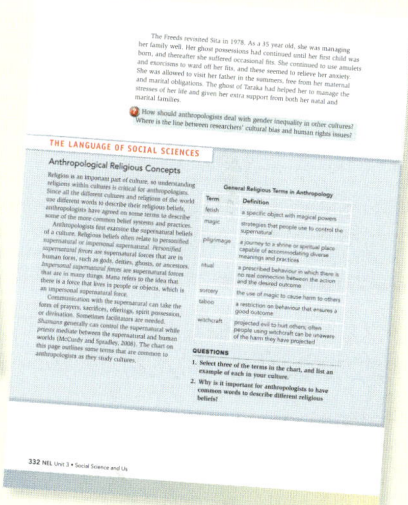

Social Science in Popular Culture

- Explores the portrayal of social science in media and popular culture—books, movies, and television—and explores how accurately—or inaccurately—social science is used in popular media.

Point/Counterpoint

- Highlights current—and sometimes controversial—perspectives with alternate ways of looking at a topical issue.

Youth Perspectives

- Follows former students of the course who have gone on to further social science education or are currently working in a social science field.

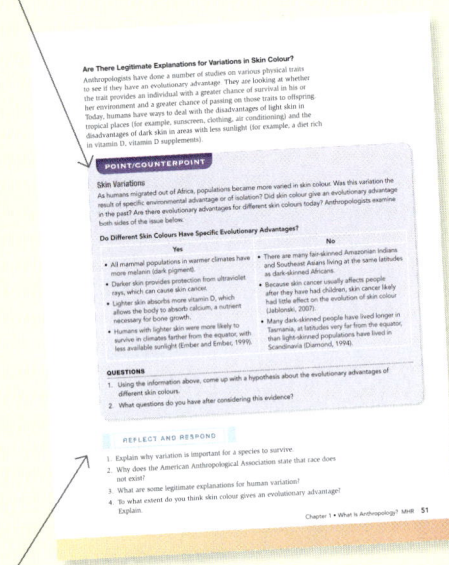

Reflect and Respond

- Questions designed to encourage you to think critically about the material you have read and which provide an opportunity for self- and teacher assessment.

Before You Read

- A prompt at the beginning of a section that helps you access prior knowledge to gain a stronger understanding of the content.

Voices

- Brief quotations that provide thought-provoking perspectives on the main subject of the chapter text.

More to Know ...

- Shows connections to what is on the page to parts of the text that you have already read, or will read later.

xvi   NEL   A Tour of Your Textbook

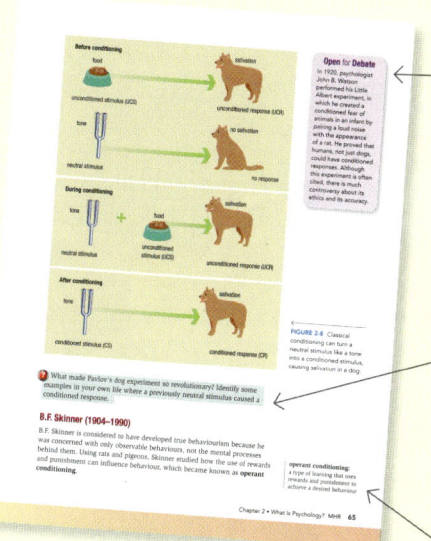

Open for Debate
- Provides further opportunities for thought-provoking discussions.

Pause and Think
- Questions within the body of the text that give you further opportunities for self-reflection and self-assessment.

Glossary terms
- Each key term is in boldface and is defined in the margin next to the term; each term is also compiled in the Glossary on pp. 454–460.

Connecting to ...
- Connects one of the social sciences to another to help you see the connections between the social science disciplines.

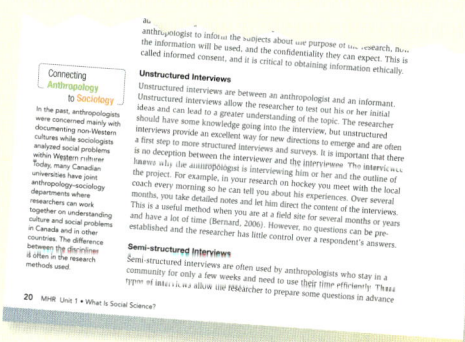

Skills Focus
- Reinforces and provides opportunities to further develop the skills learned in the current and earlier chapters.

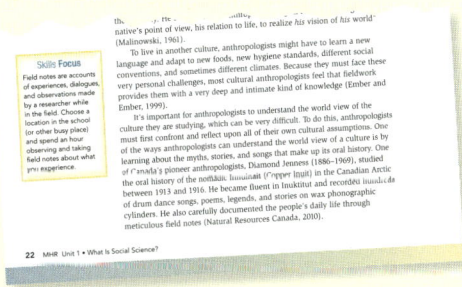

A Tour of Your Textbook   NEL   xvii

INTRODUCTION

Introduction to Anthropology, Psychology, and Sociology

Who are we? Why do we do what we do? What is the impact of our decisions? The study of social science allows insight into these and other questions that shape human nature. Social science is the organized study of people and their activities and their customs in relation to others. Much of what you hear about human behaviour is really myths and misconceptions, which are often described as common sense. Throughout this text, you will challenge these myths. The reasons why individuals, groups, and societies act the way they do is actually quite complex. Using social sciences to understand the world will provide you with insight and help you question many of the ideas you may have taken for granted.

Chapter Expectations

By the end of this chapter, you will:
- use terms relating to anthropology, psychology, and sociology correctly
- formulate effective questions to guide your research and inquiry

Key Terms

anthropology
psychology
social science inquiry model
social science
sociology

FIGURE I-1 This elderly man was rescued after being buried under rubble for three days. He was discovered by other survivors of the massive earthquake and tsunami that devastated Japan on March 11, 2011. Why do people help others, especially strangers, even if it means putting themselves at risk? Anthropologists, psychologists, and sociologists all have different answers to this question.

Spotlight on Social Science — What Would You Do?

Before You Read
Why do people have different reactions to the same situation?

On a Saturday morning in May, a 17-year-old girl lay on the ground near a west-end Montreal subway station. She was near the parking lot of a call centre, Sitel Teleservices Canada. Sitel employees saw her lying on her back, naked from the waist down. The supervisor told employees not to call 911 because he did not see any blood and thought the girl was drunk or on drugs. She lay there for almost three hours in the rain, in plain sight of employees and passersby, until one employee disobeyed instructions and called 911 on his cell phone.

The girl was taken to hospital in a coma. She had been beaten and suffered severe head injuries. The supervisor was fired, and the people of Montreal were outraged. The girl was identified three days later through a tattoo on her body, shown on a television newscast, but no arrests were made in the assault. The supervisor later issued a statement saying that he did not initially believe that the woman was in distress, or else he would have called police. In hindsight, he said, his actions were an error in judgment, but the way the media portrayed him as an unfeeling monster was unfair.

Social science encompasses a broad field. When social scientists examine a situation such as this case study, they look at the evidence from different perspectives (see Figure I-2).

> **social science:** the scientific discipline involving the organized study of people and their activities and relationships; aims to understand human society, culture, actions, attitudes, and behaviour; uses a research inquiry model

An anthropologist would ask, How did the environment influence the decisions of the people involved? What violent experiences had there been in this community? Could cultural factors have influenced decisions?

A psychologist would ask, Why did people not call for help? Why did they obey their supervisor? What factors led the girl to this location?

A sociologist would ask, What factors influenced the decisions of the supervisor, the employees who did not respond, and the employee who did make the 911 call? What were the ethnic or cultural backgrounds of the employees, supervisor, and girl? Were there any factors, such as gender, race, age, or economic status, that might have influenced the assumptions of the supervisor and employees?

> **VOICES**
>
> The Stranger is close to us, insofar as we feel between him and ourselves common features of a national, social, occupational, or generally human, nature. He is far from us, insofar as these common features extend beyond him or us, and connect us only because they connect a great many people.
>
> Georg Simmel, *The Stranger*, 1908

FIGURE I-2 Anthropologists, psychologists, and sociologists investigate the issue of helping others from different perspectives. What factors do you think influence a person's decision to help someone in need?

QUESTIONS

1. Create a graphic organizer to identify the beliefs held and actions taken from the viewpoint of each participant or group of participants in the case study.
2. Write a blog posting containing your thoughts about this case. What would you have done if you were one of the employees at Sitel?
3. If you could, what questions would you ask the participants involved?

Social Science

There are many social sciences, but they are all concerned with society and human behaviour. Social science includes **anthropology**, criminology, economics, political science, **psychology**, and **sociology**. Law and comparative religions are often considered social sciences as well. Within all of these social sciences, there are many areas of study. This course will focus on anthropology, psychology, and sociology since they relate to who you are and whom you will become. These subjects will help build an understanding of the world, and often provide career opportunities.

Social scientists use a unique vocabulary. They use the social science language and images in various forms to read, write, listen, view, represent, and think critically about different ideas and points of view (see Figure I-3).

> **Before You Read**
> Why did you take this course? List all the reasons, and then try to organize the ideas into themes.

anthropology: the scientific study of humans, including their origins; behaviour; and physical, social, and cultural development

psychology: the scientific study of the human mind, mental states, and human behaviour

sociology: the scientific study of human social behaviour, including individuals, groups, and societies

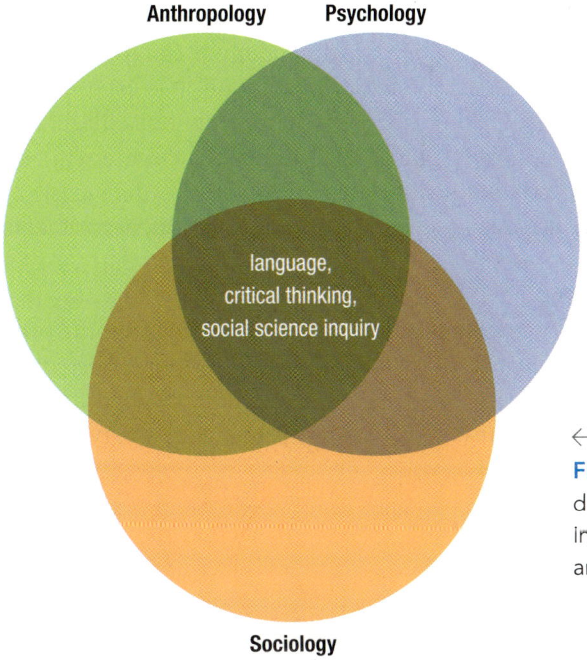

[Venn diagram showing three overlapping circles labelled Anthropology, Psychology, and Sociology, with "language, critical thinking, social science inquiry" in the centre intersection]

FIGURE I-3 Although there are important differences among the social sciences, all involve a unique vocabulary, critical analysis, and inquiry model.

An important aspect of a social scientist's job is fieldwork, which is often done outside the social scientist's usual place of work (see Figure I-4). For example, an anthropologist might observe by video the behaviour of people in a village or take an oral history. A psychologist might conduct a survey or observe people's behaviour in an airport or shopping mall. A sociologist might conduct a race-relations workshop for police.

FIGURE I-4 Fieldwork is how social scientists find primary sources for their research. Have you ever been surveyed on the phone or in person in a mall?

> **More to Know...**
> You will learn more about Chomsky's theory of linguistics in Chapter 1.

Daniel Everett, an American social scientist, travelled far from the university where he works to investigate the language of a Brazilian tribe (see Figure I-5). Everett studied the Pirahã people of Brazil and their language. According to his research, their language does not have features that linguists consider to be necessary to a language. For example, it does not have words for quantity concepts or numbers over two. It also does not have words for colour concepts or a perfect tense (in English, an example of the perfect tense would be *The boy has eaten the apple*). Everett's findings contradict the Chomskyian theory of linguistics, which includes the concept of a universal grammar. Chomsky's theory had dominated linguistics for decades. Everett argued that the Pirahã people's hunter-gatherer lifestyle did not require these concepts, which is why their language does not describe them.

Social science is always changing as we learn more about who we are, challenge previous understandings, and develop new research methods. For example, the concept of multiculturalism is familiar to many Canadians, but this idea is now being challenged in Canada and other countries. The concept of interculturalism is a new model for integration. It is especially popular in Quebec, for instance. Quebec has a strong francophone culture but has tried to integrate other minorities into a common public culture while respecting their diversity. As one politician stated, "Religious freedom exists but there are other values. For instance, multiculturalism is not a Quebec value. It may be a Canadian one but it is not a Quebec one" (Toronto Star, 2011). Anthropologists want to understand how the different cultures change and stay the same. Psychologists study how the individuals involved adapt to the pressures to conform, and sociologists study how race and class are affected by the debate.

As a student of the social sciences, you will have opportunities to connect the ideas of social scientists to your own life and community and to investigate issues that are important to you.

FIGURE I-5 Daniel Everett doing fieldwork with the Pirahã (pronounced *Pee-da-ha*) people. What questions would you pose to each of these men?

❓ Which social scientist do you think would be most interested in Everett's research: an anthropologist, a psychologist, or a sociologist? Do you think Everett's findings might have been controversial? Why? Why might the concept of multiculturalism be problematic today?

Introduction to Anthropology

Anthropology is the study of humankind. The field is divided into two areas: cultural anthropology and physical anthropology. Cultural anthropology can be divided further into social anthropology (ethnology), archaeology, and linguistic anthropology. Physical anthropology can be divided further into paleoanthropology, forensic anthropology, and primatology. There are many different anthropological schools of thought, including cultural materialism and feminist anthropology, to name just a few. This means that anthropology involves more than digging up bones or finding out where humanity began (see Figure I-6).

Anthropologists use reasoning to gain insight into how humans live, think, communicate, produce, and interact with their social and physical environments.

Studying anthropology can lead to a wide range of careers, including social science analyst, social service agency planner, archaeological fieldworker, exhibit assistant, cultural artifact specialist, museum worker, research assistant, forensic anthropologist, and art conservator, among many others.

There are many well-known anthropologists, some of whom you will study in later chapters. A few of them are Noam Chomsky, Charles Darwin, Jane Goodall, the Leakys, Margaret Mead, Edward Sapir, Marvin Harris, and Richard Less. Many anthropologists, including Jane Goodall, study primates. Goodall is best known for her studies of chimpanzees in Tanzania. Examine the two photos in Figure I-7 and consider how the study of these animals fits into anthropology.

↑ **FIGURE I-6** The Museum of Anthropology in Vancouver recently underwent a $55 million renovation. How might studying artifacts such as these totem poles give anthropologists insight into humans today?

↑ **FIGURE I-7** Humans are part of a group of mammals called primates. This group includes gorillas and chimpanzees, among others. How do you think studying these animals can help us understand ourselves?

❓ List a few more careers related to anthropology. Which one interests you most? In what ways do you think anthropologists think differently than historians or geographers?

Introduction to Psychology

Psychology is the study of the human mind and its mental states. It includes the study of characteristics of temperament and behaviour of a person or group (see Figure I-8). There are many subfields in psychology, including biological, psychoanalytic, behavioural, cognitive, and humanistic psychology. Psychologists aim to describe, predict, and control behaviour and mental processes. They study individuals as well as groups.

FIGURE I-8 What two images can you see in this figure? Why do you think this figure relevant to the study of psychology?

Studying psychology can lead to a variety of careers, including psychologist, therapist, animal care worker, teacher, human rights worker, police officer, mental health worker, social worker, marketing specialist, and forensic psychologist, to identify a few (see Figure I-9).

FIGURE I-9 Sports psychology is a growing field. How might a sports psychologist help an athlete to improve his or her performance?

(?) Select an advertisement from any medium, and pose a question about it that a psychologist might want to investigate. Do you know of any athletes who use psychology to improve their performance? What strategies do they use?

1. **Questions.** Begin with questions about a topic that interests you, and has an impact on many people. Your questions should have the potential to be answered through investigation. Select a focus area such as anthropology, psychology, or sociology. Create a central research question.

2. **Focus.** Take notes about what you already know and research what has been previously learned. Identify your sources.

3. **Formulate a hypothesis.** Turn your question into a hypothesis.

4. **Collect data.** Anthropology, psychology, and sociology use different methods to collect data, including surveys, questionnaires, interviews, observations, and statistics. Select the methods that will provide the most relevant information to confirm your hypothesis.

5. **Assemble and analyze data.** Organize your data into charts, graphs, or another format that best communicates your main ideas.

6. **Stop and check.** Have you collected enough data to confirm or refute your hypothesis? If not, return to step 4.

7. **Present results.** Draw conclusions, identify any limitations from your research, and make some recommendations about next steps. This is the *so what* part of the process. Share your findings in a presentation, either written, oral, visual, or a combination.

8. **Reflection.** Reflect and evaluate your research process and results. What went well? What would you do differently next time?

FIGURE I-12 The social science inquiry model provides steps to follow when conducting research to investigate a question.

> ### REFLECT AND RESPOND
>
> 1. Create your own open-ended questions based on the photos in this chapter. They should be questions that could lead to more research.
> 2. Create open-ended questions based on the case study at the beginning of this chapter.
> 3. Brainstorm some issues that you want to know more about in your school, your community, or the world.
> 4. Which type of questions do you think are most useful when conducting research: open or closed? Why?

UNIT 1

What is Social Science?

Chapter 1
What is Anthropology?

Research and Inquiry Skill Focus:
- Creating a Central Research Question
- Recording Data and Analyzing Information

Section 1.1 Cultural Anthropology and Understanding Human Culture and Behaviour
Section 1.2: Human Evolution and Defining Humans
Chapter 1 Review

Chapter 2
What is Psychology?

Research and Inquiry Skill Focus:
- Variables and Control Groups in Social Science
- Sources in Social Science
- Quantitative and Qualitative Research

Section 2.1: Schools of Thought
Section 2.2: Psychological Approaches to Understanding Behaviour
Chapter 2 Review

Chapter 3
What is Sociology?

Research and Inquiry Skill Focus:
- Surveys
- Assessing and Recording Sources

Section 3.1: Schools of Thought
Section 3.2: Socialization and Social Development
Chapter 3 Review

Why study social science? Social science provides you with life skills as well as a way of looking at the world around you. Social science—anthropology, psychology, and sociology—is the study of people, their actions, and customs in relationship to others. While anthropology, psychology, and sociology have different perspectives and different approaches, together they create a foundation for understanding human behaviour, cultures, and societies.

This unit will introduce you to the three social sciences by looking at each one in depth. You will learn about the development of each discipline and the work of some key anthropologists, psychologists, and sociologists whose research has been instrumental in their fields. Through case studies, classic research projects, and examining controversial issues in each discipline, you will develop an understanding of social science.

FIGURE U1-1 How do you view the world around you?

CHAPTER 1

What Is Anthropology?

Anthropology is the scientific study of the origin, the behaviour, and the physical, social, and cultural development of humans. Anthropologists seek to understand what makes us human by studying human ancestors through archaeological excavation and by observing living cultures throughout the world. In this chapter, you will learn about different fields of anthropology and the major schools of thought, important theories, perspectives, and research within anthropology, as well as the work of influential anthropologists. You'll also learn methods for conducting anthropological research and learn how to formulate your own research questions and record information.

Chapter Expectations

By the end of this chapter, you will:
- summarize and compare major theories, perspectives, and research methods in anthropology
- identify the significant contributions of influential anthropologists
- outline the key ideas of the major anthropological schools of thought, and explain how they can be used to analyze features of cultural systems
- explain significant issues in different areas of anthropology
- explain the main research methods for conducting anthropological research

Key Terms

bipedalism
culturally constructed
culture
ethnocentric
ethnography
ethnology
fossil
hominin
hypothesis
informant
kinship
objective
participant observation
radiometric dating
reflexivity
subculture
subjective

Landmark Case Studies

Richard Lee: The Dobe Ju/'hoansi

Primatology
Dian Fossey (1932–1985)
Biruté Galdikas (1946–)
Jane Goodall (1934–)
Sue Savage-Rumbaugh (1946–)

Paleoanthropology
Raymond Dart (1893–1988)
Donald Johanson (1943–)
Louis Leakey (1903–1972)
Mary Leakey (1913–1996)

Richard Leakey (1944–)

FIGURE 1-1 Paleontologist Marco Avanzini measuring fossilized footprints created 385 000–325 000 years ago by an ancestor of modern humans. Why do you think anthropologists are interested in finding out about the origin and development of humans?

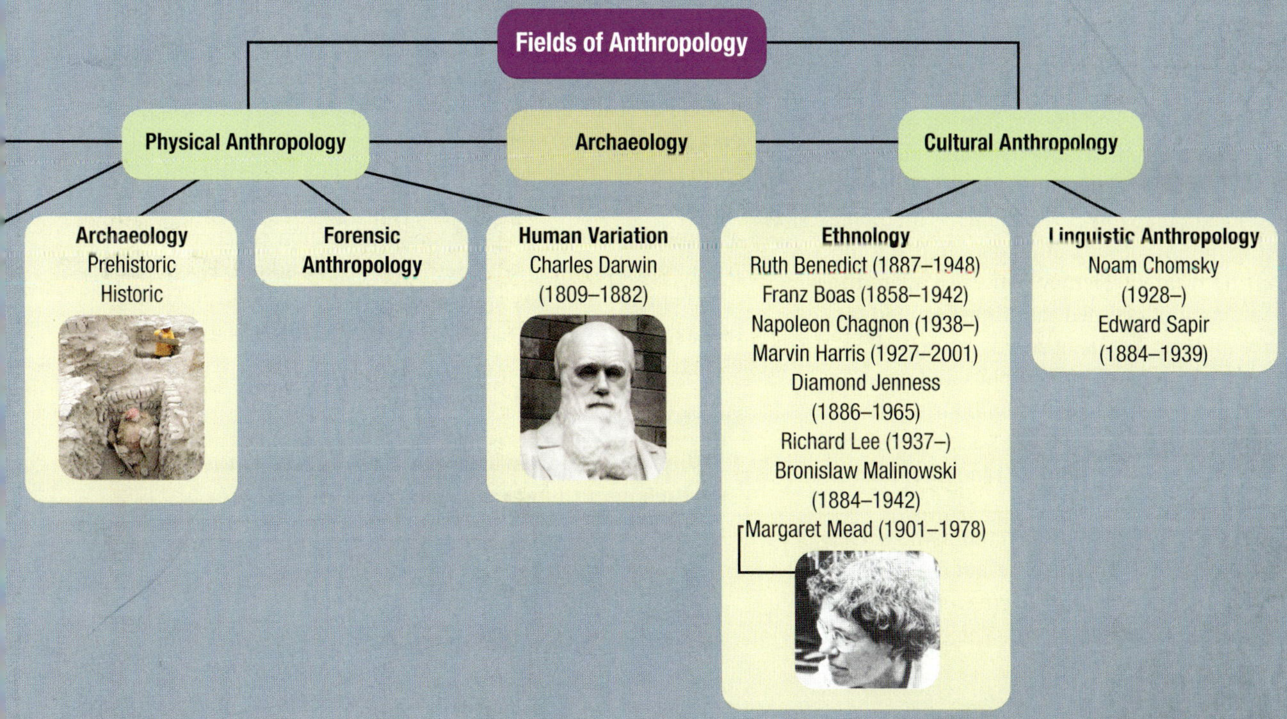

Fields of Anthropology

- **Physical Anthropology**
  - **Archaeology**
    Prehistoric
    Historic
  - **Forensic Anthropology**
  - **Human Variation**
    Charles Darwin (1809–1882)
- **Archaeology**
- **Cultural Anthropology**
  - **Ethnology**
    Ruth Benedict (1887–1948)
    Franz Boas (1858–1942)
    Napoleon Chagnon (1938–)
    Marvin Harris (1927–2001)
    Diamond Jenness (1886–1965)
    Richard Lee (1937–)
    Bronislaw Malinowski (1884–1942)
    Margaret Mead (1901–1978)
  - **Linguistic Anthropology**
    Noam Chomsky (1928–)
    Edward Sapir (1884–1939)

Spotlight on Anthropology — *Yanomamö and the Anthropologists*

> **Before You Read**
> You have just read a brief introduction to anthropology. Scan these two pages and predict what this chapter is about. Record two questions that you expect will be answered as you read.

When American anthropologist Napoleon Chagnon (1938–) (see Figure 1-2) went to Venezuela in 1969 to study the Yanomamö (sometimes called the Yanomami), isolated hunter-gatherers who live in the Amazon rainforest, he had little idea of the controversy his research would generate among anthropologists. Chagnon spent years living with the Yanomamö, participating in their culture, providing them with goods such as axes and machetes, and vaccinating them against deadly diseases. His book *Yanomamö: The Fierce People* described the Yanomamö as an extremely violent society, where aggression and conflict between men was valued. Chagnon suggested that aggression in males was both culturally and biologically determined. The males who were most aggressive had more wives and children than those who were less aggressive. Chagnon reasoned that cultural success (in this case, being aggressive and violent) led to increased genetic success (meaning that more of the children born would be disposed toward violence). Chagnon's book went on to become a best-selling anthropology text and is often studied in universities.

Fast forward to 2000 and the publication of *Darkness in El Dorado: How Scientists and Journalists Devastated the Amazon*. Author and journalist Patrick Tierney condemns Chagnon's work, criticizing his methods and accusing him of manipulating data to reach the conclusions he wanted. Tierney, who also spent time with the Yanomamö, claimed that Chagnon had incited the violence and conflict he observed by providing (or bribing) the Yanomamö with goods and creating competition between them and neighbouring tribes. Tierney has also suggested that the vaccines did more harm than good since some of the Yanomamö became ill after they were inoculated.

Did Chagnon's participation in Yanomamö society alter the behaviour of the people he interacted with? It's important to remember that Tierney studied the Yanomamö decades after Chagnon. The differences

FIGURE 1-2 Napoleon Chagnon (left) was criticized for his dealings with the Yanomamö people. To what extent is the criticism of Chagnon's work justified?

between the Yanomamö culture that Tierney observed and the one Chagnon described might not be caused only by the actions of anthropologists, but by the massive social changes caused by missionary work, forestry, gold mining, and changes to their environment.

The controversy raises questions for anthropologists, such as: How does a researcher's presence influence a society? Anthropologists agree that they must always carefully consider their impact on the people they study and try to protect the safety, dignity, and privacy of their subjects. The ongoing disagreement among anthropologists whether Chagnon's research practices were ethical, that is, whether his research adhered to accepted principles and conduct, demonstrates that what anthropologists consider to be ethical has changed over time.

QUESTIONS

1. Why was Chagnon's research criticized? Is the criticism of Chagnon's work justified? Why or why not?
2. To what extent can anthropologists conduct research ethically in another culture? Explain.

Research and Inquiry Skills

People become social scientists to understand people and cultures and to gain insight into human behaviour. To do this, a social scientist must do a great deal of research. Social scientists review case studies and other published material and do their own primary research in the field.

Creating a Central Research Question

The first step is coming up with a central research question on a topic that interests you. A research question must be testable and as unbiased as possible. We all have biases. They can come from our culture, our point of view, and our interests. Social scientists have established research methods and practices to try to reduce these biases. Here are some examples of research questions:

1. *Why are men violent?*
   This question assumes that men are violent. It would be very difficult to test since "violence" is not defined.
2. *Are men violent in all cultures?*
   This question is better since it does not assume that all men are violent. But it is better to define violence and culture more specifically.
3. *Do men in industrial countries commit more deadly violence than men in hunter-gatherer societies?*
   Phrasing the question this way provides a basis for further research. You have ways of investigating this example by counting and comparing the number of murders in different communities.

After creating a central research question, the next step is conducting a literature review to discover the research that already exists on your topic. This will allow you to refine your question and further develop a **hypothesis**.

> **hypothesis:**
> a tentative assumption made from known facts as the basis for investigation

Activities

1. In small groups, brainstorm an issue or problem in your school or community that could be investigated.
2. Once you have your list, create at least three research questions that are testable and unbiased.
3. How would you go about researching the problem? What kinds of information would you need to gather?

Recording Data and Analyzing Information

When you are doing research, you will need to collect data (small factual pieces of information) and information to test your hypothesis. Data becomes information when it is interpreted by someone. Record how you collected your data and where you found your information. Summarize the information and think about how it answers your research question.

Assessing and Recording Sources

It is very important to record where you got your information and to cite your sources correctly. In the social sciences, we generally use APA style. For more information about APA style, see Chapter 3.

Summarizing Information

Summarizing your information is critical to helping you understand what you've found and avoid plagiarism. Here are a few examples to help you:

Point-form notes
Start with a title and include subtitles to organize the information. Summarize the information in your own words. Write down where you found your information, so you will remember to properly cite it.

Mind mapping
A central idea can branch off into subtopics. This technique is helpful to see connections.

Diagrams and flow charts
These can show a process or record how information is related. For visual learners, diagrams and charts may be preferred over point-form notes.

Evaluating Your Information

When researching, it's helpful to note how the information will help you answer your research question. Doing so helps you to keep focused and avoid irrelevant research. After you finish collecting your data, you will need to analyze and synthesize it. It's also important to evaluate your sources. Note who the author is, his or her qualifications, and where it is published.

Activities

1. As you read through Chapter 1, create a mind map that organizes the main theories and ideas of all the anthropologists mentioned in the chapter.
2. Create a graphic organizer to help you understand the different schools of thought in anthropology.

Section 1.1 Cultural Anthropology and Understanding Human Culture and Behaviour

As anthropologists gather more and more information about culture throughout the world, we can see what characteristics are universally human, how cultures adapt to new challenges in innovative ways, and how culture is learned and passed on to new generations. In this section, you will learn about the different fields of cultural anthropology, different theories and schools of thought, and the tools cultural anthropologists use to conduct their research.

Cultural Anthropology

culture:
the total system of ideas, values, behaviours, and attitudes of a society commonly shared by most members of a society

What do you think of when you hear the word **culture**? Maybe you think about the ballet, the theatre, or a concert. Culture is not just the artistic activities a society considers valuable, like playing an instrument. Culture is made up of what people do, what people make, and what people believe. Culture includes all behaviour of people in their everyday lives, from daily rituals (for example, washing dishes) to beliefs about abstract concepts (for example, time), and is learned and transmitted from one generation to the next. It can be the food people eat, the clothes they wear, the shelter they live in, how they move from place to place, how they defend themselves, what they learn, and the languages they speak.

Cultural anthropologists are anthropologists who study both past and present cultures. They ask questions such as: Why is there social and political inequality? How does language affect and express culture? What can we learn about a culture from what the people leave behind? Researchers attempt to answer these questions by immersing themselves in a culture for months or years while conducting interviews and taking detailed notes as they study the history and structure of languages and the physical remains of past cultures. The mind map below (see Figure 1-3) explains the different fields of cultural anthropology.

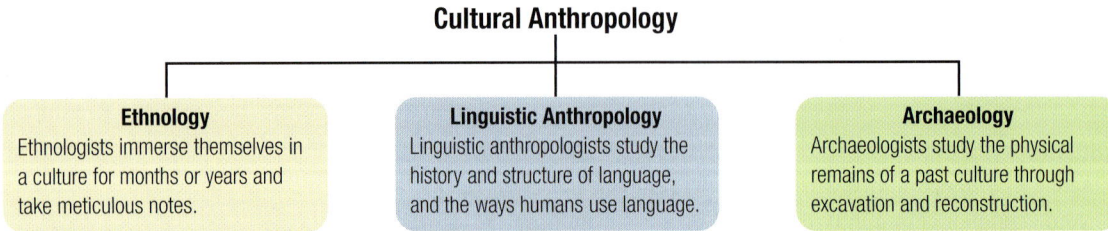

↑ **FIGURE 1-3** The different fields of cultural anthropology

↑ **FIGURE 1-4** Look carefully at the photos above. What aspects of culture can you see? In what ways are people's beliefs, behaviours, and attitudes evident?

THE LANGUAGE OF SOCIAL SCIENCES

Introducing Social Sciences

As you are introduced to social sciences in Unit 1, you may see certain terms used to describe different theories and practices of anthropology, psychology, and sociology, such as *schools of thought*, *branches*, *fields*, and *disciplines*. These terms are closely related and used often. A school of thought is a common view or approach taken by a group of like-minded people on a specific topic. A branch is a division of a subject, an area of specialized skill or knowledge. A field is a topic, subject, or area of academic interest. A discipline is a branch of learning or a field of study. Each of these terms is used to describe different elements of the social sciences and is important to understanding social science.

QUESTIONS

1. Write the following terms in your notebook: *school of thought*, *branch*, *field*, and *discipline*. As you go through Unit 1, find an example for each one.

REFLECT AND RESPOND

1. Examine an item belonging to someone in your class. Make some predictions about the beliefs and values of his or her culture based on this item.
2. Look at the images on this page. Choose two images, and develop a research question that a cultural anthropologist might ask for each one.

Research Tools of Cultural Anthropologists

Finding Informants

When anthropologists conduct their research within a community, it is impossible for them to talk to everyone from every group. They rely on **informants**, people in the community who are willing to share information about their culture and their community. Informants should be reliable and knowledgeable about what the anthropologist is studying. For example, if you were studying hockey in rural Ontario, you would want to find informants who had specific knowledge of the game, players, fans, or community volunteers. It can be very difficult to find an informant. Anthropologists have to be aware that informants will react to their presence as researchers and may be distrustful of them or unwilling to share critical information. There has to be a certain level of trust between an informant and an anthropologist. The relationship between an anthropologist and an informant is a partnership and without the help of an informant, an anthropologist cannot conduct his or her research. It is essential to choose reliable informants and to verify their information through other methods.

Interviews

Interviews are important tools used by anthropologists (and other social scientists) to understand the culture they are studying and obtain valuable information. There are different kinds of interviews, each with its own advantages and disadvantages. Before interviewing, it is important for the anthropologist to inform the subjects about the purpose of the research, how the information will be used, and the confidentiality they can expect. This is called informed consent, and it is critical to obtaining information ethically.

Unstructured Interviews

Unstructured interviews are between an anthropologist and an informant. Unstructured interviews allow the researcher to test out his or her initial ideas and can lead to a greater understanding of the topic. The researcher should have some knowledge going into the interview, but unstructured interviews provide an excellent way for new directions to emerge and are often a first step to more structured interviews and surveys. It is important that there is no deception between the interviewer and the interviewee. The interviewee knows why the anthropologist is interviewing him or her and the outline of the project. For example, in your research on hockey you meet with the local coach every morning so he can tell you about his experiences. Over several months, you take detailed notes and let him direct the content of the interviews. This is a useful method when you are at a field site for several months or years and have a lot of time (Bernard, 2006). However, no questions can be pre-established and the researcher has little control over a respondent's answers.

Semi-structured Interviews

Semi-structured interviews are often used by anthropologists who stay in a community for only a few weeks and need to use their time efficiently. These types of interviews allow the researcher to prepare some questions in advance

---

Before You Read

Why do you think police rely on informants or tips from the public when they are investigating a crime? Are all of these sources reliable? Why or why not?

informant: a reliable and knowledgeable person who provides specific information to an anthropologist studying his or her community

---

Connecting Anthropology to Sociology

In the past, anthropologists were concerned mainly with documenting non-Western cultures while sociologists analyzed social problems within Western cultures. Today, many Canadian universities have joint anthropology–sociology departments where researchers can work together on understanding culture and social problems in Canada and in other countries. The difference between the disciplines is often in the research methods used.

and end up with reliable qualitative data. The researcher goes in with an outline of what types of information are wanted, but not a strict list of questions. The interview is semi-structured because it is flexible, allowing both the interviewer and the subject to follow leads that may come up in the course of the interview and for the subject to express personal views. However, it can be easy to stray away from the topic you need information on. For your hockey research, you might want to interview the mayor, but she can't meet with you every morning. The semi-structured interview is a good method if you have only one chance to interview her.

Structured Interviews

Structured interviews are interviews that use a set list of questions that do not change. This method should be used when the researcher is very clear on the topic and there is other information that is easily available. These interviews can be conducted efficiently by non-experts, trained to follow only the instructions on the interview questionnaire. This method does not require the development of a relationship between interviewer and interviewee, and it can produce consistent data that can easily be compared between respondents. However, since the questions are set in advance, they cannot be adapted to changing situations and few are open-ended questions, so the researcher might obtain limited answers.

Counting People, Photographs, and Mapping

At the beginning of their research, anthropologists often count all the people they are studying and map their physical locations. They take photographs and draw diagrams, such as the ones shown in Figures 1-5 and 1-6, of how humans use physical space and the relationships between people in the society. Anthropologists collect this type of information on the activities of the people in the society to help them understand the society they are studying. For example, by counting the hours of work over a month of one community of hunter-gatherers in Southern Africa, the Ju/'hoansi, anthropologist Richard Lee discovered that most of the people spent an average of 20 hours a week gathering food. Women brought in 55 percent of the total calories, in addition to doing other kinds of work, including making clothing, processing food, and child care. Lee found out that the Ju/'hoansi worked no more than 40 hours a week in all tasks, which helped him to draw conclusions about the equality of labour within their society. This kind of information can be compared to information gathered through interviews or informants, which can help anthropologists verify what people are telling them.

> **More to Know...**
> You will learn more about Richard Lee and the Ju/'hoansi on pages 26–27.

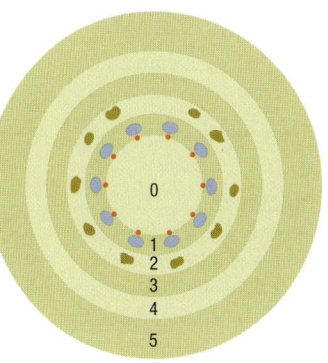

0 central plaza, *chu/o*
1 circle of huts and fireplaces, *da/tsi*
2 ash dumps
3 cooking pits
4 empty area
5 zone of defecation, *z/o*
6 the bush *t,si*

FIGURE 1-5 A plan of a Ju/'hoan village. What kind of information about people's culture and daily lives is available in this diagram? How is the information different from the information provided by the photograph?

FIGURE 1-6 Anthropologist Richard Lee interviewing Ju/'hoansi hunter about cooking debris. How does Figure 1-5 help you make sense of this photo?

REFLECT AND RESPOND

1. Create a chart comparing the advantages and disadvantages of different research methods used by cultural anthropologists.
2. Select which type of interview you would do if you were going to conduct research today in the Ju/'hoan village and explain your reasons.

Ethnology

Before You Read

Have you ever misunderstood someone trying to communicate with you? What were the circumstances and what was the result? What did you learn from the experience?

Ethnology is the study of the origins and cultures of different races and peoples. Ethnologists are concerned with topics such as marriage customs, **kinship** patterns, political and economic systems, religion, art, music, and technology. They study a culture through **participant observation**, in some cases living with a group and participating in their culture, while taking extensive notes. They use these notes to write an account of the culture, or **ethnography**.

ethnology:
the study of the origins and cultures of different races and peoples

kinship:
the relationship between two or more people that is based on common ancestry, marriage, or adoption

participant observation:
the careful watching of a group, in some cases living with its members and participating in their culture

ethnography:
the written account of a culture

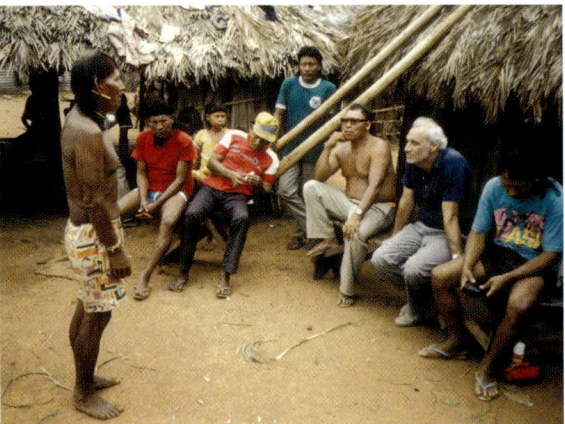

FIGURE 1-7 Living with a culture while studying its members is a common method of research in anthropology. Can you think of some of the challenges and problems of using participant observation as a research method? What are some of the benefits?

How Do Ethnologists Study Culture?

Participant observation is the main method of study that ethnologists use to gather information about cultures. Bronislaw Malinowski pioneered this method in his 1915 study of the Trobriand Islanders in the South Pacific. He immersed himself in their culture, learning their language and participating in their society. He stated that the anthropologist's goal should be "to grasp the native's point of view, his relation to life, to realize *his* vision of *his* world" (Malinowski, 1961).

To live in another culture, anthropologists might have to learn a new language and adapt to new foods, new hygiene standards, different social conventions, and sometimes different climates. Because they must face these very personal challenges, most cultural anthropologists feel that fieldwork provides them with a very deep and intimate kind of knowledge (Ember and Ember, 1999).

It's important for anthropologists to understand the world view of the culture they are studying, which can be very difficult. To do this, anthropologists must first confront and reflect upon all of their own cultural assumptions. One of the ways anthropologists can understand the world view of a culture is by learning about the myths, stories, and songs that make up its oral history. One of Canada's pioneer anthropologists, Diamond Jenness (1886–1969), studied the oral history of the nomadic Innuinait (Copper Inuit) in the Canadian Arctic between 1913 and 1916. He became fluent in Inuktitut and recorded hundreds of drum dance songs, poems, legends, and stories on wax phonographic cylinders. He also carefully documented the people's daily life through meticulous field notes (Natural Resources Canada, 2010).

Skills Focus

Field notes are accounts of experiences, dialogues, and observations made by a researcher while in the field. Choose a location in the school (or other busy place) and spend an hour observing and taking field notes about what you experience.

Early anthropologists such as Diamond Jenness felt it was important to document the way of life of what he called "disappearing cultures." His book, *The People of the Twilight* (1928), is still regarded as one of the best sources of information on the life of the Innuinait. Today, anthropologists still use oral history, working together with people all over the world to preserve both culture and the environment.

❓ What are some challenges that cultural anthropologists face? What characteristics does an effective anthropologist require?

Open for Debate

Anthropologist Diamond Jenness collected thousands of artifacts, from fish hooks to parkas, many of which were given to the Museum of Civilization in Ottawa. In some cases, museums also keep the human remains of Aboriginal people for study. Aboriginal groups object to and are deeply offended by the collection and display of these types of artifacts and have fought to have these items returned. How do you think anthropologists, Aboriginal groups, and museums should deal with these issues?

YOUTH PERSPECTIVES

What is Canadian Culture?

Understanding the world view of another culture can be very difficult. In order to do so, an anthropologist must understand his or her own culture and how it shapes how he or she sees the world. Canadian culture has always been difficult to define; individuals have different opinions about Canada based on where they live, their background, and their experiences with other culture. Read the following statements from high school students about Canadian culture. Which opinions do you agree with? Which do you disagree with and why?

I find that Canadians say "sorry" a lot! Whenever someone steps on my foot, I'm the one to say sorry.
— Ellie

I would describe the Canadian culture as an open minded culture. People accept differences and respect each other, not making fun of other cultures. — Sarah

I lived in China until my family moved to Canada when I was 11. Canadian culture is definitely more about freedom of expression and choices. — Mary

I think we Canadians attempt to seek out and incorporate the cultures of the people that make our country. For better or for worse. — Tony

When I returned to Canada from Chad (after living there for two and a half years) I noticed how much more uptight Western culture is than Chadian. For example, in Chad it is acceptable to visit any person whom you know at least relatively well without invitation or calling to inform of your visit. They will still feed you, give you water, and make you feel welcome. In Canada, going to your own family member's house without letting them know is unacceptable, let alone doing that with someone who is only an acquaintance. — Amina

As an international student, I noticed many differences such as hugs and kisses for your friends that were not considered common back in my country, Indonesia. This trip to Canada also made me understand the reason why a Canadian teacher, back at my school in Indonesia, would often end his questions with the phrase "eh." — Han Hwe

Canadians take a lot of things for granted. I was in Jamaica in December and, depending on where you are, having running water is great and leaving the lights on costs a fortune. — Mekonen

Canadians will eat ice cream in the winter. In minus 40°C weather! — Sierra

QUESTIONS

1. How would you define Canadian culture?
2. How does Canadian culture compare to another culture you are familiar with?
3. Can you identify cultural behaviour, attitudes, and values in these examples?

↑ **FIGURE 1-8** Hockey is often mentioned as an important aspect of Canadian culture. To what extent does hockey define Canadian culture?

The Problems of Participant Observation

subjective: type of conclusions shaped by a person's cultural and personal perspective, feelings, and beliefs

objective: type of conclusions based on facts and data and uninfluenced by personal perspectives, prejudices, or emotions

reflexivity: the practice of reflecting on your own world view, biases, and impact on the culture you are studying

As you read on page 22, participant observation can be a source of in-depth cultural understanding. It is also highly **subjective**, which means that a researcher's point of view and cultural background can shape his or her conclusions. To make their conclusions more reliable, researchers should use **objective** data (for example, counting populations, mapping, and semi-structured interviews), along with the notes from their participant observations. It is also important for researchers to use **reflexivity**, the practice of reflecting on their own world view, biases, and impact on the culture they are studying. Researchers should share their work with their subjects and ask them if their interpretations are accurate (Ember and Ember, 1999).

Sex, Lies, and Anthropology: Margaret Mead and Derek Freeman

Margaret Mead is one of anthropology's most influential and controversial figures. Best known for her study of Samoan adolescent girls, Mead was interested in examining whether stresses during adolescence were caused by adolescence itself or by society. Mead studied Samoan adolescent girls using participant observation, living among a small group and conducting interviews over nine months between 1925 and 1926. Mead observed that, in contrast to American adolescent girls, adolescence was a stress-free time for Samoan girls. Mead believed that this easy transition to adulthood was due to the sexual freedom Samoan girls experienced and concluded that sex roles were determined by culture, not biology. This conclusion fit with the anthropological and societal ideas of the 1920s. Women were re-evaluating their roles in North American society, and her findings were popular among women and men who wanted social change. Margaret Mead was a popular speaker and went on to publicize her work and the study of anthropology.

Derek Freeman, who began working in Western Samoa in the 1960s and studying its culture, criticized Mead's work in a book published in 1983. He concluded, based on his own research and interviews, that Samoa actually had very restrictive sexual practices. He felt that Mead had been tricked by her informants, teenage girls who were highly embarrassed by the intensely personal questions of a foreigner, citing specific rituals that indicated the importance of female virginity.

↑ **FIGURE 1-9** Margaret Mead and two Samoan girls, 1926. How did Mead's controversial work in Samoa demonstrate the problems of participant observation?

? What challenges does participant observation have for the researcher and for those who are being observed?

Anthropologist Paul Shankman published a book in 2009, re-examining Mead's and Freeman's original data and found that Samoans in comparison to other cultures are neither permissive nor restrictive in their sexual practices. However, Shankman concluded that both anthropologists were correct. Mead was working in American Samoa in the 1920s at a time when premarital sex in the United States was uncommon. By the 1960s, when Freeman was doing his fieldwork in Western Samoa, American attitudes around premarital sex had changed greatly. The researchers were coming from different contexts and had different experiences in Samoa. Mead and Freeman were both from different generations, which shaped their outlook, but they were also studying Samoa at very different times. Samoa had changed greatly in the time between Mead's and Freeman's work due to colonization, World War II, and commercialization. More Samoans had also become Christians, which influenced their beliefs about sex during that time.

Anthropology from a Distance: *The Chrysanthemum and the Sword* (1946)

During World War II, anthropologist Ruth Benedict researched Japan for the U.S. government in order to help Americans understand and defeat the Japanese army. Unable to live in Japan during the war, Benedict used all the cultural material available to her, including literature, newspapers, and films, to complete her research. She also interviewed Japanese immigrants and Japanese-Americans. She was able to make recommendations to the U.S. government to reach terms of surrender. After the war, Benedict's book was translated and published in Japan. Some scholars supported her work, but others criticized her approach. Her methods of studying a culture from a distance have been criticized, but her book, *The Chrysanthemum and the Sword*, remains a classic and best-selling work of cultural anthropology.

FIGURE 1-10 Japanese teens demonstrating street fashion. Can you draw any conclusions about Japanese culture from this photo?

Look at the photographs on this page. Can you make conclusions about the cultural attitudes, beliefs, and values of the people in these photos from these images? What might be some challenges of studying a culture only through photos? How could you overcome those challenges?

REFLECT AND RESPOND

1. Why was Mead a controversial figure?
2. How did Margaret Mead and Derek Freeman come to different conclusions using participant observation?
3. Why was Ruth Benedict's research criticized?
4. What are some of the ethical issues of studying the culture of an enemy nation during wartime?

FIGURE 1-11 Does this photo accurately represent North American culture? If this photo was the only evidence you had of North American culture what conclusions might you draw?

Landmark Case Study

Richard Lee and the Dobe Ju/'hoansi

Richard Lee, one of Canada's most distinguished ethnographers, has lived and worked with the Dobe Ju/'hoansi (pronounced *zhut-wasi*), a group of San people of Southern Africa for almost 40 years, starting back in the 1960s. (In the past, this group has also been referred to as the !Kung.) In that time the Dobe Ju/'hoansi have changed from a relatively isolated hunter-gatherer society, who foraged for food, to an integrated herding and farming society.

Lee decided to conduct his research among the Dobe Ju/'hoansi because of studies he read about evolution and human behaviour, as well as his personal interest in hunting and gathering societies. He was hoping to gain some insight into human behaviour and how our hunting and gathering ancestors may have behaved. During his first research trip, Lee studied the food gathering or subsistence patterns of these hunter-gatherers of the Kalahari through participant observation, taking detailed notes of his interactions with the Dobe Ju/'hoansi. In addition, Lee collected a great deal of objective data, such as population information, to help him complete his research.

In the excerpt below, Lee (1993) explains the practice of "insulting the meat." To celebrate Christmas, he slaughtered and cooked a large ox to share with the community. Instead of appearing grateful for the gift, as is customary in Canada, the Ju/'hoan belittled the ox, saying it was only skin and bones, and was barely enough to feed anyone.

Eating Christmas in the Kalahari

We danced and ate that ox two days and two nights; we cooked and distributed fourteen potfuls of meat and no one went home hungry and no fights broke out. But the "joke" stayed in my mind. I had a growing feeling that something important had happened in my relationship with the Bushmen and that the clue lay in the meaning of the joke. Several days later, when most of the people had dispersed back to the bush camps, I raised the question with Hakekgose, a Tswana man who had grown up among the !Kung, married a !Kung girl, and who probably knew their culture better than any other non-Bushman.

"With us whites," I began, "Christmas is supposed to be the day of friendship and brotherly love. What I can't figure out is why the Bushmen went to such lengths to criticize and belittle the ox I had bought for the feast. The animal was perfectly good and their jokes and wisecracks practically ruined the holiday for me."

"So it really did bother you," said Hakekgose. "Well, that's the way they always talk. When I take my rifle and go hunting with them, if I miss, they laugh at me for the rest of the day. But even if I hit and bring one down, it's no better. To them, the kill is always too small or too old or too thin; and as we sit down on the kill site to cook and eat the liver, they keep grumbling, even with their mouths full of meat. They say things like, `Oh this is awful! What a worthless animal! Whatever made me think that this Tswana rascal could hunt!'"

"Is this the way outsiders are treated?" I asked. "No, it is their custom; they talk that way to each other too. Go and ask them."

/Gaugo had been one of the most enthusiastic in making me feel bad about the merit of the Christmas ox. I sought him out first.

"Why did you tell me the black ox was worthless, when you could see that it was loaded with fat and meat?"

"It is our way," he said smiling. "Say there is a Ju/'hoan who has been hunting. He must not come home and announce like a braggart, 'I have killed a big one in the bush!' He must first sit down in silence until I or someone else comes up to the fire and asks, 'What did you see today?' He replies quietly, 'Ah, I'm no good for hunting. I saw nothing at all [pause] just a little tiny one.' Then I smile to myself," /Gaugo continued, "because I know he has killed something big."

"In the morning we make up a party of four or five people to cut up and carry the meat back to the camp. When we arrive at the kill we examine it and cry out, 'You mean to say you have dragged us all the way out here in order to make us cart home your pile of bones? Oh, if I had known it was this thin I wouldn't have come.' Another one pipes up,

FIGURE 1-12 Lee among the Dobe Ju/'hoansi. What did Lee learn about the Dobe Ju/'hoansi from the practice of insulting the meat?

'People, to think I gave up a nice day in the shade for this. At home we may be hungry, but at least we have nice cool water to drink.' If the horns are big, someone says, 'Did you think that somehow you were going to boil down the horns for soup?'

"To all this you must respond in kind. 'I agree,' you say, 'this one is not worth the effort; let's just cook the liver for strength and leave the rest for the hyenas. It is not too late to hunt today, and even a duiker or a steenbok would be better than this mess.'"

"Then you set to work nevertheless, butcher the animal, carry the meat back to the camp, and everyone eats," /Gaugo concluded.

Things were beginning to make sense. Next, I went to Tomazho. He corroborated /Gaugo's story of the obligatory insults over a kill and added a few details of his own.

"But," I asked, "why insult a man after he has gone to all that trouble to track and kill an animal and when he is going to share the meat with you so that your family will have something to eat?"

"Arrogance," was his cryptic answer.

"Arrogance?"

"Yes, when a young man kills much meat he comes to think of himself as a chief or big man, and he thinks of the rest of us as his servants or inferiors. We can't accept this. We refuse one who boasts, for someday his pride will make him kill somebody. So we always speak of his meat as worthless. This way we cool his heart and make him gentle."

"But why didn't you tell me this before?" I asked Tomazho with some heat.

"Because you never asked me," said Tomazho, echoing the refrain that has come to haunt every field ethnographer. (p. 187–188)

The Dobe Ju/'hoansi have changed a great deal in the years since Lee's first research study. Increased globalization, commercialization, and resource pressure have changed their way of life and made it difficult for them to maintain their language and culture. To assist them, Lee and other researchers established the Kalahari People's Fund in 1973. The fund has helped the Ju/'hoansi to establish appropriate education in their own language, retain control of land and water rights, and preserve their oral history and language through digitization and Internet access. The initial focus on participant observation has shifted to a collaborative research and development approach, which maintains the dignity, rights, and culture of the Ju/'hoansi.

QUESTIONS

1. How does the behaviour of the Ju/'hoansi in this story show us their cultural values?
2. Why is it important for a cultural anthropologist to take detailed notes during an interview?
3. What did you learn about the process of participant observation from this excerpt?
4. What assumptions were made about communication in this case? Have you ever made assumptions about something you heard but may not have understood?

Schools of Thought in Cultural Anthropology

Cultural anthropologists develop theories to make sense of the evidence they have gathered. Sometimes they start with a theory and look for evidence, but most anthropologists start with an interest in a topic and, as they research, they find that they are part of a school of thought. Anthropologists do not always agree about the meanings of culture, but the debate stimulates new research and new theories, resulting in new ways of understanding ourselves.

Cultural Relativism

Franz Boas, a pioneer of modern anthropology in the early twentieth century, promoted the idea of cultural relativism, stating that an anthropologist cannot compare two cultures because each culture has its own internal rules that must be accepted. Everyone sees other cultures through the lens of their own culture. For example, if you were born and raised in the United States, you might view Canada differently than if you were born and raised in Canada. Boaz urged anthropologists to understand cultures on their own terms and avoid snap judgments about other practices. Cultural relativism was a response to cultural evolutionism (the theory that all cultures evolve from "savage" to "barbarian" to "civilized"), which assumed an **ethnocentric** view that nineteenth-century European culture was superior to all others.

Functional Theory

In anthropology, functional theory is the idea that every belief, action, or relationship in a culture functions to meet the needs of individuals. This theory stresses the importance of interdependence among all things within a social system to ensure its long-term survival. Meeting the needs of individuals makes the culture as a whole successful. Like Boas, Bronislaw Malinowski rejected cultural evolutionism, but unlike Boas, he felt that societies could be objectively measured and compared.

Malinowski saw functional theory at work in the Trobriand Islands during World War I. Every year, there was a ceremonial exchange of a necklace and an arm band between two men on each island in the South Pacific. The jewellery was not valuable, but the exchange was a highly anticipated event (New World Encyclopedia, 2008). Malinowski discovered that the jewellery travelled the entire circle of the islands in two different directions, linking distant individuals in what he called the "Kula Ring." This exchange of jewellery was not an economic trade, but it reinforced the status of the Kula traders and allowed them to trade food and everyday objects, and maintain peaceful relationships. What seemed to be a highly ceremonial exchange had very real economic, social, and political functions, serving the needs of the individuals and the whole society (Schwimmer, 2007).

Before You Read

Have you ever eaten seal? If you lived in the Arctic, do you think you would have a different response to this question? Why or why not?

ethnocentric: believing that one's own culture is superior to all others

Cultural Materialism

Cultural materialism was pioneered by Marvin Harris in the 1960s. Influenced by economists such as Karl Marx and Thomas Maltus, the theory states that materials or conditions within the environment (for example, climate, food supply, geography) influence how a culture develops, creating the ideas and ideology of a culture (see Figure 1-13). Cultural materialists believe that society develops on a trial-and-error basis. If something is not of value to a society's ability to produce or reproduce, then it will disappear from society altogether. Therefore, institutions, such as the law, government, and religion, must be beneficial to society or they will no longer exist. One criticism of cultural materialism is that it is too simplistic and ignores spiritual considerations or that humans are thinking beings.

The Infrastructure
A society's material resources — technology, population, available land, etc.

The Structure
A society's familial, political, economic, and social systems

The Superstructure
A society's ideas, values, symbols, and religion

FIGURE 1-13 According to Harris, culture develops in three stages.

FIGURE 1-14 The stay at home wife and mother was the cultural ideal for women in the 1950s.

Harris applied the theory to the Hindu belief in the sacred cow. Among Hindus in India, the cow is a sacred animal that cannot be eaten. Harris found that cows are used in India for important agricultural work, pulling plows and hauling heavy loads. This important function influences decisions about the best way to use a cow and contributes to the belief that cows are sacred and should not be eaten.

Maxine Margolis's research in North America in 1984 supports the theory that material conditions change before ideas change. She studied women's roles in postwar America and found that, even though the cultural ideal in the 1950s was for women to stay home, material changes (for example, inflation) sent women into the workforce. Women's material activities (in this case, going to work) drove the ideological changes of the feminist movement of the 1960s, not the other way around (Margolis, 1984).

> Identify some examples of cultural relativism and cultural materialism. How does each theory help you understand your own culture?

FIGURE 1-15 An equal rights protest in the United States. How would Margolis explain the differences between Figure 1-14 and Figure 1-15?

> **Connecting Anthropology to Psychology**
>
> Much in the way feminist anthropologists examine gender relationships in different cultures, feminine psychologists examine female identity and issues faced by women. The field also highlights gender bias in traditional psychological theories and counters this bias with alternative theories.

Feminist Anthropology

By the 1970s, feminist anthropologists were re-examining anthropology to ensure that female voices were heard and included in research. They also compared cultures to see how many were dominated by men, how many were dominated by women, and how many were egalitarian. Ernestine Friedl, an American feminist anthropologist, concluded that in forager societies, the amount of freedom women had was strongly tied to their contributions to the food supply. Men and women are relatively equal in societies where women gather more of the food, but in societies where men have more control over the food resources (for example, in societies where hunting is the major food-gathering activity), men are more dominant and women have less control over their lives and choices (Friedl, 1978). Figure 1-16 demonstrates the division of labour by gender in the world.

WORLDWIDE PATTERNS IN THE DIVISION OF LABOUR BY GENDER					
Type of Activity	Males Almost Always	Males Usually	Either Gender or Both	Females Usually	Females Almost Always
Primary subsistence activities	Hunt and trap animals	Fish Herd large animals Collect wild honey Clear land and prepare soil for planting	Collect shellfish Care for small animals Plant crops Tend crops Harvest crops Milk animals	Gather wild plants	
Secondary subsistence and household activities		Butcher animals	Preserve meat and fish	Care for children Cook Prepare food and drinks Launder Fetch water Collect fuel	Care for infants

Other		Lumber
		Mine and quarry
		Make
		  boats
		  musical instruments
		  bone, horn, and shell objects
		Engage in combat
			Build houses
			Make nets and rope
			Exercise political leadership
				Prepare skins
				Make
				  leather products
				  baskets
				  mats
				  clothing
				  pottery
					Spin yarn	

↑ **FIGURE 1-16** Worldwide patterns in the division of labour by gender. What does this chart tell you about gender roles?

culturally constructed: created or shaped by a culture

Today, feminist anthropologists continue to look at how cultures determine gender roles, try to debunk gender myths, and show how our ideas about gender are **culturally constructed**, that is, created by the culture, not biology. They also look at how gender, race, class, ethnicity, and sexual orientation are constructed in various societies and the effect of those ideas on marginalized people (Lavenda and Schultz, 2010).

Postmodernism

Postmodernism is a theory that influences a number of disciplines, including anthropology. It is the belief that it is impossible to have any "true" knowledge about the world. Postmodernism rejects the idea of objective truth. What we "know" about the world is our own construction, created by society. Postmodernists try to deconstruct, or break down, what a society believes to be true. Postmodernists believe that anthropologists can't study their subjects in a detached or objective way, like a chemist studying a chemical reaction, because of the personal relationships that develop between anthropologist and informants during participant observation. Postmodernists practise reflexivity, which you learned about on page 24.

Since the 1980s, postmodern anthropologists have more and more been doing research in their own cultural settings. Some of the recent research has focused on understanding the immigrant experience in urban Canada (for example, defining of Italian cultural spaces in Toronto).

Another example of postmodernist anthropology is the research done by Canadian anthropologist and director Sam Dunn on the **subculture** of heavy metal music and heavy metal fans (sometimes called *headbangers* or *metalheads*). In his two films, *Metal: A Headbanger's Journey* (2006) and *Global Metal* (2008), he explains how his passion for heavy metal music led him to conduct his research at home and around the world. Dunn's work is an example of multisited fieldwork (fieldwork conducted in more than one location), studying a culture that crosses national and ethnic boundaries. Dunn is an insider in the headbanger culture and shows reflexivity in his documentary, frequently discussing how his own bias as a metal fan is affecting his research.

> **VOICES**
>
> Mass media communications technologies also enable people to participate in communities of others with whom they share neither geographical proximity nor a common history but an access to signs, symbols, images, narratives, and other resources with which they can convey mutual solidarity...
> — Rosemary E. Coombe

subculture: a small group within a larger group who shares a common system of values, beliefs, attitudes, behaviours, and lifestyle distinct from those of the larger group

FIGURE 1 17 Heavy metal fans, part of a worldwide community who absorb the music and transform it into a new form of cultural expression (Dunn, 2008). Do you think it is possible for a researcher who is a member of the culture he or she is studying to conduct reliable research?

REFLECT AND RESPOND

1. Women in Canada make up half of the population, yet they make up less than 20 percent of the elected government. How would a feminist and a functionalist differ in their explanations of this statistic?
2. What is the essential difference between the approach of cultural materialists and postmodernists?
3. Study the chart of division of labour in world cultures by gender (see Figure 1-16). How would a cultural materialist interpret the information differently from a feminist anthropologist?
4. If you were an anthropologist studying ethnicity, class, or gender in your community, how would you conduct your research?

Linguistic Anthropology

Linguistic anthropologists study human languages and how language affects and expresses culture. There are three areas of linguistic anthropology: historical linguistics, structural linguistics, and sociolinguistics. Some of the research in each of the three areas will be examined below.

Historical Linguistics

Historical linguistic anthropologists compare the similarities and differences of language structures so they can understand how languages are related and how people migrated in the past. This is an important field for cultures with no written language. One of Canada's early anthropologists, Edward Sapir, studied the Aboriginal peoples of Canada and recorded their languages, often with the last living speaker. Through analysis and historical reconstruction, he was able to trace the languages of Canada's Aboriginal populations and set the foundation for the understanding of the five major culture areas of Canada. Much of Sapir's work in this field has been used by Canada's Aboriginal groups to create written forms of their languages as part of their cultural revival and survival.

Using Linguistics

Widely dispersed throughout Europe, the Middle East, and North America, there are an estimated 4 million to 14 million Roma in the world. It is impossible to estimate the total population with accuracy, since many governments do not record Roma in their census figures and many Roma conceal their ethnic origin. Historically, the Romani people were highly mobile and nomadic, moving from place to place, as they were expelled from cities and countries. To study the history of the Romani people, scholars have looked to linguistics to track their migration. Recent studies have traced their origins to India. The Roma migrated from India to Europe in the eleventh century (Matras, 2002).

Structural Linguistics

Noam Chomsky is known as the father of modern structural linguistics, or the study of how sounds are put together to make meaning. He is best known for developing the theory of universal grammar: that all human children are born with internal, universal rules for grammar and that they apply these rules as they learn their mother tongue.

According to Chomsky, the reason that children so easily master language is that they have innate knowledge of certain principles that guide them. In other words, Chomsky's theory is that learning language is made possible by a predisposition that our brains have for the structures of language. However, evolutionary biologists disagree, saying that language is not an instinct encoded in the brain, but is a learned skill. For Chomsky's theory to be true, all the languages must share some structural characteristics. In fact, linguists have shown that the 5000 plus languages of the world do share rules and principles.

> **Before You Read**
> How does the slang of your peers differ from that of your parents? What does this tell you about the culture and values of each generation?

↑ **FIGURE 1-18** Road sign in Squamish and English in British Columbia. How do you think road signs like this one would help the cultural revival or survival of the Squamish people?

We often judge people on whether or not they use proper grammar, but if two people are speaking the same dialect (a regional speech pattern) and understand each other, then they are using linguistically good grammar. Take the following example:

Merle: I ain't got no shoes.

Pearl: I ain't got none either.

The two speakers understand each other perfectly, even though the sentences don't meet our expectations of standard English. In fact, the dialect they are speaking has its own internal grammar rules, which the speakers understand intuitively (Peoples and Bailey, 2003).

> ❓ Why would a linguistic anthropologist want to research texting in the twenty-first century? What are some possible research questions a linguistic anthropologist might ask teens today?

FIGURE 1-19 Does this baby already know grammar?

Sociolinguistics

Sociolinguistics is the study of how people use language within their culture to express status and context. For example, you would probably use language differently when talking to a teacher in a classroom than with your friends on the weekend.

A study by Roger Brown and Marguerite Ford from 1964 showed that how people address each other can show the relationship between them. Peers tend to address each other by their first names, while people who use a title and last name to address each other often have a business relationship. If one person uses a title and last name while the other uses a first name, there is a difference in status (for example, students and teachers). In some cases, generally among boys and men, people address each other by their last names with no title, particularly in a sports context. Some anthropologists suggest that this is a middle ground, indicating respect but not intimacy.

Sociolinguists study not only spoken language, but also body language in different cultural contexts. For example, in many First Nations cultures, it is rude for students to look a teacher in the eye. In Japan, showing your teeth is a sign of social dominance and is considered very rude. North Americans who tend to smile openly are often seen as aggressive or bullying in Japan. Many large corporations employ linguistic anthropologists to train their employees to work effectively in other cultures so that they are not misunderstood.

REFLECT AND RESPOND

1. What kinds of questions do linguistic anthropologists ask in their research? Give an example for each area of linguistic anthropology.
2. What are some challenges of studying linguistic anthropology?
3. How does language reflect status or culture in Canadian society? List examples.
4. Have you noticed miscommunication between speakers of different languages or from different cultures? Give some examples.

Archaeology

Archaeology is the cultural anthropology of the past. Archaeologists excavate physical remains of past cultures to understand and reconstruct them. Some archaeologists study cultures with no written record (prehistory) or study sites that have a recorded history to supplement their understanding of the culture. Often written histories are incomplete or contain only some aspects of society. Archaeologists work with historians and physical and cultural anthropologists to make sense of the past.

IN THE FIELD

Archaeological Services Inc.

Have you ever wondered about what kind of jobs archaeologists and anthropologists have? We usually hear about them working in universities and colleges, but not all archaeologists and anthropologists work in academic institutions. Archaeological Services Inc. (ASI) is a Canadian-owned archaeological consulting firm that works with the public and private sectors. The ASI team excavates archaeological sites and assesses their heritage value, reviews heritage planning studies, and documents archaeological features of development sites.

Ontario's cultural history dates back about 11 000 years. Archaeological sites can be found throughout the province. Some sites we know about, like the First Parliament site in downtown Toronto. Others are found accidently, sometimes when buildings are being built or torn down.

In one project, ASI excavated along the shoreline of the Niagara River in Fort Erie. Fort Erie was upgrading the town's infrastructure and redeveloping land. The municipality brought in ASI to minimize impact of their work on the archaeological sites throughout the town. ASI drilled through roads and sidewalks to study the soil and found evidence of a large settlement that existed 4000 years before Europeans arrived in North America. The archaeologists from ASI also found the Snake Hill Cemetery, a previously unknown American military cemetery from 1814. They were able to identify and exhume 28 bodies, which were then repatriated to the United States.

The staff at ASI have backgrounds in anthropology, archaeology, and geography. They interpret data using state-of-the-art techniques, including 3-D imaging to bring to life an Iroquoian village, and chemical analysis of animal and human bone samples to determine dietary trends.

FIGURE 1-20 Archaeologists from Archaeological Services Inc. working at the Snake Hill Cemetery

QUESTIONS

1. What skills do you think are important for working at Archaeological Services Inc.?
2. What are some positives of working in this field?

Prehistoric Archaeology

For civilizations with no written record, archaeology is the only way to find out how people lived hundreds or thousands of years ago.

One study looked at the spread of tobacco in the Americas. Archaeologists sifted through piles of dirt in many sites across North America for tiny tobacco seeds. They traced the spread of tobacco from Central America up the Mississippi River to Canada to about 800 CE. Tobacco did not spread to the Arctic and West Coast until the nineteenth and twentieth centuries (Collishaw, 2009). By understanding the movement of tobacco, archaeologists can understand ancient trade routes, contact between peoples, and agricultural and cultural practices of the Aboriginal peoples of North America before European contact.

Archaeology and History

Archaeology can also supplement an existing historic record by telling us about the daily life of people who may not be included in the written history. Archaeology is the recovery, documentation, and analysis of objects that remain to shed light on human prehistory, behaviour, and cultural evolution.

FIGURE 1-21 One of the best known archaeological sites in Canada is L'Anse aux Meadows. Dated to 1000 CE, it is the remains of the first European settlement in North America.

In an unusual archaeological study, William Rathje of the University of Arizona looked at modern garbage to find out if people really do what they say they do. Starting in 1973, Rathje's team examined people's garbage and excavated landfills. Their conclusions are surprising. Although people have been concerned about the amount of plastic in landfills, plastic bags, disposable diapers, and styrofoam comprise only about 3 percent of the volume, while paper products make up 40 percent. During meat shortages, consumption went up, rather than down. They also found that people consumed products considered to be negative, like alcohol and junk food, in much greater quantities than they said they did. Rathje concluded that what people say they do and what they actually do are different, that these differences are predictable, and that often people will do the exact opposite of what they say.

IN FOCUS

Kwaday Dän Ts'inchi

In 1999, three teachers were hunting bighorn sheep in Tatshenshini-Alsek Park, British Columbia, when they came across what turned out to be the mummified remains of an ancient man, preserved in a glacier. Archaeologists and the Champagne and Aishihik First Nations (CAFN) went to the site and excavated the remains for further study. First Nations people in Canada have specific beliefs about the handling of ancient human remains, and the handling of this find demonstrates how archaeologists, the British Columbia government, and First Nations worked together to ensure that cultural concerns were respected while recognizing the significant scientific information that could be discovered (Government of British Columbia, 2000). Historically, archaeologists did not always respect First Nations beliefs and values or involve them in their discoveries. Sometimes this resulted in protests and legal battles and led to repatriation policies, where artifacts and remains once part of museum collections were returned.

The CAFN elders named the ancient man *Kwaday Dän Ts'inchi*, which means "long-ago person found." Archaeologists were allowed to study the human remains for one year. No photos could be taken, and the body was kept in a locked freezer. After one year, his remains were cremated and scattered across the glacier where he was found. Several artifacts had been found with Kwaday Dän Ts'inchi, including a woven cedar hat, a walking stick, a spear thrower, an iron-blade knife, and a robe made of gopher and squirrel skins. One artifact, a leather bag, was left unopened because it was likely a sacred medicine bag (Grambo, 2006).

In 2008, researchers gathered to discuss their results. Kwaday Dän Ts'inshi was a hunter who lived about 200 to 300 years ago. From the contents of his stomach, researchers believe he was travelling. Through mitochondrial DNA testing, researchers revealed that Kwaday Dän Ts'inshi was related to 17 living people from coastal and interior First Nation groups, 15 of which are from the wolf clan. These DNA findings support the oral history of the local First Nations, confirming both the important ties between the coastal and inland peoples and the traditional clan associations. Lawrence Joe, the heritage director of the CAFN stated, "We want to be able to use the science to confirm our cultural knowledge, our beliefs, and our family relationships" (CBC, 2008). By working together with First Nations cultures, archaeologists and anthropologists have been able to learn from the past and apply that knowledge to the present.

FIGURE 1-22
The glacier in Tatshenshini-Alsek Park, British Columbia where Kwaday Dän Ts'inshi was found.

QUESTIONS

1. How can archaeology contribute to the understanding of Canada's First Nations peoples, both past and present?
2. Why is it important for archaeologists to work with groups such as the Champagne and Aishihik First Nations?

REFLECT AND RESPOND

1. What techniques do archaeologists use to learn about past or current cultures?
2. What personal qualities and skills do you think an archaeologist should have?
3. What are some ethical questions archaeologists face in their work?

Human Evolution and Defining Humans

Section 1.2

Where do we come from? How did we evolve? What makes humans unique? Physical anthropologists seek to answer these questions, constructing theories of humanity's origin, migration, and behaviour in the distant past to understand our present behaviour and characteristics more clearly. In this section, you will learn about the different fields of anthropology, how humans have evolved, and the differences and similarities of human populations.

Before You Read
What stories have you learned about where we come from? What questions do you have about them?

Physical Anthropology

Physical anthropologists want to know where humans as a species come from, how our bodies evolved to their present form, and what makes humans unique. The mind map below (Figure 1-23) explains how researchers attempt to answer these questions.

FIGURE 1-23 The different fields of physical anthropology. Subtopics include the development of evolutionary theory, the biological basis for human variation, the evolutionary influences, and human adaptability.

Physical Anthropology

- **Paleoanthropology**
  Paleoanthropologists study bone and stone remains of our ancient ancestors from millions of years ago.
- **Primatology**
  Primatologists study primates.
- **Human Variation**
  The study of the physical differences and similarities of existing human populations.

Look carefully at the following photos (Figures 1-24 and 1-25). What kind of evidence is each anthropologist examining? What kind of questions might they be asking about the evidence? What conclusions do you think they can come to from the evidence shown?

↑ FIGURE 1-24 Donald Johanson and "Lucy"

↑ FIGURE 1-25 Jane Goodall observing chimpanzees

Paleoanthropology

Before You Read
Have you ever seen a fossil? What do you think we can learn from these fossils?

Paleoanthropology is often called the "bones and stones" branch of physical anthropology. It is the study of human ancestors based on evidence from the distant evolutionary past. These human-like ancestors together with living humans are called **hominins**. Much of the evidence is in the form of preserved remains or impressions of biological matter, or **fossils**. That evidence includes skeletal remains, ancient tools, animal bones, and the remains of vegetable matter. Paleoanthropologists can learn much about our hominin ancestors by looking at very small, sometimes microscopic, details from the distant past.

hominin: a human or human ancestor

fossil: preserved remains of biological matter

What Can Anthropologists Learn from Ancient Bones?

In 1974, paleoanthropologist Donald Johanson found a skeleton in Ethiopia that was 40 percent complete. Johanson nicknamed the skeleton "Lucy," because the Beatles' song "Lucy in the Sky with Diamonds" was playing on the radio when his team made the discovery. Lucy is part of the new species *Australopithecus afarensis*, a member of the human family, or hominin, that walked the earth 3.2 million years ago. Lucy has provided anthropologists with a huge wealth of knowledge. Figure 1-26 demonstrates what anthropologists learned about Lucy from her skeletal remains.

In 2006, a discovery of another *Australopithecus afarensis* was found in Ethiopia's Afar triangle. This fossil of a three-year-old female was named Selam, and is the most complete fossil of a juvenile *Australopithecus* found to date. The find included most of the skull, both shoulders, part of the vertebral column, parts of both knees and legs, parts of the right arm, and several ribs. Selam will help researchers understand how humans came to move on two feet. Her lower body was adapted for walking upright, but her shoulder blades suggest the possibility that she was also able to climb and swing through trees. Selam also has the earliest confirmation of a hyoid bone (a bone found in the larynx that supports the muscles in the throat and tongue), important to the research into the origins of human speech.

FIGURE 1-26 Lucy's skeletal remains

Femur and pelvis: Lucy's thigh has an inward slant, a strong indication that she walked upright. The length of her femur suggests that she was about 1 metre tall, and the wear on her pelvis shows that she weighed about 27 kilograms.

❓ What are some of the things anthropologists can learn from ancient bones? How can Lucy and Selam help paleoanthropologists understand our past?

Teeth: Lucy's third molars or wisdom teeth had already erupted and showed signs of wear, indicating that she was an adult when she died. The hole where her canine tooth had been is much smaller than other specimens, one of many clues indicating that she was female.

Skull fragment: From the curve of the five skull fragments, anthropologists can tell that Lucy's brain was about 380 cm^3, the same as the brain of a modern chimpanzee and significantly smaller than that of a modern human. (Edgar, 2007)

Where Do Humans Come From?

Charles Darwin (1809–1882), was a naturalist, scientist, and author who established the concept of natural selection to explain how animals and plants evolved. In 1831, he spent four years on the HMS *Beagle* where he made observations on the wildlife and fossils he collected, mostly from the Galapagos Islands. Darwin proposed that species were forced to evolve or they would become extinct. Those that were able to adapt lived and passed down the characteristics that allowed them to survive to their offspring. It took Darwin 20 years to develop and publish his theory. He published *On the Origin of Species* in 1859, outlining the theory of natural selection, and *The Descent of Man* in 1871, applying his theory to humans. During his lifetime, the public began to accept evolution as fact.

Darwin suggested that humans first evolved in Africa. Many of his contemporaries disagreed and pointed to Asia as the place where humans first evolved. In 1924, the anatomist Raymond Dart was given a skull found by workers at a quarry at Taung, South Africa. He determined the skull to be more human than ape and that its owner walked upright but had a small brain. He named it *Australopithecus africanus* ("southern ape from Africa") and declared it to be an early form of human. He was the first person to provide evidence of the African origin of humanity (Lewin, 1998).

Louis and Mary Leakey found further proof of an African origin in 1959 when they found an australopithecine skull in Olduvai Gorge, Kenya. Using **radiometric dating** for the first time, they determined the skull to be 1.75 million years old. Mary Leakey nicknamed the fossil "Dear Boy." Soon after, the Leakeys found many more fossils of other hominins, including *Homo habilis*. Together with their son, Richard, who also discovered an almost complete *Homo erectus* skeleton at Lake Turkana, they proved humanity's African origin, helped to start the school of primatology, and generated much interest and publicity for the field of human origins.

radiometric dating: a process that is used to determine the age of an object, based on measuring the amount of radioactive material it has

FIGURE 1-27 Louis and Mary Leakey carefully excavating a site in Africa

Open for Debate
Some people do not recognize the theory of evolution since it does not align with their religious views. Some believe in intelligent design, the belief that nature is too complex to have developed through natural selection, so it must have had some form of intelligent being directing its development (Laidlaw, 2007).

? Why is finding fossil evidence important in paleoanthropology? What do you think are some of the challenges that paleoanthropologists face? What might be some of the rewards?

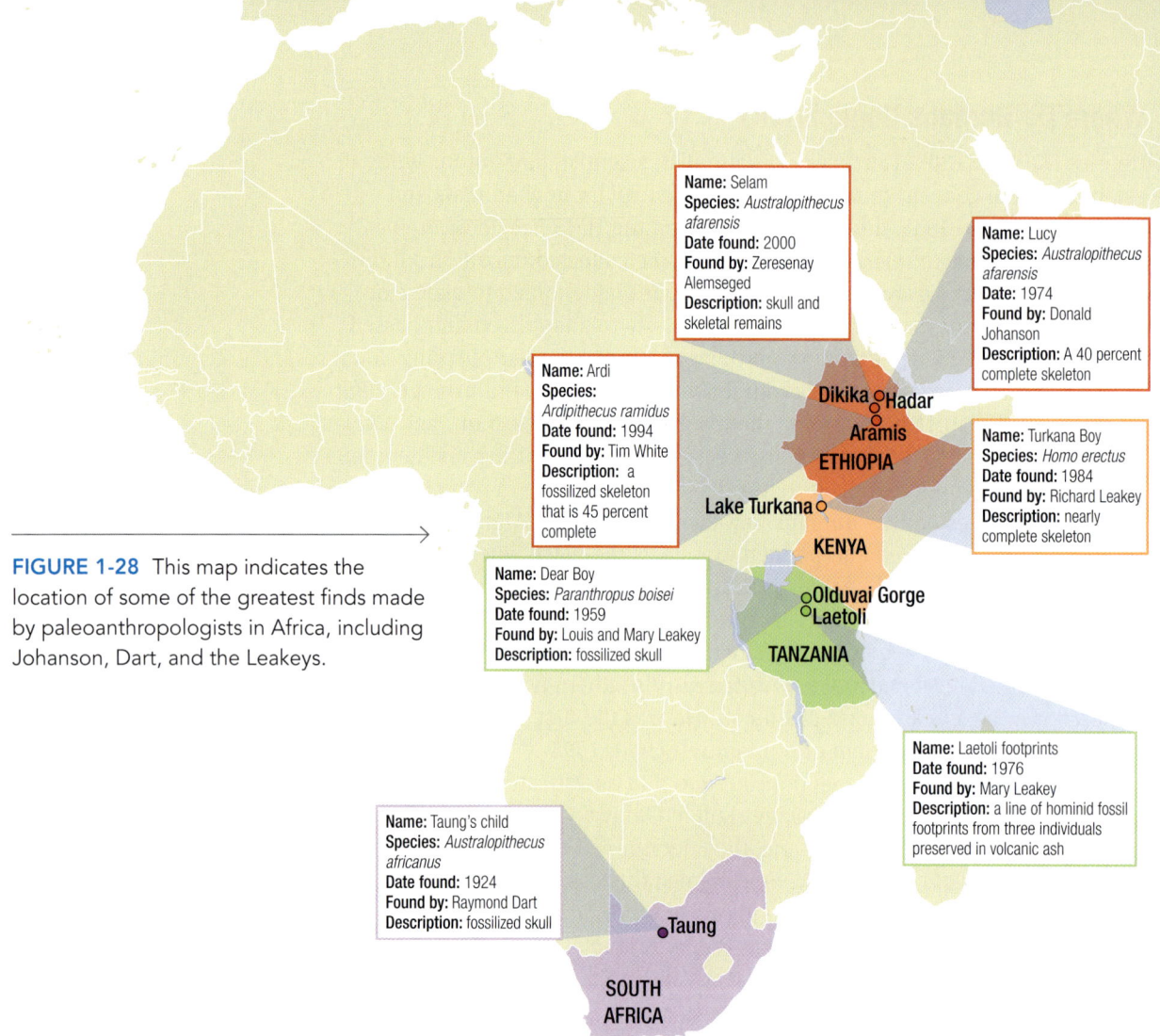

FIGURE 1-28 This map indicates the location of some of the greatest finds made by paleoanthropologists in Africa, including Johanson, Dart, and the Leakeys.

bipedalism: the trait of habitually walking on two legs

VOICES

The fundamental distinction between us and our closest relatives is not our language, not our culture, not our technology; it is that we stand upright, with our lower limbs for support and locomotion and our upper limbs free from those functions.

Richard E. Leakey, paleontologist

When Did Humans Walk Upright?

One of the major differences between humans and other primates is that humans walk habitually on two legs. This adaptation is called **bipedalism**. When anthropologists find a fossil, they look for traits that mark bipedalism, such as an S-shaped spine; a wide, flat pelvis; a slanting thigh bone; a double-arched foot; and a big toe in line with the heel. When they find these traits, they can say that the fossil belonged to a hominin, one of our ancient relatives.

One of the most important finds in paleoanthropology is Mary Leakey's discovery of the Laetoli footprints. Preserved in a layer of volcanic ash, there are three sets of footprints of early hominins. These footprints are clearly bipedal, having a strong heel strike, distinct arch, and big toe in line with the heel. These footprints indicate that bipedalism began at least 3.6 million years ago, well before the development of a larger brain in hominins.

> What are some of the things that make humans different from other primates? How do anthropologists determine whether a fossil is a hominin?

IN FOCUS

Ardipithecus Ramidus

The 2009 discovery of the ancient hominin *Ardipithecus ramidus* has pushed bipedalism back to at least 4.4 million years ago, even further back than the Laetoli footprints. "Ardi" has added more information to the debate about when human ancestors stopped living in the trees. She was bipedal but, unlike the australopithecines, had opposable big toes that allowed her to move in the trees. From her hands, paleoanthropologists can tell that she was not a knuckle walker, as our closest living relatives, the chimpanzees and gorillas, are today. The discovery of Ardi forces anthropologists to reconsider previous theories of human evolution and pushes the common ancestor between humans and apes back to seven million years ago.

QUESTIONS

1. Why is the discovery of *Ardipithecus ramidus* important to anthropologists?
2. What do Ardi's physical features tell us about her?

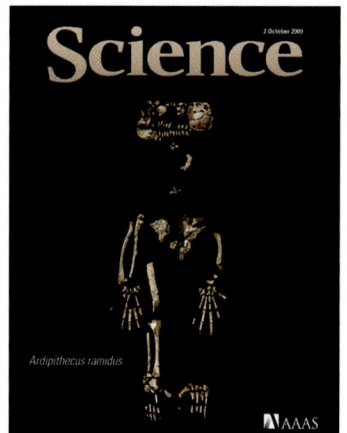

FIGURE 1-29 *Ardipithecus ramidus*. The bones were so fragile that it took scientists 15 years to carefully excavate and analyze them.

Human Evolution—A Timeline

Anthropologists frequently debate how we are related to our hominin ancestors, but there is general agreement on when the species lived and what they looked like.

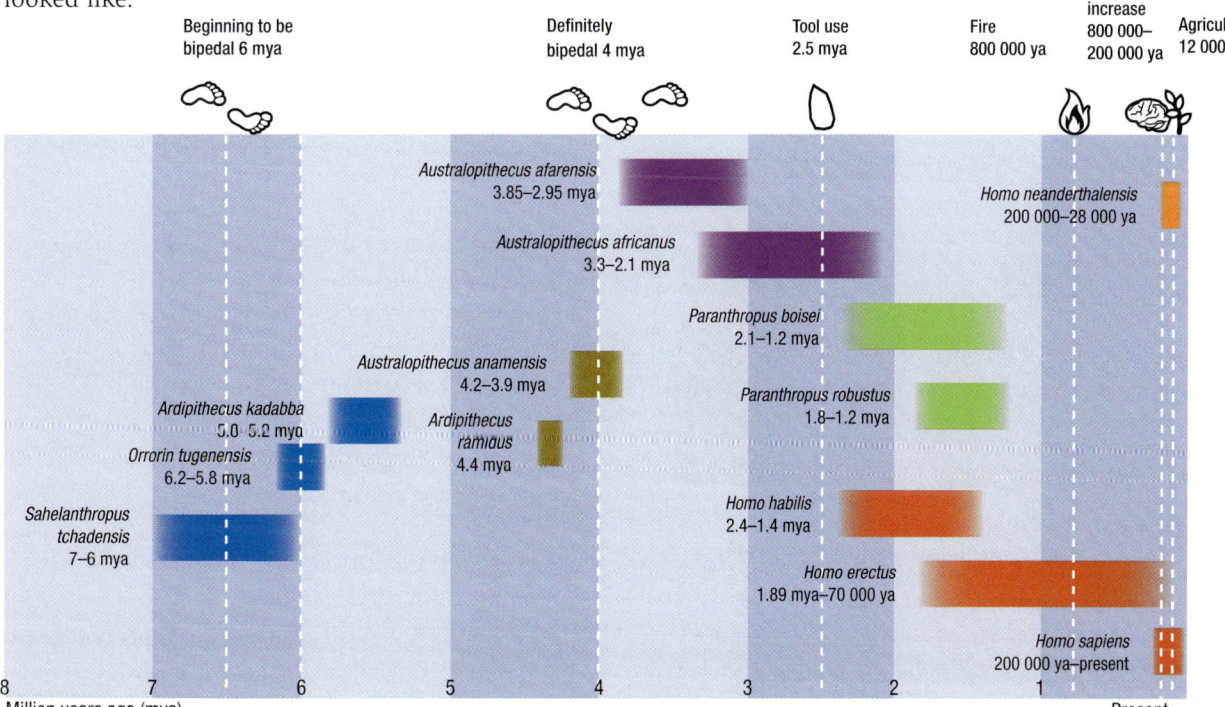

FIGURE 1-30 This timeline demonstrates when our hominin ancestors lived

Chapter 1 • What Is Anthropology? **41**

IN FOCUS: Who Were the Neanderthals?

Since the discovery of the first Neanderthal skull in the Neander Valley in Germany in 1856, anthropologists have been debating just who the Neanderthals were and what their place is in the story of human evolution. Were they less intelligent beings who lost out to *Homo sapiens*, or were they intelligent, well-adapted precursors to modern humans? Are they our direct ancestors, or did they become extinct? Some suggest that they could have been hunted by other premodern humans, while others suggest that they may have interbred with modern humans. A DNA study in the spring of 2010 found that humans and Neanderthals did indeed interbreed and that all populations except Africans have some Neanderthal genes. As more research is done, our picture of Neanderthals continues to change.

One of the most interesting finds in paleoanthropology is the discovery of a Neanderthal burial site at Shanidar Cave in Iraq. A large amount of pollen was found around a man's body from 60 000 years ago, suggesting a deliberate burial with the placing of flowers as a funeral rite. Previously, flowers in burial had been associated only with Cro-Magnons, an early group of *Homo sapiens* who lived 40 000 years ago. Pollen analysis indicates what kind of flowers they were, but we don't know for sure if the flowers on the grave were placed deliberately or if the pollen ended up there accidentally.

FIGURE 1-31 A Neanderthal female reconstruction based on both fossil anatomy and DNA analysis

What anthropologists know for sure is that:

- Neanderthals were living all over Europe, the Middle East, and parts of Asia from 150 000 to 30 000 years ago, at the end of the last ice age.
- Their bodies were well adapted to the icy environment; they were shorter, heavier, and more muscular than modern humans and used their bodies in a more rigorous way.
- Their brains are larger than modern humans, measuring about 1450 cm^3, about 100 cm^3 larger than modern humans.
- Their skulls are shaped differently than those of modern humans, with a protruding nose, heavy brow ridges, large teeth, and a little chin.
- They made and used complex stone and bone tools, and they lived in caves. (Lewin, 1998).

"Feel like going out clubbing later?"

FIGURE 1-32 The term *Neanderthal* is used to describe someone or something as outdated, unintelligent, or uncivilized. New finds in paleoanthropology continue to change our understanding of who these hominins really were.

QUESTIONS

1. How are Neanderthals different from modern humans? How are they the same?
2. How do the findings made by scientists about the Neanderthals relate to various theories of human evolution?

What Can Anthropologists Learn from Ancient Stones?

Stone tools help paleoanthropologists accurately date a site and discover more about the hominins who used them. The oldest stone tools are large cobbles or *choppers*, which are about 2.5 million years old. Anthropologists use a number of methods to find out how these tools were used and what they were used for.

Oldowan stone tool
2.5–2 million years old

Acheulian stone tool
1.5–200 000 years old

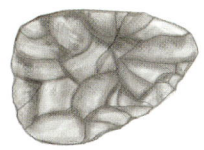
Mousterian stone tool
200 000–35 000 years old

FIGURE 1-33 Compare the three types of stone tools shown here. What differences do you notice? What conclusions can you draw about the hominins who made and used these tools?

Some paleoanthropologists are specialists in making stone tools as our ancestors might have done millions of years ago. Experiments have shown that with the oldest stone tools, the most effective part is the small flake leftover from making the large core. These specialists have discovered that the flakes are razor sharp and can be used to butcher an animal or whittle wood into sharp sticks. The chopper can also be used to cut branches or cut tough animal joints (Ember and Ember, 1999).

While experimentation can tell anthropologists what a tool *could* be used for, microscopic analysis of a tool can indicate what it was actually used for. The polish on a tool can indicate whether it was used to cut meat, wood, or plants. Another way to learn about tool use is by looking at ancient animal bones. Microscopic analysis of cut marks on animal bones can indicate whether a hominin tool was used to make the marks or whether they were caused by an animal or through erosion. It is clear that hominins at least 2.5 million years ago were cutting meat from animal bones.

REFLECT AND RESPOND

1. What are the significant contributions of the following anthropologists to the understanding of human origins:
   a) The Leakey family
   b) Raymond Dart
   c) Donald Johanson
2. What can anthropologists learn from ancient stone tools? Name three things.
3. What is bipedalism, and why is it important when studying human origins?
4. What do you think would be challenging about becoming a paleoanthropologist? What might be some of the rewards?
5. Think about a product or technology that you use everyday. How do you think an anthropologist in the future might interpret it? What do you think it might say about your culture?

SOCIAL SCIENCE IN POPULAR CULTURE

Forensic Anthropology

Forensic anthropologists help legal agencies to identify human remains after mass disasters, wars, homicides, suicides, or accidental deaths. With the popularity of shows such as *CSI* and *Bones*, more and more adolescents are thinking about a career in forensic anthropology. On television, forensic anthropologists work closely with law enforcement agencies to solve murders. Not only do they process crime scenes, but they carry out raids and interrogate and arrest suspects. These television anthropologists have access to state-of-the-art technology and are able to obtain evidence quickly, with a high degree of accuracy.

In reality, forensic anthropology is not usually as exciting or dramatic as it is portrayed on television. Forensic anthropologists are usually paleoanthropologists or archaeologists who have spent years studying human bones and fossils. Police and others will ask them to examine bones to help them solve a case. In Canada, forensic anthropology is often a part-time job. To keep impartial about the evidence they collect, forensic anthropologists are not usually involved in detective work, and it can take weeks and sometimes months to process evidence.

Most opportunities for Canadian forensic anthropologists involve investigating former war zones and genocides. Forensic anthropologists working for Physicians for Human Rights went to Rwanda after the 1994 genocide to help exhume and identify bodies thought to have been part of a single massacre. To their horror, they discovered that more than half of the bodies were infants and children and that they had been killed by a blow to the head with a machete (Thomas, 2003). While it can be rewarding to bring war criminals to justice, or to identify and return bodies to family members so that they can grieve, it can be very traumatic as well. Dean Bamber, an Edmonton anthropology graduate student who went to help with the excavations, says he will never forget seeing the bodies of young mothers with newborn infants tucked in pouches on their backs. "The worst of all was a little kid I found, maybe four years old, who was wearing a T-shirt from Queen's University," he says. "That was too much" (Sheremata, 1996).

↑ **FIGURE 1-34** Dr. Temperance Brennan, the main character of the television show *Bones*, is inspired by real-life forensic anthropologist and novelist Kathy Reichs.

Forensic anthropologists who go to war-torn countries also need a good understanding of cultural anthropology. They need to be aware of the cultural norms surrounding death. For example, bodies in Canada are usually buried face up in a coffin, but in Muslim countries it is usual to cover the bodies with a sheet and lie them on their side in the direction of Mecca, the holiest site in Islam. Knowing what normal practice in a culture is can help people to determine whether or not a death is suspicious. Cultural anthropology skills are also useful to those who interview family members about the deceased and help them to be sensitive to the cultural and religious practices of the area. Knowing whether bodies should be cremated or buried, whether religious ceremonies should be conducted, and which family members or government officials should be present are critical in restoring peace to grieving families (Thomas, 2003).

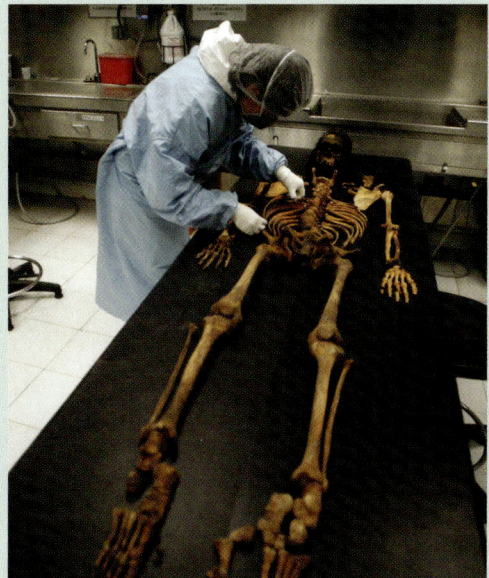

FIGURE 1-35 A forensic anthropologist examining human remains. What are the rewards and challenges of a career in forensic anthropology? How does forensic anthropology use anthropology concepts?

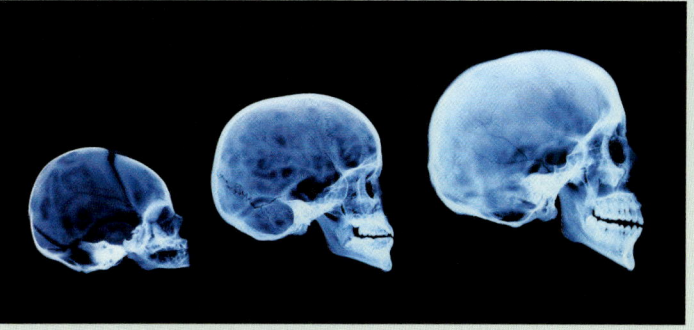

FIGURE 1-36 What differences do you notice between these three human skulls?

In Argentina, forensic investigations have been ongoing since 1984, trying to locate the thousands of people murdered by the ruthless military regime that operated from 1976 to 1983. During the regime, people would disappear suddenly and never return. Families had no idea where their missing loved ones were. A young Argentinean woman, Ivana Wolff, now training to be a forensic anthropologist states her motivation simply: "I help to identify the dead to get them back to their families. I work from the worst thing that can happen—people that are already dead—to bring joy to the living" (Myers, 2010).

Regardless of where forensic anthropologists work or whether they are investigating a single murder or a mass grave, the following 11 questions from the Canadian Society of Forensic Sciences (2007) are ones that they all use to uncover the identity of the deceased:

1. Is it bone?
2. Is it animal or human bone?
3. How many individuals are represented?
4. How long has the person been dead?
5. What is the sex of the individual?
6. What was his or her age at death?
7. What is her or his ancestry (ethnic origin)?
8. How tall is he or she?
9. Is there evidence of trauma that may assist in determining the exact cause of death (for example, homicide, suicide, accidental, natural, unknown)?
10. Are there any distinguishing features, such as evidence of medical devices, bone anomalies, bone disease, old fractures, fingerprints, or amputations?
11. What is the identity of the deceased?

QUESTIONS

1. How is forensic anthropology similar to other types of anthropology? How is it different?
2. How do the findings of forensic anthropology support or enhance the work of physical and cultural anthropologists?

Primatology

> **Before You Read**
>
> Make a Venn diagram to compare humans and animals. How are they similar and different? Add to this organizer as you read about primatology.

Humans and other primates share many characteristic features, such as grasping hands, forward-facing eyes, and a relatively larger brain. Primatologists study the anatomy and behaviours of living primates. They are not always anthropologists. They may be trained in biology or zoology, but their research is always relevant to anthropology, because they are investigating what makes us similar to and different from other primates. If we know more about our primate cousins, we can learn more about ourselves.

How Do Primatologists Study Primates?

Primatologists observe primates both in their natural habitats and in the laboratory. Pioneering work in observing primates in the field was done by Jane Goodall, Dian Fossey, and Biruté Galdikas. All were encouraged by paleoanthropologist Louis Leakey in the 1960s and 1970s. He reasoned that "if we found behaviour patterns similar or the same in our closest living relatives, the great apes, and humans today, then maybe those behaviours were present in the ape-like, human-like ancestor some seven million years ago. And therefore, perhaps we had brought those characteristics with us from that ancient, ancient past" (Goodall, 2007). Goodall went to Tanzania to observe chimpanzees, Fossey to Rwanda to observe gorillas, and Galdikas to Borneo to observe orangutans. They all lived in damp, solitary, and difficult conditions and had to wait patiently for months before they could get close enough to the animals to understand their social behaviour. Each primatologist had to learn to imitate the animals' calls and gestures and eat their food before the primates trusted her as one of their own.

FIGURE 1-37 Dian Fossey interacting with a gorilla named Puck

In some cases, this research took years. Galdikas spent over 40 years studying orangutans, arriving in Borneo in 1971 to document the ecology and behaviour of the wild orangutans. She lived in a hut, without telephones, electricity, or regular mail service as she worked. She had been told that her research couldn't be done, but four years later, Galdikas published her first of many articles about the orangutan. She has also conducted the longest continuous study of any wild animal in the world and is a world-renowned expert.

Other primatologists work in laboratory settings, observing and testing primates in motion, studying their communication patterns or teaching them to use human language. In laboratory settings, primatologists can understand specific behaviour or anatomical traits in more detail than in the wild.

How Are Humans Similar to Other Primates?

All three primatologists kept meticulous journals of primate social behaviour, getting to know the animals as individuals and giving them names. They all observed complex social behaviours and relationships very similar to humans and much more similar than anyone had previously thought. Goodall noted that chimpanzees can be cannibalistic and violent, waging war on other troops. She also witnessed chimps making and using tools by stripping the leaves off branches and sticking a branch into a termite mound to pull out the tasty insects, debunking the common theory that humans were the only primates who made tools.

Research over the last 40 years in primatology has shown us what makes humans similar to and different from other primates in social and physiological ways. Researching primates in their natural habitats has allowed primatologists to draw the following conclusions about the complex social behaviour among our primate relatives:

FIGURE 1-38 This chimpanzee is termite fishing. Why do you think it was important to find out that chimpanzees make their own tools?

- The bond between mothers and infants is important for survival in all primate species. Infants must learn much of what it takes to survive.
- Primates have the longest infant dependency period of all mammals. This is usually measured as the time until an individual can successfully reproduce.
- All primate societies have dominance hierarchies and aggression among the males for access to food and females.
- All primates groom one another. They spend a lot of time picking fleas and lice out of one another's fur. Grooming helps primates reduce stress, and it is also related to dominance hierarchies. The higher the primate in the hierarchy, the more likely he is to be groomed than to groom others.
- All primates communicate through facial expressions, touch, vocalizations, and body language. They play and laugh, show grief, become angry, and become violent.
- All primates have rotating forearms, grasping hands and feet, forward-facing eyes, and relatively larger brains.

Why is it important for primatologists to study primates? Why should scientists follow ethical guidelines when conducting experiments on primates?

> **Skills Focus**
>
> Create a central research question about humans and primates that a primatologist could investigate. Evaluate the bias of your question and consider what factors might contribute to your bias.

How Are Humans Different from Other Primates?

Anthropologists used to believe that the main difference between humans and other primates was our capacity to make and use tools. Goodall's findings and those of other primatologists have changed those ideas. Anthropologists agree that the differences between humans and other primates are small. The list below explains that there are some things that are strictly human.

- Humans are the only primates adapted to bipedalism.
- Humans have the longest infant dependency period of any primate. On average, we reproduce at about 20 years old, whereas chimpanzees reproduce at 10 years old.
- Humans are the only primates with a symbolic, spoken language and the physical ability of speech.
- Humans are the only primates who live in groups and mate in pairs. Some primates, such as chimpanzees, mate and live in groups, and others, such as orangutans, mate and live in pairs. Humans are the only primates who do both at the same time.
- Humans also develop ideas and beliefs about the world that guide their actions. Humans also have the ability to think and reflect on their own behaviour. They develop complex systems of morality and spirituality that influence and motivate behaviour.

Can Nonhuman Primates Use Language?

One of the more remarkable laboratory studies is primatologist Sue Savage-Rumbaugh's long-term study of bonobo communication. She has taught the 30-year-old Kanzi 348 graphic symbols, which he uses to communicate with her and other bonobos in his compound. He and the other bonobos can state simple sentences, respond to requests, and have conversations with their human caretakers. "Once," Savage-Rumbaugh says, "on an outing in a forest, Kanzi touched the symbols for 'marshmallow' and 'fire.' Given matches and marshmallows, Kanzi snapped twigs for a fire, lit them with the matches, and toasted the marshmallows on a stick." Kanzi can also make stone tools, draw symbols, and create music (Raffaele, 2006).

While the capacity for language of great apes is still much more limited than that of humans, the laboratory studies done by Savage-Rumbaugh and many others are proving that great apes have the capacity to learn many things previously considered to be only human (Rumbaugh, 2010).

↑ **FIGURE 1-39** Kanzi and Savage-Rumbaugh with a language board. Is there value in teaching primates to communicate with humans? Is this an ethical process?

REFLECT AND RESPOND

1. What are some of the challenges and rewards of studying primates in the wild?
2. How are humans similar to and different from other primates?
3. To what extent is the study of primates useful in understanding past hominin cultures?
4. Should primates be given basic civil rights?

Human Variation

Look around and you will notice that human beings are all different. Anthropologists study human variation, or the genetic differences between people and populations, to understand the differences between people. Anthropologists studying human variation try to find out how and why human beings are different and try to understand these differences from an evolutionary perspective.

> **Before You Read**
> Why do you think humans are different from one another?

Why Are Humans Different from One Another?

Like every other living thing on earth, humans have evolved over time in order to survive in different conditions. Evolution is the process of species' change, survival, or extinction. In *On the Origin of the Species* (1859), Charles Darwin outlined how every living thing evolves through natural selection. Natural selection involves three principles:

1. variation (Every species has a lot of variety within it.)
2. heritability (Individuals pass on traits to their offspring.)
3. environmental fitness (Individuals who are better adapted to their environment will produce more offspring and pass on their traits to the next generation.)

Variation is essential to the survival of any species. If there is a change in the available food supply, and all the individuals of a species are able to eat only the old kind of food, the species will become extinct. If some individuals are able to eat the new kind of food, they will reproduce and pass on their traits to their offspring, ensuring the survival of the species as a whole.

Do Human Subgroups Exist?

The idea of race has historically meant more than just physical traits. The concept of race is socially constructed, meaning that it is something defined by our society. The American Anthropological Association (AAA) states that race does not exist as a scientific category. More genetic variation exists within races than between them. An individual's behaviour and personality are largely conditioned by his or her culture. The idea of race has been used in the past to justify social, economic, and political inequalities and excuse hatred, cruelty, and violence. Some examples include the Nazi persecution of Jewish people, apartheid in South Africa, and the Ku Klux Klan in North America. Racial beliefs are considered by the AAA as myths and folk beliefs and have no biological legitimacy (AAA, 1998).

↑ **FIGURE 1-40** Has anyone ever made an assumption about you based on external characteristics, such as height, skin colour, hair colour, or body type?

More to Know...
See Chapter 7 for further discussion of racism in Canadian society.

Can We Study Human Variation in a Legitimate Way?

Anthropologists look at human variety and try to understand a specific trait, such as skin colour or blood type, in terms of evolutionary advantage. Blood type is an example of a trait that is easy to measure objectively. Anthropologists have found that certain blood types are connected to certain parts of the world, but blood type does not correspond to external characteristics. Anthropologists have concluded that race is a cultural myth, not a biological reality (O'Neill, 2010). In natural selection, traits develop to help individuals survive and reproduce in a particular environment, but many traits are the result of a population's isolation or migration. Many "racial" traits, such as eye colour, probably have no evolutionary advantage at all.

> Name some myths, stereotypes, or folk beliefs about race in Canadian society. Can you give specific examples? Think of an example from history where ideas about race were destructive.

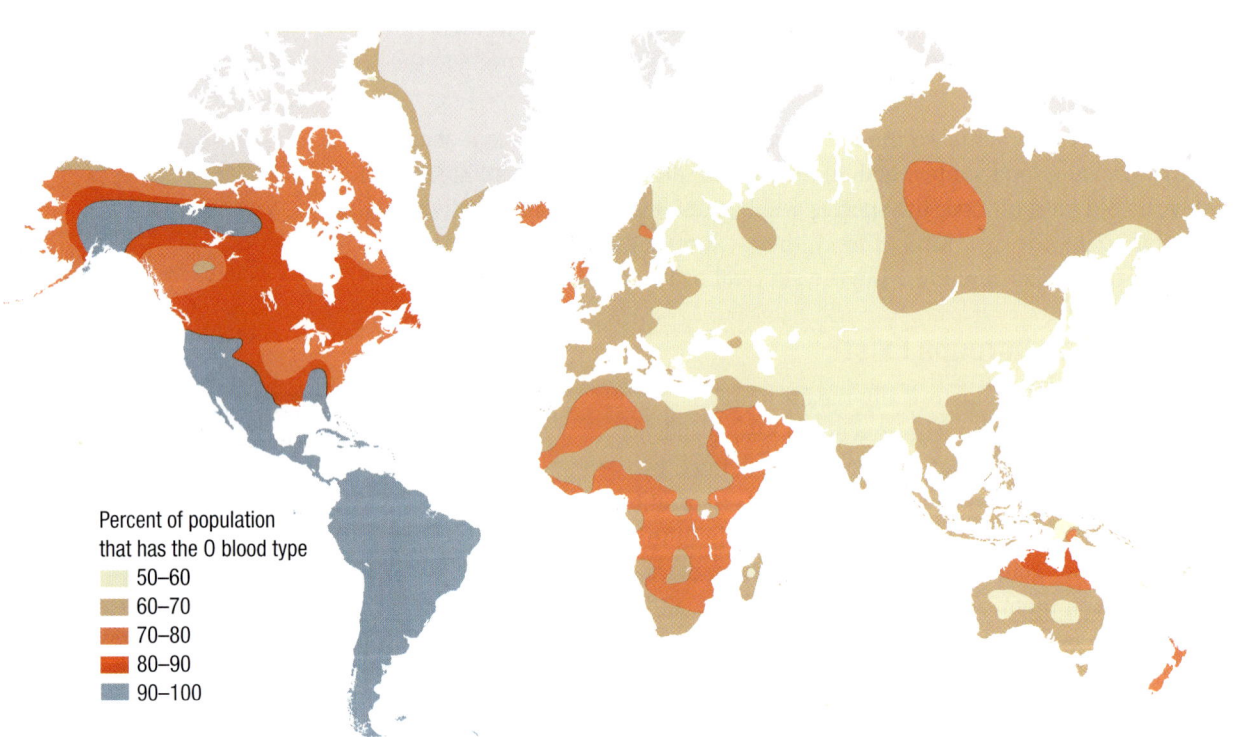

FIGURE 1-41 This map indicates the distribution of type O blood in human populations. What conclusions can you draw by looking at this map?

Are There Legitimate Explanations for Variations in Skin Colour?

Anthropologists have done a number of studies on various physical traits to see if they have an evolutionary advantage. They are looking at whether the trait provides an individual with a greater chance of survival in his or her environment and a greater chance of passing on those traits to offspring. Today, humans have ways to deal with the disadvantages of light skin in tropical places (for example, sunscreen, clothing, air conditioning) and the disadvantages of dark skin in areas with less sunlight (for example, a diet rich in vitamin D, vitamin D supplements).

POINT/COUNTERPOINT

Skin Variations

As humans migrated out of Africa, populations became more varied in skin colour. Was this variation the result of specific environmental advantage or of isolation? Did skin colour give an evolutionary advantage in the past? Are there evolutionary advantages for different skin colours today? Anthropologists examine both sides of the issue below.

Do Different Skin Colours Have Specific Evolutionary Advantages?

Yes	No
• All mammal populations in warmer climates have more melanin (dark pigment). • Darker skin provides protection from ultraviolet rays, which can cause skin cancer. • Lighter skin absorbs more vitamin D, which allows the body to absorb calcium, a nutrient necessary for bone growth. • Humans with lighter skin were more likely to survive in climates farther from the equator, with less available sunlight (Ember and Ember, 1999).	• There are many fair-skinned Amazonian Indians and Southeast Asians living at the same latitudes as dark-skinned Africans. • Because skin cancer usually affects people after they have had children, skin cancer likely had little effect on the evolution of skin colour (Jablonski, 2007). • Many dark-skinned people have lived longer in Tasmania, at latitudes very far from the equator, than light-skinned populations have lived in Scandinavia (Diamond, 1994).

QUESTIONS

1. Using the information above, come up with a hypothesis about the evolutionary advantages of different skin colours.
2. What questions do you have after considering this evidence?

REFLECT AND RESPOND

1. Explain why variation is important for a species to survive.
2. Why does the American Anthropological Association state that race does not exist?
3. What are some legitimate explanations for human variation?
4. To what extent do you think skin colour gives an evolutionary advantage? Explain.

CHAPTER 1 REVIEW

Knowledge and Understanding/Thinking

1. Look at the following statements, and determine which kind of anthropologist might have made it.
   a) Anthropologists try to understand how ideas form in a society by looking at the specific environmental resources available.
   b) No culture is superior to another; all cultures have internal rules and are logical within their environmental, historical, social, and cultural contexts.
   c) Anthropology can help us to understand how gendered groups are oppressed, and anthropologists should help activists create change in their own societies.
   d) Each element in a culture functions to serve the people in it. The anthropologists' goal is to discover the practical function of a cultural trait.
   e) Anthropologists must consider the impact of their own interactions in their research. It may be impossible to be objective, so research in one's own culture is just as valid as research in a different culture.

2. Anthropology is a discipline with many different approaches. There is a debate within the discipline whether anthropology should be more objective or more subjective. Sort the following based on whether they are more objective or more subjective and provide explanations for your decisions:
   a) primatology
   b) paleoanthropology
   c) forensic anthropology
   d) human variation
   e) archaeology
   f) linguistic anthropology
   g) ethnology
   h) cultural relativism
   i) functional theory
   j) cultural materialism
   k) feminist theory
   l) postmodern theory

3. What makes us human? How would a physical anthropologist answer this question? How would a cultural anthropologist answer it?

4. Anthropology research stirs up debate both within the discipline and in society in general. Describe two controversial issues, one in cultural anthropology and one in physical anthropology. For each issue, outline two perspectives and come up with questions that need to be asked in order to understand the controversy.

Thinking/Communication

5. Which area of research in physical anthropology do you find most interesting: paleoanthropology, forensic anthropology, primatology, or human variation? Explain why. What skills would you need to develop to pursue a career in that field?

6. Think of something in your school culture you would like to investigate. Develop a question to investigate people's attitudes, values, beliefs, and behaviours. What types of research methods would be most effective? How would you make sure that your research is ethical and reflexive?

7. Which area of research in cultural anthropology do you find most interesting: ethnology, linguistics, or archaeology? Explain why. What skills would you need to develop to pursue a career in that field?

8. What kind of material culture might future archaeologists find in your school, and what would it tell them about your culture? Choose three artifacts in your classroom, and explain what these would tell future archaeologists about your ideas, values, attitudes, and behaviours.

Communication/Application

9. Make a collage that depicts Canadian culture. Organize it to show ideas, values, attitudes, and behaviours. Demonstrate culture that is commonly shared, and show how it is passed on from one generation to the next. Include captions and explanations for your choices.

10. In this chapter, we examined multisited fieldwork, where anthropologists follow a particular culture with no ethnic or national boundaries.
    a) What other cultures could be examined using multisited fieldwork?
    b) What kind of research question would you ask to direct your research?
    c) What kind of research methods would you use?
    d) How would you know that your data is reliable?
    e) Would it be better to study a culture that you are a member of or to study a culture as an outsider? Explain.

11. Write and perform a skit or create a Facebook profile that demonstrates an understanding of a key researcher's work in anthropology. Include the following:
    a) What did the person research, and which school of anthropology is he or she in?
    b) What were the researcher's key findings or theories?
    c) How are the researcher's findings relevant to you today? Include a modern example that illustrates how his or her findings might help you understand human behaviours today.
    If performing a skit, try to make the skit memorable, using rhyme, humour, costumes, or puppets to get your message across. If you choose to create a Facebook profile, think about how to present your information in an interesting way. Don't forget to include images!

12. Look at the Web sites of universities and colleges in Ontario that offer anthropology courses. Make a poster comparing three different programs. Look at the different fields and schools of thought at each school and give an example of research being done there.

CHAPTER 2

What Is Psychology?

Have you ever wondered why you and your siblings are alike in some ways and different in others? Or why you act differently in certain situations? Psychologists seek answers to questions like these as they study behaviour and the mental processes of the brain.

In this chapter, you will learn about major schools of thought and approaches to understanding behaviour by examining various psychological theories and perspectives. You'll also learn about various types of research.

Chapter Expectations

By the end of this chapter, you will:
- understand the major theories and perspectives in psychology
- understand the major contributions of important psychologists to the study of psychology
- identify and understand the major fields of study in psychology
- understand quantitative and qualitative methods of research and when they are used

Key Terms

analytical psychology
archetypes
cerebrum
classical conditioning
client-centred therapy
cognition
collective unconscious
conditioned response
conditioned stimulus
conscious
correlation
defense mechanism
denial
displacement
ego
extinction
fixation
free association
id
identity crisis
logotherapy
neo-Freudians
neuroscientist
neurotic disorder
operant conditioning
personality
projection
psychoanalytic theory
psychodynamic theory
repression
self-actualization
superego
unconditioned response
unconditioned stimulus
unconscious

Landmark Case Studies

Mary Ainsworth (1913–1999): Infant–Mother Attachment

Behaviourism

John Watson 1878–1958
Ivan Pavlov 1849–1936

B.F. Skinner 1904–1990

FIGURE 2-1 Psychologists study behaviour to determine how why we act as we do

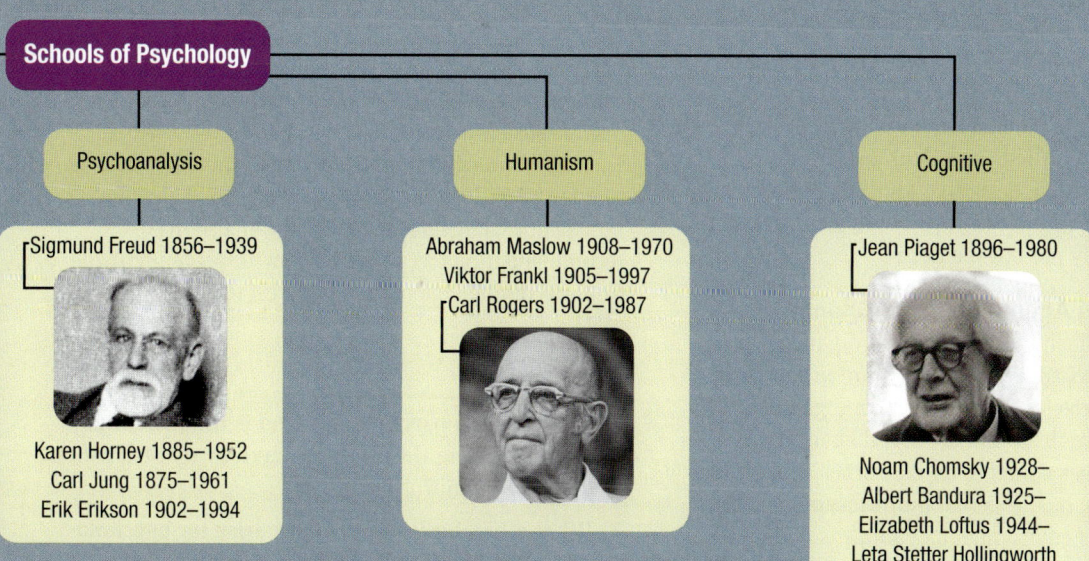

Schools of Psychology

Psychoanalysis
Sigmund Freud 1856–1939

Karen Horney 1885–1952
Carl Jung 1875–1961
Erik Erikson 1902–1994

Humanism
Abraham Maslow 1908–1970
Viktor Frankl 1905–1997
Carl Rogers 1902–1987

Cognitive
Jean Piaget 1896–1980

Noam Chomsky 1928–
Albert Bandura 1925–
Elizabeth Loftus 1944–
Leta Stetter Hollingworth 1886–1939

Spotlight on Psychology — *Flash Mobs*

> **Before You Read**
> How would you react if everyone around you suddenly froze? Why would you act that way?

At a predetermined time on January 31, 2008, 207 people throughout Grand Central Station in New York City all suddenly froze in place: one man was tying his shoe while elsewhere a couple held hands mid-walk. All the participants remained absolutely still for five minutes and then simply unfroze and went on their way again, as if nothing out of the ordinary had just happened. Reactions from bystanders varied: some people continued on as if nothing was happening, others appeared confused or fearful, while still others found the situation amusing and waited to see what would happen next. This flash mob—a spontaneous public assembly of people that perform a brief, unusual act and then disperse—ended as quickly as it began.

Since the first flash mob at Macy's department store in New York City in 2003, flash mobs have increased in popularity to include a massive pillow fight, a zombie walk, and a gathering of Santas. In November 2010, a flash mob of people singing "Hallelujah" was staged at the Welland Seaway Mall. People in the food court suddenly broke out in song while others watched in amazement. The video of this flash mob was one of the most-watched YouTube videos of 2010.

While usually just harmless fun, flash mobs have been damaging as well. In March 2010, police in Philadelphia had to crack down on violent flash mobs largely consisting of teenagers who were vandalizing property, attacking pedestrians, and fighting one another. Attacks like these have occurred around the world but luckily are not the norm.

Flash Mobs As Agents of Social Change

More recently, flash mobs have been organized for purposes such as advertising, a form of urban street art, and civic protest. Carrotmob is an organization that uses flash mobs to initiate social change by having businesses compete for consumer support (see Figure 2-2). The business that promises to make the biggest social or environmental change is rewarded with a flood of consumers who spend money at their establishment. Since its inception in 2008, Carrotmob campaigns have occurred across five continents.

FIGURE 2-2 Carrotmob is an organization that uses flash mobs to encourage businesses to make changes to improve our world.

The Psychology of Flash Mobs

Why do people participate in flash mobs? Do they act because of their sense of who they are, or do they lose themselves in the crowd?

Social psychologists who study crowd behaviour are interested in flash mobs to help them understand social behaviours including conformity. Social psychologists used to believe that crowds have no order and cause people to lose their sense of identity, allowing them to be manipulated by a leader. Now psychologists such as Steve Reicher are exploring the idea that crowds not only reflect society, but they can also create social change. So when people act in a crowd, they develop a new sense of identity as a result of their participation. Social psychologists can therefore study flash mobs to gain an understanding of our current society and how people see themselves. They can also make recommendations to police on how to prevent crowds from becoming violent and how best to handle those that do.

QUESTIONS

1. How might a psychologist who is interested in understanding flash mob behaviour research such a phenomenon?
2. What ethical questions might arise for psychologists who want to stage their own flash mobs for experimental purposes?

Research and Inquiry Skills

Variables and Control Groups in Social Science

As you learned in Chapter 1, when social scientists have an issue or a topic they wish to research, they first must develop a central research question. This question becomes the focus of an experiment, where a researcher looks at the effects of one factor on another. These factors are called variables. You need to avoid making a conclusion until you finish your research. Look at the following example of a good central research question to learn more about experiments: Does using a cell phone at school affect students' grades?

Independent and Dependent Variables

In an experiment, there is an independent variable and a dependent variable. The *independent variable* is the variable whose effect is being studied. In the central research question above, the independent variable is the use of a cell phone. The *dependent variable* is what is being measured and may change in response to manipulation of the independent variable. In our central research question, the dependent variable is the students' grades.

Control Groups

To accurately measure the results of an experiment, researchers establish a *control group*. The control group serves as a comparison to the group under study. Control groups can be made up of individuals who are not exposed to the independent variable in the same way or individuals who are fundamentally different in nature. In the cell phone example, a control group would consist of students who do not use cell phones in school.

Activities

1. For each of the following central research questions, indicate the independent and dependent variables and suggest an appropriate control group:
   a) Does playing on a sports team affect students' behaviour?
   b) Are students' attention spans affected by eating breakfast?
   c) Does wearing brand name clothing affect the number of friends a student has?
2. Write three social science central research questions on issues that are important to you. For each central research question, indicate the independent and dependent variables and a possible control group.

Sources in Social Science

When you conduct research in the social sciences, you must select from a variety of primary and secondary sources. *Primary sources* (for example, interviews, observations, surveys) are obtained from field research, while *secondary sources* (for example, research reports, newspaper articles, journal or magazine articles) summarize what other people have to say about a topic. When starting research, you begin with secondary sources to see what has already been found about your question. Then you design your own primary source to test your hypothesis.

Quantitative and Qualitative Research

Generally, the various ways in which social scientists conduct their research can be categorized into *quantitative* and *qualitative* methods.

	Quantitative Research	Qualitative Research
Purpose	• to test a hypothesis • to establish relationships between variables	• to build a hypothesis based on research data • to understand relationships between variables
Description	• closed-ended questions • numerical results	• open-ended questions • descriptions and comparisons
Examples	• surveys • laboratory-based observation	• interviews • naturalistic observation

Activities

1. For each of the following central research questions, suggest whether quantitative or qualitative research methods would be more appropriate and provide a reason explaining your decision:
   a) How is a child's academic success affected by how much time the child spends with his or her family?
   b) Is there a relationship between time spent on the Internet and number of friends?

Section 2.1 Schools of Thought

While anthropology developed as a science that studies humanity across time and place, psychology's early questions focused on the study of the mind and the behaviours that result from what goes on in it. The earliest psychological theorists asked and attempted to answer questions such as:

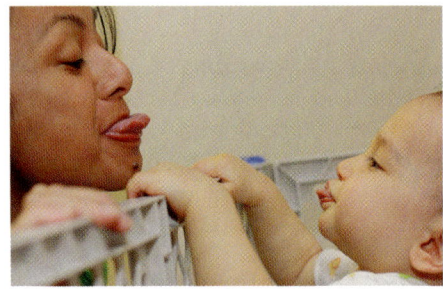

FIGURE 2-3 Depending on his or her perspective, a psychologist may view this fun game between mother and child in a variety of ways.

1. What is the mind?
2. What is its relation to the brain?
3. If the mind and the brain are not the same thing but are somehow related, how do you study what you cannot see?
4. What roles do biology (nature) and environment (nurture) play in complex human behaviours?
5. How does the mind develop and change over time?

As pioneer psychologists struggled with these questions, different schools of thought in the field of psychology arose as a result of early attempts to find answers. Schools of thought are systematic and structured ways of approaching questions related to human behaviour that have different sets of underlying assumptions. For example, *behaviourism* is a school of thought that asserts that psychology can only study and manipulate what it can *see*—behaviour. This meant that behaviourists did not attempt to study or theorize about the nature and function of the mind because they could not see inside of it. This belief defined the questions behaviourists asked and the theories they developed as a result of their research.

Other schools of thought that arose in response to these questions included psychoanalytic theory, humanistic theory, cognitive theory, and more. Each of these was based on a set of assumptions about the nature of the mind and behaviour, how they could be studied, and the role they played in producing behaviour. There is a distinction between the brain and the mind in psychology: the *brain* is what is physically inside the skull, and its study consists of understanding the functions of its various structures; the *mind* refers to the mental processes, and its study is an attempt to understand the conscious and the unconscious. Ultimately, psychologists seek to understand the brain and the mind, and how they affect and direct human behaviour.

Like other social science disciplines, insights gained from the efforts of early theorists and researchers contributes to and refines how we understand the human mind and human behaviour. As our understanding has grown, the way scholars and researchers approach their exploration has changed.

Describing how people feel, think, and act has been the mission of psychologists since the nineteenth century. In this section, you will learn about psychology's various schools of thought and the theories within them.

Psychodynamic Theorists

Early in the twentieth century, psychologists began to develop **psychodynamic theories** as a new approach to therapy, based on Sigmund Freud's **psychoanalytic theory**. These theories are based on the belief that unlocking the **unconscious** mind is the key to understanding human behaviour and relationships. Calling your new love interest by your ex's name—a *Freudian slip*—would lead a psychoanalyst to speculate that you have unresolved feelings for your ex or perhaps misgivings about the new relationship. The **conscious** mind is everything we are aware of, that which we can think and talk about rationally. Early childhood experiences are also seen as important to understanding a person's personality, motivations, and behaviours. In fact, Freud believed that human development occurs mainly in the first few years of life, as people struggle to resolve sexually based conflicts. (You'll learn more about this in Section 2.2.) Have you ever wondered what influences your behaviour?

Developmental psychologists study teenage behaviour in an effort to better understand why teens behave as they do. Some questions under study may include the following:

- How do peers influence one another's actions and attitudes?
- How do teens use technology differently than their parents?
- What factors influence teen behaviour with other peers? With adults?
- Why do teens claim to be individuals, yet all wear the same clothing?

? What other questions do you have about teenage behaviour that psychology can help answer?

Sigmund Freud (1856–1939)

One of the world's most famous psychologists is Sigmund Freud. He is well known for his conception of human consciousness as consisting of three distinct parts: the id, the ego, and the superego. The **ego** represents the rational part of the mind and operates on what Freud called the "reality principle." It often suppresses the urges of the **id**, the instinctual aspect of the mind, which is run by the "pleasure principle." As the moral centre of the mind, the **superego** acts as the mind's conscience. The ego often struggles to satisfy the needs of the impulsive id while satisfying the moral superego. Freud believed that human personality results from the ego's efforts to resolve these conflicts.

? How do the id, ego, and superego work together?

Before You Read

What have you heard about Freud? What questions do you have about Freud and his theories?

psychodynamic theory: an approach to therapy that focuses on resolving a patient's conflicted conscious and unconscious feelings

psychoanalytic theory: Sigmund Freud's theory that all human behaviour is influenced by early childhood and that childhood experiences influence the unconscious mind throughout life

unconscious: information processing in our mind that we are not aware of; according to Freud, it holds our unacceptable thoughts, feelings, and memories; according to Jung, it includes patterns of memories, instincts, and experiences common to all

conscious: information that we are always aware of; our conscious mind performs the thinking when we take in new information

ego: Freud's term for the rational part of the mind, which operates on the reality principle

id: Freud's term for the instinctual part of the mind, which operates on the pleasure principle

superego: Freud's term for the moral centre of the mind

FIGURE 2-4 The daily struggles of the ego

FIGURE 2-5 Like an iceberg, only part of our mind—the conscious—is above the surface.

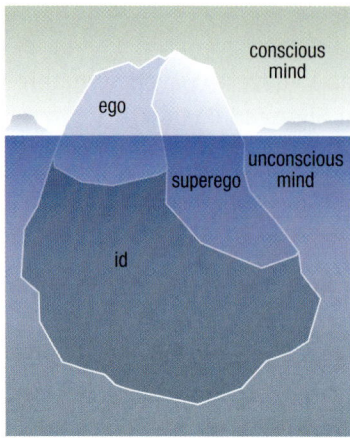

defence mechanism: the ego's way of distorting reality to deal with anxiety

repression: a process in which unacceptable desires or impulses are excluded from consciousness and left to operate in the unconscious

denial: a defence mechanism whereby a person refuses to recognize or acknowledge something that is painful

displacement: the shift of an emotion from its original focus to another object, person, or situation

free association: a method used in psychoanalysis where a patient relaxes and says whatever comes to mind

projection: a defence mechanism whereby a person attributes their own threatening impulses onto someone else

neo-Freudians: psychologists who modified Freud's psychoanalytic theory to include social and cultural aspects

VOICES

The view that women are infantile and emotional creatures, and as such, incapable of responsibility and independence is the work of the masculine tendency to lower women's self-respect.

Karen Horney (*Feminine Psychology*, 1932)

Acts of the Unconscious Mind

Freud described the mind as an iceberg (see Figure 2-5): our conscious mind is above the water; the unconscious mind is below the surface. The id is totally unconscious, while the ego and superego straddle both sides of the iceberg and therefore operate both consciously and unconsciously.

Because Freud believed that much of the human mind was unconscious, he theorized that the ego uses **defence mechanisms** to distort reality in order to deal with anxiety. The ego **represses** unacceptable feelings and memories from consciousness so that they remain below the surface. His psychoanalytic approach sought to find and interpret these repressed feelings and memories so patients can gain personal insight. To deal with painful experiences, such as the loss of a pet, the ego may use **denial** as a defence mechanism. Freud believed that people needed safe outlets to deal with unacceptable feelings of sexuality or aggression and often **displaced** their feelings onto other objects or people. For example, if you've had a fight with a friend, you may snap at your parents instead because you know they will love you despite your outburst.

To uncover the unconscious, Freud used various methods including examining dreams and fantasies and having clients engage in **free association**, where they relaxed and said whatever came to mind, regardless of how silly or embarrassing. He also identified methods of resistance and defence mechanisms. Patients would often **project** their feelings onto the therapist (also called *transference*), which allowed them to examine their feelings and gain insight into their current relationships. Freud's methods also emphasized understanding the child–parent relationship.

❓ Select any of Freud's ideas, and provide examples from your own experience that prove or disprove the theory.

Karen Horney (1885–1952)

Today's developmental psychologists believe that development is lifelong and not fixed in childhood, as Freud stated. Psychologists also believe that repression is a rare response to trauma. While many of Freud's theories are no longer seen as accurate, **neo-Freudians** often believe in the basics of psychoanalysis. Karen Horney (pronounced *Horn-eye*), for example, was a feminist neo-Freudian who followed Freud's basic concepts about the mind but disagreed on two points: she did not believe that personality is strongly influenced by sexual conflicts in childhood; she felt that Freud's theories did not accurately represent females.

The founder of feminine psychology, she argued that women were pushed by society and culture to depend on men for both love and status, since without a husband and children, they had little value in society. Feminine psychology is a field with issues unique to females, such as "female human identity" and the issues confronted by females during their lifetime. It also highlights the gender bias that exists in traditional psychological theories and offers alternative theories to counter those biases and promote new thinking. Karen Horney also made significant contributions to the study of **neurotic disorder**, a mental disorder involving anxiety and fear. Many of her contributions are still considered valid today.

neurotic disorder: a mental disorder involving anxiety and fear

> How did Karen Horney's contributions influence how women are represented in psychology?

Carl Jung (1875–1961)

Once a student of Freud's, Swiss psychiatrist Carl Jung (pronounced *Yoong*) grew to disagree with Freud on a number of key issues, including the influence of sexuality on human behaviour. He founded **analytical psychology**, a way to understand motivation based on the conscious and unconscious mind, which together form the psyche. Jung believed that achieving balance within the psyche would allow people to reach their true potential (Jung, 1964).

analytical psychology: a branch of psychology founded by Carl Jung, based on the idea that balancing a person's psyche would allow the person to reach his or her full potential

Jung on the Mind

Jung believed that there are two parts to the unconscious: the personal and the collective. The *personal unconscious* is unique to each individual, while the **collective unconscious** contains memories from our ancestors, shared by all human beings regardless of their culture. Jung observed through his practice and research that certain images and symbols tended to appear over and over again; Jung determined that these models of people, behaviours, and personalities were universal **archetypes** of the collective unconscious. Jung believed that we are born with these archetypes, as our collective unconscious contains images derived from our early ancestors' experiences.

collective unconscious: the shared, inherited pool of memories from our ancestors

archetypes: universal symbols that tend to reappear over time; includes models of people, behaviours, and personalities

Archetypes connect us to images as well as emotions. For example, the "Mother" is an archetype that represents nurturing and soothing, while the "Father" is seen as stern, powerful, and controlling. Works of fiction often include a courageous champion—the "hero"—and a deceptive "trickster"—both of which are Jungian archetypes. We tend to feel emotionally connected to these images, which suggests that they are deeply ingrained in our psyche.

Symbols that often reoccur include stones, animals, and the circle. Like the images, we tend to find these symbols in the arts and literature across the ages. Symbols can, and usually do, reflect a multitude of meanings. Stones appear in ancient religious texts, animals in cave drawings and today on sports teams. The circle symbolizes the self, completeness, or the whole.

The methods Jung used were similar to Freud's. Jung felt that examining past experiences, dreams, and fantasies was useful for understanding the unconscious self. He also used other techniques during therapy sessions, including having clients produce creative projects, such as a painting, and having them use their imagination. The goal of using imagination was to exert as little influence as possible on mental images as they flowed. Jung believed that these methods allowed the unconscious mind to express itself.

Skills Focus

If you were going to analyze the theories of Horney, Freud, and Jung, which type of research would you use (qualitative or quantitative)? Suggest one research question for each theorist.

Personality

personality: an individual's characteristic pattern of thinking, feeling, and acting

Carl Jung also contributed a great deal to the understanding of **personality**, an individual's characteristic pattern of thinking, feeling, and acting. The idea of categorizing personalities into types has been around since ancient Greek philosophers first classified them into four types based on which bodily fluids (*humors*) they believed to be in excess: yellow bile (*choleric*—irritable character); black bile (*melancholic*—depressed character); blood (*sanguine*—optimistic, cheerful character); phlegm (*phlegmatic*—calm, unemotional character).

Jung had different ideas about how to describe personality. First, he believed we are all either introverted or extroverted. Then he added his four Functional Types: thinking (uses reason), feeling (uses emotions), sensation (uses the five senses), and intuition (uses perception). Thinking and feeling are opposites of each other, as are sensation and intuition. Jung theorized that we consciously gravitated to one functional type while our unconscious gravitated to the opposite type.

Today, Jung's theories have led to the field of psychometrics, an area of study that uses questionnaires and tests to measure personality, ability, and knowledge. Katharine Briggs and her daughter Isabel Briggs Myers developed the *Myers-Briggs Type Indicator* (MBTI), a method of classifying personality that is based on Jung's personality theory. Similarly, the Canadian Personality Dimensions® (see Figure 2-6) and the American True Colors systems are based on Jung's personality theory and were developed to help understand human behaviour, motivation, and communication. For example, students take these tests to help them decide what jobs might be suitable for them, while businesses use the tests to help managers hire suitable employees or to help co-workers understand one another.

Although the MBTI is a popular tool, its validity as an adequate way to classify personality has been questioned. While the Introversion/Extroversion scale has shown some accuracy, the accuracy of the other scales have been challenged. Another criticism of the MBTI is that its answers can be easily faked to obtain a particular result. Other personality tests such as the Minnesota Multiphasic Personality Inventory (MMPI) include a scale to determine if responses have been exaggerated or faked, something lacking in the MBTI.

While not all psychologists accept psychodynamic theories, these theories have influenced humanist psychologists, as well as educational psychology and our understanding of intelligence. They are still used today to understand and help patients with anxiety disorders and addictions.

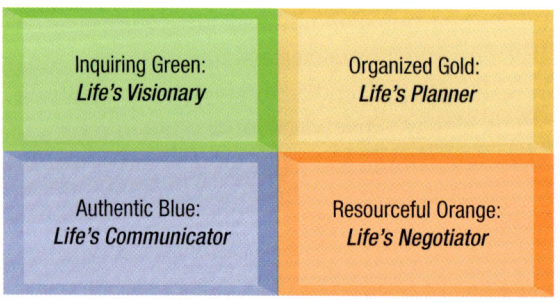

FIGURE 2-6 The Personality Dimensions® system uses flash cards and surveys to classify people into one of four dimensions.

The Psychology of Dreams

In the first half of the twentieth century, theories on why we dream were mainly of interest to psychologists like Jung and Freud, who used dreams to make diagnoses. However, the discovery of a relationship between rapid eye movement (REM) sleep and dreams in the latter half of the century peaked the curiosity of the scientific community.

Have you ever woken up in the morning and wondered if what you dreamt actually happened? You were likely experiencing an extremely vivid REM dream. REM sleep has been shown to be important in helping us consolidate the day's important events, which is why we experience an increased amount of it if we've been deprived of REM sleep. Even animals require REM sleep, indicating that it is a hard-wired need.

Dream Interpretation

The idea that dreams represent something meaningful, rather than being strange fleeting thoughts, has been around for centuries. In First Nations cultures, dream interpretation is one aspect of spirituality. The Iroquois, for example, believe that dreams are messages from the god within each person, so they go on "dream quests" for guidance. Similarly, the Odawa believe that dreams are a guide to wisdom. In Australia, Aboriginal cultures believe in "Dreamtime," an all-together-time where the past, present, and future are experienced together.

The idea that dreams can be useful in a scientific way—to help a patient overcome an obsession or phobia, for example—is relatively new. Both Freud and Jung believed in analyzing dreams as a method of understanding the unconscious. However, their beliefs about what the dreams represented were quite different.

Freud believed that the people, situations, and images in dreams represented suppressed sexual desires of the dreamer. Even those dreams that were not obviously sexual in nature revealed sexual needs upon interpretation by a trained psychoanalyst. Freud's dream theories, however, have been widely criticized and are considered to be one of his biggest failures. On the other hand, Jung believed that dreams and the symbols used in them were the unconscious, or instinctive, mind communicating with the conscious mind. Jung wrote that "dream symbols are the essential message carriers from the instinctive to the rational parts of the human mind" and that when they are interpreted, the dreamer can learn from the unconscious (1964). He cautioned the analyst to be careful, though, to interpret the dreams and symbols only in terms of that particular dream and not to generalize.

↑ **FIGURE 2-7** Freud discovered that by having his clients recline on a comfortable couch, they often revealed previously hidden memories and emotions.

REFLECT AND RESPOND

1. Give an example from your own life of how your unconscious mind had an impact on a decision. Compare it with one where you were conscious of your thinking. Why is it important to be aware of these concepts of the mind?
2. How does Freud's conception of the mind compare with Jung's ideas? Create a chart showing their ideas and how they are different and similar.

Behavioural Psychologists

Before You Read
What do you do upon hearing a fire alarm? Why? Does an infant respond the same way? Why or why not?

Behavioural psychology is another branch of psychology that was common in the first half of the twentieth century. It is based on the belief that psychologists need empirical evidence, obtained through experimentation, to understand and change human behaviour. Behavioural psychologists emphasize the importance of observable behaviours and phenomena, as well as using scientifically proven intervention procedures. Behavioural psychology can be applied to individuals with a wide variety of mental disorders, as well as to groups such as those in a workplace.

Ivan Pavlov (1849–1936)

Ivan Pavlov was a Nobel Prize–winning Russian scientist who started his career studying the digestive system. His research with dogs showed that they would drool as soon as he put food in their mouths. But he noticed that they started drooling at other times, too, for example, when they saw a white lab coat, which he and his colleagues wore whenever they fed the dogs. This observation led him to devise an experiment to see if other things could make a dog drool.

The Experiment

unconditioned response: the natural response to an unconditioned stimulus

unconditioned stimulus: a stimulus that naturally triggers a response

conditioned stimulus: an originally neutral stimulus that comes to trigger a conditioned response after being paired with an unconditional stimulus

conditioned response: the learned response to a previously neutral stimulus

classical conditioning: a type of learning where a once neutral stimulus comes to produce a particular response after pairings with a conditioned stimulus

Pavlov already knew that he would get an **unconditioned response**—drooling—when he presented the **unconditioned stimulus**—food—to a dog. To test his theory, Pavlov took a previously neutral stimulus—a bell—and began to ring it at the same time the dog received the food. After a while, the dog began to associate the sound of the bell with receiving food, a **conditioned stimulus**, since it produced the **conditioned response** (see Figure 2-8). This type of learned response is known as **classical conditioning**.

Pavlov's Legacy

But why do psychologists care whether a dog will salivate when hearing a bell? Classical conditioning has been successfully applied to many species with a variety of stimuli. This had led researchers to determine that classical conditioning is one way that nearly all organisms learn to adapt to their environment.

Its applications to the real world have been widespread. The principles of classical conditioning can be applied to a variety of areas of our health and well-being. For example, some children may demonstrate fear in the waiting room of their pediatrician's office after having received an immunization during a previous visit.

Pavlov's work heavily influenced behaviourism by showing the value of using experiments within psychology to study internal processes objectively. He also explored the idea that observable behaviour can be changed by associating stimuli with one another.

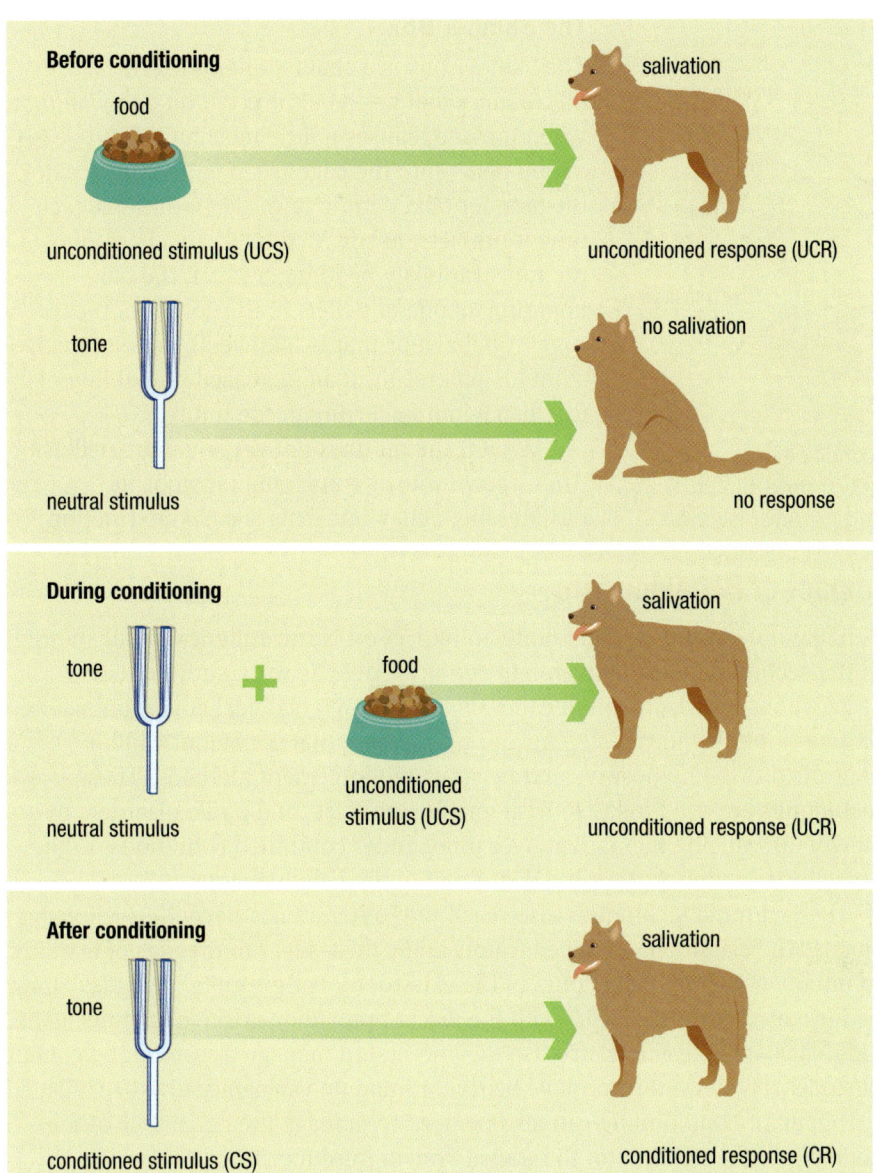

FIGURE 2-8 Classical conditioning can turn a neutral stimulus like a tone into a conditioned stimulus, causing salivation in a dog.

> **Open for Debate**
> In 1920, psychologist John B. Watson performed his Little Albert experiment, in which he created a conditioned fear of animals in an infant by pairing a loud noise with the appearance of a rat. He proved that humans, not just dogs, could have conditioned responses. Although this experiment is often cited, there is much controversy about its ethics and its accuracy.

❓ What made Pavlov's dog experiment so revolutionary? Identify some examples in your own life where a previously neutral stimulus caused a conditioned response.

B.F. Skinner (1904–1990)

B.F. Skinner is considered to have developed true behaviourism because he was concerned with only observable behaviours, not the mental processes behind them. Using rats and pigeons, Skinner studied how the use of rewards and punishment can influence behaviour, which became known as **operant conditioning**.

operant conditioning: a type of learning that uses rewards and punishment to achieve a desired behaviour

Chapter 2 • What Is Psychology? NEL 65

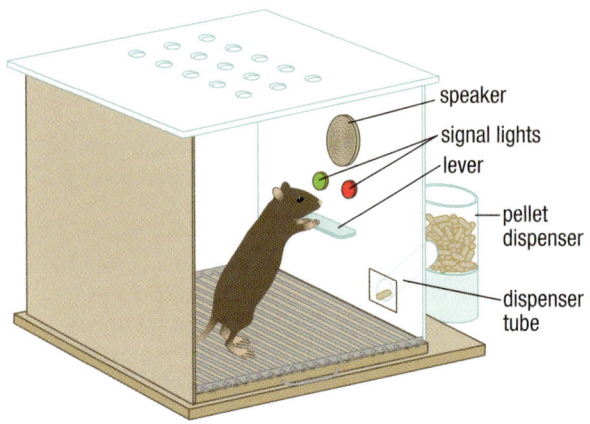

FIGURE 2-9 Skinner's operant conditioning chamber, also known as the Skinner box. Over time, the rat learns that the reward for pushing the lever is food.

The Skinner Box

The Skinner box is a chamber designed by B.F. Skinner that has a bar or pedal on one wall that, when pressed, causes a little mechanism to release a food pellet into the cage (see Figure 2-9). Inside the Skinner box, a rat is rewarded with food each time it presses the bar. Within a very short time, the rat is furiously peddling away at the bar, hoarding its pile of pellets in the corner of the cage. A behaviour that is followed by a reinforcing stimulus will result in an increased probability of that behaviour occurring in the future.

What if the rat does not get any more pellets? After a few futile attempts, the rat stops its bar-pressing behaviour. This is called **extinction**.

extinction: in operant conditioning, the diminishing of a conditioned response due to a lack of reinforcement

Impact of Behaviourism

Behavioural psychology had quite an impact on North American education in the second half of the twentieth century. Pavlov's work showed that associations between stimuli can be made through classical conditioning. Skinner took this idea a step further by showing that behaviour can be controlled by using positive and negative reinforcement methods. These techniques are used today to treat anxiety, phobias, and panic disorders by slowly introducing the patient over time, under controlled conditions, to the object or situation that causes distress until the reaction stops.

Behaviourist techniques also reach into other arenas beyond psychology, such as the classroom. Some educators apply these ideas to theories of learning to modify students' behaviours in the classroom. For example, new tasks may be introduced in small steps, with the teacher providing positive reinforcement after each step. Teachers also use this method to manage classroom behaviour of students by rewarding positive behaviours and punishing negative behaviours.

Operant conditioning can also be used to manage the behaviour of the general public. In Toronto, the transit system introduced classical music in some stations to discourage people, especially youths, from hanging around for no reason.

Connecting Psychology to Anthropology

Noam Chomsky (1928–)

Noam Chomsky has had an impact on both psychology and anthropology. A contemporary of B.F. Skinner's, Chomsky argues against Skinner's behaviourist model. Skinner's theory of stimulus response states that we learn language through association, imitation, and reinforcement. Chomsky argues that this theory cannot explain the creative use of language.

REFLECT AND RESPOND

1. Compare the techniques used in classical conditioning to those used in operant conditioning. How do they differ?
2. What assumptions are made about people in behavioural psychology? How are these assumptions similar/different to those of psychoanalysis?
3. Standing when you hear the national anthem is an example of how classical conditioning works. Provide three more examples of how classical conditioning has affected you at school.

IN FOCUS: Is It Ethical to Experiment on Animals?

Why Use Animals in Experiments?

The use of animals in scientific research has been going on since about the fourth century BCE. Animals have been used in scientific research for a number of reasons, such as to test the effects of a medication and to ensure that cosmetics are not harmful. Psychologists such as Pavlov and Skinner used animals as well. While many people have heard research horror stories about the use of animals, current techniques and practices minimize the harm and pain of research subjects far more than before.

Groups such as Pro-Test and Understanding Animal Research, and university laboratories like the one at the University of California–Los Angeles (UCLA) point out that *vivisection*, experimenting on live animals, has led to major breakthroughs. Countless human lives have been helped and saved thanks to the new understandings about biology and medicine that result from the use of animals in research. These groups and labs argue that we have a moral obligation to help humans first, especially since the animal research subjects do not have the same sense of consciousness as humans.

However, anthropological research has shown consciousness, language ability, and creativity in some animals, especially primates. Researchers are required to act responsibly when creating and conducting their experiments, and their laboratories are monitored by animal care committees (ACCs).

While alternatives to the use of animals in research do exist and are used in labs, they can be limited in scope and thus give incomplete data. In addition, in many countries, such as Canada, it is the law to test products on animals before conducting human trials in order to protect citizens from harmful products and procedures.

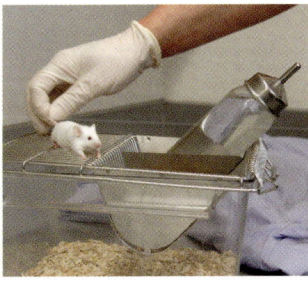

FIGURE 2-10 Animal testing has been done in psychology, medicine, and pharmacy. Does the purpose change the ethical standards?

What Are the Alternatives?

Opponents to the use of animals in research believe in practising the three Rs: refinement, reduction, and replacement. Researchers need to refine their methods to reduce or eliminate the need for using animals. According to the Johns Hopkins Center for Alternatives to Animal Testing, technologies such as magnetic resonance imaging (MRI) and X-ray techniques are some alternatives already used in labs.

Next, researchers can reduce the number of required animals to achieve the same scientific outcomes, or replace the need for animal experimentation altogether where possible. Companies such as The Body Shop and animal rights groups such as In Defense of Animals and People for the Ethical Treatment of Animals (PETA) argue that it is unethical and unnecessary to conduct research on animals since the results of these experiments are unreliable, the facilities are sometimes inadequate, and some tests are extremely inhumane. They say that after participating in some psychological experiments, the test animals were never able to function normally again. They advocate replacing animal experiments with the new available technologies as the best solution.

Experiments in the Social Sciences

In terms of the social sciences, animals are most often used to test psychological theories, but they are also used in sociology and anthropology. Animal experiments are used to try to understand the nature of behaviour, addiction, and even language. Experiments could include testing the effect of medication on cognitive ability or simulated mental illnesses such as depression, evaluating how an animal reacts to situations such as isolation, or even determining how quickly a subject learns a new skill within the limits of an experiment. The most common animals used for experiments are rodents and birds, but primates are also used.

QUESTIONS

1. Write a research question that could be used as a basis of study for this topic.
2. How would psychologists adjust their research if they could not use animals for testing?

Humanist Psychologists

Before You Read
What happens if you do not eat for long periods of time? Make a prediction about the importance of food to psychology.

While psychodynamic and behaviourist theories dominated the first half of the twentieth century, humanist psychology became an important concept in the second half of the century. It developed out of the patient relationship idea of therapy. Humanist psychologists believe that the client should be very involved in his or her own recovery, rather than relying only on the therapist's interpretation of the issues. This approach empowered the client in a way not previously practised. This approach also represented a shift in methodology because humanist psychologists favoured more qualitative, rather than quantitative, research to understand the person as a whole. Humanism rejects quantitative methodology like experiments and prefers qualitative research methods. Examples include diary accounts, open-ended questionnaires, and unstructured interviews and observations. In fact, humanism introduced and legitimized qualitative methodologies to the field of psychology.

Abraham Maslow (1908–1970)

Abraham Maslow is considered one of the founders of humanist psychology. Unlike many psychologists in the past, he was interested in studying well people, as opposed to psychologists such as Freud who were interested in sick people. He studied what he called "**self-actualizing**" people and their "peak experiences" because he wanted to understand how they achieved the status of having reached their full potential.

Maslow is most known for his Hierarchy of Needs (see Figure 2-11) to describe his theory of motivation. He based this theory on observing clients rather than on experimentation. The Hierarchy of Needs explains that basic needs must be fulfilled before higher-order needs become important. So if someone's

self-actualization: reaching one's full potential; occurs only after basic physical and psychological needs are met

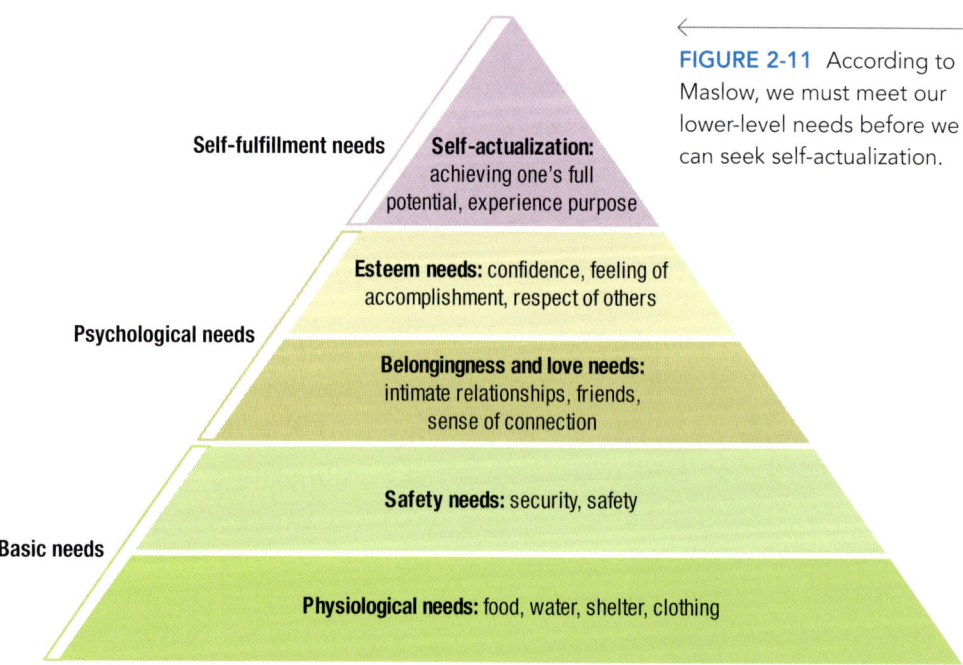

FIGURE 2-11 According to Maslow, we must meet our lower-level needs before we can seek self-actualization.

physiological needs are not met (for example, they are very hungry), then "all other needs may become simply non-existent or be pushed into the background" (Maslow, 1943). Each need must be met before moving on to the next one. For example, if our physiological needs have been met but our need for safety has not, we cannot seek to fulfill our need for love until we feel safe and secure.

Maslow's Hierarchy of Needs theory made psychologists consider peoples' needs and what happens if basic needs are not met. However, his theory has been questioned because it is not supported in scientific, experimental research. Maslow himself knew that there could be other factors that affected motivation, such as values and conditioning. Some critiques of Maslow include the assumption that you have to move step by step, as well as the fact that his concept of self-actualized individuals included only highly educated white males. Still, his theory made psychologists question their previous assumptions and opened the door to new ways of thinking about motivation.

Viktor Frankl (1905–1997)

Viktor Frankl took a different approach than Maslow. Frankl's theory and therapy grew out of his experiences in Auschwitz—a Nazi concentration camp that was set up during World War II. The conditions in Auschwitz were poor and provided little hope for its inhabitants' survival. Frankl observed the behaviours of his fellow prisoners and saw that those who survived often did so because they had something to hold on to. Some had loved ones that they hoped to reunite with, while others wanted to return to their lives to complete a project. For some, just having great faith tended to increase their chances of survival compared to those who had lost all hope. The survivors had meaning in their lives.

Frankl used this knowledge of the power of having meaning in one's life as the basis for a new form of therapy. He called his form of therapy **logotherapy**, from the Greek word *logos*, which can mean study, word, spirit, God, or meaning. It is this last sense that Frankl's theory centres on. Comparing himself with other psychiatrists, Frankl believed that everyone has an inborn inclination to seek the meaning of his or her existence. He believed that this determination existed even in the worst of circumstances. He suggested that Freud essentially proposed a need for pleasure as the root of all human motivation, while psychologist Alfred Adler proposed a need for power. Logotherapy suggests that humans are motivated by a need for meaning. Frankl believed that those people who cannot find meaning in their lives will feel empty, and this emptiness may lead to feelings of depression.

Another tenet of logotherapy is that each of us has the freedom of will. This means that you can choose how to respond to situations and thus have the power to shape your own life. This is important in helping people make changes in their lives, such as overcoming anxiety.

FIGURE 2-12 Viktor Frankl believed that we have the freedom to choose how we respond to what life throws at us.

logotherapy: a form of psychotherapy that tries to help the patient find the aim and meaning of his or her own life as a human being without accessing the medical aspect of mental health

? How do Viktor Frankl's observations about concentration camp survivors contradict Maslow's theory of self-actualization?

Carl Rogers (1902–1987)

Also considered one of the founders of humanist psychology, Carl Rogers developed **client-centred therapy**. This approach focuses on the potential of each person to realize his or her own growth in self-awareness and self-fulfillment. It differs from the approach used by psychoanalytic therapists because it focuses on the present and the future, rather than the past, and gives more value to conscious, rather than unconscious, thoughts. Rogers believed that people are basically good and have a need to self-actualize. Rogers spent the last years of his life applying his techniques to help solve social conflicts throughout the world. He was nominated for a Nobel Peace Prize for his work toward ending conflict in Ireland and South Africa.

client-centred therapy: a humanistic therapy developed by Carl Rogers in which the client plays an active role

The Client-Centred Model

In the client-centred model, the psychotherapist creates a warm environment in which clients can express any feeling or thought without fear of judgment. As clients explore their attitudes and emotions on an issue, they will discover the underlying motivations for those attitudes. By playing an active role in the discovery process, the client not only gains greater insight but also gains self-acceptance. The psychotherapist follows a predictable process and uses specific techniques but doesn't interpret for the client. Generally the client starts with more superficial concerns and then moves to deeper attitudes and concerns. Clients see how problems relate to one another and their patterns of behaviour. Then they begin to improve their self-concept, how they see themselves, and change their negative patterns.

Through this process, ways of thinking that were not available to the conscious mind become unearthed. The benefits of the client-centred approach are that the insights gained can lead to real changes in behaviour to conform to new understandings. So the client-centred approach may be seen as an effective way of improving behaviour. Because of its effectiveness, this approach has become the basis of modern psychotherapy.

↑ **FIGURE 2-13** Carl Rogers, founder of the client-centred approach to therapy, believed that clients should be able to express themselves freely during therapy.

> **VOICES**
> I hear, I know.
> I see, I remember.
> I do, I understand.
> Confucius

(?) Compare the client-centred approach to therapy to the psychoanalytic approach. Discuss the benefits and limitations of each.

(?) Consider the following situation: you've just moved to a new school and you're having trouble in Math class. Create a web diagram to show how these problems might be related and what other issues may be contributing to them.

Impact of Humanistic Psychology on Society

Humanistic psychology has not only changed the way many psychotherapists work, but has had a broader impact as well. In terms of psychotherapy, the humanist approach is now the basis of many practices since its focus on working with clients to help them come to their own understanding is preferred by both clients and therapists. Because its approaches help to create a positive environment, clients are more likely to feel comfortable enough to explore their own motivations and behaviours openly and honestly.

Humanism in Education

Humanist models of education are called *student-centred*, or open education. Like clients in humanist therapy sessions, students are encouraged to take responsibility for their learning, to be curious and creative, and to learn independently as much as possible. The role of the teacher is to understand why students behave the way they do and to learn how to help them achieve growth. As a result, students in this environment tend to be co-operative, creative, and independent learners.

The Principles of Open Education

Open or humanistic education is based on the following principles:

1. Students will learn best what they want and need to know once they learn the skills to analyze what is important to them and why.
2. Knowing how to learn is more important than acquiring a lot of knowledge.
3. Self-evaluation is the only meaningful evaluation of a student's work.
4. Feelings are as important as facts.
5. Students learn best in a nonthreatening environment.

What does open education look like in a classroom? It often looks like experiential learning, where students get to "do the discipline" rather than simply reading about it. Choice in assignments is available, and student ideas and interests are used in instruction.

(?) What are the benefits of this model in the classroom? What are the challenges in translating this model in the classroom?

Humanism in the Workplace

Approaches developed by Maslow and Rogers also have applications in the workplace. In a collaborative workplace, managers provide a positive, nonjudgmental environment where creativity, individuality, and risk-taking are valued. This work environment can improve employee motivation because each person's self-esteem needs are considered and more responsibility is given to the individual employee. This consideration of the whole person fosters self-actualization, the ultimate goal of humanist psychology.

FIGURE 2-14 What evidence does this photo provide that these people are collaborating?

REFLECT AND RESPOND

1. Are there humanist influences in the way your classroom is organized or in the way you are learning in your class? If so, what are they and how do they connect to the principles above?
2. To what extent do you agree with Maslow's assumption that people naturally want to become self-actualized? Support your answer.

Cognitive Psychology

Before You Read
Think about a time you were successful in learning something new. What method of learning helped you most: reading about it, doing it, or listening to an explanation of it? How do you know this method was successful?

cognition: the mental processes in the brain associated with thinking, knowing, and remembering

The word **cognition** refers to the mental processes in the brain. So cognitive psychology is the study and application of how the brain learns. Unlike behaviourists, cognitive psychologists believe in and consider mental states, such as beliefs, motivations, and desires. However, cognitive psychology is often coupled with behavioural psychology to create methods of treating people with some mental illnesses and neurotic disorders.

Albert Bandura (1925–)

Canadian Albert Bandura was part of the "cognitive revolution" of psychologists moving away from purely behaviourist thought. He wondered why the same situation could generate different responses from different people or even the same person. His research led him to come up with social-cognitive theory, a perspective on personality that takes a person's motivation, environment, and behaviour into account. His theory can be used to predict and change individual and group behaviour.

Bandura believes people learn behaviour by watching and then imitating others. To explore this theory, he created the Bobo Doll experiment. First, children watched a video in which an adult acted aggressively toward a rubber Bobo doll by hitting, punching, kicking, and even striking it with a mallet. He then allowed the children, one at a time, to interact with the doll. Other aggressive and nonaggressive toys were also provided in the room. Bandura discovered that instead of their aggression being let out by watching the adult, the children behaved just as aggressively (see Figure 2-15). More disturbing were the observations that the children had increased interest in using toy guns to hit Bobo, despite the guns not being used by the adult in the video, and even created new ways of acting aggressively toward the doll. The children in the control group did not view the video and were therefore not exposed to aggressive modelling. They were less likely to behave aggressively toward the doll and were not as interested in the other aggressive toys in the room, such as the guns.

? Do you think Bandura's experiment would be considered ethical by today's standards? Why or why not?

? Do you believe that Bandura's work supports the theory that playing violent video games promotes violence in children?

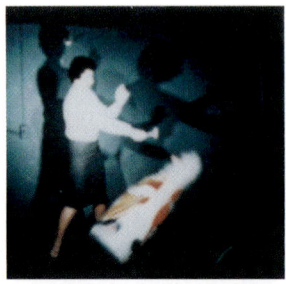

↑ **FIGURE 2-15** The top frame shows an adult modelling aggressive behaviour. The next frame shows a girl behaving aggressively toward the Bobo doll.

Elizabeth Loftus (1944–)

For the past 30 years, Elizabeth Loftus has been studying false memories and the flexibility and reliability of repressed memories. Her belief that repressed memories rarely exist and can be created through the power of suggestion has been controversial. Some victims of sexual assault who recall their repressed memories after many years are quite hurt by Loftus's claims. They feel that their painful memories are being brushed aside as being nothing more than made-up stories. Yet, there is some research that suggests that there is some truth behind false memories. Canadian doctor Laura Melnyk's findings in *The Development of Metasuggestibility in Children* indicate that children's reports of a behaviour can be influenced by the statements of others and this influence is exerted well into the school years.

Lost in the Mall?

To test her theory, Loftus and her research associate Jacqueline E. Pickrell created an experiment where participants read several stories of real events that had occurred during their childhood, as well as one fictional story where they were lost in the mall at the age of five. The results showed that 29 percent of participants remembered at least part of the false event, with 25 percent continuing to remember it in two follow-up interviews (Loftus & Pickrell, 1995).

It is important to remember that the lost-in-the-mall study is about how to plant false memories. The study proves that people can be led to remember their past in various ways, and even "remember" a past that didn't happen to them. Understanding how false memories are implanted can help psychologists understand how a person can be led to remember something that never occurred. As such, Loftus's work has had an impact in the fields of cognitive psychology as well as law in terms of the reliability of eyewitness accounts.

False Memories in the Visual Age

German psychologist Gerald Echterhoff researches false memories created by observation. Echterhoff found that for 25 percent of people, the memory of doing something can be created by watching someone else do it on TV.

Echterhoff's study involved having participants perform and read about many simple actions, such as shuffling a deck of cards. The actions that were selected were simple but not so common that participants were likely to do them every day. They then watched videos of other people doing simple actions. Some of these actions the participants had also done; some they had not. After two weeks, researchers asked the participants to identify which of 30 actions on a list they had done.

The researchers discovered that participants were far more likely to "remember" actions that they had watched than those they had read about. More surprisingly, the participants had false memories even when they were warned that this might happen in the experiment! How do these false memories occur? Echterhoff believes that seeing something happen creates that image in the brain—a sort of simulation—that then activates a representation similar to one that would occur had the individuals done the task themselves.

> **VOICES**
>
> Misinformation has the potential for invading our memories when we talk to other people, when we are suggestively interrogated or when we read or view media coverage about some event that we may have experienced ourselves.
>
> Elizabeth Loftus
> (*Scientific American*, 1997)

> **Skills Focus**
>
> What is the central research question for each of these studies? Compare their results: how are they similar and how are they different?

REFLECT AND RESPOND

1. How can we apply what was learned from the Bobo Doll experiment to early childhood learning?
2. The studies on false memory suggest eyewitnesses in court are not as reliable as we would expect. Why might these testimonies continue to be used?
3. How might technology and social media affect false memories?

Section 2.2 Psychological Approaches to Understanding Behaviour

Research in psychology attempts to make sense of our behaviour, including how we learn, how we perceive the world, and how we use language. In this section, you will learn about theories on behaviour proposed by developmental psychologists as well as the role of the brain in behaviour.

Developmental Psychologists

The human body changes throughout the course of its life, both physically and mentally. Psychologists who study human psychological development are concerned with explaining *how* we change and offer a variety of theories to help us understand what we can expect and what is happening to us at different times in our lives.

Sigmund Freud (1856–1939)

Freud's *stages of development* theory was based on his observations of how children focus on pleasure as they mature. These stages occur one after the other, but individuals can become **fixated** at the oral, anal, or phallic stage if they have not fully resolved the conflict in this stage. Freud believed that this could cause those people to over- or under-indulge in that area in adulthood, which would lead to engaging in behaviours like smoking, nail biting, or overeating.

> **Before You Read**
> How important are our childhood experiences to our psychological development? Are there other times in our lives when there are significant changes in development?

fixation:
the continued focus on an earlier stage of psychosocial development due to an unresolved conflict at the oral, anal, or phallic stage

PSYCHOSEXUAL STAGES OF DEVELOPMENT		
Stage	**Description**	**Issues in Adulthood If Unresolved**
oral (birth–18 months)	• focuses on oral pleasures, such as sucking, biting, and chewing	• can lead to nail biting, smoking, and overeating
anal (18 months–3 years)	• derives pleasure from learning to control anus (toilet training)	• can lead to concern with perfection and obsessive cleanliness (anal retentive) or extreme messiness (anal expulsive)
phallic (3–6 years)	• focuses on genitals as a source of pleasure; develops Oedipus complex (boys unconsciously desire their mothers and compete with their fathers)	• can lead to overindulgence or avoidance of sexual behaviour and weak sexual identity
latency (6 years–puberty)	• plays mainly with same-gender friends; sexual feelings are dormant	• not applicable, as sexual urges are repressed in this stage
genital (puberty onward)	• directs sexual urges toward members of the opposite sex	• not applicable, as this is the final stage

Like many of his theories, Freud's psychosexual stages have been criticized for being sexist and lacking in evidence. However, they were fundamental to Freud's theory that much of personality is developed at an early age.

Jean Piaget (1896–1980)

French psychologist Jean Piaget was a highly influential figure in developmental psychology as well as in cognitive psychology. Through his work on the Binet IQ test, he became interested in why children's answers at various ages were qualitatively different. Eventually his case study observations led to the creation of his stages of cognitive development theory. As in Freud's theory, children move through the stages in order as they grow older.

Piaget's theory is still influential today as applied to education. Cognitive development stages are taken into account when a curriculum is developed to ensure the material is at an appropriate level. Piaget's theories also extend to techniques used in the classroom. For example, high-school teachers can assume their students are moving from concrete operational to formal operational stages. So their teaching strategies will include concrete techniques, such as using graphs, charts, and step-by-step instructions, and formal operational techniques, such as having class discussions, linking broad concepts, and using explanations for problem solving.

PIAGET'S STAGES OF COGNITIVE DEVELOPMENT	
Stage	**Description**
sensorimotor (birth–2 years)	• experiences the world through senses and actions, by touching, looking, and mouthing • begins to understand that objects exist even if they can't be seen (object permanence) at around 7 months • understands some symbols, language begins
pre-operational (2–6 years)	• develops language and use of symbols, memory, and imagination • exhibits nonlogical thinking • is egocentric
concrete operational (7–11 years)	• develops logic • develops ability to link concrete objects to symbols and use them • becomes less egocentric
formal operational (12 years–adulthood)	• develops ability to logically link symbols to abstract ideas • early in this period, becomes egocentric again • not all adults reach this stage

? How might knowing the stages of development theories be helpful for parents?

IN FOCUS — Core Knowledge

While Piaget believed that children under the age of two do not have abstract ideas, studies by researcher Robert Fantz and more recently Elizabeth Spelke have shown that infants make sense of the world more quickly than Piaget thought. For example, until the 1960s it was believed that newborns could see only blurry light and dark shades. Fantz discovered that babies as young as two months old could differentiate all basic colours, and that newborns preferred their mother's face over that of a stranger's (unless either one has covered up her hair).

Elizabeth Spelke has taken Fantz's work one step further to explain why infants are able to make these distinctions. Her theory of *core knowledge* states that each of us is born with basic cognitive skills that allow us to make sense of objects, space, people, movement, and number. Therefore, because core knowledge in each of these areas is present at birth, infants are able to organize information and their perception of it.

QUESTIONS

1. How does the research of Fantz and Spelke challenge Piaget's theories?
2. What suggestions would you give to parents/caregivers based on the theory of core knowledge?

> **Open for Debate**
>
> Boomerang children—adults in their 20s who move out then come back home—are a new phenomenon in North America. Some people say they're just lazy; others argue that it's a new stage of life due to new economic and social expectations, and huge postsecondary education debts.

identity crisis: a time in a teenager's life filled with extreme self-consciousness as he or she attempts to test and integrate various roles

Erik Erikson (1902–1994)

German-born psychologist and child analyst Erik Erikson was a neo-Freudian in terms of child development and his understanding of the ego. Freud's stages of psychosexual development influenced his thinking, but he believed that humans continue to develop over their lifetime rather than just in childhood. He also differed from Freud in that he believed that individual growth depends on society, not just personal experiences. Erikson's stages of psychosocial development outline the developmental tasks that must be resolved during each stage of life.

Erikson also believed that adolescents sometimes experience what he called an **identity crisis**. What this looks like will often depend on the society in which the teenagers live and the concerns of their time period. He described it as a time when the teenager feels extremely self-conscious and engages in a lot of conflicts that were started unconsciously. This idea of an identity crisis has now become a part of the mainstream understanding of teens. For example, if at home you act like a co-operative teen but at school feel pressured to talk back to your teachers in order to be "cool," you may find yourself having difficulty determining which of these selves best represents who you are. Similarly, if your parents want you to adhere to certain cultural norms, you may find it difficult to fit in with your peers if these norms conflict with what is considered popular.

ERIKSON'S STAGES OF PSYCHOSOCIAL DEVELOPMENT		
Stage	**When Needs Are Met**	**When Needs Are Not Met**
trust vs. mistrust (birth–1 year old)	• trust is developed when needs (e.g., hunger, comfort) are dependably met	• if needs are not met, frustration and withdrawal set in
autonomy vs. shame and doubt (2–3 years old)	• supportive environment fosters autonomy	• loss of trust can lead to shame and doubt about independence
initiative vs. guilt (3–5 years old)	• initiative increases with sense of responsibility	• anxiety about initiating tasks can lead to guilt
industry vs. inferiority (6 years–puberty)	• interest develops in knowledge; awareness develops that they are productive human beings	• unsuccessful learning experiences can lead to a sense of inferiority and worthlessness
identity vs. role confusion (adolescence: teens–20s)	• increased concern for the way others see them, exploring "who am I?"	• inability to settle on an identity can lead to role confusion
intimacy vs. isolation (young adulthood: 20s–early 40s)	• well-formed identity enables the ability to form close relationships and friendships	• social isolation occurs if unformed identity limits experiences that could harm ego
generativity vs. stagnation (middle adulthood: 40s–60s)	• the middle-aged feel a need to guide the next generation	• stagnation develops out of a sense of lack of purpose
integrity vs. despair (late adulthood: late 60s onward)	• through re-examination of life, integrity is achieved if previous stages developed well	• fear of death or dependence on others can lead to despair

Gender Differences?

Erikson's stages of development may be useful for understanding major concerns as we age, but are these concerns the same for girls as they are for boys? Psychologists Mindy Bingham and Sandy Stryker think there are some differences. To illustrate their theory, they created a five-stage model for girls that is based on Erikson's stages of psychosocial development.

Bingham and Stryker's theory suggests that development is influenced by society, not just biology. Adolescents, for instance, may have different needs based on the twenty-first century economy than they did before, so their development might necessarily look different than their parents' or grandparents' development. Bingham and Stryker also emphasize that for girls, financial independence, not just social and emotional skills, is an important step in developing their sense of autonomy and self.

> **Open for Debate**
> Stage theorists don't all agree on where stages begin and end or why people behave the way they do in those stages. To what extent are stage theories helpful for understanding psychological development?

FIGURE 2-16 According to Bingham and Stryker, how might this picture be different if there were boys present or if the children were older?

STAGES OF SOCIO-EMOTIONAL DEVELOPMENT FOR GIRLS	
Stage	**Expected Resolution**
developing the hardy personality (birth–8 years old)	• feels in control of own life; is committed to specific activities; looks forward to challenge and opportunity for growth
forming an identity as an achiever (9–12 years old)	• develops steady, durable core of self as person who is capable of accomplishment in a variety of areas (e.g., intellectual, physical, social, potential career)
building skills for self-esteem (13–16 years old)	• has feeling of being worthy, deserving, entitled to assert needs and wants; has confidence in ability to cope with life
developing strategies for self-sufficiency (emotional and financial) (17–22 years old)	• has sense of responsibility for taking care of self and, perhaps, a family, based on a sense of autonomy
finding satisfaction in work and love (adulthood)	• finds contentedness in personal accomplishments and social/personal relationships

❓ According to Freud, Piaget, and Erikson, you are in the genital, formal operational, and identity vs. role confusion stages, respectively. Which of these stages do you feel most accurately represents your current stage in life? Explain. Is this true of your peers as well? What role does your culture play in your current stage of development? Explain.

> **Connecting Psychology to Sociology**
>
> According to sociologists, the most common role that we are taught from birth is how to behave according to our gender. What we believe about gender is internalized from a young age through the primary agent of socialization—the family—and is based on accepted norms of masculine and feminine behaviour as developed by family and society, and portrayed in the media. If gender is so important to our identity, why didn't psychologists recognize females in their research?

> **More to Know...**
>
> Is intelligence inherited or influenced by environment or both? Look ahead to Chapter 5 to learn more.

FIGURE 2-17 What assumptions is the cartoonist making about gifted students?

Leta Stetter Hollingworth (1886–1939)

Leta Stetter Hollingworth was an American psychologist who worked at a time when the field was dominated by men. She found that their theories, while thought-provoking, largely ignored the concerns of women. In fact, at the time, the belief was that men were more variable in their physical and mental abilities, and women were basically the same in their abilities. This was used to explain why there were more male geniuses and led to the belief that women had neither the same cognitive ability nor the same range of talents as men and would not achieve anything extraordinary. Hollingworth hypothesized, and proved, that this belief was wrong. She conducted a large study measuring the height and weight of 1000 male and 1000 female newborns, and, just as she had predicted, there was no statistical difference between the genders in these areas. Because the variability in physique was not greater in males as was once thought, Hollingworth was able to poke some serious holes in the theory that men had greater cognitive abilities.

Gifted Children

Hollingworth shifted her research focus to the cognitive abilities of children and was the first psychologist to study gifted children, defined as those who score higher than 160 IQ on the Stanford-Binet IQ test. Hollingworth conducted several studies of gifted children and believed that while their intelligence was based partially on genes, the children's potential could be truly realized only through education and their environment.

In 1936, Hollingworth began working at the Speyer School in New York City, where she initiated an enrichment curriculum known as "Evolution of Common Things." She believed that gifted children were interested in everything about the world around them. The curriculum taught them about ordinary, everyday things such as food, clothing, shelter, transportation, and timekeeping. In the end, gifted students benefitted academically more from this curriculum than from the introduction of advanced academic courses (Hollingworth, 1943).

The impact of Hollingworth's work led to a greater understanding of the needs of gifted children and their development. She observed that gifted children tended to have difficulty adjusting because either they were not challenged enough intellectually or they were often left alone by adults who assumed they could take care of themselves.

However, to be identified as gifted in most boards of education requires standardized testing. Tests work well for some people, but not all people (Sternberg, 1982). There are some concerns with the validity of the testing as there are concerns and criticisms about gender bias, as well as bias against minority races and those from socio-economically disadvantaged homes.

> **?** Make recommendations to the Minister of Education based on Hollingworth's theory. Refer to her ideas and provide one or two suggestions that would help all children learn.

> **?** How might an IQ test written in a Middle Eastern or African culture affect the determination of who is defined as gifted?

Harry Harlow (1905–1981)

Harry Harlow, an American psychology professor, was responsible for developing many of the tests using primates that are standard today. He believed that studying primates is an appropriate way to understand human behaviour because they have a number of similarities to humans and the genetic difference between humans and chimps is in fact quite small.

For some time, developmental psychologists had held the belief that infants formed an attachment to those who provided them with nourishment. Harlow wanted to find out which urge is stronger: the need for affection or the satisfaction of physical needs (specifically, food). He devised the Surrogate Mother experiment using rhesus monkeys because of their similarities to human infants' behaviours with their mothers (for example, clinging, "language" learning, nursing). He removed the young monkeys from their mothers before they had a chance to bond and kept them isolated. The monkeys were kept in a cage with two "mothers," both made of wire mesh. One of the mothers was covered with tan terry cloth; the other offered food in the form of a bottle from its breast area. Both mothers were warmed with radiant heat.

The monkeys overwhelmingly preferred the cloth mother, even though she did not provide food. When they were anxious, the monkeys would cling to the cloth mother. So Harlow's experiment showed that infants depend on their caregivers for more than just their physical needs: meeting emotional needs is crucial for attachment. The monkeys that did not receive affection early in life often experienced psychological problems later on. For instance, they behaved in ways that illustrated misdirected aggression (for example, they held themselves while rocking back and forth), and the females became either negligent or abusive mothers.

> **Skills Focus**
> Assess the evidence in this study for relevance, reliability, and bias. What conclusions can be made using this evidence? What other research could be conducted to prove/disprove this conclusion?

REFLECT AND RESPOND

1. Compare the stages of development theories using a Venn diagram. Suggest a reason why the number of stages varies by theorist.
2. What types of issues or considerations are left out of stage development theories?
3. Based on Harlow's experiment, what recommendations can be made about caring for an infant?
4. What do Harlow's findings suggest about Maslow's Hierarchy of Needs?

FIGURE 2-18 Even while feeding from the wire mother, this rhesus monkey tries to find comfort from the cloth mother.

Landmark Case Study

Mary Ainsworth (1913–1999): Infant–Mother Attachment

Noted North American psychologist Mary Ainsworth's study of child development has become the groundwork for our understanding of mother–infant separation and how it influences interactions later in life. As demonstrated by Harlow's work with rhesus monkeys, attachment to a caregiver happens early on in life and is necessary for survival. Infants usually become attached to those who are familiar and responsive to their needs. They use this attachment as a secure base from which to explore their environment. Mary Ainsworth was interested in learning more about the ways in which infants were attached to their parents.

Ainsworth began her work on attachment theory while she lived in Uganda with her husband. During the same period, psychologist John Bowlby was establishing a theoretical understanding of child–mother attachment. Bowlby believed that babies have a behavioural system, which includes behaviours such as crying, that gets the parent to stay close to the child. Ainsworth found his work of help when she devised her Strange Situation experiment to study the quality of infant–mother attachments in the 1970s.

The Strange Situation Experiment

The experiment was conducted in a controlled environment that resembled a living room in a home but had a one-way glass mirror so psychologists could observe and take notes. Typically a caregiver (for example, a mother) brought in a 12-month-old child for the experiment. The following indicates the steps:

1. A caregiver enters the experiment room with the child. They play until the child is relaxed.
2. A stranger enters the room and does not interact with the child.
3. The caregiver leaves the room, and the stranger attempts to console the child (who is usually very upset).
4. The caregiver soon returns to the room and consoles the child until the child is relaxed again.
5. The caregiver leaves the room for the second time, and the stranger again attempts to console the child.
6. The caregiver again returns to the room and soothes the child.

While the experiment is in progress, the researchers are observing through the glass and taking notes using a common language to describe certain actions. They are interested in the child's reactions to the caregiver's leaving and especially the nature of attachment displayed upon the caregiver's return. They also take note of how much exploration the child does both while the caregiver is there and absent.

FIGURE 2-19 Mary Ainsworth's classic Strange Situation experiment was important to help psychologists understand the nature of attachment between an infant and his or her caregiver.

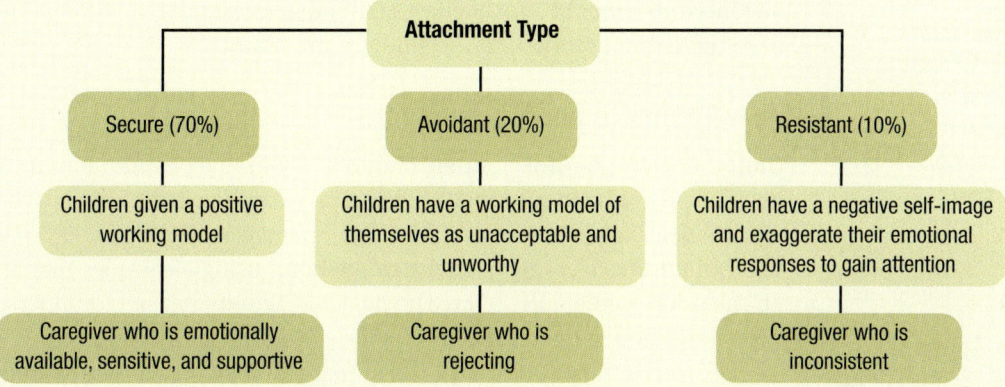

↑ **FIGURE 2-20** Ainsworth categorized infant attachment into three categories: secure, avoidant, and resistant.

Results

Based on the infant's response to the caregiver's departure and subsequent return, as well as how the child explored his or her environment, children were categorized as one of the following three types: secure, avoidant, or resistant (see Figure 2-20).

Secure Attachment

A securely attached infant happily explored the new environment while the caregiver was in the room. When the caregiver left, the infant was visibly upset but responded with happiness when the caregiver returned.

Ainsworth believed that this type of attachment forms when the caregiver is emotionally available and consistently responds to the child's needs.

Avoidant Attachment

Infants exhibiting avoidant attachment were extremely upset when their caregiver left but were ambivalent when she returned and refused to play with her. These infants were anxious about exploring their environment.

Having a caregiver who is rejecting may lead the child to have this type of attachment.

Resistant Attachment

Infants with resistant attachment did not explore very much, regardless of whether or not their caregiver was in the room. These infants showed little emotion upon the caregiver's departure and return.

Resistant attachment forms when a caregiver is at times very responsive while at other times rejecting.

Conclusions

Ainsworth's pioneering research demonstrated the profound effects of attachment on behaviour. Her work helped psychologists understand the importance of early attachment to a caregiver and has led others to study its effects in more depth. Researchers such as Bartholomew and Horowitz (1991) have concluded that secure attachment sets up positive emotional development later on in life, while failure to form attachments early in life can have a negative effect on behaviour in later childhood and throughout life. Avoidant or resistant attachment can set a child up for difficult emotional development and a negative self-concept very early in life, which can cause many problems as he or she grows.

Interestingly, rates of attachment style vary by culture. For example, similar studies have shown that children in Germany have a much higher rate of avoidant attachment than those in North America.

QUESTIONS

1. Explain to a partner the research methods used by Ainsworth. What was her central research question?

2. What is the most significant contribution Mary Ainsworth made to developmental psychology? Explain with examples.

3. Do you think that the same results would be achieved if this experiment were conducted today with people of different cultural backgrounds?

Understanding the Brain

Before You Read
What do you know about your brain? Where did you learn about your brain?

Psychologists have been interested in understanding the mind—conscious and unconscious thought—for the last century. Yet, to understand the mind, they have increasingly turned to the study of the brain.

New Technology: Windows into the Brain

Until the 1970s, **neuroscientists** had to study brains postmortem, or once people had died. Now computer technology can be used to help psychologists and neuroscientists understand how the brain works. An electroencephalogram (EEG) measures electrical activity in the brain using electrodes that are placed on the scalp (see Figure 2-21). The detected activity is used to understand where and how much brain activity is occurring.

Devised in the early 1990s, functional magnetic resonance imaging (fMRI) machines make it possible to "see" in real time what is happening in the brain by measuring blood flow to its different regions (see Figure 2-23). A patient lies down inside an fMRI scanner and is then given audio or visual stimuli. The scanner senses increased blood flow, due to the need for more oxygen, which indicates areas of the brain that are being used to process the new information. This information is displayed in the form of images.

While these technologies can be windows into a live brain, they are limited because they show only the areas of the brain being used. They still cannot answer such questions as what motivates someone or why people choose to behave differently in similar situations.

neuroscientist: a scientist who specializes in the study of the human brain

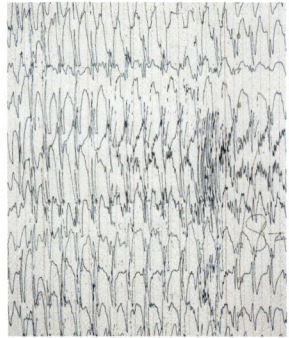

↑ **FIGURE 2-21** This EEG reading shows an absence seizure.

 How are your brain and your mind interconnected?

IN FOCUS: Phineas Gage

Phineas Gage was a 25-year-old railroad construction worker who was an expert in removing rocks using explosives to build the railroad. In 1848, he accidentally set off an explosive, which propelled a rod through his left cheek and out his skull. He was bleeding but conscious and taken to a nearby town for medical care.

This was the first case that demonstrated the relationship between the brain and behaviour. Before the accident, he had been capable and efficient with a well-balanced mind, and was looked on as a smart businessman. After the accident, his behaviour was erratic and he showed little respect for his co-workers. He was also impatient and stubborn, yet impulsive. His friends said he was "no longer Gage."

QUESTION

1. What are some environmental issues that may challenge this research?

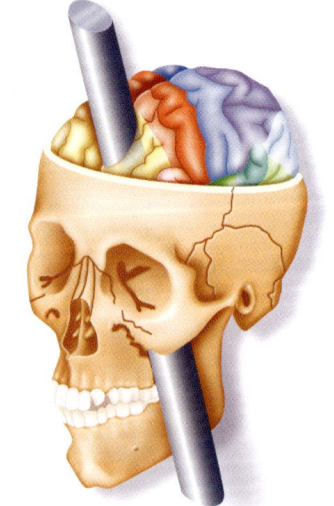

↑ **FIGURE 2-22** The reconstruction of Gage's skull by Peter Ratiu and Ion-Florin Talos.

How the Brain Works

Here's an interesting fact: while the brain is only about 2 percent of the average adult's total body weight, it uses up 20 percent of the body's energy! How does it work? The brain is made up of millions of cells called *neurons*. They store information and communicate using electrical impulses. Covering the whole brain is the cerebral cortex, which is made up of grey matter. The brain's problem-solving ability is mainly controlled by the **cerebrum**, which is divided into two regions. The left cerebral hemisphere is responsible for communication and language, logic, and mathematical abilities. The right cerebral hemisphere receives and analyzes information, so it handles facial recognition, spatial awareness, and visual imagery (see Figure 2-24). However, each hemisphere controls the muscles on the opposite side of the body.

The hippocampus is responsible for short term and long term memory. Interestingly, it is also part of the emotional system, which explains why you remember people who have affected you in some way. Psychologists are interested in sections of the brain because understanding how the brain works helps them understand principles such as conditioning and memory.

cerebrum: the largest and most developed portion of the brain, which is responsible for controlling memory, understanding, and logic

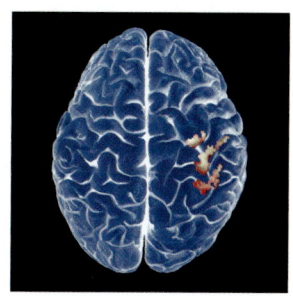

FIGURE 2-23 The fMRI image of the brain is often displayed in colour to help doctors see the active regions more easily.

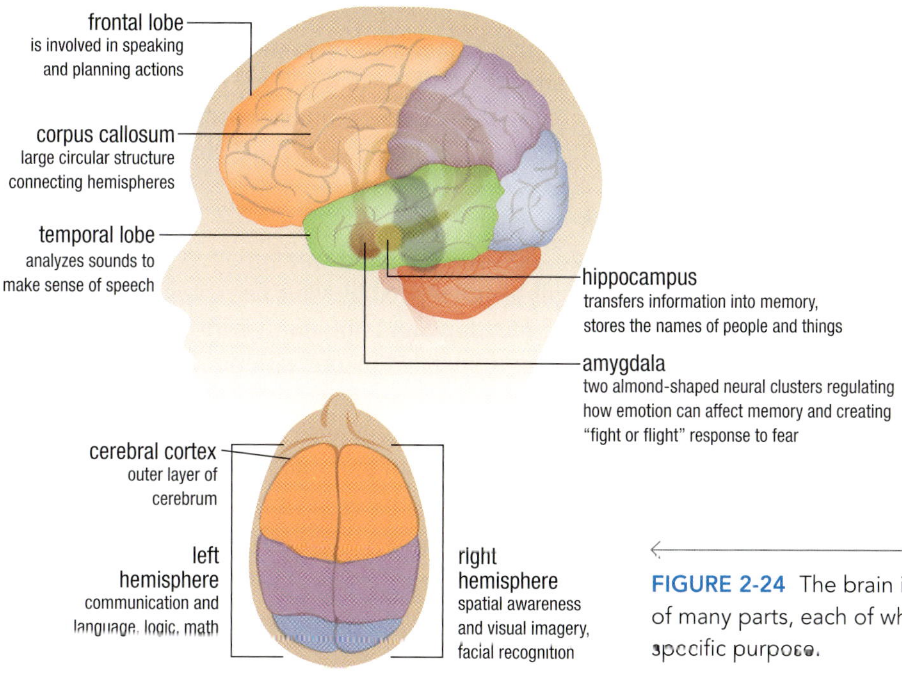

frontal lobe is involved in speaking and planning actions

corpus callosum large circular structure connecting hemispheres

temporal lobe analyzes sounds to make sense of speech

hippocampus transfers information into memory, stores the names of people and things

amygdala two almond-shaped neural clusters regulating how emotion can affect memory and creating "fight or flight" response to fear

cerebral cortex outer layer of cerebrum

left hemisphere communication and language, logic, math

right hemisphere spatial awareness and visual imagery, facial recognition

FIGURE 2-24 The brain is made up of many parts, each of which has a specific purpose.

❓ Psychologists and neuroscientists both study the brain. What is the difference between their disciplines?

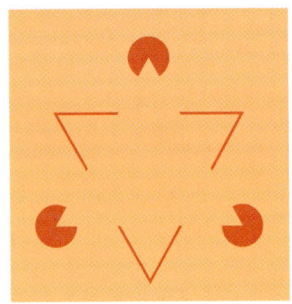

FIGURE 2-25 Our brain fills in the gaps to create a triangle when in reality one does not actually exist. What happens to the triangle when the circles are covered up?

Perception

While we're awake, our brains are constantly registering everything our eyes "see" exactly as it exists, then interpret it for understanding. This is true for each of our senses. This process of selecting, organizing, and interpreting our sensations is called *perception*. According to some psychologists, the brain naturally groups similar items together. Organizing information in this way avoids repetition and makes the brain more efficient.

Filling in the Gaps

In essence, the brain works on a set of assumptions and fills in gaps by making educated guesses. The principle of *closure* occurs when the information given to the brain is incomplete. In the example in Figure 2-25, the brain fills in the missing information. This happens especially when the shapes are familiar.

Perceptual Constancy

Another function of the brain is to maintain *perceptual constancy*. Even though our view of an object changes as we move, the brain recognizes it as unchanged. For instance, as you walk to school, the school building seems to become bigger, yet you know that the building's size hasn't actually changed. If the brain didn't instinctively understand this principle, it would have to re-evaluate the school every step you took toward it. This idea of constancy applies to size, shape, and colour. Without perceptual constancy, you would have a hard time identifying objects if your viewing angle changed.

Perceptual Sets

Look at Figure 2-26: do you see an old woman or a young woman? How you answer will be influenced by your *perceptual set*, your tendency to perceive one thing and not another. (It's actually both!) Our perceptual sets are influenced by our experiences and expectations, which in turn affect how we view the world. For example, if, in your experience, babies dressed in pink were girls, you would be surprised to learn that a pink-outfitted infant was named "Henry." Our perceptions are therefore a mix of what our senses take in and what our experiences suggest.

FIGURE 2-26 Is this a drawing of an old woman or a young woman?

REFLECT AND RESPOND

1. How might each of the following influence a person's memory of a crime:
   a) the changes in the hippocampus during heightened anxiety or stress while witnessing the crime
   b) the person's perceptual set
2. Describe a situation where your peceptual set influenced your behaviour.
3. Suggest a theory of why the brain needs to interpret what the eyes see.

Controlling the Ever-Changing Brain

Psychologists want to explore the brain so they can learn how to improve human lives. They used to believe that once the body reaches adulthood, the brain is completely developed. However, neuroscientists have recently discovered that these assumptions are false. Researchers have discovered that everything we do changes our brains. According to American psychologist and professor Robert Epstein, "[M]editation, diet, exercise, studying, and virtually all other activities alter the brain, and a new study shows that smoking produces brain changes similar to those produced in animals given heroin, cocaine, or other addictive drugs" (2007). Our brains are always changing!

Neuroplasticity is the idea that the brain is plastic and malleable. Research that challenges the idea that the brain is incapable of fundamental change was highlighted by Canadian Dr. Norman Doidge in his book, *The Brain That Changes Itself*. Up until recently, doctors had given up on people suffering from brain damage or post-traumatic stress disorder, but new research is showing that the human brain can even rewire itself. For example, one woman lost her sense of balance due to a side effect of a drug. After participating in a simple therapy, she regained the ability to balance and is now living a normal life. Consider, also, the case of Dr. Jill Bolte Taylor whose stroke caused swelling and trauma that placed pressure on her dominant left hemisphere. The functions of her right hemisphere were enhanced; among other things, she discovered new artistic talents. These feats can only be explained by the fact that the brain is resilient and adaptable.

Is Meditation the Answer?

Can we control the changes in our brains in ways that help people? Richard Davidson and his team at the University of Wisconsin–Madison wanted to find out. They studied a dozen Buddhist monks who claimed to be the happiest people on earth. These monks were not born with this frame of mind; rather they say they created their happiness with over 10 000 hours of meditation. Matthieu Richard, a French scientist who became a monk years ago, was the first test subject to "see" what happiness looks like in the brain. In the lab, 128 EEG electrodes were stuck on his head while he meditated on "unconditional loving—kindness and compassion." Intense gamma waves (brain waves of a certain frequency) that indicate extreme focus were immediately detected, when usually gamma waves are difficult to find. Davidson discovered that through their practice of meditation, these monks had altered several parts of their brains including the amygdala. This was a surprising discovery.

> **Before You Read**
> Brainstorm what you know about the brain and how the brain works with a partner. Skim the subtitles of this section and see if you can add to your list.

> **Skills Focus**
> What type of research was used in the study of the monks? How reliable is this research? Think about its strengths and weaknesses to make your judgment.

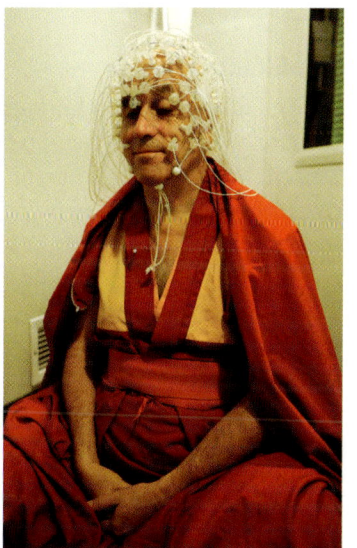

FIGURE 2-27 Matthieu Richard meditates in a soundproof room while EEG electrodes measure his brain activity.

Focusing Therapies

Davidson's study was done on highly skilled meditators. How could his findings have any significance for the rest of society? Davidson and his team had the same question. They conducted studies on short-term practitioners and discovered significant changes occur even then. For example, his team studied the effect meditation had on immune function for workers who participated in an eight-week training program in mindfulness meditation. The results indicated an increase in positive feelings and immune function. An understanding of how to intensely focus the brain could also lead to important therapies for depression, stress-related issues, and behavioural issues.

Meditation's Effects on Alzheimer's Disease

A recent study at the University of Pennsylvania demonstrated that meditation could even help improve memory in people suffering from Alzheimer's disease, a brain disorder characterized by the loss of memory, reasoning, and language. In this case, Dr. Dharma Singh Khalsa used the Kirtan Kriya form of meditation, where repetitive finger movements accompany the singing of particular sounds for 12-minute periods. Cognitive tests were performed on the 15 study participants before and after the 8-week meditation practice. A control group was instructed to listen to Mozart violin concertos twice a day for 12 minutes. Khalsa found that the meditators had increased blood flow to areas of the brain that involve retrieving memory, such as the frontal lobe regions, which resulted in significant increases in general memory and attention.

↑ **FIGURE 2-28** These people are practising meditation. Will it help improve their memory?

The Effects of Yoga

Derived from a Hindu philosophy, yoga is a series of postures and breathing exercise practices that help to achieve control of the body and mind. J. Eric Jensen, an assistant professor of psychiatry at the Harvard Medical School, conducted a study to see if yoga had an impact on the brain. Researchers used MRIs to compare subjects before and after one hour of yoga with those in a control group who sat reading quietly. Those who did yoga had increased levels of the neurotransmitter gamma-aminobutyric (GABA)—a chemical messenger in the brain associated with reducing anxiety and depression, while those in the control group had no change to their levels. The research has shown promise to improve symptoms linked with depression, anxiety, and epilepsy.

> ❓ Suggest other ways meditation could be used to help people. What other activities could people suffering from Alzheimer's disease do to exercise their brains?

POINT/COUNTERPOINT

How Does Internet Use Affect the Brain?

Can you remember a time without the Internet? While its exact origins are debatable, interest in the Internet really exploded among broader society in the early 1990s, when most people started to get a personal email address. As of 2010, about 80 percent of Canadians used the Internet, 500 million users worldwide used Facebook for social networking, and people commonly use eBay to buy and sell goods. If we now know that everything we do changes our brains, then what is the effect of using the Internet? Does it affect children the same way that it affects adults? What about the impact on future generations?

Gary Small is a neuroscientist at UCLA and director of the Memory and Aging Research Center who believes that the Internet makes us better at filtering information and making quick decisions. Moreover, he states that people with excellent technological and social skills will be important for the next generation of citizens.

On the other hand, Nicholas Carr believes that the Internet is having a negative impact on the way we process information and even how we read.

Internet Use Improves Our Technological Skills	Internet Use Makes Us Lose Focus
• Young people today are referred to as "digital natives" because of their great exposure to and familiarity with various forms of technology. This exposure can heighten certain skills, such as multitasking, decision-making, and complex thinking because the brain circuitry is rewired through repeated exposure.	• The Internet is based on interruption, with instant messaging and hopping from one Web page to the next, and as such creates a "chronic state of distraction." This is supported by current brain research showing that everything we do changes our brains.
• Studies indicate that Internet use helps the brain filter information and make quick decisions.	• Many studies indicate that we understand and remember better what we read on paper than online, but the next generation may become more adept at online reading.
• To be successful, people in the next generation will need to be good at communicating through technology as well as face to face; they will have to evaluate a situation quickly to determine the most appropriate means of communication. This is an evolutionary change for humans.	• People are losing the ability to use a "slower, more contemplative mode of thought." Research indicates that people who are better multitaskers are not as creative in their thinking skills.
• One study showed double the activity in areas of the brain that control decision-making and complex reasoning for experienced Internet users compared with beginners. This increased activity is because mental tasks that are performed repeatedly build up certain neural pathways and ignore others. (Small, 2008)	• Practice is the key. Young people spend more time surfing the Web than sitting with a book and, as a result, are not as good at focusing for prolonged periods of time.
	• The Internet is returning humans to their "natural state of distractedness"—the way our ancestors behaved before the invention of the printed page. (Carr, 2010)

QUESTIONS

1. Which opinion most reflects your point of view? Explain.
2. Pick an argument from either side. Do you think research will still show its truth in 20 years' time?

How Do We Learn Language?

> **More to Know...**
> You will study the case study of Genie, the girl isolated until age 13, in Chapter 5. Researchers wanted to see if she could learn language when she was an adolescent.

Part of human development involves learning language. Language development moves from simple to more complex. Infants begin babbling sounds as young as 4 months, and by 10 months they are babbling to match the sounds of the household language. Around their first birthday, children begin to speak in single words, and by the age of two they speak in two-word statements. This progression from babbling to speaking in multiple-word statements has led to some debate over how language is acquired.

Behaviourist B.F. Skinner argued that language development occurs through the association of words with things, imitation of sounds modelled by others, and positive reinforcement from caregivers. Noam Chomsky, whom you learned about in Chapter 1, argues that the rate at which children acquire words is too great to be explained by simple learning principles. He believes that we are biologically prepared to learn words.

A leading researcher in child development and language acquisition, or psycholinguistics, was Elizabeth Bates. Her research showed that the brain is quite flexible in terms of learning language. She studied infants who were born with brain damage and discovered that their brains can still learn language normally. She concluded that language processing can happen in many areas of the brain, not just those typically attributed to that function, and applied her findings to develop ways to help stroke victims recover language function.

However, while there are many active theories on the process, there is so far no definite scientific evidence to support how language is acquired and learned. There is agreement that it is a very complex process that involves mental activity that may not be completely understood. There is also some debate about whether there is a critical time period in which to learn language.

Does Language Affect Thought?

As representations of words, languages sound different from one another, but do they actually change the way their speakers think? Answering this question can give psychologists important insights into the nature of perception, memory, and how humans think. The Sapir-Whorf hypothesis, developed in the 1930s, states that speakers of different languages necessarily think and behave differently. Recently, this hypothesis has been supported by the work of Stanford University's Lera Boroditsky, whose studies produced some fascinating discoveries, specifically, that the way a language is structured can affect what we pay attention to.

In one experiment, native English and Spanish speakers were shown a video of a man deliberately sticking a pin into a balloon. They then watched another video in which a man moved his hand toward a balloon and appeared surprised when it popped. The Spanish speakers more easily recalled the person who intentionally pricked the balloon. The English speakers tended to remember the individuals in both videos equally; the intention of the person in the video didn't influence their memory of what they saw. Boroditsky argues that because intent matters in the Spanish language, speakers are more likely to recall an intentional act; therefore, language structure affects what we pay attention to.

The "Teen Brain"?

While psychologists and neuroscientists have learned a lot about the brain, they still have many questions. The existence of a "teenage brain" is one such mystery. Psychologists used to believe that there are windows of opportunity for a child's brain and that by the time the child reaches adolescence, his or her brain is mostly developed and will remain that way for the rest of the person's life. Recently, research on the teenage brain suggests otherwise, along with some other unexpected results. For instance, sometimes teenagers and adults use their brains differently for similar tasks, such as reading emotion. Why is this so?

Is It Biology?

Using fMRI, neuroscientists have mapped the same teenagers over a number of years and compared adolescent brains to adult ones to gather data. Recent technology seems to reveal that the adolescent brain is in a "use-it-or-lose-it" stage of development because the synapses—how neurons communicate—that are not used are removed from the brain. Crucial brain development occurs from the age of 10 to 25. Interestingly, the last parts of the brain to mature are the frontal and temporal lobes, where the prefrontal cortex is located—the part that is most responsible for judgment, reasoning, planning, organization, and even impulse control. Some social scientists argue that the late development of the frontal and temporal lobes could explain why teenagers sometimes behave erratically and make poor decisions.

Or Is It Socialization?

Is adolescence a turbulent time for everyone? Not so, according to psychologist Robert Epstein. The myth of adolescence as a universally turbulent period was spread by psychologist G. Stanley Hall in 1904, who based it on ideas that were later discredited but popular in biology at the time. Epstein argues that if the teenage brain had to go through a difficult transition, then it would be the same for adolescents around the world. Studies of teens in other cultures and pre-industrial societies show that few teens experience difficulty. In fact, studies have shown that trouble in adolescence begins when Western influences are introduced to teens in other cultures. Epstein believes that the problem in Western societies is that teens almost always spend time only with one another, and when they do interact with adults, they are treated like children rather than being taught to become adults. Finally, while brain-scan studies have shown a **correlation** between teenage brain activity and behaviour, they do not identify the cause of this relationship.

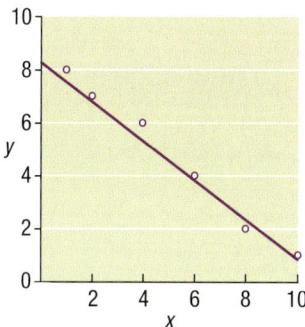
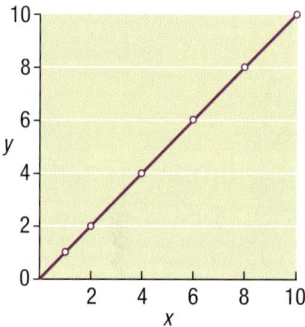

FIGURE 2-29 The graph on top shows a negative correlation between data: as one variable goes up, the other goes down. The positive correlation shown on the bottom indicates that both variables go up.

correlation: a measure that indicates a relationship between two factors but does not indicate causation; in a positive correlation, one variable goes up precisely as the other goes up; in a negative correlation, one variable goes up precisely as the other goes down

REFLECT AND RESPOND

1. Why do you think psychologists study language acquisition?
2. How do the ideas of Chomsky and Boroditsky connect to your understanding of learning new words or languages?
3. Which explanation of teen behaviour do you think is more accurate? Why? Provide some examples.

CHAPTER 2 REVIEW

Knowledge and Understanding/Thinking

1. Look at the following pictures. Which type of psychologist would be most likely to investigate the issue shown in the image?

   a)

   b)

   c)

   d)

2. What is the difference between primary and secondary sources in social sciences? Why is it important to base your research on a variety of secondary sources rather than just one or two? What criteria would you use to choose the best secondary source for your research?

3. Using a mind map or timeline, show the progression of the major schools of psychological thought.

4. Why did women become more influential in the later part of the twentieth century? What were their main concerns/topics of study? Why might that be?

5. Select one of the following, and summarize the key ideas. Place your points into two categories: Interesting and Important.
   a) brain
   b) attachment
   c) perception
   d) conditioning
   e) behaviourism

Thinking/Communicating

6. Why would it be important for a clinical psychologist to have a good understanding of developmental psychology?

7. Which area of research in psychology do you find most interesting: psychodynamic theory, behaviourism, cognitive theory, or humanistic theory? Explain why. What skills would you need to develop to pursue a career in that field?

8. Compare two areas of psychology to determine which of them has had more impact on society today. Select criteria you could use (for example, purpose, supporters, approaches) for your comparison.

9. Write down your thoughts/ideas about one of the following topics that you are interested in. What would the possible outcomes and consequences be if you were to put your thoughts into action?
   a) flash mobs
   b) logotherapy
   c) meditation
   d) yoga

10. If you were a school principal, how would you use Skinner's theory of operant conditioning to respond to one of the following issues: skipping classes, punctuality, absenteeism, or bullying? How would this differ if you used Pavlov, or Maslow's theories?

Communication/Application

11. Create a model to explain how Erikson's psychosocial theory can be applied to your own extended family. Does your family fit into the specific stages?

12. How would a humanist therapist and a behaviourist therapist each treat depression? What ideas influence their different approaches?

13. If you were a school principal, how might you use Skinner's theory of operant conditioning to help you devise a strategy to decrease the number of students skipping class? How would this strategy differ from one based on Maslow's theory?

14. Select a topic of interest in psychology, and prepare a central research question. Identify the type of research that would be required and some possible next steps.

15. Working with a partner, prepare a role play to explain operant conditioning to someone not taking this course, and give an example from your own experiences.

CHAPTER 3

What Is Sociology?

Sociology is the study of social behaviour and human groups, such as a society. A society is a large group of people who live in the same area and who share a distinctive culture and institutions. This group provides protection, stability, security, and identity to its members. Sociologists attempt to answer key questions about why certain social behaviours exist and how different societies function. They study individual behaviour within the context of groups, the behaviour of groups, and a society as a whole to understand the complex world around us, investigate existing problems, and examine issues. In this chapter, you will be introduced to sociology, the different schools of thought in sociology, and the contributions made by key theorists. You will also learn about behaviour and socialization, as well as how sociologists begin their research.

Chapter Expectations

By the end of this chapter, you will:

- summarize and compare the major theories, perspectives, and methods in sociology
- identify the significant contributions of influential sociologists
- summarize the key ideas about the major sociological schools of thought and explain how they can be used to analyze social behaviour
- identify and explain the main research methods that are used for conducting sociological research

Key Terms

agents of socialization
anticipatory socialization
bureaucracy
empirical
feral
functional differentiation
isolate
macrosociology
microsociology
norm
positivism
primary group
primary socialization
rationalization
resocialization
role
secondary socialization
social influence
socialization
survey
values

Landmark Case Studies

William Foote Whyte: Street Corner Society

structural functionalism

Auguste Comte (1798–1857)

Emile Durkheim (1853–1917)
Talcott Parsons (1902–1979)

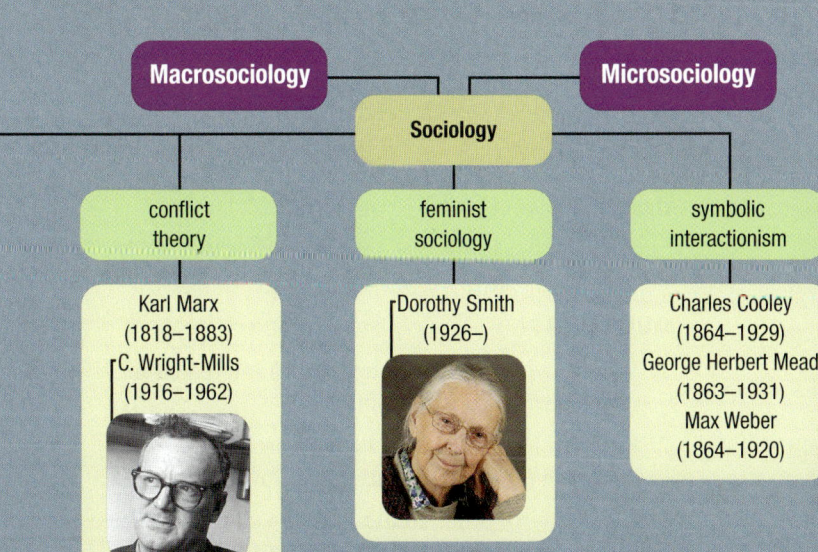

FIGURE 3-1 What can be learned by studying society?

Spotlight on Sociology

Energy Drinks and Risky Behaviour

Before You Read
Do you drink energy drinks on a regular basis? Do they affect your behaviour?

Since Health Canada lifted the ban against energy drinks in 2004, these highly caffeinated beverages have become increasingly popular, especially among young people. Sociologists have begun to study the effect of these beverages on behaviour, particularly their impact on social behaviour and peer relationships. In one of these studies, Kathleen E. Miller, a sociologist at a college in Buffalo, examined the relationship between energy-drink consumption and risk-taking among 18 to 25-year-olds. Miller's research validates existing concerns about energy-drink consumption. "The principal target demographic for energy drinks is young adults, but they're nearly as common among younger teens," she explains. "This is a concern because energy drinks typically contain 3 times the caffeine of a soft drink, and in some cases, up to 10 times as much" (University of Buffalo, 2008, para 4).

In results published in the *Journal of Adolescent Health*, Miller identified links between energy-drink consumption, risky substance use, and sexual risk-taking. Frequent energy-drink consumers (those who consume energy drinks six or more days a month) were approximately three times more likely than less-frequent energy-drink consumers or nonconsumers to have smoked cigarettes, abused prescription drugs, and been in a serious physical fight in the prior year. They reported drinking alcohol, having alcohol-related problems, and using marijuana about twice as often as nonconsumers. They were also more likely to engage in other forms of risk-taking, including unsafe sex, not using a seatbelt in vehicles, and participating in extreme sports (CBC, 2008). A total of 795 Western New York undergraduate students participated in the study (University of Buffalo, 2008).

According to Miller, frequent energy-drink consumption may serve as a useful way to identify students at risk for problem behaviours. However, it does not necessarily follow that consuming energy drinks leads to more serious health-compromising activities. Miller cautions, "It is entirely possible that a common factor, such as a sensation-seeking personality or involvement in risk-oriented peer sub-cultures, contributes to both. More investigation is needed to study these relationships further, over longer periods of time" (University of Buffalo, 2008, para 13).

As a result of several recent deaths linked to energy drinks, a number of countries have introduced restrictions on their use. Some countries, such as France, Turkey, Denmark, and Iceland, have banned the high-caffeine/taurine energy drinks altogether. Canada requires warning labels on these beverages advising that children and pregnant women should avoid drinking them and that they should not be consumed by anyone in large doses or in combination with alcohol.

↑ **FIGURE 3-2** Why might people consume energy drinks?

QUESTIONS

1. Why do you think sociologists are interested in energy-drink consumption?
2. How did Miller conduct her research? What are some possible limitations to this research?
3. Discuss with other students in the class whether there is evidence in your community of risky behaviour associated with energy-drink consumption. Is this relevant to this research topic?

Research and Inquiry Skills

Surveys

Once social scientists develop their central research question (see Chapter 1), they follow specific steps to make sure their research is completed scientifically and systematically. **Surveys** are important tools to help social scientists collect **empirical** evidence.

> **survey:**
> a set of questions used on a sample of the population study about opinions, values, or actions

> **empirical:**
> based on facts, statistics, and data

A survey is a set of questions created to find out more information about an issue, usually using a wide range of people. Surveys are examples of quantitative research and allow a researcher to gather large amounts of information at one time. They must be conducted following certain guidelines to ensure accurate results. When surveying people, it is important that you:

- be objective (Don't just select people who think as you do.)
- select people randomly
- survey a large sample of the population
- inform survey takers about the purpose of the survey
- keep the identity of the survey taker confidential

Activities

1. How would you set up a survey to obtain the most accurate results?
2. If you saw a headline in a newspaper that read "64% Admit to Cheating on High-School Test," what questions do you have about the survey?

Assessing and Recording Sources

When using secondary sources, it is important to be certain that they are reputable. Reputable sources can include textbooks; journal, magazine, and newspaper articles; and research reports. It's also important to review what the leading experts have written about the subject you are researching. Finding reputable sources is especially important when researching online. You should select Web sites that come from trustworthy organizations, such as universities and governments. After you've selected your sources, it is important to cite your sources. In the social sciences, it is common to use the style of the American Psychological Association (APA) style.

Citing a Source Using APA Style

To avoid plagiarism, you need to cite the ideas, as well as the exact words and phrases that you have taken from another source. When you are citing an idea within your report (called an *in-text citation*), include the author and date in parentheses. If it is a direct quote, also include the page number. If your statement included the author, then include only the date and page in parentheses.

The following are general rules for creating the reference list added to the end of your report:

- Use alphabetical order by author's last name.
- Capitalize only the first word of the title and subtitle and any proper nouns.
- If the source has no author, use the title first, and place the reference in the proper place alphabetically.
- Double-space your references.
- If the reference requires more than one line, indent the second and all following lines.

Follow the format and style below for each reference.

- *Books*
  Author's last name, First initial of first name. (Year of publication). *Title of book*. City of Publication: Name of Publisher.
- *Journals and Periodicals*
  Author's last name, First initial of first name. (Year of publication). Title of article. *Title of Journal or Periodical*, *volume number* (issue number), page numbers.
- *Electronic Sources*
  Authors' names/Name of Sponsoring Institution or Organization. (Date of publication). Title of article. Title of site or page. Editor. Retrieval information including date retrieved, Web site address in full.

Activities

1. Rewrite these citations correctly.
   a) *Anthropology and Education*. 36(2) 132–148. (2005). Merten, Don E. Transitions and Trouble: Rites of Passage for Suburban Girls.
   b) 2003. Worth Publishers. *Thinking About Psychology: The Science of Mind and Behaviour*. New York. Charles T. Blair-Broeker and Randal M. Ernst.
2. Select a paragraph in this chapter. Rewrite it in your own words and include the proper citation.

Section 3.1 Schools of Thought

Is understanding society important? How do we create society, and how does it affect us? Sociology developed as a discipline as scholars looked to society to understand the world around them and address social problems. Sociologists study the organization, institutions, and development of society, especially changing relationships between individuals and the collective behaviour of groups. In this section, you will learn about sociologists and schools of thought to help you understand the world you live in today.

Sociology: Past and Present

The Roots of Sociology

Ibn Khaldun was a fourteenth-century philosopher of history who wrote about the world around him. Khaldun's writings contain valuable information about the political events and social problems of the Muslim world in the fourteenth century. His work is a record of the pre-modern world and filled with observations about society and social conditions. Although sociology had not developed as a discipline during Khaldun's time, his methods and observations are very recognizable to modern sociologists, and today he is considered a forefather of sociology.

Throughout history, poets, artists, theologians, and scholars such as Ibn Khaldun have documented and recorded the political, economic, religious, and cultural practices of their society. But the discipline of sociology did not formally exist until the Industrial Revolution, a period of massive change in agriculture and manufacturing that began in England during the eighteenth and nineteenth centuries.

The changes caused by the Industrial Revolution significantly altered the social, economic, and cultural conditions in England. Every aspect of daily life was affected by these economic changes, especially how people worked and how people lived. While the Industrial Revolution benefited the middle class, significantly increasing their wealth, it had disastrous consequences for the working class. Many people lost their jobs as machines began to replace skilled workers. Those who did have jobs were often working long hours for low wages in unsafe working conditions. Child labour increased during this time, as they could be paid less than adult workers. Children were forced to work in horrible conditions. As more people moved to urban areas to find work, cities became overcrowded. Living conditions deteriorated and the crime rate rose. Many scholars began to write about and document the social problems they observed. In fact, many theories about social inequality that are still important today came out of the Industrial Revolution. You will learn more about some of these theories in this section.

> **Before You Read**
> Have you ever been in trouble for behaving in a way you shouldn't have or for saying the wrong thing at the wrong time? How do you know what is acceptable behaviour in different situations? Who decides what is acceptable behaviour?

FIGURE 3-3 The Industrial Revolution caused significant changes in England. Why did the discipline of sociology develop during this time?

Defining Sociology

Sociologists study the interactions among people living together in a society and their actions, beliefs, and behaviours in order to understand the society. Sociologists also compare and contrasts human interactions and behaviours between different societies. They examine a wide range of issues and topics to investigate problems and developing issues, including the following:

- gender roles
- criminal behaviour
- ethnicity
- family structure
- social institutions
- sexuality
- social classes

Studying society can be very complex, and sociologists often rely on knowledge from other disciplines, such as political science, economics, and history, to help answer their questions about society.

> Why do sociologists look to other fields and disciplines in order to study society? Why do sociologists study individual actions, beliefs, and behaviours if they want to understand a society as a whole?

FIGURE 3-4 What predictions can you make about what sociologists do?

Auguste Comte (1798–1857)

The term *sociology* was first used by the French philosopher Auguste Comte who defined sociology as the systematic study of society. He believed that society is constantly changing and observed that individuals and groups struggle to adapt to these changes. He believed that ultimately these changes are positive for society as a whole. Comte developed theories about social inequality that influenced other theorists, including Karl Marx. One of his most important contributions to sociology is the notion of **positivism**, the strict application of the scientific method in order to obtain concrete, measurable, and testable data to understand society.

positivism: the application of the scientific method to obtain quantifiable data in order to understand society

What Do Sociologists Do?

Sociologists observe and conduct practical research into key social issues and behaviours to explain why a society functions as it does. Sociologists must ask broad questions and look at different elements to make sense of them as a whole. The questions should be broad enough to have implications in other societies. For example, studying criminal activity in a single Canadian city will not necessarily tell us what produces criminal behaviour in other parts of the world, but it can add to research about North American crime, which can then be compared to information about criminal activity in other countries around the world.

> Why is it important for sociologists to consider how their conclusions affect other societies?

Skills Focus

According to Comte's theory of positivism, data should be testable and measurable. A good survey is made up of questions whose answers can be converted into quantifiable, or measurable, information. When writing survey questions, ensure that you will later be able to tally the results.

values:
shared ideas and standards that are considered acceptable and binding

norms:
expectations about how people should behave

role:
the expected behaviour of a person in a particular social position

Cultural Expressions

Ultimately, a sociologist is interested in the cultural expressions of a society—the shared symbols and learned behaviours that everyone in a society recognizes and understands. For example, the maple leaf and beaver are national symbols that appear on flags, logos, and money and are understood to represent Canada. Learned behaviours come from the particular **values**, **norms**, and **roles** held by members of a particular society. The values of society are shared ideas and standards that a society or a specific group considers acceptable and binding. For example, in Canada equality is a value. Norms are expectations about how people should behave in particular contexts. For example, at a concert it's expected that you will scream, cheer, and applaud loudly. But if you behaved the same way in a library, other people would find your behaviour unacceptable. The role of an individual refers to the expected behaviour of a person in a particular social position. For example, if you visit the dentist, you expect him or her to examine your teeth.

> Why do you think it is important for sociologists to study social roles? How might studying cultural symbols be useful in a multicultural society such as Canada?

Objectivity and Universality

When studying society, it is important for sociologists to approach their research objectively, set aside their own beliefs, and avoid making judgments when they encounter a situation that conflicts with their personal views. It is also important for sociologists to recognize elements of the universality of their research and break down cultural and geographic boundaries. For example, a study on parenting conducted in a remote African village can have important applications to a study on the same topic completed in a large North American city. All societies rely on some form of family structure to help teach their young the rules of society. There are some aspects of human societies that are similar in every culture. Sociologists compare societies to explain trends and behaviours and weave together the common threads among cultures in order to make sense of issues that affect all societies.

↑ **FIGURE 3-5** The beaver and the eagle are respective national symbols of Canada and the United States. What do the national symbols of the United States and Canada imply about the people who live in these countries?

← **FIGURE 3-6** An African mother and child on the left and a Canadian mother and child on the right. Why would a sociologist try to understand how families function across different cultures?

98   NEL   Unit 1 • What Is Social Science?

In the documentary *Babies*, director Thomas Balmès tracks four babies from four different cultures in their first year of life. The film is shot from their point of view and follows the babies through the year as they reach the common milestones of infancy (for example, sitting up, crawling, walking) while discovering the world around them. The result is an illustration of how all human beings are fundamentally the same, yet how our physical and cultural environment shapes us from the moment we are born.

> **VOICES**
>
> I wanted to give a baby point of view, just immerse you in a baby's world for 80 minutes.
>
> Thomas Balmès, director of documentary *Babies*

IN FOCUS — Sociologists and the Fall of the Berlin Wall

Studying historical events can be a very useful tool for sociologists who are researching issues in modern society. Events that happened in the past can have a tremendous impact on the structure of a society and how people behave. The relationship between historical events (particularly economic and political events) and social behaviour is a popular theme for many researchers.

East and West Berlin were two societies which greatly interested sociologists. After the Second World War, Berlin was divided in two, with East Berlin becoming a socialist society under control of the Soviets, and West Berlin becoming capitalist society under the occupation of the Americans, British, and French. In 1961, the Soviets built a wall to stop the exodus of East Berliners into the west and eliminate any cultural contact between the two societies. Neighbours, friends, and even family members were completely cut off from one another. Until 1989, when the wall was torn down, the people in East and West Berlin had separate political systems, economies, cultures, institutions, and experiences.

When the Berlin Wall was torn down, sociologists and the rest of the world watched, as families and the city were reunited. As the city began the process of re-unification, sociologists were interested in recording the social changes, tensions, and differences so they could later study how social change and social institutions affected behaviour. The political and economic events of the day were just as important to a sociologist as they were to a historian or an economist.

FIGURE 3-7 East and West Germans meeting for the first time in decades after the fall of the Berlin Wall. How would sociologists study the social habits and culture of occupants on either side of the wall?

QUESTIONS

1. Is it important for sociologists to understand the history of the societies they study? Explain why or why not.
2. How can historical events explain current social issues? Give an example and explain how the event affected the society where it occurred.

REFLECT AND RESPOND

1. What is positivism? Why is it an important concept in the development of sociology?
2. Give an example of a value, norm, and role. Why do sociologists examine the values, norms, and roles of the society they are studying?
3. How do other disciplines, such as history and economics, help sociologists?
4. What should sociologists consider when they approach their research?

> **Before You Read**
>
> What is the difference between a photograph of something taken from far away and one taken close-up? What kind of information can you obtain from each photo?

Sociological Schools of Thought

In sociology, schools of thought provide different ways of observing, studying, and understanding society. The schools of thought and key theorists that you will explore in the following pages are part of the foundations of sociology and have helped sociologists understand society and further develop the discipline. The chart below illustrates the different sociological schools of thought that you will learn about in this section.

School of Thought	Theorist	Purpose
structural functionalism	Emile Durkheim Talcott Parsons	• to study how social structures function to serve the needs of society
conflict theory	Karl Marx C. Wright Mills	• to study how power forms the basis of the relationships between different groups and creates social conflict
feminist sociology	Dorothy Smith	• to examine conflicts created by gender
symbolic interactionism	Charles Cooley George Herbert Mead Max Weber	• to study the individual's role and place within the wider society and how people create their world through social interactions • to examine how a physical environment and social structures determine individual behaviour

FIGURE 3-8 Pilgrims praying at Mecca, the holiest site for Muslims. How does this image reflect a macrosociologist perspective?

macrosociology: an approach of sociology that analyzes social systems on a large scale

microsociology: the study of small groups and individuals within a society

Macrosociology

All perspectives in sociology can be classified as either *macrosociological* or *microsociological*. **Macrosociology** takes a wide perspective and is concerned with studying society as a whole. Macrosociologists analyze social systems and populations on a large scale. They examine larger social institutions that individuals belong to, such as a country or a place of worship. For example, a macrosociologist studying religion would try to learn a great deal about religious worship as a large structure or institution in society.

Microsociology

Microsociologists are interested in understanding the bases of social action and interaction among individual members and their place in society. **Microsociology** is concerned with the role and interactions an individual or small group of people may have in society. For example, a microsociologist would study religious worship by looking at the role and beliefs of a single worshipper or small group of worshippers within a religion.

FIGURE 3-9 An individual praying. How does this image reflect a microsociologist's perspective?

> **REFLECT AND RESPOND**
>
> 1. Define the microsociological and macrosociological approaches to society, and suggest some advantages and disadvantages for each approach.

Structural Functionalism

Structural functionalism states that a society is stable when social institutions (for example, the family, religion, politics, schools) meet the needs of its citizens. According to this theory, these institutions, or structures of a society are interdependent and work together to meet the needs of individuals. Structural functionalists study how these structures work together to help society to function. Structural functionalism places a great deal of emphasis on the power of social structures to create harmony and happiness among its members and reflects optimism that society can meet the various needs of its members.

One criticism of this theory is that it does not account for destructive forces within society. Structural functionalists believe institutions exist because they have a positive function in society—to serve a particular need or benefit individuals. Because they believe social structures are positive for society, structural functionalists tend to overlook important issues such as poverty and racism, which often have roots within the structures of society. Focusing on the positive functions of a society can cause people to ignore social injustices.

> **Before You Read**
> Which of the following influences your life the most: religion, culture, school, or family? Explain your choice.

FIGURE 3-10 Long commutes are a source of major frustration but are an unfortunate result of the intricate road systems needed to help people get around in cities. How might a structural functionalist explain traffic jams?

Emile Durkheim (1858–1917)

Emile Durkheim, a French sociologist influenced by Comte, formally established sociology as an academic discipline. Along with Karl Marx and Max Weber, he helped to propel sociology forward, and his influence is seen today in the work of modern sociologists. Durkheim in particular is remembered for establishing the sociological method still practised today. His theories provided the foundation of structural functionalism. His work centred on the belief that society functions logically and protects the interests of its members. He was interested in studying the forces that unite individuals in society. Durkheim observed that humans are social creatures and define themselves by their social interactions at home, work, play, and worship.

FIGURE 3-11 Emile Durkheim is considered the "first sociologist." How did Durkheim's work contribute to sociology?

functional differentiation: divisions that are created to help deal with a complex environment; these divisions operate independently but are connected to one another

Durkheim also believed that society is in a constant state of flux. According to Durkheim, the constant change he observed meant that society was becoming more diverse. He viewed this diversity as positive and necessary. He called the emerging diversity in society **functional differentiation** and believed it would allow groups to work together more productively and peacefully. Through his work, he established himself as an authority on social issues and rightfully earned the title of "first sociologist."

Durkheim on Suicide

In his controversial book, *Suicide*, Durkheim attempted to answer the difficult question, Why do people commit suicide? His book was impressive for the way in which he organized, examined, and explained the statistical information he had gathered from a number of sources, including government records. He went about his research systematically and scientifically by studying what he termed *social facts* (i.e., the values, cultural norms, and social structures and trends external to the individual) about a group and then comparing them to the social facts of other groups. In the end, his work on suicide revealed that, although the decision to commit suicide is a highly personal and individual choice, the causes of suicides are rooted very deeply in society.

As you learned on page 96, the Industrial Revolution and the movement of people from rural to urban areas caused a great deal of upheaval within society. Looking at the Industrial Revolution in Durkheim's study on suicide, he described the importance of community and stability to a person's happiness. He found that during the Industrial Revolution, people were increasingly disconnected from their communities and that this social upheaval had a greater effect of suicide rates than other factors such as wealth.

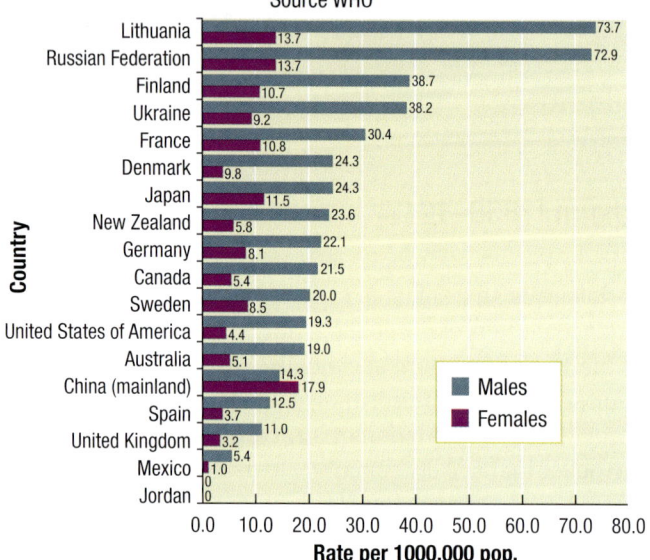

FIGURE 3-12 Suicide rates as studied by the World Health Organization. How would a sociologist use this data?

During his research, Durkheim pioneered the modern method of statistical analysis. He recorded his observations in charts and compared and contrasted these observations to identify and explain his research. Durkheim's study also suggested the infinite possibilities of sociology to provide explanations for some of the more devastating issues affecting society. By approaching suicide scientifically, Durkheim set a precedent for future generations of sociologists to follow as they conduct research into controversial issues.

> (?) What are some possible links between Durkheim's work on suicide and historical or current examples of suicide bombers?

Talcott Parsons (1902–1978)

Like Durkheim, Talcott Parsons was a structural functionalist. Responsible for developing the structural functionalist school of thought in the United States, Parsons examined social behaviour as a single entity or mass. He emphasized that all social phenomena and relationships could be explained through their functions in society. That meant that individuals and specific groups in society could be defined by the purpose that they served. He argued that if something existed in many societies, then it must exist to serve a necessary purpose. In Parson's interpretation, people act according to their values and the values of the people around them and this created stability within a society. Although he found that people acted in their own self-interest, Parsons concluded that there is a strong desire among people to get along with each other and cooperate to achieve goals based on these shared values. It was clear from his work that Parsons believed in social evolution and social Darwinism. This idea was controversial since it suggests that the negative aspects of society, such as discrimination, serve a purpose.

FIGURE 3-13 How would Parsons justify social inequality?

> **IN FOCUS**
>
> ## Herbert Spencer (1820–1920) and Social Darwinism
>
> Spencer was a British philosopher and sociologist who was an influential figure during the Victorian era (1837–1901). A supporter of Darwin's evolutionary theory (you learned about Darwin's evolutionary theory in Chapter 1), Spencer applied the theory to the study of society. He compared society to a living organism or body with the different parts (for example, the family, the economy, the political system, religion) all working together to keep it alive and functioning. He applied the notion of natural selection to society in what he called "survival of the fittest." According to his theory, the fittest people in society should survive and flourish while the weak (or unfit) either deserve to live in unfortunate circumstances or be allowed to die. For example, under social Darwinism, the poor, elderly, or disabled should not receive any financial assistance since they aren't fit enough to survive on their own.
>
> Social Darwinism was also used to justify colonialism and slavery. Some people claimed that because white people were superior to other races and cultures, they were justified in taking over other countries or enslaving people. Spencer's theory was used as a basis for some of history's most notorious figures, such as Adolf Hitler who used the theory to justify the Holocaust. Spencer's theory is also connected to the concept of eugenics, a movement that advocated for the "improvement" of the species by either selective breeding (positive eugenics) or the sterilization or killing of "undesirable" humans (negative eugenics). These concepts were also used in Canada by Helen MacMurchy, who became Ontario's Inspector of the Feeble-Minded in 1915. She led the National Council of Women to endorse sterilization as a means of preventing mothers from "filling the cradles with degenerate babies." The Alberta Sexual Sterilization Act was passed in 1928, which led to the creation of a Eugenics Board. This board had the power to order the sterilization of individuals. Between 1929 and 1972, 2822 individuals were sterilized, many of them without their knowledge, before the practice was abolished.
>
> ### QUESTIONS
>
> 1. Why is social Darwinism a problematic theory?
> 2. How is social Darwinism connected to eugenics?
> 3. Would eugenics be supported by the Canadian government today?
> 4. What lessons can we learn from theories such as Social Darwinism?
>
>
>
> ↑ **FIGURE 3-14** What does this image tell you about eugenics?

REFLECT AND RESPOND

1. Is structural functionalism a macro or micro theory? Explain your answer.
2. How did Durkheim and Parsons contribute to the theory of structural functionalism?

Conflict Theory

Unlike the structural functionalist theory, which focuses on how the structures of society work to maintain equilibrium, the conflict theory studies competition between different groups for power. This competition is a result of the constant struggle between those who have economic and political power and those who do not. The conflict theory is modelled on the work of Karl Marx. Marxist understanding of society focused on conflict within the economic system between two distinct classes, the wealthy class of owners and the poor class of workers. The imbalance between these two groups is the source of constant conflict in society. Those who have power seek to keep it away from those who do not. Institutions tend to further alienate the poor, making them feel powerless. The conflict theory generally focuses on economic conflicts between the rich and the poor, but it can be applied to gender (the power imbalance between men and women in society) and race (the power imbalance between two or more racialized groups in a society).

? How would the conflict theory explain a rivalry between a sports team that was well funded and one that did not have a lot of money?

Karl Marx (1818–1883)

Karl Marx, author of the *Communist Manifesto*, was a German philosopher interested primarily in economic history. His views and beliefs have been used as the basis for theoretical perspectives by many different disciplines, especially political science and sociology. Marx's theories concentrate on the idea of class conflict, its role in social evolution, and its usefulness in understanding social issues. Marx was living in London during the Industrial Revolution and witnessed how factory owners exploited workers who worked long hours for little pay and had very poor living conditions. He predicted that the workers would one day revolt against the factory owners.

Marx examined societies through their economic organization and found that Western society is based on a system of property ownership and labour exploitation, particularly in the capitalist economic systems. He saw that society was based on a fierce competition for power and wealth. The wealthy class would make it impossible for the poor to ever achieve economic equality, and the only way for the working class to achieve equality would be to topple the wealthy class out of power. In his view, the conflict between social classes created isolation which would lead to disruption and change. Marx saw this kind of conflict and revolution as the only way societies evolved from one system to the next. In the same way that feudal societies became capitalist, capitalist societies would become communist.

Earlier, you learned about the connection between historical events and sociology. Marx studied historical events to understand what was happening in society. From Marx, we learned that it is important to study the economy if we want to understand social changes. Sociologists have borrowed from Marx's ideas in order to explain many social phenomena. Marx's work is important to sociology because his ideas about power and exploitation help explain the existence of a number of inequalities in all human societies.

Before You Read
What causes conflict between two different people or two different groups?

VOICES
The history of all hitherto existing society is the history of class struggles.
Karl Marx, *Communist Manifesto* (1848)

More to Know...
You learned about the Industrial Revolution and the development of sociology on page 96.

FIGURE 3-15 How would Marx view the treatment of the Chinese immigrants who were enlisted to build the Canadian railway, a dangerous job for which they were paid very low wages?

Landmark Case Study

William Foote Whyte and the Street Corner Society

William Foote Whyte (1914–2000) was an economist who, through a study of a poor Boston neighbourhood in the 1930s, created the model for urban ethnography and set the standard for this methodology in sociology, becoming a pioneer in participant observation. His book, *Street Corner Society: The Social Structure of an Italian Slum*, remains one of the best-selling works to be produced for urban sociology and is a classic reference for all sociologists.

For more than three and a half years in the 1930s, Whyte lived in a poor Boston neighbourhood inhabited by first- and second-generation Italian immigrants. The neighbourhood had a high crime rate, was considered dangerous, and was often referred to as a *slum*. He called his neighbourhood Cornerville for anonymity and his research Street Corner Society. While in Cornerville, Whyte lived in the community, observing and recording the tensions between different groups in the neighbourhood. He studied two groups: "corner boys" and "college boys." The corner boys were those who hung out on street corners and around shops, while the college boys were those who wanted and had the means to get an education and to get out of the slum.

Whyte was particularly interested in finding out more about the corner boys and their relationship to other groups. The college boys enjoyed a position of privilege in the neighbourhood, and certain college boys viewed the corner boys negatively. Whyte mapped the intricate social relationships of the corner boys, recording their stories and interactions and documenting the complex nature of urban life in their neighbourhood with a great deal of accuracy. He was able to peer into their daily lives and make sense of their world.

In his study of Cornerville, Whyte demonstrated that a poor community was socially organized. He put a human face to the neighbourhood with his vivid portrayals of real people in real situations. His research changed the landscape of sociology forever. Like the pioneering work of anthropologists Malinowski and

↑ **FIGURE 3-16** Sunday morning, Napoli Square in Boston, 1950. How did participant observation help Whyte understand the corner boys?

Goodall, Whyte's study challenged the way in which society could be studied. His work not only enhanced the understanding of social groups and networks, it revolutionized the way sociologists conduct their work in the field and how sociology is studied today.

QUESTIONS

1. What did Whyte's study reveal about the social realities of living in a neighbourhood?
2. How have Whyte's methods revolutionized the way research is conducted in the field?
3. Compare Cornerville to your own neighbourhood. How are they the same? How are they different?

REFLECT AND RESPOND

1. Why did Marx focus his theories around class conflict?
2. How did studying historical events help Marx develop his ideas?

Feminist Sociology

Just as Marx looked at economic inequality, feminist sociologists examine gender inequality. In the twentieth century, female sociologists expanded their study on how men controlled women's lives—their jobs (what kind of jobs women could hold or if they could work at all), their finances (paying women less money than men doing the same job, not allowing them to have control over their own money), and their bodies (limiting their reproductive choices). They concluded that women were marginalized, deprived of power, and without equal membership in society. Examining the symbols, values, and norms of their society, they found it to be patriarchal, favouring men above women, concluding that much of society is based on male authority and constructed to favour men. Historian Gerda Lerner argues that patriarchal systems are historical. In her book, *The Creation of Patriarchy*, Lerner explains that class for men is based on their relationship to their economic role, while women's class is determined through their sexual connection to men. Many female scholars were frustrated by the double standard they experienced. They had less access to tenured positions and to funding they needed for their research. As the women's movement of the 1960s and 1970s progressed, many people began advocating for change.

> **Before You Read**
> How has the role of women changed in the last sixty years?

Dorothy Smith (1926–)

Dorothy Smith, a Canadian sociologist, contends that women have long been marginalized in society. Smith argues that sociologists should develop the discipline of sociology so it is capable of reaching and speaking to all members of society. The starting point for Smith's analysis was that culture is socially constructed, and since society is constructed to favour men, it does not operate in women's best interests. In her publication *The Everyday World Is Problematic: A Feminist Sociology* (1987), Smith examines how women are "alienated from their experience" and deprived of an authority to speak because of the ideas imposed on women in a society constructed on concepts that favour men. Smith and others like her are working toward a sociology that reflects the realities and experiences of all people regardless of race, gender, or economic status.

"Just do as you're told young lady. Don't you want to grow up to be a strong independant woman?"

FIGURE 3-17 How does this cartoon demonstrate the notion that young girls struggle to find a voice in their society?

> ❓ What does Smith mean when she says women are "alienated from their experience?"

Current Research

Feminist sociology began by studying issues relevant to upper-class white women, but as the discipline developed, feminist sociologists began to examine gender in the context of race, class, and sexualities. Sociologist Chandra Talpade Mohanty examines race within feminist theory and how Western feminism has constructed the "Third World Woman," an idea that portrays diverse women from different cultures and different countries as having one identity and implies that they all suffer from oppression in the same way. In her published work, including "Under Western Eyes: Feminist

Open for Debate

In New Brunswick, a florist refused to provide flowers for a gay couple's wedding. Is it acceptable to deny service to people because of their sexual orientation? What if it was based on race or religion?

Scholarship and Colonial Discourses" (1986) and *Feminism Without Borders: Decolonizing Theory, Practicing Solidarity* (2003), Mohanty points out the ethnocentrism of this view and explores the diverse ways women from other countries are oppressed by their geography, history, and culture.

Sociologist Judith Stacey studies the changing forms and meanings of gender, family, and sexuality, and is best known for her research on same-sex families. Her most recent research, "(How) Does the Sexual Orientation of Parents Matter?" (2001), examined 21 studies of children of gay and lesbian parents and found that such children tend to function as well as children who grow up with heterosexual parents, concluding that sexual orientation has little to do with successful parenting. The work of feminist sociologists has contributed to debates about rights of women in society and led to changes in public policy.

IN FOCUS

M. N. Srinivas (1916–1999)

Mysore Narasimhachar (M.N.) Srinivas is one of the most noted scholars on Indian sociology in the twentieth century. His work focused on the caste system in India. The caste system is a complex social system that organizes people into social classes that determine status, occupation, culture, marriage partners, and political power. Although caste-based discrimination is outlawed by the Indian constitution, caste-based barriers still exist in rural communities.

Srinivas's work challenged colonial and Western assumptions about Indian society. When Srinivas began his career, the dominant belief was that the caste system in India was rigid and unchanging, implying that Indian society did not change over time. His fieldwork proved that the caste system was a fluid and dynamic social institution that had a tremendous impact on society. In particular, he studied the importance of caste in the electoral process as democracy developed in India.

Srinivas had a tremendous impact on the development of sociology in India, moving researchers away from classic texts and into the contemporary world they were studying. "He moved sociology from the so-called 'book view' toward

FIGURE 3-18 Mayawati, Chief Minister of Uttar Pradesh, India's most populous state. Mayawati the first Dalit (a caste typically discriminated against) chief minister of any Indian state. How would Srinivas's work explain her success?

the 'field view,'" one of Mr. Srinivas's students, A. M. Shah, said. "Earlier generations explained society from descriptions in the ancient texts. M.N. Srinivas encouraged his students to look at society in the raw, to get out into the villages, hospitals and trade unions" (Bearak, 1999, para 3). Srinivas developed new ways of understanding Indian society.

QUESTIONS

1. How did Srinivas's work affect perceptions of Indian society?
2. Are there any similarities between the work of M. N. Srinivas and that of Chandra Talpade Mohanty?

REFLECT AND RESPOND

1. Why did feminist sociology develop? To what extent is it still relevant today?
2. How has the work of Mohanty and Stacey contributed to the discipline?

Symbolic Interactionism

Symbolic interactionism studies human interaction at the micro level. This approach emphasizes the individual living within a larger society. According to this theory, the individual is at the centre of understanding society, since social values and roles are formed by individual interpretation. An individual creates a sense of self by the reactions of others. Social life depends on our ability to imagine ourselves in our social roles but also the ability to see ourselves reflected in the experiences of those around us. The behaviour of others in society is deeply rooted in our response and reaction to it, and this dependent relationship is what allows society to function smoothly. Unlike both structural functionalism and conflict theory, symbolic interactionism does not focus on social systems but on the way that individuals, through their interpretations of social situations and behavioural negotiation with others, give meaning to social interactions.

We accept roles for ourselves in order to fit into the society in which live; different societies have defined these roles differently. Thomas and Znaniecki's (1918–1920) historic study, *The Polish Peasant in Europe and America*, was an early application of some of the main themes and concepts of symbolic interactionism. Thomas and Znaniecki examined Polish peasant families as they immigrated to the United States and focused on the adjustments and transformations in personality and family patterns that took place as they adjusted to North American society.

> **Before You Read**
> How does the behaviour of the people around you affect your own behaviour?

(?) How would a symbolic interactionist interpret the experiences of immigrants adjusting to life within a new society?

Max Weber (1864–1920)

German scholar Max Weber believed that social life is rife with examples of conflict and cohesion. In his writings, he laid out a theory he called **rationalization**, which he defined as social actions motivated by efficiency or benefit, rather than morality, custom, or emotion. According to Weber, rationalization helps society to function more efficiently.

Like Marx, Weber saw many faults in the capitalist system and argued that it trapped and restricted individuals. Unlike Marx, Weber thought that people could be liberated through **bureaucracy** rather than revolution. He envisioned a society in which the bureaucracies would improve social problems. In sociological terms, a bureaucracy is a form of administration that is found in organizations pursuing a wide variety of goals. According to Weber, a bureaucracy is an organization where people are given specialized tasks and where each role is supervised in a hierarchy. A person holds a job based on his or her competence. People are treated impersonally so that everyone is treated the same. Rules and regulation guide the organization and reliability is guaranteed by written communication. Weber proposed an ideal bureaucracy, but recognized that they wouldn't function this way in reality. He was aware that bureaucracies in reality could be an "iron cage," reducing people to cogs in a machine.

rationalization: social actions motivated by efficiency or benefit, not custom or emotion

bureaucracy: a large administration that pursues a wide variety of goals

FIGURE 3-19 A honeybee hard at work. How might the bee's activity be compared to the activity of workers in an office? How might this type of environment increase productivity and efficiency?

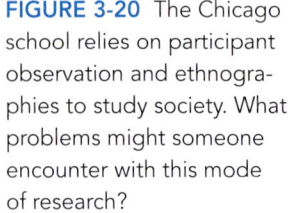

More to Know...
Research conducted on honeybees revealed that they have advanced societies with a fascinating social structure. In Weber's work on bureaucracy, he illustrates how social structures greatly influence how well a society functions.

While bureaucracies are common in our world today, they were new systems during Weber's time. The Canadian civil service is an example of a modern bureaucracy. Although bureaucracies sometimes have a negative reputation, governments often need these to provide services that meet the needs of its citizens.

Weber believed, however, that social inequalities and disparities could not be explained in only economic terms as suggested by Marx. To Weber, inequality meant unequal access to society's resources. He believed that government bureaucracies could better manage these resources by ensuring that all essential social services, such as education, would be available to all. Weber believed the bureaucracies could theoretically lessen the tensions in society and potentially eliminate existing inequality.

? How are the theories of Marx and Weber the same? How are they different? Create a chart to organize your ideas.

The Chicago School

Another perspective on social behaviour and society emerged from some American scholars at the University of Chicago. Their theories became known as the *Chicago school*. The Chicago school furthered the development of the symbolic interactionist approach, with much of the research centering on how physical environment and social structures determine individual behaviour. The researchers focused on how a community shapes how people act and behave.

Sociologists from the Chicago school were also pioneering a new and exciting way of researching social issues. They believed a great deal could be learned about society by immersing themselves in urban environments

FIGURE 3-20 The Chicago school relies on participant observation and ethnographies to study society. What problems might someone encounter with this mode of research?

and conducting ethnographies supported by participant observation. Their qualitative methodology allowed them to study urban social trends in a natural setting. Their findings were intimately linked with the subjects and groups they studied and had implications for public policies. However, relying on qualitative methods, to the exclusion of reasonable quantitative measures, later became one of the Chicago school's greatest liabilities.

Charles Cooley, George Herbert Mead, and the Looking-Glass Self

Charles Cooley studied the relationship between the individual and society in great depth. He believed that the two are interconnected and that their functions cannot be separated. One cannot be studied without some consideration of the other, because they influence each other constantly. To Cooley, the individual is just as capable of shaping society as society is of shaping the individual. One important concept attributed to Cooley is the **primary group**, which is the set of people with whom an individual has the most intimate and important interactions. The primary group typically includes family and friends. Cooley believed the constant interaction with members of one's primary group is crucial to developing a social identity. The individual becomes a reflection and representative for the primary group. The most important idea to come from Cooley's work is the *looking-glass self,* which is the way in which the individual's sense of self is mirrored and reflected by others. An avatar is an example of this idea. People create an avatar, a customized symbol, to represent themselves online. This symbol can represent what someone actually looks like but it can also represent how a person would like to be seen by others.

Cooley's colleague George Herbert Mead, added details about the importance of symbols, language, and communication in human relationships. Like Cooley, Mead believed in the looking-glass self as a way of explaining how individuals see themselves through the eyes of those with whom they interact. Mead took the notion one step further and claimed that, depending on the circumstances, the individual assumes a variety of different social roles and learns early on which "mask" to wear.

Of all the ideas to emerge from the Chicago school, the looking-glass self most came to represent the important influence of the individual on overt social behaviour. Many people can easily identify with this approach since it provides a way of placing themselves into the studies about society that can sometimes be impersonal. This concept earned Mead the title of "founding theorist for symbolic interaction." As you've read, this view sees human actions as being governed by the meanings that the individual gives to his or her particular social situation. This idea proved to be a valuable framework for many future analyses of individual **socialization** with implications in the areas of class, race, and ethnicity. Thanks to their ideas, Cooley and Mead made it possible to examine social inequalities and differences more clearly.

primary group: a set of people with whom an individual has strong emotional and personal connections

socialization: the continuing process where an individual learns the appropriate behavioural patterns, skills, and values for his or her social world

> ❓ How do Cooley's and Mead's theories highlight the role of the individual in sociology? What are the benefits of including the individual perspective when trying to understand an entire society?

C. Wright Mills and Sociological Imagination

C. Wright Mills was a sociologist who was influenced by both Marx and the conflict school and Weber's ideas. Mills's most influential work was developing the concept of *sociological imagination*, the ability to connect individual experiences to social realities. This ability is required to understand the society in which we live, including the structures and the people who live in it and the historical forces that created it. Without this understanding, individuals cannot understand either themselves or their role and place within society. Sociological imagination provides this insight, allowing an individual to recognize and understand the larger forces at work within the society. For Mills, this exchange between the individual and society is crucial to understanding the forces that shape our behaviour and our social world in general.

Mills and Parsons: Conflicting Ideas

One of the most well-known rivalries in sociology is between Parsons and Mills. Mills and Parsons (you learned about his theories on page 103) went head to head on a number of issues, mostly stemming from Mills's accusation that Parsons's ideas about society were too rigid and conservative. Mills refuted Parsons's belief that society is static and that one needs to look at it only as a whole to understand it. According to Mills, society is a living organism capable of great change and social problems such as poverty, crime, and racism can be eradicated in time. So Mills considered the suggestion that these social problems serve a function, as Parsons believed, an unfortunate error in judgment.

> **?** What are the fundamental differences between Mills's and Parsons's theories? Suggest reasons why Parsons may be too strict in his view of society. Whom does he risk leaving behind in his views? Who does not have voice in his ideal society?

REFLECT AND RESPOND

1. Create a visual timeline/graphic organizer that includes all the major theorists of sociology presented in the chapter, and indicate one important contribution made by each theorist to the study of society.
2. How does sociology attempt to break down issues of geography and culture in order to get a more accurate picture of society shared by all humans? Provide examples.
3. Inequality seems to be a key issue for many sociologists. Why do sociologists study inequality? Identify and explain the various kinds of inequality presented by two sociologists.
4. Choose a social issue (for example, crime, poverty). Create a mind map explaining the factors that contribute to a social issue, who it affects, and the agencies who deal with the issue.

Socialization and Social Development

Section 3.2

Socialization is a process where someone learns the attitudes, values, and behaviours that are valuable and necessary for the society in which he or she lives. It starts in infancy and continues throughout a person's life. Socialization and social development begin in the family but are also influenced by many forces other than your family, such as peers, school and work, media, religion, and gender. The process of learning how to behave according to the values and norms of society also includes how to behave in different situations.

> **Before You Read**
> Think about lunch time in the school cafeteria. How do you know how to behave or sit? How did you learn these "rules?" What are the consequences if you don't follow the rules? How is this similar or different from lunch in your home?

What Is Social Behaviour?

In general, human behaviour can be defined as the observable responses to external and internal stimuli. Each individual in a society responds to these stimuli simultaneously. Social behaviour is the interaction among members of the same group responding to external and internal stimuli. For example, when you are dining in a restaurant, how do you know how to behave? You might remember what you learned from your family or how you've seen people on television behave in the same situation, which would be an example of internal stimuli. You might also be guided by what other diners in the same restaurant are doing. Are they speaking quietly? Are they moving from table to table? Observing the people around you provides clues for how you should behave, which is an example of external stimuli. In this section, you will learn what influences social behaviour.

↑ **FIGURE 3-21** Families shape our social behaviours. What messages did you receive from your family about eating and dining?

What Influences Behaviour?

When studying social behaviour, it is important to understand **social influence**. Social influence is the effect of other people on a person's thoughts and actions. Social influence can affect someone directly and indirectly. For example, joining your friends at a sushi restaurant for lunch when you really want a burger is an example of a direct influence. An example of an indirect influence is basing your decision to date someone on the reactions you *think* you will get from your family or avoiding dating a specific type of person because of real or imagined family pressure. Based on these two categories, sociologists are able to measure the frequency and classify the importance of certain influences on social behaviour.

social influence: the effect of other people on a person's thoughts and actions

> **Skills Focus**
> Sociologists can measure the frequency and rate the importance of certain influences on social behaviour through surveys. They then draw conclusions by examining their data.

Connecting Sociology to Anthropology

Anthropologists look at gender as defined by a person's culture. Human societies vary in how they define what it means to be a man or a woman and what roles they view as appropriate for each gender. These ideas are not the same in all cultures, nor are they fixed at birth. How is this similar or different from how sociologists look at gender?

▲ **FIGURE 3-22** Gender influences your social behaviour. What are the risks of not conforming to the expectations attributed to your gender?

The Family

The first force to shape the individual's behaviour is the family. An individual learns values and acceptable behaviours from his or her family and often exhibits these learned values and behaviours in social settings. A person's first social interactions happen with his or her parents or caregivers. Parents and caregivers act as custodians, caring for us until we reach independence. Ideally, families teach a child how how to act and the necessary skills to act appropriately in their absence. Our social behaviours are a product of interactions, customs, and rituals observed in the home and are reflected in our interactions with others in society.

Gender

Most of us are born male or female, which is regarded as our biological sex. How we behave as either a male or a female is determined by the role given to our gender by the society in which we live. Therefore, if you live in a society that values strength in men and sensitivity in females, you are likely to internalize the qualities attributed to your gender. You will be expected to demonstrate those qualities yourself and expect to see them exhibited by others of your gender in society. For this reason, it is often said that your gender is culturally constructed, or created by forces at work in your particular society. Your gender will also influence your views and behaviours as you interact with others in society. We usually talk about biological sex and gender in terms of male and female. However, some people are born intersex and are sometime referred to as *third* (and sometimes *fourth*) *gender*. Intersex means someone who was born with both male and female sexual characteristics and organs). Definitions of *third gender* vary, but the term is used to describe people who don't identify themselves as completely male or completely female either because biologically they are both or because their gender identity differs from their assigned biological sex. You will learn more about gender in later chapters.

 How do we learn about gender roles? How do they influence behaviour?

THE LANGUAGE OF SOCIAL SCIENCES

Sex and Gender

The terms *sex* and *gender* are often used interchangeably, but each term has a distinct meaning in social science. The term *sex* refers to the biological and physical characteristics that define someone as female, male, or intersex. The term *gender* refers to socially constructed roles, actions, behaviours, and attitudes that a society considers appropriate for men and women. Our view of gender is influenced by interactions with family, peers, and culture and determines expectations for how people should think and behave, and even what they are capable of. A society's construction of gender can determine what kind of job an individual should have, what chores they are responsible for, and even what kind of toys children should play with. For example, boys are often encouraged to play with toy trucks, while girls are encouraged to play with dolls.

QUESTIONS

1. How does society inform your ideas of gender?
2. How do children's toys reflect your society's view of gender? Do toys reflect or reinforce a society's ideas about gender?

Culture

Each of us is raised in a specific culture with its own characteristics and traditions. Cultural traditions may be simple or elaborate, involving complex symbols and values. A culture can be shaped by the history and laws of a country, television that people watch, and the music they listen to. We are all affected by cultural influences and view the rest of the world from our own cultural perspective. A person can also be influenced by more than one culture. In Canada's multicultural society, individuals can be influenced by the culture of their relatives and ancestors. They are also influenced by Canadian culture. They may have to adjust their cultural views to be able to function and make sense of the social norms and values around them.

↑ **FIGURE 3-23** How do our cultural traditions help shape our social behaviours?

Open for Debate

In 1990, RCMP officer Baltej Dhillon won the right to wear a turban rather than the Stetson hat traditionally worn as part of the RCMP uniform. (Dhillon is Sikh and wears a turban for religious reasons.) His story led to a national debate about religious freedom and Canadian identity. Some people objected to allowing this change in the RCMP uniform, claiming that the Canadian Mountie is a national icon and the Mountie's uniform should not be changed to accommodate someone's religious beliefs. Others supported the move, arguing that freedom of religion and multiculturalism are fundamental Canadian values. In a multicultural country like Canada, how do we balance competing cultural traditions?

Media

Think about all the media you access in a day: television, newspapers and magazines, radio, the Internet, and social networks. How difficult would it be to avoid any media for one day? The media have an important influence on social behaviour. New research suggests that Facebook friendships may improve real friendships. The findings were released in a study in 2009 and stated that 27.6 percent of American social media users said that their offline relationships are actually benefiting from online interaction using social media. People are using technology to shape new forms of human communication that are fascinating to sociologists. In all its forms, the media can help us understand social behaviour. While not all the world shares the same access to media, media have given the whole world access to how others around the world live. We will look more closely at this relationship in later chapters.

❓ Identify the major forces that influence social behaviour, and provide an example for each. Are there other factors that influence your behaviour? Explain and provide examples.

Different Cultures, Different Greetings

We have seen how family, gender, culture, and media influence how we function and interact with the world. Most of the time, we can apply what we've learned at home with a great deal of success to social situations. Sometimes, however, our understanding about how something is supposed to work in society may come into direct conflict with how it actually works. Consider something as simple as the act of greeting one another. Most countries around the world have a specific ritual or custom for greeting one another in different situations. A person growing up in that society learns very early in life how to greet someone, usually taught by parents, guardians, or elders in an attempt to prepare that child for the future.

For example, in India, people greet one another by pressing their own hands together close to the chest and slightly bowing or nodding. Sometimes handshakes are also exchanged, but men will rarely ever greet a woman in this manner unless she initiates the handshake. In North America, the handshake is the most common way to greet another person in public. The handshake seals many deals or agreements and is extended to people regardless of their age or station in life. Young children in North America, as a result, are often taught to have a firm handshake in order to show confidence and self-assurance. The handshake is also used in Nigeria to greet other people, along with a smile. In other parts of the world, it is customary to kiss and hug close friends and relatives. The greeting customs from around the world are as diverse as the cultures to which they belong.

Consult the chart below for more global greetings:

Culture	Greeting
Polynesian	• Place the other person's hands on your face and stroke.
Tibetan	• Stick your tongue out at the person you wish to greet.
Inuit	• Rub noses with the other person.
Western European	• Kiss the other person on the cheek.
Massai (tribe in Kenya)	• Spit on the other person, and when greeting an elder, spit in your hand before you offer it up to be shaken.

FIGURE 3-24 The traditional Tibetan greeting. How might this greeting be viewed by someone living in North America?

The chart above describes generalizations about greetings throughout the world. It's important to remember that these are generalizations about what people in other cultures do. Not everyone in Tibet will greet you by sticking out their tongue and if you meet someone from the Massai tribe in Kenya, you probably shouldn't spit on them. As we interact with other cultures, we also need to acknowledge that an action or gesture that is acceptable in one culture could be offensive in another.

IN THE FIELD

Social Worker Egerton Blackwood

Egerton Blackwood was always a good listener. Growing up in Ottawa, Blackwood's friends came to him for help with their problems or just for a sympathetic ear. After completing an undergraduate degree at the University of Ottawa, Blackwood began volunteering at a distress centre where he could put those listening skills to good use. He quickly realized he wanted to have a career helping people and went back to school to pursue a Masters degree in social work. Blackwood then went on to work with the Peel Children's Aid Society before moving on to his current position as a social worker with the Toronto District School Board.

Social work is a profession that puts social science knowledge and methods into practice to help people solve problems in their relationships, face illness and disability, and resolve social problems. Some social workers help families adopt children or find foster homes for neglected and abused children, while others work in public health to help seniors and their families assess and arrange for services. Social workers who work in schools like Egerton Blackwood often work with parents, guardians, teachers, and other school officials. They help students deal with stress or emotional problems and address problems with misbehaviour and discipline. Social workers also conduct research and develop policies to promote social change. Educational requirements for social workers vary from province to province, but social workers usually have an undergraduate degree in social science or from a social work program at a university.

As a social worker, Blackwood develops programs and collaborates with the community to meet the needs of both elementary and secondary students. Since he works with students in all grade levels, he can watch students grow up and be involved in their lives throughout their education.

By far the most difficult challenge he has faced in his career was the murder of Jordan Manners in May 2007. Blackwood was the social worker for the school where Manners was shot and killed, as well as other schools in the surrounding area. Since he knew the students best, he was called in to work with the police, school trustees and superintendents, teachers and other staff, to help students cope with the tragedy and its aftermath.

FIGURE 3-25
Egerton Blackwood with students planning a *Shoot With This* production.

Blackwood began developing an innovative program alongside Dameion Royes, CEO and president of BigItUp International. BigItUp provides financial and other support to various literacy and educational programs in Canada. Together Blackwood and Royes created the Shoot With This program. The program works to empower and motivate at risk youth by giving them resources to learn about video and photography. Taught by talented individuals who have experiences similar to their own, students learn how to plan and make a film, as well collaboration and conflict resolution skills. Many of the films have been shown in film festivals and the photos shown in galleries across the city.

Navigating through the bureaucracy of a large school board can be frustrating, but Blackwood thinks that it's worth it for the opportunity to help students. In his opinion, social work is a career for those who are good listeners, are empathetic, and non judgemental, and who recognize the need to be open minded and like people. He believes that social work will continue to change as institutions work together with the community to make a positive difference in the lives of others.

QUESTIONS

1. What skills are important for a career in social work?
2. How is sociology connected to social work?

Measuring Social Behaviour

So far, you have examined a number of important influences on social behaviour, as well as the greeting rituals of several different cultures. Can these influences be measured quantitatively or observed qualitatively? Sociologists agree that behaviour can be measured and observed with a certain degree of accuracy. Social interaction is a very important part of an individual's daily life. In fact, very few of us actually want to live in isolation. People continually develop new relationships. As an individual goes through different stages of life, such as high school, post-secondary school, and entering the work force, they interact with new people. Social networks, such as Facebook, MySpace, and Twitter make isolation less likely since staying connected to others is easy as long as your computers and cell phones are turned on.

> ### Skills **Focus**
> Sociologists rely on two research methods (quantitative and qualitative) in order to gather data for their studies. When studying social behaviour, it is important to determine whether the influences are direct or indirect. How would you go about studying those influences using one or both of the research methods available to sociologists?

FIGURE 3-26 How do you manage your social relationships?

REFLECT AND RESPOND

1. Provide an example of how each factor (i.e., family, gender, culture, media) influences your social behaviour.
2. Why is the family crucial to our understanding of social behaviour?
3. How is our gender culturally constructed?
4. Can a person be influenced by more than one culture? Looking at how a culture influences behaviour, what kind of challenges do people living in multicultural societies face?
5. How does symbolic interactionism influence family decisions?

Socialization

In order to thrive as members of a particular society, individuals learn to think and act as others do in their society. Learning what is acceptable and unacceptable in one's society is part of the journey to becoming a well-adjusted adult and a participating member of that society. The process by which the individual learns the behavioural patterns, skills, and values of her or his social world is called socialization. Socialization begins at birth and continues throughout an individual's life. Earlier in the chapter, you learned about values and norms. Now we will consider the process by which those values and norms are internalized by the individual. Socialization occurs in every culture. The values and norms of each society may differ, but the process of socialization is the same. Socialization is the process of learning the following elements:

- basic skills (for example, how to take physical care of oneself)
- socially accepted goals (for example, employment, marriage)
- roles and behaviours (for example, how to act in specific conditions)

Before You Read
Have you ever done something because your friends encouraged you to do so? What was the result? Why did you do or not do this activity? What did you learn about yourself?

FIGURE 3-27 What did you learn as a child about being an adult?

primary socialization: the process of learning the basic skills needed to survive in society

secondary socialization: the process of learning how to behave appropriately in group situations

anticipatory socialization: the process of learning how to plan the way to behave in new situations

resocialization: the process by which negative behaviour is transformed into socially acceptable behaviour

❓ What is the ultimate goal of socialization? Why is socialization so important? How can it be both positive and negative?

The Categories of Socialization

The process of socialization is often divided into distinct categories. **Primary socialization** is responsible for teaching the individual the basic skills needed to survive in society. These skills may include hygiene, eating with utensils, how to use language, and how to dress appropriately. **Secondary socialization** is responsible for teaching individuals how to act appropriately in group situations, such as at places of worship or school. **Anticipatory socialization** is concerned with teaching the individual how to plan ahead behaviour for new situations. For example, using your prior knowledge about certain social settings, you should be able to think ahead and anticipate the type of clothing, language, and behaviour required for an occasion. Finally, **resocialization** refers to the process by which an individual learns to transform old, sometimes unacceptable, behaviour into new, socially acceptable behaviour. For example, a criminal released from prison is given the opportunity to practise new behaviour or a new employee completes a training session to prepare him or her for a new job.

More to Know...
Abraham Maslow's Hierarchy of Needs (see Chapter 2) provides us with a road map of the ultimate goal of socialization, which is becoming a self-actualized human being capable of living harmoniously in society.

❓ What steps might a prisoner have to take to become resocialized? How does an individual learn to internalize the values of his or her society?

IN FOCUS: Female Violence and The Murder of Reena Virk

On November 14, 1997, 14 year-old Reena Virk was headed back to her foster home when a group of acquaintances invited her to a party in a nearby park. Once there, the group swarmed Virk, punching and kicking her, burning her, and trying to light her hair on fire (Steinberg, 2009). Although severely injured, Virk was able to get away from the group, walking over a bridge in an attempt to reach a bus stop to make her way home (CBC, 2009). Two of her attackers, later revealed as Warren Glowatski, 17 and Kelly Ellard, 15, dragged Virk back into the park, beating her again and drowning her. Police didn't find her body until eight days after she was attacked.

Virk's murder made headlines across the country after it was revealed that seven of the eight adolescents involved in her death were girls. Six girls, ages 14 to 16 were charged in the initial beating and sentenced to one year. Glowatski was convicted of second-degree murder in 1999, while Ellard was convicted in 2005 of second-degree murder (CBC, 2009).

Virk's case was seen as an example of the rise of girl on girl violence in North American society. Statistics were cited that indicated that violence by adolescent girls was on the rise and "experts" indicated female violence was caused by an increasingly violent culture, by angry girls no longer willing to channel their aggression in socially acceptable "feminine" ways, such as gossiping (CBC, 2008). Stories about Virk appeared in national newspapers and covered nationally on television, giving the impression that Canada was in the middle of an epidemic of female teenage violence. Even the federal government weighed in, indicating concern about the rise of female participation in violent activities.

In the years since Virk's murder, criminologists and sociologists examined the crime and the public's reaction to it. Using Statistics Canada data, they found that youth rate of violent crime dropped 5 percent in 1999, the fourth year in a row that the number declined (Statistics Canada, 2000). Although some statistics did indicate a rise in minor or moderate assaults by adolescent girls (in 1980, 710 women were charged compared to 4434 in 1995–1996), social scientists indicated that this increase reflected a change in policy and practices rather than a change in the behaviour of adolescent girls.

Why was there a discrepancy between what the media reported and what criminologists and sociologist concluded? Some argued that the media and the public were engaged in a "moral panic," reflecting an anxiety about the changing world and female roles with Canadian society. Barron and Lacombe also argue that the perception of an increasing problem can lead to changes in educational and legal priorities, such as more punitive policies for young offenders and zero tolerance policies in schools (Barron and Lacombe, 2005). Sociologists and criminologists examining the Reena Virk case were not only looking at the event itself, but also about the wider implications and meaning of the event on society.

QUESTIONS

1. Is it important to understand socialization in this case? Why or why not?
2. Why did the media and criminologists have different perspectives on the meaning of this event?

↑ **FIGURE 3-28** Reena Virk's parents leaving court

120 NEL Unit 1 • What Is Social Science?

Socialization and Gender

From their very earliest social interactions, boys and girls tend to display differences in behaviours, attitudes, abilities, and interests. As you learned on page 114 when examining gender and behaviour, children are encouraged to play with gender-specific toys. Typically, young girls play with dolls while young boys play with toy cars and trucks. These forms of play represent the typical play for children growing up in North America and the Western world. Not all cultures around the world designate child's play to dolls for girls and toy cars for boys. In many parts of the world, children's first toys have little to do with their gender and more to do with religious traditions or the harsh economic realities their families face, which in many cases means toys of any kind are hard to come by.

Sociologists studying gender generally consult different cultural models and experiences to determine how gender roles are transmitted to children from diverse cultural backgrounds. The findings for such studies suggest the same results—that gender is socially constructed and gender roles are internalized very early on in the process of socialization. Interestingly, the biological distinctions between male and female behaviours are not labelled right or wrong, better or worse. Therefore, any labels we use to describe male and female behaviours are learned. The first lessons about gender are taught at home by family. Later, as children age and their world expands, their religion, peers, school, and media reinforce or introduce new information about what it means to be male or female.

In an article for the Globe and Mail, clinical psychologist Gregory Lehne discusses the idea of forcing a child to play with a certain kind of toy:

> Some parents may raise a concerned eyebrow when their sons want to play with dolls or their daughters want to play with army figures, but those who try to push their children into gender stereotypes may do more harm than good. "It's fairly common that children experiment with cross-gender behaviour in their play. It helps them understand their own gender role better, as well as the gender role of other kids. (Globe and Mail, 2010, para 5)

Abnormal Socialization

Ideally, children should be raised in a nurturing environment that promotes physical, emotional, and intellectual development. Children also need the attention, encouragement, and stimulation of a caregiver to develop healthy self-esteem and become productive, well-adjusted members of society. Sadly, some children are raised in very unfortunate circumstances where they may be completely neglected and, in even rarer situations, are outright abandoned by their parents and left to fend for themselves in the wild. In these cases, the crucial socialization that occurs in the first years of life is missing, resulting in rather disastrous consequences for the children.

More to Know...

Margaret Mead examined a number of distinct features about American and Samoan adolescent girls and concluded that gender roles are socially constructed and relative to the culture in which they are exhibited.

VOICES

Many parents are quick to try to change any atypical gender behaviour in their kids for fear that their children will be bullied at school or the target of ridicule from peers.
Gregory Lehne

FIGURE 3-29 How are gender roles taught?

Child Abuse

There are devastating consequences for children raised in abusive homes. In cases of child abuse, children do not learn normal and healthy behaviours. The root causes of abuse are varied: the abusive parents may have been abused themselves, lack appropriate parenting strategies, or be unable to deal with their own frustrations and anger. Whatever the reason, the results are devastating and life-altering for the children living through abuse. Neglect and abuse can take on many different forms.

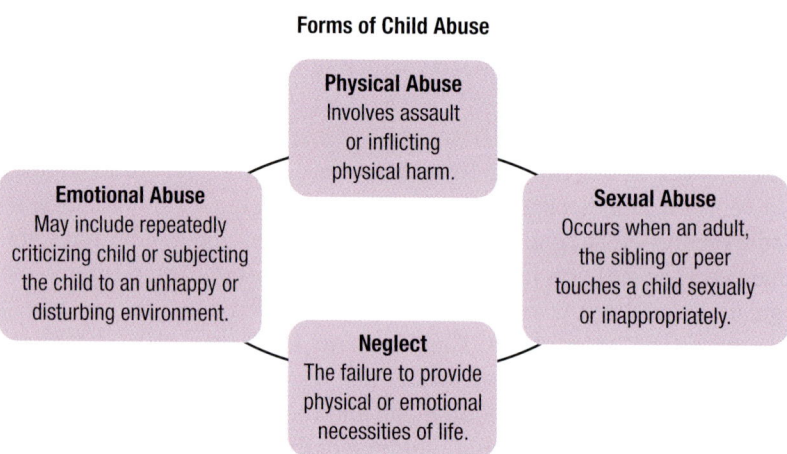

Forms of Child Abuse

- **Physical Abuse** — Involves assault or inflicting physical harm.
- **Sexual Abuse** — Occurs when an adult, the sibling or peer touches a child sexually or inappropriately.
- **Neglect** — The failure to provide physical or emotional necessities of life.
- **Emotional Abuse** — May include repeatedly criticizing child or subjecting the child to an unhappy or disturbing environment.

Feral Children

feral: unwanted child deserted at a young age and raised by animals

Ferals are children deserted at a young age and raised by animals. These children are of particular interest to psychologists and sociologists alike. Sociologists who have studied feral children discovered that they appropriate the behaviours of the species that raised them and can perfectly imitate their gestures and sounds. In 1991, a disturbing discovery was made in Ukraine, where an eight-year-old girl named Oxana Malaya was found exhibiting dog-like behaviour. The neglected child of alcoholic parents, Oxana, also known as the "Ukrainian Dog Girl," spent much of her life between the ages of three and eight living and interacting with the dogs that lived in a kennel in the family's yard. Her five years of interaction left her fearful of humans. When she was discovered, she barked like a dog and preferred to move around on all four limbs. She drank from a bowl and viewed the world from the viewpoint of a dog.

FIGURE 3-30 Feral children lack basic skills because they are raised by animals. If a child's only interactions are with animals, what behaviour is he or she learning? What behaviour is he or she unable to learn? Why is the socialization of children so important?

By the age of 26, Oxana could speak and many of her behaviour problems improved. Oxana resides at a home for the developmentally delayed, where she helps look after the cows in the home's farm. She has stated that she is happiest when among dogs. By studying feral children, sociologists concluded that children need to learn social skills at a young age. It is during this critical period that children are able to develop and internalize social behaviours most readily.

Isolated Children

Isolates are children raised in near isolation within human households. The most famous isolate case was a young girl named Genie who was discovered living in California during the 1970s. Genie had lived most of her 13 years in severe isolation. Confined to a darkened room, Genie was constantly strapped to a potty chair with little to no human contact. When police discovered her, she could not speak and could barely walk or eat. Despite intensive rehabilitation, Genie was never able to make a full recovery from the trauma she lived through. You will learn more about Genie in Chapter 5.

In July 2005, another isolate case emerged in Plant City, Florida. Authorities were called in to investigate a woman and her two grown sons living in a quiet neighbourhood. Some neighbours suspected that the conditions in the home were unsafe. When authorities entered the home to investigate, they found a three-year-old girl lying on a mattress, her emaciated body covered in feces, insect bites, rashes, and sores, and her hair crawling with lice. She was naked except for a soiled diaper. Police removed the girl from the home. It was later discovered the girl's name was Danielle and that she lived most of her three years in a darkened room, lying on the dirty mattress. Danielle promptly received medical treatment and was adopted by a loving family in October 2007. Her birth mother was forbidden to see her. Although she still does not speak, she is learning to listen and can understand simple commands. She can walk, is almost fully toilet trained, can chew and swallow, and is learning about emotions, including what it means to be loved. To sociologists, Danielle's story is an opportunity to study the dangerous effects of improper or lack of socialization in a young child's life.

> **More to Know...**
> You learned about the concept of the looking-glass self on page 111. The image reflected to feral children is so limited that they are unable to develop a self-concept beyond imitating the sounds and gestures of the animals that raised them.

isolate: child raised in near isolation within a human household

FIGURE 3-31 How do children such as Danielle offer sociologists the opportunity to learn more about the importance of socialization?

> **Connecting Sociology to Psychology**
> You might see the connection between the isolates you've just read about and Harlow's Surrogate Mother experiment you learned about in Chapter 2. This classic experiment demonstrates the important role that social interaction plays in the development of healthy relationships. How does Harlow's experiment relate to Genie and Danielle?

❓ What do the cases of Oxana, Genie, and Danielle tell you about the importance of socialization in the early years of life?

Agents of Socialization

Before You Read
Recall something that you do because it's part of your family's tradition, such as a holiday get-together, special event, or dinner. Share with a partner to see how your traditions are similar to or different from the traditions of other families.

The people and institutions that shape an individual's social development are known as **agents of socialization**. Throughout your life, you will encounter situations where you will rely heavily on certain individuals and groups to help shape your behaviour and beliefs. These groups teach you how to participate. The role that these agents play is significant to your social, emotional, and physical development. Different agents of socialization have different levels of influence, depending on your age and stage in life. For example, when you were a young child, you relied on your parents to guide and shape your responses. As you get older, you may rely on your friends more than your parents to help you with what is happening in your life at the moment. The following are agents of socialization that have the most influence on you a different point throughout your life and help you to navigate the complex social world in which you live:

- family
- peer groups
- workplace
- media
- religion

agents of socialization: people and institutions that shape an individual's social development

The Primary Agent of Socialization: The Family

The primary agent of socialization is the family. The family is responsible for meeting an individual's most basic needs and providing the beliefs needed to survive in this world. It is within the family structure that you are first introduced to right and wrong, proper and improper, appropriate and inappropriate. The family teaches the individual about social behaviour. The family is the primary agent of socialization because it shapes behaviour throughout life, starting from the day an individual is born, especially during those crucial early years of development.

Family Structure and Socialization

In the past, a traditional and idealized family structure was made up of a father, a mother, and children. The family has undergone significant changes in the last 50 years. Families are more diverse than they have ever been, with divorce, remarriage, and same-sex marriages having a notable effect on how we define Canadian families today. There is no such thing as a typical family. There have been many changes to the structure and makeup of what is considered a traditional family, but all families are equally important for socialization.

FIGURE 3-32 Why is family so important for socialization?

According to the Vanier Institute of the Family, a family is any combination of two or more people who are bound together over time by ties of mutual consent, birth, and/or adoption or placement and who, together, assume responsibilities for some or all of the following:

- physical maintenance and care of group members
- addition of new members through procreation or adoption
- socialization of children
- social control of members
- production, consumption, and distribution of goods and services
- affective nurturance (love)

TYPES OF FAMILIES	
Family Structure	Definition
nuclear family	• a family that consists of spouses and their dependent children
extended family	• a family system in which several generations live together in one household
lone-parent family	• a family that consists of one parent living with one or more dependent children
blended family	• a family in which divorced partners with children from a previous union remarry
same-sex family	• a family that consists of two individuals of the same gender, with or without children

? What defines a family? What does the family teach an individual? Why are families so important for socialization?

Secondary Agents of Socialization

The secondary agents of socialization are the non-family people and institutions that teach an individual social behaviours and norms, such as schools, workplaces, peers, media, and religion. Typically, secondary agents of socialization begin to have an influence once a child enters school. Once there, the influence of school life and peers becomes increasingly more important as a socializing agent for the child. Increasing exposure to media further socializes the individual. Religion also provides a strong influence and can continue to do so throughout a person's life.

School

Schools transmit knowledge and skills to students. The education system in North America sets out to teach students a curriculum, a set of standard knowledge and skills that everyone should know. This is what you learn in class and what you are tested on. Schools also socialize students through a hidden curriculum as well. The hidden curriculum models a certain set of beliefs and attitudes and endorses specific behaviour in different situations. The hidden curriculum can often create advantages for some students and disadvantages for others. In order to function in groups, students need to internalize and demonstrate important behaviours such as punctuality, self-reliance, teamwork, competitiveness, and obedience. The goal of schools is to teach these skills and reinforce these values with praise and positive reinforcement.

↑ FIGURE 3-33 How do schools transmit knowledge and skills?

Peer Groups

Perhaps the most important lessons from school are learned from and through your peers. Peers are people of the same age. The influence of the peer group is especially pronounced during adolescence, sometimes becoming more important than the family as a major agent of socialization. The adolescent peer group creates the opportunity to learn such skills as communication, collaboration, and compromise. Often referred to as the *social curriculum of schools*, peer interactions provide ample opportunity for the individual to learn about gender and culture and to establish relationships with others from a variety of social and ethnic backgrounds. The adolescent peer group is primarily responsible for teaching the individual about sexual relationships and, in some cases, stands in direct opposition to the values taught by the individual's family. The adolescent peer group is highly susceptible to the influence of media. In some cases, this reliance on the media for values and beliefs can have negative implications.

FIGURE 3-34 The adolescent peer group is a powerful influence. How do your peers influence you?

The Workplace

School is a very important agent of socialization for children and youth. But as they become adults, it is the workplace that becomes important. In much the same way that school is an important place where students learn how to behave in certain situations and work with others, the workplace is very important for adults to understand.

Children first learn about work at home through chores, play, and observation. Parents and other close adults help shape the values and attitudes of children toward work (Feij, 1998). In Grade 9, many students across Canada participate in "Take Our Kids to Work" Day. The purpose of this day is to give students a chance to explore their future and help them to understand a parent's role in making a living and supporting a family. Many students who work part-time or have co-op placements have first-hand experience of the workplace already.

> Identify and explain the goals of schools in socializing young children. At what point do peer groups exert more influence over the individual than family?

Media

Mass media includes television, radio, movies, books, and the Internet. The power of media to influence and shape behaviour is a fascinating subject for sociologists. Media can be particularly influential in a child's socialization. For children today, television viewing and playing video games have become part of the day's routine. Many children spend considerable amounts of time in front of the television while busy parents work or tend to the household. The consequences to a child's development are clear: time spent watching television means time away from others, playing and interacting, building social skills and relationships. As children get older, they spend more time online and visiting social networking sites. Perhaps the most pervasive messages to come from media are in the form of advertisements about what to wear, how to act, and what to aspire to. There is evidence that suggests that young people learn from the values, beliefs, and behaviours exhibited by television characters (Valkenburg, 2004). To some people, the media stands in direct opposition to the family, challenging the very values that the family tries to instill in its children.

Although studies have not linked exposure to violence to violent acts by males, the media does normalize violence, making it appear to be part of our culture. On television, males are shown committing most of the violence. Advertisers use violence to sell products to men, such as video games.

However, the influence of mass media is not entirely negative. New technologies have exposed people to other cultures and ideas and provided an outlet for creativity and expression. Mass media has also created new ways to connect with people around the world.

FIGURE 3-35 How does the media influence behaviour?

Religion

While fewer people are part of organized religious traditions today, religion continues to be an important agent of socialization for a number of reasons. Most religions have moral codes and often set standards of behaviour that they expect their members to follow. Religion can also teach people responsibility to others and the importance of charity, whether monetary donations to the poor or volunteering time and effort in social institutions such as hospitals.

REFLECT AND RESPOND

1. List the agents of socialization and give an example of how each one has influenced your social behaviour.
2. Does the socialization you experience in school prepare you for the workplace?
3. There is a lot of discussion and concern about how the media influences young people today. In your opinion, how important is the media in socializing children? Is the media always a negative influence? Why or why not?
4. If fewer people belong to organized religions than ever before, why do sociologists study their influence on socialization?

CHAPTER 3 REVIEW

Knowledge and Understanding/Thinking

1. Define the terms *values*, *norms*, and *roles*, and describe the purpose of each in any given society.

2. Explain how sociologists conduct their research. Describe the initial steps of the sociological inquiry model, and suggest a possible topic sociologists might study.

3. Define the term *social imagination* and explain why it is important for understanding individual problems that are affected by social institutions. How can this help sociologists understand social issues such as poverty or unemployment?

4. Compare and contrast the ideas of Marx, Durkheim, and Weber in one of the following areas:
   - inequality
   - society's responsibility to its members

5. Identify the difference between direct and indirect social influence, and suggest an example for each.

Thinking/Communication

6. Describe and summarize the three main schools of thought (conflict theory, structural functionalism, symbolic interactionism) to analyze social behaviour differently. Write a brief statement explaining which of the schools of thought you find the most convincing.

7. Why are objectivity and universality important concepts for sociologists to understand?

8. How might society go about resocializing the victims of abnormal socialization in each of the following examples:
   a) feral children
   b) isolated children
   c) victims of child abuse

9. Identify and summarize the key ideas for feminist sociology. How is it connected to the conflict theory?

Communication/Application

10. Using a current or historical event with which you are familiar, write a research question that a sociologist might ask about the event and suggest an appropriate research method with which to gather data. Write out a response to your research question.

11. Identify the social groups in your school. List several characteristics, norms, and values of at least two groups. To which groups do you belong? What sociological theory best explains how these groups operate?

12. Write an updated editorial about the contributions of one of the sociologists featured in this chapter and his or her relevance to sociology today.

13. Create a dramatization that reflects the categories of socialization and includes at least two agents of socialization for one of the following situations:
    a) a holiday meal with your family
    b) getting caught breaking a rule at school or at home
    c) dealing with a difficult customer at your part-time job
    d) responding to an invitation from a friend for an event you don't want to attend

UNIT 2

Social Science and Me

Chapter 4
Anthropology and Me

Research and Inquiry Skill Focus:
- Creating a Research Plan

Section 4.1: Culture and Identity
Section 4.2: Anthropology and Behaviour
Section 4.3: Ethical Issues in Anthropology
Chapter 4 Review

Chapter 5
Psychology and Me

Research and Inquiry Skill Focus:
- Creating a Research Plan in Psychology
- Analyzing and Interpreting Research Information

Section 5.1: Development of Self
Section 5.2: Psychology and Behaviour
Section 5.3: Ethical Issues in Psychology
Chapter 5 Review

Chapter 6
Sociology and Me

Research and Inquiry Skill Focus:
- Gathering and Processing Information

Section 6.1: Sociology and Identity
Section 6.2: Sociology and Behaviour
Section 6.3: Ethical Issues in Sociology
Chapter 6 Review

Why do you need to know about social science? Social science is an interconnected subject that allows you to develop the tools to explore the human condition, human behaviour, and society. You will develop an understanding of yourself, how you think, how you live, and how you interact with others and the world.

Understanding and applying the ideas of the three social sciences is crucial to developing critical thinking skills. You will apply your knowledge to develop an understanding of the factors that influence your identity. As you learn more about each of the social sciences, you will research a topic of interest to you and apply the social science inquiry skills that you develop along the way. As you read each chapter in this unit, stop and ask yourself, "How does this connect to my own experiences? What is similar, and what is different, and why?"

FIGURE U2-1 What aspects of your culture are an important part of your identity? How do you define yourself? How do you know what factors influence your decisions?

CHAPTER 4

Anthropology and Me

Anthropologists wrestle with fundamental questions about what it means to be human. They examine how cultures shape our identities, and how our worldview influences our behaviour. In this chapter, you will learn about human cultures and behaviours and why they are important to anthropology. You will also learn about the importance of ethics in the social sciences, how ethical practices developed within anthropology, and ethical issues facing anthropologists.

Chapter Expectations

By the end of this chapter, you will:

- use an anthropological perspective to assess how diverse factors influence and shape human behaviour and culture
- explain from an anthropological perspective how various factors influence and shape an individual's behaviour and culture
- describe the effects that diffusion, assimilation, and multiculturalism have on culture
- explain how studying cultural systems of different times, places, and groups helps anthropologists understand human behaviour and culture in the present
- explain ways in which culture is an agent of socialization
- correctly use terms relating to anthropology
- create appropriate research plans to investigate selected topics

Key Terms

bilineal	identity moratorium	polygyny
bridewealth	liminal stage	potlatch
circumcision	lineage	reciprocity
clan	matrilineal	redistribution
emic perspective	meta-analysis	rite of passage
etic perspective	monogamy	ritual
euphemism	naive realism	self-enhancement
explicit cultural knowledge	patrilineal	taboo
fetish	perception	tacit cultural knowledge
globalization	polyandry	technological diffusion
horticultural	polygamy	wage labour

FIGURE 4-1 Look at the photos, and try to draw a conclusion about what is going on. What questions might an anthropologist ask the people in these photos? What is the danger of drawing conclusions about a society based only on these pictures?

Landmark Case Studies

Steel Axes Among the Yir Yoront
Death Without Weeping
Shakespeare in the Bush

Key Theorists

Laura Bohannan
Rachel Burr
Amber Case
Gary Fine
George Gmelch
Bronislaw Malinowski
Gerald Murray

Nancy Netting
Rebecca Popenoe
Ken Pryce
Nancy Scheper-Hughes
Lauriston Sharpe
Claire Sterk

Spotlight on Anthropology — *Cyborg Anthropology*

> **Before You Read**
> How often do you use technology in a day?

"We are all cyborgs now," argues Amber Case, in a TED talk in January 2011. Case is a cyborg anthropologist who examines the way humans and technology interact and evolve together. The word *cyborg* often conjures up scary science fiction images of half human and half machine monsters. A 1960s paper on space travel defined a cyborg as an organism to which components produced from outside the organism have been added for the purpose of adapting to new environments (Case, 2011). For example, space suits and scuba gear are technologies that allow the person wearing them to adapt to environments they would otherwise be unable survive, transforming them into cyborgs.

Cyborg anthropologists study interactions between humans and non-human objects and try to understand the effect of technology on culture. As technology has evolved, culture evolved alongside it. The amount of time spent online, using cell phones, or using other digital devices like mp3 players, as well as the number of devices we carry around with us are part of this cultural shift. In his book *The Cyborg Handbook*, Chris Hables Gray said "I think about how almost everyone in urban societies could be seen as a low-tech cyborg, because they spend large parts of the day connected to machines." (p.373.) How we interact with technology is important to understanding our culture.

Case explains that our tool use is an extension of our mental self. We are all carrying around a virtual bag of information with us. If we printed out all the information contained in our desktops or our cell phones, it would be an enormous pile of paper and information. If we lose our information, it often feels like a part of us has gone missing. The information that we carry around with us has led to the creation of a digital self. In the same way we maintain our physical self by showering, brushing our teeth, and getting dressed, we also maintain a digital self; an online presence that requires maintenance because people are interacting with it even when we're offline.

Case argues that as more and more humans adopt technology, time and space are being compressed. People are communicating rapidly. We have the power to connect with family and friends anytime and anywhere and expect immediate responses to our emails, calls, and texts. Case speculates that this is leaving little time for self-reflection.

Like all anthropologists, cyborg anthropologists gather information through participant observation and fieldwork. Case observes how people participate in digital networks, how they project their personalities through digital networks, and how they use technology to work, for leisure, and how they communicate (Case, 2011). "This is the first time in the entire history of humanity that we've connected in this way. And it's not that machines are taking over; it's that they're helping us to be more human, helping us to connect with each other. The most successful technology gets out of the way and helps us live our lives … And so this is the important point that I like to study: that things are beautiful, that it's still a human connection; it's just done in a different way. We're just increasing our humanness and our ability to connect with each other, regardless of geography. So that's why I study cyborg anthropology" (Case, 2011).

FIGURE 4-2 Amber Case, cyborg anthropologist. Do you think modern humans have become cyborgs?

QUESTIONS

1. What evidence does Case present that we are now cyborgs?
2. Do you agree with her point of view that technology is making us more human? Why or why not?

Research and Inquiry Skills

Creating a Research Plan

All research is driven by a purpose; it begins with an interest that leads to a question. Research questions are often vague at the beginning and become more specific. Research can also change direction as the researcher collects and analyzes data and information. It's important to analyze your information as objectively as possible and avoid making judgments or drawing conclusions before the research is complete.

Creating a research plan is an important part of the research process. Your research plan explains the basis of your research and communicates your research ideas to other people. It also explains your research methods. As you learned in Unit 1, you start with a central research question and hypothesis. When you create your research plan, you also choose how you will conduct your primary research and design the questions you will ask. It's also important that your research meets ethical guidelines and standards. A research plan is a way to demonstrate that your research is sound and credible. After completing your research, you compare the information you gathered to that of previous sources and present your findings.

Locating and Assessing Secondary Sources

Before beginning any primary research, you should find out what research has already been done on your topic by looking at reliable secondary sources. How do you know if a source is reliable? You should always ask the following questions of any print or online source:

1. Is it accurate? Who wrote it? Is the author qualified? Is the material written in a professional manner?
2. Is it an authoritative source? Who published the document? Is it from a preferred and credible source, such as the government, a university, a museum, or a professional association?
3. Is it objective? Why was it written? How detailed is it? What opinions are expressed?
4. Is it current? Is the information up to date? If there are links included, are they credible?
5. Does it cover the topic fully? Is there a fee to view the whole page? Is the information cited correctly?

As you learned in Chapter 3, once you have found good sources, you need to cite them using an appropriate bibliographic format. Social science uses APA style.

Research Methods

In cultural anthropology, participant observation and the semi-structured interview are the basic research methods. You need to decide what type of method is appropriate for your question.

Participant Observation

- You can conduct this method in person or online (for example, chat rooms, social networking sites). Be sure to verify that people you interact with online are who they say they are.
- This method can be time consuming and may involve risks for you as the researcher.
- Accurate note-taking is important, but online research is often already transcribed. You always need to do an analysis and a summary.

Semi-structured Interview

- Preparation should include creating open-ended questions or topics related to your research to generate discussion and uncover the subject's concerns.
- New areas of investigation can emerge during an interview.
- Accurate note-taking is essential since an interview or a social interaction can't be repeated. Record and analyze the information as soon as possible.

Ethical Guidelines

Your research must be conducted with ethical integrity and be as unbiased and accurate as possible. Social scientists must follow the ethical guidelines of their disciplines. You'll learn more about ethical guidelines in anthropology in Section 4.3, but there are a few principles that are important to all social science research. A researcher must be open and honest with research subjects about what he or she is researching, and research subjects must give informed consent to participate. (*Informed consent* is voluntary agreement by a person who understands, in his or her own cultural terms, the researcher's purpose.) A researcher must also protect the confidentiality of any information shared by the research subjects, and must protect the dignity, safety, and privacy of research subjects at all times. Research must be ethical to be credible.

Activities

1. Create a research plan for an issue you are interested in investigating. How will you go about your research?

Section 4.1

Culture and Identity

ritual: prescribed behaviour in which there is no real connection between the action and the desired outcome

Culture is made up of elements that societies produce and teach. From the arts and languages, to **rituals** and roles, to history and economic structures, culture helps form our identities and shows us how to function within society. Cultures are not static; they adapt over time in response to internal or external changes, such as new technologies or changes in climate or population. Anthropologists study how people respond to cultural change. Through fieldwork and participant observation, anthropologists learn not only about the culture they are studying, but also about themselves and their own culture.

How Does Culture Shape Identity?

You are born with certain features as determined by your DNA, and you are probably aware of differences between your family and your friends' families. These things certainly have an impact on who you are, but culture shapes our identity in ways that we may not be aware of.

Before You Read
How do you think your culture has influenced your identity?

In Chapter 1, culture was defined as what people do, what people make, and what people believe. These three ideas cover most of our daily activities. The most important of these three is what people believe because it influences what they do and what they make. We sometimes focus on behaviour that seems different to us or the strange objects of people in faraway places, but these are merely the expressions of what those people believe and how their ideas shape their identity, behaviour, technology, and art.

Consider the following statements:

- Two men holding hands in public indicates that they are equals and friends.
- If my father dies, it is best that my mother marry my uncle.
- Family compatibility is more important than romantic love when choosing a marriage partner.
- Fat women are more desirable than thin women.
- Homosexuals should be allowed to legally marry.
- A tattoo indicates that you are a responsible adult.
- The best way to gain status in society is to give away a lot of material goods.
- Family and parental wishes should always be more important than personal desires or needs.

FIGURE 4-3 What cultural expectations do you think are influencing these expressions of identity?

All of the above beliefs are from specific cultures that we will examine in this chapter. They are all examples of cultural beliefs. People know this information to be true because it is true for all or most people in their society. By looking at many cultures, we can become aware of some of our own cultural assumptions and different ways of knowing the world and the people in it. In this chapter, we will look at some different ways that culture affects growing up, race, gender, class, family, and language.

Canadian Culture and Identity

Understanding your own culture is vitally important to understanding other cultures. But what is Canadian culture? Is it made up of hockey, snow, maple syrup, Tim Hortons, Margaret Atwood, and the Group of Seven, or is it something more difficult to explain? Canadians often struggle to define Canadian culture, and sometimes it is easier to explain what we are not.

Although First Nations and Inuit peoples inhabited Canada long before European settlers arrived, early Canadian culture was shaped by the two founding nations of Canada, France and England. These two cultures shaped our system of government, laws, economy, and art. First Nations and Inuit cultures became increasingly important to Canadian identity in the mid- to late twentieth century as government policies surrounding assimilation changed. Previously, the Canadian government tried to assimilate First Nations and Inuit peoples into European culture through relocation, residential schools, and other policies designed to sever First Nations and Inuit peoples from their culture. Aboriginal ways of knowing have affected our Constitution, attitude to the environment, and education and justice systems. The other major influence on Canadian culture is the United States. As Canada became more independent from Britain, the United States became an increasingly greater influence. Canadians often compare their politics, economy, history, music, television, and authors to American politics, economy, history, and arts.

Canada is also defined as a multicultural country. The arrival of immigrants from many countries prompted the Canadian government to introduce the Multiculturalism Act in 1971, a policy of multiculturalism within a bilingual framework. The Multiculturalism Act acknowledged the "freedom of all members of Canadian society to preserve, enhance, and share their cultural heritage" and led to greater recognition of Canada's diverse ethnicities and cultures. However, some argue that this policy has made it harder to define Canadian culture and participate in it. They also point out that multiculturalism as a policy separates people into different groups and emphasizes differences over similarities.

Literature is often used to define a culture. At the end of the twentieth century, Canadian literature included writers of backgrounds who were neither English nor French. Writers such as Wayson Choy, Michael Ondaatje, and Joy Kogawa provided a new lens on Canada and Canadian culture. Other forms of diverse cultural expression also emerged in the other arts from artists such as rapper K'naan, filmmaker Deepa Mehta, and photographer Yousuf Karsh.

> **Connecting Anthropology to Sociology**
>
> Sociologists compare societies to explain trends and behaviours. They weave together the common threads among cultures in order to make sense of issues that affect all societies. How is this different from the way anthropologists look at culture?

> **Skills Focus**
>
> Prepare questions for a semi-structured interview about Canadian culture. Create open-ended questions to generate discussion and understand the subject's concerns and ideas.

> **VOICES**
>
> You only know [Canada] by being away.
>
> K'naan (born Keinan Abdi Warsame in Somalia, immigrated to Canada at age 13

REFLECT AND RESPOND

1. What is Canadian culture for you?
2. How would an anthropologist research Canadian culture differently than a psychologist or a sociologist?
3. What does K'naan mean when he says, "You only know [Canada] by being away"?

Rites of Passage

Before You Read

Do you think a ceremony is helpful in life transitions, such as birth and death?

rite of passage: a ceremony, ritual, or event that marks an individual's passage from one stage of life to another

All human beings are born, grow, and become adults, but cultures look at this process in many different ways. A **rite of passage** is a ceremony, ritual, or event that marks a change in life or status. Most cultures have ceremonies to mark birth, adolescence, marriage, and death, but cultures vary enormously in how they mark these occasions. In Canada, a funeral may last only a few hours and only close friends or family members might be expected to actively mourn for more than one day. In other cultures, mourning rituals last longer. For the Maori of New Zealand, a funeral involves a large gathering of the extended family for a week or more to give speeches, celebrate, and mourn the deceased. In Judaism, the parents, spouse, siblings, and children of the deceased directly observe a seven-day mourning period called *shiva*. Mourners are not supposed to work or attend school during this time. For both the Maori and Jewish people, the structure of the ritual allows families to mark the passing of the deceased before continuing with their own life. Rites of passage exist to help individuals move from one stage of life to another, reduce stress, create emotional bonds, and strengthen the fabric of society.

In Canada, common rites of passage include some of the following:

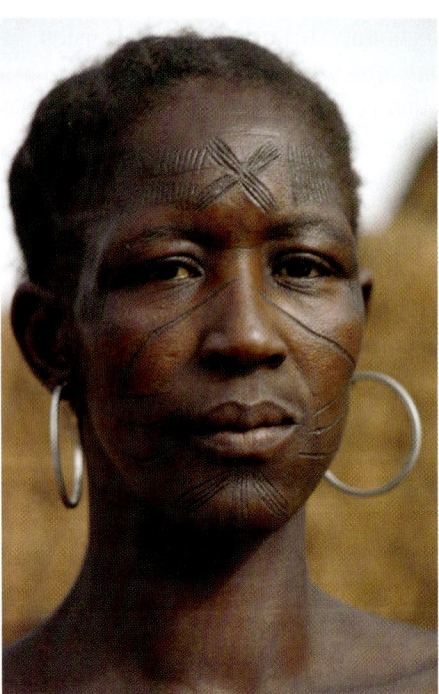

FIGURE 4-4 This African woman has undergone scarification (an age-old practice in some parts of Africa where young women are deliberately scarred in elaborate patterns) as part of her rite of passage to adulthood. How do Canadian teens mark their transition to adulthood?

- reaching puberty
- taking religious initiations (e.g., bar/bat mitzvah)
- going on a first date
- getting a driver's licence
- graduating high school
- drinking alcohol
- having the first sexual experience
- moving from one's parents' home
- graduating from a postsecondary institution
- getting a job
- getting married
- buying own home
- having children

? In your opinion, which rite of passage is the most important for Canadians? Are there different rites of passage for the transition to adolescence and to adulthood? Should rites of passage occur in a specific order? Why or why not?

Three-Stage Process

Throughout history, rites of passage have occurred in very similar patterns across cultures. In his book *Rites of Passage*, first published in 1908, Charles-Arnold van Gennep demonstrated that most cultures have rites of passage that follow a similar, three-stage process of segregation, transition, and incorporation, and reintegration (see Figure 4-5).

FIGURE 4-5 Three-Stage Process

Segregation

In the first stage, a person undergoing the rite of passage is separated from the rest of society and from his or her original status. This segregation often includes a geographic change as well as a change in physical appearance, such as body paint or special clothing (Irwin, 2008).

Transition

The transition stage, also called the **liminal stage**, in a rite of passage can last for a few hours, days, months, or years. In this stage, the person going through the rite of passage is becoming his or her new self and learning the new role. Often there is learning, guidance, or instruction from a mentor who has completed the rite, but in some cultures, such as Aborigines of Australia, the individual is expected to be alone in the wilderness, seeking guidance from the spirit world. In other cultures, such as the Kikuyu of Kenya, the initiates live together in a special dwelling for one year, have instruction from the elders, and perform specific duties.

In Amish cultures, adolescents have to participate in *rumspringa* before being considered an adult member of the Amish community. *Rumspringa* is a Pennsylvania Dutch term, loosely translated as "running around." The *rumspringa* period begins when an Amish youth turns 16. He or she hasn't been baptized yet and isn't subject to the church's rules about permitted and forbidden behaviours. During *rumspringa*, Amish youth go on their own in the outside world, in many cases for the first time. This can include going to a movie theatre, taking driving lessons, going to parties, and even having sex. *Rumspringa* ends when a youth agrees to be baptized into the church and to take up the responsibilities attendant on being an adult member of the Amish community.

Incorporation and Reintegration

The individual is reintegrated into regular society in his or her new role. Sometimes he or she is marked by tattoos, scars, body paint, or new clothing. In other cases, the individual gives up something to symbolically indicate that one role has ended and another has begun. The individual is expected to assume new tasks and is formally recognized by the society in his or her new status.

liminal stage: the second stage in a rite of passage, when the initiate is in a state of transition between the old and the new

Male Rites of Passage

Rites of passage are often undertaken to indicate a transformation from child to adult. These rites of passage occur at a specific point in a person's life. In North America, some common rites of passage are getting a driver's licence or going on a first date. Male and female initiation rites around the world can be quite different. Male rites of passage are more common than female rites, along with a longer period of adolescence. Male initiation rites are sometimes more painful and traumatic, especially among societies that engage in warfare regularly. These rituals often involve scarification (deliberate scaring), beatings, fasting, genital mutilation, tattooing, and intimidation by threats and stories. These hardships are thought to strengthen boys and assist in transforming them into men.

Maasai Circumcision

The Maasai people live in eastern Africa, in what is now Kenya and northern Tanzania. They remain a culturally distinct people and are still herding cattle, though they now have some income from tourism and craft sales. Tepilit Ole Saitoti underwent the rite of passage to become a Maasai warrior in the 1960s. In his autobiography, *The Worlds of a Maasai Warrior*, originally published in 1986, he describes the process and the ceremony. Young men are circumcised as part of a ceremony. The **circumcision** is performed by an elder with ritual knives. The initiate must sharpen the knives himself and bring a ritual cowhide from a cow that had been slaughtered during his naming ceremony. Ice-cold water is poured over his head, a ceremonial paint is splashed on his face, and the circumcision is performed. The warrior must lie on his bed until the bleeding stops and must not let any blood fall on the ground. As you read the passage below, think about how Tepilit's rite of passage conforms to the three-stage process.

> In two weeks I was able to walk and was taken to join other newly circumcised boys far away from our settlement … On our way to the settlement, we hunted birds and teased girls by shooting them with our wax blunt arrows. We danced and ate and were well treated wherever we went. We were protected from the cold and rain during the healing period. We were not allowed to touch food, as we were regarded as unclean, so whenever we ate we had to use specially prepared sticks instead. We remained in this pampered state until our wounds healed and our headdresses were removed. Our heads were shaved, we discarded our black cloaks and bird headdresses and embarked as newly shaven warriors, Irkeleani.
>
> As long as I live I will never forget the day my head was shaved and I emerged a man, a Maasai warrior. (p. 70–71)

Open for Debate

For some, male circumcision is a cultural ritual. For others, it is a cosmetic procedure. Medical bodies argue that circumcision reduces disease. Recent research concluded that it is an effective strategy in HIV prevention. But there are also groups who oppose it. To them, circumcision is mutilation that has harmful long-term effects. Circumcision is usually performed on newborns and infants who cannot consent. Should circumcision be performed on a child who cannot consent?

circumcision: the surgical removal of the foreskin of the penis; often performed as part of a ceremony at birth or during adolescence

↑ **FIGURE 4-6** Tepilit Ole Saitoti. How are Tepilit's experiences of becoming a man different from those of young men in Canadian society today? Are there similarities?

❓ What were the three stages of the rite of passage for this Maasai warrior?

Female Rites of Passage

Rites of passage for girls are quite different than those for boys, and less common. The male rites are often a test of strength and involve more physical and emotional hardship. For many females, the transition from childhood to adulthood revolves around first menstruation. This is a time in a female's life when she is often then considered ready for marriage and child-bearing. Rites for girls often include instruction in responsibilities of womanhood and being a wife and mother. In some parts of North America, a debutante ball is a common rite of passage in which girls participate. At a debutante ball, girls are introduced into society as potential marriage partners. Although both boys and girls attend, it is considered a more important event for girls.

Different religions also have rites of passage for adolescents. For example, Jewish girls participate in a bat mitzvah at age 12 to indicate that they are responsible for their actions and decisions. This rite of passage involves a ceremony at a synagogue, where the 12-year-old girl reads from the Torah, and is usually followed by a celebration.

Mescalero Apache Puberty Rites

The Mescalero Apache, who live in south-central New Mexico, have puberty rites for girls that re-create and emphasize traditional culture. Once a year in early July, all girls who have had their first menstruation in the previous year gather around a large teepee. The girls wear special clothing to indicate their status as reincarnations of White Painted Woman, a spiritual being who gave many good things to the people. Over four days and nights, the girls are blessed by singers, relatives, and friends. All attendees participate in songs and dances dedicated to the four directions. On the fourth day, singers tell of Apache history, and girls are reminded of their ancestry and obligations as "Mothers of the Tribe." According to ethnographer Claire Farrer, "almost invariably, the girls report having been changed, not only into social women but also at a very basic level. They are ready to put aside their childhoods and become full members of their tribe and community" (Bailey and Peoples, 2003).

↑ **FIGURE 4-7** These Mescalero Apache girls are dressed for the four-day ceremony celebrating the attainment of womanhood. Do you think a ceremony such as this helps young people to assume adult responsibilities?

> ❓ What are the differences in attitude and gender roles between the rites of passage? In what ways is this ritual different from the Maasai boys' initiation? Are there comparable ceremonies for girls in contemporary Canadian society?

While some male and female rites can be different, some rites are the same for everyone. Many Aboriginal peoples participate in a vision quest as a rite of passage into adulthood in order to grow spiritually. Individuals isolate themselves in the wilderness for a number of days. The person usually does not eat and sometimes does not drink during this time. The vision quest is a psychologically and physically difficult period of reflection, contemplation, and confrontation with the deepest parts of the soul. The vision quest concludes when the participant receives a vision, which often manifests as an animal guide that imparts wisdom and assistance. Though a vision quest is a profound, intense, and solitary experience, the goal of the quest is not merely personal; it is also for the strengthening and benefit of the entire tribe.

Body Modification and Body Art

Body modification and body art are a part of cultures around the world. In many cultures, body modification and body art are a part of rites of passage and can take the form of tattoos, piercings, and decorative scarring and branding. In North American culture, tattoos and piercings are one way to express identity. Piercings are the most popular form of body modification among young people and have moved from ears to other parts of the body, such as eyebrows, navels, and genitals. Decorative scarring and branding are forms of body modification that involve burning skin to create elaborate patterns in scar tissue. It's not for those who are queasy, as it involves heating bent pieces of sheet metal to 982° Celsius and pressing them into the skin to leave elaborate scars.

Tattoos go back many centuries. The earliest evidence to date was found on a 5300-year-old man, Ötzi, whose mummified body was found lying high in an Alpine pass in 1991. The mummy was adorned with 57 tattoos on different parts of his body. Tattoos represent a complex connection of the art to gender, youth culture, ethnicity, and even prison life (Kuwahara, 2005). Tattoos are also a way of telling a story. Some people adorn themselves with tattoos to tell a story of a time during their lives. Diane Pacom, a University of Ottawa professor who specializes in youth culture says tattoos "go from marginal to mainstream … because we live in a society where we don't have rituals any more. People, in many ways, are desperate to ritualize their lives."

Modern tattoos began in the Pacific region as a way of expressing connections to land, family, and spirit. When castaway Irish James O'Connell landed on the Pacific Islands in the 1830s, he received a full-body tattoo in Pohnpei on the Caroline Islands. While on the Caroline Islands, the tattoo gave him status; in New York, women and children ran screaming from him in the streets. O'Connell became the first man to display his tattoos for money (Ellis, 2008). Tattoos became trendy in Europe for a brief time, and many nineteenth-century European aristocrats had tattoos. But soon tattoos became associated with sailors, working-class people, and criminals. Western society began to see tattoos as a sign of deviance.

> Tattoos were once seen as a sign of deviance. Do some people still feel this way? Is there a difference in opinion between generations about where and when tattoos are acceptable?

↑ **FIGURE 4-8** What do tattoos and piercing say about this adolescent?

Tattoos in Polynesian Culture

The word *tattoo* comes from the Samoan word *tatau*. In many Polynesian societies, men underwent a painful and lengthy tattooing process to indicate their status as adults. In Samoa, at adolescence, men of the chiefly or noble rank would have the *pe'a*—an intricate tattoo covering their body from waist to knee—applied. The process would begin with payment of mats to the *tufuga* or tattoo artist, a hereditary position of great respect. The tattoo required the support of family during the three-month application process and for up to one year afterward until the healing was complete. Once the tattoo was complete, the man's family threw him a party, and the *tufuga* smashed a water gourd to mark the end of the ordeal. Infection, illness, and death were real possibilities for those getting the *pe'a*. If a man cried out in pain, shied away, or had second thoughts during the process, the tattoo would not be finished and the man would be reviled, permanently marked by the unfinished tattoo.

Christian missionaries tried to dissuade Samoans from continuing what they considered to be a barbaric practice. Samoans had it done secretly for many years, but now many people choose to get the *pe'a*. Modern tools are used, the application takes just over a week, rather than months, and any man may choose to get it. However, the *pe'a* still has similar meanings of status and responsibility in today's society, and few men choose to get one without the support of their families.

Read the following excerpt from an interview for a documentary called Skin Stories with Tupuola Savea, a Samoan man who decided to get a tattoo in the 1960s. What does his *pe'a* mean to him?

FIGURE 4-9 Lome Fa'atau, a Samoan rugby player, displays his *pe'a* in a game against England in 2003. His *pe'a* took nine days to complete. How is the meaning of the *tatau* different for Samoans today than in the past?

> If you do have a tattoo in my opinion, you are responsible for serving the people of the village, the country, the family, and the church. Things like you can do by working or by speaking. [...] When I got my tattoo done, I feel like a man. I'm a gentleman. When I did have one, I feel responsible for the family, for anything that a gentleman can do. That's why it is from my heart. (PBS, 2003)

Another Polynesian people, the Maori of New Zealand/Aotearoa traditionally used chisel tattooing: they would cut a groove into the skin and put ink made from burnt kauri gum into it, so the tattoo would also be a raised scar. Facial tattoos—*moko*—indicated rank in society and ancestry. If only one side of your family had rank or high status, only one side of your face would be tattooed. A great chief could be identified by his *moko*, and a person with no rank would not have one (Whitmore, 2008).

Women in Samoan and Maori culture would also get tattoos. Their tattoos would not be as extensive as those of the men but would also show that the women were of high rank or status. Maori women tattooed their lips and chin in a dark blue until the 1970s. In Samoa, women tattooed their legs from the knees to the upper thighs, but the tattoos covered much less area than the men's tattoos.

Connecting Anthropology to Psychology

Developmental Tasks of Adolescence

Many psychologists create and test theories of human development. These theories are frequently stage model theories, in which people must accomplish the tasks of a stage to move on to the next one. Erik Erikson developed the comprehensive psychosocial stage model theory, which describes the tasks of every stage of life from infancy (trust versus mistrust) to old age (integrity versus despair). The task at adolescence, according to Erikson, is becoming aware of one's own uniqueness and future roles. Erikson and other psychologists have been criticized because their theories do not apply to all cultures. Anthropologists use the theories as a basis for understanding and comparing cultures or for framing research questions.

identity moratorium: a status in which the adolescent is in crisis and unable to accomplish tasks necessary to becoming an adult, and explores other youth subcultures

Coming of Age in Contemporary Canadian Culture

Most cultural anthropologists argue that adolescence is culturally constructed by Western culture. Historically, adolescence wasn't recognized as a stage of development; individuals were considered children until they became adults. It wasn't until the turn of the twentieth century, when child labour laws ended and mandatory education was put into practice, that adolescence emerged. Adolescence is associated with puberty, but in Canada and other Western nations, it is intended to be a period of time to learn adult skills before becoming an adult. Many non-Western societies have a much shorter learning period and an initiation ceremony, or children gradually learn adult skills by working with their parents. In Canada, some of the following developmental tasks must be accomplished by adolescents in order to become adults:

- developing and understanding potential—a unique set of abilities, limitations, talents, and possibilities
- finishing school, choosing a career, and getting a job
- gaining independence from parents, both emotionally and financially, by moving away from home
- choosing a mate and starting one's own family
- identifying with a worldview or ideology (political, religious, etc.)

When one or more of these tasks are not accomplished, teens can get stuck in an **identity moratorium**. In an identity moratorium, adolescents are unable to accomplish tasks necessary to becoming an adult and explore subcultures usually associated with youth. These subcultures are focused on behaviour, language, lifestyle, and body decoration. Some subcultures can be relatively harmless, such as hippies, punk, grunge, or hip hop. Or they can be helpful to society, such as social movements like environmentalism. Other youth subcultures can be damaging and lead to gang membership, crime, suicide, or substance abuse. Youth subcultures were not really known before the beginning of compulsory schooling in the twentieth and twenty-first centuries (Ervin, 2001).

Extended Adolescence Among the Inuit

Typically, adolescence has been defined as the period of a person's life between the ages of 13 and 19. But as you've learned in this section, passing through adolescence is marked by certain rites of passage, such as graduating from postsecondary school, finding a job, or becoming financially independent. As the job market changes, requiring graduate degrees and postgraduate programs, postsecondary schooling can extend into a person's 20s. With high unemployment and the number of students graduating with large student-loan debt, some studies have placed the age of adulthood in Western nations as late as 35 years old. Extended adolescence refers to this later transition to adulthood.

The Inuit of the Central Arctic give us a dramatic illustration of how extended schooling has created problems. The Inuit had a culture without adolescence. Prior to the 1950s, most young people lived with their parents and learned the skills of adulthood at home. Sometimes a young man would live with his prospective bride's family for a year as a trial marriage. Boys were recognized as adults at their first seal kill. Young people generally learned skills early on and married at a young age, as early as 14 for girls and around 18 for boys.

In the 1950s, the Canadian government moved the Inuit into settlements where they could receive services such as health care, education, social services, and economic development. Children were sent to school where they learned southern values and curriculum. The traditional ways of knowing and living were threatened as they moved from a seasonally nomadic life to one based on permanent settlement. Adults no longer took their children on hunting trips or taught them skills at home.

It is much more difficult for Inuit youth to fulfil the tasks of adulthood than for their peers in Southern Canada. Jobs are not available in the North, and strong family ties keep Inuit youth from migrating south for work. Inuit youth often spend their leisure time in cafes or at hockey rinks. Some try to go back to hunting and fishing, but they aren't inclined to listen to their elders, and adults do not know how to connect with youth when they are in school for most of the day. For many youth, the extended period of waiting for adult responsibilities can lead to substance abuse, violence, and epidemics of suicide, leaving whole communities shattered and grieving. Most Inuit become effective adults in their communities, but the path to adulthood has become much more difficult than it was in the past (Ervin, 2001).

> **More to Know...**
> You will learn more about residential schools and the effect on First Nation cultures in Chapter 7.

> **VOICES**
> Inuit youth should have a voice. We have a lot to say. We know what we need; we just need to be given a chance.
> Anna

FIGURE 4-10 Inuit youth in Arctic Bay have been connected via the Internet since 1998. They can learn about their own culture and connect with other youth in distant communities. Do you think the Internet can help them to make the transition to adulthood more successfully?

? How was adolescence different for Inuit youth before 1950 than it is today? How does Anna's statement reflect the challenges for Inuit youth accomplishing the developmental tasks of adulthood? How did the actions of the Canadian government threaten Inuit culture?

REFLECT AND RESPOND

1. How is tattooing in traditional Polynesian culture different from tattooing among young people in modern Canadian society?
2. How does the three-stage process apply to the following rites of passage:
   a) the Maasai circumcision rite for boys
   b) the Mescalero Apache initiation rite for girls
   c) the Samoan tattoo ceremony
   d) a rite in contemporary Canadian society

Gender and Culture

> **Before You Read**
> How is gender portrayed in commercials and on television programs?

Anthropologists make a distinction between sex and gender. Sex is generally the biological characteristics such as XX or XY chromosomes, genitals, and other physical characteristics determined by a person's genes. Gender is defined by a person's culture, not just biology. Anthropologists make this distinction because human societies vary so much in how males and females perceive each other, how they define what it means to be a man or a woman, and what roles they view as appropriate for men and women. These ideas are not the same in all cultures, nor are they fixed at birth. Anthropologists do not ignore biological differences, but culture determines how biological differences are interpreted; this is why anthropologists (and other social scientists) say that gender is culturally constructed.

Gender is culturally constructed by:

- the symbols associated with gender, such as particular clothing
- the classifications of what is inherently male or female (some cultures minimize these; others emphasize them)
- the relative values of the genders (some cultures see genders as equal to each other; other cultures value one over the other)
- behaviour patterns, including what activities are appropriate for each gender (Bailey and Peoples, 2003)

FIGURE 4-11 What symbols and gendered behaviour are evident?

❓ What are some examples of gendered symbols, classifications, values, and behaviour patterns for men and women in Canadian society?

Female Identity and Culture

We evaluate and assess female identity every day, in subtle and unsubtle ways. There are expectations about how a woman should look, act, and behave and what she should want. Assumptions are made about women based on the way they dress as "girly" or "sporty." Many people make choices based on these expectations and strive to meet the ideals set out by their culture. Western culture assumes that women are more nurturing, emotional, and caring than men. Does this mean that women are better suited to nurturing and caring careers, such as nursing and child care? How do we view men who take on these careers and women who take on careers that are identified as more masculine? How does your culture shape your gender identity? Sometimes gender identity is hard to see in your own culture because you take it for granted. It can be useful to look at other cultures to understand how people view their roles as women or men in their society.

FIGURE 4-12 What symbols and behaviour patterns of gender are evident in this photo?

❓ What are the cultural expectations of women in Canadian society? How do your cultural expectations of education and career influence your sense of self, male or female?

Body Image in Niger

One of the most variable ways that we construct our sense of self is through our personal body image. In Canada and most industrialized nations, the ideal body image for girls and women is very tall and very thin. This is a very recent cultural phenomenon. In fact, for most of human history, the ideal female body image has been plump or even fat. Body image can be recognized as a cultural construct by looking at differences between the ideal body shape in different cultures.

Anthropologist Rebecca Popenoe lived for four years among desert Arabs in Niger, a country south of Algeria and north of Nigeria. In this society, and in much of the Western and Central Sahara, the fat female form is celebrated, desired, and actively pursued. When women step on a scale in the local health clinic, they usually pick up items, such as a shawl or a purse, in order to weigh more. Girls are fattened on a porridge of millet and milk from the time they lose their first teeth until adolescence. After puberty and usually in early marriage, women eat a dry couscous, which is supposed to maintain the fat figure. Stretch marks are desired and sung about in a love song as a "waist lined with stripes." Women there say that "anyone can get stretch marks on their stomachs" but that stretch marks on your arms and legs are a real achievement. Upper-class women spend as much time as possible sitting or lying down, letting female servants fetch water and do the cooking.

FIGURE 4-13 Which woman is more beautiful? Your opinion depends on your cultural ideals.

Popenoe had some difficulty getting women to talk about fat for several reasons. They were religious and proud women who would rather discuss matters that they felt would give them status in the eyes of a Westerner. They didn't want to discuss the fattening of their daughters because to talk about fattening was to risk casting the evil eye on the girls and could cause them to lose weight or become ill. The other reason why women were reluctant to discuss fat was because fat was linked with desire and sex. In a sexually restrictive society, discussing sexual matters, including fat, is not a topic of casual conversation. Perhaps the most revealing part of Popenoe's study, published in 2005, was her own struggle with fitting in as a thin woman in a society that idealized fatness:

> I could pile my hair on top of my head as women did there, waltz about draped in desert finery, rub indigo on my lips, and put kohl around my eyes—even carefully veil my body and hair before older men. But to gain weight to comply with a foreign aesthetic felt like betraying myself and giving up my identity in a way that none of those other adaptations to local culture did. My own body ideal was just as much a construct as fatness was here, but it was too deeply integrated into my self-image to give up. (p. 16)

The fat body ideal among Nigerian Arab women is perhaps just as destructive to health as our current waif-like body ideal. The plump ideal is common in societies where food is scarce because it is associated with status, wealth, and reproduction. In many ways, their body ideal reflects the values of their societies. Elite Arab women depend on a former slave population to do housework and on men, who are herders and traders, for money and food.

FIGURE 4-14 Miss World 2001, Abgani Darego of Nigeria, was the first black African to win the contest. Many people in the region felt that she would not win because she was too thin to be attractive.

> **Connecting Anthropology to Psychology**
>
> Mental illnesses such as anorexia, bulimia, and body dysmorphic disorder are related to our culturally constructed body image. Psychologists seek to understand the causes and find treatments for these illnesses.

When women drink the milk that men produce and eat the grain that they buy with trade earnings, they become symbols of their husbands' economic success.

By contrast, in the West, both women and men are expected to contribute to the economy as workers and consumers. They strive to have bodies that are sleek, efficient, and machine-like. This conflicts with other realities of our culture—sedentary jobs, cars, and the pressure to indulge in fast food. In our society, women who fail to meet unrealistic body ideals often see this failure as their own fault. In Niger, if women fail to get fat, their failure is seen as a case of jealousy, the evil eye, or illness. Thin women are not considered desirable or fully mature, but they do not engage in the same kinds of destructive behaviours and self-loathing that many Western women do when they fail to meet the ideal body image of their culture.

Culture constructs our sense of self and our understanding of our gender in very deep and personal ways. The Nigerian body image is an extreme one, just as our own ideal of thinness is, and both ideals shape how women and girls see themselves and their worth in society. What is important to recognize is that both ideals are culturally constructed and are not unchanging biological forces. Indeed, the Western ideal of thinness is beginning to be recognized in the Sahara while Canadian women are fighting for more representations of "real" women in the media.

> **?** Why do you think the fatter female shape is desirable in Niger? How does culture construct an ideal body image? Give examples from Nigerian and Canadian societies.

Male Identity and Culture

As a society, we don't devote as much time to analyzing male gender roles as we do to analyzing female gender roles, but male identity is just as culturally constructed as female identity. What it means to be a man (and how masculinity is defined) varies enormously across many cultures. There are some tasks that, historically, were predominantly done by men in all societies, such as hunting, mining, woodworking, and warfare. As societies industrialize and become part of the global market, divisions of labour change and these distinctions of gender shift. These changes can be particularly destabilizing for men, who may lose power and authority and be forced to seek wage work instead of relying on their land and kinship ties.

Gender roles in Canada are changing with respect to child care. Traditionally, women were solely responsible for the care of babies and young children. But with the increasing number of women in the workforce and support from the Canadian government, men are taking on increasingly more responsibility for child care in their families. Currently, about 80 percent of Canadian men take some form of leave at the birth of a child, and in Quebec, men can take 5 additional weeks of leave with Employment Insurance benefits, along with the 35 weeks of parental benefits available to either parent offered by the federal government.

MALE PARTICIPATION IN CHILDCARE		
	2008	1976
Stay-at-home dads	11%	1%
Dual income households	2005	1986
Men	2.5 hours housework/ child care	2.1 hours housework/ child care
Women	4.3 hours housework/ child care	4.8 hours housework/ child care

(Statistics Canada, 2009)

Defining Masculinity

Which is more masculine: hunting, writing poetry, or wearing a skirt? In fact, all of these are viewed differently in different societies. In a few societies, hunting is a female activity. The Agta women in the Philippines regularly hunt in groups and kill wild deer and pigs. They generally contribute about 30 percent of the wild game to their communities. Writing poetry, while not considered an exceptionally manly behaviour in Canada, is nonetheless usually considered romantic and attractive by many girls. In Japan, poetry is the domain of women and girls, and boys who write poetry are considered not only unmanly, but supremely unattractive as potential boyfriends. In Persian or traditional Iranian culture, poetry is always associated with wrestling. Wrestling matches are combined with long poetry recitations, and poetry is considered as manly as wrestling.

Wearing a skirt in Canadian society is generally not considered manly. It's normal for women to wear pants, but it is unusual to see men wearing skirts. There are many societies in which men have worn and still wear a skirt-type garment; in fact, there is even a movement of men who wish to wear men's unbifurcated (undivided) garments, or MUGs. They describe themselves as wanting to be free from the "tyranny of trousers." There are many cultures in which men wear skirt-type garments (for example, the Scottish kilt, Polynesian sarong, Moroccan *djellaba*, Greek *fustanella*, Japanese *hakama* and kimono, Burmese *longyi*, Fijian *sulu*) and are considered no less manly than those who wear pants. In fact, in Bhutan, all men are required by law to wear a *gho* (a knee-length robe belted at the waist) or face a hefty fine.

FIGURE 4-15 How does this photo challenge assumptions about clothing and gender?

> How is masculinity culturally constructed in Canadian society? What are some of the rules that boys learn to follow in order to be accepted as men? How are these rules changing?

Have you ever found yourself at a school dance and wondered why the girls were dancing and the boys were not? Is there something inherently unmanly in dancing? Why are some kinds of dancing considered more masculine than others? In fact, dancing is considered the height of manliness in many cultures and in many contexts in Canadian culture. For example, male hip-hop dancers express their masculinity through physical stamina and dance competition. Some female hip-hop dancers participate in this culture but are in the minority in this male-dominated arena. The extremely popular Bollywood movies highlight male dance scenes, and often the leading man is judged on his dancing abilities. Until recently, in many First Nations cultures, dancing was seen as a predominantly male sphere (see Figure 4-16). Women were not allowed to dance in the physically expressive ways of the male dancers and had constrained movements until the twentieth century.

Sometimes, certain foods are connected to ideas about masculinity. In Mexico, sea turtle eggs (which are illegal to consume) were supposed to increase a man's sexual potency. Eating illegal seafood in Mexico was also considered a mark

FIGURE 4-16 Men competing in the fancy dance competition.

> **Skills Focus**
>
> As an anthropologist conducting fieldwork, you choose a target population, such as male or female hip-hop dancers, and a focus, such as gendered self-image. Then, as a researcher, you get to know your group and let them direct the research as much as possible, expressing their own thoughts and feelings.

of high status since it was expensive. Since the illegal market for seafood put the already endangered sea turtle population at further risk, in 2005, Wildcoast, a small conservation organization, launched a media campaign featuring a Playboy model saying, "My man doesn't need to eat turtle eggs, because he knows they don't make him more potent." With the support of World Cup soccer players and Baja's governor, the market for sea turtle eggs began to decline (Bahnsen, 2007). A culture's idea of what is manly can have a dramatic effect on both the economy and ecology.

Alternate-Gender Identity

In Chapter 3, you learned that gender could be defined by more than male or female and that some people are born intersex, and are part of a third (and sometimes fourth) gender. Third gender can can include people who are intersexed (i.e., having both male and female sexual characteristics and organs), transgendered (i.e., having a gender identity that differs from their assigned biological sex), or homosexual (i.e., being sexually attracted to people of the same gender).

In Western culture, we have historically determined gender through biology, but other cultures (for example South Asian, African, Polynesian) have a long history of recognizing alternate-gender identities. In many North American Aboriginal cultures, third- or fourth-gendered people were historically accepted and recognized as a distinct group who fulfilled valuable and necessary roles within society. When Europeans arrived in North America, they imposed Western views about gender and sexuality on Aboriginal societies and this aspect of Aboriginal culture (among many others) was lost. Third gender people faced discrimination and violence, could not live openly as they once did, and no longer had the status in society they once did (O'Brien, 2009). As part of the larger movement to reclaim their cultures, Aboriginal peoples adopted the term *two-spirited* to refer to Aboriginal people of alternate gender. Serena Nanda identified some widespread features of two-spirited people in First Nations groups:

FIGURE 4-17 Third-gender individuals at an awareness rally in Nepal to mark World AIDS Day

- occupation—a preference for the work traditionally done by the opposite sex or for work set aside for third- or fourth-gender identity people
- transvestism—a preference for the dress of the opposite sex or a combination of male and female garments
- spiritual power—possession of special powers believed to come from a spirit combined with personal experience
- same-sex relations—formation of sexual and emotional bonds with members of the same sex who were not of the third or fourth gender (Bailey and Peoples, 2003)

Anthropologists find in general that societies that are not focused on population growth and maintenance are more supportive of blurred gender roles, but this is not always the case. Some societies that are very strict about heterosexual relations are relatively permissive about homosexual behaviour. The Siwan of North Africa, for example, expected all men to engage in homosexual behaviour, and fathers arranged for their unmarried sons to be given to an older man in a homosexual arrangement until their late teens when they would marry women. The Etoro of New Guinea prohibited heterosexuality for 260 days a year but permitted homosexual relations among men any time and believed these relations made the crops grow (Ember and Ember, 2009).

IN FOCUS: Pink Shirt Day

In the small town of Cambridge, Nova Scotia, in 2007, a Grade 9 boy wore a pink polo shirt on the first day of school. He was bullied by several students, who threatened violence and repeatedly called him a homosexual. Two Grade 12 students, David Shepherd and Travis Price, decided to take action. They went to a nearby discount store and bought 50 pink shirts. They emailed all their friends, asking them to wear the shirts the next day in support of the Grade 9 student. The next day, practically the whole school was wearing pink. The Grade 9 student (who was never identified by the media) wasn't bullied again after that day. "If you can get more people against them … to show that we're not going to put up with it and support each other, then they're not as big as a group as they think are," he said (CBC News, 2007). Pink Shirt Day or Day of Pink is now a worldwide phenomenon. Every year, schools around the world encourage students to wear pink one day to take a stand against bullying and discrimination.

FIGURE 4-18 Children participating in Pink Shirt Day. How does Pink Shirt Day illustrate our cultural construction of gender?

QUESTIONS

1. How did Shepherd's and Price's actions end the bullying of the Grade 9 student? Why do you think their plan worked?

REFLECT AND RESPOND

1. How much of your self-image is tied up in your gender? Give examples from the section to support your answer.
2. How do anthropologists know that gender is culturally constructed?
3. What behaviours are exclusively male or female? Make a list of "female" jobs and "male" jobs around your home. How did this designation take place?
4. What is meant by the third or fourth gender, and how is it constructed in North American Aboriginal societies?

Section 4.2 Anthropology and Behaviour

How do cultural factors influence and shape our behaviour? People's behaviour has a lot to do with what they know or what their culture has taught them. To understand why people behave the way they do, we must understand their worldview. Worldview is influenced by our physical environment and our cultural and social structures, such as marriage, kinship, and political and economic structures.

Physical Environment and Culture

Before You Read
What changes do you make to your morning routines as the weather changes?

In Chapter 1, you learned how humans have physically evolved to adapt to their environments. Physical anthropologists study how humans have adapted to the environment and since the 1950s have focused on the study of physiological response to environmental stresses and how different populations have adapted genetically (Moran, 2005). But it is culture that helps people to adapt to their physical environment much more quickly than evolution does. Cultural anthropologists look at how weather is understood in different cultures. For example, we see that different cultures give different meanings to rain. In the Judeo-Christian tradition, rain was seen as part of God's anger. Even in Shakespeare's *The Tempest*, rain is associated with danger. For the Anasazi, a Navajo culture, rain is sacred since it is necessary for survival. Cultural anthropologists also look at how the climate creates elements of culture and provides practical tools for survival.

Cold Climate Adaptation

The Canadian climate varies greatly from coast to coast and from season to season. The Canadian Arctic is an example of an extreme environment where it would be difficult to survive without strategies in place for housing and clothing. Instead of developing a heavy coat of fur or blubber to adapt to Arctic environments, Inuit people created warm and waterproof sealskin clothing, snowhouses (*igluit*), and other cultural ways of surviving in an extreme environment. This knowledge was learned and passed on to children to help them to survive. As the Inuit came into contact with Europeans, their cultural ways of survival changed. So the Inuit today use different cultural products to adapt to their environment, including snowmobiles, nylon parkas, and central heating. As we saw in Section 4.1, cultural change can be destructive, but most Inuit consider snowmobiles and central heating to be helpful to their survival and not destructive to their culture.

↑ **FIGURE 4-19** How has culture helped the Inuit to adapt to their environment?

Hot Climate Adaptation

Just as the Inuit have developed strategies to survive in cold climates, people in hot climates have developed ways to survive in extreme heat. The Bedouin are a nomadic people who live in the deserts of the Middle East in an intensely hot environment. Their cultural adaptations include loose and light clothing to protect them from the sun and sand in the daytime and the cold at night. Prior to the twentieth century, Bedouins moved frequently to find new pastures for their sheep, goats, and camels and to collect plants for medicines and food. By not staying too long in one place, they did not overtax any resources or deplete water or plant supplies. As governments force them to settle in one place and military threats increase, the nomadic lifestyle is disappearing, and the culture is forced to adapt. For example, Bedouin females in the Sinai used to be able to roam widely and visit other women when their main job was herding the sheep and goats. Now that the Bedouin are living in larger settlements, women are more likely to be indoors in a courtyard home with running water and without much reason to leave. While they are free from prying eyes within their home, more people are scrutinizing their movements in the village and they may be accused of having secret relationships with men just for walking alone. One woman describes the change:

> Before, people were better. They would see each other often and go out to herd and to collect water together. Today, there is none of this. Each one is in their house, sitting. And that is it—because there are many people around. Nowadays, a month or two or four pass, but you do not see your close neighbours. (Gardner, 2000)

FIGURE 4-20 Bedouin men in the desert. How has forced settlement changed Bedouin culture?

REFLECT AND RESPOND

1. How does the environment influence the cultures of the Inuit and the Bedouin? What other factors have influenced these cultures?
2. Identify positive and negative impacts of technology on the Inuit and Bedouin cultures.
3. What environmental factors can you observe today that anthropologists will likely study in the future?

Technology and Culture

> **Before You Read**
> How has technology affected your culture? How has culture influenced your use of technology?

Since the first stone tools and fur clothing, humans have been using technology to adapt to their environment. Most human societies today have incredibly complex technologies, including airplanes, water purification systems, factories, and cell phones. When a society adopts a new technology, then ideas, language, social structures, and ultimately culture also change.

Technological diffusion is the adoption by one culture of a technology invented by another culture. To be adopted into the culture, the innovation must become known, be accepted by many people, and fit into an existing system of knowledge. Other factors that influence how quickly or whether an innovation will be accepted are whether an authority endorses it, when it is introduced, whether it meets a perceived need, if it appeals to people's sense of prestige, and how well it fits with local customs (McCurdy and Spradley, 2008).

technological diffusion: the adoption by one culture of a technology invented by another culture

Air Conditioning and the End of the Front Porch in North America

Air conditioning revolutionized how people live. The ability to control indoor climates has changed the way buildings are built, where people live, and how they interact with one another. In particular, air conditioning has changed the culture of the front porch, particularly for women in North America. Before air conditioning, the front porch was not just a decoration on the front of a home, but a social place where women would talk to neighbours, catch up on news, and do work such as knitting. The porch provided a cooler place to sit on hot summer evenings, and allowed women to talk with one another and with other people (Beckham, 1988).

People are still cooling off, catching up on news, and doing work, but technology has changed how these things are done. North Americans have become more isolated from their physical neighbours, while the Internet has created new virtual communities that are not dependent on physical proximity. In many communities, neighbours are connecting through neighbourhood forums, blogs, and other types of social networks.

↑ **FIGURE 4-21** An American front porch in 1942. How is this scene different from or similar to a modern front-porch scene?

❓ Brainstorm how neighbourhoods and communities have changed as a result of technology.

Digital Technology

Anthropologists are currently studying digital technology's impact on cultures and subcultures. Some recent research studies include:

- hacker or blogger culture
- the greater popularity of instant messaging and texting over cell phones among teens
- the culture of online poker
- reasons that Google is unpopular in China
- the effect of laptops on doctor–patient interactions
- cultures of digital immigrants (those who had to learn digital ways as adults) and digital natives (those who grew up in a digital environment)

Landmark Case Study

Steel Axes Among the Yir Yoront

The Yir Yoront are an Aboriginal people of Australia. For centuries, they had made and used stone axes, necessary for just about all of their daily activities, including chopping firewood, building shelters, making tools, gathering plants, fishing, and hunting. Axes always belonged to men. If a woman needed to use an axe, an event that occurred several times a day, she had to borrow one from a man, usually her husband, who never refused. Children and younger men also had to borrow axes from their fathers or older brothers. So the axes reinforced kin relationships, social status, and hierarchy for the Yir Yoront.

When European missionaries arrived in the area in the early twentieth century, they started giving out a number of goods that they felt would improve the Yir Yoront's way of life. None was more popular than the short-handled steel axe. This tool allowed people to complete tasks more quickly than they could with a stone axe. Women and younger men gained prestige previously unavailable to them by owning their own steel axes, and they no longer needed to borrow axes from older men.

While steel axes appeared to be an improvement, these tools had far-reaching and destructive effects on the entire culture. They upset the traditional relationships between men and women, old and young, and trading partners, and whole groups, for whom the dry season festivals became less profitable without the trading of stone-axe heads. Within a few years, the Yir Yoront ceased to be a self-sufficient band and became completely dependent on the missionaries for handouts (Sharp, 1952).

However, some modern technologists and cultural ethnographers might see the shift from stone axes to ones made of steel as the Yir Yoront connecting to world trading networks. The Yir Yoront accepted a new technology that fit with their existing views and it changed their culture. Technology writer and Wired magazine co-founder Kevin Kelly has written extensively on technological change and its impact on society. Kelly would theorize that stone axes were probably still being made today. In a test of whether people were still using older technology, Kelly took a page from an 1895 catalogue and found that all of the products were still being made new today. He argues that cultures change and humans change, but culture also accumulates knowledge and in many cases, preserves it.

FIGURE 4-22 How was this Yir Yoront man's life changed by the introduction of European steel axes?

QUESTIONS

1. Organize the arguments for and against "helping" the Yir Yoront, including the impact on their culture, in a T-chart or Venn diagram.
2. What lessons can anthropologists learn from the Yir Yoront?

REFLECT AND RESPOND

1. How did front porches in the 1940s and 1950s serve a similar purpose to social networking sites today?
2. Reread the definition and factors affecting technological diffusion. Explain how these factors apply to the case study of steel axes among the Yir Yoront.
3. What other areas of research in digital culture can you think of? Write three possible research questions to investigate how digital technologies have changed or are changing culture. How would you collect your data in a reliable and ethical manner?

Language and Culture

Before You Read
Does language influence your culture, or is language just a reflection of culture? How have words changed to reflect equality in society? Brainstorm words that have changed to become more inclusive, such as firefighter instead of fireman.

Language and culture are intimately tied together, and one of the most important jobs of anthropologists is to understand the language of the people they are studying. This often requires an anthropologist to seek out the help of an insider to the culture he or she is studying to act as a partner in the research process. Understanding a culture be extremely challenging if the language is unwritten or if no translators are available. Teaching your language to another person makes you more conscious of how words are used and sentences are structured. If outsiders aren't regularly attempting to learn the language, native speakers may not be able to explain the subtleties of their language. Even for speakers of the same language, the same words may have completely different meanings. For example, when Canadians call someone a "hard case," they generally mean someone who is tough or angry. When New Zealanders call someone "a hard case," they mean a real character, an eccentric or funny person.

? Have you ever encountered a linguistic and cultural misunderstanding? How can such a misunderstanding be overcome?

Sapir-Whorf Hypothesis

The Sapir-Whorf hypothesis is the theory that language not only labels reality but also shapes our cultural reality. Since people think in a language, the way the language is structured can influence their thoughts. If there is a word for a concept in one language that doesn't exist in another language, then people who have that word might be more likely to think of the concept more often. For example, the Hanumbo of the Philippines have 92 words for rice, while English has a lot of words to describe cars (e.g., convertible, four-door, coupe, four-wheel drive). Does having many words for rice or cars influence people to think about these concepts more often, or does the language simply reflect the culture and environment? One of the problems with the hypothesis is that it's very difficult to prove whether language influences culture or culture influences language.

perception: the process of how an individual takes in information visually and with the other senses.

FIGURE 4-23 What colour is this bus? If you were paying attention to North American culture, you would say yellow, but it is really orange.

Colour **perception** is another area where language and culture intersect. In English, there are generally six colour terms (i.e., red, orange, yellow, green, blue or purple). Other colours, such as baby blue and mauve, are considered variants of the basic colours. In Liberia's Bassa culture, there is only one word for all the warm colours between yellow and reddish purple, and another for the cool colours between green and bluish purple. Among the Shona people of Zimbabwe, there are three colour words (one that indicates orange, red, and purple; one that indicates blue and green-blue; and one that indicates yellow and yellow-green). We all see the same colours, but different cultures just have different names them.

The English Language

Much study has been done on how language influences our ideas of time. English speakers are highly concerned with time and when things happen. The English language has many words for time and many ways to talk about the past, present, and future. We tend to have almost an obsession with punctuality and scheduling. By contrast, in the Hopi language, only the concepts of now and becoming exist. If one is weaving a mat now, one is preparing materials that will become a mat, whenever that will be. The past is more like a stream; many deeds of the past were done to prepare for the present and continue accumulating to become the future. If a Hopi is planning a meeting of many people, the meeting will start when everyone gets there, which is when it has become a meeting. English speakers may get frustrated trying to find out when Hopi events begin because events start when everybody gets there; the event is becoming until all are assembled. To people without clocks and who live in close proximity to one another, this system is more useful and makes more sense than abstract notions of time.

Anthropologists also look at how the English language is used. One way that language is revealing of culture is in the use of **euphemisms**. A euphemism is a word or set of words used to describe an uncomfortable or inappropriate concept in a polite or socially acceptable fashion. The use of euphemisms can reveal what things are rude or taboo to discuss in certain situations. In Canada, we say we are going to the bathroom or the restroom even if there is no bath and we have no plans to rest. While saying *toilet* would be more precise, we often choose a euphemism. We also refer to our preference for a certain part of poultry as *white meat* or *dark meat* since it is considered rude to say *breast* or *leg* at the table. The following chart shows some common euphemisms:

euphemism: a word or set of words used to indirectly describe an uncomfortable or inappropriate concept or idea in a socially acceptable way

Euphemism	Meaning
passed away	died
let go	fired
friendly fire	gunfire shot accidentally by one's own troops or allies in war
collateral damage	death or injury to civilians or noncombatants during wartime
the Final Solution	the phrase used by the Nazis for the planned genocide of Jewish people in World War II
preowned	used or second-hand
powder your nose	visit the bathroom

❓ Find examples of political euphemisms in a recent news article. Brainstorm other examples of euphemisms in everyday language.

Body Language

Body language is probably one of the most important areas of communication, especially for anthropologists. You may run into trouble if you think that you can rely on gestures and body language to communicate your ideas when learning a new language. A smile can be interpreted as submissive or aggressive depending on the culture. In Japan, it's considered rude and aggressive to show your teeth to someone else. In many cultures, a smile can mean a person is submissive to an authority, not necessarily that the person agrees or understands what is being said. There are very few gestures that have universal meanings among cultures. One of them is the eyebrow flash. This is a very brief raising of the eyebrows.

In many cultures, greetings can be complicated. The French are famous for kissing one another on the cheek, but there are rules for doing so. One must never kiss the actual cheek, but the air beside it. Women kiss one another on the cheek and men may kiss women, but men do not kiss one another. In some regions, people give two kisses; others give three or four. Sometimes the number of kisses depends on your degree of intimacy or friendship with the other person. The way we greet people can communicate very powerful messages about who we are and the nature of the relationship between individuals.

Gestures are often misinterpreted due to cultural differences. For example, the OK sign and the "thumbs-up" gestures in North America are generally positive, but in many other countries these gestures can be very rude and equivalent to the middle-finger gesture. Eye contact in general Canadian society is usually accepted and encouraged. Avoiding eye contact is generally seen as a sign of deception or evasion. Among many First Nation peoples, however, avoiding eye contact with a teacher or parent is polite while making eye contact with an authority figure is rude and aggressive.

Distance between speakers varies enormously by culture as well. In North America, we generally follow the following guidelines:

- public (between audience and speaker): 3.7–7.6 m
- social (in business and between strangers in public places): 1.2–3.0 m
- personal (between friends and family members, between customers waiting in line): 0.6–1.2 m
- intimate: less than 0.3 m; romantic or best friends: whispering and touching involved (Sheppard, 1996)

In many countries, the accepted distance is smaller or greater, leading to misunderstandings and misinterpretations of behaviour. (Maginnis, 1995).

FIGURE 4-24 Nelson Mandela, with his grandson, exhibiting the eyebrow flash

Skills Focus

If you were to study the distance between speakers in a particular culture, how would you begin your research? Create a research plan outlining your plan.

> ### REFLECT AND RESPOND
>
> 1. Explain how language may influence culture in terms of colour and time. What can happen when cultures with different languages come into contact?
> 2. How important is body language to effective communication? Give examples of how smiling, kissing, gestures, and social space can cause misunderstandings.

Economic Systems and Culture

All human societies depend on economic systems to produce the resources that they need and to distribute those resources to people. All humans have technology to assist them in this, such as stone tools, computers, and oil wells. All societies divide the labour, some along gender or kin lines, others in more complex ways.

Before You Read
How does a society's economy influence its culture?

Foraging Societies

Humans have spent almost all of their time on earth as foragers, or hunter-gatherers. For this reason, foragers are one of the most studied groups in anthropology. They tend to be more mobile to access the resources that change with the seasons. For example, Canada's Aboriginal peoples of the subarctic, such as the Mistassini Cree in the 1970s would normally hunt and fish intensively in the fall and winter, and gather berries and participate in cash-generating activities, such as guiding, in the summer. They moved to different camps in the summer, fall, and winter to take advantage of the resources available. In foraging societies, labour was divided along gender lines; men did most of the hunting and boat building, while women did much fishing, child care, and fur processing (Ervin, 2001).

Among foraging societies, from the Inuit of the Arctic to the San of Southern Africa, goods are distributed by **reciprocity**, or sharing. Reciprocity is the generalized giving of resources, with the expectation that sometime in the future the giver will be on the receiving end. Since people move so frequently, goods are not stored or hoarded. Personal accomplishments are devalued, and food is shared among many and consumed as soon as it is collected. In foraging societies, all members of society contribute to the survival of the group, and there are few, if any, status divisions.

reciprocity:
an economic system of formal and informal sharing among members of a society to distribute resources fairly

Horticultural Societies

Horticultural societies practise agriculture but without irrigating or cultivating the soil. The people in these societies generally use up the soil in one area for a few years and then move to a new area. The Huron or Wyandot, a matrilineal society in Ontario, were horticultural people. The men would clear a field, and the women would burn and remove the stumps and then plant corn, beans, and squash. People lived in longhouses, where they would store the corn for the winter. Men would often be away hunting to supplement the diet, which was 65 percent corn. Every 12 years, the entire village would have to be moved when the soil was exhausted. The arrival of the Europeans ended this practice with their refusal to acknowledge shared land use and built fences around the land.

Many horticultural societies use the economic system of **redistribution**. In this system, the goods produced are collected centrally and then handed out. Redistribution is carried out by an individual or a government motivated to gain or maintain status. In New Guinea, people would give many gifts away to shame their rivals and gain prestige. At one event in the 1970s, hundreds of pigs, thousands of dollars, cows, birds, a truck, and a motorbike were given away. Redistribution is similar to the **potlatch** ceremonies on Canada's West Coast.

horticultural:
a form of semi-nomadic agriculture

redistribution:
an economic system of collecting resources centrally and handing them out them among members of a society

potlatch:
a sacred ceremony of First Nations peoples on the Northwest coast of North America in which property is given away to enhance status

> **Open for Debate**
>
> In the twentieth century, unions provided security for industrial workers. As the factories moved to less developed countries, union membership dropped. Some argue that unions are not necessary in the new global economy. Others argue the unions protect workers by ensuring that people are paid a fair wage and work in a safe environment. Are unions necessary? Should consumers boycott products made in sweatshops?

wage labour: work for which wages are paid

↑ **FIGURE 4-25** How is this workplace similar to or different from that of your parents/ grandparents?

globalization: the process by which economies, societies, and cultures become integrated through a worldwide network

Agricultural Societies

When humans started doing intensive agriculture, the structure of societies changed. Once people stopped moving so much, they started to irrigate and fertilize their fields, which led to surplus crops. They could store their extra crops in case of a bad harvest in the future. Societies shared less and divided into social classes, with populations of peasants supporting classes of nobles, priests, and kings in ancient Mesopotamia, Egypt, China, and South America. Merchant and craft classes also developed, since not everyone needed to be involved in food production. Some First Nations peoples were agricultural at the time of European exploration, while many others were strictly foragers. Until the 1920s, Canada's economy was based on agriculture and natural resources (for example, mining and fishing).

Industrial Societies

Industrial societies have less than the majority of the population working to produce the food and goods needed for subsistence, with most people working in **wage labour** (a system in which people are paid for their work, not their products) and producing goods in factories. The Industrial Revolution started in England in the eighteenth century, but Canada was an industrial nation from the nineteenth century until the 1970s. No longer directly involved in their own subsistence, families sold their labour to earn a wage to then buy their food from someone else. Factories and farms relied increasingly on machines, and with the increase in the efficiency of shipping by rail and sea, the specialization of labour became possible. Industrial societies have a market economy where price, supply, and demand are often more important than kin networks and individual prestige. Industrial societies are complex and large; people living in close proximity often don't know one another.

Postindustrial Societies

Since the 1970s, Canada has had a postindustrial economy. In this economy, a majority of the population does not work for subsistence or in industry producing things; rather, most people work in the service sector, producing information or providing a service. Wage labour is still a big part of the system, but those jobs don't pay as well and are often part-time, such as those in retail or food service, or they are temporary or contract work without security and benefits, such as those in the high-tech sector.

In the postindustrial economy, information is the product that is bought and sold. In the industrial age, if you wanted to buy music, you would go to a store and buy a record. The price of the record would reflect the cost of producing the physical object. Now when you want to buy music, you go online and buy a digital file. There is no physical object; you are purchasing only the information.

The postindustrial economy is also a global system, with items being transported over vast distances. Your T-shirt could have had its cotton grown in India and been sewn in China, printed in Mexico, and designed and sold in Canada. This process is called **globalization**, and it affects everyone in the world.

Distribution Types in Canada

While the Canadian economy operates largely on a market system (an economic system where supply and demand determine what is produced), there are many important elements of reciprocity and redistribution in modern Canadian society. Think about taxes: a central agency (in this case, our government) collects money from everyone who works or buys products and redistributes those resources to pay for health care, roads, water systems, and education.

Reciprocity is also alive and well in Canadian society when we give gifts. For example, when two people get married, their family or friends often hold a wedding shower to provide the couple with items that they will need to begin their life together. Occasions such as weddings provide the opportunity for resources to be shared among friends and family.

The Potlatch

Canada's Northwest Coast peoples held potlatches, important sacred and ceremonial feasts, in the winter season, when all the hunting, gathering, and collecting of food had been completed. Potlatches were held to mark an important event, such as honouring the dead or witnessing the inheritance of names and privileges. Hundreds of guests would be invited, and they would dance, sing, and participate in a ceremony that lasted for many days. At the potlatch, the host chief would give out a vast amount of material wealth, in order to increase his prestige and status.

The potlatch was banned from 1884 to 1951 by the Canadian government, but many groups continued holding them in secret until the 1920s, when the Canadian government began an aggressive campaign to assimilate Aboriginal peoples into mainstream society and to eliminate Aboriginal culture and practices. Today the potlatch is enjoying a revival, and First Nations peoples are continuing the elaborate ceremonies and gift giving of pre-European times.

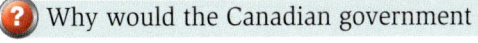 Why would the Canadian government try to stop potlatches?

> **REFLECT AND RESPOND**
>
> 1. In a chart, compare foraging, horticultural, agricultural, industrial, and postindustrial societies.
> 2. What is the impact on a culture when the economic system changes?
> 3. How do you think making a living for yourself will be similar to or different from how your parents make a living? Use economic evidence to support your ideas.
> 4. Rank agricultural, industrial, and postindustrial societies according to their impact on Canada today. Explain your reasoning.

The Impact of Globalization on Cultural Systems

Before You Read

How has globalization affected your community? Consider where people in your family work, the media, and your consumer choices.

As people and cultures become part of the global market system, there are many effects on individuals and culture, both positive and negative. The world has become more connected through the integration of our economies and financial systems, our cultures, and technology. What we're able to buy, how we are able to buy things, and how we speak to people around the world have all been affected by globalization. From sweatshops to fast food, from technology to education, globalization has a dramatic effect on everyone.

Sex Workers in Sosua, Dominican Republic

The Dominican Republic has been a popular tourist destination for many North Americans and Europeans for most of the last century. However, recent globalizing forces have had profound effects on Dominican women. Tourists used to stay at small hotels run by local people, spent money in local restaurants and bars, and bought local products at the stores. Now most tourists come on all-inclusive vacations that they pay for in Canada, Germany, or the United States. They stay in giant hotels that were built with imported materials and filled with imported furniture, fabrics, and other items, providing no work for locals. A tourist who used to put between $1000 and $2000 into the local economy, now spends only $100 locally. Europeans and North Americans hold most of the management positions, leaving the lowest paid service jobs for Dominicans. Many Dominicans have found themselves struggling to gain employment and make ends meet.

Many Dominican women have been attracted to Sosua, where many of the big resorts are located, in hopes of starting a relationship with a wealthy foreigner who will marry them and help them emigrate. They see such an alliance as a better chance than waiting in long lineups for visas in Santo Domingo. There are few job opportunities for women in the Dominican Republic. Jobs as a domestic (maid), hairstylist, or waitress pay only 1000 pesos ($83) per month, which is enough for a woman with a supporting husband, but not enough for a single mother. Sex workers often charge 500 pesos for one encounter. The aspirations and hopes of financial advancement that bring women to Sosua are usually unfulfilled and leave women worse off than they were before (Brennan, 2002).

FIGURE 4-26 Slum housing on the banks of a river, San Pedro de Macoris, Dominican Republic. What pushes women in the Dominican Republic to work in the sex trade?

The Kayapó: Resisting and Harnessing the Power of Globalization

The Kayapó are one of many indigenous peoples of the Brazilian rainforest. They continue to live mainly as hunter-gatherers and horticulturalists and see the forest as part of themselves. They have been actively resisting the destruction of their forest and lands by the Brazilian government and corporations. In the 1980s and 1990s, there were several threats to their way of life including:

- the corruption of some of the Kayapó leaders, who sold logging rights for cash
- the announcement by the Brazilian government declaring large tracts of Kayapó land open for settlement
- gold mining sponsored by the Brazilian government on their territory
- the dumping of radioactive waste in their territory
- the threat to the food and water sources of the Kayapó posed by a project to build dams on the Xingu River, which would flood much of their forest
- a constitutional change stating that any Kayapó able to bring a legal action to court was assimilated into Brazilian society and couldn't be considered Kayapó or represent the Kayapó community

FIGURE 4-27 Kayapó men performing a ritual. How are indigenous peoples affected by globalization?

The Kayapó began their resistance with armed attacks on settlers, who all fled. The Kayapó leaders then went to Brasilia (the capital) to pressure the government to return their stolen land. They also attacked and captured the two illegal gold mines. The government gave up the title and 10 percent of the profits from the mines to the Kayapó and legally demarcated the gold mine area so there would be no further encroachment.

The Kayapó used the money from the mines to buy a plane and hire a pilot. With the plane, they were able to patrol their borders for squatters and other encroachment, but they were also able to use it for trade and for transport to medical facilities.

There is still dispute among the Kayapó about the logging concessions and the pace of development. Many people feel the mines should have been shut down, while some Kayapó have opened their own mines. Some have also purchased homes, ranches, and their own airplanes with mining or logging money. By 2006, many had abandoned some of the more destructive practices of development in favour of sustainable cultivation of nuts and crops (Turner et al., 2006).

As a united group, the Kayapó have staged sit-ins to protest the dumping of radioactive waste and pressured the government to have the constitutional clause dismissed. They ensured strong rights in the new constitution for themselves and other indigenous communities. In 1988, Kayapó leader Payakan went on a world tour to gather support for a protest against the dam project on the Xingu River. Payakan managed to get the plans for the dams and worked to get environmental, animal, and human rights nongovernment organizations (NGOs) in North America to work together to help him stop the dam. With the NGOs, he was able to raise over $100 000 and generate an enormous amount of publicity in the media, creating a strong international

More to Know...
You learned about the Yanomamö in Chapter 1.

presence for the Kayapó. He held international meetings and managed to get the World Bank to cancel the loan for the dam.

The Kayapó also gained support from Sting's Rainforest Foundation, which raised $2 million by 1992, helping to reserve an area the size of Britain for the Kayapó. The Kayapó continue to patrol their reserved land as well as fight the government on dam projects. They were even able to help the Yanomamö when they were attacked by the government.

The story of the Kayapó resistance shows us that indigenous peoples are not just victims of globalization, but can be and are active participants in the solutions. The Kayapó were able to unify and mobilize First-World activists to work together to harness political power and news media to address concerns about the environment. With effective transportation and communication, the Kayapó are working toward a sustainable future in the modern world. Anthropologists can help to catalyze awareness of the value of traditional cultures in the First World and connect indigenous peoples to the support that can help them sustain their culture (Turner, 1993).

Globalization: Connecting the World

Globalization is not just destructive to culture; it also has positive effects. Globalization connects humans around the world, breaks down cultural barriers, and exposes people to ideas and products they may not have access to before. It has an effect on larger issues, such as international relations, the economy, and the environment, as well as the smaller aspects of daily life. For example, globalization has changed the kind of food we eat compared to fifty years ago. In most cities there are restaurants representing ethnic cuisines from around the world, such as Indian, Japanese, Thai, and Ethiopian. Ingredients important to different food cultures are available in most grocery stores.

As the population of the world increases, and technology becomes smaller and more accessible, people are using it to connect in ways unimagined before. Technology has also led to the creation of a global information system, where information can flow easily between borders and in remote location. This technology has facilitated communication between people from different parts of the world, allowing people to interact in ways they may not have been able to before. For people living under oppressive regimes, the Internet has provided people with access to information that may have been censored and provides forums for people to communicate what is happening in their country.

In 2011, countries in the Middle East and North Africa exploded in protests against dictatorships that controlled the region for decades. Despite restrictions on the media in these countries, protestors were able to communicate what was happening through Twitter, Facebook, and photo sharing Web sites. The protestors were also able to obtain information about other protests in the region and observe the reaction of the rest of the world. In one example of this, software developer Virender Ajmani created a tool using Google Maps that allowed people map the protests and what was happening in different parts of the country. Protestors could send a tweet containing information or photos and it would be uploaded to a map. People outside the country could also use the map to relay information to the protestors (Brown, 2011).

FIGURE 4-28 A young woman named Neda was shot and killed in the Iranian election protests in 2009. Her murder was caught on a cell phone camera and was circulated around the world. Neda became a symbol of the demonstrations and a rallying point for those opposing the regime. To what extent has globalization helped the protests in the Middle East and Northern Africa?

Adapting Products

Globalization also has an impact on industry. There are now worldwide production markets and trade. People now have access to products made throughout the world and have the ability to obtain products previously only available in other countries, adapting the product to suit their unique needs. Jan Chipchase, an anthropologist who used to work for Nokia, studies the stuff in our lives. Specifically he studies what stuff we carry around. He has found that the absolute essentials that people of all genders in all cultures carry with them are keys, a wallet, and a cell phone if they own one. These represent people's basic needs. The keys represent shelter, and to some degree transportation, especially in North America. The wallet holds money which can buy food and other necessities. . The cell phone represents safety and community. His work as an anthropologist is not only to study our stuff, but to look at how people use the stuff they do carry, and he found an extraordinary example of how rural Ugandans are turning mobile phones into ATM machines. Sente is a Ugandan word that means money, but it also means to send money as airtime. Figure 4-29 illustrates how this works.

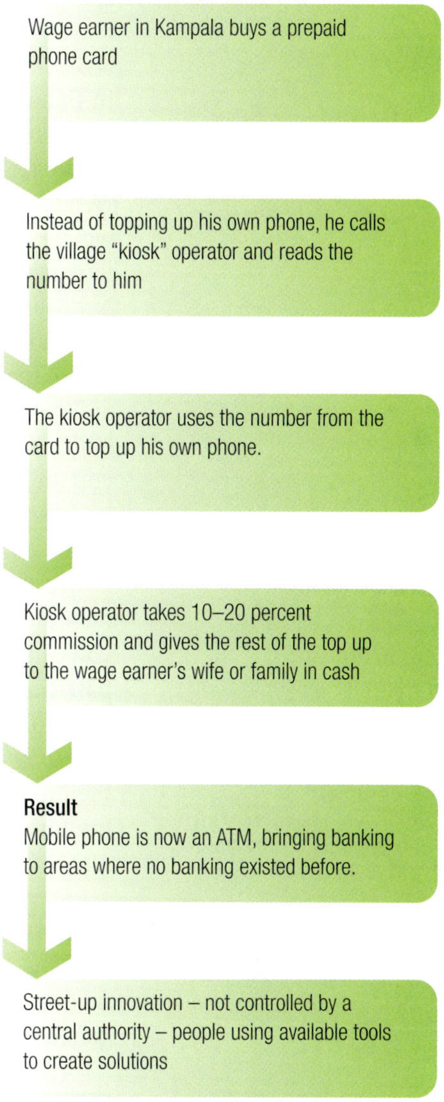

Creating Complex Tools

Globalization has also allowed us to make products and tools that are more complex. A hammer could be made by one person, using materials available locally. Can we do this with the products we use in our daily life? Think about a tool you may use everyday, like a computer mouse. British scientist and author Matt Ridley argues that no one person can make this tool. The president of the company that makes them knows how to run a company and the person on the assembly line knows how to assemble them. But neither of them knows how to gather and produce all the necessary materials to create it.

A computer mouse represents an incredibly complex system of accumulated ideas. No one person alone can make most of the mundane objects of our culture. They are a result of both accumulated knowledge and the exchange of ideas between cultures. As the world's population continues to grow, and communications continue to increase in speed and accessibility, ideas are exchanged ever more rapidly, creating a global society that is connected, innovative and using more and more of our specialized skills together to create solutions.

- Wage earner in Kampala buys a prepaid phone card
- Instead of topping up his own phone, he calls the village "kiosk" operator and reads the number to him
- The kiosk operator uses the number from the card to top up his own phone.
- Kiosk operator takes 10–20 percent commission and gives the rest of the top up to the wage earner's wife or family in cash
- **Result** Mobile phone is now an ATM, bringing banking to areas where no banking existed before.
- Street-up innovation – not controlled by a central authority – people using available tools to create solutions

FIGURE 4-29 This flow chart illustrates how a cell phone can be adapted into an ATM.

> **REFLECT AND RESPOND**
>
> 1. Does globalization affect cultures positively or negatively? Support your answer with examples.

Culture as Agent of Socialization: Kinship Systems

Before You Read
Whom are you related to? How do you know you are related to them?

In Canadian culture, we define ourselves and others by our jobs, our interests or hobbies, our taste in music or clothing, and our social roles, including family relationships. However, our personal success is not related to how well we get along with our family. Often we mark ourselves on how independent we are. Many Canadians would not consider themselves successful adults if they were living in their parents' home or relying on assistance from relatives, but in many cultures, living harmoniously with your parents or in-laws is considered a sign of successful socialization.

In many societies, family relationships define how individuals see themselves and others in their society. The study of these relationships is the study of kinship systems. In all societies, including our own, *kinship systems* determine whom you are related to, to whom you must show respect, and who owes respect to you. We may think of our biological family as unchangeable and common across cultures, but the anthropological record tells a different story.

Anthropologists recognize different patterns of descent, or how people trace their ancestry. Ancestry often determines inheritance, loyalty, obligations, who you can marry, and kinship groups. There are three main patterns: **matrilineal**, **patrilineal**, and **bilineal**.

Most Canadians trace their ancestry in a bilineal way. They recognize that they are related to both their mothers' and fathers' families and trace their ancestry in both lines. Since the number of ancestors multiplies rapidly the further back you go in generations, bilineal societies often do not track or remember ancestors much beyond great-grandparents.

In matrilineal societies, such as the historical Huron or Wyandot of Ontario, ancestry is traced through only the mother's line, while in a patrilineal society, only the father's ancestors are recognized as family. In most patrilineal and matrilineal societies, families live in extended family groups—with many generations together.

matrilineal:
a kinship system in which people trace their ancestry through their mothers

patrilineal:
a kinship system in which people trace their ancestry through their fathers

bilineal:
a kinship system in which people trace their ancestry through both their mothers and fathers

FIGURE 4-30 A Minang woman. The Minangs of West Sumatra, Indonesia, are the world's largest matrilineal society, in which property is inherited through female lineage. If the Canadian system of property inheritance was changed to the Minangs system, how would our lives be different?

Patrilineal Case Study: The Bhil in India

The Bhil people in India are an agricultural and patrilineal society that, like many patrilineal societies, recognize **lineages** and **clans**. The lineage is the group of men descended from a common ancestor whom all are related to, who holds land rights and can make marriage decisions. The clan, among the Bhil called the *arak*, is a much larger group of many lineages together. Individuals may not be able to trace the exact relationships in a clan, but it is recognized that they are related and may not marry within the same *arak*.

When anthropologist David McCurdy studied the Bhil in the 1980s and 1990s, the villagers didn't believe him when he told them that he did not have an *arak*. They protested with some shock, "[T]hen how do you know if you have not married your own relative?" All Bhil automatically get their *arak* from their father, so knowing their *arak* is like knowing who their parents are.

Marriages among the Bhil are arranged. This is preferred by the Bhil since arranged marriages strengthen kin networks and reinforce social strength, security, and reputation for everyone involved. When a girl is around 15 years old, her father consults all of his male relations. They help to spread the word that his daughter is available for marriage, loan him money, and provide labour for the wedding. Each family prepares a special meal for the bride. The lineage also provides similar financial and labour services in matters of land obligations and funerals.

After members of the lineage spread the word, they bring back suggestions of eligible men to the girl's father. They provide information about a candidate's character, appearance, reputation, and *arak*. Once a suitable candidate is found, arrangements are made for the wedding, including at least 11 days of wedding feasts and other preparations, the payment of the bride price from the groom's father to the bride's father, and other rituals, including a mock battle between the groom and the bride's brothers. Once the couple is married, the bride's family owes respect to the groom's family, and the families will exchange mutual hospitality in the future.

In the 1990s, wage labour came to Bhil society and many young men left the farms to work in cities or migrated as far as North America, Europe, or Asia. The new economic realities had the potential to break down traditional kinship ties since the ties are based on economic dependence on one another rather than on an external employer. In addition, kinship obligations would be difficult to maintain due to the long hours spent at work and the long distances between relations. However, the Bhil are still arranging marriages, family loyalty is still considered very important, and gifts and favours are still expected to be given freely within the lineage. The Bhil continue to send money home when they are away. The kinship system has not been replaced but has simply been stretched to Europe, Asia, and North America, and helps people deal with changing times (McCurdy, 1997).

? How is the Bhil system of kinship different from your own family system? In what ways are the two systems similar? What impact has immigration and/or emigration had on extended families?

---

lineage: all the male relatives in a family that can be traced back to one common direct ancestor

clan: a group of several lineages in a patrilineal or matrilineal society in which people are related but cannot always trace exact relationships

Bilineal Case Study: The Dobe Ju/'hoansi Three Systems of Kinship

The Dobe Ju/'hoansi of the Kalahari are hunter-gatherers with bilineal descent. They keep track of all of their relatives on both their mother's and father's sides. Richard Lee found that they, in fact, have three systems of kinship.

The first system is much like the one we use in Canada and includes those to whom you are related by blood or marriage. These are your parents, brothers, sisters, grandparents, wife, husband, etc. Some relationships are friendly or joking, and others are respectful or avoidance relationships. For example, you would joke with your grandparents and avoid or show respect to your parents.

The second system is a naming one, in which anyone with the same name as you is related to you as well. For example, if a man had the same name as you, you would address him as either *!kuma* (young name) if he was younger than you or *!kun!a* (old name) if he was older than you. In the same system, you would address any man with the same name as your father also as "father." As you can imagine, the two systems would frequently be in conflict. According to the first system, you must have an avoidance relationship with your father, but if your husband's brother, with whom you should have a joking relationship, has the same name as your father, how would you know how to act with him?

To sort out which system takes precedence, the Ju/'hoansi have a third principle, that of *wi*. According to *wi*, in determining what two people should call each other, the elder of the two always decides which naming system should prevail. A very old man once told Lee that he knew he was the oldest person alive because everyone who had *wied* him was dead and he had *wied* everyone alive now.

These three systems tie the Ju/'hoansi society together in the following ways:

1. The systems ensure that almost everyone in the society is linked through kinship ties and obligations.
2. A person always has kin of one sort or another that he or she can go visit or live with temporarily or permanently. The Ju/'hoansi frequently change camps if the food source at one camp is dwindling or if there is an argument between individuals, and the kinship systems structure this frequent movement.
3. By allowing people to move to visit their relatives, the kin systems ensure that all members of the society have access to the available food and resources. (Lee, 1993)

↑ **FIGURE 4-31** Ju/'hoansi man and child. Children are frequently named after their grandparents with whom they have a joking or affectionate relationship.

❓ How does your kinship system determine your sense of self? What do you think are the advantages and disadvantages of systems like those of the Bhil and the Ju/'hoansi?

Marriage, a Cultural Universal

Almost all cultures of the world have the cultural institution of marriage. As with many other cultural institutions, marriage varies enormously from one culture to the next. In fact, it varies so much that it is hard to define marriage in a way that fits all cultural variations. Anthropologists generally agree that marriage defines social relationships to provide for the survival and socialization of children. Marriage also:

- defines the rights and obligations of the two people to each other in terms of sex, reproduction, work, and social roles
- creates new relationships between families and kin groups

In Canada, marriage began to change in the late 1960s. Before that time, marriage was what we considered as traditional: men supported a wife and children, the marriage reflected religious traditions, people primarily married others in their own social groups (i.e., ethnicity, religion, class), it was very difficult to get divorced, and children born outside marriage faced social stigma. Since the late 1960s, more couples have chosen common-law relationships, although most couples do marry (in 2006, 69 percent of Canadians were married, 16 percent were common law, and 16 percent were lone parents).

More couples are now interracial (3.9 percent in 2006 compared to 2.6 percent in 1991) and interfaith (20 percent in 2001 compared to 15 percent in 1981). In 2006, 17 percent of same-sex couples were married. Recent legal changes to allow same-sex marriage mirror a societal shift in the acceptance of homosexuality. However, same-sex unions still reflect and fit into traditional anthropological definitions of marriage. Even though fewer same-sex couples choose to have children, many of them have children from previous marriages, choose to adopt, or use some kind of reproductive technology to have and raise children. The greatest change in Canadian marriage is not a result of increased divorce, same-sex unions, or even the choice of more couples not to get married, but of the choice of more couples not to have children. Without children, one of the functions of marriage does not apply, but the other two are still valid.

How people meet and begin dating has also changed. In 2010, 17 percent of the couples who married in United States had met each other on an online dating site. How do you think technology has affected marriage and relationships?

No Marriage in the Na Society

Chinese anthropologist Cai Hua documented the Na, a society that doesn't have formal marriage relationships. The Na are an ethnic minority of Tibetan-style Buddhists in the Yunnan province in China. Their language has words for mother and children but no word for father or marriage. Women live with their brothers and other maternal relations. The men help to raise their sister's children. At night, the men visit women at their homes for sexual relations. There are no words for illegitimate, promiscuity, infidelity, or incest; however, there are rules forbidding sex with anyone living in the same household. There is no jealousy among partners, and both men and women are free to ask or refuse a partner. Couples often set up their "dates" during the day by exchanging belts or going to the movies.

> **Before You Read**
> What do you know about marriage in other countries or cultures? What is similar or different in your examples?

↑ **FIGURE 4-32** How has marriage changed and stayed the same over time? What do the changes indicate about our society's attitude to marriage?

FIGURE 4-33 The Na people of Yunnan province are sometimes described as having a "walking marriage." Do you think they are an exception to the marriage universal?

The Han Chinese have been trying to get the Na to change their sexual behaviours since 1656 but without much success. Communist China tried to force the Na to marry in 1974 by passing a number of laws pressuring women to marry the fathers of their children or go without grain rations, and by prohibiting the nighttime visits. These measures worked to some degree, but it wasn't until the 1980s and 1990s through the Chinese education system and movies that the Na started to feel ashamed of their culture and wanted to become more like the Han Chinese (Geertz, 2001).

> To what extent does the Na system meet the requirements of the functions of marriage? Do you agree with Hua that the Na have no marriage?

Arranged Marriage

The relative importance of the three functions of marriage varies from one society to the next. In Canadian society, the couple's obligations to each other are the focus, rather than having children or family ties. This is reflected in the care that couples put into writing their vows, the fact that marriage is usually arranged by the couple themselves and families come into the picture later, and the decision of many couples not to have children or to leave the question of children open at the time of marriage. Arranged marriages are marriages set up by someone other than the people getting married. According to Reva Seth (2008), arranged marriages have a 5 to 7 percent divorce rate versus 50 percent for nonarranged marriages in the United States and 33 percent in Canada.

In many societies, the child-rearing, economic, and kinship functions are much more important than a couple's personal desires. In societies such as the Bhil of India, marriages are arranged by the parents or other adults. As in most societies with arranged marriage, the Bhil feel that the joining of two kin groups through marriage is much too important to leave to the whims of romantic love. In many societies, marriage is the first step, with the presumption that love will grow afterward.

Although globalization is increasing, marriages in many cultures are often still arranged, but there are changes. The prospective bride and groom often get the chance to meet even a few times in a chaperoned setting, and a prospective partner can often be refused. In a recent study of Indo-Canadian marriages, Nancy Netting at the University of British Columbia (2006) concluded that Western ideals of romantic love are meshing with traditional family values in Indo-Canadian families. She found through a series of interviews that many young Indo-Canadians are negotiating both arranged and love marriages and finding common ground between the two systems. They often did not date until after moving away from home to go to college or university. However, most of them still considered an arranged or introduced marriage acceptable if they could not find their own partner or if dating did not work out for them. Since many young Indo-Canadians' own parents' marriages were arranged, they could see the value and potential success of the system. They especially valued the close family ties, extended family households, and parental support in maintaining the marriage.

FIGURE 4-34 A Bhil wedding. How is the meaning of a wedding in Bhil culture similar to or different from that in Canadian culture?

IN FOCUS Indo-Canadian Arranged Marriage

In her 2006 study, Nancy Netting interviewed a number of young Indo-Canadians, including Jaya, Ravinder, Anjali, and Avtar about their feelings on arranged marriage. "I want the marriage my parents have. They're more in love now—you would never know they were ever, ever arranged. They're the happiest couple I've ever met," says Jaya of her parents' arranged marriage. In North America today, in order to find suitable spouses for their children, Indian families use a modified version of the traditional arranged marriage. As Ravinder put it, "It's not called *arranging* any more; it's called *suggestion*." When a daughter's education is completed or a son has a steady income, parents put the word out, letting relatives and friends know their child is ready to marry. Sometimes they place an ad in an Indo-Canadian newspaper or on a Web site; at times they seek candidates from families in other countries or India itself. Almost always the search is limited to Indians of the same religion, caste, and mother tongue. Suggestions, with photographs and resumés, soon arrive; parents and youths select the most promising candidates for further examination. Detailed background checks rule out those whose families have financial or personal scandals, mental illness or suicide, or alcoholism or other addictions.

If a prospect looks promising, a formal introduction takes place between the boy and girl, usually with both sets of parents present. After a group conversation and tea drinking, the two young people are allowed to go somewhere together, perhaps out for coffee. It is now accepted that if the two feel no romantic spark during this meeting, negotiations will terminate. Yet mutual attraction, although necessary, is not sufficient; there must be a family-to-family bond as well. Anjali explained: "If there's any chemistry there, then it's there, and it's got to be both ways. It's not just between two people, it's between two families, and even larger than that for me, it's important for my grandparents that he be [in the same caste from the same area of India]—maybe not [as important] to my parents, but to my extended family."

FIGURE 4-35
Why might people agree to an arranged marriage, and what factors might their parents consider in the selection?

Once the two young people agree to consider the match, they usually have a longer time to get to know each other than their parents did. They can go out together but not date casually as do many North American couples. Instead, their whole community knows they are considering each other as potential lifetime partners. As Avtar put it, "[T]his is not a disposable relationship. After two, three months with an introduced Indian girl, there would have to be something drastic for us to break up."

Their meetings are filled with interview-type questions: Could you live with my parents? Would you treat a son and a daughter differently? Have you had a previous relationship? (and possibly) Would you agree to an HIV test? Usually the decision is made within a few months. In theory, it is up to the couple, but in practice there is often pressure to accept (Netting, 2006).

QUESTIONS

1. How is this account of arranged marriage different from and similar to the account of a Bhil arranged marriage on page 167?
2. How is a modern Indo-Canadian arranged marriage similar to and different from a Canadian love marriage? Would you want to marry a person that your parents disapproved of? Explain why or why not.
3. What are the strengths and drawbacks of arranged marriages?

Types of Marriage

monogamy:
a relationship where an individual has one partner. Serial monogamy refers to monogamous relationships that occur one after another.

polygamy:
a form of marriage that involves multiple partners

polygyny:
a form a marriage between one husband and multiple wives

polyandry:
a form of marriage with one wife and multiple husbands

In Canada, the only legal type of marriage is monogamous, that is, between two partners. While our culture values **monogamy**, because of North Americans' high divorce and remarriage rate, we frequently are described as being serial monogamists. We may have only one partner at a time, but we can change partners over our lifetimes.

Polygamy is a marriage involving more than two people. There are two types of polygamous marriage: **polygyny** between one man and several women, and **polyandry** between one woman and several men. Polyandry is practised in less than 1 percent of the world's cultures, but polygyny is relatively common and permitted in about 80 percent of human cultures. Many monogamists think that polygamous marriages are about having sexual access to many partners, but a closer examination of polygamous societies shows that economic and social reasons are more useful in understanding why these marriages occur.

Polygyny

Polygyny is permitted in most of the world's cultures, but most men in polygynous societies have only one wife. In some polygynous cultures, many men have no wives at all (Bailey and Peoples, 2006). In Islam, a man may have up to four wives, but few Muslims practise polygyny because Mohammed also exhorted men to treat their wives equally and "deal justly with them all," something that is emotionally and financially difficult to do. The other reason could be that a man would realize he could not love all his wives equally and thus it would not be fair to him or his wives.

bridewealth:
a cultural system where the groom (or the groom's family) must pay a father in order to marry his daughter

In many cultures, extra wives are both a symbol of wealth and a means to acquiring wealth. In some cultures that have a **bridewealth** system where a man must pay the bride's parents to marry her, the cost of acquiring many wives may be prohibitively expensive. In many herding and agricultural societies, wives and children provide the labour to work the fields, increasing a man's wealth and status, and the children and grandchildren provide for his old age. In some societies where men engage frequently in warfare, there is a surplus of women and polygyny is one way to ensure that all women are married and cared for by husbands.

The advantages of polygyny for men may seem obvious, but women also report advantages. African women generally prefer a polygynous marriage to being childless and unmarried or bearing children outside marriage. They get the benefit of their husband's labour for chores and tasks that only men are permitted to do. Many wives report that they also enjoy the company of their co-wives in sharing the work of producing, processing, and preparing food and caring for children. As women in Africa are increasingly educated, many are rejecting polygyny and, as in North America, are waiting until they are in their 30s before seeking marriage and children (Kilbride, 1996). Other researchers have found polygynous families to be a definite stress on women, one that consistently produces low self-esteem, depression, and psychological distress (Profanter and Cate, 2009).

↑ **FIGURE 4-36** Family gathered to eat. What type of family is this?

❓ What differences would a woman in a monogamous marriage with children experience in a polygynous African society?

IN FOCUS

Canada's Polygamous Community: Bountiful British Columbia

When Debbie Palmer was 15, she became the sixth wife of the 55-year-old leader of the polygamous community of Bountiful, British Columbia. The town of Bountiful, a small community of about 1000 people, has been a polygamous community since the 1950s, when it was founded by breakaway members of the Mormon church, the Fundamentalist Church of Jesus Christ of Latter-Day Saints (FLDS), who believed that a man must have at least three wives to get into heaven. The mainstream Mormon church renounced polygamy in 1890, after U.S. federal law outlawed polygamy in 1862. Members of the FLDS believe polygamy is a tenet of their faith.

In 1988, Debbie Palmer ran away from Bountiful with her eight children and wrote her memoirs, *Keep Sweet: Children of Polygamy*, exposing many of the abuses of the community's polygamous system.

In 1990, a number of women who had fled Bountiful demanded an investigation. The RCMP carried out an investigation, but no charges were laid. In 2004, another investigation led to allegations of child abuse, forcible marriage, and sexual exploitation. The RCMP investigated the community for sexual exploitation and polygamy between 2004 and 2008 but concluded that it couldn't lay charges (Fong, 2009). In Canada, polygamy has been illegal since the 1950s, but up to that point, no one had been charged with the offence. Two studies were commissioned in 2006 by the Department of Justice and the Status of Women Canada, and came to different conclusions. One study stated that Canada should make polygamy legal in order to better protect women and children who are living in polygamous unions, and the other study urged the British Columbia government to pursue charges immediately, which it did (CBC, 2007).

Winston Blackmore and James Oler, leaders of the church in Bountiful, were brought to court on charges of polygamy in September 2009, but the judge dismissed the case, stating that the provincial government did not have the authority to pursue the charges. The men claim that polygamy is part

↑ **FIGURE 4-37** Winston Blackmore with six of his daughters and some of his grandchildren. How is this family similar to nonpolygamist families?

of their religion and should be legal. They declare that Canada's Charter of Rights and Freedoms will protect them. In 2010, the British Columbia government opened a hearing in the British Columbia Supreme Court to determine if the law is constitutional before reopening a criminal case against Blackmore and Oler. The issues relate to a conflict between freedom of religion and equality of the sexes. The ruling in 2011 is expected to be appealed to the Supreme Court of Canada. Lawyers for the provincial and federal governments have argued that polygamy has created a long list of problems in Bountiful, including child brides, teenage pregnancy, the trafficking of young girls to meet the demand for wives, the subjugation of women, and the expulsion of boys to reduce competition for brides. Lawyers for the Bountiful defendants argue that the actions of the British Columbia government amount to religious persecution. Because of the possibility of other religious groups wanting to practise polygamy, this case will set a precedent beyond British Columbia.

QUESTIONS

1. In what ways is polygyny in Bountiful, British Columbia, different from or similar to polygyny in other parts of the world?
2. Do you think polygamy should be legal in Canada? Why or why not?

Polyandry

Polyandry, or the marriage of one woman to several men, is extremely rare, but it has been noted in a few societies. It is practised in some places in India, Nepal, Tibet, Sri Lanka, and Bhutan. Some societies practise fraternal polyandry, that is, the marriage of a woman to a man and his brothers. All partners in the marriage have their own separate residences, and the men work together to support their wife and any children she bears. They make no distinction of paternity, and any sons will inherit the land that the brothers already own. The eldest brother is the authority in the household, and the younger brothers and the wife must respect his decisions. The wife has an increased workload since she must look after all the husbands and all the children, and she does not increase her status by having multiple husbands as men do in polygynous unions.

This particular type of polyandry is thought to exist because of lack of cultivable land. It works to limit population growth and keep the land from being divided up. In the high Himalayas, there is very little land suitable for agriculture, so if land were divided among brothers and inherited by their sons, it would take only a few generations before the land was divided so much as to be insufficient to support any one family. Having only one wife for three brothers puts a cap on the population and ensures that there is enough land to support the entire population.

Polyandry is defined as the simultaneous bond of one woman with more than one man, in which all parties involved have sexual rights and economic responsibilities toward one another and toward any children that may result from the union. Using this definition, Katherine Starkweather (2010) identified 52 polyandrous societies, more than have been historically recognized in previous literature. A recent study (2010) shows that polyandry has been practised around the world, among hunting and gathering people, as well as horticulturalists and pastoralists. It seems that polyandry is a means by which societies, and individuals in them, can respond to different environmental and social constraints.

FIGURE 4-38 Kundar Singh Pundir, left, and his brother Amar, right, share Indira Devi, centre, as their wife. What do you think are the advantages and disadvantages of this type of marriage?

> ### REFLECT AND RESPOND
>
> 1. How do your cultural expectations of marriage influence your self-identity?
> 2. How might your self-identity be different if you lived in a society without marriage or with a polygamous marriage system?

Family Roles and Culture

Family members all have roles within the family, for example, mother, father, son, daughter. These roles carry particular meanings in every society and influence people's behaviour. As you can imagine, roles vary from one culture to the next. For example, in the Na culture, many of the roles that we associate with the father would likely be associated with the uncle, or specifically the mother's brother. Roles also change over time, as we have seen in Canadian society with mothers entering the workforce and fathers taking on more responsibilities in the home, such as housework and child care.

All family members have obligations to their families. These can be members of the nuclear family or extended family, which includes uncles, aunts, cousins, and grandparents. In many societies, the extended family plays a much more active role than in Canada. Canadians often hire nonfamily members to do many tasks. Consider who in your family is (or was) responsible for the following tasks:

- repairs to the household
- looking after young children
- cleaning dishes
- earning money to provide food
- paying for a wedding
- preparing meals
- paying for postsecondary education
- studying and attending school

> **Before You Read**
> How do you think family roles influence self-concept and people's actions?

> **More to Know...**
> You learned about the Na people on page 169.

FIGURE 4-39
How are family roles in Canada changing?

Self-concept in Western and East Asian familes

In a cross-cultural **meta-analysis** (a study combining the results of many other studies) of Asian self-identity, Canadian researchers Hamamura and Heine (2007) found that East Asians and Westerners tend to view themselves differently, and those differences have an important effect on family roles. In both cultures, people perceive themselves positively; they tend to like themselves and feel that they are good people in general.

However, there is a great deal of **self-enhancement** in Western society. Westerners tend to see themselves more positively than they really are. For example, a bad mark on a school assignmentcan be considered a minor mistake, the teacher's fault, or a case of bad luck in some way. The bad mark can be seen as a minor setback, not as a reflection of ability or and future progress.

> **meta-analysis:**
> a study combining the results of many other studies

> **self-enhancement:**
> the belief that you are more competent and generally better than your actions and behaviour indicate

Chapter 4 • Anthropology and Me NEL **175**

Landmark Case Study

Death Without Weeping: Poverty and Family Roles

"Why do the church bells ring so often?" Nancy Scheper-Hughes asked her host Nailza de Arruda after she moved into a corner of her hut in Alto do Cruzeiro, a slum in Northeast Brazil in the summer of 1965. Nailza replied "It's nothing, just another little angel gone to heaven" (Scheper-Hughes, 1992, p. 268).

As a Peace Corps volunteer, Scheper-Hughes was trying to help the mothers and children of the Brazilian slum, but continued to be puzzled by the question of the mothers' seeming indifference to child death. She returned to Brazil in the 1980s as an anthropologist to try to understand the same question. Alto do Cruzeiro is one of three shantytowns surrounding the market town of Bom Jesus da Mata, in the sugar plantation zone of Northeast Brazil. Scheper-Hughes lived with some of the poorest and most marginalized women in the world. Life expectancy is only 40 years in the Northeast, mostly due to high infant mortality—116 deaths per 1000 live births. Compare this to Canada's infant mortality rate of about 5 in every 1000 births (Statistics Canada, 2010). On a personal level, this means that the average mother in Alto is pregnant 9.5 times, and suffers 3.5 child deaths, and 1.5 stillbirths in her lifetime.

Women in Alto do Cruzeiro have few choices in their lives. They do not have access to the traditional supports available in the rural farm villages, such as stable marriages, extended family households, and subsistence gardens. They live in difficult conditions and work on sugar plantations as unprotected labourers clearing or weeding, as domestic servants in the homes of the rich, or washing clothes on the riverbanks. They cannot bring their children with them to work and so are unable to breastfeed. Frequently, few other family members are available to care for their children during the day. Without stable marriages or extended family support, a mother's only choice is often to leave an infant alone with the door locked and hope for the best.

In these desperate conditions, Scheper-Hughes (1992) found some explanations for the mother's neglect. The mothers viewed the babies as having "an aversion to life that made their death seem wholly natural, indeed all but anticipated." (p. 270) If a mother had already come to think that her child wasn't going to live, it was very difficult for her to do anything to save the child, even if the measures needed to save the child were simple. Scheper-Hughes learned, "the high expectancy of death, and the ability to face child death … produced patterns of nurturing … the survivors were nurtured, while stigmatized, doomed infants were left to die." (p. 342)

Women in the Alto categorize child death into roughly three groups: natural causes such as diarrhea or disease, deaths resulting from the evil eye, sorcery or other magic, and the ill-fated hopeless cases categorized as "child sickness" or "child attack." These folk diagnoses help the mother to decide if an infant is worth her limited nurturing resources.

After her study was published, some criticized Scheper-Hughes of painting an unflattering portrait of poor Brazilian women. In response, she acknowledged that the choice the these women faced were not easy. "I have described these women as allowing some of their children to die, as if this were an unnatural and inhuman act rather than, as I would assert, the way

In many Asian cultures, the concept of shame would strongly motivate you to try to avoid getting a bad mark in the first place. Self-concept is closely tied to a person's family roles and obligations. Making a mistake has consequences not only for the individual but also for his or her family. To be considered a "good person," you must avoid humiliation for you and your family, so it is better to prevent any mistakes and save face. Some Westerners may perceive East Asians to be overly concerned with what others think, while some East Asians may perceive Westerners as overly conceited and self-absorbed. These perceptions are based on different cultural ideas of family roles.

any one of us might act, reasonably and rationally, under similarly desperate conditions. Perhaps I have not emphasized enough … the poverty, deprivation, sexism, chronic hunger, and economic exploitation. If mother love is … a seemingly natural and universal script, what does it mean to women for whom scarcity, loss, sickness, and deprivation have made that love frantic and robbed them of their grief, seeming to turn their hearts to stone?" (Scheper-Hughes 1989).

FIGURE 4-40 A shanty town in Rio de Janeiro, Brazil. How might conditions in this kind of environment contribute to high infant mortality rates.

The situation in Brazil is not unique; throughout much of human history women have had to give birth and to nurture children in situations that made it difficult for children to survive. In Scheper-Hughes's opinion, selective neglect and passive infanticide are active survival strategies (Scheper-Hughes 1989).

Primatologist Sarah Blaffer-Hrdy researches a wide range of mothering behaviours in many species, from humans and primates to insects and birds. She finds that "a broad continuum of maternal responses, ranging from self-sacrifice to infanticide, can be documented across traditional cultures. Mothers in a wide range of contexts invest selectively in infants according to birth order, sex, or maternal circumstances" (Hrdy, 1992). Mothers try to ensure their own and their offspring's survival, and are sometimes forced to decide which offspring will survive. Cultural beliefs in many cases help to make that decision easier to bear for the mothers, as they do in the chronic poverty of the slums of northeast Brazil.

QUESTIONS

1. According to Scheper-Hughes, why do mothers seem indifferent to the deaths of some of their infants in the slum of Alto do Cruzeiro? What evidence does she present to support her point of view?

2. Can you think of examples of neglect or selective infanticide in Canadian society? Are the circumstances similar to this case?

3. According to Scheper-Hughes and Hrdy, is mother love universal? Explain your answer.

REFLECT AND RESPOND

1. Connect the ideas of this research about family roles to your own family using a mind map or reflective journal.
2. What questions would you like to research based on these ideas?

Section 4.3 Ethical Issues in Anthropology

Ethics are a very important part of all the social sciences. Ethical practices require thought before action. In anthropology, there are established ethical guidelines that all researchers must follow for their research to be valid. These guidelines exist to help anthropologists conduct their research and provide guidance in complex situations. As the discipline developed, the concept of ethics and formal guidelines developed along with it. What ethical issues do you think anthropologists might face when creating their studies and reports?

Attitudes of Anthropology

One of the most important concepts of cultural anthropology at the heart of the discipline is that anthropologists doing fieldwork are learners and their informants are the teachers. Anthropologists must enter into fieldwork with an attitude of humility and openness and a willingness to learn. They have to assume that they know nothing, and that even their most basic and unconscious actions must be considered and relearned.

This attitude is reflected in the tools that anthropologists use, including the semi-structured interview. A semi-structured interview is a long list of open-ended questions that anthropologists generate based on the research question that they start with and their current knowledge about the culture. The interview is semi-structured because, during the interview, people may not want to talk about the topic of interest to the anthropologist and other topics of more interest might come up.

In the interview, the anthropologist and the informant will likely become more aware of their own **explicit** and **tacit cultural knowledge**. Explicit cultural knowledge is information about a culture that is easily explained, such as kin networks, common stories and myths, and histories. Tacit cultural knowledge is the knowledge that we are unaware is cultural and that we assume everyone else shares. Use of personal space or proper behaviour are generally tacit; that is, everyone in the culture understands the rules and believes that these are universal. Since the anthropologist also has tacit knowledge, it is necessary to adopt a position of complete ignorance and openness in order to understand the informant's point of view.

How Fieldwork Transforms

Fieldwork requires anthropologists to re-evaluate all of their own tacit cultural knowledge. Anthropologists are almost always outsiders to the cultures they are studying. Even when they do fieldwork in their own society, they are usually stepping outside their own gender, class, or social boundaries and are going to be considered outsiders. Can an outsider ever understand what it is to be someone else? Anthropologists would argue that being an outsider, or having an **etic perspective**, gives them a unique view that an insider would

---

Before You Read
When entering a new school or job, what attitude do you think is most appropriate? What about when visiting a culture that is new to you?

explicit cultural knowledge: information about a culture that is easily explained and described

tacit cultural knowledge: information about a culture that the people within the culture or organization know but have difficulty explaining

etic perspective: the point of view of an outsider to a culture

not necessarily have. Those with an **emic perspective**, or insider's view, generally believe that all people define the real world of objects, events, and creatures in the same way as they do. This belief is called **naive realism**, and it is universal. It is only when cultures come into contact that we become aware of our own particular beliefs and view of reality.

emic perspective: the point of view of an insider of a culture

naive realism: the belief that everyone else defines the world in the same way you do

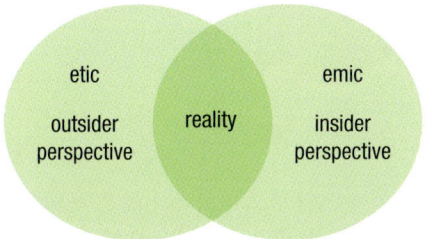

FIGURE 4-41 Apply this diagram to an everyday situation in your life.

Ethical Guidelines of Anthropology

The American Anthropological Association (AAA) sets out very clear guidelines for ethical anthropological research. While the guidelines state that anthropologists need to be open, ready to learn, and as aware of their own tacit cultural knowledge as possible, there are also specific guidelines to make sure that the subjects of study are not being harmed in any way. Consider the following guidelines for anthropological research set out by the University of Toronto's Department of Anthropology:

- Researchers must reveal to subjects that they are doing research.
- Subjects must be free to avoid contact with the researcher if they so choose.
- Subjects must give their informed consent; they must know as much as possible and in their own cultural terms about what the researcher is doing
- Subjects must be given the opportunity to provide feedback on manuscript.
- Researchers must assure the confidentiality of any information shared with them.
- There must be no harm to the dignity, safety, and privacy of informants.
- There must be no secret research for governments or private companies; all research must be published in an academic publication.
- There must be a clear purpose to the research: the researcher must have a question that he or she is attempting to answer and is not intruding on the subjects' lives for no reason.

REFLECT AND RESPOND

1. What are the advantages and disadvantages of semi-structured interviews as a research tool?
2. How do explicit and tacit cultural knowledge differ?
3. What is meant by the *etic* and *emic perspectives*? How do they help anthropologists understand the cultural reality of their subjects?
4. How are these guidelines similar to or different from guidelines for research in psychology and sociology?

Landmark Case Study

Shakespeare in the Bush

This excerpt from anthropologist Laura Bohannan's article "Shakespeare in the Bush" was originally published in 1966. She was living among the Tiv in West Africa and discovered, to her disappointment, that none of the religious rituals that she had hoped to observe would be performed during the rainy season. To pass the time, the villagers drank homemade beer and told stories. When Bohannan was asked to tell a story from her culture, she decided to retell *Hamlet* in hopes of proving to a colleague back home that Shakespeare is universal:

FIGURE 4-42 A chief of the Tiv nation in Nigeria, alongside his mother. How might his view of the world be different from yours?

> I began in the proper style, "Not yesterday, not yesterday, but long ago, a thing occurred. One night three men were keeping watch outside the homestead of the great chief, when suddenly they saw the former chief approach them."
>
> "Why was he no longer their chief?"
>
> "He was dead," I explained. "That is why they were troubled and afraid when they saw him."
>
> "Impossible," began one of the elders, handing his pipe on to his neighbour, who interrupted, "Of course it wasn't the dead chief. It was an omen sent by a witch. Go on."
>
> Slightly shaken, I continued. "One of these three was a man who knew things," the closest translation for scholar, but unfortunately it also meant witch. The second elder looked triumphantly at the first. "So he spoke to the dead chief saying, 'Tell us what we must do so you may rest in your grave,' but the dead chief did not answer. He vanished, and they could see him no more. Then the man who knew things—his name was Horatio—said this event was the affair of the dead chief's son, Hamlet."
>
> There was a general shaking of heads round the circle. "Had the dead chief no living brothers? Or was this son the chief?"
>
> "No," I replied. "That is, he had one living brother who became the chief when the elder brother died."
>
> The old men muttered: such omens were matters for chiefs and elders, not for youngsters; no good could come of going behind a chief's back; clearly Horatio was not a man who knew things.
>
> "Yes, he was." I insisted, shooing a chicken away from my beer. "In our country the son is next to the father. The dead chief's younger brother had become the great chief. He had also married his elder brother's widow only about a month after the funeral."
>
> "He did well," the old man beamed and announced to the others, "I told you that if we knew more about Europeans, we would find they really were very like us. In our country also," he added to me, "the younger brother marries the elder brother's widow and becomes the father of his children. Now, if your uncle, who married your widowed mother, is your father's full brother, then he will be a real father to you. Did Hamlet's father and uncle have one mother?"
>
> His question barely penetrated my mind: I was too upset and thrown too far off balance by having one of the most important elements of *Hamlet* knocked straight out of the picture. Rather uncertainly I said that I thought they had the same mother, but I wasn't sure—the story didn't say. The old man told me severely that these genealogical details made all the difference and that when I got home I must ask the elders about it. (p. 28–29)

QUESTIONS

1. How does Bohannan's experience illustrate the importance of the anthropologist as learner?
2. What tacit cultural knowledge was revealed by Bohannan and the Tiv elders?
3. Create a Venn diagram, similar to the one on the previous page, inserting the details of this exchange. Sort events and opinions into etic and emic perspectives. What is the reality of the situation?

Anthropology's Ethical Transformations

Anthropology has a long history of ethical abuses and questions. Early anthropologists worked with European colonial powers as translators and facilitators, allowing the European nations to more effectively exploit and assimilate the "savage" peoples. In the early days of anthropology, cultural evolutionism (the theory that all cultures evolve from "savage" to "barbarian" to "civilized"), and anthropologists put much effort into explaining why cultures were "backward" or "uncivilized." Even Bronislaw Malinowski, who rejected cultural evolutionism, wrote in his 1929 article "Practical Anthropology" that anthropologists' findings should be used by colonial administrators to solve problems involving "savage law, economics, customs and institutions." (p. 23)

Archaeology and physical anthropology are not immune to ethical problems. Many archaeological treasures of the world are in museums of Europe and North America because archaeological teams dug them up in the early twentieth century and took them to Britain, France, or Germany. There is an ongoing issue in North America about returning human remains to living Aboriginal populations for appropriate burial according to ancient customs. As you saw with the feature about Kwaday Dän Ts'inchi in Chapter 1, these types of issues can be resolved when anthropologists work together with Aboriginal people to do archaeological and anthropological work that is both sensitive to the people's wishes and informative for both cultures.

In Canada, early anthropologists, such as Edward Sapir, Marius Barbeau, and Diamond Jenness, worked hard to record Aboriginal cultures before they disappeared. While they wanted to understand Aboriginal peoples and languages, they did not work toward the preservation of the living cultures, and most of their reports, artifacts, and photographs ended up in a museum, not in the Aboriginal communities. Their paternalistic attitude was rejected by more recent anthropologists who work with communities to provide information about cultural and ecological patterns to help them plan for the future.

Anthropologists and the Military

In the United States, Margaret Mead and Ruth Benedict both worked for the U.S. military. As you learned in Chapter 1, Benedict conducted her famous *Chrysanthemum and the Sword* study to help the American military during World War II. Mead wrote a 1942 analysis of U.S. military culture called *Keep Your Powder Dry*. She concluded that several ideologies were important to Americans in supporting any military effort:

- Aggression is a response; Americans should not be the primary aggressors.
- The use of violence is okay as long as it's for altruistic purposes (for example, saving lives) and not selfish purposes.
- Conflict is a finite task: the military should finish the task and walk away.

Mead's study of the military, which was commissioned by the military, allows us to understand how it functions and why citizens support some conflicts but not others.

> **Before You Read**
> How do you think anthropological research could be used for military or hostile purposes? Are there some types of research that shouldn't be done?

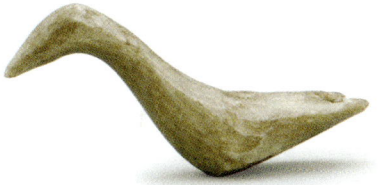

FIGURE 4-43 Loon, child's toy collected by Diamond Jenness. This artifact is in the Museum of Civilization in Ottawa. Do you think it should it be returned to the Copper Inuit? Why or why not?

> **More to Know...**
> You learned about Margaret Mead and Ruth Benedict in Chapter 1.

FIGURE 4-44 Do you think anthropologists need to work with the military to make interactions between the military and civilians successful?

The U.S. military held Iraqi prisoners captive at a prison called Abu Ghraib in 2004 and subjected them to sexual shaming, including being tied up together naked and forcing women to expose their breasts in front of men. This torture was based on the 1973 book *The Arab Mind*, which explained that Arab men were so preoccupied with sexual honour that they would do anything to prevent shameful photos of them being shown to family and friends. However, more recent cultural anthropology reveals that any affront to their honour must be avenged by blood; this is a widely known concept in Iraqi society called *al-sharaf*, or upholding one's manly honour. After the Abu Ghraib incident, the Iraqis became even more anti-American and political support for the provisional government evaporated (McFate, 2005).

POINT/COUNTERPOINT

Should Anthropologists Work with the Military?

Anthropologists have often worked with the military during wars and other conflicts. Their involvement has raised many ethical issues. As you look at the arguments on each side, consider whether you think anthropologists should never, sometimes, or always share their knowledge and skills with the military.

Yes	No
• If anthropologists don't work with the military, cultural sensitivity will be lacking in nontraditional wars where civilians on both sides are involved.	• Anthropologists will be seen as spies by field subjects and not trusted with information.
• The military will use bad or incomplete anthropological information, as in the case of the torture at Abu Ghraib prison.	• No control over how their research is used could lead to the oppression or annihilation of the people under study.
• Ruth Benedict's research led to appropriate terms of surrender being offered to the Japanese in the Second World War.	• The American Anthropological Association (AAA) has condemned secret research since it does not allow for informed consent.
• Mead's 1942 study of U.S. military culture can help us understand current attitudes.	• Franz Boas criticized those working with the military saying they "have prostituted science by using it as a cover for their activities as spies." (p. 27)
• In the Vietnam War, anthropologists commissioned by the United States government recommended nonmilitary approaches using existing factions within Vietnam as allies. This approach would have dramatically reduced casualties on both sides.	• Other anthropologists criticize the military as using knowledge as a weapon of war.
• By assisting governments to understand one another, anthropologists can help nations avoid diplomatic or military conflicts entirely.	• The AAA condemned the use of anthropological knowledge in torture and condemned the American involvement in Iraq in 2006.

QUESTIONS

1. Using an organizer, determine where you stand on this issue, including only the three best arguments for each side.
2. What advice would you give to an anthropologist asked to assist the Canadian military in Afghanistan?

Fieldwork in Contemporary Culture and Subcultures

Early anthropologists generally studied cultures different from their own and tried to understand their point of view. With increasing globalization and rapid cultural change around the world, anthropologists have shifted some of their focus to study contemporary urban cultures and subcultures using anthropological methods. Anthropological approaches can be revealing of our own beliefs and practices.

Baseball Magic

Bronislaw Malinowski had a hypothesis that people are more likely to believe in magical or supernatural forces when the outcome of events is important and more risky. The Trobrianders that he lived among in New Guinea would perform specific rituals before going out into shark-infested waters of the open ocean, but no such rituals were performed when fishing in the calm lagoon.

George Gmelch, a former professional baseball player turned anthropologist, went on the road with amateur and professional baseball teams in the 1990s. Hitting and pitching in baseball involve greater risk and less certainty of success than fielding. A batter will be successful fewer than 3 times in 10, while a fielder will be successful more than 9 times in 10. According to Gmelch's research, batters and pitchers have elaborate and specific rituals, **taboos**, and **fetishes** that they use, while fielders do not.

Rituals are not rational behaviours, and many are quite bizarre. A personal ritual that Gmelch observed was drinking iced tea and eating a tuna-fish sandwich before a game. As part of his elaborate pregame rituals, Wade Boggs had to eat chicken before every game and leave the house at precisely 1:47 p.m. for a 7:05 p.m. game. Some rituals were more commonly practised by players, such as tapping the plate three times before each hit, adjusting a ball cap, or sitting in the same spot on the bench.

Taboos are restrictions on behaviour that help ensure a good outcome. Some baseball taboos include not letting a pitcher touch your bat, because he might pollute it with his worse batting skills, and not watching movies in the 24 hours before a game.

Fetishes are specific objects that are believed to have magical powers. Some of the fetishes among pro baseball players are specific sweaters or shoes, which are always worn during a game, and a coin or unusual stone found before a hitting streak. Glenn Davis chewed the same piece of gum during winning streaks, saving it under his cap until the streak ended (Gmelch, 2006).

Gmelch demonstrated quite clearly how people in a society that prizes rationality and scientific explanations can very quickly become superstitious when it is important that they be successful at a task involving a high degree of chance. The subculture of professional baseball players can be understood in anthropological terms.

> In what other subcultures of Canadian society do you think Malinowski's hypothesis might apply? Can you think of rituals, taboos, and fetishes in your own life?

Before You Read
Is it easier to study an entirely different culture or your own?

taboo:
a restriction on behaviour to help ensure a good outcome

fetish:
a specific object believed to have magical powers

VOICES

Magic enables man to carry out with confidence his important tasks, to maintain his poise and his mental integrity in fits of anger, in the throes of hate, of unrequited love, of despair and anxiety. The function of magic is to ritualize man's optimism, to enhance his faith in the victory of hope over fear. Magic expresses the greater value for man of confidence over doubt, of steadfastness over vacillation, of optimism over pessimism.

Bronislaw Malinowski
Magic, Science and Religion

Cultural Diffusion: Japanese Hip-Hop Culture

As globalization continues to dissolve borders between countries and cultures, anthropologists are becoming more interested in looking at how cultures spread around the world. Generally, people do not adopt a culture entirely; rather, they adapt parts of it and fit these in with local conditions and sensibilities.

This adaptation of culture is illustrated by Ian Condry's work on the hip-hop subculture in Japan. Hip hop began as a North American genre of music but since the 1980s has spread to other countries, including Japan. Condry has been doing regular fieldwork in Japan since the mid-1990s in clubs, recording studios, and anywhere that Japanese hip-hop fans gather. There are several elements of North American hip-hop culture—fashion, DJs, rap music, graffiti, and break dancing—that are present at Japanese all-night dance clubs. There are, however, some unique features in Japanese hip-hop culture:

- Japanese hip-hop fans generally live at home with their parents.
- Both hip-hop fans and artists went through Japanese school and participate in Japanese daily life.
- Japanese hip-hop fans and artists speak only Japanese.

In some ways, Japanese hip-hop artists are imitating North American hip-hop style, such as the rapper pose with microphone against the mouth, finger under the nose, head bobbing and arm waving, and using English phrases. In other ways, these artists are creating a uniquely Japanese culture. Most of the lyrics are in Japanese, and some of the themes found in song lyrics reflect local culture, such as expressing or an imagined love with a girl on a train and retelling an ancient story of a double-suicide pact. Most themes, however, are about youth speaking for themselves.

The hip-hop revellers arrive on the last subway train of the night around 1:00 a.m. when the clubs open, and head home on the first morning trains, after the clubs close at 5:00 a.m, commuting in opposite direction to the many adults coming into the city to work (Condry, 2002).

FIGURE 4-45 Japan's popular hip-hop group Rhymester expressing Japanese culture hip-hop style. What elements of hip hop and Japanese culture are evident?

REFLECT AND RESPOND

1. Does adopting a North American music style make Japanese youth more American? Does playing Pokémon, singing *karaoke*, and reading *manga* make Canadians more Japanese? What do these actions mean for North American culture?

2. Arjun Appadurai, an anthropology professor and globalization expert, has stated that "our sense of self comes from who we imagine ourselves to be rather than where we are." How can this be said to be true of Japanese hip-hop artists and fans? Is this true for you? Give specific examples from your own experience to support your answer.

3. How can anthropological methods be applied in the context of subcultures and globalization? Are there subcultures in your community or school that could be studied in this way? What are some of the ethical concerns of doing this type of research?

Research Dilemmas

Research can often create a moral dilemma for anthropologists. Since morality varies from one culture to another, full participation in another culture will almost always involve some moral compromise. Anthropologists cannot keep themselves separate from their subjects. The only way to become integrated and accepted into a community is to become involved in it as much as possible. Anthropologists must consider some important questions: How much should I try to fit in? Should I intervene if there is something I can do to help?

> **Before You Read**
> Have you ever faced a situation at school or at work in which your morals or ethical values were challenged? How did you respond?

Personal Belief Dilemmas

As you saw in Section 4.2, Rebecca Popenoe had to decide whether she was willing to gain weight in order to fit in with the local culture. She did not have to do so in the end and was accepted to some degree, but the Arab desert women of Niger still considered her a bit of an oddity.

One of the main issues in ethnography is that, to gain the trust of informants, anthropologists must appear to be more sympathetic to the people being studied than they may be in reality. For example, Gary Fine did field research (1992) in a group called "Victims of Child Abuse Laws." These were adult child abusers who felt that they had been unfairly targeted by social workers and laws. As the parent of two young children, Fine felt personally less sympathetic than he led his subjects to believe in order to gain their trust so that they would tell him their point of view. He came to believe that some of them were unfairly accused, that others were in fact child abusers, and that the group had serious boundary issues. Fine's other fieldwork among amateur mushroom collectors and fantasy role-play gamers involved less revulsion, so he didn't need to pretend as much. Certainly all anthropologists are interested in their subject populations; they just may not be as interested as they pretend to be.

Ken Pryce studied West Indian (Caribbean) communities in Bristol, England, in the 1970s. He had to decide whether to become baptized in the community church. He was not a man of that faith and was not intending on becoming a long-term member of the church, but much of the community life of the group under study occurred in and revolved around the church. In the end, he decided to become baptized, and his informants became much more open and willing to talk about their lives with him. The baptism was essential to his becoming accepted in the community.

> ⓘ Should anthropologists ethically be allowed to participate in a culture that is contrary to their own values? Were Pryce's actions ethical?

Moral Dilemmas in Cultural Anthropology

An anthropologist may be in a situation to be able to save someone or a group of people from harm. Should he or she do so? Is it against the guidelines? Should an anthropologist ever interfere?

To some extent, it's impossible for an anthropologist not to interfere and the answer frequently depends on the specific fieldwork situation. In some situations, it may not be a good idea to either disclose the goals of your research or interfere if doing so would cause someone to be harmed. You would likely lose the trust of your informants. In other cases, interfering may prevent harm. For example, if you were studying youth culture among the Innu and you were aware that young people were sniffing glue, you should probably notify the local community leaders about the situation to try to help. In applied anthropology research, the explicit goal is to understand the culture and community to bring about a specific, positive change. Anthropologists are often faced with intensely personal and emotionally charged dilemmas, and they must make the best decision for their research and for their subjects.

Walking the Streets: Ethnography of Prostitution

Anthropologists are most likely to encounter ethical dilemmas when studying populations who, by definition, are engaging in illegal or questionable activities in the shadow economy. Anthropologists often study prostitutes, crack addicts, street children, and other marginalized populations in order to try to help them or to help understand them so that government and other organizations can provide appropriate help that meets their needs.

Anthropologist Claire Sterk walked the streets with prostitutes in New York and Atlanta in the 1990s and came to understand their lives from their perspective. She started out by hanging around, and once she talked to some of the prostitutes about her research, she started building trust by giving rides, providing child care, or buying groceries. Sometimes she would listen for hours to stories unrelated to her research in order to establish rapport and position herself as the learner. Many women were flattered that they had something to teach.

Sterk often found herself in ethically uncomfortable positions. She would hear stories of pimps or customers abusing women, customers forcing unwanted acts, and boyfriends who had unrealistic expectations of women providing money to support their drug habits. Once she was threatened by a crack-house owner and had to leave a scene before violence erupted. She was sometimes asked to hold drugs or money stolen from a customer. In these cases, she would usually re-explain her researcher role and often would just have to leave a particular scene.

Sterk would be subject to the same uncomfortable conditions as her subjects—freezing weather, no access to a washroom, no restaurant access, and harassment by customers and police. She had to be careful to express empathy, not opinions. She lost a lot of trust one day when she said she felt sorry for a woman who was in a particularly abusive situation. She was interpreted as being judgmental and implying that the woman was a failure, when, in fact, her intention was to express her concern. Sterk also had emotional reactions to situations that were at odds with her researcher role: she almost adopted one woman and her family, had an intense hatred for a crack-house owner, and was angry with a woman whose partner was HIV-positive and refused to use a condom. To deal with her own emotions, she had to take breaks from the scene to regain her researcher perspective.

> ❓ What are the dangers and risks in this kind of research? What are the benefits? Do the benefits outweigh the risks? Can anthropology provide insights that other types of research might not?

When Should an Anthropologist Intervene?

In 1996, Rachel Burr went to Vietnam as part her PhD in anthropology. Through fieldwork, Burr spent two years studying street children to understand local perceptions of childhood.

Before leaving for Vietnam, Burr spent a great deal of time thinking about her ethical responsibilities as an anthropologist. With her background as a social worker, she wondered about whether she could avoid intervening in a situation in which she could help (Burr, 2002). But becoming involved with the people she was studying could also violate ethical guidelines within anthropology.

Burr faced her greatest ethical dilemma doing participant observation in a reform school for boys aged 12 to 17 years old. The boys were injecting heroin, sharing needles, and giving themselves tattoos. In addition she suspected that some of the boys were having sex (Burr, 2002). Burr and her colleague from a local NGO noticed that many of the boys had lesions on their skin and were concerned about the possibility that some of the boys could have HIV. At the time of Burr's study, local beliefs about HIV were similar to North American ideas about HIV in the 1980s. People believed that the only people who were at risk of being infected were drug addicts and prostitutes. Burr and her colleague approached the police in charge of the reform school to have the boys tested (Burr, 2002). Since at the time people believed that children did not get AIDS, the police refused.

Burr was faced with a difficult decision: withdraw from the school in protest, challenging the authority of the police or continue with her fieldwork and ignore a potential serious health risk to the children at the centre. Weighing her options, Burr felt that the first option would do more harm. Withdrawing from the school would have embarrassed the police and left the school without any support services since no other NGOs were permitted to work there (Burr, 2002), nor would it have led to the boys being tested.

Ethical guidelines in anthropology have evolved over time. In the past, in the early development of the discipline, anthropologists focused on maintaining distance between themselves and the people they studied in order to be "objective." As anthropology evolved, researchers began to acknowledge that they could never truly be objective and began to practice reflexivity in their work. Part of the current discussion around ethics is a debate about the level of involvement an anthropologist can have. In her article, Burr argues that anthropologists should be more proactive and intervene in certain cases. A year after leaving Vietnam, Burr found out that 50 percent of the boys in the reform school tested positive for HIV (Burr, 2002). Reflecting on her own experience:

> Now that the true extent of the children's rate of infection is known, I wish more than anything that I could have somehow convinced the police that it was worth doing HIV tests. In the eyes of some anthropologists, such action would have meant I was crossing an unacceptable line between being an anthropologist and becoming a social activist. In retrospect I believe that the social activist route would have been preferable.

More to Know...
You learned about reflexivity in Chapter 1.

? Do you think Burr acted in an ethical way? Was her research valid? Explain. What would you have done in her situation?

FIGURE 4-46 What does the cartoon suggest about researchers and research ethics?

Connecting Anthropology to Psychology

Psychologists must follow the same ethical guidelines as anthropologists in housing and working with nonhuman primates. The Harlow experiments, discussed in Chapter 2, clearly demonstrated the negative effects of primate isolation. Because of the startling results of Harlow's research, nonhuman primates are almost never socially isolated in a lab setting any more.

Moral Dilemmas in Physical Anthropology

It is not only cultural anthropologists who have to deal with ethical dilemmas. Physical anthropologists, primatologists, and archaeologists are often faced with difficult questions to which there are no easy answers.

Primatology

Primatologists have to be concerned with treating nonhuman primates fairly, whether in the lab or in the field. A lot of the early research involving close relationships with non-human primates that was done by Jane Goodall, Biruté Galdikas, and Dian Fossey would not be allowed today. In the lab, researchers must provide animals with not only big enough living spaces, but enough appropriate stimulation and activities within those spaces. The most appropriate stimulation for primates is other primates. Like us, nonhuman primates are highly social animals that will exhibit signs of depression if isolated from others. If animals must be isolated for a time, usually due to illness, then researchers are ethically obligated to interact more with them to prevent further stress. However, since many diseases (including measles, tuberculosis, and herpes) can be transmitted between humans and other primates, researchers must be careful to protect themselves and the animals from disease.

In the field, primatologists need to be concerned about human, as well as nonhuman, behaviour. Primatologists must follow local laws and interact with local populations in a respectful and responsible manner. Long after the research is complete, local people will still be living with the nonhuman primates, and a field researcher has an ethical obligation to share knowledge and promote conservation of endangered species. Dian Fossey's murder is a stark reminder that local people, researchers, and nonhuman primates are interconnected, and that field researchers have ethical obligations that extend to all primates, human and nonhuman.

Many organizations advocate for human rights for all primates. They feel it is not enough to have ethical guidelines for the treatment of primates in the lab and field, but that apes deserve the same rights as humans. Instead of being property to be bought and sold, these primates need guardians who will ensure that they are free from torture, imprisonment, and unnecessary death. In 2008, Spain was the first country to extend primates a limited form of rights. In Germany and New Zealand, there are more strict limitations on the use of primates in experiments.

> Are ethical research guidelines enough to protect nonhuman primates, or should human rights be extended to them? Should primates be used in research at all? Is the knowledge gained worth the risks?

Human Variation

Human variation, like many areas of anthropology, has had a questionable ethical history. Early researchers spent years cataloguing "racial" differences in anatomy, brain size, physical strength, and other characteristics that were believed to make some races inferior or superior. The Nazis twisted these ideologies to suit their own racist purposes. They conducted hundreds of studies on "groups whose value cannot immediately be determined" (Schafft, 2007, p. 100). Anthropologist Gretchen Schafft's book argues that anthropologists were responsible for developing theories of race that influenced Nazi policies.

Recently, Schafft found a box of undisturbed anthropological documents (hair samples, fingerprints, drawings, questionnaires, pictures, and file cards of research subjects) at the Smithsonian archives. The documents had been seized from the Nazis by American soldiers at the end of the Second World War. She refused to let other researchers use the data to study the migration patterns of the time because the data had been collected through cruel means, for inhuman purposes, and was not very reliable. For example, Nazi researchers had made sweeping generalizations about Russians based on starving people in prisoner-of-war camps that could not reliably or ethically be used today (Schafft, 2007).

? Should anthropologists study race? What are the risks and benefits?

The American Anthropological Association (AAA) declared that physical race does not exist and that racial differences are the result of cultural and historical factors. Anthropologists who study human variation, however, study how populations are physically different in many ways, including what are typically considered racial differences. Forensic anthropologists can reconstruct what a person looked like and often determine ancestry from skeletal remains, suggesting that racial characteristics are real. However, characteristics associated with different races are based on environmental adaptations. Archaeologists studying human remains, especially in North America, rely on physical differences in tooth shape, skull shape, and other features to identify if the person was Aboriginal. If so, the remains must be returned for proper funerary rites. There are physical differences among individuals and commonalities in groups of any species, and race is culturally constructed in every society to some degree.

> **More to Know...**
> See further discussions of race in Chapter 1 and Chapter 7.

REFLECT AND RESPOND

1. Describe the personal belief dilemmas encountered by Popenoe among the Niger women, Fine among sex offenders, and Pryce in a West Indian church community. Do you think they did the right thing? Was the knowledge gained by their research worth compromising of values?

2. What risks are involved in researching illegal activities? Do you think the rewards are worth the risk? Explain your answer.

3. What moral dilemma did Burr encounter in Vietnam? Should anthropologists intervene more strongly on behalf of their subjects? What are the consequences of intervening and not intervening? Make a T-chart to show both sides of the argument.

4. Should human rights be extended to nonhuman primates? Why or why not?

5. Since archaeology deals with the past, does it face ethical questions to the same extent as other branches or anthropology?

6. Explain some of the historical events that have made studying human variation a controversial area in physical anthropology.

Applied Anthropology

Before You Read
Brainstorm examples where having first-hand experience of a situation has helped you understand a concept more clearly. How might this idea connect to anthropology?

Applied anthropology uses anthropological methods and knowledge to do research with the intent to improve people's lives and their environment. Rather than interfering with cultures or imposing solutions from outside, applied anthropology seeks to learn from people's experiences and improve their lives in specific ways. Applied anthropology studies are usually shorter than classic ethnology studies—weeks or months instead of years. This shorter time frame minimizes interference in communities, but also has been criticized for causing applied anthropology studies to lack the depth of a traditional study. The research in many ways is secondary to the community goals, which helps to avoid ethical dilemmas, such as when and how to intervene in a potentially harmful situation. Since intervening is part of the goal, the research is helping to ensure that the end result is culturally appropriate and desirable for all parties.

Medical Anthropology: Goats in Malawi

Anthropologist Sonia Patten was part of a project to improve child nutrition in Chewa communities in Malawi. Her team felt that adding goat milk to children's diets would provide additional calories and protein, and improve overall child health. Children in these villages were usually breastfed until two or three years old, but after weaning, their diet consisted only of maize gruel, a nutritionally inadequate porridge, leading to swollen bellies, slow growth, diseases, and sometimes death. The Chewa were also familiar with keeping goats for meat. Since the goats would be sold if money was needed, the Chewa often called the goats "walking bank accounts."

Patten's job was to understand the cultural differences in health beliefs and community structures to ensure that the project was successful. Other team members had expertise in biomedical and health aspects of the project, including child health and goat breeding.

Patten started with a survey and held village meetings to get information, permission, and support for the program. She did not go into communities that did not request the program or whose leaders were corrupt or otherwise difficult to work with. She gathered information about women's daily activities, the meaning and use of goats, the relations between men and women, and the way children were fed.

Patten discovered that women were the ones who fed the children, but men were the ones who typically owned property such as goats. The team decided that goats needed to be owned by the women for the project to work. The women were very positive about this, but the men were skeptical. They felt that social relations would be disturbed if valuable animals belonged to women. They were persuaded by the arguments that the goats would not be sold for money, that the women would have to do the extra work of caring for and milking the goats, and that the milk would be for the children, not the women. In the end, the men all recognized child nutrition as a serious problem in their community and wanted to fix it. In each of the communities, the headman agreed to resolve any disputes over ownership of the goats in favour of the women.

Since one of the women's concerns was with animal theft, they decided to bring the goats with them to the field, build pens, and bring them inside at night. Two local women were hired to collect data as the program was being implemented. This was important to help provide an insider's perspective on any issues during implementation.

The project team started distributing goats. Since most women wanted them, priority was given to women with seriously malnourished children under the age of five and grandmothers of AIDS orphans. Women had to return the first offspring of the goat to the project but could keep or sell all others. The female goats would produce additional milk, and the male goats could be sold for meat. The women also received a bucket, pan, and measuring cup and instructions on milking and caring for the goats.

There were weekly checkups to measure the children's height, weight, and arm circumference, to check on the health of the goats and children, and to provide assistance if needed. Many women objected to the researchers' measuring of a child's height, which seemed to them like a coffin fitting, so the researchers had to estimate height to be sensitive to this concern.

In 2004, two-thirds of the women still had the original animals; the other goats had died of disease or injury, but their offspring survived. Women were using the money from selling surplus goats to purchase fertilizer for maize crops, cooking oil, salt, and clothing. Some villages had set up community policing to help with the theft issue.

This project continues to have a profound effect on the whole community. It is helping not only to improve child health, but also to improve individuals and communities by giving them more control over their own resources. By having an anthropologist on the team, the project was able to be implemented in culturally appropriate and successful ways, and the team was able to solve problems in a timely and appropriate manner.

FIGURE 4-47 Women walking down a road in Malawi.

How does this case avoid or deal with some of the ethical issues common to ethnology? Can you think of potential ethical issues for this project? How has the social structure and balance of power between genders been affected?

Ecological Anthropology: The Domestication of Wood in Haiti

In the 1970s, Gerald Murray was doing ethnological fieldwork on Haitian farmers. At that time, the Haitian government was concerned about deforestation because peasants were cutting down forests to use for construction and charcoal, and none of the government's conservation programs were working. Murray found in his research that Haitian peasants who owned their own land and practised cash cropping felt that the government trees were taking away from their potential to earn cash because they had to plant them on their land. In 1980, he was asked to lead a reforestation project based on his research.

Murray decided to distribute fast-growing wood trees that would resist drought and provide harvests in four years. By growing trees for wood and charcoal, the peasants would be able to meet their own needs for these products without cutting down the remaining wild stands. He also decided on lightweight micro-seedlings, which were lighter and more compact, reducing the fuel costs and the human workload in planting. He also taught border planting and intercropping strategies, so that the trees would take minimal land away from their normal cash and food crops.

Murray also made sure that the farmers would want to plant and care for the trees in the long term. It was vital that the trees belonged to the peasants, not the state. Since Haitian farmers are fiercely independent and suspicious of the government, they needed assurance that the state would not come in and steal their land or their trees. They could harvest the trees whenever they wanted or needed to, but had to cut these trees, not the natural stands, to meet the project goal of conservation.

Between 1981 and 1985, Murray expected to be working with 2000 peasants and to plant 1 million trees. By 1985, 75 000 peasants were participating, and they had planted 20 million trees. In evaluating the program, he discovered that peasants were harvesting the wood more slowly than expected. They were banking some trees against crop failure or other unexpected expenses, adding the trees to their existing cash crops.

FIGURE 4-48 Haitian farmer

The anthropological approach not only provided an insider's view of the problem, which led to appropriate and sustainable solutions, but also the project provides an interesting analogy for one of anthropology's oldest questions: why did humans switch from foraging to agriculture?

The global tree crisis can be compared to the global food crisis in the Palaeolithic era, which led foragers to become farmers. The problem of not enough trees in Haiti was not solved by conservation, but by domestication. Peasants already cut and sold natural stands of wood, and they already planted and sold food crops. The move to planting and selling wood was a small evolutionary step and may have been similar for our foraging ancestors.

> How does this case avoid or deal with some of the ethical issues common to ethnology? Can you think of potential ethical issues of this project?

Applied Policy: Improving Immigrant Services in Saskatoon

The anthropological approach can be used to understand and improve institutional policies and practices right here in Canada. The Saskatoon Open Door Society commissioned anthropologist Alexander Ervin to investigate how successful its policies and programs were in helping immigrants settle in the Saskatoon area. The society especially wanted to know what immigrants thought of its programs and what needs were being unfulfilled. The organization felt that the government put too much emphasis on statistics, such as how quickly immigrants found jobs and got off social assistance. The Saskatoon Open Door Society felt that these statistics didn't tell the whole story and wanted to understand the immigrant experience in a more holistic way.

By speaking with immigrants over one year, Ervin was able to come to several conclusions about their issues and needs. Participants were concerned about getting jobs, but they were also looking for more meaningful and fulfilling jobs that would give them personal satisfaction and meet their goals of supporting their families and bringing loved ones to Canada. As a result of the research, the agency was able to get more resources to teach employment skills, establish a job-finding centre, and integrate technology use in the English-as-a-second-language training. Educational upgrading and recertification, however, remain areas of need for refugees and immigrants across Canada.

The second area of need was for immigrants to have a sense of well-being and good physical and mental health for themselves and their families, especially their children. Because of these findings, the agency was able to bring in community health workers to provide counselling and classes on a variety of health issues. The agency also now provides discussion groups on parenting and family adjustments to the new country.

While this type of research does not have the same focus as traditional ethnology, it can help to produce solutions to problems in many different types of communities by focusing on bridging the gap between the etic (outsider) and emic (insider) perspectives.

REFLECT AND RESPOND

1. Does applied anthropology have the same ethical issues as traditional approaches?
2. Create a chart examining the ethical elements of the studies about the goats, wood, and immigrants from pages 190–193 to show how these types of studies overcome, do not overcome, or may overcome some of the problems of traditional approaches.

CHAPTER 4 REVIEW

Knowledge and Understanding/Thinking

1. Explain the three-stage process of a rite of passage. Give an example of the three stages in a rite of passage discussed in this chapter or from your own experience.

2. Complete a chart outlining how certain factors (language, technology, gender roles, climate, kinship structures, marriage systems, and economic structures) influence behaviour and culture. Explain how anthropologists can better understand their own present culture by studying other cultures in other places and times. Refer to explicit and tacit cultural knowledge in your answer.

3. What are the ethical guidelines for conducting research in cultural anthropology? How much do you think an anthropologist's presence will affect peoples' behaviour? What should an anthropologist do to minimize this influence?

4. Describe the effects of diffusion, assimilation, and multiculturalism on culture, using an organizer.

Thinking/Communication

5. Anthropologists have found that cultural diffusion happens more quickly if an authority endorses a new cultural element, the timing of the element's introduction is appropriate, the element meets a perceived need, the element appeals to people's sense of prestige, and the element fits well with local customs. Use these criteria to explain the rapid adoption of:
   - steel axes among the Yir Yoront
   - goats in Malawi

6. Select a country, industry, or people, that has been affected by globalization. Has globalization been a positive or negative force? Create a T-chart to show both sides of the issue.

7. Are tattoos part of the identity moratorium for teenagers in Canada? Explain why or why not. How does this practice in Canada differ from that in traditional Polynesian societies?

8. You are a representative of a cultural agency, making a presentation to the government for funding. Explain how culture is an agent of socialization, with references to the concepts of diffusion, assimilation, and multiculturalism.

9. Does applied anthropology overcome some of the ethical issues of traditional ethnology? What advantages and disadvantages does applied anthropology have?

Communication/Application

10. Do Canadians believe in magic? Give examples of rituals, taboos, and fetishes commonly used in Canadian society.

11. Create a rite-of-passage ceremony that would be appropriate to your culture. Meet the purposes and follow the three stages.

12. Study the language of a subculture in your school or community. Are there particular language patterns, words, or euphemisms used? What trends do you notice?

13. Create a research plan to investigate an online community. Choose a particular cultural factor to investigate (e.g., technology, kinship, gender, language).
    a) Write a research question.
    b) Explain your method:
        - Will you access only public Web sites?
        - Will you conduct semi-structured interviews? Online or in person?
        - Will you develop open-ended interview questions?
        - How will you take notes?
        - How will you ensure your research is ethical according to the guidelines on page 179?

14. Rate the following secondary sources. How useful would they be in your research on youth gang subcultures in Canada? Use the criteria on page 135 to evaluate them.
    a) A Wikipedia entry on gangs with a warning stating that there are not enough citations
    b) A Web page from Simon Fraser University called "Youth Gangs" under the heading "Security and You," providing information to students about the dangers of youth gangs in British Columbia
    c) A book entitled *Young Thugs: Inside the Dangerous World of Canadian Street Gangs*, published in 2007
    d) A book entitled *Comparative Youth Culture: The Sociology of Youth Cultures and Youth Subcultures in Britain, America, and Canada*, published in 1985
    e) A Web site—The National Gang Centre—providing news updates on gang activity across the United States
    f) A journal article published in 2006 in the *Canadian Journal of Urban Research* entitled "Immigration, Social Disadvantage, and Urban Youth Gangs: Results of a Toronto-Area Survey"

CHAPTER 5

Psychology and Me

How are you a product of both your genes and your environment? The development of who you are as a person is influenced by a number of factors, including your DNA and how you are raised. While some behaviours are learned, others are innate. Behavioural change is not an easy thing to achieve, but there are some strategies that can help alter the way we behave. In this chapter, you will have a chance to examine yourself and reflect on some of the possible reasons for your behaviour, as well as factors that you can control. You will also learn about the various ways the development of your sense of self and your behaviour can be influenced. Finally, you'll examine ethical issues related to the study of psychology.

Chapter Expectations

By the end of this chapter, you will:
- explain how various influences contribute to an individual's psychological development
- understand how aspects of heredity and environment combine to create personality and account for differences in personality
- create a research plan and analyze research methods such as a questionnaire

Key Terms

attention deficit/hyperactivity disorder
attribution theory
cognitive dissonance
cyberpsychology
DNA
drive reduction theory
extrinsic motivation
extroversion
factor analysis
fundamental attribution error
gender identity
heredity
instinct theory
intelligence
intrinsic motivation
introversion
negativity bias
phobia
post-traumatic stress disorder
psychotic disorder

Landmark Case Studies

Genie: The Story of an Isolate Child
Philip Zimbardo: Stanford Prison Experiment

FIGURE 5-1 Our behaviour is influenced by both genes and the environment. How does each play a role in your life?

Key Theorists

Alfred Adler
Thomas J. Bouchard
Carlo DiClemente
Paul Ekman
Hans Eysenck
Victor Frankl
Howard Gardner
Fritz Heider
Abraham Maslow
Stanley Milgram
Walter Mischel
James O. Prochaska
Philip Zimbardo

Spotlight on Psychology

Obedience

> **Before You Read**
> Do you always do as you're told? What motivates you to obey an order?

Social psychologist Stanley Milgram knew that social pressure could influence a person's behaviour. He wanted to see to what extent people could be pressured to act against their beliefs because they were told to do so. In 1961, he conducted an experiment that ended up shocking its participants as well as everyone else.

The Experiment

Volunteers were recruited to Milgram's lab at Yale through newspaper ads and were told they were participating in an experiment to understand the effect of punishment on learning. The volunteers were told they were "teachers" and were given word pairs to teach and then test the "student's" memory of the second word in the pair. The student was in a room opposite that of the teacher, hooked up to an electric shock machine. If the student got an answer wrong, the teacher was instructed to provide a shock by flipping a switch.

A panel in front of the teacher showed that he or she could deliver shocks from 15 to 450 volts, and was labelled with terms such as *moderate shock* (120 volts) and *strong shock* (150 volts). The shocks started at 15 volts (slight shock) and increased in strength by 15 volts at a time. Each time a shock was administered, the student made a grunting noise.

By the time a moderate shock was delivered (the eighth time the switch was flipped), the student could be heard crying out in pain and the teacher was showing signs of stress, such as sweating and trembling. When teachers asked to stop the experiment, an authority figure in a white lab coat would make comments such as "It is absolutely essential that you continue."

One crucial fact about the experiment was hidden from the teachers: the students were really actors and were just acting as if they were receiving electric shocks!

Results

The experiment revealed that, despite wanting to stop much sooner, about 68 percent of people acting as teachers obeyed the authority figure's urging to continue the experiment to the end. They did so regardless of the fact that, before the experiment, they had been given a 45-volt shock so they knew what the shocks felt like.

Lesson Learned?

Researchers have done similar studies to see if they could replicate Milgram's results. In 2010, researchers in France made the experiment look like a TV game show. The "Game of Death," featured 80 contestants shocking another contestant (an actor) whenever the contestant got an answer wrong. Participants were told ahead of time there was no prize because the show was a pilot. They were, however, encouraged by the announcer (authority figure), the audience (group pressure), and dramatic music to continue until the other contestant stopped screaming in pain (either because he or she appeared dead or unconscious).

In the end, 16 of the participants stopped before the lethal dosage of voltage; however, 80 percent of the participants went to the end. The show's producers—and the French people—were shocked by these results. Sociologist Jean Claude Kaufmann suggests that these results illustrate that television has a powerful influence over people's willingness to obey.

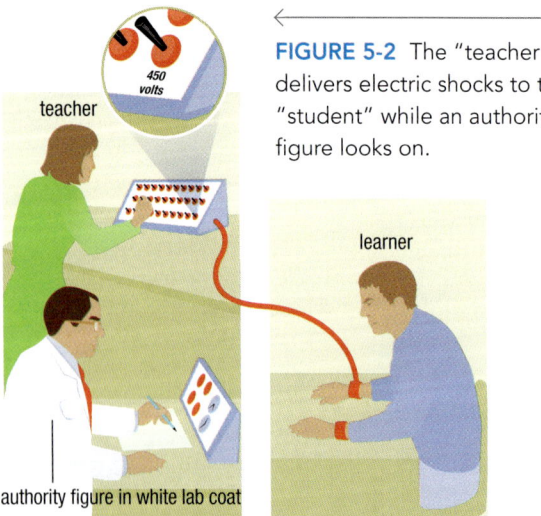

FIGURE 5-2 The "teacher" delivers electric shocks to the "student" while an authority figure looks on.

QUESTIONS

1. What is the significance of using shocks to punish the students for wrong answers?
2. What ethical issues might there be with Milgram's experiment and the "Game of Death"?
3. How are the conclusions of the Milgram experiment transferable to other aspects of society, such as the workplace?

Research and Inquiry Skills

Creating a Research Plan in Psychology

Conducting research in psychology includes common expectations and procedures. These processes are likely more similar to research you have done in Science than in History or Geography. It is important to follow the steps completely so that you get an understanding of how a psychologist conducts his or her research.

- **Introduction:** Outline the *purpose* of your research. What are you trying to accomplish? Create a *hypothesis* that describes what you think the outcome of your research will be.
- **Method:** Select the type of research that will be the most appropriate to answer your question. Research methods commonly used in psychology include questionnaires, interviews, case studies, and observation. Explain the *design* of your research methods, including who your *participants* will be. What are the dependent and independent variables? Explain your design by illustrating the *procedure* you will use so anyone else who wishes to re-create your experiment may do so.
- **Results:** Illustrate your results in a way that is meaningful to others, such as with a chart, graph, or other display.
- **Discussion:** Explain how you have interpreted your results, based on the purpose of your research. Also explain any problems or shortcomings that exist in the design, and make suggestions for improvements.

Developing Research Tools

To gather data, you may develop research tools, such as surveys, questionnaires, or even interview questions. Many questionnaires include basic information, such as age and sex to help classify information. Questionnaires may offer open-ended or close-ended questions. An open-ended question does not offer any choices. An example of an open-ended question is, "What is your favourite after-school activity?" A close-ended question would provide examples from which to choose, for example, "Which of the following after-school activities is your favourite: baseball, dance, art, gymnastics, or football?" You would then have to choose one of the options provided.

Activities

1. What would be the shortcomings of primary research on the impact of Internet use, if you:
   a) survey students only in your school?
   b) interview only Grade 11 students?
2. What factors can you use to decide which method of research is best? Go through the decision-making process and provide reasons for each of your decisions while working toward your finalized research data.
3. With a partner, determine something you'd like to study and follow the steps noted to the left. Create a survey or questionnaire to gather your data. If possible, conduct the research and outline your results. *Note:* At all stages of research, ethical guidelines must be followed. For example, you should not deceive anyone involved in the experiment, as Milgram did in his experiment. You must get *informed consent* from everyone involved in the study so that participants understand what will happen during the experiment.
4. What challenges might you face if you use only open or closed questions in your questionnaire? Create a T-chart to compare each type of question.

Analyzing and Interpreting Research Information

One job of social scientists is to analyze and interpret the research data that they have gathered. For survey data, you can create graphs to compare the data. For interviews or observations, you will have to sort the data into different categories. As you examine the research results, look for common themes or patterns. Did a majority of participants react a certain way? Is there a correlation—a relationship—between an aspect of the research and the behaviour of the participants? Are there inconsistencies or disagreements? If there are inconsistencies, you will probably have to do more research, perhaps by conducting more surveys or interviews, or changing your questions. In order for you to establish a correlation, there needs to be a direct connection between the variables.

Activities

1. What was the purpose of Stanley Milgram's experiment? Was that purpose achieved?
2. Look at the results of your research from your earlier experiment. Do you see a correlation in the data?

Section 5.1

Development of Self

How do we become who we are? Is our personality within us when we are born, or is it shaped by the influential people in our lives? These questions have provided social scientists with much to ponder.

Before You Read
Which seems to have more impact on your life, what you have inherited from your parents or the environment in which you live? Provide an example to support your thinking.

The Influence of Heredity and Environment

Researchers aim to understand to what extent **heredity** and environment play a part in shaping us. Is there a part of us that is always inherited and another part that is determined by our experiences?

Heredity

heredity:
physical characteristics and aspects of personality and behaviour that are passed down genetically from your relatives

DNA:
Deoxyribonucleic acid; the molecule that carries genetic information in all living systems and provides the most basic explanation of the laws of genetics

If both your mother and your father are left-handed, are you more likely to be left-handed as well? Left-handed parents are more likely to have left-handed children, and it has been shown that handedness runs in families. Heredity refers to physical characteristics and aspects of personality and behaviour that are part of your genetic structure; you inherit these attributes from your relatives (see Figure 5-3). However, when psychologists study heritability, they understand that they are dealing in statistics—that is, the extent to which a characteristic varies within the population, which can be attributed to genes—based on common environments. The Human Genome Project, coordinated by the U.S. Department of Energy and the National Institutes of Health, over a period of 13 years, identified all 3 billion **DNA** (deoxyribonucleic acid) subunits and determined that humans share 99.9 percent of the same nucleotide bases (the structural units of DNA). Despite this commonality in genetic makeup, psychologists do not believe that our personalities and behaviour are 100 percent dependent on our genes.

Environment

Many factors in your environment can have an influence on your development. Family, peers, and socio-economic status can all play a role in a child's development. For example, parents may encourage a child to read daily and model reading themselves, both of which can contribute to a child's love of reading early on in life. Similarly, if a child's peers all enjoy a particular TV character, the child is more likely to watch and enjoy that character on television.

The Edith Experiment

In the 1950s, Aaron Stern designed an experiment to prove that the right environment and strategies could create a genius. His daughter Edith, born in 1952, was the subject of this experiment. He played classical music to her and showed her flash cards from infancy. By the time she was 5, she was able to read the entire Encyclopedia Britannica, and, at the age of 18, she obtained a PhD.

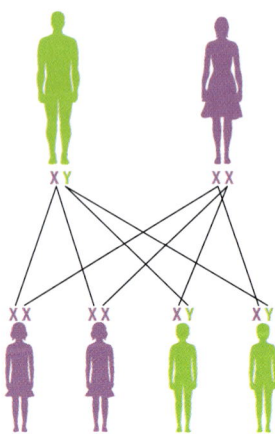

↑ **FIGURE 5-3** Although you do inherit some characteristics from your parents, you don't inherit them all.

? Does Aaron Stern's experiment with Edith prove that a genius can be made? What factors should we consider before coming to this conclusion?

Twin Studies

In the search for understanding what is inherited, psychologists have often turned to studying twins—two people who are born from the same pregnancy. There are two types of twins: identical, or monozygotic, twins and fraternal, or dizygotic, twins. Researchers study both types of twins to help them understand heredity. Initially, the theory was that any differences between twins would have to be explained by environmental factors. However, newer research suggests that there are other variables to consider. Specifically, females are more likely to display differences that are linked to genetics because they have two X chromosomes, while males have one X and one Y. In females, to avoid duplication, one of the X chromosomes is often dominant. So it's possible that the X chromosome dominant in one twin sister is not the same X chromosome dominant in the other twin sister, and thus the twins may have some genetic differences.

Twins Raised Apart

There have been numerous studies of twins to determine what aspects of personality are inherited. However, many twin studies are based on siblings who were raised together. In 1979, Thomas J. Bouchard began a long-term study of twins who were raised apart to try to determine just how much twins' similarities are based on genetics. He discovered astonishing similarities.

The "Jim Twins" were Bouchard's first twins in the study. Jim Lewis and Jim Springer were separated at 4 months and reunited at 39 years of age. Their similarities were eerie: they both had interests in carpentry and mechanical drawing, drove the same blue Chevrolet, had dogs named Toy, chain-smoked the same brand of cigarette, got headaches at the same time of day, had married and divorced a woman named Linda and remarried a woman named Betty, and vacationed at the same beach in Florida. Other psychologists have argued that these similarities, while fascinating, are not actually representations of genetic similarity. However, on personality tests, the Jim twins scored the same as someone who took the same test twice. Although most of the twins in the study were not as similar as the Jim twins, Bouchard has since studied hundreds of twins and concluded there is a genetic component to personality and behaviour.

FIGURE 5-4 Like the Jim Twins, Paula Bernstein and Elyse Schein are identical twins that were separated at birth and share a number of similarities.

The Limitations of Twin Studies

Even with the information learned from twin studies, psychologists can still discuss heredity and its link to behaviour only in terms of tendencies. Because behaviour involves multiple genes, it is even more difficult for researchers to determine which behaviours have genetic tendencies. Research has shown that some characteristics have a strong chance of being inherited. For example, your height and weight are more likely to be in line with that of your parents'. Some intellectual and emotional characteristics, such as shyness and extroversion, are likely to be passed on by parents to their children.

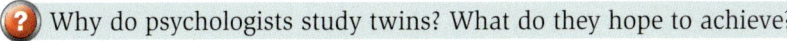
Why do psychologists study twins? What do they hope to achieve?

FIGURE 5-5 What assumptions does the cartoonist make about technology, age, and intelligence?

"I'm sorry, but I'm not allowed to sell you that smart phone without first verifying your IQ."

The Roots of Intelligence Testing

Is intelligence, like height, a trait that runs in families? English scientist Sir Francis Galton—Charles Darwin's cousin—was determined to find out. Galton believed that children inherit everything from their parents and that those born with desirable qualities such as high intelligence should mate with one another. This began the eugenics movement (from the Greek word "eugenes," which means "well-born"). By applying the ideas of Darwin, Galton believed that science could be used to increase the proportion of persons with better than average genetic abilities. He developed various measures for assessing mental abilities. Although his methods were not successful in determining intelligence, they were influential in the work of French psychologist Alfred Binet, who applied the idea that intelligence could be measured to create an intelligence test. Binet's intelligence test was revised by Lewis Terman of Stanford University and became known as the Stanford-Binet intelligence test, which is widely used today.

Defining IQ

intelligence: a person's ability to solve problems and reason effectively; a social construct used to explain why some people are better than others at cognitive tasks

The Stanford-Binet IQ test is a standardized test, which means that it is first given to a representative sample of people. The results of this group are then used as the basis of comparison for others taking the test.

The majority of people (68 percent) have an IQ between 85 and 115, with an average IQ being 100 (see Figure 5-6). Superior intelligence is noted for those achieving a score above 120. An IQ below 70 indicates developmental disability, a condition where a person has limited mental abilities, making it difficult to complete certain tasks.

More to Know...

To what extent are IQ tests fair and accurate? What effect does knowing one's IQ have on a person? Look ahead to Section 5.3 for more information.

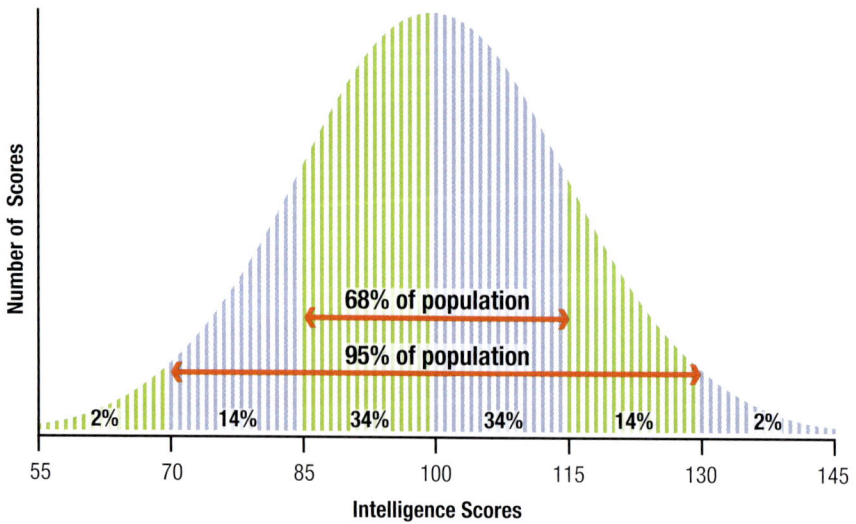

FIGURE 5-6 This is a bell curve that shows the historical definition of intelligence using the Stanford-Binet IQ test. Where do most people fall on the graph?

Studying Genetic Influences

Tests of intelligence like the Stanford-Binet, which measure verbal and mathematical aptitude, have been used to compare data in studies that are designed to assess intelligence. As discussed earlier, one way to study the hereditary aspect of intelligence is to study identical twins because of their genetic similarity. However, because most twins grow up in the same home, and therefore share the same environment, psychologists can't determine whether it is genetics or environment that has the greater influence on twins who have similar intelligence quotients (IQs), or scores on tests that measure intelligence. However, studies do show that even identical twins who were raised in different homes have a statistically significant similarity in their IQs. Interestingly, when IQs of adopted children are compared against those of both their adoptive and biological parents, their scores more closely resemble those of their biological parents.

> **?** What ethical concerns are raised by IQ tests when they are used to determine admission to certain programs? Is there any role for IQ tests in society?

Open for Debate

From 1980 to 1999, Robert K. Graham operated a sperm bank that housed specimens of university students and scientists, and advertised that its clients were more likely to produce intelligent babies. If it were possible to genetically engineer our babies to have specific traits such as high intelligence or athleticism, should we have the right to do so?

Environmental Influences on IQ

Factors such as nutrition, the type of schooling, and home life can influence IQ scores. Moreover, over the past few decades there has been a steady increase in IQ scores in the United States, a trend known as the *Flynn effect*. This increase is difficult to credit to genes because the gene pools have presumably not changed over the course of generations, so psychologists believe that environmental factors must be playing a role. However, theorists can only guess at what those specific factors are (see Figure 5-7). Finally, another look at twin studies shows that identical twins who grow up together have very similar IQ scores, more so than those who grow up apart. This suggests that environmental factors play a role in a person's intelligence.

However, there are issues with the Flynn effect. In some countries, the effect seems to have slowed or even stopped. What might account for this change?

Skills Focus

What is a possible hypothesis that you might want to investigate based on the Flynn effect? How could you test it?

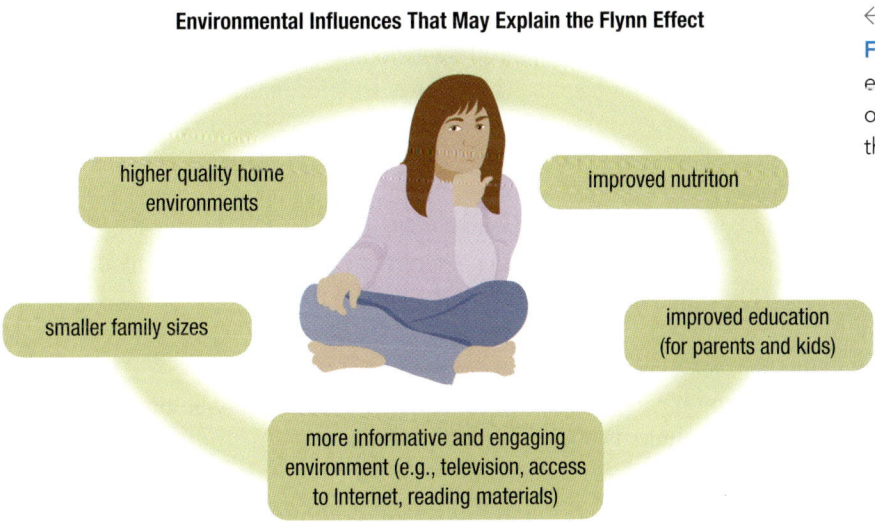

FIGURE 5-7 How does the Flynn effect influence a child? Which of these do you think has the most influence?

FIGURE 5-8 Children in a Romanian orphanage in the 1990s.

Romanian Orphans

One interesting study on the effect of environment is ongoing in Romania. The Romanian government used to house all orphans in large institutions (see Figure 5-8). For this study, developmental psychologists convinced the government to place randomly selected orphaned infants into the care of willing foster homes. So far, the results have been clear: "Despite adequate nutrition, children remaining in an institution throughout infancy and the preschool years had smaller head circumferences and less brain activity than the foster children. When intelligence was assessed, the institutionalized children had an average IQ of 64 (indicating mental retardation [sic]), whereas the foster children, on average, had IQs in the normal range" (McDevitt & Ormrod, 2007).

So environment does make a difference. But so do genes. The issue of nature versus nurture in the role of intelligence does not have a clear winner: both are important factors. What psychologists are still trying to determine is just how much influence each exerts.

> Is it fair to assume that since people in developing countries tend not to do as well on Western IQ tests that they have a poorer quality of life? Why or why not? What other factors need to be considered?

The Link Between Heredity and Environment

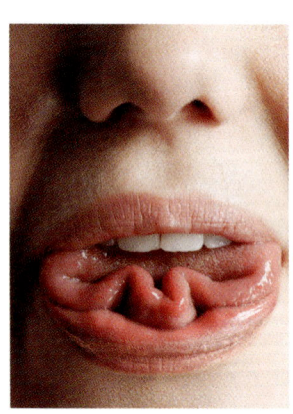

FIGURE 5-9 Physical abilities such as curling your tongue can be inherited.

Are you born with a desire to be on stage? Is your shyness a product of your environment? As you have seen in our exploration of heredity and environment, the answer to how our personalities are formed is extremely complex. Psychologists do not have an exact answer, but they do have some ideas.

The formation of who we are involves a complex combination of inherited and environmental factors. The debate about nature versus nurture is not exactly the way psychologists see their work. Rather, research shows that any psychological trait can be heritable; it's how each of us chooses to show these traits that accounts for differences in us all.

For example, researchers have discovered that genetics play a role in whether a person is likely to be religious, but the religion that person believes in is largely based on environmental factors. The same is true for many of our behaviours as well. Just because you're able to wiggle your ears or curl your tongue (see Figure 5-9) doesn't mean you're going to entertain your friends with this trick. Your choices influence how you use your inherited traits. So, while heredity may be the basis for who we are, our personal choices and environment account for how we express ourselves and who we become as individuals.

Sibling Differences

Do you ever feel as if your sibling is an alien from another planet? How can two people who have the same parents and share the same environment be so different? Psychologists have used twin and adoption studies to look at personality traits and have determined that genetic influences account for nearly 50 percent of differences in traits such as extroversion and emotional instability. Psychologists believe that the other 50 percent can be explained by differences in their unique experiences outside the home. Additionally, children are influenced by how they react to experiences with their parents. For example, if you're easygoing, you may view a scolding as a natural consequence to misbehaviour; however, if your sibling is a little more high-strung, he or she may not take the punishment so well.

Applying Our Understanding: Behavioural Genetics

As scientists learn more about our genetic code, behavioural geneticists are looking for a possible link between genes and psychological issues such as mental illness and developmental difficulties. They are finding that, to varying degrees, there is an interaction between heredity and environment (see Figure 5-10).

> **Skills Focus**
>
> What research method would be the most appropriate to test the impact of heredity and environment? Why?

> **More to Know...**
>
> To learn more about mental illness and treatments, look ahead to Section 5.2.

Psychological Issues Ranked from Most to Least Heritable

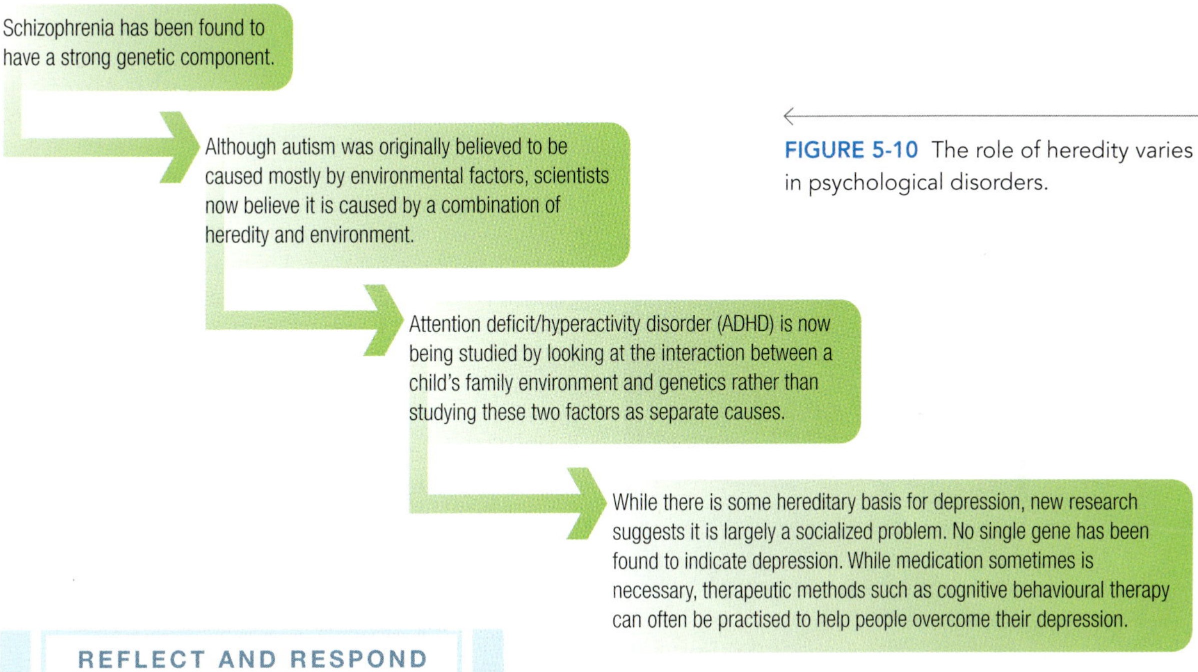

- Schizophrenia has been found to have a strong genetic component.
- Although autism was originally believed to be caused mostly by environmental factors, scientists now believe it is caused by a combination of heredity and environment.
- Attention deficit/hyperactivity disorder (ADHD) is now being studied by looking at the interaction between a child's family environment and genetics rather than studying these two factors as separate causes.
- While there is some hereditary basis for depression, new research suggests it is largely a socialized problem. No single gene has been found to indicate depression. While medication sometimes is necessary, therapeutic methods such as cognitive behavioural therapy can often be practised to help people overcome their depression.

FIGURE 5-10 The role of heredity varies in psychological disorders.

REFLECT AND RESPOND

1. Create a chart of the benefits and limitations of twin studies. What value do twin studies have to psychology? Include any ethical concerns that may arise with this type of research.
2. If there are genetic tendencies for behaviour, does that mean we will necessarily act in a certain way? In other words, do we have a choice about how we behave or is our behaviour predetermined?
3. Some have called the eugenics movement "scientific racism." Explain whether you agree or disagree with this description.
4. Brainstorm aspects in your environment that may have influenced the development of your personality. Use a graphic organizer, such as a web diagram, to help gather your ideas.

Landmark Case Study

Genie: The Story of an Isolate Child

The story of "Genie" is of particular importance to understanding the influence environment has on an individual's development. Genie is an example of a child who suffered acute social deprivation, otherwise known as an *isolate*. She grew up without any significant human contact and had minimal language acquisition.

Living in Isolation

In 1970, 13-year-old Genie was discovered in Los Angeles, California. For over 12 years she had been kept locked in a room, strapped to a potty chair. At night she would be moved and tied into a sleeping bag set into an oversized crib with a metal screen on top. As a result, she could not walk properly or chew solid food, was not toilet trained, and often spat and sniffed. While she understood some words, her own vocabulary was limited to two words—*stopit* and *nomore*—and experts later learned that she had been beaten if she made noise. She was also physically frail: at 4½ feet tall, she weighed just 59 pounds.

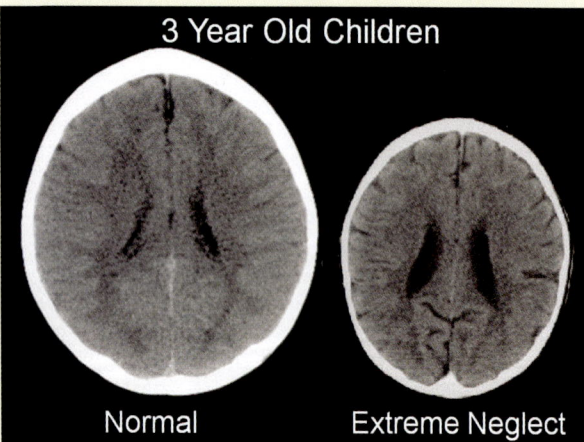

FIGURE 5-11 These images illustrate the impact of neglect on the developing brain. The CT scan on the left is from a healthy three-year-old child with an average head size (50th percentile). The image on the right is from a three-year-old child following total global neglect during early childhood. The brain is significantly smaller than average and has abnormal development of cortical, limbic, and midbrain structures.

A New Start

Apart from the terrible story of abuse, Genie was of interest to psychologists who were debating the nature of learning. The National Institute of Mental Health provided funding so that psychologists could study Genie. Given a nurturing environment, could Genie be taught to speak and live as others did?

At first, under the care of psychologist James Kent and teacher Jean Butler, among a team of others, Genie's language and motor skills improved. She was curious and wanted to learn the name for everything around her. Also, her nonverbal communication skills were brilliant. For example, when she was tested on her ability to see patterns and make sense out of chaos, she scored extremely high. A year later, therapist David Rigler took her on as a foster child; his wife Marilyn became Genie's new teacher.

Genie's brain was also studied. Scientists conducted tests that measured brain activity while she performed specific tasks. They discovered that she had almost no left-brain function. (Research suggests that left brain functions include controlling the right side, as well as language and logic.) In fact, her tests resembled those of children whose left brains had been removed!

Genie's learning improved only partially. At her best, she could say a few words that related to what she wanted to say, but she never could put these words into a proper sentence. Also, when she spoke, her words were difficult to understand and sounded like short, high-pitched squeaks.

Funding for the research was pulled in 1975, and the Riglers decided to discontinue their fostering. Genie was then shuffled between numerous foster homes, where she was poorly treated and eventually regressed back to her old mute ways.

Environment, it seems, is definitely an important aspect of learning and social development, but it is not the only piece of the puzzle.

QUESTIONS

1. Identify some of the ethical issues that relate to Genie's case management, and explain why they raise ethical concerns.
2. What tentative conclusions can be made about the importance of environment in human development?
3. What questions would you like to ask Genie if you could?

Personality

Do you know someone who makes his or her presence known wherever they are—be it at school, at a party, or at work? Most people would say that this person has a strong personality. Each of us has a distinct personality that shows our characteristic pattern of thinking, feeling, and acting. Your personality is what makes you, you! Read on to learn more about personality.

Categorizing Personality

As we have begun to study, the nature versus nurture debate plays a large role in psychologists' efforts to understand the development of personality. Throughout the twentieth century, psychologists have created various systems to measure and categorize personality. One such important researcher was Hans Eysenck, who began his research in the 1940s. He believed there were two dimensions for categorizing personality: a person's level of **extroversion** or **introversion**, and a person's level of neuroticism or stability (see Figure 5-12). He tested his theories on 700 patients at a military hospital. By studying a person's responses to a series of questions, Eysenck could predict the person's personality by plotting the intersection of the two dimensions.

> **Before You Read**
> Alexander (Sandy) Nininger was a quiet man who liked to sip tea, listen to classical music, and go to the theatre. When he entered the United States military, he became a fierce soldier and was awarded the Congressional Medal of Honour for his tremendous fighting in World War II. Could anyone have predicted this side of his personality before the war?

extroversion: directing one's interests outward, especially toward social contacts

introversion: directing one's interests inward

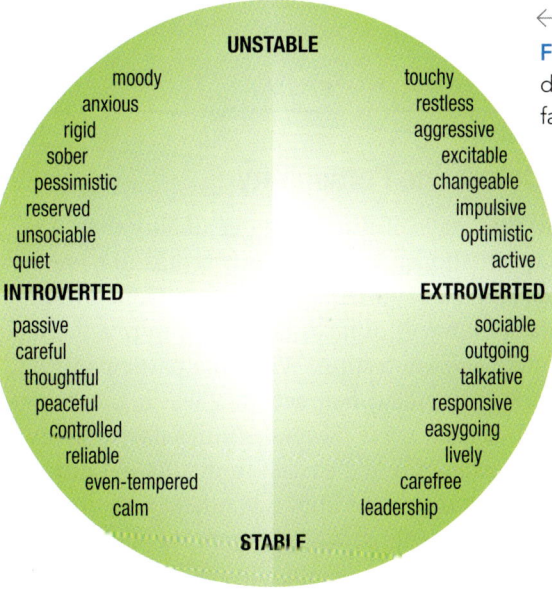

FIGURE 5-12 Examine the diagram, and see where you would fall using these criteria. What aspects of your personality do these dimensions not explain? What environmental factors might cause you to exhibit behaviours in one of the other categories?

Further research revealed that those dimensions rarely predicted how people react to situations. In a series of studies, Walter Mischel used personality scores to determine how people could be predicted to act in certain situations. In 1968, he published his research showing that only 9 percent of the differences between how people act in situations could be accounted for by their scores on tests of personality. What do you think might account for this difference between the description of a personality and behaviour?

> Eysenck's tests were conducted at a military hospital; what effect might this have had on his results?

> **VOICES**
> It's not who I am underneath, it's what I *do* that defines me.
> Batman, from the film *Batman Begins* (2005)

> **More to Know...**
> Recall Jung's system of describing personality in Chapter 2. His understanding was later used by Katharine Briggs and Isabel Myers to create a popular personality test, known as the Myers-Briggs Type Indicator.

Predicting Personality

Elements of personality are still under debate. Psychologists generally organize personality traits into the Big Five factors of personality (see chart below). While not perfect, the Big Five dimensions are psychologists' best attempt at grouping personality traits.

Predicting aspects of someone's personality is very complex. While there have been various methods created to predict personality, there is no definitive tool yet. Today, psychologists tend to use a statistical technique called **factor analysis**. In this strategy, subjects respond to a series of written questions that ask how they would react in hypothetical situations. The psychologist looks for patterns when analyzing the data. These patterns (or factors) then form the basis for predictions of how personality and behaviour are linked.

factor analysis: a statistical technique that identifies patterns of related test items (factors)

Connecting Psychology to Sociology

Sociologists look at behaviour differently. The theories of collective behaviour are often applied to violent or aggressive groups or events, but not all collective behaviour is negative. It can also be used to explain acts of kindness, generosity, and altruism. Psychologists tend to look at individual behaviour. What impact does this have when you are trying to make predictions about human behaviour in general?

THE BIG FIVE	
Trait Dimension	Description
openness	imaginative/independent vs. practical/conforming
conscientiousness	organized/careful vs. disorganized/careless
extroversion	outgoing/energetic vs. shy/reserved
agreeableness	friendly/helpful vs. cold/unkind
neuroticism	anxious/insecure vs. calm/secure

Using Facial Patterns to Determine Personality

Psychologists are also trying to find ways of predicting personality that could be applicable to everyday situations. A British study seems to have established a link between people's facial patterns and their personalities. Participants were shown composite images of faces and asked to rate them on the Big Five scale. The results were interesting. While the participants could predict personality with some accuracy, their accuracy was higher when evaluating female faces and with certain traits. Several studies have shown that extroversion and conscientiousness are the easiest to predict in both male and female faces. There remain questions about whether there are cross-cultural differences in facial expressions, which psychologists hope to learn more about through ongoing research.

❓ Reflect on your own personality based on what you have learned and include whether you agree or disagree and why.

Introversion

Everyone has felt the need for some alone time at various points in their lives. But is it unusual to feel that way all the time? About 1 in 5 people (20 percent) are introverted. Introverted individuals find it draining to be around people all the time and require time on their own as they find their energy from within. Do you have a friend who doesn't like talking on the phone? She or he may be an introvert, so don't take the lack of phone time as a sign that your friend doesn't care about you. In fact, many introverts tend to prefer communicating through email or online social networks. An introvert is also more likely to think before acting and to develop ideas privately. But we live in a society of extroverts who expect others to be as outgoing as they are. While an extrovert is seen as a *people person*, an introvert is often described as a *loner* by the extroverted. In a society that expects people to behave as extroverts, life can be challenging for more solitary introverts.

FIGURE 5-13 What feelings do you expect the lone person in the middle to be feeling? What reasons might there be for this situation?

Highly Sensitive People

It is estimated that about 15 to 20 percent of people can be classified as Highly Sensitive People (HSP), and of these HSP, 70 percent are introverted. An HSP needs minimal auditory stimuli (having the TV on as background noise is a no-no), and he or she can be extremely sensitive to other people's moods. An HSP is not likely to enjoy spending a long time at public events among a bunch of strangers, but a smaller social gathering with friends he or she knows well is paradise.

Overcoming Shyness

While introverts find other people draining, people who are shy are anxious or nervous around other people. Psychologist Jerome Kagan has been researching child development for over 40 years. His work with Nancy Snidman has shown that shyness in adults begins very early in life. When subjected to unfamiliar stimuli, infants who are highly reactive will cry and thrash their limbs; these infants tend to become shy adults. So shyness may have a biological root that begins very early in life. However, how these children behave later on can be influenced by how their parents respond to them. If the parents act in a protective manner, their child's shy tendencies are enhanced, whereas if the parents encourage their child to be more outgoing and sociable, the child's shy tendencies are not as strong later on. While there might be a biological root to shyness, it seems that environmental influences play a role in the ultimate outcome.

Perfectionism

Perfectionism, as an aspect of personality, can be both a positive and a negative. While it can help a person achieve excellence, it also has the potential to lead to some serious negative consequences (see Figure 5-14). Perfectionists are people who tend to set unrealistically high expectations of themselves and are then overly critical when they fail to meet those goals. They also believe that if something is not done perfectly, then it wasn't worth doing at all. In fact, they often view their mistakes as evidence that they are unworthy of love or rewards.

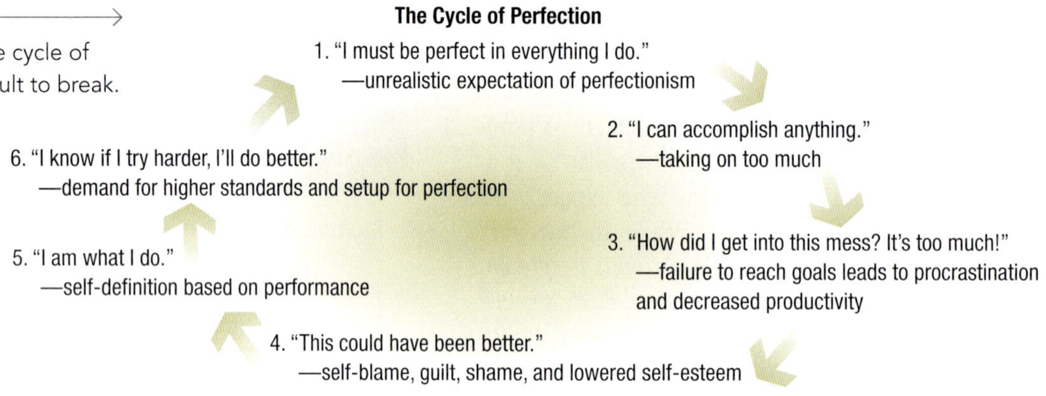

FIGURE 5-14 The cycle of perfection is difficult to break.

The Cycle of Perfection

1. "I must be perfect in everything I do."
   —unrealistic expectation of perfectionism
2. "I can accomplish anything."
   —taking on too much
3. "How did I get into this mess? It's too much!"
   —failure to reach goals leads to procrastination and decreased productivity
4. "This could have been better."
   —self-blame, guilt, shame, and lowered self-esteem
5. "I am what I do."
   —self-definition based on performance
6. "I know if I try harder, I'll do better."
   —demand for higher standards and setup for perfection

Perfectionism Versus Striving for Excellence

Setting high standards for yourself is healthy and does not mean you are a perfectionist. True perfectionists set standards that are unreachable and become depressed when they fail at a task. While many people see mistakes as opportunities for learning and growth, perfectionists see these as signs that they are unworthy. Perfectionists also tend to have an all-or-nothing mindset. For example, given a goal to read 100 books in a year, perfectionists would be disappointed if they read only 99, while most people would be pleased to have come so close to such a large target. Perfectionists don't enjoy the ride; they see only the final destination, and if they don't get there, they feel as though they've failed.

Procrastination

A perfectionist's attitudes can have some negative consequences, including depression, anxiety, and frustration. Perfectionists are also often procrastinators, as is evident in the cycle above, since procrastination is often a symptom of perfectionism. Procrastination—the decision not to act—is something that everyone does at some point. According to the Procrastination Research Group at Carleton University, chronic procrastination is often due to lack of confidence or fear of failure. It can also be a part of a cycle of stress and anxiety, in which people procrastinate because they are stressed and then become more stressed and anxious as they have less time to complete their tasks. The research also suggests that breaking down tasks into smaller manageable parts is the most effective way to avoid procrastination.

Perfectionism in Youth

Like other aspects of our personalities, perfectionism typically develops at an early age. Often it is related to significant events or responses from parents. For example, perfectionism can develop if a child's parents are perfectionists and are more critical than encouraging (e.g., by expressing disappointment when a report card full of A's includes one B+). Some researchers suggest that perfectionism could be caused by being first in the birth order (see page 212 for more). However, while there is some evidence to show that perfectionism may be affected by environmental influences in childhood, the exact roots of perfectionism are not completely understood and are still under study.

Serious consequences of perfectionism can also develop. For instance, children who are perfectionists are prone to depression. Studies show perfectionism could also be related to anxiety disorders in youth because of constant worry about being perfect or performing well (e.g., on a sports team or academically). There is also evidence that perfectionism can even lead to eating disorders, especially when the child suffers from low self-esteem.

Perfectionism in Young Athletes

Youth sports psychologists note that perfectionism is an issue among young athletes, often due to the fear of failure. Dr. John Dunn and his colleagues at the University of Alberta concluded that these athletes are prone to fits of anger and demand too much of themselves in response to the expectations of parents and coaches. When he studied young hockey players, he discovered that one way to improve anger issues was to lower the players' standards to more realistic, achievable goals. Dunn suggests that parents and coaches give praise whenever the child is working hard and giving his or her all; high-fives should not be reserved for meeting a particular goal.

Moderating Perfectionism

The good news is that perfectionist attitudes can be changed. Since perfectionism relates to a way of thinking, there are a few strategies that can help moderate perfectionism:

1. Remember that everyone fails at some point; it's normal to experience both success and failure.
2. Get rid of anxiety and anxious statements, such as "It's all my fault" and "If I make a mistake, my friends will hate me." When you have such thoughts, stop and challenge them.
3. Use hardships as opportunities to learn and change.
4. Take things one step at a time; don't think about how large a project is, just think about doing it bit by bit.

How might you help a friend who seems to be a perfectionist?

Wanting his picnic with Gwen to be perfect, Hal made sure they would not be bothered by ants.

FIGURE 5-15 What does this cartoon suggest about perfectionists?

Birth Order

> **Skills Focus**
>
> What conclusions can you make about environment and heredity? What questions do you have that require more research? Write your questions as research questions and underline the independent and dependent variables.

Another way to understand personality is to look at the order in which people were born into their family. The first psychologist to examine how birth order affects personality was Alfred Adler in the 1920s. Adler believed that the personality of a first-born child is not the same as that of a middle child. Psychologists such as Dr. Kevin Leman continue to study this phenomenon in an effort to not only understand behaviour, but also help people improve their parenting and marriages, and even select more appropriate careers.

Personality Attributes According to Birth Order

Dr. Leman's research was used to evaluate all of the literature on birth order, which was then presented as a combined set of birth order categories (see the chart below).

ATTRIBUTES BY BIRTH ORDER	First-born	Middle-born	Last-born	Only Children
Personality	• are responsible, reliable, and well-organized • are perfectionists and critical • tend to be high achievers and natural leaders	• are compromising and diplomatic and avoid conflict • are loyal and have many friends • often feel forgotten so they are mavericks and secretive	• are attention-seeking • are manipulative and charming • are precocious • love people and are engaging and affectionate • love surprises	• are comfortable with those older or younger than themselves • are thorough and self-motivated • are high achievers who can't bear failure
Careers	• tend to go into fields that require higher education (e.g., medicine, law, engineering)	• tend to like jobs that use their great mediating skills (e.g., law enforcement, nursing, firefighting)	• tend to like outdoor and artistic professions (e.g., journalism, art design, sales, athletics)	• tend to go into fields that require higher education (e.g., medicine, law, engineering)
Famous People	• Bill Clinton • Oprah Winfrey	• Charles Darwin • Donald Trump	• Jim Carrey • Ellen DeGeneres	• Leonardo da Vinci • Tiger Woods

The Limitations of Birth-Order Categories

While interesting to study, it is important to note that the categories noted in the above chart are highly variable and are influenced by a number of factors: the number of years between siblings' ages, how parents treat each child, gender, if a sibling looks or has abilities very different from the others, multiple births (e.g., twins, triplets), adoption, the death of a sibling, as well as class differences.

It is also wise not to place too much importance on the order in which you entered your family. While interesting to ponder, birth order alone does not determine personality. As we have seen throughout this chapter, a number of factors influence who you are as an individual and more research is needed.

> **REFLECT AND RESPOND**
>
> 1. Create a T-chart showing the pros and cons of being introverted.
> 2. Does the description of your place in the birth-order category accurately reflect your personality? Why might this be?

Sex and Gender Differences

As we have seen, a genetic female has two X chromosomes, while a genetic male has one X chromosome and one Y chromosome. This is what determines a person's sex. However, some people are born exhibiting sexual characteristics of both sexes, and are considered to be intersexed. It is important to note the difference between sex and gender. While a person's sex is genetically determined, a person's gender—the way they are viewed as male or female—can be influenced by both biological and social factors.

In 1992, John Gray's book *Men Are from Mars, Women Are from Venus* popularized the notion that each gender is unique by nature and therefore needs to learn about how the other thinks to live together in harmony. Yet, based on what we learned about personality earlier in this chapter, is it fair to assume that people's behaviour can be explained by their gender? What roles do biology and the environment play in these differences?

The Influence of Biology

Neuroscientists have been searching for explanations for sex differences in the brain. Is there a reason that men and women tend to estimate time, do mental mathematical calculations, and orient objects in their minds differently? Neuroscientists have noticed several differences in the brains of men and women. For example, they have discovered a region of the cortex that is larger in men than in women, and some areas of the frontal and temporal lobes that are larger in women than in men. The corpus callosum connecting the right and left brain hemispheres tends to be larger in women, but men seem to have more neurons in the cerebral cortex. Neuroscientists believe that these differences in the brain are evidence for a biological explanation for some of the differences between the personalities and behaviour of men and women.

Experiment: Gender Roles or Obedience?

How often do people behave the way they think they should? Conduct the following experiment to find out. Be sure to get permission before you conduct this experiment.

Select a well-used set of doors—perhaps the entrance to your school or a local mall. On one door post a sign marked "Men Only," and on the other door post a "Women Only" sign. Consider adding an image of a male or female to each door. Ensure the door closes so the sign can be read. A door that stays open will have the sign facing the incorrect way. Observe the doors from a place that will not be obvious. Decide on the length of time you will make your observations—perhaps over a lunch period or before school—and record your observations. How often do people go through the "correct" door?

More important, what does this experiment prove? Does it show how often people stick to their assigned or perceived gender roles, or does it demonstrate how obedient people are?

> **Before You Read**
> Brainstorm examples where you have been treated differently because of your sex (e.g., at home, work community, etc.) and suggest possible reasons for this treatment.

> **Connecting Psychology to Anthropology**
> Anthropologists make a distinction between sex and gender because human societies vary so much in how males and females perceive each other, how they define what it means to be a man or a woman, and what roles they view as appropriate for men and women. How is this different and similar to how psychologists look at gender?

> **Open for Debate**
> In one study, it was found that 50 percent of children aged 9 to 18 try new identities, such as the opposite gender, on the Internet. They try a new identity mostly to see how others will react, but they may do so also to compensate for introversion or to help form relationships. Why might people try on these new identities in the virtual world?

More to Know...
Look back to Chapter 2 to learn more about how the brain works and what the different parts of the brain help us do in our daily lives.

Neurosexism

Australian psychologist Cordelia Fine questions how much neuroscience can really contribute to our understanding of sex. Findings about brain differences in men and women can lead people to overlook just how much similarity exists between sexes, as evidenced by their behaviours. Fine is concerned about *neurosexism*—the idea that any perceived difference between the sexes is due to brain differences. We need to keep in mind that we still have so much to learn about how the brain (synapses) enables the mind (personality) and that using neuroscience to make assertions about sex differences is premature. She also worries that if we look to neuroscience too much, without remembering that social context, place, and historical period all influence behaviour, then we don't have to take responsibility for rectifying gender inequality.

Gender Identity

You know whether you're a boy or a girl. Your sex was genetically determined before you were born. But what may not be so clear-cut is your **gender identity**—your sense of being male or female. What is involved in the creation of a gender identity? How do you know that girls are expected to act one way and boys to act in another?

When you pass a baby in the street, how do you know if the baby is male or female? What clues about its appearance help you make this determination? If you were to stop and meet the baby, would you behave the same or differently toward a baby boy as you would toward a baby girl? What are the words you would use to describe the gender of each child? The answers to these questions are based on your perceptions of gender, which you have acquired over the course of your life.

gender identity: an individual's sense of being male or female

The Formation of Gender Identity

Besides your obvious physical traits, what makes you male or female? How do you know what is expected of you as a member of this gender? According to *social learning theory*, children's gender-specific behaviours are established by their observation and then imitation of the behaviours modelled by the people around them, usually their parents (see Figure 5-16). Adults then give positive or negative feedback for these behaviours, for example: "Michelle, you're such a good helper in the kitchen." "Boys don't play with dolls, Fawad."

Gender schema theory includes the basic tenets of social learning theory but suggests that children view themselves through a "gender lens" based on their cultural learning of what it means to be male and female. Children develop *schemas*—concepts—of how each gender should act and think through language, dress, toys, and social learning. They then compare themselves with their concept of gender and modify their behaviour to fit the schema as necessary. For example, a three-year-old boy's gender schema may lead him to change his caring, sweet behaviour because boys are supposed to be tough and strong. Interestingly, even in families where parents make an effort to avoid gender-specific stereotypes, children still tend to organize themselves into "boy worlds" and "girl worlds."

FIGURE 5-16 What does this photo indicate about this little girl's gender schema?

Gender Roles

When children imitate the gender-specific roles modelled for them, they are often imitating traditional gender roles set out by society. These expectations about the way men and women should behave vary across cultures and have certainly changed over time. Where it used to be the norm that a woman stayed home to raise her children while her husband went into the workplace, we now see many two-parent income earners and even fathers who stay home with the children while the mothers become the breadwinner of the family. There are also single-parent families in which one parent fulfills both roles simultaneously.

> **More to Know...**
> To learn more about gender roles in other societies and cultures, look at Chapter 6.

IN FOCUS — A Question of Circumstance?

In Afghanistan, a person's gender may sometimes be determined by his or her family's needs. In Afghan culture, it is important for a family to have at least one boy to inherit his father's wealth and pass the family name on to. He has many privileges that his sisters do not have, such as being allowed to play sports, have a part-time job outside of school, and go outside the home alone. Households that have only girls are pitied by their communities, and the failure to have sons is blamed on the mother.

For many families in this position, the solution is simple: one of the girls must become a boy. Mehran Rafaat was a girl until she was six years old, when her parents decided that she would dress as a boy. Her father took her to get her hair cut and to buy boys' clothing, and from that day on, everyone—from her friends at school to visitors to her family's home—treated her like a boy. Her family gained respect from the community, and Mehran could even escort her sisters to the market to help with the shopping, as often girls were not permitted outside without a male escort. Her parents will decide when it is time for her to be a girl again; in most cases, this occurs when the bacha posh (meaning "dressed as a boy") reaches puberty.

FIGURE 5-17 What differences are there between boys and girls? Why is this relevant?

QUESTIONS

1. How are gender roles part of your experience as a student today? What would happen if you challenged the expectations of your peers or others about gender?

REFLECT AND RESPOND

1. Create a mind map showing the various influences on gender identity.
2. What issues might an intersexed person face when forming his or her gender identity?
3. Explain how positive and negative reinforcement of behaviours can influence gender identity and gender roles.
4. Why might gender roles evolve over time? Suggest some other ways that these roles have changed and have not changed in the twenty-first century.
5. What changes in gender roles do you hope to see achieved in this century?

Section 5.2 Psychology and Behaviour

In Chapter 2, you learned about the basics of psychology and theories about human behaviour. So far, in this chapter, you have learned about some of the ways that your genetics and environment can influence who you become. In this section, you will explore the influences on human behaviour in more depth.

Psychological Influences on Behaviour

Behaviour is influenced by a variety of factors (see Figure 5-18). A person who is motivated by external rewards will complete a task for a different reason than someone who has a desire for achievement. A person's specific attitude about something can lead him or her to act in a particular manner once faced with the situation. The way we view the behaviour of others can also influence our behaviours. Finally, psychotic and neurotic disorders can influence the way a person acts.

Before You Read
What factors do you think influence the way you behave? Ask a classmate to make some educated guesses about your behaviour(s) and what influences them.

FIGURE 5-18
Your behaviour is influenced by a number of factors.

> REFLECT AND RESPOND

1. Examine the behaviour of someone close to you. Make a prediction of the factors that influence this behaviour.

How Does Motivation Affect Behaviour?

Have you ever watched an elite athlete and wondered why he or she put so much effort into the sport? What motivates your parents to get up each day and go to work? Although motivation is not something that can necessarily be seen, we often make inferences (conclusions) about the reasons behind a person's actions. When psychologists talk about motivation—the need or desire to do something—the focus is on how someone is motivated. Psychologists have offered various theories in an attempt to understand motivation, including looking at biological factors or genetics, cognitive reasoning, and achievement motivation.

Before You Read
Make a list of all the reasons you do each of the following activities: eat, do your homework, meet an athletic or academic goal, and get a part-time job. Are there patterns in your list?

Biological Explanations for Motivation

Review the list you made earlier. Did any of your reasons for motivation have to do with a biological necessity? Look again at the eating example. Some of the reasons we eat are because we are hungry and because we need food to nourish our bodies in order to survive. Did you come up with any other reasons?

Early Ideas

Biological explanations for motivation were made popular in the first half of the twentieth century by **instinct theory**. Instincts are involuntary and unlearned processes that direct behaviour. Animals know instinctively that when they feel thirsty, they need to drink. Babies are born with the instinct to root and suck. Psychologists such as William McDougall created lists of instincts that within a few years topped 10 000! Also, Sigmund Freud's ideas about the unconscious were influenced by this understanding of motivation. However, much like Freud's other theories, instinct theory failed to explain human motives; rather, lists like McDougall's simply named, rather than explained, human behaviours. Psychologists argue that while genes do predispose us to particular behaviours, we cannot ignore the role of psychological wants when exploring motivation.

Even though it is no longer used, instinct theory was the basis for other ideas such as **drive-reduction theory**. We each have biological drives, such as thirst and hunger. You may be hungry first thing in the morning, but if it's noon and you have still not eaten, your hunger drive will increase and you will be motivated to reduce it by getting some food. The problem with this theory is that it doesn't explain why our drives don't run our lives. Why, for example, does a hungry person wait until the table is set and everyone is seated to eat his or her food? Psychologists realized there was something more to motivation than instinct or drive.

Theories Based in the Brain

Philosophers suggest that we use reason to make everyday decisions. Author Jonah Lehrer argues that emotion is attached to our decisions, even when we don't know it's there, which means that rational thought is not always part of the equation. This suggests that it's our unconscious mind that rules our decision making. Lehrer demonstrates that if conscious reason were all we had, it would be impossible to make solid decisions in nanoseconds; instead we use "gut feelings" for some important decisions. Imagine deciding to eat a ham sandwich versus a turkey sub. You likely would make this decision very quickly based on a desire for ham.

Cognitive Explanations: Rewards and Punishments

When psychologists consider cognitive explanations for motivation, they look at both extrinsic and intrinsic forms of motivation. **Intrinsic motivation** comes from within you or for reasons you have internalized, such as wanting to do something meaningful or wanting to get better, while **extrinsic motivation** refers to doing a task due to external factors, such as rewards or the threat

FIGURE 5-19 Hayley Wickenheiser was the captain of Team Canada's Olympic gold-winning hockey team. What motivated her to achieve this success? What activity motivates you? Why?

instinct theory: the theory that involuntary and unlearned processes direct our behaviours

drive-reduction theory: the idea that our physiological needs create drives that need to be reduced, which motivates us to satisfy this need

intrinsic motivation: desire to perform a task for its own sake

extrinsic motivation: desire to perform a task due to external factors, such as a reward or the threat of punishment

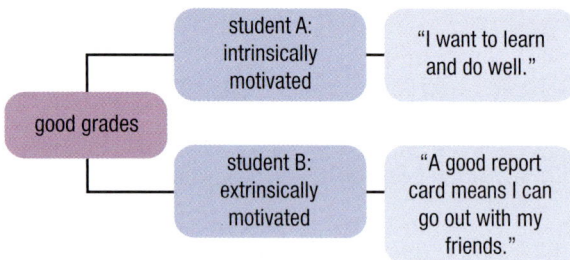

FIGURE 5-20 Which student do you think is likely to get the better grades, student A or student B?

of punishment (see Figure 5-20). For example, you probably don't enjoy cleaning your room, but knowing that a messy room might keep you from going out with your friends, you're more likely to tidy up. Recall what you learned about behaviourist psychology in Chapter 2 and how rewards and punishments are used to change behaviour.

Intrinsic Versus Extrinsic Motivators

Some researchers argue that intrinsic motivation is a better motivator than extrinsic motivation. For example, business innovators are discovering that traditional bonus plans based on performance (extrinsic) are not as effective at getting employees to improve their work as once thought. Google has implemented the 20 percent time plan, where its engineers are allowed one day per week (20 percent of company time) to work on their own projects. This type of intrinsic motivation has been highly successful and has kept employees excited about new projects.

In addition, some research suggests that rewards can backfire and actually reduce motivation. Psychologists Mark R. Lepper and David Greene studied motivation in three- and four-year-olds who liked to draw. Some of the children had been told they would be getting a reward after the activity, while others were given a reward as surprise. Over the next several days, those children who had expected a reward were the least motivated to draw again, while those who received a surprise reward were the most motivated to do so.

The Negativity Bias

When considering the use of extrinsic rewards, we need to keep in mind the **negativity bias**: bad news or events tend to have more impact than good ones. This concept explains why, in an average marriage, it takes five compliments to make up for one mean comment. Moreover, when people's minds wander, they tend to remember the negative events of the day. Therefore, motivation that uses the threat of punishment has the potential for negative consequences. If you're stuck at home because you didn't clean your room, you're probably not too happy with your parents, and you certainly won't find the intrinsic motivation to clean it the next time.

> What might B. F. Skinner think of the latest research about how rewards and punishments affect human behaviour?

Achievement Motivation

Each of us has a need to master certain skills and to achieve certain goals. You may be the video-game queen or the king of the basketball court; you might be an excellent speller or know three languages. Although you might receive some extrinsic motivation, these skills aren't motivated by biological needs; those who have high levels of achievement motivation simply have a desire to accomplish a goal at a high standard.

Open for Debate
Should students be paid to participate in their co-op placement? How would this impact the value of the experience?

negativity bias: the tendency to recall and react to unpleasant events more easily than positive ones

Among the first to discuss motivation was Alfred Adler, the psychiatrist who was also the first to study birth order. Adler believed that there is a universal drive in all humans called *striving for perfection*. He felt that this fundamental urge to achieve our potential motivates all of our actions.

This idea is echoed in Abraham Maslow's "self-actualization" stage, the pinnacle of his Hierarchy of Needs. In Chapter 2, you learned that the needs described at each level are actually motivations for behaviour. Once our basic needs are met, it is assumed that we are able to move up the hierarchy to more complex needs. Maslow understood these needs as motivations because they explain when and why people seek satisfaction for needs. While his hierarchy helps explain why some needs are more compelling than others, Maslow's theory does not explain all aspects of motivation. For example, hundreds of firefighters went into the burning buildings of the World Trade Center in New York City on September 11, 2001 to help those trapped inside. They gave up their need for safety—what need was satisfied in exchange?

> **More to Know...**
> To see a detailed description of Maslow's Hierarchy of Needs, see in Chapter 2.

Achieving Goals

Achieving goals is an important part of human nature and leads to success in and outside of school. There are short-term goals and long-term goals. Short-term goals are often stepping stones to achieving longer-term goals. For example, you may have a long-term goal of attending college or university. A short-term goal could be achieving the grades necessary in the prerequisite high-school courses. How has the education system helped or not helped you to set goals and achieve them? What role does motivation play in this scenario?

Psychologists like those at the University of Ottawa's Laboratory for Research on Achievement, Motivation, and the Regulation of Action are studying how personality and motivation interact to affect goal achievement. When they conclude their studies, they hope to be able to "generate evidence-based guidelines to promote achievement and well-being across time, situations, and contexts." So, if a rock climber wished to keep motivated enough to train for a climb of Mount Everest, the guidelines generated by this group would be able to help that person set and achieve the short-term goals to help achieve this long-term goal.

REFLECT AND RESPOND

1. Which explanation for motivation makes the most sense to you? Explain your reasons using examples. Compare your answers with others.
2. Using your understanding of motivation, suggest a way to motivate someone to change a behaviour such as eating healthier or to start something new like a food drive.
3. Using the idea of negativity bias, connect a personal experience to the theory. Suggest a way to overcome this experience. How might this influence your behaviour in the future?
4. Create a plan to make a change in your community. What can you do to motivate others to participate? How does this connect to the need to complete community hours to graduate in Ontario?

Before You Read

When you see a police officer in uniform or someone smoking, how do you feel? Have you always felt that way? Do you feel differently depending on the situation? What created your attitude?

cognitive dissonance: the theory that people are motivated to reduce the discomfort they feel when their behaviour doesn't match their attitude

How Does Attitude Affect Behaviour?

The way in which you perceive and react to a situation is influenced by a variety of things, including your attitude. Your beliefs and feelings guide your responses toward certain people and events; your attitude is reflected in your behaviour. For example, if you're a person who believes in fairness, you're unlikely to cut in line at the cafeteria. What contributes to our attitudes toward certain things and people?

How Are Attitudes Formed?

Attitude formation is an important concept in the study of social psychology. While there can be genetic links to attitude formation, a person's environment seems to be a key component. Yet the link between attitudes and behaviour is complex.

Psychologist Leon Festinger coined the term **cognitive dissonance**, which theorizes that we feel a level of discomfort when we realize that our behaviours don't match our attitudes. To relieve this discomfort, we usually change our attitude. Imagine that you have started to date someone who likes to go fishing—something that you have no interest in. When asked to help promote a school fishing trip, you agree to put up signs about how much fun it would be. According to the theory of cognitive dissonance, you are now more likely to believe that fishing is an enjoyable activity because your behaviour (putting up the posters) indicates that this is your belief, so in order to relieve your discomfort, you must adjust your attitude.

Types of Attitudes

Social psychologists often classify attitudes as positive and negative. However, it is possible for someone to be ambivalent, meaning they have both a positive and a negative attitude at the same time.

Implicit and Explicit Attitudes

When we think of attitudes, we often think of our *explicit* attitudes—those that are based on our conscious thoughts and beliefs. However, we can also have *implicit*, or unconscious, attitudes; these attitudes are expressed automatically and unconsciously. When expressing these attitudes, we are often unaware that we have them or that we are expressing them (see Figure 5-21). For example, there is a tendency for the heads of large corporations to be tall men. Leadership is often associated with strong physical presence, which includes a taller-than-average height. This attitude is not one that most of us explicitly hold, but unconsciously, this may lead a company to pass up a shorter, more qualified candidate for a taller, less-qualified one. Think back to the question at the start of this page. Do you hold implicit attitudes toward police officers?

FIGURE 5-21 What is your attitude toward each of these images? Do you know how you got that attitude?

Can Attitude Predict Behaviour?

Psychologists are still studying the relationship between attitude and behaviour. The problem is that there are times when we don't act the way we think, as you saw in the cognitive dissonance example. Also, there are various factors that influence our behaviour. Sometimes we behave differently because of the social situation we are in; a person who does not want to smoke might try it if he or she felt pressured by friends. However, researchers have discovered that while general attitudes don't predict behaviour, attitudes to specific situations do. For example, just because you care about the environment (general attitude) doesn't mean that you'll recycle. However, if you truly believe that recycling is important (specific attitude), you are more likely to toss your can into the blue bin.

The Marshmallow Experiment

In the 1960s, Walter Mischel conducted a series of experiments at Stanford University that have often been referred to as the "Marshmallow Experiment." He wanted to see if four- and five-year-olds could delay gratification for 15 minutes if they were promised a reward. Mischel explained to each preschooler that if he or she waited for a while without eating the marshmallow, that child would receive a second marshmallow. He then left the child alone in a room without much stimulus. He also interviewed these same children 18 years later. He discovered a statistical correlation between success later in life and the 30 percent of children who had delayed gratification (i.e., did not eat the marshmallow while he was gone). So, it seems your attitude can have a huge influence.

FIGURE 5-22 Can this little girl stop herself from eating the marshmallow?

Dr. David Walsh continued conducting the Marshmallow Experiment to develop theories about how to help people develop self-discipline. He believes that parents need to set limits and stick to them. This goes against the dominant message in North American culture that essentially says, "Go ahead, eat the marshmallow now!" This attitude makes it difficult for people to delay gratification. Where once you had to save your pennies to buy something you really wanted, now you need only show your credit card to get it now, and pay later. However, if you don't have the resources to pay the bill when it comes, you may be in trouble!

Skills Focus

What was the purpose of interviewing the children in the Marshmallow Experiment 18 years later?

(?) How do attitude and motivation interact to influence your behaviour?

Can Attitudes Be Changed?

Social psychologists have been studying attitude-change theories since the 1950s. By understanding how to effectively change attitudes we can open people's minds to new ideas and improve lives. Using experimental techniques, largely begun by Carl Hovland and his associates, many psychologists have tested four major categories of theories (see Figure 5-23).

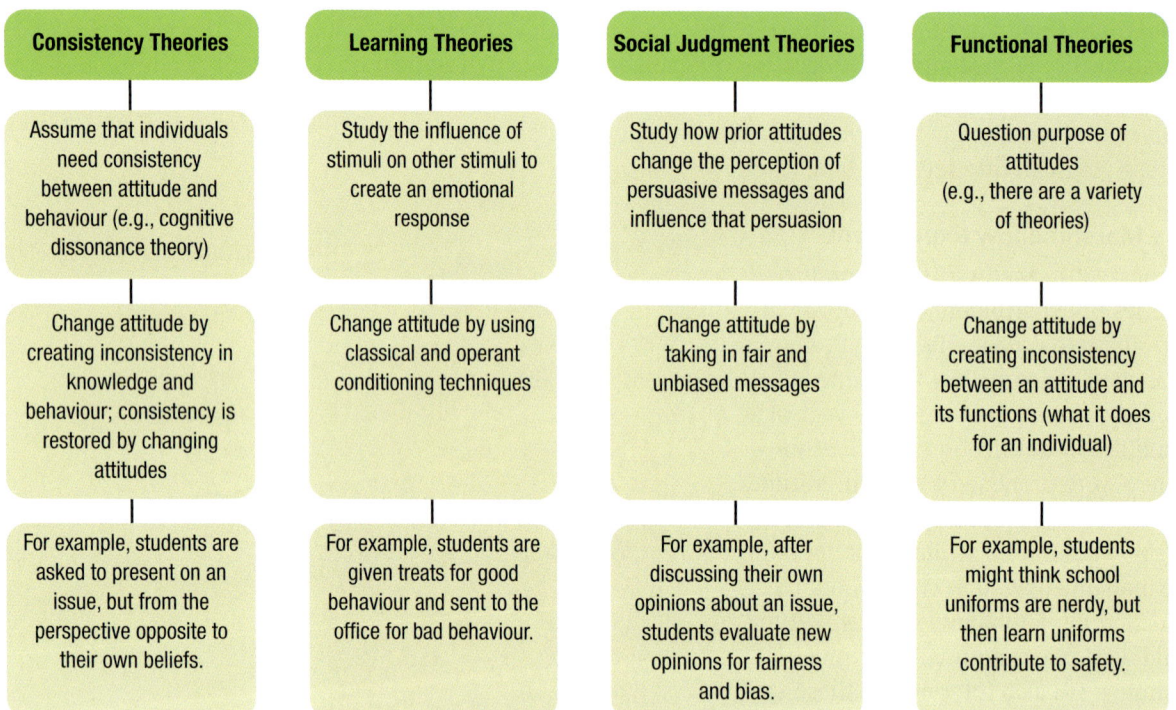

FIGURE 5-23 Attitudes can be changed in a variety of ways. Provide a personal example for one or more of these theories.

Using attitude-change theory effectively can yield great results. For example, judges of a particular orchestra once held the belief that women were not as talented at playing the cello as men were. As such, they didn't often hire a female cello player for their ensemble. However, when auditions were held with a screen in front of the judges, they were more likely to select a female cello player as the best candidate. Which of the four theories above was used to change this attitude?

Another example of an attempt to change attitudes is used in commercials. Foreign aid groups attempt to shock viewers through their imagery and words about the extreme poverty in developing countries. Instead of thinking this is someone else's problem, our attitudes are changed to make us feel that we should be the ones to take action. Which of the four theories above was used to change these attitudes?

> Which theory of attitude change do you think would most likely change your attitude? How can you test your hypothesis? Consider examples such as attitudes toward school administration, the police, and post-secondary plans.

The Psychology of Marketing: How It Can Change Our Minds

Marketing experts utilize research on how to change attitudes in order to sell their products. One company is using research literally—it is conducting social psychology experiments to change attitudes and behaviour in a positive way. In its "Fun Theory" experiments, Volkswagen got people to change their behaviour because it was fun to do so. For example, in one experiment it got a number of people to choose the stairs instead of the escalator by making the steps into piano keys that produced sounds as people stepped on them (see Figure 5-24).

FIGURE 5-24 When these stairs were converted into piano keys, 66 percent more people chose the steps over the escalator than had done so before.

Government Campaigns

Government campaigns in Canada have also changed our attitudes about garbage and recycling. Campaigns focused on how to recycle and why it was important. According to a 2007 Statistics Canada survey, 95 percent of Ontario households now have recycling facilities, up from 74 percent in 1994, and of those households 98 percent recycle some or all of their recyclable waste. Most people said they recycled because they felt a sense of social responsibility and they wanted to reduce the amount of waste going to landfills.

In addition, Canada was one of the first countries to pass a law against smoking in public places. The Canadian government then spent millions of dollars for its intensive Stop Smoking Canada campaign. Canada was ranked first in an international ranking of cigarette package health warnings after this campaign but dropped to 15th spot out of 18 countries in 2010. Part of the reason is that the packaging had not changed in a decade and the impact lessened. However, in 2011 the federal government introduced new packaging in an attempt to address this issue.

> **VOICES**
>
> The greatest discovery of our generation is that human beings can alter their lives by altering their attitudes of mind. As you think, so shall you be.
>
> William James, psychologist

REFLECT AND RESPOND

1. What is one attitude you would like to see changed in your school? How might you suggest changing it?
2. What challenges might you expect to meet if you were to try and make this change in attitude?
3. Suggest five questions for a survey or other research method that determines attitudes about recycling or any issue in your community and how those attitudes have changed over the past ten years.
4. Plan your own fun theory experiment to see if you can change behaviour in your school. Be sure to get the necessary approvals for this experiment before you begin.

SOCIAL SCIENCE IN POPULAR CULTURE

Behavioural Profiling

In the context of the law, behavioural analysis, also called *profiling*, is the art of using behavioural sciences to understand and catch criminals and terrorists, and has been used by the FBI since the 1970s. It is based on the assumption that a person's thoughts direct his or her behaviour, and that studying a crime from a psychological perspective can provide investigators with clues about the perpetrator's personality type. The popular TV show *Criminal Minds* features FBI agents in the Behavioural Analysis Unit (BAU) who catch serial killers among other criminals, by using behavioural profiling techniques. While on this show crimes are usually solved within hours of the agents' arrival, in reality, criminal profiling takes much longer.

To create a criminal profile, investigators can take one of three approaches. By profiling historic and political figures such as Adolf Hitler and Saddam Hussein, investigators hope to understand their behaviour and motivations. Investigators can also profile criminals'

FIGURE 5-25 The members of the BAU on the show *Criminal Minds* create psychological profiles of criminals, much like the real members of the BAU.

common characteristics by looking for patterns in the personalities, behaviours, and backgrounds of criminals who have committed similar crimes. They do this by looking at childhood experiences and examining the results of personality tests, such as the Minnesota Multiphasic Personality Inventory (MMPI). A third method of profiling involves looking at characteristics of the crime scene itself to gain clues about the criminal's standard operating procedures, such as a kidnapper's repeated use of a van to capture victims.

Criminal profiling has been successful in some cases, and less so in others. For example, Dr. James A. Brussel provided a very specific profile of the "Mad Bomber," a man who had been terrorizing New York for over 16 years in the 1940s and 50s. According to the profile, the Mad Bomber would be an unmarried Roman Catholic of Eastern European descent, living in Connecticut with parents of siblings. Dr. Brussel suggested that he would be dressed in a tightly buttoned, double-breasted suit

---

Before You Read

Have you ever gone to an event expecting certain behaviours or activities, but it turned out to be something quite different? Why was it different than you expected?

attribution theory: the belief that a person's behaviour is the result of his or her disposition or an external situation

fundamental attribution error: the tendency to overestimate the impact of personal disposition and underestimate the impact of social influences when analyzing the behaviours of others

Social Thinking

Ever wondered if that hug from a friend is more than just a friendly gesture? Or if your quiet classmate is really shy? It is not unusual to wonder why people act in certain ways. Psychologist Fritz Heider studied the ways people explain the behaviours of others and came up with **attribution theory**, which states that we link the behaviours of others to their disposition or to an external situation. Given this, your interpretation of a person's behaviour can be different than your friend's view.

How Do We Explain Behaviour?

Research has shown that we are more likely to attribute a person's behaviour to his or her internal disposition rather than to the situation. Arriving at a social gathering to see your usually quiet classmate being the life of the party would likely surprise you. But just because she is quiet in class does not mean that she is shy in all situations. This underestimate of social influences and overestimate of personal disposition is known as the **fundamental attribution error**.

Interestingly, when explaining our own behaviour, we do not make the fundamental attribution error; we understand that our own behaviour changes according to the situation we're in.

when caught. Sure enough, when George Metesky was arrested he not only fit the psychological profile, but also was wearing a suit as predicted!

In the case of the "Boston Strangler," the profile suggested that there were two killers, one of whom was a single man with a deep hatred for his mother that was directed at other women. The second killer in the team was profiled as a homosexual who knew his victims. Albert DeSalvo was arrested for the crimes after confessing and was later convicted. He worked alone, was married, and showed no signs of rage toward his mother. Interestingly, Dr. Brussel was a member of the profiling committee in this case; however, he disagreed that there were two killers committing the crimes.

The FBI

The Federal Bureau of Investigation (FBI) really does have a BAU—actually there are three units, each with a specific focus—as part of the National Center for Analysis of Violent Crime. Its mission is "to provide operational support for complex and time-sensitive cases and other matters through the application of investigative case experience, education, specialized training, and research." The BAU teams can provide services such as threat assessment, profiles of unknown offenders, crime analysis, and media strategies.

The FBI also has a Behavioral Sciences Unit (BSU) whose special agents and veteran police officers have advanced degrees in psychology, sociology, criminology, and conflict resolution. This unit educates domestic and international law enforcement officers, U.S. military and intelligence officers, and others about behavioural analysis and its applications.

Behavioural Profiling in Canada

The Royal Canadian Mounted Police (RCMP) has a Behavioural Sciences Branch based in Ottawa that consults with other RCMP branches and police organizations in criminal investigative analysis, geographic profiling, and truth verification. It also maintains the Violent Crime Linkage Analysis System (ViCLAS) and the National Sex Offender Registry. Specially trained investigators monitor the ViCLAS to analyze and interpret entries to look for patterns and linkages so they can help identify serial crimes and offenders.

QUESTIONS

1. How can knowledge of psychology help police in investigations? Are there any drawbacks to using psychology in this way?
2. What are the possible drawbacks of using a criminal profile?

Examining Stereotypes

Stereotypes—our preconceived beliefs about someone or a group of people—can provide us with shortcuts to information about people and our world. For example, you may have the stereotype that teachers are intelligent. John Bargh, a professor at Yale University, conducted several studies to test the theory that stereotypes can influence our behaviour, with surprising results.

In one study, participants were given word puzzles to unscramble containing words that related to the group they were unknowingly placed in; for instance, the designated "polite" group had such words as *behaved*, *courteous*, and *patiently*; the "rude" group had such words as *disturb*, *bother*, and *bold*; and the neutral group had neutral words. When the participants had completed the task, they had to find the experimenter, who was in conversation and kept them waiting 10 minutes. While only 18 percent of those in the polite group interrupted the conversation, 64 percent of the rude group interrupted, and 36 percent of the neutral group did so. Bargh showed that people could be unconsciously cued to have certain beliefs and behave toward others in accordance with those beliefs.

> **More to Know...**
> You'll learn more about the effects of stereotypes in Chapter 6.

FIGURE 5-26 Would you be surprised if this boy was the life of the party at your next social gathering? Why or why not?

Positive Attraction

How you see other people affects how you react to them. Think about how you act when someone enters the room smiling or grimacing. Do you react the same way to both expressions?

Finding Meaning

In one social psychology study called "Meaning as Magnetic Force," researchers found that people are attracted to those who have found meaning in their life. Participants who had a strong sense of meaning were thought to be more likeable, better potential friends, and more desirable conversation partners.

Viktor Frankl was the first psychologist to popularize this idea in 1946 when he said that the search for meaning is a basic human drive. It is an interesting extension that we seek to associate with those who have a strong sense of meaning. Think about examples in your own school. Who are the leaders of the student council or athletic teams? What attributes attract others to them? Is there any evidence that they have found meaning for themselves?

> **More to Know...**
> You learned about Viktor Frankl in Chapter 2.

The Truth Behind Our Facial Expressions

The way you see someone has the potential to affect how you behave around her or him. As you have learned, we tend to credit internal dispositions as the reasons behind people's behaviour. There are other clues, too. Facial expressions, for example, can involve tiny movements called *microexpressions*, each with its own significance. These microexpressions occur at 1/15 to 1/25 of a second and cannot be seen by the naked eye; they can be viewed only in a picture on video. Taken together, these facial expressions can act like a window into a person's thoughts and feelings. So being experts at reading facial expressions could immensely help police investigators, psychologists, and judges who evaluate the behaviours of others.

Psychologist Paul Ekman created the Facial Action Coding System (FACS) in the 1960s in an effort to understand and codify all human facial expressions (see Figure 5-27). Today, about 500 people in the world have received FACS training. This skill has reached the mainstream media in the form of the TV show *Lie to Me*, in which investigators use their understanding of facial expressions to see through people's lies.

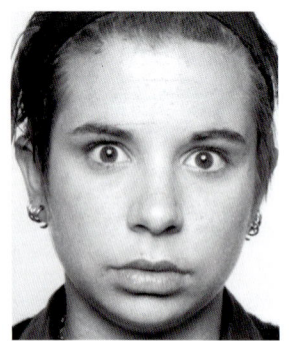

Fear
Upper eyelids raised

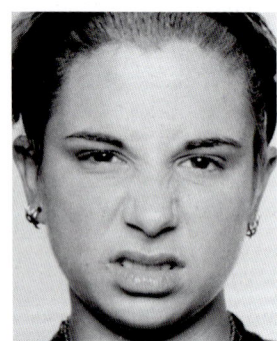

Disgust
Nose wrinkled

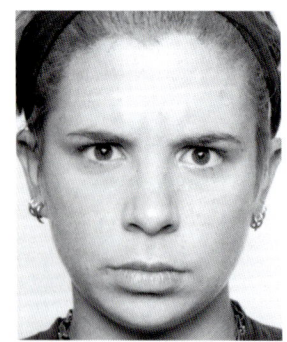

Anger
Jaw thrust forward

FIGURE 5-27 Each facial expression that was catalogued has a description of its distinguishing characteristics. This picture shows the same female with three different expressions. What subtle differences do you see?

> ❓ Why is it important to understand facial expressions? What benefits are there for people who have developed this skill? How can cultural differences affect the interpretations of expressions?

How Do We Change Our Behaviour?

Psychologists Carlo DiClemente and James O. Prochaska have identified five stages of change. Their model, the Transtheoretical Model of Change, is based on a study that involved 872 people who were trying to quit smoking. According to this model, change does not happen in one step and people must progress through each stage in order to successfully change their behaviour. The stages of change are precontemplation, contemplation, preparation, action, and maintenance (see Figure 5-28).

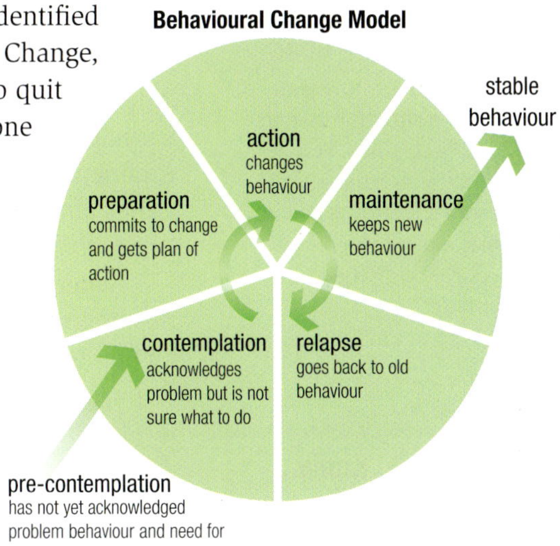

Let's look at an example of how this model works. Let's say you have an addiction to playing video games. At the precontemplation stage, you don't see your video-game playing as a problem and may get defensive if your parents tell you to quit.

As your grades start to suffer, you start to become more aware of the effect that playing video games is having on your life. You enter the contemplation stage and may weigh the pros and cons of stopping your game playing. You can be in this stage for quite some time before taking action.

Once you have decided to stop playing video games, you have entered the preparation stage. At this stage, you are likely taking small steps toward making the change, such as talking about it to your friends and family.

When you believe you have the ability to change your behaviour and take active steps toward making the change, you have reached the action stage. You may use a variety of methods to help you sustain your motivation to avoid video games and seek support from others to help you along.

To achieve the fifth stage, maintenance, you need to successfully avoid temptations to return to your bad habit. It's important to remind yourself why you stopped playing video games in order to avoid a relapse. Preparing coping strategies to deal with situations where you might want to play video games is an important part of this stage.

If you continue maintenance long enough, you will reach another stage—transcendence. If you reach this stage, you'll find it hard to imagine how important video games once were to you. You will have transcended your old bad habits to become a new you.

FIGURE 5-28 Changing behaviour is a complex process that tends to follow a series of steps.

Skills Focus

Suggest a possible hypothesis and research method to change behaviour.

REFLECT AND RESPOND

1. Select one of the studies in this section and connect it to your personal life. Do the study's conclusions seem consistent with your own experiences?

2. Working with a partner, observe the facial expressions of other students and try to determine what they are feeling. If possible, look at people from a culture different from your own. What evidence do you have about their feelings? If possible, try to verify your interpretations. How can this information help you understand these people's behaviour?

How Does Mental Health Affect Behaviour?

Before You Read
Think about how you handle situations when you feel happy. How might you handle the same situation when you feel upset? Why does your mood affect how you act?

Mental health is as important as physical health to one's well-being. Psychologists study what is normal, as well as what causes anxiety. Mental illness affects people of all ages and cultures, and does not discriminate based on educational or income levels. About 20 percent of Canadians will experience mental illness. Psychology tries to understand these mental health issues and find therapies and approaches to resolve any problems that arise. You will study different types of disorders as an introduction to mental health.

Generally, psychologists categorize mental health issues into two categories: neurotic disorders and psychotic disorders. As you learned in Chapter 2, a neurotic disorder is an emotional disorder that can have physical, mental, or physiological symptoms. A person with a neurotic disorder is still able to think rationally and function socially.

More to Know...
To learn more about mental health, review a copy of the *Diagnostic and Statistical Manual of Mental Disorders*, Fourth Edition (DSM-IV).

Psychotic Disorders

Psychotic disorders can be devastating. This term indicates severe mental disorder characterized by a break from reality. It can involve hallucinations and/or delusions, and it impairs the sufferer's ability to cope socially, academically, or in daily living. Schizophrenia, a disorder of delusional thinking, disturbed perceptions, and inappropriate emotions and actions, is an example of a mental illness that falls into this category.

While each mental illness has different roots and causes, researchers are still trying to discover exactly what causes mental illness so they might find cures. They have, however, discovered one disturbing trend: those who live in urban areas are statistically more likely to have a psychosis. They believe that poverty and poor social cohesion are contributing factors. These issues cause stress, and stress aggravates existing mental health issues.

psychotic disorder: a broad term that indicates severe mental disorder characterized by a break from reality

Neurotic Disorders

Phobias fall in the category of neurotic disorders because, while encountering the sources of your fears might be terrifying, they do not greatly interfere with your life. A phobia can cause some physiological reactions, such as increased heart rate or sweaty palms, and fear. There are various types of phobias. For example, some people have a fear of spiders while others are afraid of heights or enclosed spaces.

phobia: anxiety about a specific object, activity, or situation

Psychologists view the causes of neurotic disorders as either learned or biologically based. For example, you may not have a fear of planes, but if the thought of dying in a plane crash enters your mind, you may become anxious. Eventually, every time you think of planes, you may come to experience fear and anxiety. Biological reasons for phobias can be attributed to genes or even evolution. A certain degree of fear of everyday objects such as snakes and insects was required for our ancestors to survive.

Treatment for neurotic disorders depends on the symptoms presented and the problems that are caused by those symptoms. Common treatments include psychotherapy and cognitive behavioural therapy, as well as psychoactive drugs. Music therapy and relaxation exercises are newer treatments.

↑ **FIGURE 5-29** Some people have phobias of thunder and lightning and become anxious during a thunderstorm.

Post-traumatic Stress Disorder

Post-traumatic stress disorder (PTSD) is a type of anxiety disorder whereby a person relives a traumatic event through recurrent memories, including flashbacks and nightmares. PTSD commonly leads to insomnia and depression, and can result in increased aggression. It often occurs with other problems such as alcohol abuse. For example, 60 to 80 percent of Vietnam veterans who sought help for PTSD also had alcohol abuse issues. When people are dealing with alcohol abuse in addition to PTSD, treatment can be more complex.

PTSD was initially known as *shell shock* when it was first discovered as soldiers returned from World War I. However, PTSD as a diagnosis did not occur until veterans from the Vietnam War successfully argued that a description be included in the American Psychiatric Association's *Diagnostic and Statistical Manual of Mental Disorders* (DSM). While PTSD is commonly associated with veterans because of the violent events they suffer, it can be experienced by anyone, adult or child, who undergoes a traumatic event.

post-traumatic stress disorder (PTSD): a type of anxiety disorder characterized by the reliving of a traumatic event through flashbacks and nightmares

Treatment for PTSD

Although the prevalence of PTSD among soldiers may not be as widespread as was once thought, PTSD is still a very real disorder faced by both war veterans and those who have experienced other types of trauma.

While there are various therapies available to help those with PTSD, there are few that are very effective. Among the most successful ways to treat PTSD is cognitive behavioural therapy and the use of medication. Group therapy can also help those with mild or moderate symptoms. A PTSD therapy commonly used by the military is exposure therapy. In this therapy, a person is asked to imagine the traumatic event in as much detail as possible and then verbally describe the image or memory. This procedure is repeated until the stress has been reduced.

However, more research is needed to understand the best treatment immediately following a traumatic event, such as a hurricane or rape. One such approach is critical incident stress debriefing, in which people are encouraged to talk about their feelings immediately after a traumatic event. However, this approach has been shown to actually increase the rates of PTSD, perhaps because people are not given the opportunity to naturally process all of the emotions experienced. Another approach, psychological first aid, involves talking about the impact the event has had and how to cope with feelings and reactions, in order to encourage natural coping and resilience skills. Although still being researched, this method is looking more promising.

Virtual Therapy

One new therapy being tested with American veterans of Iraq and Afghanistan is Virtual Iraq. In this form of exposure therapy, veterans enter a 3-D virtual-reality simulation of urban combat, wearing a headset to see and hear, and may ride or drive in a simulated convoy (see Figure 5-30). This simulation provides hands-on experience similar to what the veterans experienced in combat. The hope is that this virtual experience will help them to work through their combat trauma by making an emotional connection to the memory, so that they can gradually face the traumatic experiences that underlie their distressing

FIGURE 5-30 Clinical psychologists are testing the Virtual Iraq simulator to help veterans struggling with PTSD.

> **Skills Focus**
>
> How could you evaluate the results of the virtual Iraq method of therapy? What are the limitations of such therapy outside military situations?

attention deficit/ hyperactivity disorder (ADHD): a type of developmental disorder characterized by inattention, impulsiveness, and overactivity

memories. As well as using the simulator, they work with a psychiatrist to discuss what happened to cause the trauma and participate in a support group to complete their therapy. Eventually, this form of therapy might be applied to others with PTSD to help them work through their traumatic events.

Attention Deficit/Hyperactivity Disorder (ADHD)

Attention deficit/hyperactivity disorder (ADHD) is a problem based in the brain, but shows up in how a person acts. The main components are inattention, impulsiveness, and overactivity and usually begin by the age of 7.

ADHD is more common in boys than girls by a ratio of 2:1. Symptoms can include any of the following: procrastination, impulsiveness, accident proneness, boredom, nervous energy, difficulty sleeping, and an inability to finish projects. It is important to keep in mind that anyone can experience these symptoms sometimes and this does not mean they have ADHD. ADHD is usually diagnosed by a psychologist or psychiatrist, although there is no single test for ADHD.

Research suggests that key cognitive or thinking skills are slower to develop in many children with ADHD. These skills are key to managing and regulating behaviour and play an important role in performing many tasks necessary for academic success. The tasks that can be affected include organizing materials, getting started on and finishing schoolwork, remembering homework, memorizing facts, writing essays or reports, completing long-term projects, being on time, controlling emotions, and planning for the future. Positive traits are also associated with ADHD, including creativity, linking various ideas together, and looking at the big picture without getting bogged down.

Causes

Studies have shown a possible correlation between mothers who consume alcohol and smoke during pregnancy and children with ADHD. There is limited research to suggest an accident or use of food additives and sugar as causes. Attention disorders often run in families so there are likely genetic influences, as well as environmental ones.

Treatment

Typically, medication has been used to treat the symptoms of ADHD and many children have shown improvement. However, some are worried about the potential for abuse of these drugs. Another form of treatment involves behavioural interventions such as the use of positive and negative reinforcement, setting behavioural goals, and parental training programs for how to positively respond to their child's behaviour. Studies are ongoing to determine whether drug, behavioural, or a combination of treatments is most effective.

> **REFLECT AND RESPOND**
>
> 1. In what other areas could virtual therapy benefit the recovery process?
> 2. How does an understanding of mental illness help governments take action for our Canadian military?

POINT/COUNTERPOINT

Addiction

According to the American Psychological Association, addiction is a condition where a person must use a substance to avoid psychological and physical withdrawal symptoms. Addicts are not only dependent on a substance, but also build a tolerance to the substance so they need increasing amounts of it to satisfy their addiction.

A 2002 study by Statistics Canada found that 2.6 percent of Canadians were addicted to alcohol, while fewer than 1 percent were addicted to illegal drugs (Statistics Canada, 2003). Addiction also affects about 23.2 million Americans. The prevalence of heavy, frequent drinking among youth 15 to 24 years of age was 3 times higher than for adults 25 years and older (11.7 percent versus 3.9 percent) in 2009. This tendency among youth is of concern since it could lead to addiction.

Treatment usually requires that a patient enter a rehabilitation program that combines withdrawal from the addictive substance and therapy. Yet, whats exactly is addiction? Is addiction an uncontrollable disease or a choice that people make? Psychologists Shepard Siegel and Robert V. McDonald argue that addiction is a disease, while psychologist Gene Heyman maintains that it is a choice. (See chart below).

Is Addiction a Disease or a Choice?

Addiction Is a Disease	Addiction Is a Choice
• Addiction is a disease that begins voluntarily, such as trying that first cigarette, but at some point it becomes involuntary. • Once a person is addicted, quitting becomes difficult because of both external cues and internal responses that prepare the body for the addictive substance (Siegel, 2004). • Like Pavlov's dogs, environmental cues (e.g., specific music that is always played while a person takes drugs) trigger a response in the body that prepares it to receive the drug. • Taking a small amount of the drug can signal the body that a larger amount is coming, setting up internal triggers for drug use. • Withdrawal symptoms (e.g., nausea, fever) occur if larger amounts of the drug are not taken since the body has started compensating for the effects of the large amount. • Treatment must take into account the body's physiological reactions and internal triggers (Siegel, 2004).	• Addiction is a choice and most addicts stop abusing substances because they choose to stop. • When faced with a decision between buying drugs or keeping their family and job, most addicts were able to stop using drugs. • Addicts make a choice about how they are going to think about taking their drug. Alcoholics can choose not to worry about their health in 20 years as they consume their next drink, or they can start to think about the long-term consequences of their actions. • As people get older, they start to recognize the consequences and to weigh them against their priorities. • Treatment programs need to focus on teaching addicts to make the right choice in the moment. Programs that reward success (e.g., Alcoholics Anonymous) are also beneficial (Heyman, 2009).

QUESTIONS

1. Explain whether you feel heredity or environment plays a more important role in addiction. Provide evidence to support your view.
2. Determine what further actions should be taken by our levels of government to support those who face addiction. Use your answer from question 1 to help explain your position.

New Research in Mental Health

Before You Read
Skim the subtitles that follow and suggest how these topics relate to mental health issues.

Over the last century, our understanding of mental health issues has expanded greatly. However, discoveries are still being made, including new understandings of previously described disorders and mental illnesses that exist because of the realities of today's society.

Nature-Deficit Disorder

Do children go outside to play anymore? Would it matter if they didn't? According to University of Illinois psychology professor Frances Kuo, "nature-deficit disorder" is real and is a problem that increases as people in society have less access to the natural world. In her research, Kuo discovered that a lack of nature in children's lives can lead to obesity, attention deficit disorders such as ADHD, and depression. On the other hand, there is a tendency for elderly people to live longer when they live near a park or green space.

Some studies show promising signs that immersing children with ADHD in natural environments calms their symptoms. Their impulsivity and inattention decrease after exposure to natural views and environments. Interestingly, the results are not affected by age, gender, or income group.

↑ **FIGURE 5-31** Spending time outdoors is important to our mental and physical well-being.

Sensory Processing Disorder

Sensory processing disorder (SPD), also known as *sensory integration disorder* and *sensory integration dysfunction*, is a disorder in the processing of sensory information, which includes a cluster of symptoms that develop in childhood, mostly in boys. Although not yet recognized in the *Diagnostic and Statistical Manual of Mental Disorders*, people with SPD have difficulty taking in or interpreting inputs from the five senses, as well as responding appropriately to such input. For example, a child with SPD may object to new foods, shy away from cuddling, and/or find loud sounds extremely distressing. SPD can impair a person's daily functions and can lead to severe problems ranging from low self-esteem and difficulty with relationships to behaviour and learning problems.

At this time, the disorder is diagnosed using the Sensory Integration and Praxis Tests, developed by Dr. A. Jean Ayres. However, because the disorder has not yet been recognized in the DSM, it is difficult for researchers to obtain funding and for others to take it seriously. The SPD Foundation has been lobbying for this disorder to be included in the forthcoming DSM-V in 2012.

There is no simple remedy for dealing with SPD. One strategy that seems to be successful uses sensory integration activities: as children's neurological systems develop, they do fun activities with objects that cause them difficulty. It is important to recognize SPD early and have children work with an occupational therapist and a psychologist to help their neurological development.

Open for Debate
Many new tests now exist to predict the onset of dementia, especially Alzheimer's, later in life, but doctors still can't stop it from happening. Would you want to know if you were likely to develop a neurological disorder?

❓ What changes would you recommend to increase awareness of nature-deficit disorder and SPD in schools?

Hoarding

TV shows such as *Hoarding: Buried Alive* and *Hoarders* have brought to light a disorder that affects 2 to 5 percent of Canada's population. Hoarding is more than just being too messy to clean up your home. Recently, "hoarding disorder" was recognized as an indication of obsessive compulsive disorder (OCD) and was recommended for inclusion in the DSM-V.

Compulsive hoarding is defined as excessively collecting items and not being able to throw them away. The home of a compulsive hoarder is so cluttered that walking through it can be like navigating an intricate maze (see Figure 5-32). People with this disorder become emotionally attached to their items—mostly books, magazines, papers, clothing, or bags—and find it scary when asked to throw them away. Often they are generous people who buy items for others or feel they are being environmentally friendly by "recycling." Moreover, their homes become hazardous to their health as rodents and insects move in and mould grows, and can even become potential fire hazards. Hoarding has been known to end marriages and alienate friends.

FIGURE 5-32 Compulsive hoarding can become not only a health and safety issue, but also the source of marital and family conflict.

Most hoarders don't recognize their behaviour as problematic. As such, many don't seek treatment until they are faced with the threat of eviction or divorce, or a cleanup order from the department of public health. However, there is hope for hoarders. Quebec psychologist Kieron O'Connor is researching the use of virtual reality as a form of therapy for hoarders. This new field in psychology—called **cyberpsychology**—studies the ways in which the Internet influences people, and even how techniques such as virtual reality can help treat mental illness. Virtual Iraq, which you learned about earlier on page 229, falls under this category. The generic home cyberenvironment is filled with images of the patient's home. Then the patient practises throwing items out and seeing what a clutter-free home looks and feels like. After a while, patients are able to move from virtual reality to their real home. They are often surprised to see what their home looks like without all that clutter. While this study is ongoing, the technique looks promising.

cyberpsychology: a new field of psychology that studies the influences of technology on people and the ways it can be used to treat mental illness

More to Know...

In 1998, the Tragically Hip filmed the video for their hit song "Poets" in Kingston, Ontario. The location was the small home of an animal hoarder who kept over 100 cats. Animals are among the more common of the items hoarders tend to collect. While the cats at this particular home are well cared for, this is not often the case when it comes to animal hoarding.

> **REFLECT AND RESPOND**

1. What are the advantages of using virtual technology as part of a patient's treatment?
2. How might having a psychotic disorder affect other factors that influence behaviour? For instance, how might a psychotic disorder affect your motivation?
3. The symptoms of diseases like nature-deficit disorder and SPD are general and quite similar to other illnesses. Why might this cause a problem for diagnosing these diseases?

Section 5.3 — Ethical Issues in Psychology

Much like in anthropology, ethics are an important aspect of doing research in psychology. Because experiments are often conducted on people, it is important to take care not to inflict any undue harm on the participants. Ethical guidelines also apply to research using animals. Codes of Ethics are often revised to meet the changing needs of the discipline and society.

Introduction to Ethics in Psychology

> **Before You Read**
> Have you ever been caught accidentally plagiarizing? Why is plagiarism an important issue for social science researchers?

The Canadian Psychological Association (CPA) publishes the Canadian Code of Ethics for Psychologists in Canada. As of 2010, the CPA was reviewing the code. The Canadian Code of Ethics for Psychologists, Third Edition, published in 2000, begins with four principles that psychologists and researchers should take into account in a balanced way in order to make ethical decisions. Each principle is followed by the applicable ethical standards. The following is a list of these principles and some of the ethical standards that psychologists must adhere to.

CANADIAN CODE OF ETHICS FOR PSYCHOLOGISTS: Third Edition, 2000

I. Respect for the Dignity of Persons

- **I.7** Make every reasonable effort to ensure that psychological knowledge is not misused, intentionally or unintentionally, to infringe on human rights.
- **I.20** Obtain informed consent for all research activities that involve obtrusive measures, invasion of privacy, more than minimal risk of harm, or any attempt to change the behaviour of research participants.

II. Responsible Caring

- **II.2** Avoid doing harm to clients, research participants, employees, supervisees, students, trainees, colleagues, and others.
- **II.17** Not carry out any scientific or professional activity unless the probable benefit is proportionately greater than the risk involved.
- **II.46** Use a procedure subjecting animals to pain, stress, or privation only if an alternative procedure is unavailable and the goal is justified by its prospective scientific, educational, or applied value.

III. Integrity of Relationships

- **III.31** Not exploit any relationship established as a psychologist to further personal, political, or business interests at the expense of the best interests of their clients, research participants, students, employers, or others …

IV. Responsibility to Society

- **IV.15** Acquire an adequate knowledge of the culture, social structure, and customs of a community before beginning any major work there.

Think back to Milgram's obedience experiment at the beginning of the chapter. Did Stanley Milgram follow the CPA's Code of Ethics? What is the likelihood that his experiment would be performed by a psychologist today?

REFLECT AND RESPOND

1. Do you agree with all the principles? What others could be added?

Issues in Ethical Experimentation

A key element in psychology is its use of experiments to support ideas and further knowledge. However, unlike experiments in a chemistry lab, psychological experiments are often performed on human beings. In the past, some of these experiments were not ethical. As you read about some of these unethical experiments, imagine you were there too.

Why Experiment?

As you learned in Chapter 2, there are a variety of ways that social scientists can gather data to test a hypothesis. Psychologists can use quantitative methods, such as laboratory-based experiments, or qualitative ones, such as unstructured natural observation. Although used often, experiments are by no means the only way psychologists can gather research data. In fact, when experiments use human subjects, there is the potential danger of harm to the participants. Why, then, are experiments the method of choice, and how can psychologists ensure that they are safe?

The Benefits of Empirical Research

Sometimes the only way to understand a situation is to study it by reconstructing it, or an aspect of it, in a controlled environment. For example, to study the effects of alcohol reflexes, a researcher can provide the alcohol in a safe setting where the participants can't harm themselves. The researcher can use the findings to explain how a person's reflexes may be affected in a real-life situation, such as driving. It would be unethical to test the effect of alcohol on driving in a real-life setting.

Experiments also allow a researcher to manipulate a variable of interest while controlling other variables. Another benefit is that the experiments can be re-created by other psychologists using the same conditions to establish their validity. Psychologists have learned a lot about the human mind and behaviour over the past century, and significant advances have been gained because of experiments.

> **Before You Read**
> What would happen if psychologists didn't experiment to make discoveries?

> **More to Know...**
> Learn more about issues in animal experimentation in Section 2.1 and Section 4.3.

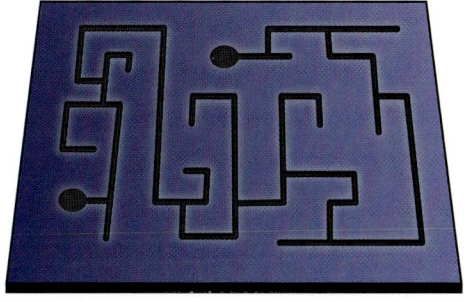

↑ **FIGURE 5-33** This classical pencil-maze experiment is used to study learning processes. For this experiment, the participant is blindfolded and must learn how to trace a path through the maze properly while researchers analyze the learning involved.

Benefits to Others

Psychologists are not the only beneficiaries of research, however. Educators have improved teaching practices based on new understandings of childhood brain development and learning styles. Moreover, research data has helped teachers gain a better understanding of ADHD, depression, and other issues faced by the students in their classrooms.

Research in psychology can also have a more universal impact. Marketing experts study the purchasing patterns and buying habits of the public and how to maximize these habits. Advertisers also employ psychologists to suggest methods of marketing to consumers so that consumers remember their products as they shop. Do you believe psychologists should be involved in such practices?

> ❓ In what other areas can an understanding of psychology be of value?

Unethical Experiments

The early days of psychology saw some experiments go too far. There was little regard for the people involved in the experiment or for the foreseeable harm that resulted. The following table lists 10 of the most unethical experiments in psychology's history.

TEN UNETHICAL EXPERIMENTS IN PSYCHOLOGY'S HISTORY	
Study	**Description**
Little Albert, 1920	In an attempt to understand the nature of fear, psychologist John Watson exposed Albert, a nine-month-old boy, to a variety of white objects, such as rabbits and cotton wool. The boy played with these items for two months and exhibited no fear. Watson then started making loud noises behind Albert's back as he played, causing him to cry and show fear. Albert began to associate those items, and eventually anything white and furry (even Santa Claus), with fear. Watson did not have the opportunity to desensitize Albert of this fear after the experiment. (See Open for Debate in Chapter 2, page 65 for more.)
Landis's Facial Expressions Experiment, 1924	Graduate student Carney Landis of the University of Minnesota was studying how facial expressions relate to emotion and whether specific expressions were common to everyone. Participants had black lines drawn on their faces, to make changes in expression easy to see, and were then given various stimuli meant to elicit specific reactions. At one point, the participants were given a live rat and told to behead it. One-third did so, but because most people had no prior experience, the rats suffered. Landis decapitated the animals of those who refused. In the end, the study showed no proof that people have common facial expressions and the rats were killed for no reason.
The Monster Study, 1939	Wendell Johnson of the University of Iowa conducted a speech experiment on 22 orphaned children with normal language development. Half were placed in the negative speech therapy group, where they were belittled for every speech error and told they stuttered. Many of them suffered negative psychological effects, and some actually developed speech problems that persisted throughout their lives.
Learned Helplessness, 1965	Psychologists Mark Seligman and Steve Maier experimented on three groups of dogs placed in harnesses. Group 1 dogs were released unharmed after a time. Group 2 dogs were leashed together in pairs, and one dog per pair received shocks that could be ended by pressing a lever. Group 3 was set up like the second except the shocks did not end by pressing a lever; they were random and seemed inevitable. Because the dogs in group 3 had no power to change their situation, they experienced "learned helplessness" and even showed symptoms of clinical depression. Later these dogs were put in another box from which they could easily jump out to escape. When shocked, instead of jumping out of the box, the dogs in group 3 just gave up.
David Reimer, 1965–2004	A botched circumcision when he was eight months old resulted in Bruce Reimer's penis being burned off. Psychologist John Money recommended that his parents raise him as a female, "Brenda." Dr. Money claimed that gender is a matter of socialization but failed to tell Bruce's mother that this had never been proven. After years of feeling "wrong," Brenda discovered the truth and began to live as "David." He faced deep psychological issues, including depression, and eventually committed suicide. (See Chapter 6 for a complete explanation.)

Study	Description
Monkey Drug Trials, 1969	C. R. Schuster and T. Thompson designed an experiment to help understand the effects of drug and alcohol abuse, in which monkeys and rats were trained to inject themselves with a syringe and left with large stocks of alcohol, morphine, cocaine, codeine, and amphetamines. Some monkeys tore hair from their bodies, broke their arms while attempting escape, suffered convulsions, and broke their own fingers off (probably from hallucinations). Others died from the drugs. Schuster went on to work as the Director of the National Institute on Drug Abuse in the 1980s.
Stanford Prison Experiment, 1971	Psychologist Philip Zimbardo recruited university students to create a mock prison. He randomly divided them into two groups: guards and prisoners. Throughout the experiment, his research team watched as the guards became increasingly cruel in reaction to the prisoners' acts of rebellion. The guards used a "divide and conquer" tactic, which pitted the prisoners against one another. After just a few days, the prisoners showed signs of depression and other psychological issues. The experiment had to be ended far earlier than expected due to the extreme conditions. (See page 238 for more details.)
The Aversion Project, 1971–1989	In an attempt to root out homosexuality from its armed forces, South Africa's apartheid army performed forced "sex-change" operations on about 900 white gay and lesbian soldiers. Other atrocities included chemical castrations and electric shock. The head of the top secret study, Dr. Aubrey Levin, later worked at the University of Calgary's medical school. In 2010, he faced over 20 charges of sexual assault by former patients of his psychiatry practice.
The Surrogate Mother Experiment, 1971	To understand the effects of social isolation, Dr. Harry Harlow separated infant rhesus monkeys from their mothers shortly after birth. He put the infants alone in steel cages and then offered them surrogate mothers: one made of wire that offered milk at times, the other covered in soft cloth. The infants preferred the cloth mothers until they were hungry and then went to the wire ones. While his experiment showed that attachment did not depend on feeding alone, many of the monkeys left the experiment exhibiting psychotic behaviour. Harlow's colleagues questioned the necessity of the experiment. (See Chapter 2.)
Milgram Study, 1974	Psychologist Stanley Milgram conducted an experiment on obedience where a volunteer "teacher" was told to provide shocks in increasing increments when the "student" (an actor who was part of the experiment) provided a wrong answer to word-pair questions. How far would the teacher go if asked to do so by an authority figure? To Milgram's surprise, about 68 percent of teachers shocked the students to the full extent of 450 volts, which they believed would cause severe pain or even death. (See page 198 for more on Milgram's experiment.)

While these experiments are shocking and arguably should never have been conducted, the results are significant. Psychologists now have codes of ethics largely because of these experiments, which made them question how they conduct research.

The results of these experiments have given us the basis for a number of other theories in psychology. But is it ethical to use information gathered from an unethical experiment? Some argue that using the findings validates the experiment at some level. How could you change each experiment to make it more ethical?

> Rank the experiments in the table from 1 to 10 in order of least to most unethical. Establish a set of criteria such as the number of people affected and the degree to which the participants' lives were affected to help you make your decisions.

Landmark Case Study

Philip Zimbardo (1933–): Stanford Prison Experiment

In 1971, psychologist Philip Zimbardo conducted his famous experiment where prison life was re-created in the basement of Stanford University's Psychology Department building. He and his team were curious to understand the psychological effects of acting as a prisoner or prison guard.

The Experiment

Volunteers for the experiment were obtained through ads in the newspaper. After interviewing the applicants, the team selected 24 American and Canadian university men based on their psychological and physical health; the team started with 18 participants and used the rest for backup. The participants were paid $15 per day during the experiment.

The participants were randomly divided into two groups: guards and prisoners. The "prisoners" were first arrested and handcuffed at their homes by real Palo Alto, California police, exactly the way any other suspect is arrested, and then taken to the police station where they were fingerprinted, formally booked, and put in a holding cell. At this point, the prisoners were blindfolded and taken to "Stanford County Jail," the experiment prison in the basement of the university.

Prison life was set up to be degrading to the prisoners from the moment they arrived. The prisoners were strip-searched and sprayed with lice spray. Thick chains were locked around their ankles, they were dressed in smocks without undergarments, and stockings were put on their heads to simulate closely shaved hair. Prisoners were called by identification numbers instead of their names to make them feel anonymous. In the prison, there were no windows or clocks so the prisoners had no sense of time.

Three "guards" were on duty at all times, rotating in eight-hour shifts. They wore khaki uniforms and sunglasses with mirrored lenses, which helped to give them a sense of anonymity. They had whistles and billy clubs borrowed from the police department. They were allowed to create all the rules and routines in the prison.

The Results

The researchers gathered data by videotaping everything and using an intercom system that was in all the rooms. The experiment was planned to run for two weeks, but it had to be stopped after only six days because of the reactions of the subjects involved.

The Guards

At first, the prisoners weren't taking the situation seriously and the guards were trying to determine what to do. However, within three days the guards had created an elaborate system of total control that included increasingly creative methods of taunting and harassing the prisoners. They woke prisoners up in the middle of the night for arbitrary reasons such as "counts" (saying their prisoner number), made them to do endless push-ups, and made them scrub toilets with their bare hands. It was later discovered that similar tactics had been used by Nazi guards at concentration camps during World War II.

Zimbardo observed three types of prison guards: fair guards who followed the prison rules, "good guys" who did small favours for the prisoners, and hostile guards who created new and horrible ways to punish the prisoners. A third of the guards fell into this last group, even though the personality tests that were done before the experiment did not predict this hostile behaviour.

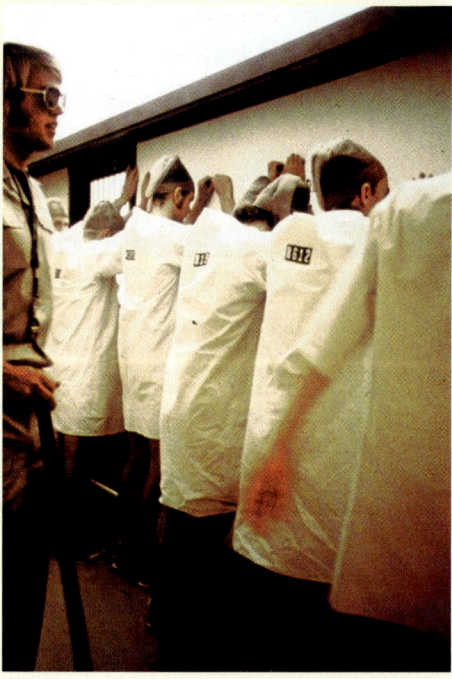

FIGURE 5-34 What does the body language of the guard and the prisoners tell you about how they felt about themselves during the experiment?

Coping in Prison

The researchers also noted that the prisoners, who felt completely powerless and lost their identity, had different coping styles. There were a couple of times when prisoners rebelled against the guards, but their actions only made matters worse and resulted in the guards' creation of a privilege system to create distrust among the prisoners.

Some prisoners broke down emotionally, including one who developed a psychosomatic rash on his entire body. Some prisoners tried being extremely well behaved by doing everything that was demanded of them. Most shocking was how quickly healthy, intelligent men became so completely emotionally isolated and depressed.

In fact, the prisoners became so immersed in their roles that none thought to demand to be released, even though it was just an experiment from which they could withdraw at any time. They all tried to get early release as "prisoners" rather than leave as students.

↑ **FIGURE 5-35** Blindfolded, this "prisoner" is taken from his home to the experimental prison at Stanford University.

When Zimbardo ended the experiment, he held group sessions where everyone spoke about what they experienced. While all of the prisoners were relieved that the experiment was over, some of the guards were upset that it ended early. They also discussed the moral issues faced in the simulation by both the guards and the researchers themselves.

Connections in the Real World

In real prisons, the guards are people who are trained to work with far more numerous, often hardened criminals. The power dynamics described in this experiment are, to some degree, necessary to maintain control in an environment that could become dangerous if chaos were allowed. Yet, are there times when that control is taken too far?

One of the most shocking examples of prisoner abuse occurred at Abu Ghraib prison in Iraq. Pictures emerged of American troops humiliating and abusing the inmates. As guards taunted them, prisoners were made to line up naked with bags covering their heads and then were forced to do tasks that were beyond the range allowed by international laws. Zimbardo's experiment illustrates how the guards' behaviour can happen without proper oversight.

QUESTIONS

1. What elements were set up to make the "prisoners" feel confused and dehumanized?
2. Did Zimbardo's experiment follow the CPA's Code of Ethics? Do you think such an experiment would be allowed to take place today? Why or why not?
3. What does this experiment show us about what people are capable of doing? How does this relate back to Milgram's experiment on obedience?

Ethics in Research

Whenever psychologists conduct research, they must follow the guidelines established in the Code of Ethics. Secondary-school students also have a responsibility to act ethically when doing research (see Figure 5-36). But do students always act in ethical ways?

Moral Illiteracy

The Josephson Institute publishes a Report Card on the Ethics of American Youth every two years. The 2008 edition wasn't good news. After surveying almost 30 000 students, the Institute reported that American youth are lying, cheating, and stealing in record numbers. About 45 percent of boys and 26 percent of girls admitted to stealing from a store in the past year, while 64 percent of students admitted to cheating on an exam. About 83 percent of students lied to their parents. The Josephson Institute expressed concern with the apparent widespread "moral illiteracy" of American youth. Is the situation in Canada similar or different?

FIGURE 5-36 Just like social science researchers, students have a responsibility to conduct their research ethically.

Plagiarism and Cheating on Tests

Plagiarism—copying someone else's work—is on the rise in Canada and the United States. The Canadian Council on Learning released a 2006 study on academic dishonesty, which was conducted by the University of Guelph and Rutgers University. The researchers asked 20 000 first-year university students at 11 institutions about their behaviours in secondary school. Shockingly, 73 percent of the respondents admitted to seriously cheating on their written assignments, and 58 percent cheated on a test. At the University of Waterloo between 2003 and 2006, there was an 81 percent increase in the number of plagiarizing and cheating incidents.

Students know that cheating is wrong, so why do they do it? According to the study, students cited such reasons as fear of failure and ease of access to material. The sharp increase in academic dishonesty since the late 1990s occurred at the same time as increased use of the Internet, an observation also noted by university professors. However, students also stated that they at times had different definitions than their teachers of what plagiarism meant.

Implications of Dishonesty in Research

While cheating and plagiarism appear to be on the rise, it's important that researchers conduct investigations as ethically as possible. Think about the implications of falsifying data in a drug trial, for example. A harmful drug could be approved for use based on this false data and could cause serious harm to others. While the research you're doing is not a matter of life or death, it's important to consider the potential for harm if you falsify your research results or plagiarize content from others. Would you want your hard work copied by someone surfing the Internet?

> What would you expect the 2010 results on the Josephson Institute's Report Card to look like? Do you think the percentage of students lying, cheating, and stealing rose or fell?

Creating an Ethical Experiment

One of the ethical standards in the CPA's Canadian Code of Ethics for Psychologists is that researchers must avoid foreseeable harm to their subjects. How do psychologists know that they have done this? Ethical guidelines for experiments have been published as far back as 1901. These standards have changed throughout the last century, but the message is the same: there are rules/guidelines that all psychologists must follow.

Ethical Experiment Checklist

Researchers ask themselves a number of questions about the potential harm to human participants prior to engaging in an experiment. The following is a sample of such questions:

- ☐ Is the experiment necessary to prove a significant hypothesis?
- ☐ Would the experiment cause harm to the participants?
- ☐ Do you have informed consent from the participants?
- ☐ Do you have informed consent from parents if the participants are under the age of 18?
- ☐ Have you considered if the experiment is appropriate, given the culture and customs of the participants?
- ☐ Have you had a peer review of the experiment (in school, this would be the teacher)?
- ☐ Have you debriefed the participants (explained the purpose of the experiment to them) after the experiment is complete?

> **Skills Focus**
> Would this checklist change depending on the type of research method you use? What might be added for an interview, questionnaire, or case study?

You can use this checklist as an ethical check on your own research. Once you have designed an experiment, go back and use the checklist to make sure it is ethical. Then ask a peer to check for you before checking with teacher. It may be necessary to make changes in questions or participants.

FIGURE 5-37 What are some of the limitations of doing social science research on the Internet?

Ethical Experiments on the Internet

Psychologists are discovering the great advantages of conducting experiments on the Internet. They are able to reach a broad range of participants quickly and with far less expense than a lab experiment, which involves paid assistants and the cost of running the lab. In particular, the breadth of the data can be expanded since researchers at small schools can access larger numbers of participants on the Internet. The Internet also provides opportunities to observe social behaviour as researchers can study the behaviours of people in chat rooms and message boards, which would otherwise not be observable in a laboratory setting. The trend emerging from the early research is that Internet studies yield the same conclusions as studies done in the lab (Krantz and Dalal, 2000). However, there are new ethical issues that come with the territory of doing this kind of research.

The Code of Ethics still applies to Internet experiments, but it can be more difficult to follow. For example, how can researchers ensure that participants truly understand what they are signing up for and thus obtain informed consent? Also, how can psychologists ensure confidentiality for participants' personal information? Another issue of concern with online research is that the researcher is less likely to know if the research experience is causing harm to a participant and intervene to stop it. On a professional level, how can they ensure their work is not stolen by unethical colleagues? These issues are significant not only because of the ethical dilemmas they pose, but also because they can affect the validity of the data gathered. Just because someone clicks on a button indicating that the person is a married female doesn't mean that a 14-year-old boy isn't inputting the information!

A paper by Kraut et al. (2003) suggests pretesting survey questions and informed-consent statements with others to ensure that they are suitable. They also suggest discussing Internet-based research with technical consultants prior to beginning such research. Using the Internet for psychological research is still a fairly new endeavour, and much is to be learned about how to utilize the Internet in an ethical manner.

REFLECT AND RESPOND

1. Besides those in the Ethical Experimental checklist, what questions other than the sample ones listed above should researchers ask themselves prior to conducting experiments on human subjects?
2. Do you believe it is acceptable to use knowledge that is gained through previous unethical experiments? Why or why not?
3. Suggest three survey or experiment topics that you think would be suitable for conducting on the Internet. Explain your reasoning as well as the possible limitations of using this type of research.

Issues in Ethical Testing

Can a test reveal your intelligence? Tests to measure intelligence have been around for over a century, but their validity is something that continues to be questioned. Issues such as what is innate ability versus what has been learned through environment also challenge our notions about what these tests reveal. Even the developer of the first intelligence test believed that it had limits because intelligence was too broad to quantify with a single number and can change over time.

Before You Read
What conditions are necessary for you to learn?

Tests of Intelligence

Developed in 1916 when Lewis Terman adapted Alfred Binet's original intelligence test, the Stanford-Binet Intelligence Scales have been a widely used method of measuring intelligence for many years. This test was originally designed to measure the intelligence of special-needs children in France, but today it is more widely used among the general population.

Each edition of the test is quite different from the last. The fifth version of the test, Stanford-Binet 5, was published in 2003 and has little resemblance to the original test. For instance, the original test consisted mainly of word pairs and measured only general intelligence; the Stanford-Binet 5 has other components, such as toys, and measures general intelligence as well as quantitative reasoning and nonverbal IQ. How, then, is it possible to compare today's scores to earlier ones? How do our educators know if our system is improving? Researchers are still seeking the answers to these questions.

Concerns about Intelligence Tests

The validity of the results obtained is just one of many concerns that have been raised about intelligence tests. In 1981, Harvard Professor Stephen Jay Gould's book *The Mismeaure of Man* argued that intelligence tests are based on faulty assumptions that are then used as the basis of scientific racism. For example, he believed that the test questions were culturally and socially biased. He felt that quantifying intelligence as a number served to rank individuals to prove that some races, classes, and sexes are innately inferior.

In fact, the United States enacted an immigration law in 1924 based on the results of testing done by psychologist Henry Goddard. His findings showed that those of Hungarian, Italian, and Russian descent were "feeble-minded." Because of this, the number of immigrants allowed in from those countries was significantly reduced. In hindsight, even Lewis Terman—the originator of the Stanford-Binet intelligence test—came to realize that the test scores actually reflect people's education as well their familiarity with the culture assumed by the test.

Progressive Matrices Test

Another type of IQ test is Dr. John C. Raven's Progressive Matrices, developed in 1938. This multiple-choice test asks subjects to fill in a missing item that completes a pattern within a matrix (see Figure 5-38). It was designed to measure abstract reasoning regardless of schooling,

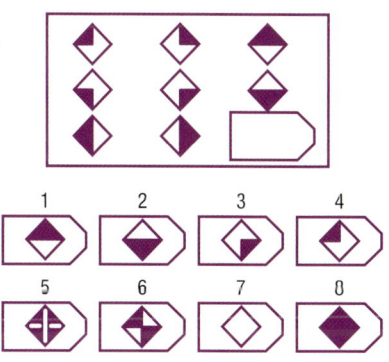

↑ FIGURE 5-38 Which of the eight boxes is the missing piece of the pattern? How does this measure intelligence? How might this question have more or less cultural bias than questions on the Stanford-Binet test?

so socio-economic background is not a factor in determining a person's ability. Environmental factors such as culture should not influence the results either since the images chosen include designs from various cultures. However, the test does bring to mind one question: considering the differences between Raven's test and the Stanford-Binet models, what defines intelligence?

Multiple Intelligences

When we think of intelligence, what we often think of is really academic intelligence. In 1983, Howard Gardner proposed a new way of thinking about human intelligence. He argued that everyone, to varying degrees, has what he called *multiple intelligences* (see chart below). A test based on Gardner's theory focuses on each person's unique intelligence profile. Understanding which intelligences are your strengths can help you understand how you learn, and can in turn help you learn better. Multiple intelligences are also important to consider for children with special needs who might score poorly on the Stanford-Binet test but excel in the arts.

One criticism of this theory is that there has not been any published research showing the validity of the model, nor are there fully worked-through tests to identify and measure each of the different intelligences. However, Gardner believed that such testing could lead people to be labelled in a negative manner. Another criticism is that the intelligences are more talents or personality traits rather than true intelligences. Nonetheless, the model has gained popularity among many educators as a tool to help students.

The first seven intelligences were in Gardner's original theory, and the last one was added later. Which intelligence do you feel best describes your learning style? Are learning styles this distinct or are they a combination of styles?

> **VOICES**
>
> The empires of the future will be empires of the mind.
> Sir Winston Churchill

GARDNER'S MULTIPLE INTELLIGENCES THEORY		
Intelligence Type	**Description**	**Potential Career Choices**
visual-spatial	picture smart—learn best by using pictures or other observed things	graphic designer, tour guide, architect, surgeon
kinesthetic	body smart—learn best by moving their bodies	professional athlete, sports analyst, masseur, firefighter
intrapersonal	self smart—learn best by working on their own	entrepreneur, social worker, researcher, theorist
interpersonal	people smart—learn best by working with other people	therapist, actor, politician, hotel manager, police officer
logical	number smart—learn best by experimenting, seeing numerical patterns, and using logic	accountant, air-traffic controller, Webmaster, data analyst
linguistic	word smart—learn best by thinking in words rather than pictures	journalist, librarian, lawyer, screenwriter
musical	music smart—learn best by using sound as they transfer information	musician, music teacher, composer, DJ
naturalistic	nature smart—learn best through hands-on activities, especially outdoors in the natural environment	landscaper, farmer, biologist, zookeeper

Emotional Intelligence

Emotional intelligence (EQ) is the ability to recognize, use, and regulate your emotions. Emotionally intelligent people are able to manage their emotions and use empathy to understand other people's emotions. This helps them manage conflict. Some psychologists argue that people with a high EQ are more successful in their careers and personal relationships. Various tests to measure EQ have been created, but EQ has yet to be included in a standard IQ test.

> **?** Is it fair to measure everyone using the same test, regardless of their culture, linguistic ability, socio-economic background, and urban or rural residence?

Studying the Unstudiable

Sometimes psychologists have a difficult time studying aspects of the psyche because it would be unethical to conduct the necessary experiments on humans.

"The Forbidden Experiment"

Two hundred years ago, the early French psychologists who studied Victor, a feral child who had grown up alone in the woods, called their study "The Forbidden Experiment." Even then they knew that it would be unethical for psychologists to create an experiment that involved separating a child from his or her parents to understand the nature of learning. They can study only those rare children who are separated from their family without scientific intervention.

Fighting over Genie

The case of 12-year-old Genie, about whom you read earlier, represents a more recent example of a child whom psychologists studied that would have been unethical to create in an experiment. Many psychologists were interested in the opportunity to study her learning and language acquisition because it occurred so late in her development. Since she had been abused by her parents, she needed a new place to live. While she stayed at the hospital, her psychologist, James Kent, became her surrogate parent. A year later, she moved in with her teacher, Jean Butler, who largely kept Genie away from the other members of her team. When Genie began to hoard items in her room, she was moved again. This time, her therapist, David Rigler, and his wife, Marilyn, Genie's new teacher, became her new foster parents. She lived with them for four years. All of these foster parents cared about Genie, but they also studied her and hoped to gain recognition for their results. Was there a conflict of interest when those who were studying her also took care of her?

↑ **FIGURE 5-39** Victor, a feral child, was part of "The Forbidden Experiment." Why was his life of interest to psychologists?

> **More to Know...**
> Look in Chapter 3 and Section 5.1 to learn more about Genie's incredible story.

Surveys at School

What types of information are ethical to allow in surveys of students at school? Are there topics that are forbidden when working with school children? Surveys can be an excellent tool for quickly gathering information from a large group of people. While psychologists use surveys for their research, other groups in society do so as well. The results can be used to help these groups improve their services to meet the needs of their members.

Student Surveys

In November 2010, the Ottawa-Carleton District School Board was supposed to conduct a survey of students and parents, similar to a survey conducted by the Toronto District School Board in 2006. Students from Grades 7 to 12 were to answer the questions on their own. The board hoped that the results would be used to help make decisions about what programs and services it would offer and how funds would be used, all to help better serve its diverse student population.

The survey consisted of 43 multiple-choice questions that included topics about home life, academic achievement, ethnic background, religious affiliation, socio-economic status, bullying, and even sexual orientation. However, some people thought the questions were too personal for the younger Grade 7 students. The board had to delay the survey's start date because of a complaint to the Information and Privacy Commission. The Toronto District School Board survey had not collected data on sexual orientation for students in Grades 7 and 8. Still, students did have the option not to participate, but only if their parents let the school know in writing.

> **More to Know...**
> Other organizations survey students as well. In their ongoing survey of Ontario students in Grades 7 to 12, the Canadian Centre for Addiction and Mental Health (CAMH) follows trends in student mental and physical health. Their 2009 report revealed an increase in students rating their mental health as poor.

FIGURE 5-40 Should children be surveyed by their schools on topics such as sexual orientation and socio-economic status? If you think surveys at school are appropriate, suggest what age students should be to be asked more personal questions.

REFLECT AND RESPOND

1. Would the student survey described above be considered ethical according to the CPA's Code of Ethics for Psychologists? Are there portions that would be considered unethical?
2. What benefits would this data have for school boards? What are the disadvantages for students to participate in the survey?
3. Relate the story of Genie to CPA's Code of Ethics, and suggest a plan to care for a child like her should this situation ever occur again.

POINT/COUNTERPOINT

Gender and the Classroom

In recent years, educators have become increasingly concerned about the gap between girls' and boys' achievement. In the 1980s, educators were concerned about girls, who were not excelling in math and science. Now the concern is about boys' literacy, which is lagging behind that of girls.

Many theories have been suggested about how to fix the gender gap in learning. One idea that is gaining support is to have single-gender classrooms. Some schools have already moved to this model; while there are separate secondary schools, often the discussion is about elementary classrooms.

Should Schools Be Segregated By Gender?

Gender Segregation Improves Learning	Gender Integration Is Better
• The U.S.-based National Association for Single Sex Public Education argues that separating girls and boys will allow each group to learn using the most appropriate methods.	• University of Alberta professor Heather Blair, who specializes in elementary education, argues that the perceived crisis in boys' literacy is due to their performance on standardized tests, which don't consider nontraditional literacies, and that boys don't really learn much differently than girls. In her six-year study that followed boys from Grades 4–10, she learned that they are "multiply-literate." For example, they tend to explore digital literacies before girls and may actually be ahead of girls their age in that sense.
• The latest research in neuroscience indicates that boys and girls have differences in the sequence of their brain development. For example, boys develop spatial skills four years earlier than girls do, while the area of the brain involved in language develops four years earlier in girls. Therefore, boys and girls may not be ready to learn about geometry or poetry at the same grade level (Sax, 2005).	
• Single-sex classrooms lead both boys and girls to pursue their true academic interests, without worrying about how they will be stereotyped. Girls in these classes are more likely to pursue math and science classes (Sax, 2005).	• In parts of Canada, single-sex classes were introduced in the 1980s and 1990s to address low take-up of—and achievement in—math and science among girls. Research indicated that single-sex schooling did not necessarily result in learning gains (Demers & Bennett, 2007).
• Research indicates that boys and girls generally have different learning styles. For example, boys often enjoy more hands-on learning activities and talk through their learning while many girls prefer a quiet environment and don't need to move around much.	• Another concern about separating boys and girls is socialization. Will they feel comfortable around each other later in life if they don't spend significant amounts of time together, such as in classrooms, as they grow up?
• The essential-difference view argues that boys and girls should be educated separately for reasons of biology. For example, boys don't hear as well as girls but have visual systems that can see action better than girls'. This means that getting through to boys requires a louder volume and a faster-paced presentation (Sax, 2008).	• A different solution is to alter the teaching methods that are used. In many Ontario schools, differentiated instruction models are one way of improving learning. Differentiated instruction means the teacher gets to know the children in the classroom and uses a variety of strategies to help all students learn. Instead of treating boys like boys and girls like girls, teachers treat each student like an individual with different learning needs (Martino, 2008).

QUESTIONS

1. Select the best two arguments from each side. Prepare to participate in a debate about the issue, or write an argumentative paragraph.

Should We Change People Based on Psychological Beliefs?

Before You Read
List the people whose advice you would listen to based on their authority.

Psychological research offers a wealth of information about human nature, which can have an influence on policies and the way others are treated. Therefore, it is important to make responsible decisions based on strong evidence. Historically, however, some decisions were made without enough evidence to support them. These decisions were based on beliefs rather than evidence and had a significant impact on society.

Left Is Not Right

For centuries, left-handedness was considered strange and something to be discouraged. As far back as the ancient world people believed the left was associated with evil. For example, in Latin the word for left is "sinister" (in English). Common expressions still continue a belief that left is wrong; consider that some people describe something bad as being "gauche," the French word for left. Even the word *right* means *correct*! So, it is not a surprise that, there were dramatic attempts to alter this trait in the 1900s. When the Palmer Method of teaching handwriting became popular, so did the belief that left-handedness should be changed. In the 1960s, teachers tied children's left hands behind their backs to force them to use their right hands. What message did this action send to those children?

FIGURE 5-41 In the past, this little girl would have been taught to write with her right hand instead of her left.

Homosexuality

In the 1950s and 1960s, there was a lot of emphasis on being "normal." Part of what defined normalcy was strict gender roles, including sexuality. Homosexuals were labelled as deviants and thought of as weak-minded and susceptible to such influences as communism (a concern and source of fear at the time). People thought homosexuals were untrustworthy and immoral, even a threat to national security.

In 1948, Dr. Alfred Kinsey conducted the largest study of human sexuality, *Sexual Behavior in the Human Male*. His results led him to conclude that "Males do not represent two discrete populations, heterosexual and homosexual ... Only the human mind invents categories and tries to force facts into pigeonholes. The living world is a continuum in each and every one of its aspects."

Homosexuality as a "Disorder"

The psychiatric community supported these social views, and the medical community believed that homosexuality was a psychiatric problem. In fact, until 1973 homosexuality was defined as a mental illness in the APA's *Diagnostic and Statistical Manual of Mental Disorders*. The belief was that homosexuality was caused by an event in childhood or by domineering mothers and weak fathers.

This was despite the fact that well-respected sexual researcher Dr. Alfred Kinsey's 1948 study of human sexuality concluded that sexuality could not be defined as either "gay" or "straight." He believed that sexuality ranked on a continuum from "exclusively heterosexual" on one side and "exclusively homosexual on the other; in between were categories such as "predominantly heterosexual, only incidental homosexual" on the other, with "equally heterosexual and homosexual" and other categories in between.

Homosexuality was removed from the DSM in 1974 after gay rights groups protested at APA conferences from 1970 to 1973. Kinsey's research was also influential in making this happen.

Homosexuality in the Canadian Military

In 1961, Carleton University psychologist Robert Wake was hired by the Canadian military to create clinical tests that would distinguish whether a person was gay or straight. Nicknamed the "fruit machine," Wake hooked up participants to a machine that monitored pupil dilation, perspiration, and other physiological signs as he ran tests, such as saying words linked with homosexuality and showing photos. However, his efforts were unsuccessful and his device made it to only the pilot stage of research.

Yet the social damage was done. Homosexuals knew they needed to keep their sexuality a secret at the risk of losing their jobs, friends, and families. Between 1959 and 1968, a committee of RCMP officers and representatives of National Defence, External Affairs, and the Privy Council investigated over 9000 men and women in the civil service and armed forces who were suspected of being gay or lesbian. As a result, hundreds of people lost their jobs, most without any real explanation. Today dismissal for reasons of sexuality is illegal.

> What impact might the negative use of psychology have on people? Is it right to use our beliefs to try to change people?

Advertisements for Children

Anywhere you look, advertising is sure to be found; it's become a fact of life in North America's consumer culture. Children aged 2 to 11 in Canada watch an average of 14 hours of television per week (Statistics Canada, 2006). According to the American Academy of Pediatrics, children in the United States see an average of 40 000 ads on TV per year. What we see in advertisements is no accident; everything about an advertisement has been carefully planned. Ads are meant to stick in your head, whether through humour or annoyance, so you remember the products in the ads the next time you're out shopping. Moreover, the advertising industry is targeting children as never before; in 1990, advertisers in the United States spent $100 million on marketing to children, which increased to $2 billion by 2000. Data from Schor 2004 indicates that this number has grown to $15 billion. While figures are not available for Canada, we can assume that the amount of advertising directed at children has grown here as well. The effects of increased marketing to children are shown by research indicating that children as young as two years old can develop brand loyalty (see Figure 5-42).

↑ **FIGURE 5 42** Companies are increasingly targeting their advertising to young children so that they will buy more "stuff." What does this illustration show about the children's response to this type of promotion?

Using Psychology

Advertisers employ psychologists to advise them on how to achieve their goal. These psychologists give advice about children's development, as well as insight into their social and emotional needs, to help advertisers understand how to effectively target children at different ages. Psychologists analyze children's dreams and fantasy lives, their artwork, and their behaviour. Are these psychologists behaving ethically? In 1999, this issue was brought to the attention of the American Psychology Association by a group of U.S. mental-health professionals. While at the time the APA ruled that advertisers' employment of psychologists was ethical, the APA is now reviewing the matter.

Standards in Advertising

Although a lot of ads on television are geared to children, there are very specific standards in the Broadcast Code for Advertising to Children (Children's Code). It explicitly states what advertisers are and are not allowed to do. For example, advertisers may not use subliminal messaging or encourage children to directly purchase a product or to ask their parents to do so. However, they can make children want to buy things using creative strategies such as "pester power" to get children to nag their parents to buy products. The Children's Code also outlines a process for filing complaints by consumers. So, if advertisers do step over the line, they must face consequences.

> **?** Connect the ideas of the Canadian Code of Ethics for Psychologists to the Broadcast Code for Advertising to Children, and suggest other standards.

Memory Alteration

As technology improves and we are able to do more with smaller machines, the possibility of altering the human brain by technological means is becoming greater. If having a perfect memory were possible, is it something you'd like to have?

Would a Perfect Memory Be Beneficial?

Wouldn't it be amazing to remember everything? No more forgetting to do your homework! Scientists believe that it might be possible some day to use implants to record everything that happens. Someone who might be hoping for such a device is 47-year-old Michelle Philpots, who suffered severe head injuries in two separate road crashes and has been left with no short-term memory since 1994. She cannot remember anything beyond 24 hours and at times does not recognize her own family. She uses navigation devices to go outside.

However, Jill Price doesn't think a perfect memory is such a good idea. The "girl who can't forget" says she can remember everything about her life since she was a young girl. While she can remember all the significant events of her life, she can also remember every nasty thing that was said to her and every bad thought she's had. Imagine never being able to forget what your friend said in anger.

Rethinking Memory

Perhaps our failing memory isn't such a bad thing. Dalhousie University professor Tracy Taylor-Helmick argues that intentional forgetting has a purpose: to forget information that isn't needed any more so as to make space in our brains for new, relevant information. If psychologists like Taylor-Helmick are correct, would it be ethical to change our biological memories? Yet, isn't there a duty for science to help people whose memories are failing terribly, such as those whose brains have been affected by accidents or Alzheimer's disease?

> **More to Know...**
> See Section 2.1 to learn about how memories can be influenced.

FIGURE 5-43 Jill Price, the woman who can't forget, can remember everything since she was 8 years old. The daily diary that she kept between the ages of 10 and 34 helps researchers confirm the events that she remembers seconds after being asked.

Neuroethics

At times, technological possibilities advance faster than our social ethics. Neuroethics is a growing field in ethics that tries to understand the ethical issues involved in using new technologies that enhance the brain, and to resolve these issues.

Researchers are studying a variety of uses for nanotechnology—microscopic biotechnology—including improving human health care. One such application is the possibility of using nanotechnology to improve our memories. What are the implications of using nanotechnology for this purpose? For example, how would society decide who gets to use this technology: would it be for only the extremely ill (and how would we define that?), those who could afford it, or anyone who wants it?

There are other social questions that arise as well, such as how old should a person be to receive nanotechnology, and would nanotechnology affect education? In terms of research, how will psychologists and other researchers know when it will be safe to begin human trials of this technology? Will those who do not have these procedures be considered inferior? Clearly, much is still to be learned about this new form of technology.

> **REFLECT AND RESPOND**
>
> 1. Create a T-chart that compares the ways psychological research has helped and hurt Canadians.
> 2. Make connections to your own ability to remember people, events, and facts. What changes would you make to your abilities if you could?
> 3. What other issues do you think might arise by using nanotechnology?

Ethics and Mental Illness: Helping Those in Need

Before You Read
What are some possible exceptions to the idea of "you do the crime, you do the time"?

A diagnosis of mental illness often changes how an individual is viewed by others. This is because of the stigma that is associated with mental illness, often born of ignorance or lack of knowledge. The response of the psychiatric field as well as wider society has created this problem; it also has the power to make the changes required to reduce this stigma.

Mental Illness in Prison

The Annual Report of the Office of the Correctional Investigator reports that about 20 percent of prison inmates have mental illnesses that need treatment. Seven to nine percent of these inmates have a serious mental illness such as major depression, schizophrenia, or bipolar disorder. What's more, the number of mentally ill inmates in federal prisons has doubled in the last 10 years.

The Canadian Mental Health Association (CMHA) points out that there is no national strategy for mental illness or mental health, and, as a result, the prison system is forced to take on the issue. Unfortunately, the prison system is ill equipped to handle the large number of mentally ill offenders. In fact, inmates who exhibit symptoms of their illness, such as being too noisy, harming themselves, or attempting suicide, are often punished rather than given psychiatric help. Punishments such as isolation can trigger psychosis, which makes the situation worse.

IN FOCUS   Ashley Smith

Nineteen-year-old Ashley Smith was an inmate at Kitchener's Grand Valley Institution when she strangled herself using a strip of cloth while guards watched in October 2007. The correctional officers had been instructed by their superiors not to enter her isolation cell while she appeared to be breathing.

At the age of 15, Smith threw apples at a letter carrier in her hometown of Moncton, New Brunswick. When she breached her probation, she was sent to jail. While in custody, she kept misbehaving, lengthening her imprisonment. At 18, she was put in the federal system and moved from province to province. During her incarceration, there were over 170 "use-of-force" events where she was pepper-sprayed or injected with drugs to control her behaviour. She was confined to a windowless room for 23 hours a day and often attempted suicide as a method of sensory stimulation. Like others in the correctional system, Smith's increasingly bad behaviour was deemed deviant rather than symptomatic of her mental illness.

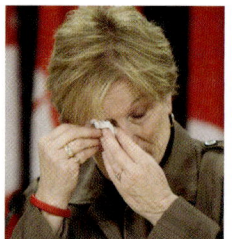

FIGURE 5-44 Coralee Smith, mother of Ashley Smith, wipes a tear while talking about the death of her daughter in a federal institution during a news conference in Ottawa.

Smith's case highlights the difficulties of mentally ill inmates in Canadian prisons today. Guards are trained in security, not in psychology. While psychologists do work in prisons, they are usually there for assessment purposes, not for treatment, and there are long waiting lists for mental-health programs that do exist. Prisoners are released after their time has been served even if they have not accessed the programming necessary for their rehabilitation.

QUESTIONS

1. Think back to the guards in the Stanford Prison Experiment. What similarities do you see between their treatment of prisoners and the way in which Ashley Smith was treated in prison?

Moving Forward: Veterans Get Help

It is well documented that veterans of war and peacekeeping missions are susceptible to post-traumatic stress disorder (PTSD), a mental illness that is triggered by a traumatic event. People dealing with PTSD experience feelings of anger, guilt, and fear, and their behaviour can become erratic. They also typically experience memory loss and nightmares. They can have difficulty functioning in their day-to-day lives, which has consequences for their families as well. The strain on family relationships can be stressful for everyone, and children often begin to suffer emotionally.

More to Know...
Look back to Section 5.2 to learn more about PTSD.

Getting Help

In the past 15 years, there have been advances in our understanding of PTSD and how to treat it. PTSD has also become more high profile because of Canada's long-term involvement in Afghanistan and the many returning veterans. This attention has helped promote more research and has resulted in improved treatments. However, many veterans still have difficulty getting diagnosed properly. Treatment is also an issue due to the large number of people with PTSD and the difficulty of getting into residential programs.

Shawn Hearn suffered PTSD after a tour of duty in Bosnia in 1994. Frustrated by the lack of help and resources provided by the medical system, he helped found Operational Stress Injury Social Support (OSISS), a program designed to help soldiers help one another overcome the effects of battlefield trauma. The program connects veterans and members of the military to resources and peer support. Part of its mission is to educate others in the Canadian Forces about stress injuries incurred on the job.

Honour House, in New Westminster, British Columbia, provides short-term accommodations for families visiting troops and first responders who are in rehabilitation in Vancouver. It is the first house of its kind, illustrating the changing understanding of the needs of patients and families. Our attitudes about helping those who have been through traumatic wartime experiences are slowly changing.

FIGURE 5-45 Honour House in B.C. is a place where veterans' families can stay while they get help.

REFLECT AND RESPOND

1. List all the ethical issues/problems in the Ashley Smith case. Next, label who was responsible for each issue: the prison guards, the Correctional Service of Canada, the Canadian government, or Ashley.
2. What recommendations would you make to ensure that a case like Ashley Smith's does not occur in Canada again?
3. How does society's attitude toward mental illness influence individual behaviour? Why is it important that we take care of our mentally ill citizens?
4. Is PTSD something that is unique in North America? Look for examples from other countries of this condition and note any similarities and differences.

CHAPTER 5 REVIEW

Knowledge and Understanding/Thinking

1. For each of the following scenarios, explain which area of the Code of Ethics relates and why:
   a) Parents ask for a medication traditionally prescribed for ADHD to increase their child's competitive advantage for gaining admission into better universities.
   b) A company asks you to complete a survey in the mall without your parents' knowledge or permission.
   c) Parents allow their children to be part of a paid study on whether they can avoid temptation.
   d) As a research assistant for a psychology professor, you learn that another research assistant has faked the research data because he or she ran out of time.
   e) A teacher conducts an experiment in class on a student without his or her knowledge to model an example.
   f) Parents want to hire a psychologist to help them raise their child to be a professional athlete.
   g) A student used the survey data of a friend who took the Social Sciences course last year rather than developing his or her own question and gathering survey data.

2. For each of the following scenarios, provide a psychological explanation(s) from a psychologist or a specific theory:
   a) Mr. Williams, the manager of a grocery store, has decided to make the self-checkout machine play funky music as people pay for their items in order to encourage customers to use it more often.
   b) Andrea has difficulty even beginning a project because the pressure is so great to make it as good as possible.
   c) All her life, Fatima has felt extremely shy but doesn't know where that feeling came from.
   d) Miguel, who was in a bad car accident a few months ago, is having nightmares and mood swings.

3. How is psychology being used in real-world applications? Using the headings below, create a chart that includes the various examples from this chapter.

Example	Type of Psychology	Applications	Impact	Ethical Implications

4. Explain how heredity, environment, birth order, and gender can affect personality. Discuss the arguments against the effects of these ideas as well.

Thinking/Communication

5. Create a graphic organizer that illustrates how motivation, attitude, perception, and mental health affect behaviour. Demonstrate relationships among factors and include examples and psychologists.

6. How would behaviourists respond to the debate of nature versus nurture? How would developmental psychologists respond? Communicate your ideas in a poster or position paper.

7. Select one of the criteria in the Canadian Code of Ethics, and explain why it is included. Discuss the potential problems that might occur if it were not included.

8. Suggest an experiment that you would like to conduct in order to answer a question you have related to psychology. Explain how it would meet ethical guidelines today, referring to the Canadian Code of Ethics.

9. "If a system of death camps were set up in the United States of the sort we had seen in Nazi Germany, one would be able to find sufficient personnel for those camps in any medium-sized American town." (Stanley Milgram, 1979). Explain whether you agree or disagree with this statement using evidence from this chapter.

Communication/Application

10. Select a psychologist or study mentioned in Chapter 5, and write a blog responding to the ideas involved and the impact of these ideas. Your blog must include the following sections:
    - a clear title
    - a response
    - a photo or image that represents your ideas
    - appropriate language for your purpose and audience
    - appropriate language or terminology associated with the research of the psychologists or specific study
    - a personal example (or one of a friend) to show how psychology and your life today are connected

11. You have been appointed to a government committee on childhood obesity. Use what you have learned in this chapter and your own research to suggest how to motivate Canadians to become more active and eat healthy foods.

12. Create a survey on a topic of significance at your school. Consider the use of open-ended and closed questions, your wording, and the appropriateness of questions. Use the Ethical Experiment Checklist on page 241 to review your survey before you use it.

13. Prepare a presentation to an ethics panel to explain one of the experiments in this chapter, how you can improve on what was done, and why it is necessary to do this research.

CHAPTER 6

Sociology and Me

Understanding how people behave in groups and form a social identity is of great interest to sociologists. In this chapter, you will learn about social belonging and examine how groups are formed, including the impact of technology on groups. You will look at collective behaviour and how conformity, alienation, obedience, and aggression play a role in this behaviour. You will also consider the ethical dilemmas that exist in the discipline of sociology. Finally, you will practise the research skills employed by sociologists to ethically gather evidence and data for their studies.

Chapter Expectations

By the end of this chapter, you will:
- identify and describe the major influences that contribute to an individual's sociological development
- explain why behavioural responses vary depending on the context and the groups involved
- analyze the role of major influences on social behaviour

Key Terms

acting crowd	expressive crowd	riot
altruism	groupthink	sanction
casual crowd	homophily	scapegoat
census	informal group	secondary group
chaperone	Islamophobia	sexism
classism	mass hysteria	smart mob
compliance	mob	social identity
conformity	obedience	social role
conventional crowd	panic	solidarity
dehumanize	prejudice	stereotype
demography	prosocial behaviour	threshold
differential association	racism	upstander
discrimination	review of literature	virtual community
dyad		

FIGURE 6-1 Is it possible to retain your individuality in such a large crowd?

Landmark Case Studies

Henri Tajfel: The Social Identity Theory
Stanley Milgram: Subway Experiments
The Clark Doll Experiment

Key Theorists

Albert Bandura
Kenneth Clark
Mamie Clark
Robin Dunbar
Erving Goffman
Mark Granovetter

Charles Hofling
Irving Janis
Muzafer Sherif
Henri Tajfel
Scot Wortley

Spotlight on Sociology

Group Conflict: Sherif's Robbers Cave Experiment

Before You Read
Have you ever been a part of a competitive team? How did you feel about your opponents?

In the summer of 1954, Muzafer Sherif conducted an important study to learn about the way in which groups develop and function. The study took place in a summer camp in Robbers Cave State Park, Oklahoma, where 22 11-year-old boys were taken as part of this unique social experiment. Before the trip, the boys were randomly divided into two groups. Sherif hoped to discover how prejudice and conflict developed between different groups of people.

When the boys arrived, the two groups were housed in separate cabins and, for the first week, did not know about the other group. During this time, the boys began to develop strong bonds with the others in their group. Eventually, each group choose a name for itself, which it stencilled on its shirts and flags: one group was known as the Eagles and the other as the Rattlers.

Once the groups were established, the experiment moved into its second phase. For the first time, the two groups were allowed to meet and it wasn't long before conflict emerged. At this point, the experimenters set up a series of competitions between the two groups to intensify the conflict. In the end, the Rattlers won, intensifying the conflict. The groups shouted insults at each other and refused to eat in the same room together.

With conflict between the groups successfully established, the experiment now moved into its final phase. Sherif's research team wanted to know if peace between the Eagles and Rattlers was possible.

First, the team tried some simple activities, such as having the two groups watch a film together, to see if the groups could overcome their differences, but that failed. The experimenters then tried a new approach: they took both groups to a new location and gave them a series of problems to solve. In the first problem, the boys were told that vandals had sabotaged their drinking-water supply. Faced with the prospect of having no water to drink, the groups worked together successfully to unblock a faucet. That was the first sign of co-operation Sherif's team had seen from the boys.

For the second problem, the boys were told they could watch a movie if they agreed on the choice together. The Eagles and Rattlers reached a consensus and agreed on a movie. Soon after, a truce was called and the boys were once again eating together.

Sherif reached an important conclusion as a result of this study. He argued that groups naturally develop their own culture, structure, and boundaries. He likened the group to a country. Each country has its own culture, government, and legal system, and it draws boundaries to separate itself from other groups. Therefore, attacking any part of the country's system will certainly result in conflict.

FIGURE 6-2 The boys at Robbers Cave built strong relationships among their group members.

QUESTIONS

1. What ethical concerns do you have about this experiment?

2. Do you see any connections between this case study and your school or community? What connections do you see to local and world events?

3. Map the social bonds of your friends and social groups.

Research and Inquiry Skills

Gathering and Processing Information

Sociologists consult several sources of information when conducting their research. A sociologist begins with a **review of literature**, which is a search for and examination of credible, reputable studies conducted by others in the discipline. The literature may include journals, books, and statistical records. The review of literature reveals whether a topic is worthy of research. Typically, after a review of literature, the sociologist may refine the original research question and formulate a hypothesis.

Criteria for a Good Hypothesis

A good hypothesis:
- must be a clear answer to the question posed, not a statement of the topic or evidence
- must be an answer that summarizes a definite point of view and is supported by arguments and evidence
- must be testable
- enables predictions that can be experimentally assessed (using primary research methods)

Activities

1. For each of the following statements, decide whether it is a good or poor hypothesis. Give reasons to support your answer.
   a) In Canada, there are many different religions that influence children.
   b) Video games have a positive educational impact on teenagers.
   c) Television makes children into consumers for toy manufacturers.

The Limits of Sociological Research

Limits to sociological research include the following:
- Human behaviour is complex and making generalizations and predictions based on a sample is difficult.
- The presence of researchers can affect what is being studied.
- Society is continually changing, so it is hard to compare studies over time.
- It is difficult to remain neutral when studying part of your own society.
- Some research questions violate ethics and cannot be researched.

Testing a Hypothesis

With the review completed, it is time for the sociologist to begin testing the hypothesis and gathering data. Data is gathered from a number of sources, such as public and historical records, census information, newspapers, magazines, and electronic media.

The sociologist also develops his or her own tools to test the hypothesis. These tools are known as primary sources. Primary sources may include surveys and interview questions, which you learned about in Chapter 2.

Synthesizing Research

After completing secondary research and conducting primary research to test a hypothesis, it's time to put all the information together. The sociologist synthesizes the findings and formulates a conclusion. To do this, he or she might consider the following questions:

- Did the results support or contradict the hypothesis?
- Were the results affected by *confounding variables* (variables not controlled in your research design)?
- Were the results affected by such factors as the sample size of your primary research?
- Compare results to the existing body of research on the topic.
- What steps should be taken next (for example, more research, change in policy)?

After the research is complete, it should be shared with others. This can be done using a variety of methods, which you will learn about in Chapter 8.

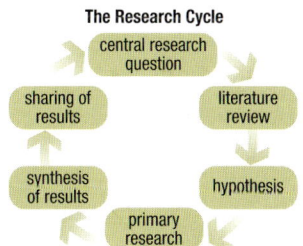

FIGURE 6-3 Researchers follow a number of steps from forming their initial central research question to sharing the results of their study.

Activities

Using the Robbers Cave experiment as a guide, answer the following questions:

1. What steps would you take to discover how conflict develops between two groups? What sources of information would you consult before conducting your study?
2. What is a possible hypothesis for more research about conflict?

Section 6.1 — Sociology and Identity

Sociologists view identity as a mutual relationship between an individual and society. As individuals, we influence society through the creation of groups and networks. Society, in turn, influences us through common language and shared meanings. Sociologists are interested in understanding these social structures and how they influence how identity is constructed.

Social Identity

In Chapter 3, you learned that socialization is the process by which individuals learn the beliefs and values of their society, enabling them to become well-adjusted members of that society. By internalizing the values of the group to which one belongs, an individual also develops a self-concept and begins to establish his or her place in the larger world.

This emerging **social identity** allows a person to interact socially with a number of people in a variety of different situations. The challenge becomes knowing when and how to act in these various situations. The greater the number of interactions, the more a person is able to develop his or her approach to social interactions, or social identity. This in turn creates a reciprocal relationship between the individual and society.

When studying the emergence of the social identity, it is important to acknowledge the many elements that work together to establish identity. These elements include gender, culture, age, and social class. Throughout the course of one's life, these elements aid in the formation of social identity.

Social Identity and the Life Cycle

A concept that sociologists return to over and over again is that social identity is not static. It changes and grows along with the individual throughout his or her life and is influenced by life experiences. Life stage is a key determinant of social roles and identities. For many sociologists, the key to understanding the emergence of a specific behaviour or role in society is to study its progress throughout a person's life. Sociologists assume that individuals will pass through different stages in their life, and while doing so, the individuals are meant to accomplish certain developmental tasks. Much like Erikson's or Piaget's stages of development, which you learned about in Chapter 2, stages of the life cycle refer to developing social skills and abilities that form your behaviour in society.

Life Stages and Developmental Tasks

The table on page 261 provides a guide for the major life stages through which many people pass and the possible connections to an emergent social identity for individuals. The importance of socialization is clearly seen as individuals are constantly asked to develop, examine, and re-examine the crucial roles they play in the family and in society at various stages of development. Not

> **Before You Read**
> Have you ever been in or observed a social situation in which you or someone else was uncomfortable? How did you or the other person respond? How could it have been handled differently?

social identity: the way you define yourself to the world and to yourself

FIGURE 6-4 Social identity is a complex structure. What elements are involved in its formation?

FIGURE 6-5 How does social identity change throughout the course of one's lifetime?

everyone passes through all these stages, however, nor will the stages necessarily occur in the same order. Many people today may never get married; others will get married but not have children, while still others will get married to someone who already has children. Many of these life stages have been altered by greater choices in career and lifestyle, and have also been influenced by socio-economic circumstances, as well as cultural background.

There are several elements that reappear routinely throughout the life cycle; these include gender, culture, and social class. Each person fashions a unique social identity out of these experiences. So, long before we learn anything from society, we are learning from our formative experiences of belonging to a family. We, in turn, take those lessons and translate them into a broader identity that will serve us in the "real world."

> **Connecting Sociology to Psychology**
>
> Psychologists Freud and Erikson also looked at the life cycle. Freud's stages of development theory was based on his observations of children's focus of pleasure as they mature. Erikson believed that individual growth depends on society, not just personal experiences. Sociologists look at different factors such as how culture, class, and status are confirmed.

LIFE STAGES

1. Young Single Adult
- Establishing one's independence as an individual and setting life direction
- Planning and obtaining an appropriate education
- Establishing one's social class and status
- Developing love relationships in connection to one's identity
- Acknowledging cultural traditions of the family

2. Newly Married Couple
- Determining social and gender roles
- Further establishing social class and status
- Developing conflict-resolution strategies
- Deciding on parenthood
- Teaching cultural traditions of one's family to spouse

3. Family with Young Children
- Fully integrating gender roles and expectations of parenthood
- Acting as the primary agent of socialization for children
- Passing along cultural traditions to offspring
- Confirming social class and status
- Integrating important agents of socialization (for example, school, religion)

4. Family with Adolescents
- Further integrating agents of socialization (for example, peer groups)
- Establishing balance of autonomy and control for adolescents
- Coping with strong social influences on the family (for example, media)
- Ensuring cultural traditions are maintained by all members of the family

5. Family in Mid-life
- Launching grown children (sometimes relaunching them more than once)
- Incorporating new members through social institutions such as marriage
- Maintaining cultural traditions of the family while expanding traditions to include new members
- Aging and possibly developing alienation between older and younger generations

6. Family in Later Life
- Adjusting to retirement and possible changes in social status and class
- Maintaining love, sex, and marital relationships
- Reintegrating important agents of socialization (for example, religion)
- Passing along cultural traditions to future generations

Landmark Case Study

Henri Tajfel: The Social Identity Theory

Sociologists have long known that humans are a social species. We seek interaction with others whenever possible and use those experiences to shape our future responses and behaviours. Who we are is formed by our gender, class, age, and culture. Our daily interactions with others, where we learn about important social roles and values, also have a great influence. Our behaviour within a group can also influence our attitudes and behaviours. The study of group behaviour is an integral part of sociology. Observing group behaviour and interactions between members of a group can reveal important information about individual motivation and social values.

For example, one can learn a great deal about **conformity**—the process by which one changes one's thoughts, feelings, and behaviour to meet the expectations of a group or authority figure—by simply observing how individuals interact with members of their group. Ultimately, when studying group behaviour, sociologists aim to discover the nature of the group relationship and the amount of influence it exerts on our attitudes and identities as individuals.

FIGURE 6-6 Paul Klee's painting *The Rose Garden*

Tajfel's Experiment

Social psychologist Henri Tajfel set out to study group influence on individuals. He began his investigation with a simple question: What would happen when individuals stood together for 30 seconds while looking at a painting? Tajfel wanted to investigate the notion that individuals are capable of forming a group in a short period of time. Furthermore, he wanted to know if these groups could have any lasting implications on actions and behaviours of the individual.

In his experiment, a group of 14- and 15-year-old boys were shown a series of pictures of well-known art pieces by Paul Klee and Wassily Kandinsky (see Figures 6-6 and 6-7, respectively for examples). The boys were then told they would be grouped based on their preference for one or the other artist. What the

FIGURE 6-7 Wassily Kandinsky's painting *All Saints I*

boys were not told was that the whole process was a ploy meant simply to create competition and, more importantly to establish the notion of "us" and "them" between the two groups.

For the final task in this experiment, each boy was taken to a cubicle where he was given the task of

FIGURE 6-8 No two groups are alike. What advantages are there to being part of a group? Does being a member of a group mean that it is impossible to live with other groups in a noncompetitive manner?

distributing "play money" to the other participants. The boys were provided with only two pieces of information about the person receiving the money: a code number for the boy and the group to which the boy belonged.

Tajfel wanted to discover how the boys would distribute the money. He set out questions to help gather data, for example: Did the boys distribute the money to ensure their group would profit? Did they distribute it fairly, disregarding their own group's welfare? What patterns for distributing the money were established?

The Results

Tajfel and his research team believed that it was possible for a group to form instantaneously without so much as a word exchanged between members of the group.

After reviewing how the money was distributed, Tajfel concluded that the boys did, in fact, favour their group over the other group. This study was conducted many times, and the results were the same every time. Even though they stood to gain nothing by favouring their own group, the boys consistently chose to favour their group members. This discovery carries powerful implications for society at large, where there are many advantages to group favouritism because it is part of our need for protection, acceptance, and security.

Conclusions

Tajfel's study, along with others like it, has helped to establish a direct link between social behaviour and social identity. Theories such as Tajfel's *social identity theory* suggest that group membership helps to shape one's identity. Belonging to a group also means protecting the core beliefs of the group and ensuring its future survival. That typically means putting down an opposing group or any other group that might threaten the group's existence.

In the end, Tajfel's experiment proved that, with minimal prompting, individuals are willing to join groups and, once a member, internalize the group's core beliefs as their own.

QUESTIONS

1. Create a comparison chart noting the similarities and differences between Tajfel's work and the experiment at Robbers Cave.
2. What did Tajfel's team discover about group membership and social identity?
3. Tajfel used paintings to group his subjects. What other prompts would you consider using to conduct a similar experiment? Explain your choice.
4. When protecting his or her group, is a group member doing this to protect his or her position? Are the actions motivated by a personal agenda for a more altruistic goal?
5. In some instances group membership is extremely important because of its ability to provide protection as well as identity. Provide an example of when this might occur.

> **REFLECT AND RESPOND**

1. What role does socialization play in the development of social identity?
2. How might a person's life stage help or hinder a healthy social identity? Provide examples.
3. What stage seems the most difficult emotionally? Financially?

Role Theory

> **Before You Read**
>
> Brainstorm the different roles you play in society (for example, student, child) and the influences on your behaviour in each of these roles.

In Chapter 3, you learned about the micro- and macro-approaches to sociology. In this chapter, you will use microsociological theories to help explain the give-and-take relationship between the individual and society. You also know that microsociology focuses on the individual's behaviour in society. To add to this understanding, symbolic interactionists such as Erving Goffman set out to understand individual behaviour in relation to social roles people willingly and unwillingly play in society.

Social Roles

social role: expectations attached to particular social positions

Social roles have expectations that are attached to particular social positions. According to Erving Goffman, *all* human behaviour is acted. He claimed that people manipulate their appearance in order to present a specific kind of self, depending on the audience. For example, some positions in society are very clear, such as the role of a teacher. Most of us can describe, with certain accuracy, the rights and duties associated with this position. Teachers deal with students, parents, colleagues, and administrators, each of whom has different expectations for the teacher. The teacher consolidates all of these expectations and acts accordingly. In a sense, the teacher plays the same role consistently, but the scene may change, which may require a slight change in the teacher's approach or behaviour. The same can be said about the student's role or the parent's role.

Sometimes we are able to play the role willingly and, at other times, we do so reluctantly. The most common role that we are taught from birth is how to behave according to our gender.

FIGURE 6-9 William Shakespeare wrote, "All the world's a stage, and all the men and women merely players." Why might sociologists believe this to be true?

> **?** How can your role as student help influence your social identity long after you leave the formal school setting?

Gender Roles

Gender is one of many identities an individual is expected to enact throughout his or her lifetime. What we believe about gender is internalized from a young age through the primary agent of socialization—the family— and is based on accepted norms of masculine and feminine behaviour as developed by family and society, and portrayed in the media.

Gender socialization occurs as the child ages. Initially, very young children are not able to distinguish the differences between masculine and feminine roles. That's why it is not uncommon to see preschoolers playing with members of the opposite sex or with toys not associated with his or her particular gender (for example, a girl playing with trucks and a boy playing with dolls). It isn't until they begin to mature that school-aged children develop an understanding about the differences between the sexes. As children grow, they continuously re-examine and make adjustments to their attitude toward both sexes. They eventually come to appreciate the company of the opposite or same sex and may seek out intimate relationships as a result.

FIGURE 6-10 Teachers are expected to understand their role in the classroom and to act accordingly. What role does the student play in this situation? How have the roles of students and teachers changed since this photo was taken?

Gender roles are not the same today as they were in the first half of the twentieth century. Economic and cultural globalization has had a significant impact on redefining gender roles. Factors such as greater educational opportunities for women, dual-earner families, and access to contraceptives have all shifted traditional roles. The ideal of the man as the breadwinner is also changing, which is having an impact on the expectations of men. For these reasons, sociologists are careful to distinguish between *gender roles* and *gender behaviours*. At one time mothers stayed home with their children while fathers worked long hours, each taking on a particular role that was expressed with particular behaviours. For example, the housewife may have deferred all important financial decisions to her husband. Today, many spouses see their contributions to the household as equal. More women than ever before are in the workforce and are equal partners in earning power. It is also becoming more common for fathers to be full-time caregivers of their children.

FIGURE 6-11 Social roles determine identity. Will this woman's gender affect the role she plays in this instance?

Examining Gender Identity in Children

In the 1977 classic study by Peter J. Burke and Judy Tully entitled "The Measurement of Role/Identity," the two researchers studied a group of middle-school children in an attempt to discover what the group had to say about gender identity. Burke and Tully asked the children to complete the following statement: "Usually [boys/girls] are …." Then they selected items that sufficiently described the differences between boys and girls. Examples such as *weak* versus *strong* and *emotional* versus *not emotional* were used to describe females and males. The study found that children with cross-sex identities (boys who thought of themselves in ways similar to the way most girls thought of themselves and vice versa) were more likely to have low self-esteem.

FIGURE 6-12 How do same-sex couples challenge the idea of traditional gender roles?

> Why do children respond to gender roles? How might a parent's positive reinforcement for a girl playing with a doll cause the child to want to continue to receive praise? Does this reinforce the idea that playing with dolls is something that is proper?

Dating and Courtship in the Digital Age

Along with other social trends, mate selection undergoes noticeable changes from one generation to another. These trends tell us a great deal about gender values for that particular generation. For example, during the Victorian era young ladies, under the watchful eyes of **chaperones**, accepted "invitations" by eligible gentlemen. In some parts of the world, parents have played an instrumental role in the dating and courtship process, from choosing prospective mates to arranging contracts with the suitor's family. In Canada, free-choice mate selection is the most common method, although some cultures maintain some element of parental involvement. Recently, an interesting phenomenon has been growing in many societies around the world: digital dating.

chaperone: an older or married woman who accompanies or supervises a young unmarried woman on social occasions

FIGURE 6-13 The digital age offers many new ways to find love.

Chapter 6 • Sociology and Me NEL 265

homophily:
the tendency to associate with those who are similar to us

More to Know...
You can read more about courtship and marriage from an anthropological perspective in Chapter 4.

Skills Focus
Write a hypothesis for an investigation of the influence of technology in courtship and relationships. List the primary and secondary sources you would use to test this hypothesis and explain your reason for using each source.

The Influence of Technology on Traditional Courtship

Choosing a mate based on similar characteristics is known as **homophily** and has long been a part of mate selection. People gravitate toward those who are similar to them, particularly in terms of core values and education. The availability of online dating has made it possible to track factors that lead to the selection of a mate and reveals that homophily is quite prevalent. In particular, people look for a mate whose level of education is similar to their own. The Internet allows one to broaden this search to include the entire online world to find the "perfect" partner.

A fascinating trend is emerging among young singles in traditional cultures such as that of India: where once arranged marriages were the norm, they are much less common today. This change has been developing rapidly over the last two decades, and the pivotal force behind the change has been technology.

Today, many young couples share their experiences of love online and swear by its effectiveness. A study out of the University of Washington showed that young East Indians involved in arranged relationships were using cell phones as a way of getting to know each other better. This is quite different from the traditional method of meeting your spouse for 20 minutes and getting married a short time later.

The use of email and social networking sites, such as Facebook, has also changed the landscape of dating and courting. Today, many prospective mates can be found on sites dedicated specifically to finding suitable cultural matches. Often, parents create profiles for their adult children in an attempt to find the perfect match.

Many sociologists see this as a natural shift and a response to the changing lifestyles of young singles today. Fewer people are getting married in their early 20s, and more are choosing lifestyles and careers that involve travel away from the places where they grew up. For these reasons, many young adults are less likely to participate in traditional social networks close to home, where they would traditionally meet a mate, and are turning to alternative technology-based methods of meeting people. The prevalence of technology in our daily lives has also created a shift in social attitudes to online dating. It is quickly becoming an acceptable practice, especially among women.

REFLECT AND RESPOND

1. Are there still some roles that are/should remain gender specific (for example, combat roles in the military)? Provide evidence for and against this idea.

2. How has technology changed the dating process in the last 20 years? Is it a positive change? Interview or survey people from different generations to hear their stories about dating when they were younger. Alternatively, compare how dating is depicted on television shows from the 1960s to the present.

3. In your opinion, how will multiculturalism and the large influx of new immigrants from around the globe change the notion of gender in Canadian society in the next 10 to 20 years?

IN FOCUS: David Reimer: The Boy Who Lived as a Girl

Winnipeg twins Bruce and Brian Reimer were born in Winnipeg in 1965. At the age of six months, both boys were circumcised due to recurring urinary infections. The procedure went horribly wrong and Bruce's genitals were damaged beyond repair. His parents spent months consulting with countless doctors, but they all agreed that the situation was hopeless. One night, Bruce's parents saw a television profile of Dr. John Money of Johns Hopkins University in Baltimore. Money claimed that boys could be raised as girls if taught early enough. Janet Reimer, Bruce's mom, thought it was worth exploring, and the family went to Baltimore to see Dr. Money, who decided that Bruce was a perfect candidate for a gender reassignment.

Dr. Money believed that while genes are important, a baby is essentially gender-neutral for the first two years of life. During these critical two years, the child's upbringing and how he or she is nurtured determines whether the child feels masculine or feminine. Dr. Money indicated that Bruce was young enough that he could be raised as a girl and recommended that parts of Bruce's genitals be removed. His parents were to treat him as a female thereafter and not to divulge anything to anyone. They went home with a girl they called "Brenda."

Despite their best efforts to raise Bruce as a girl, the transformation was anything but smooth. On the outside, Bruce looked like a girl: he wore dresses and makeup. But his mannerisms were not very feminine. He also didn't like playing with the other girls and was known to get into fights at school. "Caveman," and "freak" were common nicknames.

As Bruce reached puberty, his thick neck and shoulders revealed a more masculine physique. It became increasingly clear the experiment was not working. Dr. Money pressured the Reimers to take the final step and allow surgeons to create female genitals for Bruce. Finally, the Reimers decided to tell their son the truth.

The Aftermath

On learning of his past, Bruce decided that he no longer wanted to live as a female. He cut his hair and began dressing as a boy again. He changed his name to "David" (see Figure 6-14).

Initially, David Reimer told his story only from the shadows; he refused to talk about it if his identity were revealed. That changed in 2000 when David gave permission to American author John Colapinto to write a book about his life: *As Nature Made Him: The Boy Who Was Raised as a Girl*.

Because of the surgical procedures he endured, David was unable to father his own children, although subsequent reconstructive surgeries allowed him to have a normal sex life. He did get married, was a stepfather to his wife's three children, and seemed to be happy. Sadly, he committed suicide in 2004 after his wife requested a separation.

FIGURE 6-14 In his teens, Bruce Reimer reclaimed his masculine identity and became known as "David."

QUESTIONS

1. What can we learn about gender roles from David's story?
2. Despite all the attempts to socialize Bruce as a girl, the experiment failed. What does this failure say about the power of biology versus socialization?
3. Would you consider Dr. Money's methods ethical? Organize ideas both for and against in terms of how social scientists conduct research.

Identity and Discrimination

Before You Read

Identify yourself with all the labels that people place on you by looking at you (for example, *student*, *athlete*, *shy*, *artistic*). Then in a separate list, add the labels that cannot be seen. What does this say about you?

Society and its institutions, such as the government and law enforcement, are responsible for ensuring everyone's rights regardless of age, sex, race, or sexual orientation. In Canada, our rights and freedoms are written into the laws that govern our society. The Canadian Charter of Rights and Freedoms demands that the government treat all individuals, and, by extension, the groups to which they belong, equitably and fairly. In Canada, men and women enjoy the following fundamental freedoms equally:

- freedom of conscience and religion
- freedom of thought, belief, opinion and expression, including freedom of the press and other media of communication
- freedom of peaceful assembly
- freedom of association

Stereotypes, Prejudice, and Discrimination

Despite the Charter, **discrimination** of all types exists in Canada as it does in less equalitarian societies around the world. Most forms of discrimination begin with stereotypes, which seem to endure from one generation to the next. A **stereotype** is an exaggerated view or judgment made about a group or class of people.

For example, assuming certain tasks can be accomplished only by men because women lack the physical strength is a gender stereotype. Likewise, assuming that all members of a racial group are likely to excel at a specific task is an example of a racial stereotype. Stereotypes tend to highlight a specific behaviour observed, in limited and infrequent form, about one group by another. Stereotypes may seem harmless enough; after all, they are merely exaggerated opinions. However, they may extend beyond opinion and form the basis for more severe beliefs such as **racism**, **sexism**, or **classism**. Stereotypes may turn into **prejudice**. Figure 6-15 outlines some examples of discrimination.

discrimination: the act of treating groups or individuals unfairly based on their race, gender, or other common characteristic; can be overt or systemic

stereotype: an exaggerated view or judgment made about a group or class of people

racism: erroneous judgment, assumptions, opinions, or actions toward a person or group, based on the belief that one race is superior to another

sexism: attitudes or behaviours based on predetermined ideas of sexual roles that discriminate against others because of their sex

classism: systemic or personal actions that discriminate against persons according to their socio-economic level, which leads to human needs being unmet

prejudice: an individual judgment about or active hostility toward another social group

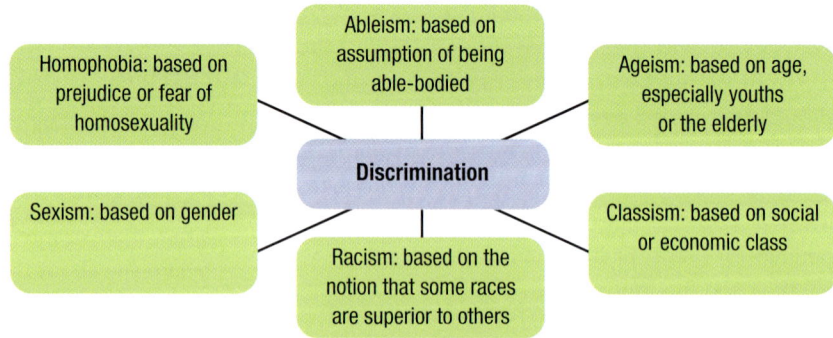

↑ **FIGURE 6-15** Discrimination comes in many forms. Identify an example for each type shown.

268 NEL Unit 2 • Social Science and Me

Prejudice is an individual judgment about or active hostility toward another social group. Prejudice is not illegal, but it is unethical. Moreover, the effects of prejudice on the victim are serious. Often times, the victim of prejudice feels isolated and fearful. The victim inevitably suffers a loss of self-esteem and likely refrains from engaging in social situations in which he or she feels threatened or judged. When the victims of prejudice are children, they may also experience a decline in academic achievement and become emotionally withdrawn. Finally, people acting on their prejudice can lead to discrimination.

Discrimination is the act of treating groups or individuals unfairly based on their race, gender, or other common characteristic. The chart below explains two forms of discrimination: overt and systemic.

> **VOICES**
> Our lives begin to end the day we become silent about things that matter.
> Martin Luther King Jr.

Overt Discrimination	Systemic Discrimination
Intentional actions that are taken against an individual or group because of some distinguishing characteristic they possess.	Subtle and unintentional discrimination against a person or group where the consequences or outcome are not fully understood by those taking action.
For example, an employer refuses to hire a woman for a traditionally male job even though she is more qualified and better suited to the position.	*For example, a physically disabled job candidate may not be able to accept a job because the building is not wheelchair-friendly.*

It's a Colourful World

It is hard to believe that such a basic product as crayons could highlight the extent of subtle prejudice in our society. While the iconic colours have remained, three times in the company's history Crayola has found itself in the position of having to change the name for some of its crayons. In 1958, "Prussian Blue" was changed to "Midnight Blue," and in 1962, "Flesh" was changed to "Peach." The 1962 change came off the heels of the civil rights movement led by Martin Luther King, Jr., in the United States at the time. Finally in 1999, with mounting pressure from Aboriginal groups, Crayola changed the name "Indian Red" to "Chestnut." In each case, the names were changed to reflect a new generation of consumers who were more culturally aware and diverse.

(?) Why might *flesh* as a colour have been changed to *peach*? What assumptions had been made by Crayola before the name change?

Upstanders

When faced with any form of discrimination, it is important to act rather than ignore. An **upstander** is one who stands up for what he or she believes in and responds to something when it happens. Being an upstander is not always an easy task. A student acknowledged, "One time, a handicapped student fell in the middle of the hallway and couldn't get up. I didn't do anything about it because no one else was stopping to help." History has many examples of both upstanders and bystanders, but if we want a society where all are included, we all need to work toward that goal.

FIGURE 6-16 Ira Bleiweiss is an upstander who is trying to teach others about tolerance by taking out billboards around Houston urging the message of peace.

upstander:
a person who takes action, particularly when the easiest or most acceptable course is to do nothing, when he or she believes something is right

Defining New Ways to Discriminate in a Post-9/11 World

Arguably, one of the most important events in American and Western history was 9/11. It has been said that the coordinated attacks by al-Qaeda extremists on the World Trade Center in New York and other strategic locations in the United States on September 11, 2001, changed the world forever. This event certainly changed the way many have come to view Islam and Muslims, as many experienced racism, prejudice, and descrimination. It is also responsible for popularizing a form of discrimination known as **Islamophobia**, which is racism that leads to prejudice against and fear of Islamic beliefs and Muslims. Since 9/11, peaceful, law-abiding Muslims have come under attack by those fearful and suspicious of their culture and religious beliefs. Terry Jones, a Florida preacher, made headlines in 2010 for his outspoken opinion on Muslims. He planned to make September 11 "International Burn a Qur'an Day," where everyone was asked to set fire to the Qur'an—Islam's book of religious teachings. Although he eventually backed down, Jones demonstrated the dangerous power of Islamophobia. Making generalizations does not benefit anybody.

Islamophobia: racism that leads to prejudice against and fear of Islamic beliefs and Muslims

> **VOICES**
>
> America and Islam are not exclusive and need not be in competition. Instead, they overlap, and share common principles of justice and progress, tolerance, and the dignity of all human beings.
>
> Barack Obama

❓ Why might people be reluctant to respond to Islamophobic comments or actions?

The Discrimination Against Obese People by Doctors

Overweight people have been the target of scrutiny for a number of years. Many people believe that these people lack willpower and thus overeat and don't exercise. While these beliefs may be applicable in some cases, they are certainly not true of all people who deal with a weight problem.

In one American study, 620 doctors were asked to describe obese patients. They used terms such as *awkward*, *unattractive*, and *ugly*. They also described them as unlikely to comply with treatment, which influenced the way they treated these patients.

Another study showed that the higher a patient's body mass, the less respect a doctor had for the patient. Less respect from a doctor for a patient leads to less time spent with the patient and less information offered by the doctor. This leads to a cycle where the patient does not get the help needed to manage his or her weight due to obesity.

Given the attitudes of doctors toward obese patients, it is not surprising that others in society have a negative feeling toward the obese.

REFLECT AND RESPOND

1. What do you think the consequences would be if the Charter did not exist?
2. Why is it difficult to act as an upstander? What can be done to encourage others to help those in need?
3. "Obesity is the same as race—an inheritable trait over which individuals have no control." Explain why you agree or disagree with this statement.
4. How might a sociologist help gauge public opinion about obese people in other fields besides medicine?

What Causes Prejudice and Discrimination?

Sociologists look for answers to the troubling question of what causes prejudice and discrimination in the process of socialization and conformity to group behaviour. There are also a number of valuable theories that aim to explain the unfortunate origins of discrimination.

Learned Theory

Prejudice and discriminatory behaviour are not innate to our species. They are learned behaviours that individuals acquire through socialization. Children learn by observing their parents and often imitate the behaviours they see. Many of the behaviours parents demonstrate are meant to help their children function and get along in society as they age. Unfortunately, not all lessons learned at home are positive. In some cases, prejudicial views are passed along from parent to child. Often, children carry those views with them until the rebellious adolescent years when some will abandon the ideas and beliefs of their parents in favour of ideas and beliefs shared by peers.

The family is not the only agent of socialization carrying potentially negative ideas that can lead to intolerance. The media are also responsible for portraying both positive and negative views of race, gender, and sexual orientation. Images in media have been known to spread stereotypes. For instance, advertising has steadily depicted white people in key roles, with minorities included only as tokens—where one minority is included to represent all.

Our language is also riddled with inappropriate terminology. For example, we have only recently begun to use the term *firefighter* in place of *fireman* and *mail carrier* in place of *mailman*. The antiquated terms taught entire generations of children to make certain assumptions about gender roles and career choices. It is through these means—family and media—that some might have learned and retained prejudice and discrimination.

Competition Theory

Canada was initially inhabited by Aboriginal peoples and then by immigrants. Although it advocates the policy of multiculturalism, prejudices exist against visible, non-white immigrants within the country. According to the competition theory, the key reason some people come to distrust immigrants is economic competition. This idea should remind you of Marxist notions of competition between groups for economic power that you learned about in Chapter 3. The same holds true here. Whenever an economic crisis is felt by society, some people assume, incorrectly, that immigration policies and immigrants are responsible. The unemployed may come to believe that newcomers have taken their jobs, creating a sense of competition between groups. Others still believe that any large influx of new Canadians places undue strains on our social and health services and contributes to the social and economic hardships of the country. Combined, these unfounded assumptions may lead some to hold deep resentment toward immigrants and may account for certain prejudice and discrimination in society.

> **Before You Read**
> Discuss with a partner how understanding the causes of discrimination could affect society. Why do you think discrimination and prejudice exist at all?

FIGURE 6-17 What do new family sitcoms such as *Modern Family* teach their audiences about tolerance and acceptance?

SOCIAL SCIENCE IN POPULAR CULTURE

Little Mosque on the Prairie

In the first episode of *Little Mosque on the Prairie*, a lawyer named Amar is travelling from Toronto to the fictional town of Mercy, Saskatchewan. He stands in line at the airport, talking to his mother on the phone about his decision to become the Imam—the prayer leader—at the mosque in Mercy. The woman in line in front of him hears the words "(career) suicide," "bomb," and "Allah," and alerts airport security. Moments later, Amar is dragged away by security guards.

Little Mosque is a sitcom airing on CBC, and is one of the most popular Canadian shows on TV. It explores the relationships between the Muslim and Christian communities in Mercy. Many of the events in the show, including Amar's detention at the airport, are inspired by real experiences of Muslims living in Canada. For example, the airport scene echoes the experience of some Muslims travelling after September 11, 2011, when airport security was tightened and fear and prejudice against Muslims began to increase.

Although the show uses humour to comment on current events, *Little Mosque* is not a political satire. It is a social comedy, and its humour comes from the misunderstandings and relationships among the characters. Comedy is an effective tool for exploring social issues because it brings issues out in to the open, where they can be discussed. By poking fun at Islamophobic beliefs and actions, *Little Mosque* leads viewers to question their own views and behaviour. However, the show's main goal is to be entertaining. Although the culture clash between Muslims and Christians is central, the comedy comes from the relationships among neighbours, and families. Those issues are universal, which is in part why the show appeals to such a large audience.

One of the key themes in the show is that the Muslim characters face the same challenges as anybody else, so they are humanized. In many other TV shows and movies, and even in other media such as the news, Muslims are often portrayed as extremists or terrorists. *Little Mosque* provides a more balanced view of Muslim

FIGURE 6-18 Some of the cast and crew on the set of *Little Mosque on the Prairie*. Zaib Shaikh (Amar) is the only Muslim actor in the cast. What unique challenges might Muslim actors face?

characters. It also teaches about some aspects of Muslim culture, and in this way reduces the fear and prejudice associated with Islamophobia. Anybody who has ever felt like an outsider, whether because of their religion or not, can identify with the characters.

A recurring theme in the show is the challenges the Muslim families face to fit in with the local culture. Halloween becomes "Halal-oween" in one episode, and when some of the female characters take a swimming class that turns out to be taught by a man, one woman comes to class in a swimsuit version of a burqa—the "burquini."

FIGURE 6-19 Zarqa Nawaz, the creator and producer of *Little Mosque on the Prairie*, accepts the Canada Award at the 2007 Gemini Awards Gala. What role do you think popular culture plays in promoting or discouraging discrimination?

One challenge the show faces is maintaining a balance between funny and offensive. Many of the issues addressed are highly sensitive, and the actual experiences they are based on are sometimes matters of life and death. The writers and producers must be sensitive to Muslim and non-Muslim perspectives. The response to the show from Muslim and non-Muslim communities has been generally very positive. However, the show has been criticized for not representing secular Muslims and for portraying the Christian community in Mercy as prejudiced and intolerant.

Overall, however, the response to *Little Mosque* has been very positive. It has the highest ratings of any CBC sitcom in the last 15 years. The first episode of the show had 2.3 million viewers, a huge audience for a Canadian show. Although the ratings have fallen since the first season, the show began its fifth season in January 2011. The show has also received international attention. The show's creator, Zarqa Nawaz, was awarded a media award by the Muslim Public Affairs Council, as well as a humanitarian honour called the Search for Common Ground award. The show also won a Canada Award for promoting racial tolerance (see Figure 6-19).

The show is now broadcast in Dubai, Finland, France, French-speaking Africa, Israel, Gaza, Switzerland, Turkey, the United Arab Emirates, and the West Bank, as well as across Canada. When French broadcaster Canal Plus picked up the show, it made it free to all viewers in the hope that it would help ease tensions between Muslim and non-Muslim communities in France. American journalist Katie Couric discovered *Little Mosque* after stating that America needed a Muslim *Cosby Show*. She invited Zaib Shaikh, the actor who plays Amar, to the CBS Evening News to discuss the social impact of the show.

QUESTIONS

1. Do you think humour is an effective tool for reducing discrimination? Why?
2. What other ways could popular culture help to reduce Islamophobia?

scapegoat: a specific person or group of people who become the target of hatred or blame for the hardships of others

▲ **FIGURE 6-20** Nazi propaganda posters against Jews carried powerful messages. What sociological reasons might explain why many did not challenge the propaganda?

Frustration–Aggression Theory

Sometimes the shortcomings an individual experiences in his or her financial status provide a reason to resent groups in society that may appear to have greater access to wealth and prosperity. For those in low-income situations, unable to get ahead financially, the frustration is unmistakable. This frustration is often displaced and turned into outward aggression toward the rival(s) who an individual feels is responsible for holding him or her back in life. People in this situation will act on their frustration by lashing out against those who represent "others." Perhaps one of the most sinister outcomes of this theory is the creation of a **scapegoat**. Scapegoats are a specific group of people who become the target of hatred and blame for the majority class in society. Perhaps one of the most infamous examples is that of the treatment of people of Jewish descent in Nazi Germany (see Figure 6-20), which led to the Holocaust and the extermination of six million people of Jewish descent. The Nazis also scapegoated other groups including the disabled, Jehovah's Witness, and homosexuals. Genocide is a concept defined in the 20th century to acknowledge the systemic murder of people based on a deliberate and systematic destruction, in whole or in part, of an ethnic, racial, religious, or national group.

Ignorance Theory

Lack of personal and social experience can cause people to make incorrect assumptions about a specific class or group in society. When we refuse to learn about a group, we remain unaware of how and why they function as they do. Without adequate knowledge, we may view the group's behaviour and customs as strange or odd. These beliefs may become the basis for later discrimination toward the group. According to the *ignorance theory*, it is the fear of unfamiliar cultural practices that guides discriminatory behaviour. You might say that those inflicting the discrimination are making value judgments based on their own culture. It is also easier to unite against a common enemy. When one group targets another to blame the other for something, the focus is taken away from the first group and any faults they might have. It is easier to focus on someone else's faults than to change your own behaviour(s). In this way, ethnocentrism is a leading cause of discrimination. Ethnocentrism is the practice of evaluating other cultures based on the customs and behaviours of one's own culture, which is considered superior to others'. Often the judgments made about other cultures may be negative and derogatory.

REFLECT AND RESPOND

1. For each of the four theories, create a short case study that incorporates the key components of the theory with an instance of discrimination.

2. Explain where the role of upstander would make a difference in each of your case studies.

3. Explain which theory gives the best explanation for the Holocaust, and explain your reasoning.

POINT/COUNTERPOINT

Do Parents Have the Right to Teach Their Children Antisocial Beliefs?

Do parents have the right to raise their children with a specific set of beliefs even if it goes against the norms of society? For example, in a 2008 case in Winnipeg, two children were dressed by their parents in outfits that included swastikas and pro-Nazi slogans. The daughter went to school with racist writings and symbols on her skin. When asked about these markings, she indicated that "black people didn't belong" and "this is a white man's world." She showed strong beliefs against black people and even suggested methods to kill them. The courts removed the children from the parents and put them into foster homes and in 2010 made this decision permanent.

The removal of the children has been hotly debated: Does the government have the right to remove children from their parents if they are being taught hateful ideas?

Yes	No
• While parents do have the right to their religious beliefs, if this causes emotional harm then these rights may be suppressed.	• Parents have the right to raise their children as they choose.
• The welfare of the child must be considered first and foremost and just because someone is the biological parent of a child does not mean he or she is the best person to raise the child, especially if he or she teaches hateful attitudes.	• Freedom of expression and religious freedom mean parents can believe what they want and pass on their beliefs to their children.
• We have laws to protect against the abuse of children and teaching children hateful attitudes is considered abuse.	• The state cannot interfere with parents' rights to raise their children just because they disagree with their values or religious beliefs.
• Tajfel's study, along with others like it, has helped to establish a direct link between social behaviour and social identity. Therefore, children who are exposed to antisocial ideas may incorporate these ideas into their identities and behaviours.	• Children do not always accept the values of their parents, as they are individuals with freedom of thought, and thus the beliefs of the parents do not constitute abuse.
• It is important to educate children on tolerance and acceptance. In extreme cases where the opposite has been taught it is important that these ideas be reversed at a young age when attitudes can be more easily changed.	• Bill Whatcott, an anti-gay Christian activist, argues that if you're going to target neo-Nazis who haven't actually hit or sexually abused their children, who's to say conservative Christian evangelicals aren't next? He believes that removing children from their parents can lead to other serious emotional and social challenges.
	• Who decides what is considered "antisocial"? It would be hard to draw the line and children could be dragged through the foster care system while allegations are sorted out.

QUESTIONS

1. What advice would you give to the family involved in the case noted above?
2. What are the potential consequences for removing children from the family home? How might this have a larger impact on society?
3. The little girl in the case above indicated that she believed that this is "a white man's world." What does this belief indicate about her view of society?

Section 6.2

Sociology and Behaviour

Understanding people's behaviour is an important part of understanding society. Sociologists are interested in why people behave the way they do and how our relationships and the people around us influence our individual and collective behaviours. Sociologists also study how these behaviours are shaped by our society and how our behaviours define the society in which we live. How is this distinct from how psychologists study behaviour?

FIGURE 6-21 These Chinese passengers wait for trains in China's southern city of Guangzhou. What could be learned from studying this crowd?

● Social Belonging and Groups

You are part of many different groups. Family, friends, teams, and the people you work with are all groups that you interact with daily or regularly. The feeling of belonging to a group is an essential element of living in society. Social belonging is based on the **solidarity** of the group. Solidarity refers to the ties that unite members of a group. It is from these group ties that individuals come to experience social belonging. Sociologists study different types of groups to better understand social behaviour. The most intimate of all groups is a **dyad**, a group consisting of two members, for example, a married couple or two friends. Less personal relationships are defined as **informal groups**, which are gatherings of people in which member interaction is not governed by explicit rules. For example, neighbours who exchange small talk are an example of an informal group.

A small group whose members have a personal and often emotional relationship with one another is known as a primary group. The family and close friends are examples of a primary group. Typically, the primary group is the most influential group to which one can belong. This group is deeply invested in and concerned for its members. The members of this group know one another's personalities and share in one another's triumphs and failures. The ties within this group are very strong. The primary group also has the

---

Before You Read

What do you do that makes you similar to your family or peers? Why does this make you similar?

---

solidarity:
the ties that unite members of a group

dyad:
a group consisting of two members

informal group:
a less intimate gathering of people in which member interaction is not governed by explicit rules

power to persuade its members and expects a certain degree of conformity to its rules and beliefs. Parents restrict certain behaviours of their children, claiming these restrictions are in the best interest of the family, and friends may influence the music you listen to or the type of clothes you wear. The primary group exerts a great deal of influence over the individual and helps shape and define his or her attitudes.

FIGURE 6-22 The family is the most important primary group. What role are the parents playing in socializing the children?

A **secondary group** is an impersonal or formal gathering of people in which the individual's role is measured by his or her contribution to a common goal or purpose. A school sports team is an example of a secondary group. Quite often, secondary groups are large, and therefore intimate details are not usually shared among their members. Small talk and occasional discussions are more likely among members of these groups. As a result, a secondary group exerts less influence than a primary group on an individual's behaviour.

Lastly, a **virtual community** is a group of individuals who communicate over the Internet. This type of group has become the subject of many recent sociological studies as more people interact via social networks such as Facebook. The primary function of the virtual community is to communicate. Its members want to communicate globally with like-minded individuals for a variety of reasons, namely, social support, companionship, or the exchange of information. Since face-to-face communication is rare, members of the virtual community have found creative and innovative ways to express themselves, such as new forms of language. For the virtual group, acronyms such as *lol* have the same meaning as laughing out loud while standing in a room with a group. The virtual community creates dependency among its members. At any given time and on any given day, members of the virtual community have access to you. The ability to chat at three o'clock in the morning Toronto time with a friend from Mumbai is a form of communication that has far-reaching implications for how we see ourselves now and in the future. As such, this communication can also be part of a person's primary or secondary group.

? How do you connect in the virtual community that is different from or similar to how you connect to your parents? What impact does this connection have on your relationships?

secondary group: a large, impersonal gathering of people in which members' roles are measured by their contributions to a common goal or purpose

virtual community: a group of individuals who communicate online

IN FOCUS: The Social Network

Today we use the term *social network* to refer to online social connections and relationships, such as Facebook, but sociologists have been referring to social networks for a long time. Social networks can refer to individuals who are linked together by one or more social relationships (virtual or not). Humans have always enjoyed a multitude of social relationships. Think about your social network: How many friends do you have? How many people do you interact with on a regular basis?

According to anthropologist Robin Dunbar, the answer might be 150. Through studying primates and their social behaviour, Dunbar came up with a theory that states that there is a limit to the number of stable social relationships that a person can maintain. He observed that brains are larger in primates who live in larger groups. Humans, with the largest brains, also have the largest groups. Dunbar calculated the ratio of brain size to group size in 36 other primate groups and applied it to humans, concluding that human brain capacity allows us, on average, to have meaningful social relationships with about 150 people at one time. This is called the Dunbar number. (Dunbar also concluded that the range could vary from 100 to 231 people.)

We can see the Dunbar number in various societies from both the past and the present. In a survey of 21 hunter-gatherer societies, the average group size was 148.4 people. Militarily, from the Romans to present-day regiments, the number of people in a fighting unit varies from 160 to 200. It has been found that this size of regiment is the most functional. The ideal size for a Hutterite colony (a religious community with many colonies in Western Canada) is 150. As soon as the number of people in a colony exceeds that, the colony divides in two. The Hutterites believe that in groups larger than 150, "people become strangers to each other." The Swedish company Gore Associates, makers of Gore-Tex, builds company plants with 150 parking spaces. As soon as people start parking on the grass, the company knows it's time to open a new branch.

In a recent study conducted by *The Economist* magazine, the Dunbar number was put to the test

FIGURE 6-23 Online social networking is gaining in popularity. Is this access to social networking universal in your community or the world? What impact will widespread social networking have on relationships in the future?

to see just how online social networks are changing the way people network. Dr. Cameron Marlow, Facebook's resident sociologist was asked to do the math. He found that the average number of friends people have is 120, with women having slightly more friends on average than men, which is consistent with Dr. Dunbar's hypothesis. The range of online friends is large, and many users have 500 or more. Interestingly, people usually interact with a much smaller group on a regular basis: between 6 and 26 for women and between 4 and 17 for men. This finding would suggest that, despite our technological advances, there is a limit to the number of interactions with which our brains can keep up.

QUESTIONS

1. How do social media, such as Facebook and Twitter, relate to the Dunbar number? To what extent does technology increase the number of people with whom we can have social relationships?

2. Has online social networking really changed the way we form groups? What is the process of forming an online friendship? How do you know you can trust the person at the other end of the connection?

3. Can virtual relationships be as strong as face-to-face relationships? What do virtual relationships lack?

The Power and Influence of Groups

Every group we belong to has expectations of how we should and shouldn't behave. Groups exert a great deal of influence over the individual behaviour of their members. Most groups rely on roles, norms, and **sanctions** to shape the behaviour of their members. But not all groups have the same roles, norms, and sanctions.

The group sets out guidelines for the social roles being enacted among its members. In formal groups, such as school or the workplace, the rules that govern these roles may be very explicit and written into a code. The role an individual has in a group is typically attached to a specific function. Most of us readily accept the roles expected by a group because we have had practice with roles as part of our socialization.

Groups also establish guidelines for appropriate behaviour among their members. These behaviours are called *norms*. Society as a whole relies on norms to keep order. Groups develop norms that reflect those of society to help govern their members as well. Although the norms vary from group to group, the underlying purpose of group norms is the same: to keep order and ensure a certain level of behaviour.

Finally, the group is responsible for imposing sanctions for proper and improper behaviour. A sanction is a reward or punishment that encourages certain kinds of behaviour and discourages others. Sanctions are typically used to encourage members to conform to group expectations. Most groups impose informal sanctions such as a word of caution for unwanted behaviour or a pat on the back for doing something right. More formal sanctions, such as expulsion and imprisonment, are extremely rare among groups.

Gangs

A gang is a group of people associating for antisocial and often criminal purposes and activities, but it has the same characteristics as other groups. Often members hold specific roles, and they are expected to behave according to certain rules. A gang can also hold a great deal of influence over its members by pressuring them to commits acts in order to stay in the gang and sanctioning those who do not conform to expected behaviour.

This group provides identity, a sense of power and purpose, as well as protection. Loyalty and respect for its rules are the most important rules for many of today's gangs. Gangs appeal to youth who have unpleasant memories of their home life. Most gang members have been isolated and alienated from their families, culture, school, community, and religion (Adler, 1984). Other research connects gang membership to the lack of employment opportunities, particularly for those around the age of 16 since that is the age when many youth get their first job (Seals, 2009).

sanction:
informal or formal penalty or reward to ensure conformity within a group

↑ **FIGURE 6-24** Groups teach their members about social roles. What messages are these girls learning?

↑ **FIGURE 6-25** Groups teach their members about norms. What might be the sanctions in this community for not following the norms?

> **REFLECT AND RESPOND**

1. Look at Figures 6-24 and 6-25, and suggest one specific way membership to that particular group might influence an individual's behaviour.
2. How might a group foster conformity among its members?

Before You Read
Why do schools have practice fire drills and lockdowns?

panic:
a highly emotional and irrational response on the part of an individual or a group to a dangerous or harmful social event

↑ **FIGURE 6-26** As each goose flaps its wings it creates an "uplift" for the birds that follow. By flying in a V-formation, the whole flock adds 72 percent greater flying range than if each bird flew alone.

More to Know...
You learned about the frustration–aggression theory on page 274.

riot:
civil disorder stemming from a social grievance, caused by a disorganized crowd exhibiting aggression, who may turn to acts of violence, vandalism, and destruction of property

 Collective Behaviour

Collective behaviour is social behaviour by a large group that does not reflect existing rules, institutions, and structures of society. The group engages in this kind of behaviour to accomplish a specific goal or outcome. Unlike the primary group, the collective is not interested in establishing personal or intimate relationships with its members. Collective behaviour is spontaneous, usually in response to a social crisis or natural disaster. The collective behaviour of the group doesn't conform to established norms, but the behaviour isn't out of the ordinary either; it occurs in situations where the established norms are unclear.

An example of collective behaviour is a **panic**. A panic is the irrational reaction of people to a dangerous situation (or a situation they perceive as dangerous). A famous example of a panic is the reaction to the 1938 radio broadcast by Orson Welles of the H.G. Wells's classic *The War of the Worlds*. People listening to the broadcast believed that they were hearing a news report of an invasion of aliens from Mars. Some people, believing that Earth was under attack, packed and fled their homes. Others hid themselves in cellars and basements. At the time, it was reported that this behaviour was widespread. However, research indicates that the panic was greatly exaggerated: at most, 12 percent of the radio audience believed the story might be true, and much fewer panicked. The assumption is that people panic in life-or-death situations, such as fires and natural disasters. In fact, empirical studies about people caught in disasters indicate that most people behave rationally and don't panic.

There are many sociological theories that help explain the concept of collective behaviour. In this section, you will explore the *convergence theory* and the *rational decision theory*.

Convergence Theory

The convergence theory assumes that when a collectivity, or large group of like-minded individuals, comes together, collective action is the most common outcome. Individuals in a collectivity are behaving according to their own beliefs but do so with the protection of others behaving in the same manner. When applied to the frustration–aggression theory you learned about in Section 6.1, collective behaviour can explain why **riots** and racial violence occur. For example, members of a collectivity may be part of the same social class, ethnicity, gender, or age group and, as such, may find it easy to act out because their frustrations are the same. How collective behaviour presents itself in society is dependent on the individual society. Of course, when the collectivity gains momentum and popularity, sometimes its origins become unclear or distorted. As history has shown, sometimes the collectivity may degenerate into extreme violence, for example, the Nazi Party's hold over Germany during World War II. The consequences of that collective behaviour led to the Holocaust.

❓ Identify a fad or craze that has influenced your generation, and describe the collective behaviour connected to it.

The Rational Decision Theory

Like the convergence theory, the rational decision theory assumes that people make rational decisions whether or not to participate in collective behaviour. The motivating factor for the individual is almost always based on self-interest. According to sociologist Mark Granovetter, individuals have a specific number or percentage of other people who must already be engaged in the group before they will join. He calls this number the individual's **threshold**. The individual tends to favour larger groups over smaller ones and more organized groups over less organized ones. When these conditions are met, the individual is more likely to participate in collective behaviour. There is also the sense of not being held responsible because everyone else is taking part in the activity. The lack of consequence(s) can also be a strong motivator for people to follow a group mentality. In other words, most of us would like to know that the benefits outweigh the costs of joining a group.

People enter into collective behaviour carefully and consider all the possible consequences ahead of time. Granovetter suggests that individual thresholds widely differ. Collective behaviour cannot develop without low-threshold individuals to get it started, and development will stop if the group lacks an individual with the necessary threshold to move the group to the next stage if needed. In other words, most collectives need a leader, and leaders will carry the group forward so long as the threshold remains within his or her comfort zone. When the group becomes too large for the leader, he or she may choose to cut ties with the group. For example, in a riot, the decision to participate is dependent on what everyone else is doing. If a leader or instigator begins rioting, some people will follow, which will encourage other people to join. However, if the riot becomes too violent or excessive, many people will begin to withdraw from it.

Prosocial Behaviour

The theories of collective behaviour are often applied to violent or aggressive groups or events, but not all collective behaviour is negative. It can also be used to explain acts of kindness, generosity, and **altruism**. Altruism is the basis of many modern religions and **prosocial behaviour**.

Prosocial behaviour is a form of altruism in which individuals or groups in society demonstrate empathy toward and care for the welfare of others without regard for their own personal gain. In some cases, those engaged in prosocial behaviour may be aware of the dangers to themselves but continue to practise the behaviour nonetheless. Several explanations exist for the origins of prosocial behaviour, but ultimately what is of interest to the sociologist is that this type of behaviour is exhibited in all societies around the globe and that it contributes to social cohesion.

Prosocial behaviour reminds us that not all social interactions are based on selfish personal goals. In fact, one need not look too far for examples of prosocial behaviour in our own society. Natural disasters tend to bring out feelings of empathy for the victims. When the impoverished country of Haiti was devastated by a powerful earthquake in January 2010,

threshold: a level or point at which something would or would not happen; a tipping point

FIGURE 6-27 Women were a significant part of Egyptian protests in 2011. The huge number of protesters taking to the streets demanding government reforms created a tipping point for women's civic participation in a country where it was risky and dangerous to demonstrate against the authorities.

altruism: the principle of unselfish regard for the needs and interests of others

prosocial behaviour: a form of altruism in which individuals or groups demonstrate empathy toward and care for the welfare of others without benefit to themselves

VOICES

There can be no question that women have been an integral part of th[e] [Egpytian] revolution, standing and dying alongside men in the streets. Nor can there be much remaining doubt ... that equality and representation is a value intrinsic and endemic to the Muslim people, as exemplified in the slogan of the Egyptian uprising "Freedom, Democracy, and Social Justice".

Janine Moussa, International human rights consultant

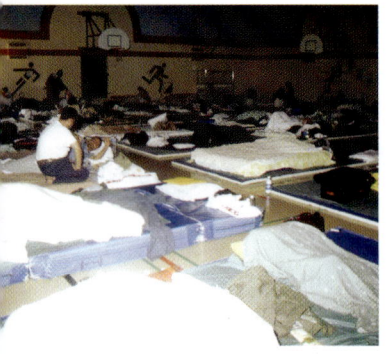

FIGURE 6-28 Stranded passengers start waking up on Thursday morning September 13, 2001 in Gander, Newfoundland in the gymnasium of Gander Academy, an elementary school. The town of 10 000 people was strained to the limit by the unexpected arrival of literally thousands of passengers but all were eager to help.

the world quickly responded with aid. Sending supplies, donating money, or volunteering are examples of prosocial behaviour and collective solidarity.

Tragedies also demonstrate prosocial behaviour. On September 11, 2001, following the attacks on the United States in New York and Washington, all American airspace was shut down and planes had to be diverted. In total, 39 planes with 6500 passengers landed in Gander, Newfoundland, a town with a population of about 10 000 people. Gander had few hotels, so schools were closed to house passengers, and churches and individual families opened their doors. Everyone chipped in over four days, providing food, shelter, access to telephones, and the Internet. One Gander citizen who housed and fed a family for four days insisted she and others did nothing out of the ordinary. "This is the way everybody is (ABC, 2001)," she said simply.

Mass Public Grief

Emile Durkheim was among the first social scientists to recognize the power of collective solidarity. He used the term *collective solidarity* in relation to a community's response to crime. To him, collective solidarity could be seen through a community's ability to overcome the negative consequences of crime. The same can be said about mass public grief, which is the collective experience of grieving publicly for someone whom most of the mourners have never met. Typically, this form of public grief is associated with celebrities or public figures. Mourners gather in a public place of great significance to the deceased, sometimes along the funeral route, and make shrines of flowers and artwork, and light candles in honour of the deceased. Being in close proximity to others who feel the same affinity toward the public figure has been known to have a healing effect. In addition to honouring the deceased, these public outpourings of grief help people make sense of death. Most recently, the untimely deaths of Princess Diana, once married to the heir to the throne of England, and legendary musician Michael Jackson brought together mourners the world over. News of their tragic deaths spread quickly through the media and Internet.

Mass public grief can also be a response to the impact of war on a country. Every November 11, people across Canada participate in Remembrance Day ceremonies where they acknowledge the people who fought and died in wars past and present, by reciting prayers and poems and laying wreaths. We also acknowledge when a Canadian solider is killed in action by gathering along the Highway of Heroes as the body is transported from Trenton to Toronto to watch the motorcade, as a way of honouring the soldier for his or her service.

FIGURE 6-29 Flowers left in memory of Princess Diana's death on August 31, 1997. Why do people feel the need to acknowledge tragedy in this manner?

> ### REFLECT AND RESPOND
>
> 1. What motivates an individual to participate in collective behaviour?
> 2. Why is the concept of threshold important to understanding collective behaviour?
> 3. Choose an example in recent history that highlights the positive side of collective behaviour, and describe how large groups can bring about positive social change.

Crowds

Crowds are large numbers of people, in close proximity, gathered for a specific reason. Sociologists study crowds to better understand the nature of collective and group behaviour and to examine what happens when large groups living in society come together in a variety of instances and for a number of reasons. There are many different types of crowds. For example, a **conventional crowd** is a large group of people gathered for a clear purpose who display the expected behaviour for that situation. A town meeting is an example of a conventional crowd. You would not expect to see inappropriate behaviour at such a gathering. A **casual crowd** is a group of people who do not appear to have a common goal other than being in the same location at the same time. Shoppers taking advantage of sales at the mall are an example of a casual crowd. An **expressive crowd** is a large number of people at an event who display emotion and excitement. People gathered at a baseball game or rock concert are examples of an expressive crowd. An **acting crowd** is a group of people fuelled by a single purpose or goal. Peaceful protestors outside a government building are an example of an acting crowd. However, the acting crowd can be easily incited to become a **mob** or riot with little provocation.

Mobs

Sometimes collective behaviour can be threatening. The law enforcement perspective is that any group has the potential to become a dangerous and angry group. The consequences of large groups escalating their activities to include violence and damage to public property are a frightening prospect for many city officials who oversee large public gatherings. A mob is a large disorderly crowd and on its own is frightening enough, but mobs can easily lead to riots. A riot is civil disorder stemming from a social grievance and caused by a disorganized crowd who usually exhibits aggression and may turn to acts of violence, vandalism, and destruction of property.

In 2010, the Canadian government hosted the G20 Summit. While world leaders met to discuss international and global issues, the streets of Toronto became a battlefield where protestors and police squared off (see Figure 6-30). Thousands protested in what was supposed to be a peaceful demonstration by concerned citizens but turned into a riot. A small splinter group broke away from the larger group. Its members set police cars on fire and damaged public property. The riot was quelled before anyone could be seriously hurt. The police reacted by arresting and rounding up many protestors, including some who were peaceful and nonviolent. Of more than 1100 people arrested, more than 700 were released without charges. Of the 320 people charged, 12 pleaded guilty and remain before the courts. After the G20, many people accused the police of excessive force, and video surfaced of officers beating protestors. The G20 riots support what sociologists know about collective behaviour: even in the most peaceful society, disorder and violence can erupt in the right circumstances.

Compare the collective behaviour of the G20 protestors and the police. What were the similarities and differences?

Before You Read

Discuss with a partner what you have observed about people's behaviour in crowds. Consider sporting events, shopping malls, and school assemblies for examples. What hypothesis can you make about crowds?

conventional crowd:
a large group of people gathered for a clear purpose who behave according to expectations

casual crowd:
a group of people in the same place at the same time but who do not have a common goal

expressive crowd:
a large number of people at an event who display emotion and excitement

acting crowd:
a group of people fuelled by a single purpose or goal

mob:
a disorderly crowd of people

FIGURE 6-30 Riot police in downtown Toronto during the G20 Summit in June 2010. What role did the police have in maintaining civil order?

IN FOCUS: The Expressive Crowd: SARS-Stock

SARS (Severe Acute Respiratory Syndrome) is an infectious disease that killed 800 people around the world and 44 in Toronto in 2003. It was first diagnosed in November 2002 and was extremely infectious. Some people wore face masks in an effort to reduce catching the illness, but also increased the fear of all. The World Health Organization posted an advisory against travel to Toronto, which had big impact on tourism. Trip cancellations amounted to an estimated $39 million in lost hotel revenue in April 2003 alone.

FIGURE 6-31 Hundreds of thousands enjoy music in the hot sun at SARS-Stock in Toronto.

To help restore faith in the city, some local community members and politicians decided to organize a concert to show the world that Toronto was safe. Known as "SARS-stock" and "SARSapolooza," the July 2003 11-hour concert was organized in a month. It was one of the largest mass gatherings in North America. Tickets were only $25 in order to attract a large number of people. Several thousand of Toronto's health care workers received free tickets to the concert from the Ontario government in appreciation for their tireless work during the SARS crisis. The age of concert goers ranged in age from preteen to over 60.

Almost 450 000 people spent the day at Downsview Park. Among the 15 performers were top acts such as the Rolling Stones, Jann Arden, Jim Belushi and Dan Aykroyd, Justin Timberlake, Blue Rodeo, AC/DC, and The Guess Who. In order to keep order, there were 20 000 workers including police, security, and EMS workers. Aside from the revenue from tickets, at least $3.5 million was invested by the federal government, $2 million from Ontario and the rest from corporate sponsors, with Molson leading the pack. The performers were paid, although organizers would not say how much. Organizers had hoped to draw up to 150,000 Americans to the concert, but only 45,000 tickets were sold south of the border and CNN was the only U.S. television network to cover the event.

The gates opened at 10:00 a.m. and the day was sunny and hot. A water cannon sprayed water to cool the crowd. There were very few problems and no arrests. Although there was food choice, there were long lines for everything, and people waited patiently in the queue. Many fans were in distress from heat stroke and dehydration, and hundreds were treated at the site. Police said at least 25 people had to be transported to hospital, most suffering from the heat, dehydration, or minor injuries. Similar gatherings, like Woodstock '69, were not so peaceful and resulted in riots and violence.

FIGURE 6-32 The day after the concert. Did the city accomplish its goal of showing that Toronto is a safe place?

QUESTIONS

1. After reading about SARS-Stock, what can you say about the mood and actions of the crowd at the concert?
2. How was the festival an example of an expressive crowd?
3. Imagine you have been asked to gauge public opinion for an upcoming concert similar to this. Develop two survey questions that might help you understand what type of people the festival would attract.

Fear and Collective Behaviour

In some instances, collective behaviour is motivated by real or perceived events of a frightening or harmful nature. The resulting social behaviour is known as panic or **mass hysteria**. As you learned on page 280, panic is a highly emotional and irrational response on the part of an individual or a group to a social event that may be construed as dangerous or harmful. Similarly, mass hysteria is the irrational reaction to a perceived danger but is always widespread. Typically, instances of mass hysteria tend to accompany acute medical and health issues, such as pandemics. A pandemic is the rapid spread of an infectious disease among people across a country or several countries. In 2009, the World Health Organization declared an H1N1 flu pandemic. As reports of deaths began appearing in the media, people began to demand access to a vaccine. When the vaccine was made available to the general public here in Canada, people spent hours waiting in line to receive it (see Figure 6-33). About 10 percent of the Canadian population was infected by H1N1, and over 400 people died (Public Health Agency of Canada, 2010). Although there was fear, fewer than 40 percent of Canadians were immunized.

mass hysteria: the widespread irrational reaction to a perceived danger

↑ **FIGURE 6-33** Canadians line up to receive the H1N1 vaccine.

? How can you explain the reactions of the Canadian public to the H1N1 pandemic? How can this be useful to the study of collective behaviour?

Smart Mobs

A relatively new phenomenon to grip society and collective behaviour is the use of technology to instigate group action. When technology and groups come together, they form a **smart mob**. A smart mob is characterized by a large group of strangers who use electronic media, such as cell phones and social networking sites, to organize and stage surprise public gatherings in which a specific behaviour is enacted for a specific period of time, after which the group disbands. According to Howard Rheingold, author of *Smart Mobs: The Next Social Revolution*, (2002) "flash mobs are not just a passing fad but are a demonstration of the ability for groups of people to organize collective action in the face-to-face world in ways that they were unable to do before the combination of the Internet and mobile telephones made it possible."

Sociologists are interested in the impact of technology on social relationships and, for this reason, are particularly interested in smart mobs. Smart mobs have now gone further than just staging a social action among strangers—some people have started smart mobs to stage a marriage proposal!

smart mob: a large group of strangers who use electronic media to organize and stage surprise public gatherings

More to Know...

Flash mobs are a type of smart mob. You learned about flash mobs in Chapter 2.

↑ **FIGURE 6-34** A smart mob in a hotel lobby in San Francisco. The members met up in the lobby, pretended to sleep, and then left.

REFLECT AND RESPOND

1. Where would individual responsibility have more impact, on smart mobs or on other forms of collective behaviour? Explain.
2. How are smart mobs similar to and different from other forms of collective behaviour?
3. Explain why an acting crowd can become a mob or riot.

Conformity

Before You Read

Using a rapid writing strategy for the amount of time specified by your teacher, write everything you know or have experienced about conforming; for example, with peers, at a mall, or at a wedding. Be prepared to share parts of your writing.

More to Know...

You will learn more about conformity in Chapter 8.

Skills Focus

As a sociologist, if you were to perform a study on conformity, how would you conduct your research? Propose a hypothesis to start your thinking. What ethical factors should you think about before you start?

As you learned at the beginning of this section, an individual can belong to many different groups and these groups are organized according to certain norms and expectations of how members of the group should behave. Individuals often feel the need to conform to the norms and expectations of society. Conformity is the process by which an individual will alter or change his or her thoughts, feelings, and behaviour to meet the expectations of a group or authority figure. Conformity can occur as the result of both direct and indirect social pressure. Individuals often feel the urge to conform in order to fit in or avoid rejection and criticism from members of their group. But fitting in can also stifle individuality and personality.

Conformity can be both positive and negative, and sociologists study both forms in order to understand society. To some extent, conformity is a necessary element to keep society functioning safely. Most often, the fear of being left out or behind is a powerful motivator for an individual to change his or her behaviour so that it imitates the behaviour of others in society. In this instance, conformity is a positive social force. For example, at one time it was unusual for people to recycle. Now there is an expectation that people will recycle items instead of throwing them in the garbage. However, when an individual is coerced into a specific form of behaviour that is detrimental to him or her and hurtful to others, that is conformity at its worst. An example is a young person who commits theft or violence to maintain membership in a gang. Whether willingly or by coercion, all humans have and will choose to conform to a group's expectations at some point.

↑ **FIGURE 6-35** What do these photos suggest about an individual's behaviour in society?

❓ To what extent is conformity negative? When can conformity be positive? Organize your ideas into a T-chart.

Conformity in Individualistic Cultures

In an individualistic society such as Canada, conformity suggests something negative. Yet Canadians often pride themselves on being agreeable and getting along with others. Is getting along with others conformity? Or is this behaviour an example of **compliance**? Is there a difference between compliance and conformity? The simple answer is yes. One can be compliant but not conform. Compliance is social behaviour by an individual that may be contrary to his or her beliefs but is exhibited nonetheless in order to achieve rewards and avoid punishments. Outwardly, compliance resembles conformity. For example, students follow school attendance rules even if they would rather skip class. In this case, students attend class to avoid punishment or to receive the benefit of coming to class and getting the needed information to get higher grades. In all its forms, conformity is a fundamental social process without which people would be unable to organize or function effectively in society. In order for large groups of people to coordinate their behaviour and actions, they must adhere to standards of behaviour that make one another's actions predictable and recognizable by all members.

Conformity is the process by which groups are able to establish boundaries. Through conformity, the members of social groups, such as families, peers, and even countries, are able to distinguish themselves as separate entities. The conformity to certain beliefs in these groups clarifies acceptable and unacceptable behaviours for their members. For example, schools expect students to show up for class on time. Those who do not are subject to punishment. Students are expected to conform to the school schedule. Peer groups can also expect their members to conform by wearing certain clothes or listening to a particular kind of music.

compliance: social behaviour by an individual that may be contrary to his or her beliefs but is exhibited nonetheless in order to achieve rewards and avoid punishments

Conformity in Collectivistic Cultures

Conformity takes on a different meaning in collectivistic cultures. From an individual's home life to public social behaviour, conformity takes precedence over individuality. Actions, language, and dress are all determined by society. People are expected to adhere to these "rules" of behaviour; not meeting these expectations has far more serious consequences than in individualistic cultures.

Many people point to Japan as an example of a collectivistic culture where conformity is vitally important. Political and historical events, as well as Japan's geography, contributed to the importance of collectivity within Japanese culture. Japan is surrounded by ocean on all sides, which limits the living space, forcing the Japanese people to live in close proximity to one another. The Japanese have had to relinquish some claims for personal space and rely on predictable behaviours to which the group conforms to maintain harmony and order.

Although Japan might have historically been defined as conformist, Japan is changing, allowing for more individual expressions of identity. When studying a culture, social scientists must not rely on the impressions they have of other countries or draw conclusions based on what a society used to be like. It's important to remember that you cannot assume

FIGURE 6-36 Japanese commuters rush to make the train in Tokyo. How is their experience similar to or different from your experience of using any form of transit? Can you draw any conclusions about a society based on this behaviour?

knowledge about another society; it's impossible to understand a society without studying it, and even then the understanding may be limited. A sociologist studying conformity in modern Japan might want to research the differences between urban and rural populations or the behaviour and attitudes of different generations. What other areas should sociologists examine if they want to study changing attitudes of conformity in another culture?

> List circumstances in which it is acceptable to conform in public. What is compliance? Provide an example.

Breaking Social Norms: The Breaching Experiments

Until now, we've been examining accepted conformity within groups. What do you think would be the result of purposefully breaking the rules or norms of a group? Sociologist Harold Garfinkel was interested in that question and conducted research in order to find out. Underlying his research is his interest in understanding how people make sense of their society and learn about the world around them. At the root of his work is the analysis of human interaction and social norms. In his renowned breaching experiments, Garfinkel studied the results of intentionally breaking a social norm and then analyzed people's reactions to this breach. His experiment tested the unwritten rules of a society and how people responded to those who broke these unwritten rules. Some examples of breaching experiments include walking backward up a flight of stairs in a public space or standing to eat a meal in a restaurant.

FIGURE 6-37 Social breaching experiments test our beliefs about how things should function. How would you react if you encountered one of Garfinkel's breaching experiments?

Part of undertaking breaching experiments is to discover how people in society might react when social norms are broken. Reactions might include confusion, anxiety, anger, or laughter. Garfinkel quickly discovered that society resists breaches in social order and quickly attempts to reconstruct order when a social norm has been broken. For example, it is generally accepted that on an escalator, you stand on the right and leave the left available for those who wish to walk up or down. Now imagine you encounter the following situation: you are trying to walk up the left side and are faced with someone standing facing backward. The general idea is that many people would make amends for the person's behaviour and walk around him or her. The reaction might include displeasure at this rudeness and ignorance of the "way things work." Some of the people on the escalator might say something in anger, or curse. Breaching experiments ultimately show how people take for granted the unwritten social norms and come to expect that certain things will always function in a specific manner.

> What is the purpose of breaching experiments? What can they tell us about conformity? What are some other examples of unwritten social rules? What is a possible experiment that you could develop to test them?

Landmark Case Study

Stanley Milgram: Subway Experiments

Subways have long been considered ideal places to observe social interaction by researchers because they are places where people of all classes, ethnicities, and religions are forced to look at others for minutes or even hours at a time without speaking to them. During the 1970s in New York, a famous breaching experiment was led by Dr. Stanley Milgram. He got the idea from his mother-in-law, who complained that passengers would not give up their seat for her on the subway. Etiquette in Western society specifies that people are supposed to give up their seats on public transit for the elderly, people with disabilities, people who are weak, and pregnant women, but otherwise the seating is first come, first served. Milgram used his students as researchers. At first, they resisted participating since they knew giving up a seat for people who appeared to be able to stand was not done in New York (Luo, 2004).

The researchers boarded crowded subway trains in pairs, with one acting as an observer and the other asking others to give up their seats. The researcher asked riders to give up their seats by asking, "Excuse me. May I have your seat?" The passengers were healthy, able-bodied men and women. The passengers were not given a reason; they were simply asked if they would give up their seat. The sole purpose of the experiment was to test the unwritten rules, or norms, that govern social behaviour on the subway. The results showed that an astonishing 68 percent of riders, when asked, gave up their seats willingly. When Dr. Milgram undertook the experiment himself (see Figure 6-38), he recalls, "Taking the man's seat, I was overwhelmed by the need to behave in a way that would justify my request, my head sank between my knees, and I could feel my face blanching. I was not role-playing. I actually felt as if I were going to perish (Luo, 2004)." In another variation, the researcher, holding a paperback mystery novel, asked, "Excuse me. May I have your seat? I can't read my book standing up." With this request, only 38 percent of passengers gave up their seats.

Part of the research involved the reactions of the researchers themselves. Thirty years later, they remember vividly their feelings in conducting the experiment. Dr. Kathryn Krogh, now a clinical psychologist, recalls, "I was afraid I was going to throw up (Luo, 2004)." Dr. Harold Takooshian, another former student, said he kept feeling there was something unethical in what he was doing, almost deceiving riders, so he developed a card that he would slip to them afterward that explained they had just participated in an experiment. It also made the task slightly easier.

In 2004, *The New York Times* attempted to replicate the experiment. The journalists experienced similar inhibitions about asking people to give up their seats. Although they did not conduct the experiment using sound sociological research methods, their results suggest New Yorkers are now less resistant to breaking social norms, since 13 of 15 passengers gave up their seats.

In the end, Milgram's experiment uncovered valuable information about the unwritten social rules and norms that govern urban life and how we take them for granted to help maintain order until they are violated. Takooshian reflected that "Milgram's idea exposed the extremely strong emotions that lie beneath the surface. You have all these strangers together. That study showed how much the rules are saving us from chaos (Luo, 2004)."

FIGURE 6-38 Dr. Stanley Milgram riding the subway in his breaching experiment.

QUESTIONS

1. What fundamental social beliefs do breaching experiments test?
2. Why were the researchers in Milgram's experiment reluctant to participate?
3. Write a hypothesis about breaching experiments for your school or community.

Groupthink

Imagine a situation in which a group is working together to come to an agreement about a project. The majority of the group has made a decision that may not be perfect, but its members have all finally agreed to it. What happens when one of the group members has a better alternative? How likely would it be for him or her to be heard? How likely is it that his or her suggestion will be adopted once the others have made a decision? The answers to these questions were highly debated and studied by psychologist Irving Janis in his 1972 study on groupthink. **Groupthink** refers to the effects of collective pressure on the decision-making abilities of individual members of a group. Many groups value independent thought by their members, but on rare occasions, the pressure for a group to arrive at a consensus may silence opposing opinions and evidence presented by individual members. This is the process of groupthink. It is so powerful that individuals within the group prefer to remain silent than stir up conflict by stating their opinion. Groupthink in sociology is a tendency within organizations or society to promote or establish the view of the predominant group. This situation typically occurs in groups that are highly cohesive, or close. In his study, Janis identified eight symptoms for the participants in groupthink. Figure 6-40 shows a few of the effects of groupthink that help sociologists understand conformity.

> Describe an instance in which your contributions to a group were not acknowledged. How did you respond? Did you give in to the group or did you speak up?

Obedience

Obedience is a routine occurrence in social behaviour. Obedience is the act or habit of doing what one is told, usually by someone in authority. A dog is often trained to be obedient to its owner; in the military a recruit is trained to be obedient to a commanding officer. Obedience is different from compliance and conformity. Compliance is behaviour influenced by peers, and conformity is behaviour that matches that of the majority and can be influenced by peers. Obedience is about power, about submitting to authority. Most people comply with the rules of society and obey authority without question in order to avoid public sanctions or punishment. You've learned about the most famous obedience experiment performed by Milgram in Chapter 5. In this section, we will consider other equally important studies that help shed light on why people willingly subject themselves to higher authorities in society.

↑ **FIGURE 6-39** Conformity can stifle independent thought among the members of a group.

groupthink:
the effects of collective pressure on the decision-making abilities of individual members of a group

Pressure:
Individual applies direct pressure to any member who disagrees with the group.

↓

Self-censorship:
Individual of groupthink would rather censor himself or herself than disagree with the group.

↓

Morality:
Individual does not question the ethical or moral decisions of the group.

↓

Stereotypes:
Individual develops stereotypical views of outside groups who don't share the same belief as his or her group.

↓

Mindguard:
Individual sometimes appoints himself or herself as protector of the group from outside information and sources that might break up the group.

↑ **FIGURE 6-40** The effects of groupthink, which may lead to conformity.

obedience:
the act or habit of doing what one is told or submitting to authority

Charles Hofling's Obedience Study

In 1966, psychiatrist Charles Hofling conducted an important experiment about obedience in the medical profession. Sociologists have since applied Hofling's findings to the study of obedience in society with great success. Hofling extended Milgram's obedience experiment, which you learned about in Chapter 5, to the field of medicine. Hofling wanted to know if nurses would carry out the orders of doctors whom they did not know and had never met in person.

The experiment involved 22 night nurses on duty at a hospital. Hofling created a character known as Dr. Smith for the experiment. Dr. Smith's job was to phone each of the nurses during one of their shifts at the hospital. Then Dr. Smith asked each to check on the availability of a fake drug called Astroten. Next Dr. Smith asked the nurse to administer 20 mg of the drug to a phony patient called Mr. Jones. When the nurse checked the dosage on the bottle of Astroten, he or she realized that the maximum recommended dosage was only 10 mg. When the nurses reported the error to Dr. Smith, they were assured it would be fine to administer the drug, despite said the information on the label. Dr. Smith pretended to be in a hurry and told the concerned nurses that he would sign the authorization form when he came in to do rounds and would check on Mr. Jones at that time. The nurses were watched to see what they would do by Hofling's researchers who were disguised as hospital staff on the floors where the nurses worked.

FIGURE 6-41 Following orders is important within the medical profession. Have you ever disobeyed a doctor's orders?

The dilemma for the nurses was whether to follow Dr. Smith's orders and risk the patient's life or administer the wrong dose and break three hospital rules: accepting orders over the phone, delivering a dose that was over the maximum limit stated on the label, and using an unauthorized medicine (Astroten). Although the medication was not real, the nurses thought it was. The results of the experiment were shocking: 21 out of 22 nurses administered Astroten as they were instructed by Dr. Smith. Hofling concluded that people will reluctantly question authority figures and would rather be wrong than disobey orders.

This experiment revealed the dangers of the medical profession, where a doctor's orders are not to be questioned. Even though the nurses knew they were not supposed to take instructions by phone and despite the fact that the drug exceeded the recommended dosage, they obeyed the authority of a doctor they had never met before.

However, there were ethical concerns with this experiment. The nurses were deceived and did not give informed consent. As well, there was the psychological harm, as the nurses admitted to feeling shame and guilt that their professionalism had been damaged.

REFLECT AND RESPOND

1. Why do people conform? Why might they choose not to?
2. What other factors may have influenced the nurses' decision to administer the drug in Hofling's experiment?
3. Reflect on how you have responded to groupthink in your life. Next, research an example of groupthink in history and the consequences.

Aggression

Before You Read
What frustrates you? How do you calm down after getting angry?

More to Know...
There have been several important studies about aggression. Albert Bandura's Bobo Doll experiment is one of the most important. You examined this experiment in Chapter 2.

differential association: the theory that individuals learn the values, attitudes, techniques, and motives for criminal behaviour through interaction with others

dehumanize: to deprive people of their human qualities; to degrade or deny the humanity of another person

Aggression is any action that is intended to injure, harm, or inflict pain on another living being or group of beings, either human or animal. It can take on many forms, from direct physical confrontations to more subtle forms involving verbal hostility. The concept of aggression can include many categories of behaviour (for example, verbal aggression, road rage, child abuse, war). No age group is exempt from aggression; throughout the life cycle, unique brands of aggression pop up, challenging the individual's progress and development. Frustration is a precursor for aggressive behaviour. Most people will agree that there is plenty to frustrate them throughout the day; traffic, rude drivers, and long lineups are just a few things that can cause frustration in a typical day. Learning to keep frustration in check is a life-long process. Eventually, most people learn methods that work for them. Unfortunately for some, learning to blow off steam is a monumental task and one that is not easily accomplished. Aggression is the result of the inadequate diffusion of frustration by an individual.

Sociologists look at the effects that variables such as class, power, and living conditions have on the behaviour of individuals and how they contribute to aggression and violence. Edwin Sutherland's theory of **differential association** explains that aggression and violence are learned behaviours. If a person associates with people who accept criminal behaviour, he or she learns to do so as well. Some sociologists believe that living without a community, perhaps in an urban or crowded area without connections to the people around them, allows people to commit aggressive actions. Dehumanization is a part of aggression. To **dehumanize** someone else is to deny his or her human qualities, making it easier to commit violence against that person. Sometimes this happens at an individual level, but it can also happen on a larger scale. For example, slavery systematically dehumanizes people by viewing slaves as property instead of people. This view makes it easier to buy and sell slaves, to injure and murder them, and to deny them basic human rights.

Bullying

Aggression among peer groups is not a new phenomenon and has gained the attention of psychologists and sociologists alike. In recent decades, the increase in peer aggression among adolescents has created great awareness for issues of bullying. In bullying, the victims may experience overt or subtle forms of aggression. They may be faced with overt, physical confrontations by their aggressor, or they may become the subject of malicious rumours or subtle gossip. Either way, bullying has devastating effects on its victims from anxiety to depression and, in some cases, suspension of daily activities and even suicide. There are also criminal consequences for bullying, whether it be in the schoolyard or workplace, as bullying is a type of harassment, which is considered a criminal act.

Bullying happens in many different forms. It's doing, saying, or acting in a way that hurts someone else or makes him or her feel bad on purpose. Some kinds of bullying are:

- verbal bullying (name-calling)
- physical bullying (punching, pushing)
- social bullying (leaving someone out of a game or group on purpose)
- theft (stealing someone's money or property)
- cyberbullying (using computers, the Internet, mobile phones)

A Canadian student is bullied every seven minutes. Barbara Coloroso, in her book *The Bully, The Bullied, and the Bystander* (2008), notes, "Bullying is not about anger, it's about contempt—a powerful feeling of dislike toward somebody considered to be worthless, inferior, and undeserving of respect. Rabbi Lerner calls it 'desanctification, not being able to see the divine in the other.' Pierre Teilhard de Chardin called it 'dehumanization,' not being able to see the humanity in the other (p. 101)." The Canadian organization PREVNet (Promoting Relationships and Eliminating Violence) has asked many children about their experiences with bullying and victimization. A substantial number of children report that they have been victimized or have bullied others.

Bullying is about power and aggression, but it is also about relationships. Sociologists examine bullying not just to understand the impact of it on children and on schools, but also because of its long-term effects on society. Studies have found that people who are bullies as children may be more likely to engage in antisocial behaviour in adulthood, behaviours that include sexual harassment, spousal abuse, or gang-related behaviours (Craig and Pepler, 2007).

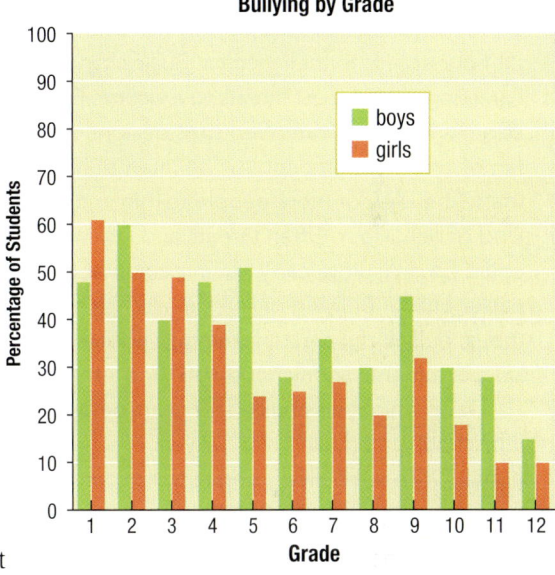

FIGURE 6-42 Percentage of students who reported being victimized within the previous two months. What conclusions can be drawn from this data? What patterns can be seen when looking at age groups and gender?

Virtual Aggression

Among today's technologically savvy teens, a method of bullying has emerged that uses technology to harass and intimidate victims. This category of bullying is called cyberbullying, and it has become an increasingly challenging issue as technology becomes more and more a part of everyday life. University of Toronto professor Faye Mishna has studied cyberbullying, and suggests that one in five kids have been bullied online. The effects of this form of aggression have devastating results. In cyberbullying, the bully targets the victim using interactive technological devices. It may take the form of a compromising picture of the victim circulated among his or her peers, or it may be as invasive as chain emails sent to the victim's home computer. A simple email or message board posting can lead to criminal consequences, including up to 10 years of jail time. It's important to think about the consequences of posting something negative online.

IN FOCUS

Cyberbullying

Internet use among adolescents has reached an all-time high. Most adolescents have access to email and the Internet on a daily basis, in addition to smartphones, Twitter, and Facebook. There are many avenues for students to communicate with one another. But this technology has also made it easier for students to bully their classmates. Before the Internet, bullying was something that happened mainly at school. But technology has allowed bullies 24-hour access to their victims. Bullies can send harassing emails, post threats to a victim's Facebook page, and even create Web sites designed to make fun of and threaten people. The Internet has also made it easier for more people to join in on this kind of behaviour. Often threats and ridicule that could be difficult to carry out in person become easier online. Bullying online can also be anonymous; bullies can create fake email addresses and post comments anonymously on Web sites.

David Knight was bullied for years before he left school, completing his final year of school at home. Once the bullying began to happen online, it became unbearable. "Rather than just some people, say 30 in a cafeteria, hearing them all yell insults at you, it's up there for six billion people to see. Anyone with a computer can see it," says David. "And you can't get away from it. It doesn't go away when you come home from school. It made me feel even more trapped" (CBC, 2005). David's classmates had created a Web site that specifically targeted him and was filled with hateful comments. Although still trying to recover from the effects of bullying, David has done remarkably well since finishing high school; he has learned how to fly so he can one day join the Canadian Armed Forces as a pilot.

FIGURE 6-43 The use of technology to enact bullying has become increasingly popular. What can be done to stop this?

The Internet is not just a venue for bullies. Some groups are using online resources to fight back against bullying. In 2010, the media began to report on a number of teen suicides in the United States. The teens who committed suicide were gay or lesbian or had been accused of being gay or lesbian by the people bullying them. In response, activists developed the *It Gets Better Project* through YouTube. The project was made up of a series of videos created by adults, in which they explained the harassment they had suffered as teens and how their lives had improved as they got older. The Web site also provides a forum for teens to seek help and encourages them to do so. The project has hundreds of videos and inspired campaigns worldwide, including the *It Gets Better Canada Project*. Although there are critiques of this campaign, it has been highly successful and inspired other campaigns.

QUESTIONS

1. Why does the Internet make bullying easier for bullies?
2. How does a victim of cyberbullying challenge a faceless bully? What kind of protection can a victim of cyberbullying count on?

REFLECT AND RESPOND

1. Why do sociologists study aggression?
2. What steps should your school take to combat bullying? What role can you take?
3. Suggest a hypothesis about bullying in your school or community. What primary research can you do to support your hypothesis?

Ethical Issues in Sociology

Section 6.3

In Chapter 4 and Chapter 5, you learned about ethical issues in anthropology and psychology, and the importance of ethics to valid social science research. Ethics are equally important to sociologists, and there are many similarities between the ethics of sociologists and those of anthropologists and psychologists. In this section, you will learn about ethics and ethical issues within sociology and how sociologists follow ethical guidelines in their work. All social scientists are required to follow these ethical guidelines, but there are differences in how they conduct their field research and how data is collected and used.

Ethical Guidelines in Sociology

Ethical guidelines within sociology were created to help sociologists carry out their research professionally and with integrity to ensure honesty, truthfulness, and harm reduction. Research within sociology is so varied that it is difficult to have formal rules that will apply to every situation. Organizations such as the Canadian Sociological Association (CSA), the American Sociological Association (ASA), and the International Sociological Association (ISA) have established standards to help sociologists make ethical judgments about their research and their research subjects. For their work to be considered valid, sociologists have to demonstrate that they have followed the spirit and principles of these guidelines in setting up and carrying out their research. These organizations view the way in which sociological research is designed and used as equally important to the proper treatment of research subjects.

Ethical Guidelines in Research

Like any other scientific field of research, sociologists adopt rules and regulations to guide their work. These guidelines help to strengthen the discipline. The International Sociological Association's (ISA) Code of Ethics provides sociologists with specific guidelines to help direct sociological research. It also suggests appropriate modes of behaviour for sociologists. Highlighted below are some of the core rules for sociologists to consider.

According to the ISA:

- Sociologists are expected to co-operate on the basis of scientific correctness alone, without discrimination on the basis of factors such as age, sex, sexual preference, ethnicity, language, religion, or political affiliation.
- Group work, co-operation, and mutual exchanges among sociologists are necessary for sociology to achieve its ends. Sociologists are expected to take part in discussions on their own work, as well as on the work of other sociologists.

> **Before You Read**
> Keeping in mind what you already know about sociology, what ethical guidelines would you suggest for research in this field? Keep reading to see how accurate your guidelines are compared to those practised by sociologists in the field.

FIGURE 6-44 All sociologists must show integrity, commitment, and truth in their work. Why are these ideas important?

FIGURE 6-45 All people have their own realities and biases that inform their point of view. It's important for researchers to recognize their own biases. How does your race, gender, class, religion, and sexual orientation influence your view of the world? If we can never be free of our biases then what hope do we have to produce meaningful research?

- Sociologists should be aware that their assumptions may have an impact on society. They must keep an unbiased attitude as much as possible, while acknowledging the uncertain and relative character of the results of their research. Sociologists should not conceal their own ideological position(s). No sociological assumption should be presented as absolute truth.
- Sociologists should act with a view to maintaining the image and the integrity of their own discipline; this does not imply that they should abandon a critical approach toward its fundamental assumptions, its methods, and its achievements.

? What is the purpose of a code of ethics?

Ethical Guidelines for Research Subjects

Ethical guidelines within sociology were created to help sociologists carry out their research with integrity but also to protect research subjects. Since sociological research is focused on the individuals and groups that make up society, it is very important that sociologists behave responsibly toward the people and groups they are studying. You learned about informed consent for anthropologists in Chapter 4. Informed consent is also an important ethical practice for sociologists. Research subjects should know who the sociologist is, his or her qualifications, and the goals of the research, as well as who is sponsoring the research. However, there are some cases where deception or providing research subjects with incomplete information may be necessary. Research conducted within academic and other institutions is subject to thorough ethical review processes where committees weigh the value of the research to society against the risks subjects may take by participating under conditions of intentional deception. The Canadian Sociological Association has many guidelines for how sociologists should work with research subjects. The following are a few important considerations for sociologists as they undertake their work:

- Sociologists enter into personal and moral relationships with those they study. They have a responsibility to respect the rights and be concerned with the welfare of all the populations affected by their work.
- Researchers must not exploit individuals or groups for personal gain and must recognize the debt incurred to the communities in which they work.
- Researchers must respect the rights of citizens to privacy, confidentiality, and anonymity, and the right to not be studied. The protection of research subjects does not absolve researchers of the responsibility of exposing physical, mental, sexual, or other abuse.
- Research should be based on the freely given informed consent of those studied and researchers must inform research subjects that they have the right not to answer particular questions or to withdraw without penalty at any point in the research process.
- Researchers should not misuse their positions for fraudulent purposes or as a pretext for gathering intelligence for any organization or government.

> **Skills Focus**
>
> When synthesizing research, it is important to keep in mind the ethical guidelines in your research. Refer to the questions on p. 259 and explain how they relate to the guidelines. What are some possible reasons to start over at this point?

Ethical guidelines also apply to how research is used. Sociologists must make sure that their research doesn't further the power of states, institutions, and corporations over the lives of people. Sociologists must also release the results of their research publicly, except in cases where doing so would put research subjects in danger.

Sociology Is Inclusive

As you learned earlier in this chapter, discrimination is the act of treating groups or individuals unfairly based on a common characteristic that they share. When studying and learning about society, care should be taken not to exclude or overlook issues of race, ethnicity, religion, gender, sexual identity, or age in any important discussion about social behaviour. In fact, sociologists should go beyond the traditional categories listed above and extend their research to investigate other marginalized groups that may be subject to discriminatory acts. For example, people with different sexual orientation or marital or parental status as well as those challenged by mental health issues or physical disabilities should also be represented in studies about society. In addition to considering inclusion and equity, sociologists must take special care to avoid personal bias from influencing their research. Sociologists are well aware of the important role group differences play in shaping social values, norms, and behaviour, and often their research requires them to draw comparisons or highlight differences between specific groups in society. Although highlighting differences can be problematic, sociologists take great care to avoid inequitable treatment, although in some cases this cannot be prevented.

FIGURE 6-46 When conducting research, why is it important to consider a wide range of participants?

A Matter of Choice

A famous 1993 photo by Kevin Carter depicts a young frail Sudanese girl crawling to an aid station for food. Standing behind her is a vulture waiting for her to die so that it can eat her. Later, Carter claimed that he waited 20 minutes for the vulture to move or spread its wings. He decided to take the picture, after which, Carter claims, he scared the vulture away and left without helping the young child. No one knows what became of the girl. Carter went on to win the very prestigious Pulitzer Prize for the photo. Although this was a journalistic decision, it had an impact on how we understand the world. Was it ethical for Carter to wait before taking action? At what point does a person's sense of being human and helping others come into play?

What Is Old Is New Again

Society is constantly changing. What was once popular can become quickly outdated and obsolete especially in these fast-changing technological times. The same can be said about sociological studies and the statistical analyses they produce. Some statistical information is notorious for becoming quickly outdated. In sociology, things change quickly. While underlying issues and topics may remain unchanged, the attitudes toward them may have changed dramatically in as short a time as a decade. Take gender roles as an example. Sociologists will often have a reason to study gender roles, but what they discover from one study to the next might show profound changes.

> **Connecting Sociology to Anthropology**
>
> Anthropologists also have a code of ethics. The American Anthropological Association has stated that physical race does not exist, and racial differences are a result of cultural and historical factors. What lessons can sociologists learn from this idea?

Landmark Case Study

The Clark Doll Experiment (1939)

Starting in 1939, Dr. Kenneth Clark and his wife, Dr. Mamie Clark, conducted a study about the racial biases among children in the United States. The Clark Doll experiment, as it became known, tested young black children to determine how race related to their self-image. The experiment consisted of showing each child a white doll and a black doll and giving instructions to the child in a particular order.

This experiment was conducted at a time when some schools in America were segregated by race. Drs. Kenneth and Mamie Clark studied students from segregated schools and compared their results to those of students who attended integrated schools. To conduct the experiment, the researchers placed a white-skinned plastic doll and a black-skinned plastic doll in front of black children aged six to nine and gave the children the following instructions in this order:

- Show me the doll that you like best or that you'd like to play with.
- Show me the doll that is the "nice" doll.
- Show me the doll that looks "bad."
- Give me the doll that looks like a white child.
- Give me the doll that looks like a coloured child.
- Give me the doll that looks like a Negro child.
- Give me the doll that looks like you.

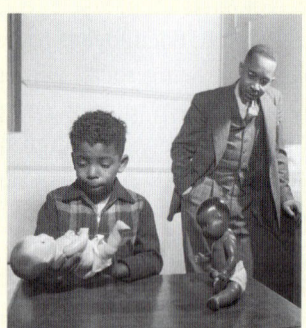

↑ **FIGURE 6-47** Dr. Kenneth Clark with one of his subjects. What other questions would you have liked to ask the child?

Results

In many of the studies conducted, the last question seemed to cause the most anxiety among the young subjects. Many of the children subjected to the test consistently chose the white doll as the "nice" doll, so by the time the last question was asked, they were obviously anxious. Some began crying and ran away. In a related task, Dr. Kenneth Clark also asked the children to draw a picture of themselves. Many chose a shade of brown much lighter than their actual skin tone. The Clark Doll studies found that children attending segregated schools were more likely to pick the white doll as the "nice" one. The Clarks concluded that the children had internalized racism caused by the discrimination that occurred through segregation.

By 1950, the Clarks' research had become involved in the *Brown v. Board of Education* case that was being presented to the United States Supreme Court. In 1954, the court ruled on the case and determined that segregation in public schools was unconstitutional, citing the Clarks' research. The Clark Doll experiment was not without controversy, however. Some allege that the experiment wasn't rigorous enough to draw a valuable conclusion. Some also claim that the Clarks were motivated by their own biases in wanting to prove that black children had internalized the racism experienced by segregated schools.

For these reasons, sociologists sometimes retest an old hypothesis or revisit past studies in an attempt to discover what's new or what's changed. Data can also be reused with a new hypothesis. Data collection can be reduced and different combinations using the data can yield interesting results. For the more ambitious researcher, there are always the classics. In some cases, there may be a need to re-open and reconstruct some of the landmark case studies in sociology. Imagine someone retesting Durkheim's theory on suicide for example! While the prospect may appeal to some, the practice may pose some ethical issues. What if the original study contained questionable methods or equally questionable results? In some cases, the original experiment was too contentious to begin with. Whatever the reasons for reconstructing classic studies, one must consider the ethical issues involved. If society is constantly changing, so too are the attitudes and language surrounding social issues.

CNN Doll Experiment (2010)

Seventy years after the original Clark Doll experiment was administered by the Clarks, CNN and Anderson Cooper repeated the experiment on a new generation.

In an attempt to discover whether much had changed in the last 70 years, CNN hired child psychologist Margaret Beale Spencer from the University of Chicago, along with two testers and one statistician, to design an updated experiment. They invited 133 black and white children from urban and rural areas in the U.S. states of New York and Georgia. The children belonged to two different age groups; early childhood (between 4 and 5) and middle childhood (between 9 and 10).

Instead of dolls, this experiment presented students with five illustrations of a child. The illustrations were identical except for the skin colour of each child and the skin colours ranged from white, to darker shades of brown and black. The testers asked the children a series of 22 questions similar to the questions asked in the Clark Doll experiment, asking the children to point out which of the children are "smart," "dumb," "nice," "mean," "good," "bad," "good looking," and "ugly."

FIGURE 6-48 Two of the children who participated in the 2010 experiment. Where do we get our ideas about race?

Results

The results of the test showed that many of the white children had high rates of white bias, where the children identified their own skin colour with positive attributes and darker skin with negative attributes. Seventy-six percent of the older white children selected the two darker shades as being the "dumb" child and sixty-six percent of the younger white children selected the two darker shades as being the "mean" child. The results also showed black children tended to describe their own skin colour with positive attributes.

There was also a number of children from both races and age groups that refused to answer particular questions, saying they didn't know enough about the illustration to answer.

QUESTIONS

1. What do the results of the Clark Doll experiment tell us about studying racial bias in 1939?
2. What ethical concerns might arise from an experiment such as this?
3. What other research would you like to see, in response to the 2010 experiment?
4. How is the 2010 experiment different from the 1939 experiment?

REFLECT AND RESPOND

1. Who ensures that the code of ethics is followed?
2. What does "maintaining the image and the integrity of their own discipline" mean with regard to sociologists?
3. Why is it important to have ethical guidelines regarding research subjects? What are some potential issues that could arise if these guidelines were ignored?
4. When studying people who are in trouble, how should a sociologist behave? How might intervening to help affect the boundaries of the research? What are the ethics of not intervening?

The Challenges of Class in Sociology

Before You Read

Describe your community using a sociological lens. Consider socio-economic status, racialized, and ethnic factors, as well as access to community supports and structures (for example, schools, transit, community centres). How might you acquire your observations?

Sociologists are very interested in the impact of crime, outcomes for children, and mental health on neighbourhoods and communities. Your involvement in your community can be a measure of your social happiness and lifestyle. Sociologists study organization, practices, changes, and problems in an urban area and then make suggestions for policy changes. Your neighbourhood indicates more than just where you live; it can suggest your level of education, how much money you make, even how healthy you are. Sometimes people define themselves by the neighbourhood they live in or the one where they grew up.

Individuals can also be defined by other people based on where they live; sometimes we make assumptions about other people based solely on their address. An example of this is the experience of Evon Reid. In 2007, Reid, a University of Toronto honours student, applied for a job with the Ontario government. He met the qualifications for the job and felt he had a good chance of being called for an interview. Instead, Reid received an email that clearly was not intended for him that said, "This is the ghetto dude that I spoke to before," from the person handling his job application (Deibel, 2007). Reid hadn't met or spoken with the person who sent the email and concluded that the person might have made a judgment about him based on his address, a community in Scarborough. "The community I live in has one of the highest levels of youth unemployment in Canada. I'd hate to think that this (memo) accounts for that (Deibel, 2007)." It is ironic that the provincial government was indeed trying to recruit employees such as Reid to diversify its staff. Reid did later get a job with a Member of Provincial Parliament and went on to law school, while the writer was disciplined.

Neighbourhoods change all the time. It's important for sociologists to study how people actually live and not base conclusions on outdated information. It is also important that they do not generalize current information to single persons. Sometimes, because of their economic circumstances, people have no choice but to live in areas that may be unsafe or that may have poor access to social services. As well, some neighbourhoods that appear to be safe may have problems that aren't immediately visible.

Sociologists routinely conduct studies about the places in which people live. These studies have the potential to create a very emotional response in residents because of the concept of *neighbourhoodism*—the idea that one neighbourhood can be generalized based on a few statistics or a study. Sociologists must be guided by clear objectives and practise responsible and ethical research by following ethical guidelines. For many people, their home is a safe refuge from the outside world, and urban sociologists could inadvertently say or do something to upset the residents of a neighbourhood by their work. When working in this environment, sociologists should be aware that some residents feel a strong sense of loyalty toward their neighbourhood and may not be happy about the sociologist's presence.

FIGURE 6-49 Sociologists often study neighbourhoods to learn about communities.

The Invasion–Succession Model

A popular theory used by urban sociologists to study the inner workings of a neighbourhood is the invasion–succession model. According to this theory, the neighbourhood is like a biological ecosystem. The residents there are the local species of the ecosystem. When people are looking for a new home, they begin with an idea of where they would like to live (for example, close to grocery stories, schools, or highways) and then they consider what features they would like their neighbourhood to have. For example, young couples starting out may want a neighbourhood with an active nightlife. A young family may prefer a neighbourhood with schools that have a large number of resources and several parks. Middle-aged buyers might want a quiet neighbourhood. A symbolic interactionist would say that people like to see themselves reflected in the neighbourhood.

So, because of these personal buying decisions and trends, neighbourhoods begin to take on a homogeneous appearance, one in which all their inhabitants resemble one another in the areas of family structure and socio-economic status. For the most part, life in the neighbourhood can be very tranquil for the homogeneous "species" that resides there. Sometimes, however, members of the "species" may move to other neighbourhoods. This creates vacancies for new groups to potentially move in. Interestingly enough, when sociologists have studied the phenomenon of the "second species" moving in to a homogenous neighbourhood, they found that the original group made room for them and the two distinct groups coexisted peacefully. However, when a "third species" entered the neighbourhood, the response was quite different. The status of the third group was quite clearly subordinate to the second group.

In the end, the first and second groups exerted pressure on the third group to assimilate and be absorbed into the daily life of the neighbourhood. In the worst cases, the third group was driven out. In other studies, the last group moving in changed the face of the neighbourhood so much that the original residents moved out. Research in Canada has shown that a neighbourhood is more likely to lose a visible minority group rather than the loss of whites. For example, more than 50 percent of neighbourhoods that consisted of groups of British or French origin, Europeans, and Asian had changed over a five-year period such that they now only had people of British/French origin and Europeans or only those of British/French origin. As you can see, studying group behaviour can be exciting and challenging.

> Reflect on the community in which you live. Has there been change over the last decade? If so, how has your community changed? (Consider ethnicity, age, family structure, etc.)

Demographic Studies and Sociology

Although completely separate fields, **demography** and sociology have a great deal in common. Demography is the study of the structure and development of human population. The data it yields is an important source of information to sociologists to show how a society's population is living. Demographic information is gathered for a view of how a society's population is living.

More to Know...
You learned about symbolic interactionism in Chapter 3.

FIGURE 6-50 Some sociologists see neighbourhoods as a social ecosystem. What assumptions can you make about the people living in this neighbourhood?

demography: the statistical study of the structure and development of human population

FIGURE 6-51
Demography can help us understand communities and the individuals who live in them.

census:
an official periodic count of a population including information such as sex, age, education, and occupation

FIGURE 6-52 Several organizations banded together to save the long-form census.

Governments and independent researchers are interested in this kind of data. Having a firm understanding of how society functions amounts to the same concern for both sociology and demography—an understanding of people.

Urban concentration, or population density, is an important theme for demographers. The increase in the number of people living in urban areas was a large part of the development of urban sociology. Aging is another area of concern for demographers since it leads to changes in the economy and employment. Aging is of interest to sociologists, who consider the effects on social attitudes and behaviour that may occur among the elderly. So, even though the two are separate disciplines, they share an equally keen interest in society and social behaviour. The connection is made between demography and sociology because both fields stand to lose a rich source of statistical information in Canada.

In a recent decision, the federal government decided to eliminate the mandatory long-form **census** in favour of an optional census. In a census, information about a specific population is gathered and recorded. In Canada, a census is issued every five years and is delivered to individual households in a given area. Many groups, including sociologists, have come to rely on the valuable information provided by the long-form census. Some argue that without it, valuable information about society will be lost. The census informs sociological understanding of different populations within Canadian society, including urban life, and, without it, there will be tremendous problems when studying urban neighbourhoods.

Census

The census is vitally important for carrying out ethical and accurate research. It provides intimate glimpses into neighbourhoods and households and creates a huge archive of information that sociologists can examine to compare how society has changed and how it has stayed the same. Eliminating the census, or making it voluntary, can undermine the quality and accuracy of data and make it impossible for sociologists to draw solid conclusions between the past and the present.

The information collected in a census directly affects how programs and policies are funded. For example, decisions about library programs and services are determined by the income, languages, and education levels of the neighbourhood where a library is located. Census information affects business, transportation, and the building of homes and schools. It can also determine which programs are needed within particular communities, such as French-language programs or immigrant settlement services.

The census not only determines where funding should go and which programs are needed within certain areas, but also whether programs already in place are working. Because the census tracks information over time, examining the census over a period of years can provide a reliable picture of how effective certain policies are. It allows tax dollars to be used more effectively and in the most appropriate areas.

The census is valid, accurate, and objective because trained statisticians/demographers know how to draw samples from a population that is representative and generalizable statistically. Making it mandatory ensures that they are able to do this. Once census information is provided voluntarily, it cannot be considered as accurate. In a voluntary census, some people would be more likely than others to complete it, so it may provide researchers with an inaccurate view of a neighbourhood. A voluntary census also makes it difficult to gauge whether a policy has been effective, since the people who it helped may not be those who choose to fill out the census.

The Canadian Sociological Association (CSA) wrote to Minister Tony Clement about the cancellation of the Canadian long-form census in 2010 to highlight its concerns. The CSA represents the interests of sociologists in Canada and considered the issue very important to sociology. The following is an excerpt from the letter:

FIGURE 6-53 The census provides information about housing needs.

> Long-form data are used by businesses, provinces and municipalities, economists, urban and community researchers, policy analysts, sociologists, and other scholars in the humanities and social sciences (including geographers and historians). Religious and ethnic groups are also users. They all rely on the mandatory long-form census for solidly representative and accurate data—especially when data are disaggregated to community or minority-group levels. Whatever the unit of analysis, an accurate statistical portrait of the population—one that allows for cross-tabulation—is required. This cannot be provided by the voluntary NHS [National Household Survey] because bias—due to the under-representation of specific groups—is likely. Aboriginal people, recent immigrants, low-income families, and perhaps even busy professionals may fail to respond to the survey.
>
> The loss of comparable, longitudinal, long-form data seriously impairs our ability to monitor change in the social indicators that inform policies and programs related to immigrants, visible minorities, the poor, ethnic groups, Aboriginal peoples, disabled people, or women (e.g., the value of unpaid work in the home).... Considering the importance of long-form census data to our members and to Canadian society at large, we ask that you reverse your decision to replace the mandatory long-form census with the voluntary National Household Survey. Our understanding of Canada and its diversity depends on it.

REFLECT AND RESPOND

1. What is the purpose of census gathering?
2. Explain how a sociologist or school of sociology would explain what happened to Evon Reid.
3. Identify a change in your community, and explain it using the ideas of urban sociology.
4. What is the long-term impact for social scientists and society at large with the cancellation of the long-form census? Why would the Canadian Sociological Association write a letter protesting the issue?

The Danger of Value Judgments

> **Before You Read**
> With a partner, share an experience you have had within a health care system. Was the experience positive or negative?

Sociologists must be careful not to apply value judgments to the social issues they study. The primary goal of any sociologist is to report without bias and as accurately as possible. This may require redefining simple terms to encompass a wider range of meaning than usual. This is why it is important for the researcher to properly operationalize some of the terms used in his or her research. As long as the researcher is clear about his or her definitions and adheres to the definitions he or she provides then the research may not be value-free, but at least it is transparent and honest. For example, when conducting a study on the future of the Canadian family, a sociologist must begin with a basic definition for the term *family*. For some sociologists, that may mean the nuclear family. Based on that definition alone, any subsequent research would produce a one-dimensional view of the future of Canadian families. But when the researcher expands his or her parameters to include lone-parent families and same-sex families, he or she has transformed the study into something much more comprehensive. Of course, the difficulty for most sociologists is the dilemma of studying a society where their own personal beliefs may be a factor. Suspending our values and beliefs is a challenging task for anyone and one that requires a conscious effort on the part of social researchers. One area that is easily given to value judgments is health.

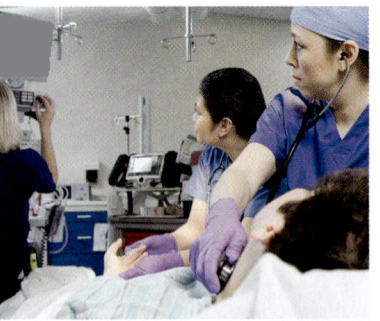

↑ **FIGURE 6-54** What are legitimate health care issues for Canadians?

Health and Sociology

As with the definition of *family* mentioned above, the definition of *health* can be complicated. Like gender, health is socially constructed. Around the world, people seek help for health issues daily, but a look at patients in a doctor's office in Toronto versus one in Dubai will tell you that not all health issues are the same, nor is the value given to certain health issues. So a broken arm, a broken denture, and liposuction are all considered issues of health care, but the value placed on each of those needs is constructed by society.

How does health become a social construction? Like every other norm and value in society, it begins with socialization. Depending on your family and cultural background, certain conditions are labelled important health issues while others are considered unimportant. For example, proper nutrition is important the world over, but many North Americans do not consider it to be a direct health care issue. Nutrition is a contributing factor to potential health problems, but we would not eat a carrot to prevent Alzheimer's disease or to cure a headache. In Asian cultures, a great deal of importance is placed on herbal remedies and acupuncture to cure severe and chronic illnesses, but in North America, these are seen merely as alternatives to common medical practices. Another example is birth control as a legitimate health concern for the sexually active. Some forms of birth control require a doctor's appointment and a prescription. For some religious groups, abstinence and natural family planning are the accepted form of birth control and, therefore, not a health care matter at all. As you can see, the sociologists conducting research in this area would have to redefine their terms carefully to ensure that their notions of health care did not intentionally or unintentionally exclude large groups of people who view health care differently.

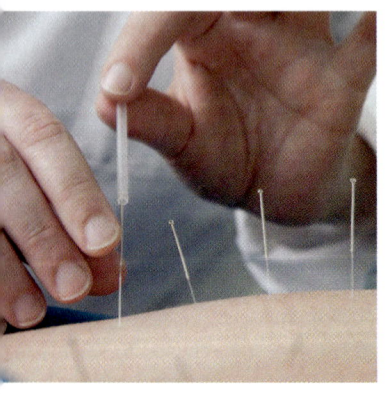

↑ **FIGURE 6-55**
Acupuncture is a time-honoured medical practice in many Asian countries. Why does health mean different things in different cultures?

The main factors that shape the health of Canadians are not medical treatments or lifestyle choices but rather the living conditions they experience. According to a report entitled "Social Determinants of Health: The Canadian Facts (2010)," the following are factors in whether or not you will be healthy:

- income and income distribution
- education
- unemployment and job security
- employment and working conditions
- early childhood development
- food insecurity
- housing
- social exclusion
- social safety network
- health services
- Aboriginal status
- gender
- racialized status
- disability

> **Open for Debate**
> A growing number of women and men are turning to the ancient art of acupuncture, which involves the use of thin needles inserted into the skin in the fight against facial wrinkles and other signs of aging. Is this a health care issue or a luxury? What does this say about ageism?

The Sick Neighbourhood

In their studies, sociologists encounter socio-economic disparities about poverty and health. Consider the extensive two-year project by the Toronto-based environmental group Pollution Watch. Its report compared federal data on low-income households and industrial air releases to determine whether residents of the Great Lakes Basin were more likely to experience health problems as a result of living in such a highly polluted area. The case of the sick neighbourhood indicates why sociologists must constantly look for new approaches to help understand and make recommendations for policy changes.

Research by the Pollution Watch group revealed that many of Toronto's poorest residents live near industries that emit the highest levels of toxic chemicals and pollutants into the air. While lower rental costs attract them to these neighbourhoods, this situation has created additional problems for low-income families who already face diminished health from stress, bad nutrition, diabetes, and poor dental care. The report revealed that children and the elderly are particularly vulnerable to the pollutants released in urban areas, despite the fact that the pollutants are within the legally allowed limits. While not all low-income communities had a high rate of chemical emissions, the study exposed a definite correlation between poverty and pollution.

This example shows that sociologists need to broaden their scope of research in order to get a complete picture of how social issues connect to our environment. In this situation, what are the obligations of sociologists studying the groups affected by the pollution? Looking back at the ethical guidelines you learned about at the beginning of this section, how should sociologists approach research subjects? How should their research be used?

↑ **FIGURE 6-56** What is the connection between poverty and health?

REFLECT AND RESPOND

1. What kind of difficulties might sociologists encounter when researching social issues such as health and poverty?
2. Why is understanding bias important to conducting research ethically?

The Ethics of Racial Profiling

> **VOICES**
>
> Racial profiling is any action undertaken for reasons of safety, security, or public protection that relies on stereotypes about race, colour, ethnicity, ancestry, religion, or place of origin, rather than on reasonable suspicion, to single out an individual for greater scrutiny or different treatment.
>
> Ontario Human Rights Commission

Racial discrimination is an issue related to power and the inability for some segments of society to have equal access to what that society offers. Here we will examine the concept of power in the context of ethical and responsible social practice. The issue of racial profiling has its roots in law enforcement and criminal behaviour. These are areas of extreme interest and relevance for sociology.

Understanding how deviant behaviour is defined and dealt with is of primary concern to many sociologists and social psychologists. Deviance in sociology refers to behaviour that contradicts cultural norms, including breaking laws, which is why crime is studied to see how the rules are created, changed, and enforced. Sociologists believe that social control is the way that members of a society attempt to persuade each other to comply with the society's norms. Social controls influence behaviour constantly because they are internalized and come into play every time a person has a deviant impulse. Social control theory argues that deviance is largely a matter of failed social controls. Deviance is behaviour that violates the norms of the social group in which the behaviour occurs. Crime is an act that violates a criminal law, or fails to follow the norms of the society.

Racial profiling is especially hurtful to the communities labelled for their alleged criminal activity. The assumption is that certain ethnic groups are more commonly involved in criminal activities and, as a result, come under more scrutiny by law enforcement agencies such as the police. The practice has become so widespread that the Ontario Human Rights Commission has highlighted non-police related examples of what it considers racial profiling. Here are some examples:

FIGURE 6-57 What is the impact of racial profiling on different groups?

- A private security guard follows a shopper because he believes the shopper is more likely to steal from the store.
- An employer wants a stricter security clearance for a Muslim employee after the events of September 11, 2001.
- A bar refuses to serve Aboriginal patrons because of an assumption that they will get drunk and rowdy.
- A criminal justice system official refuses bail to a Latin American person because of a belief that people from her country are violent.
- A landlord asks a Chinese student to move out because she believes that the tenant will expose her to Severe Acute Respiratory Syndrome (SARS) even though the tenant has not been to any hospitals, facilities, or countries associated with a high risk of SARS.

POINT/COUNTERPOINT

Racial Profiling

The sociological impact of racial profiling includes the overrepresentation of racial minorities in the criminal justice system and negative perceptions of racial minorities by the police, justice system, and Canadian society. It has been suggested that racial discrimination, leading to higher arrest and imprisonment rates, fulfils its own prediction in producing the appearance of a statistically significant racial difference in offending (Harris, 2003; Hudson, 1993). As a result, issues of systemic and personal discrimination lie at the heart of the debate over racial profiling. Criminologist Scot Wortley outlined the reasons for and against collecting data based on race in a presentation to Toronto police (see chart below). He obtained these arguments by using trained social scientists to develop and analyze the data, establishing benchmarks, and evaluating the impact of data collection.

Should Society Collect Data Based on Race?

For	Against
• Collecting this kind of data provides transparency of police actions to the public.	• Collecting data about race could compromise security and public safety as it could lead to stereotyping.
• It might eliminate or reduce some forms of racially biased policing.	• The data could easily be misinterpreted.
• Being aware of the data could help improve minority perceptions in police practices.	• Collecting this data is too expensive and takes funds from other needed areas.
• Studying the data could reduce racial disparities in arrests and in other statistics.	• The data is too difficult to collect properly.
• Addressing racial profiling issues could improve minority recruitment in the police force.	• Collecting this kind of data could increase the number of civil claims as those falsely charged may sue police.
• Wortley argues for more research and more data collection by police forces, saying the refusal to deal with it will ensure that the issue of racial discrimination continues to haunt law enforcement agencies for decades to come.	• In England, police routinely record the racial background of everyone stopped and searched by police. Statistics from 1997–98 found that black people were stopped and searched at a rate of 142 per 1000. Whites were stopped and searched at a rate of just 19 per 1000.
	• Racial profiling is based on the assumption that members of certain ethnic groups are disproportionately more likely to be involved in certain criminal activities. If this practice is widely entrenched or officially sanctioned, it also follows that members of nontargeted groups can also expect less police scrutiny.

QUESTIONS

1. Assess the merits or shortcomings of racial profiling using evidence to support your view.
2. Should a police force collect data based on race? Why or why not?
3. If a police force were to gather this kind of information, what guidelines would sociologists say are important to follow? What would a sheet look like to collect necessary data for criminals who are arrested? For each item provide a justification and how the data could be used to improve public safety or police performance.

Racial Profiling: An Issue of Human Rights

Jacqueline Nassiah was shopping for a bra in 2003 when she was stopped by a security guard in a Mississauga Sears store and accused of stealing an item worth less than $10. The black woman was searched twice, subjected to racial taunts by a police officer, and questioned for several hours, before being released without charge. The officer refused to look at all the evidence, including a security tape, "assuming that the white security guard was telling the truth (Cotroneo, 2007)," Nassiah stated.

In 2007, the Ontario Human Rights Tribunal ruled that Nassiah was the victim of racial profiling. This was the first time the Ontario Human Rights Tribunal had declared racial profiling contrary to the Ontario Human Rights Code, and ordered the Peel Police to pay her $20 000. The police force was also ordered to make systemic changes including training. The police officer transferred to the Sudbury police department.

Nassiah received no apology from Sears or the Peel police. "With the outcome I see that justice has been served and I'm glad for that," Nassaih said at a press conference Thursday. "But the fear, it has changed my life." While the decision shows that the Ontario Human Rights Tribunal obviously takes racial profiling very seriously, there is still much to be done to avoid the repetition of such a scenario in the future.

FIGURE 6-58 Jacqueline Nassiah at a press conference after the Ontario Human Rights Tribunal decision.

REFLECT AND RESPOND

1. Why are sociologists interested in racial profiling?
2. What details of the Nassiah case would a sociologist find interesting? What role did race play in this case? Explain your answer.

Communication Technology and Sociology

Technology is not something new. In the nineteenth century, the camera, the phonograph, and the telephone were invented, and the twentieth century saw the development of computers and cell phones. However, the pace of technological change has increased and its impact on our lives, particularly our social lives, has never been greater. In our recent history, there have been powerful moments when technology has helped bridge the divide among peoples of the world, such as the televising of the Olympics. Sometimes we are able to connect with others through technology during catastrophic moments of history as well, such as the events of September 11, 2001. Certainly, when natural disasters and world events are broadcast through mass media of all kinds (radio, television, and the Internet), we are grateful for the opportunity to witness these moments "firsthand."

Although technology can help facilitate communication, countries can use their authority to control the content and flow of that communication. Recent examples include the cutting off of all computer and telephone communications in Egypt by the Egyptian government when Egyptians began mass protests in 2011. Critics of technology prefer to concentrate on the negative implications and criminal activity spawned from personal electronic devices such as the cell phone, which in some cases is the weapon. As you learned in a previous case study in this chapter, cyberbullying is on the rise. So as long as technology continues to be a major force in social behaviour, sociologists will have to find a way to use and study it in order to understand its effects on the individual and society as a whole. How sociologists use technology is just as much a part of the discussion over ethics as any other component of their research.

> **Before You Read**
> Using a T-chart, brainstorm all the ways you use technology and how technology influences you within a single day.

FIGURE 6-59 How is the widespread use of technology changing sociological methods?

Video Surveillance

Camera surveillance is found in public spaces such as streets and parks; semi-public spaces such as shopping malls, universities, schools, buses and taxis, and airports; and private spaces such as homes. Although surveillance cameras are everywhere, with demands from police and businesses for more, there is no evidence to demonstrate their effectiveness. The Surveillance Camera Awareness Network (SCAN), based at Queen's University, provides research on surveillance cameras in Canada, including their use and effectiveness. Surveillance camera effects are shaped by both the social and technological environment. Operator training tends to focus on technical skills rather than the interaction of human operator and the camera, which would include the social implications of the surveillance on those whose images are captured and the role of stereotypes, prejudice, and bias in the operators' work.

> **Open for Debate**
> Canada has not yet passed legislation that explicitly addresses public camera surveillance. Various federal and provincial freedom-of-information and privacy statutes provide broad authority for information collection in the name of law enforcement, but it is unclear whether these statutes are capable of specifically authorizing public camera surveillance. Do we need more protection from our government?

FIGURE 6-60 Should you have the right to know you are under surveillance?

In a study entitled "Views from Behind the Camera's Lens: Exploring Operator Perceptions" (Derby, 2009), camera operators at eight sites in Ontario and Quebec, chosen for their diversity, were interviewed. The researchers conducted interviews in a semi-structured format, using open-ended questions, with an interview guide. At the end, participants were asked if they wanted to add more information. On average, interviews took 135 minutes, which produced 400 pages of transcripts. The study found that there were no accountability structures in place to address potential problems (including racial profiling and sexual voyeurism). Accountability rested solely with the individual camera operator. One subject said, "Since 9/11 you become more aware of Middle Eastern people; tend to watch them a little, pay closer attention to them because you never know when something's going to happen here (Derby, 2009, 42)." The research concluded that surveillance camera technology is socially constructed by the camera operators and their effectiveness on reducing crime or increasing safety is limited by this variable. While it should be noted that not all racial or ethnic stereotyping resulted in heightened scrutiny or negative consequence, this does not take away from the fact that some groups are disproportionately monitored by camera operators.

Social Networking

Technological innovations such as email, smartphones, and social networking sites have made it possible to stay connected constantly. The use of Facebook and other virtual social networking sites has meant that we can connect with thousands of "friends" online. We can update our location and upload photos and videos to the world every minute of the day. People choose what information to share online, which in theory allows us to control the amount of surveillance we're subject to. Anders Albrechtslund calls this *participatory surveillance*. Social networking can also mean restricting our privacy, so we should be aware of what the public knows about us.

However, people are increasingly being defined by their online profiles. Employers can search our public identity and online profiles may influence whether we get an interview or whether they will hire us. Social networking sites also provide data for government agencies, marketers, or police since they are easily searchable. Police also use YouTube to solve crimes by posting surveillance footage. Hille Koskela (2004) introduced the concept of *empowering exhibitionism* to describe the practice of revealing your personal life. By sharing their lives, people claim "copyright" to their own lives as they engage in the self-construction of identity. Social networking can also be used to make political or social changes. A 2009 study showed that people who use social networking sites have social networks that are 20 percent more diverse than people who do not use the Internet at all.

Visual Sociology and YouTube

A recent phenomenon known as *visual sociology* has sociologists running for their cameras. The International Visual Sociology Association (IVSA) has a strong following. Its membership attends annual conferences to discuss current scholarship in the field of visual sociology. Its guiding purpose is "to promote the study, production, and use of visual images, data, and materials in teaching, research, and applied activities, and to foster the development and use of still photographs, film, video, and electronically transmitted images in sociology and other social sciences and related disciplines and applications" (IVSA).

IVSA topics for discussion include looking at how sociology has historically been informed by experts and shifting research to be more collaborative to engage subjects not previously engaged in the research. Some argue that the people that sociologists study should be represented without the expert voice of social scientists interpreting their experiences. Instead, researchers can work with the participants and include visual evidence to change research as well as the environment where the research takes place. Visual research methods empower young people and minimize the power relationships. This research also allows access to parts of their lives that are usually not available and leads to drawing out greater oral details.

The Life in a Day project between YouTube and Academy Award–nominated director Ridley Scott is a feature documentary that was created from scenes filmed by anyone with access to video-making equipment. Participants were invited to film something of their day on Saturday, July 24, 2010. Pieced together, this film is a time capsule of one particular day and how different people experienced it in different ways.

FIGURE 6-61 Visual sociology combines the traditional methods of sociology with new and emerging technology in order to take a "snapshot" of society.

REFLECT AND RESPOND

1. Select two types of technology that affect your life, and write a blog about how they are socially constructing who you are today.
2. Where do you stand on surveillance in your life? Organize an information campaign on whether we need greater protection from video or Internet surveillance.
3. Select a topic of interest for which using photography might be an appropriate research method, and identify a possible hypothesis.
4. What was the hypothesis in the study about video surveillance? What could you have as an alternative hypothesis?
5. How is the Life in a Day project useful to sociologists?

CHAPTER 6 REVIEW

Knowledge and Understanding/Thinking

1. Describe one way in which each of the following shapes social behaviour:
   a) culture
   b) religion
   c) economics
   d) technology

2. The ISA Code of Ethics requires that sociologists "not conceal their own ideological position(s)." What is meant by that? Are sociologists not supposed to suspend their own bias and be as objective as possible?

3. Define discrimination and explain how physical and intellectual disabilities can be grounds for discriminatory actions. Describe an overt and a systemic example for each.

4. Using the rational decision theory of collective behaviour, list the possible steps that might be taken by a group of students who are unhappy with an administrator's decision to cancel student-led activities. Who might emerge as the leader of the collective, and what must happen for the group to become organized and succeed in its appeal to the school board to have student privileges reinstated? Think of a typical high school (grades 9 to 12).

5. Create a list of five professions that rely on strict obedience from their members. Rank the professions from 1 to 5 (1 representing the most obedient members). Explain the benefits and drawbacks of choosing a profession from your ranking. Explain your answer.

Thinking/Communication

6. Describe the relationship between social identity and current dating practices and create a hypothesis for this relationship that could be researched.

7. Devise a short scenario for one of the following theories of discrimination:
   - competition theory
   - frustration–aggression theory
   - learned theory
   - ignorance theory

8. In what types of groups is "groupthink" most likely to happen? Create a case study that would adequately outline the process of groupthink for an individual member of a group. Use Janis's symptoms as a guide.

9. Build an organizer that identifies both positive and negative examples of collective behaviour.

10. Using the Clark Doll experiment as a guide, suggest an experiment you would use to test racial bias in Toronto today. If you are going to use dolls, what might the dolls look like? Remember to represent the multicultural makeup of Toronto in your experiment.

11. For sociologists, what purpose is there in using information collected through the long-form census? Write a question about gender that you think might appear on a census form.

12. Review the invasion succession theory used to study urban neighbourhoods and explain how you could apply the model to residents of a condominium complex.

13. Predict what you feel will be the next ethical question facing sociologists, keeping in mind the changes in technology and the evolution of the global community.

Communication/Application

14. What expert in the field of sociology might you consider interviewing for an in-depth look at gender? Draft one crucial interview question you might ask him or her.

15. Create a dictionary for the ten most commonly used acronyms (for example, BFF) on social networking sites. Then explain what conclusions sociologists would make about society today based on your dictionary.

16. Choose a well-known public figure, past or present, who exemplifies prosocial or upstander behaviour. Give reasons that his or her behaviour is a model for society, and write a convincing statement justifying your choice.

17. Devise a "breaching experiment" that would test the social norms for using electronic devices in public spaces. Establish clear steps for the experiment and suggest possible reactions by society to the breach.

18. Within the context of collective behaviour, use smart mobs and mass public grief as the basis for a written comparison about the positive and negative implications of technology for social behaviour and social norms.

19. Draft a short outline for the ethical guidelines of using technology in social relationships. Include at least three points in your draft.

20. Review all the key experiments and landmark case studies highlighted throughout the chapter, and choose one. Decide whether the experiment or study has any ethical faults, and suggest ways in which the violations might be corrected.

UNIT 3

Social Science and Us

Chapter 7
Anthropology and Us

Research and Inquiry Skill Focus:
- Evaluating Sources

Section 7.1: Understanding Cultures
Section 7.2: Canadian Cultures, Past and Present
Chapter 7 Review

Chapter 8
Psychology and Us

Research and Inquiry Skill Focus:
- Presenting Research in Psychology

Section 8.1: Influence of Others on Self
Section 8.2: Personality and Environment
Chapter 8 Review

Chapter 9
Sociology and Us

Research and Inquiry Skill Focus:
- Writing Reports

Section 9.1: Identity in Different Contexts
Section 9.2: Canadian Social Structures and Institutions
Chapter 9 Review

How does social science help us understand society? Using social science skills to understand ourselves and people who are different than us allows us to better understand our own experiences and relationships. Understanding the complex relationships and forces that connect people makes it possible to respond to the world around us.

Each of the three social sciences takes different approaches to understanding society. Using the lenses of anthropology, psychology, and sociology we can refine our critical thinking skills to better understand the issues that surround and affect us, and to challenge the status quo and common assumptions about each issue. Rather than being a passive observer of the world, we can find ways to get involved—to affect change—whether it be in our own family, community, or further afield.

FIGURE U3-1 What issues are important to you? What influences you to take action or to affect change on an issue? How do you know what factors influence your decisions?

CHAPTER 7

Anthropology and Us

In the past, cultural anthropologists looked to small, rural, and cohesive communities in other countries to understand how cultures function. Anthropologists have since turned to communities in their own area to understand social practices and customs. In Canada, anthropologists study how Canada's many cultures define themselves and interact with one another. They use anthropological methods and theories to understand how legal and religious practices are changing. They try to understand how ideas of race and discrimination affect how people interact with one another. Anthropologists also study digital culture and how it is reshaping the multicultural landscape in Canada.

Chapter Expectations

By the end of this chapter, you will:
- explain ways in which culture is an agent of socialization
- explain how studying cultural systems of different times, places, and groups helps anthropologists understand human behaviour and culture in the present
- describe the effects that assimilation and multiculturalism have on culture
- use an anthropological perspective to assess how diverse factors influence and shape human behaviour and culture
- use terms relating to anthropology, psychology, and sociology correctly
- assess various aspects of information gathered from primary and secondary sources

Key Terms

acculturation
bicultural identity
cargo beliefs
frame of reference
hypodescent
informal justice system
institutional completeness
interculturalism
multiculturalism
placemakers
restorative justice
sapienization
social customs
social shield
supernatural
symbolic ethnicity
transnationalism
true mobiles

FIGURE 7-1 What is Canadian culture? How is it changing? What do you think each of the people in these photos would say about Canadian culture?

Landmark Case Studies

James Gibbs: The Kpelle Moot

Key Theorists

Mehrunnisa Ahmad Ali
Michele Byers
Slavenka Drakulić
E.E. Evans-Pritchard
Ruth Freed
Stanley Freed

James Gibbs
Neeti Gupta
Keith N. Hampton
Peruvemba Jaya
Katrina Jurva

Mikel J. Koven
Stephen Leavitt
Pavna Sodhi
Evangelia Tastsoglou
Tricia Wang

Spotlight on Anthropology — Canada's Residential Schools

Before You Read
How does racism affect culture?

Canada's residential schools are a tragic example of the effects of racism on culture and have left Canada with a devastating legacy. Between 1892 and 1969, the Canadian government carried out an official policy of assimilating Aboriginal children through educational institutions known as *residential schools*. The government forcibly separated Aboriginal children from their families and forbid contact for months at a time. Children were required to live at the schools, far away from where their families lived, and forbidden to speak their language, allowed to speak only English or French. They were also prevented from participating in their traditional spiritual practices. At the schools, living conditions were poor and the mortality rate was high due to outbreaks of tuberculosis. Some Aboriginal children were also abused, physically, sexually, and emotionally, by those in charge at the schools.

As these facts became public, the government faced increasing pressure to close the residential schools. The last school closed in 1996. The residential school system had long-term effects within the Aboriginal community. In addition to coming to terms with the individual effects of physical and sexual abuse, former students felt that they lost key elements of their cultures and identities with the loss of traditional languages and traditional ways of life. Consider the perspectives expressed in Figure 7-2 on the cultural effects of residential schools.

QUESTIONS

1. What was the function of the residential schools? What was the impact on Aboriginal peoples?
2. Do the perspectives expressed here give a fair representation of this issue? Give reasons to support your answer.
3. Why are the children who attended residential schools called the "lost generation?"

↓ **FIGURE 7-2**

> I want to get rid of the Indian problem. I do not think as a matter of fact that the country ought to continuously protect a class of people who are able to stand alone.... Our objective is to continue until there is not a single Indian in Canada that has not been absorbed into the body politic and there is no Indian question, and no Indian Department, that is the whole object of this Bill.
> — Duncan Campbell Scott, 1920, head of the Department of Indian Affairs 1913–1932

> After a lifetime of beatings, going hungry, standing in a corridor on one leg, and walking in the snow with no shoes for speaking Inuvialuktun, and having a heavy, stinging paste rubbed on my face, which they did to stop us from expressing our Eskimo custom of raising our eyebrows for "yes" and wrinkling our noses for "no," I soon lost the ability to speak my mother tongue. When a language dies, the world it was generated from is broken down too.
> — Mary Carpenter, 1995

> We believe firmly that the time has come to resolve a fundamental contradiction at the heart of Canada: that while we assume the role of defender of human rights in the international community, we retain, in our conception of Canada's origins and makeup, the remnants of colonial attitudes of cultural superiority that do violence to the Aboriginal peoples to whom they are directed.
> — Royal Commission on Aboriginal Peoples Report, 1996

> We don't have the closeness of family any more. A lot of the grandparents and a lot of the parents who went to residential school lost that familial sense of belonging. In the course of having grown up like that, you always try to emulate the people that raised you. If you were raised in coldness and detachment, you're going to carry those same ways of raising your own children in that atmosphere.
> — Grant Severight, survivor, St. Philip's Indian Residential School, Kamsack, Saskatchewan

> The government now recognizes that the consequences of the Indian residential schools policy were profoundly negative and that this policy has had a lasting and damaging impact on Aboriginal culture, heritage, and language. [...] The legacy of Indian residential schools has contributed to social problems that continue to exist in many communities today. [...] Therefore, on behalf of the government of Canada and all Canadians, I stand before you, in this chamber so central to our life as a country, to apologize to Aboriginal peoples for Canada's role in the Indian residential schools system.
> — Prime Minister Stephen Harper's apology for residential schools, June 11, 2008

Research and Inquiry Skills

Evaluating Sources

Do you believe everything you read or hear? Why are some sources more reliable than others? As an anthropologist or any other kind of researcher, you always need to evaluate your sources. When evaluating a source, a social scientist asks: Who wrote this? When? Why? Can I trust the person? What is his or her perspective, bias, worldview, and goals? Whether it is a village midwife in a remote community, an online gamer blogging about his experiences, a Wikipedia entry, or the textbook you are currently reading, every source has a purpose and perspective. As a researcher, you need to understand who the source is and determine if the information provided is going to help you draw conclusions.

Evaluating Primary and Secondary Sources

As you've learned in previous chapters, bias is a particular viewpoint or way of seeing an event, person, or thing. In the primary sources about residential schools (see page 318), it is clear that the Canadian government's bias against Aboriginal peoples led to the racist policy of residential schools. Bias can change, as seen in Prime Minister Harper's 2008 apology.

Frame of Reference or Worldview

Your perspective is shaped by your **frame of reference** or worldview. This is your total life experience that includes all of your cultural beliefs and learning. When evaluating sources, it's important to determine how the authors' experiences might have shaped their perspective, as well as your own frame of reference.

> **frame of reference:**
> a person's total life experience, including cultural beliefs and learning

Accuracy and Reliability

A person's bias affects how accurately he or she reports events or views of other people. People select information, highlighting some facts and ignoring others, to support their own bias. When evaluating sources, you should consider the following:

- How accurate is the source when compared to other sources on the same event?
- What information is the source leaving out or including?
- How can a researcher overcome this problem?
- Whose voices are present? Whose voices are missing?

With a primary source, a researcher needs to consider the personal bias of the speaker, but how do you know whether a secondary source is reliable? As you learned in Chapter 4, there are simple ways to check. Who is the author? When was it written? Are there citations? What is the author's bias or purpose in writing? All sources, whether print or online, need to be evaluated for reliability.

FIGURE 7-3 Before and after photos of a student at a residential school, published in a government report on the success of residential schools. These photos are seen quite differently today. If you only had the after photo as your evidence, how would this impact your research?

Relevance

When conducting research, you need to have your central research question in mind so that you can select the information that is most relevant and helpful in answering your question. Since there might be a great deal of information available on a topic, a guiding question is essential to determine whether the source is relevant. Your task as a researcher is to understand the whole story as accurately as possible. To do so involves carefully evaluating as many points of view as possible before coming to your conclusions.

Activities

Read the primary source accounts about residential schools in Canada on page 318, and evaluate each source.

1. How do you think the residential school experience changed the frame of reference or worldview of its survivors?
2. Do you think the schools have an effect on the frame of reference of the survivors' children and their families? Why or why not?
3. How does Campbell Scott's perspective affect his accuracy in his view of Aboriginal peoples?
4. What other sources (both primary or secondary) would you need to answer the question, What effects can racist policies have on culture?

Section 7.1 Understanding Cultures

Hockey and maple syrup are often given as examples of Canadian culture, but do these examples help us understand Canadian culture? Understanding the culture of any country or group of people is not simply a matter of knowing the symbols or foods, although those things are part of culture. Culture is who a people are, and there are distinct differences within a country as well as among countries. In this section, you will learn about different elements of cultures, including **social customs**, technology, legal systems, and religions, and how they help anthropologists understand cultures.

social customs: expected and ideal behaviours of a society

Social Customs, Manners, and Values

Social customs are one of the most obvious differences among cultures. When you go to another country, how will you greet people? How do people dress, and are there any formal rules for clothing? What are appropriate topics for small talk? Anthropologists doing field research must first learn the expected behaviours to fit in as much as possible with the culture, and then they must try to understand what these behaviours mean to the participants and how they reflect that culture's values. In the next few pages, you will look at how customs become apparent when cultures meet and how digital technology is interacting with Canadian social customs to change Canadian culture.

As you grow up, you learn social customs from your parents and peers through the process of socialization. How to eat, body language, and values such as "use a fork and knife" and "treat all people equally" are examples of social customs that many Canadians learn, but social customs are not the same in all cultures. While all people have customs around eating, the customs vary by culture. Which hand you use to eat, what utensils you use, how you sit, and what you say before, during, and after a meal are all ways that eating customs vary in every culture. Anthropologists call the learning of social customs **sapienization**, the process of learning "a uniquely human way of life centred on marriage, the family and the household" (Bodley, 2000). Sapienization helps to create permanent human societies that provide for their members.

When anthropologists go into a culture to study it, they, like children, must learn the basic social customs and manners of that society. They often notice that certain objects, ideas, or practices are valued more highly or are more central in some cultures than in others.

> **?** What do you think are the central ideas, beliefs, and objects in Canadian society?

Before You Read
How do cultural practices, such as holidays or meals, shape your behaviour?

Connecting Anthropology to Sociology

Sociologists look at socialization as the process by which the individual learns the behavioural patterns, skills, and values of her or his social world. Socialization begins at birth and continues throughout an individual's life. What is the impact if you change cultures? Does this mean that socialization is fixed and cannot change?

sapienization: the process of learning uniquely human social customs centred on marriage, the family, and the household

Social Customs in Conflict: Teeth

There is no better way to understand how culture is learned and what beliefs your own culture has than by travelling. When she first travelled to the United States, Slavenka Drakulić, a Croatian writer, was amazed by toothpaste:

> When I first visited the United States in 1983, I loved to watch TV commercials. This is when I noticed that Americans were obsessed by their teeth. Every second commercial seemed to be for toothpaste. Where I come from, toothpaste is toothpaste. I couldn't believe there were so many different kinds. What were they all for? After all the purpose of it is just to clean your teeth. In my childhood there were two kinds, mint flavour and strawberry flavour …
>
> Needless to say, in every commercial for toothpaste at least one bright, impressively beautiful set of teeth flashes across the screen, but this image is not confined to selling toothpaste. As we all know, beautiful teeth are used to advertise beer, hair shampoo, cars, anything. … The foreigner soon learns that they stand not only as a symbol for both good looks and good health, but for something else as well. (1996)

As Drakulić started observing the connection between Americans and their teeth, she discovered the connection between good teeth and money. Her friend's son had just had braces put on his teeth, and instead of feeling pity, as she did, the boy's mother was proud that she could afford the "torture device" and felt that the pain would be worthwhile for the status and social acceptance the straightened teeth would provide the boy as an adult.

When she returned to Eastern Europe, Drakulić started noticing the state of the teeth of her friends and acquaintances: "On the bus from the airport I met one of my acquaintances, a young television reporter. For the first time I noticed that half of his teeth were missing and that those which remained looked like the ruins of a medieval town. I had known this guy for years, but I had never thought about the state of the inside of his mouth before, or if I had, I'd considered it totally unimportant (1996)."

As Drakulić continued observing, she discovered that nobody in Croatia was particularly concerned with the state of his or her teeth, from television reporters to national politicians. Under the old Communist regimes, dentistry was free and of low quality, but in the post-Communist Croatia of the late 1990s, there were both state and private dentists available. Even so, many people who could afford private dentistry did not consider it important. Drakulić sees this as the result of a "specific culture of thinking" that was fostered by Communism. She states: "Individual responsibility, including the responsibility for oneself, is an entirely new concept here [in Croatia]. As absurd as it may sound, in the old days one could blame the Communist Party even for one's bad teeth. Now there is no one to blame, but it takes time to understand that (1996)."

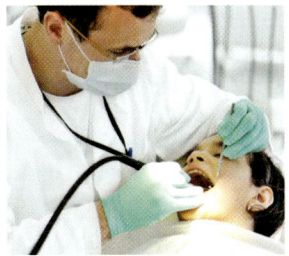

FIGURE 7-4 What does this photo tell you about Canadian culture?

❓ What do the social customs around teeth and dentistry reveal about North American culture? What did Drakulić learn about her own culture by examining another? What can we learn about our own culture by looking at the perspective of an outsider?

Open for Debate

Ontario Premier Dalton McGuinty says school boards should be open to the idea of allowing students to use cell phones in the classroom. Teachers could use cell phones to show students how to access information online, for example. Do you think cell phones should be used as a tool in classrooms?

Technology and Canadian Culture

As digital technology becomes more widespread in Canada, it has an increasingly greater effect on culture and social relationships. Not only is our experience of culture and language changing, but our culture also influences how we use technology, what technologies we adopt or choose to avoid, and how we interact with one another both online and face to face. The shift is reflected in school policies on cell phones from the late 1990s and early 2000s compared to the policies in place today. Many schools have banned the use of cell phones and even installed cell phone jammers to prevent students from using their phones at school. While there are certainly negative effects of digital technology in schools, including distracting students in class, giving students a means of cheating on tests, and allowing cyberbullying, there are also positive effects. Students and teachers can use their phones to do research and collaborate with other students and teachers online. As this technology becomes inescapable, many schools are re-examining their policies.

? Do you think cell phones should be jammed in schools? Why or why not? When is it rude or wrong to answer your cell phone or check your email?

Wi-Fi and Social Interactions

A 2008 study of Wi-Fi users in coffee shops in two American cities by researchers Keith N. Hampton and Neeti Gupta revealed some surprising results about how public access to Wi-Fi is changing North American culture. The researchers were interested in finding out how Internet access affected social interactions within a public space. They wanted to examine if Wi-Fi users were interacting digitally only with the people they knew already or whether people were accessing the Internet in public in order to interact with more people outside of their pre-established relationships. The study observed and interviewed customers in coffee shops over four months. Observers spent 120 hours in four cafes in Boston and Seattle. A total of 30 hours were spent directly observing in two-hour time blocks systematically distributed across the hours of operation—one-third on the weekends and the rest on weekdays. The researchers also conducted 20 unstructured exit interviews.

Hampton and Gupta observed and labelled two distinct groups of Wi-Fi users: **true mobiles** and **placemakers**. Both groups were in public places using Wi-Fi, but for different reasons. The true mobiles would normally be working in public for the whole day one or two days a week, instead of in their home office or their regular office. They made serious efforts to avoid social interaction with other customers by using their phones or laptops as **social shields** to avoid interacting with other people. Many reported going to the coffee shops in order to be able to focus on their work and to avoid the distractions of their regular work space. The true mobiles are examples of how public spaces are no longer used for social purposes but to ensure privacy.

The placemakers used the coffee shops for social interaction and potential social encounters on a daily basis. They would talk about what was on their laptop, engage in conversation with patrons and staff, make eye contact with other people, and were not observed to use their laptops as shields. They were

"I can never remember. Does the cell phone go on the left or the right?"

↑ **FIGURE 7-5** What customs have developed around cell phone use?

true mobiles: people who access the Internet in public to specifically avoid social interactions

placemakers: people who access the Internet in public to create social interactions

social shield: a device or object used to avoid interactions with other people

using the Internet to create local, place-based interactions, in fact, reclaiming public space to make more connections with their local community.

The results from this study show that public Internet access is creating places where people have face-to-face encounters and places where people are cut off from others in their separate private world (Hampton and Gupta, 2008).

> ❓ Are students using their digital devices as true mobiles or as placemakers (or neither) in the classroom? What social shields do you notice people using in your school or community? Examine the validity of this research. Explain.

FIGURE 7-6 Is this group more likely to be true mobiles or placemakers?

Twitter Dialects

The idea that technology makes our language less diverse was studied by a computer scientist, Jacob Eisenstein, at Carnegie Mellon University. In fact, he found that regional differences may even evolve and expand due to technology. Eisenstein collected one week's worth of messages that were marked with their location on Twitter in March 2010 for a total of 380 000 tweets from 9500 users. The assumption had been that mass media would reduce regional differences since we all watch the same movies and TV programs, but Eisenstein found that well-known regional phrases thrived on Twitter.

University of Toronto sociolinguistics professor Sali Tagliamonte noted, "What the Internet offers is variation in the way words are spelled, and that shows us another dimension of language and how people use language to differentiate themselves from another." New York City tweeters use *suttin* instead of the more commonly used *sumthin*, and there are various spellings of *for sure*, including *fo sho*, *fsho*, and *fasho* depending on the region (Khan, 2011).

Technology in the Doctor's Office

When anthropologist Tricia Wang took her grandmother to a doctor's appointment, she noticed the doctor's frustration when using new netbooks issued by the office. In a brief discussion with the doctor, she drew the following conclusions about the integration of the technology:

- *Spatial layout of material objects matters.*
  The doctor had to work on the netbook at a counter with her back to the patient and was frustrated with the lack of face-to-face interaction. She had to keep switching back and forth between computer and patient.
- *Extent of digitization of information matters.*
  The reason why the doctor had to work at the counter and not on a cart or hold the netbook on her lap was because the old paper files were not yet digitized. The doctor had to use paper files and the netbook, and interact with the patient at the same time.
- *Human connection matters.*
  The doctor felt that the netbook was not an improvement because it seriously decreased her face-to-face time with her patients.

- *Mobility is neutral.*
  Having the netbook did not significantly reduce the doctor's workload or things to carry around, since the paper files were still needed and the room's layout compromised the doctor–patient interaction.

Mobile devices are always introduced into existing social experience, which must be considered. The interaction between the existing social space and the new device is where culture happens (Wang, 2009).

> As discussed in Section 4.2, to be adopted by a society, a technology must become known, be accepted by most people, and fit into existing systems of knowledge. Which of these is the problem in the adoption of netbooks in this doctor's office?

FIGURE 7-7 How might technology impact this doctor?

POINT/COUNTERPOINT

Digital Technology and Culture

Digital technology can have a profound affect on how people do their job, who they interact with and how they interact with them, and the different issues and events they are exposed to.

Is Digital Technology Substantially Changing Culture?

Yes	No
• Technology is used in the medical field to streamline medical resources to improve health care and efficiency.	• Technology is only a means of communication and can be intrusive.
• New tablet computers are much less intrusive than paper or laptops.	• Technology is useful only as far as it can be integrated into existing culture and meets a real need. For example, older doctors may be left behind, further challenging people's access to medical services.
• Recent large-scale or impromptu protests have been largely facilitated by social networking.	
• Millions of people join activist groups online, signing petitions, sending Tweets, texts, or emails, which are much faster than writing a letter and easier than attending a protest or rally.	• Protests in the past spread quickly without the aid of social networking.
	• Few people who join online activist groups take direct action or give much money to a cause.

QUESTIONS

1. Develop a research question around the integration of new technology in the classroom, the workplace, or at home. What methods would you use to investigate it?

REFLECT AND RESPOND

1. What are some negative effects of digital technology in the classroom? What are some positive effects?
2. Which types of Internet users do you think are at your local coffee shop? What results do you think you would find if you repeated Hampton and Gupta's study of Wi-Fi users in your community?

Legal Systems and Cultural Values

All societies need a way to create social control and to deal with aggression and violence. Societies have developed many different ways of resolving conflicts, from social pressure to complex legal systems.

Justice takes many forms in different cultures and changes over time. **Informal justice systems** are used in many nomadic or semi-nomadic societies, or in remote areas where access to a central justice system is difficult. Social pressure and avoidance are enough to prevent and deal with most cases of aggression. As you've learned, among the Ju/'hoansi of Southern Africa, if two individuals are having a dispute, one of the most likely outcomes is that one person will move away for a while to a different camp. With no formal leader to adjudicate disputes, all members of the community put social pressure on those who become arrogant or think they are better than others.

> **Before You Read**
> What do you know about the Canadian legal system? What do you know about another legal system? Why are there differences in legal systems?

informal justice system: a system of social pressure to control behaviour, used most often in nomadic or nonhierarchical societies

> **More to Know...**
> You learned about the Ju/'hoansi in Chapter 1.

FIGURE 7-8 *Gacaca* are village courts in Rwanda, used to resolve disputes. Gacaca means "on the grass" in the Kinyarwanda language because Gacaca were originally met on the grass. Gacaca have been modified and adapted in order to deliberate on Rwandan genocide cases. Why would this approach be adopted in response to this serious crime?

When everyone knows everyone else, social pressure is often enough to prevent aggression or deal with it effectively if it does occur. If social pressure is not enough, a community may take collective action. Franz Boas recorded an example of community action among the Inuit in the nineteenth century. A man murdered three people in an argument over a woman. The headman asked every man in the community if the murderer should be killed. They all agreed, so the headman went deer hunting with him and shot him in the back (Boas, 1888). This is an example of capital punishment, which is a method of punishment used by many cultures at different points in history.

As societies increase in size and complexity, they often develop more complex and formal justice systems involving codified laws; courts; specialized occupations, such as judges, lawyers, and police; as well as formal punishments, such as fines and jail. These impersonal systems usually develop because societies grow so large that people don't know one another any more. These systems are more likely to occur in hierarchical societies with social classes and centralized power (Ember and Ember, 1999).

> **?** What is the difference between formal and informal justice systems? What are some possible advantages and disadvantages of each?

Restorative Justice Systems

restorative justice:
an approach to justice that focuses on restoring harmony and balance to the community by focusing on the needs of both the victim and the offender instead of punishment

Many societies have practised and continue to practise **restorative justice** as part of their informal systems of law. Restorative justice is an approach that restores harmony and balance to the community by focusing on the needs of both the victim and the offender instead of punishing offenders based on legal principles. With restorative justice, the offender publicly acknowledges the wrongs committed and repairs the harm caused by his or her crime before being reintegrated into the community. The community has input into the punishment because the offender's actions harmed the community as a whole.

Landmark Case Study

James Gibbs: The Kpelle Moot

Anthropologist James Gibbs studied the Kpelle people of central Liberia. He observed the proceedings in a moot or informal court. The Kpelle also have a formal court system that is coercive and arbitrary in its use of justice. The formal system is useful for dealing with assaults, possession of illegal materials, and thefts by unrelated individuals. It is not helpful in dealing with domestic issues such as marriage, inheritance, and divorce, where the relationship must continue after the case and there are issues of power and control that might influence the outcome. The coercive and arbitrary nature of the court generally drives disputants apart.

The moot, by contrast, has the goal of airing disputes and restoring harmony. It is usually composed of related kin from the same village and presided over by an elder chosen by the complainant. The moot is much more effective than the formal system at dealing with domestic disputes, such as spousal mistreatment or inheritance of wives. The following excerpt is a transcript of a moot in the late 1950s:

FIGURE 7-9 A moot or informal court would often take place in a home such as this one. What features seem similar to or different from courts with which you're familiar?

Wama Nya, the complainant, had one wife, Yua. His older brother died and he inherited the widow, Yokpo, who moved into his house. The two women were considered legally sisters since they were married to the same man. After Yokpo moved in, there was strife in the household. The husband accused her of staying out late at night, of harvesting rice without his knowledge, and of denying him food. He also accused Yokpo of having lovers and admitted having had a physical struggle with her, after which he took a basin of water and "washed his hands of her."

Yokpo countered by denying the allegations about having lovers, saying that she was accused falsely, although she had in the past confessed the name of one lover. She further complained that Wama Nya had assaulted her and, in the act, had committed the indignity of removing her headtie, and had expelled her from the house after the ritual hand-washing. Finally she alleged that she had been thus cast out of the house at the instigation of the other wife who, she asserted, had great influence over their husband.

Kolo Wa, the Town Chief and quarter elder, and the brother of Yokpo, was the mediator of the moot, which decided that the husband was mainly at fault, although Yua and Yokpo's children were also in the wrong. Those at fault had to apologize to Yokpo and bring gifts of apology as well as local rum for the disputants and participants in the moot.
(Gibbs, 1963, p. 3)

Aboriginal Sentencing Circles

The Royal Commission on Aboriginal Peoples began investigating alternative approaches to Aboriginal justice in 1991, after Judge Barry Stuart called in the community elders in the case of Philip Moses. This system has similarities to the Kpelle moot. Many commissions and studies have found that Aboriginal peoples in Canada were jailed at up to eight times the rate of non-Aboriginals (Lilles, 2002). Aboriginal peoples make up 3 percent of the Canadian population but make up almost 20 percent of the total federal prison population. Jail time did not seem to be solving the many problems within the community, so the judges started turning to the community to help solve the problems.

> **VOICES**
>
> Recognizing the uniqueness of each community, and the uniqueness of each dispute, warrants departing from the audacious presumption of the formal justice system that "one process fits all forms of disputes"
>
> –Judge Barry Stuart

Why is a moot successful in resolving domestic disputes? According to Gibbs, the key features of a moot that make it more successful than the formal court system in handling domestic disputes are as follows:

- **Informal setting**

  The moot is generally held in the home of an elder or key community leader. The participants are all crowded together, sometimes spilling onto the porch: complainants, mediators, witnesses, and spectators are all side by side. There is no special clothing for or separation between participants as there would be in a formal courtroom, which helps people to be less inhibited and to speak freely.

- **Supportiveness of assembled group**

  The group is assembled by an elder and joined in a prayer with chanting. The participants are supported by all those present, and there is an acknowledgement that the problem is real and requires support. All participants are encouraged to speak freely without social sanction in the moot.

- **Full airing of grievances**

  All participants are encouraged to speak, including witnesses and other community members who may be only indirectly affected by the issue. All issues are deemed relevant, and all problems are aired. Anyone present may question the complainants, and the complainants may question anyone else. This exchange frequently results in a type of catharsis for the participants and a more acceptable solution since all parts of the problem are discussed.

- **Ritual apology and token restitution**

  At the end, there is a ritual apology by the one most in the wrong, but all parties share blame and some may even voluntarily accept blame in the matter. All make a small gift of restitution that is of some value but not enough to cause further resentment and grievances.

- **Consensus**

  All parties agree to the final resolution; it is not imposed by the outside. The moot is a process for all to come to agreement to restore social harmony and deal with anti-social behaviours in a positive manner, not a punitive one.

QUESTIONS

1. Compare a moot court and a traditional court.
2. Moots are not always successful in achieving resolution and social harmony. Under what circumstances do you think a moot would be unsuccessful?
3. How does the legal system of the Kpelle act as an agent of socialization?
4. Are there similar institutions or procedures in Canadian society? How would you investigate them?

Not only have many Aboriginal offenders and communities benefited from sentencing circles, but the idea has spread through Canadian society. In 1999, the Supreme Court ruled that judges had a duty to consider an Aboriginal offender's background in sentencing. The *Youth Criminal Justice Act* of 2003 has restorative practices, such as sentencing circles and community justice forums, at its heart. Restorative circles are an option now for many adults and youth alike, regardless of culture.

There are three fundamental principles of the sentencing circle (Lilles, 2002):

1. An offence is a breach of the relationship between the offender and the community.
2. The stability of the community is dependent on healing that breach.
3. The community is better positioned to heal the breach than the formal justice system.

FIGURE 7-10 What do you think is the goal of a sentencing circle?

The circle can include anywhere from 15 to 50 individuals including the judge, prosecutors, the offender, the victim, the families, elders, and any community member who feels affected by the offence (see Figure 7-10). It is generally run by a respected community leader, and the discussion can go for hours with a full airing of grievances and perspectives. There is usually a "talking piece," often an eagle's feather that symbolizes leadership and vision for many Aboriginal peoples. When one person is holding the talking piece, the rest are silent and attentive. Unlike the arrangement of a courtroom within a formal justice system, the circle emphasizes the equality among all the parties. This equality can lead to a more appropriate sentence that genuinely heals the offender and the community.

Read the following account of a sentencing circle:

> The victim was a middle-aged man whose parked car had been badly damaged when the offender, a 16-year-old, crashed into it while joyriding in another vehicle. The offender had also damaged a police vehicle. In the circle, the victim talked about the emotional shock of seeing what had happened to his car and his costs to repair it (he was uninsured). Then, an elder leader of the First Nations community where the circle sentencing session was being held (and an uncle of the offender) expressed his disappointment and anger with the boy. The elder observed that this incident, along with several prior offences by the boy, had brought shame to his family. The elder also noted that in the old days, the boy would have been required to pay the victim's family substantial compensation as a result of such behaviour. After the elder finished, a feather (the "talking piece") was passed to the next person in the circle, a young man who spoke about the contributions the offender had made to the community, the kindness he had shown toward elders, and his willingness to help others with home repairs.

Having heard all this, the judge asked the Crown Council and the public defender, who were also sitting in the circle, to make statements and then asked if anyone else in the circle wanted to speak. The Royal Canadian Mounted Police officer, whose vehicle had also been damaged, then took the feather and spoke on the offender's behalf. The officer proposed to the judge that in lieu of statutorily required jail time for the offence, the offender be allowed to meet with him on a regular basis for counselling and community service. After asking the victim and the prosecutor if either had any objections, the judge accepted this proposal. The judge also ordered restitution to the victim and asked the young adult who had spoken on the offender's behalf to serve as a mentor for the offender.

After a prayer in which the entire group held hands, the circle disbanded and everyone retreated to the kitchen area of the community centre for refreshments. (Bazemore and Umbreit, 2001)

While the sentencing circle comes from Aboriginal traditions, it is not a universally traditional process. Communities are encouraged to develop meaningful processes within their own communities that achieve the goal of healing the breach between offender and community. Community Justice Forums (CJF) are a form of sentencing circle. They give everyone a chance to hear and to be heard and give those involved a deeper understanding of the incident and why the harm occurred. In a CJF, those who committed the act own up to it, and the outcome is decided by those who were most affected by the offender's actions. The benefits of a CJF are that victims and offenders receive closure and healing and bonds between people can be restored and created faster and often at less of a cost than a traditional court system. The RCMP has the following guidelines for those who wish to qualify for a CJF:

- The offender must take responsibility for his or her actions and be willing to participate voluntarily.
- Victim involvement is essential to the process.
- Criminal cases are referred to the process by the police or Crown.
- The facilitator must feel that the case is suitable for a CJF. (RCMP, 2010)

Open for Debate
Critics of sentencing circles feel they are too soft on criminals, that equal treatment under the law is not being upheld because sentences can vary widely for the same crime, that the evidence is mixed about their actual effect on crime rates, and that circles are used inappropriately for more serious crimes.

REFLECT AND RESPOND

1. How is the sentencing circle similar to and different from the Kpelle moot?
2. What are the advantages and disadvantages of sentencing circles?
3. What would you need to find out to be able to assess the effectiveness of restorative justice practices in Canada today?
4. How are sentencing circles changing Canadian culture? Can you think of examples of restorative justice that you have encountered in your school, community, or family?
5. Would sentencing circles be helpful in your school? Why or why not?

Religion and Ritual

Religion is a human universal. People have been practising religion for at least 60 000 years. One definition of *religion* is cultural beliefs of the **supernatural** that people use to cope with the problems of existence (McCurdy and Spradley, 2008). The supernatural is all of the things that are beyond the known laws of nature. What is considered supernatural varies a lot from one society to another. For example, floods, earthquakes, and volcanoes are natural occurrences, but all have been seen as at least partly supernatural in most cultures.

Purposes of Religion

Anthropologists agree that religious beliefs serve at least three functions for human societies:

- Religious beliefs help people to understand ultimate questions such as: Why are we here? What is death? Why does evil happen to some and not others?
- Religion satisfies psychological needs common to all people in the face of uncertainty.
- Religion provides community and affirms a person's place in society, making its believers feel part of a community and giving them confidence.

Stanley and Ruth Freed: Taraka's Ghost

Ghost possession is a common occurrence in North Indian villages. It is a serious condition that can cause illness or death. In Hindu belief, ghosts stay for 13 days in the cemetery, and then they are judged by Yama in the land of the dead according to karma, the sum of their good and bad deeds. Some ghosts linger longer, and these are often the tortured spirits who died due to disease, accident, suicide, or murder.

This is the case of Sita, a 15-year-old bride, who was possessed by the ghost of her cousin, Taraka, who committed suicide by drowning. Stanley and Ruth Freed first met Sita in the 1950s, but ghost possessions have been observed since then among both men and women. The Freeds also documented several cases of young men being possessed by ghosts when under the stresses of school examinations and finding employment. Read the following description of Sita's possession. As you read Sita's story, think about how ghost possession as described here fulfils the three purposes of religion: ultimate understanding, psychological needs, and providing a place in community.

> Despite the heat, she [Sita] complained of feeling cold, so some women covered her with quilts. She moaned, breathed with difficulty, and then collapsed in a semiconscious state.

Before You Read

How do religion and/or ritual shape your culture and beliefs? Share with a partner examples of your experience.

supernatural: all of the things that are outside known laws of nature

More to Know…

For an example of how a belief in the supernatural helps with uncertainty, see "Baseball Magic" in Chapter 4.

Connecting Anthropology to Psychology

Psychologists look at stress as well. How would they assess this situation differently? What would Freud suggest about Sita?

The spectators accepted that a ghost had possessed her and tried a variety of standard curing techniques. These ranged from engaging the ghost in conversation, identifying it, and trying to satisfy its wishes or demands so that it would leave voluntarily, to attempting to drive it away with verbal abuse and, if necessary, physically painful or unpleasant measures (applied to the victim but aimed at the ghost). First the women propped Sita up in a sitting position and wafted smoke from some moldering cow dung under her nose. She jerked violently, so they had to restrain her. Then they shouted at the ghost: "Who are you? Are you going?" The ghost, speaking through Sita, promised to leave, and the women released the girl. (Freed and Freed, 1985, p. 84)

However, the ghost possessions kept occurring. Sita would fall, moaning, into a semiconscious state. The ghost would then announce itself and talk to Sita's in-laws. Eventually, the ghost identified itself as Taraka, Sita's cousin who had recently died. Taraka had become pregnant due to an affair with a village boy. Her parents married her quickly to her fiancé, but she was returned when the pregnancy was discovered. Her father was angry with her and told her to commit suicide. While Sita was with a group of friends, Taraka approached her and asked Sita to leave with her. When Sita refused, Taraka threw herself into a well and drowned. Sita blamed herself for Taraka's death. At about the same time, one of Sita's schoolmates was raped by a schoolteacher. The girl's father became enraged, blamed her, and raped and murdered his own daughter. Because of the untrustworthy schoolteacher, Sita was taken out of school, which ended her dream of becoming a teacher. Another of Sita's friends died of typhoid and malaria just after she had begun sexual relations with her husband. Sita, as the eldest daughter, had also lived through the death of nine infant siblings.

FIGURE 7-11 Women at Udaipur market. How does culture shape these women's perspective?

Taraka's ghost refused to leave Sita, and her in-laws were unable to drive out the ghost on their own. Sita's father-in-law called in different exorcists to cure her. The exorcists would come in, examine Sita, and call on various gods to assist them with the exorcism. However, Sita's possession went on for three years. For Sita, sex, marriage, childbirth, and lack of education became associated with death and tragedy. And it was just shortly after marriage that Sita's ghost possessions began. At best, for a North Indian girl of her caste, marriage would mean moving to a new village, more supervision by in-laws, and caring for an unknown husband and family. For Sita, the prospect of marriage had become something much more frightening, resulting in her ghost possession.

❓ How does ghost possession fulfil the three purposes of religion described on page 330?

Skills Focus

Assess the reliability of the Freed's account of Taraka's ghost, considering frame of reference, accuracy, and relevance. With this analysis, what else would you need to know to make a final assessment of this source? What can anthropologists learn about the social science inquiry model through assessing the reliability of other sources?

The Freeds revisited Sita in 1978. As a 35 year old, she was managing her family well. Her ghost possessions had continued until her first child was born, and thereafter she suffered occasional fits. She continued to use amulets and exorcisms to ward off her fits, and these seemed to relieve her anxiety. She was allowed to visit her father in the summers, free from her maternal and marital obligations. The ghost of Taraka had helped her to manage the stresses of her life and given her extra support from both her natal and marital families.

> **?** How should anthropologists deal with gender inequality in other cultures? Where is the line between researchers' cultural bias and human rights issues?

THE LANGUAGE OF SOCIAL SCIENCES

Anthropological Religious Concepts

Religion is an important part of culture, so understanding religions within cultures is critical for anthropologists. Since all the different cultures and religions of the world use different words to describe their religious beliefs, anthropologists have agreed on some terms to describe some of the more common belief systems and practices.

Anthropologists first examine the supernatural beliefs of a culture. Religious beliefs often relate to personified supernatural or impersonal supernatural. *Personified supernatural forces* are supernatural forces that are in human form, such as gods, deities, ghosts, or ancestors. *Impersonal supernatural forces* are supernatural forces that are in many things. *Mana* refers to the idea that there is a force that lives in people or objects, which is an impersonal supernatural force.

Communication with the supernatural can take the form of prayers, sacrifices, offerings, spirit possession, or divination. Sometimes facilitators are needed. *Shamans* generally can control the supernatural while *priests* mediate between the supernatural and human worlds (McCurdy and Spradley, 2008). The chart on this page outlines some terms that are common to anthropologists as they study cultures.

General Religious Terms in Anthropology

Term	Definition
fetish	a specific object with magical powers
magic	strategies that people use to control the supernatural
pilgrimage	a journey to a shrine or spiritual place capable of accommodating diverse meanings and practices
ritual	a prescribed behaviour in which there is no real connection between the action and the desired outcome
sorcery	the use of magic to cause harm to others
taboo	a restriction on behaviour that ensures a good outcome
witchcraft	projected evil to hurt others; often people using witchcraft can be unaware of the harm they have projected

QUESTIONS

1. Select three of the terms in the chart, and list an example of each in your culture.
2. Why is it important for anthropologists to have common words to describe different religious beliefs?

IN FOCUS: The Hijab

FIGURE 7-12 How is the hijab a symbol of both religion and culture?

The hijab is a headscarf traditionally worn by Muslim women. The Qur'an requires that women dress moderately and scholars have interpreted that to mean that clothing must cover a woman's body, with the exception of her face and hands. Muslim women have the choice whether to wear a hijab; the Islamic religion doesn't compel women to wear the garment in order to be Muslim. However, cultures where Muslim women live do have rules about what women must or must not wear.

Under the Taliban in Afghanistan, women were not only required to wear the hijab, but also the burqa when out in public. The burqa is a garment that covers a woman from head to toe except for a small area around the eyes, which is covered by netting so the woman can see. Those who didn't wear the burqa were subject to violent punishments. The restrictions on clothing under the Taliban were also accompanied by laws forbidding women to be educated, to work, or to go out in public on their own. To most outside of Afghanistan, wearing religious clothing like the hijab was connected to the oppression of women. Other Muslim countries, such as Iran, still require that women wear a hijab in public.

While some countries require women to wear a hijab or a burqa, others ban religious clothing in public, such as Tunisia, Turkey, and Morocco. France has received a great deal of media attention for its laws banning religious clothing. Some countries forbid the hijab based on reasons of secularism, claiming that religious clothing has no place within a secular society. Others argue that the hijab is a tool used to oppress women. Still other believe that religious clothing presents a safety or security threat. The Canadian Charter of Rights and Freedoms guarantees full religious freedom.

Separating religious, political, and social beliefs is also tricky. Wearing a hijab identifies a woman as a Muslim and is generally considered a religious practice. However, there are many Muslim women who wear a hijab not because of their religion, but because wearing one is a social practice. Many Muslim women wear the hijab as a political statement of their feminism or their religious devotion or both. For these reasons, Muslim women can also choose not to wear the hijab. Religion is often deeply embedded in the social and political beliefs of a society. The following quotes are from Canadian adolescent girls about their feelings on the hijab.

> *The Islamic veil, my hijab, means much to me. It represents my piety and modesty. It elevates my status, for people no longer judge me for my appearance, but rather for my character. Therefore I do not see how it is a symbol of oppression, especially because I myself, and myself alone, choose to wear it.*
>
> Jinan Zeitoun, age 17

> *To many who don't practise Islam, the veil may seem oppressive to women. On the contrary, many women see it as empowering. They feel like they are seen for whom they actually are. They are not objectified. They choose how they want to be seen. The main aspect of the hijab is modesty, which first comes with manners. It is true that I've not veiled, but I do consider myself to be modest in manner, which is the essential thing. Regardless, I do hope to take the veil one day. In Islam, women are encouraged to represent their religion in this way. When I do wear the hijab, it will be for myself. It will not be forced upon me by culture.*
>
> Hajar Tohme, age 18

QUESTIONS

1. To what extent is the hijab a reflection of culture?
2. Is wearing the hijab empowering or oppressive?

Cargo Beliefs in New Guinea

In New Guinea, cargo cults developed in the 1940s and the 1950s. People abandoned their gardens and built imitation airstrips and control towers so that cargo planes from their ancestors could arrive. Since they believed Europeans were allied with the dead ancestors, they attempted to imitate European behaviours to gain approval and "cargo," or wealth, from them.

The Bumbita Arapesh of East Sepik province in Papua New Guinea believe that ancestral spirits help to take care of the farmers. According to their beliefs, crops grow only with magical assistance from the ancestors. This belief is part of the reciprocal economic system, where the more you give away, the more important you are. If your crops are good, it is because your ancestor was very important and gave you magical help in producing those crops. When Europeans arrived in New Guinea with vast quantities of trade goods, the logical explanation for the amount of wealth they had was that they were allied with the ancestral spirits.

These **cargo beliefs** provide a ready explanation for Western wealth and imagined good fortune in terms that maintain the New Guineans' traditional beliefs. Cargo beliefs provide a way for the Bumbita to understand the social forces beyond their control. They help people deal with the personal grief of losing a parent. The Europeans are seen as ghosts of their own dead parents, with whom they can resolve their feelings of guilt or from whom they can expect valuable gifts. However, when the cargo fails to arrive, many people start to feel a sense of moral failure when it is clear to them that their own parents or other ancestors have failed to bestow cargo (Leavitt, 2000).

Cargo cults were outlawed in 1975, and New Guineans today know where goods come from and have had direct experience with jobs, cash cropping, and schooling. Papua New Guinea also has an independent government, and people buy many goods themselves, but cargo beliefs persist. While no active cults exist, the ideology continues today. Stephen Leavitt explains why that might be:

FIGURE 7-13 New Guineans dressed as ancestral spirits. How does the worship of ancestors help to affirm these people's place in society? How can it help them deal with economic uncertainty?

cargo beliefs: religious convictions in Papua New Guinea that ancestors will reward the living with goods as a token of their love and approval

> The powerful appeal of cargo ideology can be seen when set against the backdrop of its alternative. ... Much of one's life is determined by world events completely outside one's own control. Each Bumbita household's yearly income is determined largely on the basis of coffee prices on the world market.
>
> Contrast this scenario with the one offered by the insistence on Europeans as intimately associated with spirits of the dead. The ultimate source of global wealth is the local spiritual world, which has always presided over the success or failure of wealth in produce. Differences in access to the spirit world can be explained by requisite access to secret knowledge, something that has always been relegated to particular people at particular stages of life. It offers, in essence, the key ingredient to any religious orientation—the promise that one's world holds moral significance. (Leavitt, 2000)

Today, many historians and anthropologists argue that the term *cargo cult* describes too wide a variety of phenomena to be of any practical value. Further, some theorists believe that the very notion of a cargo cult implies an explicit transfer of Western prejudices upon supposedly "primitive" people.

> ❓ How do cargo beliefs fulfil the three purposes of religion described on page 330? What terms from the chart on page 332 do you think apply to this study? Explain how. What can we learn about our research practices from this study?

Witchcraft Among the Azande

E.E. Evans-Pritchard was one of the first British anthropologists to study other cultures as a complete system without assuming their inferiority to Western culture. To study the Azande people of Sudan, he undertook a journey of seven weeks by train, boat, and steamer and three weeks on foot. He recorded the Azande people's own words and wrote about the things they were interested in. He discovered that witchcraft, or *mangu*, was of principal interest to the Azande. At the time, use of witchcraft and magic were often used by Europeans to justify the inferiority and exploitation of African peoples. Pritchard set about to see how the ideology of witchcraft shaped people's behaviour and beliefs as a cohesive and rational system.

The Azande people of Sudan explain misfortune by witchcraft. When misfortune strikes, it is believed that someone used witchcraft to do it. If, for example, a grain warehouse falls on someone, killing him or her, people know that it is probably the termites that ate the wood that caused it to collapse. They understand that since people often sit under the grain warehouse in the shade to socialize and pass the time, and since termites frequently weaken the wood that holds the granary up, it is likely that one might be killed while sitting under it. However, why a particular person was sitting under it on the particular day that it collapsed would be explained by witchcraft. Where some people in our own society might explain such an event as bad luck or the will of God, in Azande society, it is clearly a case of witchcraft since misfortune resulting in death is most particularly the result of witchcraft.

The Azande believe that all people have some witchcraft in them. The key to dealing with witchcraft is to consult an oracle who can rub a board or poison a chicken to determine whether witchcraft is involved. If it is, then one must consult the witch doctor (a name given by the white colonials) who can prescribe various spells or procedures to protect against it, destroy it, or use medicine to send it back to the sender. The powers of witch doctors allow them to see the evil intentions of others. In Azande society, there are no actual witches. Witchcraft is considered a psychic act; anyone with negative or jealous thoughts can create it and send it out into the world. It is the witch doctor's job to control it and moderate its effects.

In Evans-Pritchard's revolutionary work, he discovered how African religious beliefs are anchored in social structures and help people to manage the darker side of human nature. Hatred, jealousy, and spite are expressed and managed by the ideas and practices of witchcraft.

> ❓ How does the belief in witchcraft fulfil the three purposes of religion described on page 330? What terms from the chart on page 332 do you think apply to Azande beliefs? Explain how. What are some examples you know people use today to ward off back luck (such as knocking on wood)?

FIGURE 7-14 Azande witch doctor from Sudan. Why did white colonials name the person who controlled and moderated witchcraft a "witch doctor?" What does this term imply about how the colonials perceived the person in that role?

The Toronto Jewish Film Festival

Can a film festival constitute religion and/or culture? One ethnologist, Mikel J. Koven, studied the Toronto Jewish Film Festival (TJFF) to find the answer. The TJFF is held every year in May for one week at several locations in Toronto, including the Bloor Street Cinema in the heart of the old Jewish area of Toronto. The location is nostalgic for the older filmgoers who can revisit the old neighbourhood and old friends. It is located in the heart of Toronto's Jewish culture: even if few Jewish people live there any more, the location is the physical manifestation of the community feeling.

▲ **FIGURE 7-15** Is the Bloor Street Cinema a sacred site of pilgrimage?

Koven concludes that the festival is a liminal experience for the community. It involves a separation from regular life for the one week of the festival. Especially for nonreligious Jews, it is a way to connect with their community. Attending the TJFF is neither completely religious, as going to synagogue is, nor completely cultural, as going to a movie is, so it is outside of regular experience.

Like other liminal experiences, the festival is transformative. The films are part of a community learning experience. Cultural myths are confirmed and discussed at the TJFF. What does the Holocaust or Israel mean to the modern Canadian Jew? In the coffee houses after the films, in the car on the way home, or any time during the week, it's a safe time to discuss, question, and debate what it means to be Jewish. People are constructing their culture with the film festival as a catalyst. In Canada, being Jewish includes many voices from immigrants. Executive director Helen Zukerman explains: "When we previewed the film *Bene Israel* (1996) about the East Indian Jews, it blew me away! Well then we find out that there's a congregation, in Toronto, of East Indian Jews. So we contacted them, and they came to the film. I mean here are Jews ... wearing saris and they're praying in Hebrew" (Koven, 1999).

> **More to Know...**
> You learned about liminal stages in Chapter 4.

For Koven, the festival is a location of religion and culture that is created each year by the participants. It, in turn, transforms them by reaffirming their Judaism and by asking them to question what it means to be Jewish in Canada in the twenty-first century.

? Does the Toronto Jewish Film Festival fulfil the three purposes of religion described on page 330? What terms from the chart on page 332 do you think apply to this topic? Explain how.

REFLECT AND RESPOND

1. Compare and contrast any two of the studies on pages 330–336. What terms or concepts are important to each one?
2. Are there practices in your life that meet some of the purposes of religion? Brainstorm some cultural or social events, locations, or philosophies that take the place of religion in your community.
3. How would you investigate the location or event from question 2? What sources would be important to consult? What theories and terms would be most important to investigate?

Canadian Cultures, Past and Present

Section 7.2

Canada is a multicultural country. Canadians value **multiculturalism** and consider it a key part of Canadian identity. In an Angus Reid poll, 66 percent of Canadians responded that multiculturalism was a source of national pride (Angus Reid, 2010). But if Canada is made up of many cultures, does that mean that there is no central Canadian culture? When people think about multiculturalism, they think about cultural products, such as movies, books, and food, or cultural events, such as parades and festivals. From an anthropology perspective, culture is the everyday, lived experiences of Canadians. To determine what Canadian culture is, anthropologists examine local communities and the everyday experiences of the people who live in them. An anthropologist studying Canadian culture might ask: What does multiculturalism mean to people in their everyday lives? How do the different cultures live and work together? How is our culture as a nation changing? An anthropologist might start with data about the Canadian population, like the data in the chart below from Statistics Canada, before beginning his or her research. This chart compares the data from 2001 to what statisticians estimate for 2017.

multiculturalism: an ideology that states that all cultures are of equal value and should be promoted equally within the same nation. In Canada, multiculturalism is a policy that protects ethnic, racial, linguistic, and religious diversity.

	2001	2017
Canadians who are members of a visible minority	13%	20%
Immigrants as a proportion of the Canadian population	18%	22.2%
Number of black people in Canada	671 000	948 000 to 1.17 million
Number of people whose first language is not English	5.3 million	6.8 million to 9 million

(Source: Statistics Canada, 2006)

Race: Myths and Reality

As you have learned in previous chapters, our concept of race is based on physical traits caused by biological variation and is culturally constructed by the society in which we live. Race is generally understood as physical differences that are assigned to a person by an outside group, although, as we saw in Chapter 1, according to the American Anthropological Association (AAA), race has no biological validity. Ethnicity is your understanding of who you are based on your ancestry or a feeling of belonging to a group. Your race is not usually something you can change about yourself, especially since it is determined by an outside group, but you have a choice in how you define your ethnicity. The same person could identify his or her ethnicity as Canadian, African, African-Canadian, Jamaican, or Jamaican-Canadian depending on the context.

Before You Read

Explain the difference between *race* and *ethnicity* to a partner, and determine why they are not the same.

Cultural Anthropology Perspective

Cultural ideas about race and ethnicity can and do change, and they are frequently based on political or economic ideologies that help to keep some groups in power and exclude others. Many racial ideas start out as folk beliefs or myths that help to explain human variation, but they can quickly turn into justifications for controlling or even eliminating a specific population, as in the cases of slavery in the United States and the Nazis' attempt to eliminate the Jewish people and other races they deemed undesirable. Different cultures have different ways of constructing race; how North American cultures determine race is not the same as how other cultures define race.

> What are some of the problems with racial classifications?

Race in Brazil and the United States

Sometimes to understand an issue at home, it's useful to look at constructions of race and ethnicity elsewhere. The United States and Brazil are both countries that were originally populated by Aboriginal peoples and colonized by European immigrants who brought people forcibly from Africa to become slaves. Today, both Brazil and the United States have had a degree of intermarriage between populations. Both countries are struggling with issues of racial intolerance and inequality. Both systems of race labelling serve to perpetuate the systems of inequality and make people think that race has something to do with personal abilities. Despite their similar histories, the two countries construct race in different ways.

One system of racial classification in the United States is called **hypodescent**. In this system, children of mixed-race couples are identified as members of the ethnic group that is less privileged in society. Hypodescent is based on power imbalances within society. In the United States, this classification system has generally applied to the children of black and white mixed-race couples. This means that one black ancestor is enough for someone to be classified as black, even if the rest of the family tree is white. For example, if one of your grandparents is black and the other three are white, you are still classified as black. When someone is said to be *passing*, it means that a person has some African heritage but looks more European and is treated as white by others in society. The term implies that the individual is not white; he or she just looks white but is in fact black. This term shows how much this American system of classification relies on knowledge of ancestry and has little to do with actual appearance.

hypodescent:
a system of racial classification where children of mixed-race couples are identified as members of the ethnic group that is less privileged in society

FIGURE 7-16 How is race a cultural construction?

> Why did this classification system develop? Are there economic or social explanations that played a role?

Brazil has a system of *tipos*, or types. These types are not based on ancestry but on physical appearance. In Brazil, there are many more gradations of black and white than in the United States, which include hair colour and type and facial features such as nose, lips, and skin colour. In Brazil's classification system, it is possible that members of the same family could all belong to different racial categories. Look at the following chart to understand the differences in the cultural construction of race in Brazil and the United States.

Brazilian Tipos (male/female)	Physical Characteristics	Brazil	United States
louro/loura	straight blond hair, blue/green eyes, light skin, narrow nose, thin lips	white	white
branco/branca	light skin, any colour hair that is not tight curly, not a broad nose or thick lips, any colour eyes	white	white or Hispanic
moreno/morena	brown or black hair that is wavy or curly but not tight curly, tan skin, not a narrow nose or thin lips	white	black
mulato/mulata	tight curly hair, slightly darker skin than a morena	black	black
preto/preta	dark brown skin, broad nose, thick lips	black	black
sararo/sarara	tight curly blond or red hair, light skin, blue/green eyes, broad nose, thick lips	neither white nor black	white
cabo verde	straight black hair, dark skin, brown eyes, narrow nose, thin lips	neither white nor black	black

(Source: Fish, 1995)

FIGURE 7-17 How would you racially classify these students at a Brazilian college? Your answer would depend on your cultural heritage.

? What aspects of U.S. or Brazilian race classifications surprised you? Why? How do you think racial classifications are made in Canada?

Race in Canada

Canada's construction of race is similar to that in the United States, although not quite as strictly defined. Black people are not the only people who experience racism in Canada. Racism is not always between white people and minorities; it can exist between people belonging to different minority groups as well. However, the theory of hypodescent applies especially to blacks in Canada. Many new Canadians of African descent find their sense of self rewritten by Canadian cultural ideas of race. Awad Ibrahim, a professor at the University of Ottawa, explains, "I was not considered 'black' in Africa, though I had other adjectives that patched together my identity, such as 'tall,' 'Sudanese,' 'academic,' 'basketball player,' and so on. In other words, except in South Africa, race is not the defining social identity in Africa (2003).

According to Ibrahim, when youth come to Canada from Africa, they "become black" through culture, such as rap and hip-hop music, television, and movies. They would not necessarily have worn the same clothes or listened to the same music in Africa, but to integrate into Canadian culture means learning "black culture," which is often narrowly defined as rap, hip hop, and the associated culture (Ibrahim, 2003).

People who consider themselves Jamaican or Somalian, Catholic or Muslim, or any number of other descriptors find themselves all called "black" when they arrive in Canada. They are also usually associated with negative stereotypes of black people in North America, such as being school drop outs, belonging to low-income families, and participating in criminal activities (Ali, 2008). These stereotypes are untrue and unfair, but they are a common perception. In contrast, if a Canadian who is black goes to Haiti, he or she would be called a "noir blanc" or a "white black." *White* refers in this case to the ethnicity as Canadian, not the physical appearance (Fish, 1995).

History of Black People in Canada

The first black person to arrive in Canada was Mathieu Da Costa, a free man who was a translator for Samuel de Champlain in the early 1600s. As people settled in New France, French colonists brought black people with them as slaves. The largest group of black immigrants came from the United States after the American Revolution (1775–1783) because they were promised freedom, rights, and land in Nova Scotia after they fought for the British during the war. Following the War of 1812, Canada became the destination of choice for tens of thousands of escaped slaves on the Underground Railroad. Although slavery was still permitted in the British colonies, Canada was seen as a safe haven for black people fleeing slavery. Slavery was abolished in Canada in 1834. Although slavery was not as widespread in Canada as it was in the United States (the Canadian climate and agriculture made owning slaves less desirable), black people were still subject to racism, discrimination, and violence here.

Many of the former soldiers of the American Revolution had helped build the town of Shelburne in Nova Scotia. But in July 1784, unemployed white soldiers turned violent against the black community in Shelburne, destroying property and homes and beating men and women. This was Canada's first race riot. In 1991, there was a race riot at Cole Harbour High School involving 50 students of both races, mobilizing the black community to demand reforms, which came in 1995 when the Nova Scotia government established a fund for anti-racism education. While conditions have improved at the school (*Ottawa Citizen*, 2007), there was a brawl involving 14 students and the police in May 2009 (CBC, 2009). The idea that Canada was a safe haven for black people has not always been historically accurate. From discrimination in the past, such as Viola Desmond's arrest for sitting in the white section of a movie theatre in 1946 and the immigration policy that favoured white immigrants, to discrimination in the present, such as the harassment in 2010 of a mixed-race couple from Nova Scotia by the Klu Klux Klan, it is clear that discrimination still exists.

FIGURE 7-18 Painting of a black family in Bedford Basin, Nova Scotia circa 1835. How does this image compare to the experience of black people in Canada at that time?

> How do you define yourself in terms of race and ethnicity? How would your definition of yourself be different if you moved to another country? Since black people have been in Canada since the 1600s, why is it common practice to ask people who are non-white where they are from?

Physical Anthropology Perspective

Physical anthropologists who study human variation look at physical differences in human populations and how those differences help people to survive. As you learned in Chapter 1, some features, such as skin colour, are adaptive; that is, they help the population to survive in a given environment. Others, such as eye colour or shape or hair curl, don't really serve any purpose but are a result of geographic isolation.

Body Build and Climate

Physical anthropologists have found that average body types are linked to climate (see Figure 7-19). In areas with a warmer climate, more members of a population are tall, with long limbs and low body weight. In colder areas, people tend to be shorter and heavier. A tall person with long arms and legs can keep cool more effectively than other body types in a hot climate while a short, stocky build is good for conserving energy in a cold climate.

FIGURE 7-19 The jumping Samburu dancers of Kenya and the Inuit of the Canadian Arctic both exemplify the relationship between body build and climate.

Fingerprints

If you were to classify the populations of the world according to fingerprints, you would see quite a different picture from traditional skin colour classifications. Fingerprints are made up of arches, loops, and whorls. Most Europeans and Africans have the same type of fingerprints: their fingerprints have many loops (Diamond, 1994). Another group includes Jewish people and some Indonesians, while Australian Aborigines, whose fingerprints are made up predominately of whorls, would be in a third group by themselves. Much like blood type, fingerprints serve no particular adaptive function and are a result of geographic isolation (Diamond, 1994).

FIGURE 7-20 Fingerprint with loops (left) and one with whorls (right). Which one is more likely to be European? Australian Aboriginal?

Sickle Cell Anemia

Sickle cell anemia is a rare genetic disease affecting less than 1 percent of the world's population. In people who have the condition, some of the blood cells are sickle- or crescent-shaped rather than round. This shape makes it difficult for the cells to process oxygen, making it difficult for people with these cells to run and leaving them weaker and with a shortened lifespan.

One of the reasons why sickle cell anemia is so rare in most human populations is because, like many genetic diseases, it's not very adaptive for survival under most environmental conditions. However, it is more common in areas where there is a lot of malaria. In these areas, nearly 20 percent of the population have sickle cell anemia. The sickle shape of the blood cell makes it more difficult for the malaria parasite to infect the cell, making it less likely that the infected person will die from malaria. In regions with a higher chance of contracting malaria, people with sickle cell anemia are more likely to survive, reach puberty, and pass the anemia on to their offspring.

Lactose Intolerance

All mammals produce lactase in infancy. It is an enzyme that helps digest milk sugars or lactose, but mammals usually stop being able to produce lactase as soon as they stop drinking their mother's milk. Most human adult populations are lactose-intolerant, as is normal for mammals. In some human populations, such as northern Europeans, most people produce lactase in adulthood. These populations tend to come from cooler climates farther from the equator, where there is less sunlight. Like vitamin D, lactose helps your body absorb calcium. Other cultures, typically those closer to the equator, developed cultural ways of making lactose digestible, such as adding bacteria to yogurt, cheese, sour cream, or other low-lactose dairy products.

Theoretical Perspectives of Ethnicity

Social scientists have developed many theories of how people form their ethnic identity, particularly in the case of bicultural ethnicity. Are there similarities between how Indo-Canadians, Chinese Canadians, and Finnish Canadians develop their identities? What effect does racism have on identity formation? Of course, everyone has a sense of ethnicity, but there is a fiction in Canada that if you are white and English-speaking that you are not "ethnic." Everyone in Canada has an ethnicity, whether it be Québecois, Ojibway, or Ukrainian Canadian, and many people have multiple identities. As mixed marriages continue to increase—up to 40 percent of all marriages in Toronto and Vancouver involve partners from different ethnic backgrounds (Dib et al., 2008)—multiple ethnic identities are far more likely to increase than decrease. Stage-model theories and acculturation theories have been proposed as a result of research with a variety of ethnic communities in Canada and elsewhere.

Stage-Model Theories

Many different stage-model theories have been proposed to explain how individuals develop a sense of ethnic identity. J.S Phinney (1993) describes the following three stages:

Unexamined Ethnic Identity

An individual does not see a difference between himself or herself and the dominant society. The individual believes that she or he is part of the dominant group. This stage is illustrated by the Clark Doll experiment of 1939, in which black children were given a black-skinned doll and a white-skinned doll and asked to choose which they liked best and which looked like them. Almost all the children picked the white doll as the best one and were reluctant to choose the black doll when asked to pick the doll that looked like them.

> **Connecting Anthropology to Psychology**
>
> Many stage-model theories of ethnic identity arose from Erikson's stage-model theories of development. Anthropologists use these frameworks, or models, to analyze the cultures they are studying.

> **More to Know...**
>
> You learned about the Clark Doll experiment in Chapter 6.

Unexamined ethnic identity
↓
ethnic identity search
↓
ethnic identity achievement

FIGURE 7-21
J.S Phinney's stage model theory

Ethnic Identity Search

This stage usually begins with an event in a person's life that causes that person to question whether he or she fits into the dominant society. The catalyst could be an act of racism that a person experiences or an individual's growing sense of exploration and desire for knowledge. This catalyst could lead an individual to become more involved in his or her ethnic community, take a course, or reject the dominant society and its values.

Ethnic Identity Achievement

In the final stage, an individual resolves all previous conflicts and forms an identity that includes elements of both (or all) of his or her cultures.

Criticisms of stage-model theories argue that they are too rigid, are based on particular groups, and may not apply to all situations. Critics point out that many people may never go through all the stages, or they may stay in one stage their whole lives.

Acculturation Theory

In contrast to the stage-model theories, the **acculturation** theory does not try to demonstrate that all minorities go through the stages. It tries to understand how people view themselves in terms of their ethnic identity at the time of the study. John Berry's (1989) acculturation model describes people as belonging to one of four categories:

- assimilation (associating with the dominant culture)
- integration (accommodating both cultures)
- separation (rejecting the dominant culture)
- marginalization (relating to the culture of origin) (Sodhi, 2008)

While the two theories seem similar, there is a fundamental difference. The stage-model theory assumes that people must progress through all of the stages with ethnic identity achievement as the desired goal, but acculturation seeks only to identify which category an individual is in at the time of the study. In acculturation theory, an individual does not move through the categories, and there is no "progression."

FIGURE 7-22 Which stage of ethnic identity formation do you think this family is at? Justify your answer.

acculturation: the meeting of two or more cultural groups and the resulting cultural changes to each group

More to Know...

You will learn more about John Berry's work from a psychological perspective in Chapter 8.

> **REFLECT AND RESPOND**
>
> 1. How do physical and cultural anthropologists differ in their views on human variation?
> 2. Why is human variation important to the survival of the human species? What do you think would happen if all humans were identical?
> 3. What is the essential difference between Phinney's stage-model theory and Berry's acculturation theory?
> 4. Which theory do you think best describes individuals who have two cultural identities?

Canadian Multiculturalism

Before You Read
Is multiculturalism successful in Canada? How would you prove it?

A policy introducing multiculturalism was announced by the Canadian government in 1971 in order to recognize the reality of Canada's diversity but also to reverse earlier attempts to assimilate immigrants. It was introduced in response partly to the troubled English–French relations of the time, as well as to different ethnic spokespersons who argued that assimilation was both unfair and a failure. Immigrants had survived the Depression and fought for Canada and should still be Canadian even if they were neither English nor French. Some Canadians were opposed to multiculturalism because they thought it would divide Canadians rather than unite them. Others worried that the British heritage of English Canada would be reduced, and some people in Quebec feared multiculturalism would spoil Quebec's efforts toward separatism.

In October 2010, German Chancellor Angela Merkel stated that Germany's attempt to create a multicultural society had "utterly failed" (Siebold, 2010). Her statement sent shock waves around the world and stirred up more controversy in Canada. Does Canada's multiculturalism policy promote diversity and tolerance and give youth an enhanced sense of self-esteem, or does it impose an ethnic subculture on groups to keep them out of positions of power and privilege? This question is a topic of much debate among social scientists and politicians in Canada.

Urban Youth and Multiculturalism in Toronto

In 2008, Mehrunnissa Ahmad Ali conducted a study with youth in two Toronto high schools. The schools she studied had no white students, and all the subjects were children of at least one immigrant parent. The average income of the neighbourhood where the schools were located was below the low-income cutoff point. The low-income cutoff is a number that defines where poverty ends. This number is based on the percentage of income that individuals and families spend on the basic needs or necessities. Students lived in high-rise apartments around the school and shopped at nearby low-budget stores. The study followed 39 students for 3 years, from Grade 10 to Grade 12.

Ali found that the students firmly believed in the ideology of multiculturalism because that was their experience of the world. Multiculturalism defined their school and neighbourhood, provided a vision of Canada, offered opportunities for intercultural engagement, and fit with their ideology of equity and justice. One student, Didi, explains:

> For example, in school we all get along with one another. We hang out with various types of people, and it is very multicultural. We accept many cultures, religions, food, and many other traits from cultures. I have eaten foods from many cultures. In school, I am not racist. I hang out with many other cultures. (Ali, 2008)

Another student, Mina, feels that this will likely continue into the labour market:

> If I look at my school, no one looks to what skin colour you are or what religion you are. They don't care about that. Like, when I met my friends, that's not the question I asked them or they asked me. ... I think if you are going for a job, then I don't think people look at skin colour here 'cause everyone's from a different culture, a different country. No one's Canadian here, original Canadian, so really, very few people. ... (Ali, 2008)

However, as students moved in circles outside their neighbourhood, they often encountered discrimination and racism from the wider Canadian society. They started to notice that their parents and friends' parents had only low-level jobs; they encountered suspicion from security guards and police discrimination as well. They started to become aware of stereotyping of their neighbourhood. One student, Blue Flag Baron, explains:

> I've talked to people that are, like, my friends, living in [a suburb in the Greater Toronto Area], and they just give me this awkward look, when they're like, yeah, where do you live again? I'm [from the neighbourhood], and they're just, like, their jaw drops completely, and they're, like, "You come from that area?" And then they totally get a different perspective of you, they think that you're this gangster person, and you're going to shoot everybody. (Ali, 2008)

Open for Debate

In 2011, a Toronto school board considered opening an alternative school for Portuguese students in an effort to reduce drop-out rates. Portuguese students have the highest drop-out rates of any single ethnic group. For some, separate schools are a way to tailor education to specific needs. For others, separate schools stigmatize students. Will a separate school address a persistent student achievement problem? Or will it lead to segregation? Should students have the opportunity to attend an alternative school?

Ali concludes that the equality among all of the cultural groups in the school and neighbourhood has led the students to believe that there is no racial hierarchy in Canadian society. The reality around them, reinforced by official endorsement of multiculturalism, has led them to believe that their own situation applies to Canada as a whole. They are self-assured and aspire to higher education and higher status jobs than their parents have. Ali speculates that these students could be deeply disappointed with some Canadians' racist attitudes when they start to compete with the dominant white majority for education and jobs.

❓ Do you agree with Ali's conclusion? Why or why not? Apply the stage-model theory or the acculturation theory to these students. What stage(s) or category (categories) do you think best describes them?

FIGURE 7-23 Do all of these youth have the same opportunities in Canadian society?

English Canada: Diverse, Imperial, or Invisible?

There have not been many studies of the ethnicity of English-Canadians because English-Canadians are considered the dominant group. They have historically been the ones in power and historically been the majority in Canada. However, whom we call English-Canadians are often not actually English at all. The vast majority of settlers before the twentieth century were Irish, Scottish, Welsh, or American, not people from England proper. With the exception of American Loyalists, who were affiliated with Britain, many of these immigrants were fleeing English imperial oppression in their own homelands, and many would have been insulted to have been called English or even British (*Encyclopedia of Canada's Peoples*, 2008).

Today, a person calling himself or herself an English-Canadian is just as likely to have more non-English–speaking ancestors than English ones. The idea that English-Canadian culture is a stable majority culture is proven false by how easily other cultures' products and ideas, such as pasta, reggae, and yoga, are adopted in Canada. Many immigrants don't assimilate into an English-Canadian culture; they prefer to identify as Canadian, not English-Canadian.

The darkest period of Canadian racism was during the height of British imperialism in the late nineteenth and early twentieth centuries. Prior to this period, Canadian policies had been relatively inclusive and anti-racist for the time, abolishing slavery, accommodating French language and religious rights, and establishing treaties with the First Nations as relatively sovereign and powerful groups (Saul, 2008). It was during the period of imperial superiority that the Canadian government introduced the Chinese head tax, interned many cultural groups including Ukrainians, Germans, and Japanese in camps, and established residential schools, among other racist policies. Most of these policies have been reversed, and apologies and compensation have been offered after years of negotiations.

With the establishment of multiculturalism as policy in 1971 and the Charter of Rights and Freedoms in 1982, Canadians are legally guaranteed freedom from discrimination. But many of the old power structures and attitudes remain, perpetuating the myth that "white" people are a stable majority, invisible, and without ethnicity. English-Canadians are changing as well and are increasingly influenced by American culture.

↑ **FIGURE 7-24** Which of these images do you think best captures the culture of English Canada, and why?

> Do English-Canadians have an ethnicity? If so, how would you describe it? Can the stage-model theory or acculturation theory be applied to English-Canadians? Why or why not?

French-Canadian Culture

French-Canadians have the distinction of being the oldest European settlers in North America, and, until recently, French-Canadian culture has been relatively homogenous. Since the 1960s, immigration from French-speaking countries such as Haiti, Vietnam, Morocco, and Tunisia has forced the Quebec government to look at how it defines itself and what it means to be French-Canadian. This change is happening not only in Quebec, but also in the many francophone communities across Canada.

Intercultural or Multicultural?

The Quebec government, in response to public concerns over accommodation of religious minorities, set up the Bouchard-Taylor Commission, which released its report in 2008: *Building the Future: A Time for Reconciliation*, advocating that the government adopt a specific policy of **interculturalism**, not multiculturalism. Since Canada became a British colony, the French population has struggled to retain its cultural identity. Particularly in Quebec, the importance of preserving and protecting French culture, such as language and religion, has become a political issue. The Bouchard-Taylor Commission was created in response to insecurity stirred up by distortions in media reports on individual cases of accommodation. Public hearings were held across the province over many months and exposed many anxieties felt by Quebecers of French-Canadian descent about the apparent threat of accommodation to their identity. The chart below compares the Quebec policy of interculturalism to excerpts from the *Canadian Multiculturalism Act*, 1988.

interculturalism: a proposed policy in Quebec emphasizing cultural and economic integration of immigrants and French-language learning

Interculturalism	Multiculturalism
Often mentioned in academic papers, interculturalism as an integration policy has never been fully, officially defined by the Québec government although its key components were formulated long ago. This shortcoming should be overcome, all the more so as the Canadian multiculturalism model does not appear to be well suited to conditions in Québec, for four reasons: (a) anxiety over language is not an important factor in English Canada; (b) minority insecurity is not found there; (c) there is no longer a majority ethnic group in Canada (citizens of British origin account for 34 percent of the population, while citizens of French-Canadian origin make up a strong majority of the population in Québec, i.e., roughly 77 percent); (d) it follows that in English Canada, there is less concern for the preservation of a founding cultural tradition than for national cohesion. To summarize, we could say that Québec interculturalism institutes French as the common language of intercultural relations; cultivates a pluralistic orientation that is highly sensitive to the protection of rights; preserves the creative tension between diversity and the continuity of the French-speaking core and the social link; places special emphasis on integration; and advocates interaction. (Bouchard-Taylor Report, 2008)	It is hereby declared to be the policy of the Government of Canada to (a) recognize and promote the understanding that multiculturalism reflects the cultural and racial diversity of Canadian society and acknowledges the freedom of all members of Canadian society to preserve, enhance and share their cultural heritage; (c) promote the full and equitable participation of individuals and communities of all origins in the continuing evolution and shaping of all aspects of Canadian society and assist them in the elimination of any barrier to that participation; (d) recognize the existence of communities whose members share a common origin and their historic contribution to Canadian society, and enhance their development; (e) ensure that all individuals receive equal treatment and equal protection under the law, while respecting and valuing their diversity; (g) promote the understanding and creativity that arise from the interaction between individuals and communities of different origins; (i) preserve and enhance the use of languages other than English and French, while strengthening the status and use of the official languages of Canada; and (j) advance multiculturalism throughout Canada in harmony with the national commitment to the official languages of Canada. (*Canadian Multiculturalism Act*, 1988)

❓ What are the major differences between the two policies? Do you agree with Bouchard and Taylor that an interculturalism policy is needed? Explain why or why not using specific examples to support your position.

Religious Accommodation in Quebec: Myths and Reality

The Bouchard-Taylor Report set out to dispel the myths inflated by the media and public perception surrounding some of the specific incidents of accommodation that prompted the commission in the first place. In a sampling of 21 of these stories, only 6 incidents were reported accurately. Bouchard and Taylor detailed the other 15 in the report. The Mont-Saint-Grégoire sugarhouse was one of the incidents discussed in the report.

The Mont-Saint-Grégoire Sugarhouse

FIGURE 7-25 How did bias influence public perception of the sugarhouse incident?

A sugarhouse is a small house where sap is collected and turned into maple syrup. Often sugarhouses are tourist destinations, with tours, outdoor activities, and a restaurant on site. The following is the widespread perception of what happened at the Mont-Saint-Grégoire sugarhouse in March 2007.

A group of Muslim customers arrived one morning at the sugarhouse and demanded that the menu be altered to conform to their religious standards. All of the other customers were therefore obliged to consume pea soup without ham and pork-free baked beans. In the afternoon, the same Muslims entered the crowded dance hall and interrupted the festivities to recite their prayers. The customers in the dance hall were expelled from the sugarhouse.

The story described in the previous paragraph was the one that was presented in the media. However, this is what actually happened. One week before the outing, a representative of Astrolabe, a Muslim association, met with the sugarhouse's owners to discuss certain changes to the menu, which would apply solely to the members of the group. The modified menu excluded pork but included halal sausage and salami provided and paid for by Astrolabe. This arrangement having been made, the association reserved one of the four dining rooms in the sugarhouse for its exclusive use. On the appointed day, after the meal, about 40 members of the group moved several tables and chairs in the room reserved for them for a short prayer. The management of the sugarhouse wanted to free up the room as quickly as possible (business was brisk and nearly 300 customers were waiting to be seated) and proposed to those individuals who wished to pray that they use instead the dance hall, which was almost empty at that time. The dance hall can accommodate roughly 650 people, and 30 customers were then in the room, some of whom were waiting to be seated in the dining room. Several young girls were dancing to popular music. The management of the sugarhouse interrupted the music so that the Muslim customers could say their prayers, which took less than 10 minutes. The music then resumed. According to the management, no one was expelled from or asked to leave the dance hall (Bouchard-Taylor, 2008).

> ❓ What role did the media have in perpetuating the misunderstanding, and what impact would this have on the Muslim community?

Francophone Communities Outside Quebec

Of course, if Quebec does adopt an official policy of interculturalism, it would not apply to the 980 300 francophones (or 14.5 percent of all francophones) living in Canada outside of Quebec (Dallaire and Denis, 2005). Several studies have been conducted on the integration of francophone immigrants within these communities. While the percentage of immigrants within these populations has increased from 6.2 percent in 1991 to 10 percent in 2006, it is uncertain how well these immigrants are becoming integrated into the existing francophone communities. Immigrants tend to settle in the core of Canada's cities, while the existing French-speaking populations tend to be in the suburban areas (Corbeil and Houle, 2010). Other studies have looked at how black francophones are in a double minority position in Ontario: they struggle to be accepted in francophone communities and often resort to black English (such as rap) as a resistance tool (Ibrahim, 2003; Madibbo, 2006).

As demonstrated in an ethnology of francophone youth in Alberta, Ontario, and New Brunswick, the development of a strong francophone identity is strongly related to the degree of immersion and geographic density in youths' home communities. Youth from New Brunswick, where there are strong and densely populated Acadian areas, were found to have the strongest sense of francophone identity. Alberta has more widely distributed francophone communities, and its youth had the weakest sense of a French identity. Ontario, mixed in geographic distribution, is in the middle in terms of youths' sense of francophone identity, even though Ontario currently is home to the largest number of francophones outside Quebec (Dallaire and Denis, 2005).

> What are some of the challenges for francophones outside Quebec? Does the information presented in this section provide evidence for or against multiculturalism? Explain.

First Nations Communities in Canada: Kitchenuhmaykoosib Inninuwug

In her film *Third World Canada*, filmmaker Andrée Cazabon examines the conditions of First Nations children in Ontario. Cazabon spent one and a half years in Kitchenuhmaykoosib Inninuwug (KI), a First Nations community in Northern Ontario. In one of the most difficult scenes in the documentary, a five-year-old boy named Tyler graphically describes his father's suicide. Tyler and his brother Kyler watched their father hang himself in their home. Cazabon almost cut the scene, "but Chief Donny (Morris) told me I had taken a lot out already," she said in an interview. "He said: 'If it makes people uncomfortable to watch this film, they should try living it'" (*Toronto Star*, 2010).

In Cazabon's film, we learn that the people of KI rally together to help the eight orphaned children. Tikanagan, the family services agency of the 30 most northern communities in Ontario, works with the community to find appropriate placements within the community and with family when possible. As the film unfolds, it becomes clear that caring for eight more children is going to be tough for a community that has already suffered a lot of suicides and can't even accommodate all the children who have parents within the community. Some of the orphaned children need professional mental health services and must leave the community to access them, further separating them from their family and familiar environment. Even in these circumstances, children can be on a waiting list to see a counsellor for up to two years.

VOICES

We extend to all Canadians the invitation to support us as we bring our community up to the standards enjoyed in the rest of the country. We ask for the recognition and the fulfillment of commitments made to our forefathers so we can build a brighter future for our children and our culture.

Kitchenuhmaykoosib Inninuwug Assessment Report 2009

Suicide is the most common cause of death in KI, and children such as Kyler and Tyler grow up thinking that it is the normal way to die and that it is the way that adults deal with their problems. This problem is made worse by the fact that suicide is a taboo subject for the community elders. They will not talk about it, and few in the community have the experience or expertise to deal with the magnitude of the problem. Not only is suicide emotionally devastating, but the funeral costs can be economically devastating. Indian and Northern Affairs Canada pays $1400 for a funeral, but the actual cost can be over $20 000.

There is a shortage of housing in KI, as in most First Nations communities across Canada. Aboriginal communities are currently experiencing a baby boom, and the largest proportion of the Aboriginal population is under 25 years old. The band can afford to build only three to five houses each year, but there are over 200 people on a waiting list for housing in KI alone. Housing materials must be imported from the south, and residents often can't afford to build on their own. Residents are not allowed to log on the Crown land adjacent to the reserve, but some community members have gone ahead anyway and built their own houses, risking arrest.

The land in KI is rich in minerals, but the residents are not benefiting from any potential resource development. The Ontario government in 2006 gave a mining licence to a platinum mining company without consulting the KI residents, as it is required to do under a Supreme Court ruling. The chief, four council members, and one resident stopped the mining company from entering KI traditional lands but were arrested and sentenced to six months in jail. They were released after two months following a decision by the Court of Appeal for Ontario (Cazabon, 2010).

One result of the trial and incarceration of the band council was that a drum group started again in the community. Some people were opposed to this group because they felt that it conflicted with their Christian beliefs. The drum group, Awakening Spirits, is small, but those involved feel that getting back to traditional practices will help the community to heal and provide hope for the youth.

FIGURE 7-26 People from Kitchenuhmaykoosib Inninuwug protesting in support of their land rights. Why is land such an important issue for people in KI?

REFLECT AND RESPOND

1. Do you think, based on the evidence presented, that Canada's multiculturalism policy is successful? What information would you need to determine whether or not multiculturalism is successful in Canada?

2. Choose two sources in this section, and explain how the bias of each source influences his or her statements.

3. Which theory of ethnic identity formation do you think is most valid? Explain with reference to the case studies presented.

4. How might the tragedies in Kitchenuhmaykoosib Inninuwug relate to the legacy of residential schools?

Constructing Identity in a Multicultural Society

As you learned, culture is the attitudes, beliefs, and behaviours of a society. These are all learned from infancy, taught to us by our parents, and reinforced by our experience in our society through school, the workplace, and other social institutions. In a multicultural society, sometimes a family's attitudes, beliefs, and behaviours are not the same as those in the wider society. First-generation parents often have different beliefs and behaviours than their second-generation children are exposed to in schools and other institutions. When parental values are not reinforced in the general culture, conflict can arise between parents and children.

Much research has been done in anthropology to try to understand the individual and cultural process and effects of growing up with two (or more) identities. A lot of the research focuses on case studies, some of which will be examined here. By looking at individuals' specific case studies, you can get some idea of the challenges and benefits of growing up in two cultures.

Indo-Canadian Youth Create Bicultural Identities

A recent study of second-generation Indo-Canadian youth by Pavna Sodhi found that young people needed a zone of proximal development (ZPD) or safe third space between cultures in which to explore and create a **bicultural identity**, ethnic identity achievement (Phinney, 1993), or integration (Berry 1990, 1997). For Sodhi, the third space is "a safe, mutually respectful, genuine, and comfortable environment, which encourages an individual to be proud of his or her ethnic heritage and, in turn, integrate it into individual identity" (2008).

Figure 7-28 illustrates how bicultural identity development is a lifelong process, occurring at all stages of life (represented by the ovals) and developed or hindered by events and situations in the family, dominant culture, ethnic community, and peer groups (represented by the rectangles) (Sodhi, 2008).

The Southern Ontario Indo-Canadian youth in Sodhi's study found the following events and situations to be most prominent in developing their bicultural identities:

- Parents and the extended community often pressured youth to become doctors, dentists, or lawyers because it "attests to their success as immigrants" (Sodhi, 2008). Parents were often uneducated about different but equally lucrative and prestigious careers, and youth felt embarrassed or ashamed when they did not meet their parents' educational and career goals.
- Parents' expectations around dating and arranged marriage were another site of negotiation for youth, particularly the parents' and community's expectations of an elaborate wedding to show off parental status.
- Youth who had the support of the ethnic community, and particularly a peer group, were often better able to negotiate a more stable bicultural identity.

> **Before You Read**
> How might growing up in two cultures affect your sense of identity?

↑ **FIGURE 7-27** Comedian Russell Peters. His performances revolve around ethnic identity and his experience growing up as an Indo-Canadian.

bicultural identity: a sense of oneself as being strongly rooted in two cultures

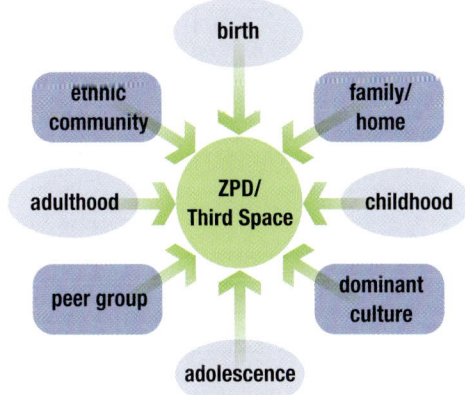

↑ **FIGURE 7-28** Bicultural identity formation

Chapter 7 • Anthropology and Us

- Youth with mental health issues were less likely than the general population to seek help outside of the family because of stigma and cultural values. If it became known in the community that a child had mental health issues, it was a source of dishonour to families.

In all of these situations, youth have the opportunity to create a third space or ZPD in which to develop their bicultural identity. Intergenerational communication is vital to this process. Parents value many aspects of Canadian culture, but they may not transfer this appreciation to the young person if their communication is too often negative. Generally, both children and parents wish to continue their culture and adopt the best of both cultures.

> **?** How is Sodhi's concept of the ZPD or third space different from the stage-model and acculturation theories? How can her theory apply to other cultural groups in Canada?

Perceptions of Physical Discipline

Is the endorsement of physical discipline among recent immigrants to Canada an imported cultural value or a result of the stresses of immigration? It has been well documented that immigration creates many additional challenges for parents, including adapting to a new culture, low socio-economic status, and dealing with the conflicting values of two cultures. A recent study (Hassan et al., 2008) assessed and compared Afro-Caribbean and Filipino parents' and children's approval of physical discipline in Montreal. It's important to note that children are more likely to approve of physical discipline if they have experienced it in some form.

The study found that immigrant parents and children, especially among Afro-Caribbean families, were more likely to approve of physical discipline, while second-generation (born in Canada) children were more likely to disapprove of physical discipline. This study and many others suggest that parental use of physical discipline is a cultural norm, since children brought up in Canada who had longer exposure to Canadian culture were more likely to disapprove.

When we look at cultures around the world, ideas of appropriate discipline of children vary widely from no physical discipline and minimal supervision among the Blackfoot of Hawaii to Kuwaiti parents' approval of beatings and Palau parents' approval of caning but not hitting a child with an open hand (Hassan et al., 2008). In Canadian society, our definitions of what is considered reasonable force to correct a child have changed considerably over the last 100 years.

The findings of this study have important implications. While native-born Canadians might perceive the actions of immigrant parents who physically discipline their children as abusive or overly harsh, if physical punishment of children is a cultural norm, then education would be more appropriate than punitive or legal measures. It is important to consider each case individually and not jump to conclusions about any particular group or incident. Considering the facts and the context of a particular case is always more useful than generalizations.

More to Know...
See Chapter 4 for an analysis of Indo-Canadian youths' negotiations of dating and arranged marriage.

Skills Focus
There is a belief that the expression *rule of thumb* originated in a British law that stated that a man could beat his wife with a stick no bigger than his thumb, demonstrating a historical definition of *reasonable force*. However, there is no evidence that such a law ever actually existed. The myth of the law probably began with the rise of feminism in the nineteenth century, and most references to it are found in the 1970s (Quinion, 1999). What might be the biased origin of this myth? What evidence would you need to consider?

IN FOCUS: Corporal Punishment Laws in Canada

In Canada, Section 43 of the Criminal Code regarding corporal punishment states that a parent, teacher, or person in place of a parent may use "reasonable force" as a form of discipline. Over the last 50 years, the definition of *reasonable force* has changed considerably in Canadian society. Most notably with the Supreme Court decision of 2004, which held that "Section 43 ensures that the criminal law applies to any use of force that harms a child, but does *not* apply where the use of force is part of a genuine effort to educate the child, poses no reasonable risk of harm that is more than transitory and trifling, and is reasonable under the circumstances" (Department of Justice Canada, 2004). The Supreme Court also stated that corporal punishment is not appropriate for very young children or teenagers. In an attempt to address the issue of corporal punishment, the United Nations Committee on the Rights of the Child (the committee responsible for monitoring compliance with the Convention on the Rights of the Child) had urged Canada to ban the use of it, which led to the Supreme Court decision.

There is no provincial legislation on the use of corporal punishment in schools, but most school boards have banned its use, and it is not generally used in Canadian schools. The Toronto District School Board banned corporal punishment in 1971, and most boards in Ontario banned it by the end of the 1980s. The Edmonton public school board banned the use of corporal punishment in 2004 (Reilly, 2008).

Anthropological evidence suggests that physical punishment trains people to accept higher levels of societal aggression. In a cross-cultural study of 186 different societies, Jennifer Lansford and Kenneth Dodge found that corporal punishment was more common in societies that support violence and engage in frequent warfare (2008).

Different research looked at the corporal punishment in the British upper class through extensive forms of beating at well-known English private boarding schools in the 1950s and other forms of ritual. This ritual corporal punishment as

↑ **FIGURE 7-29** Until recently, corporal punishment was permissible in Canadian schools. Why did this change?

a form of authority was eventually outlawed in Britain but was experienced by many children in former British colonies that adopted these practices (Benthall, 1991). The adoption of corporal punishment is a form of cultural transmission that has had long-lasting impact and negative consequences for the children of these countries.

Spanking children is rare among hunter-gatherers (Konner, 2005). Yet many American states, as well as Australia, Jamaica, and Malaysia, continue to permit corporal punishment in schools and homes. In 2001, an initiative was begun, called the Global Initiative to End All Corporal Punishment of Children, that aims to speed the end of corporal punishment of children across the world. In Thailand, where corporal punishment is banned, a teacher at a Catholic boarding school was secretly videotaped hitting dozens of students on the buttocks with a cane wrapped with electrical wire because the students did not clean their living quarters in 2010. The teacher was fired.

QUESTIONS

1. Do you agree with the Supreme Court's decision regarding Section 43 of the Criminal Code? Why or why not? What experiences and values helped shaped your opinion?

2. How does the information in this feature support the idea that corporal punishment is a cultural practice?

3. Now look at this issue from a psychological point of view. According to theories of reinforcement, what is the most effective method to reinforce behaviour? Apply this knowledge to the issue of corporal punishment.

Greek and Jewish Youth in Halifax

While much research has been done on ethnic communities in large urban centres, not as much has been written about smaller cities or beyond the second generation of immigrants. For second-generation Sri Lankan Tamils in Toronto, it is possible to be Tamil while still participating in the mainstream culture because there is a large and active Tamil community with many cultural products and activities available on a daily basis (Amarasingam, 2008). In smaller, less diverse communities, there may be fewer opportunities to connect to people from the same culture, making it more difficult to maintain a bicultural identity.

A study by Michele Byers and Evangelia Tastsoglou examined this issue by examining the Greek and Jewish communities in Halifax. Both communities are relatively small. Each community is made up of around 2000 people, within a mostly white Anglo-Saxon society. Both communities are tightly knit and have their religion and culture intertwined. Both the Greek and Jewish communities are also "invisible" or "optional" minorities within the dominant culture. One young man commented on his tightly knit community:

> More or less because we are a small community we are holding on to it. So in New York, like I said before, you run into a Greek, they're just like, hey, you're Greek, okay, see you later. But if I ran into a Greek I've never seen before here in Halifax, I'd be like, hey, what's your number, let's get together, you know, come down to the hall, the church, come dance with us, you know. (Byers and Tastsoglou, 2008)

FIGURE 7-30 Teenagers participating in a Greek festival. To what extent does participating in these events maintain a sense of identity?

The study found that both communities placed a heavy emphasis on marrying within the culture and/or religion, but since the communities were small, many young people were faced with the decision whether or not to move away from Halifax to find a suitable mate. One youth commented on the pressure to find a mate within the community:

> I do notice, though, that when it comes to dating a Jewish girl, my parents are a lot more accepting, sure, stay out late, here, take the car, here's some extra cash, take the Jewish girl out, whereas if it's a normal girl, it's, like, have a good time, get out of here, don't do anything stupid, and come home alive. (Byers and Tastsoglou, 2008)

Most of the participants felt a responsibility to maintain the culture but also felt that there weren't as many options as in the larger centres, particularly if they wanted a more secular ethnic identity. All of the Greek culture in Halifax revolved around the church, and much of the Jewish community's activities took place in the synagogues. It was difficult to have a nonreligious sense of ethnic identity.

The authors concluded that these Jewish and Greek youth were able to preserve their ethnic identity in the smaller Canadian city partly because their community was smaller and more tightly knit. However, they were generally uncertain about being able to continue their culture, especially if they stayed in Halifax and/or did not marry another member of the same culture.

> **?** Are these youth able to achieve a bicultural identity? Why or why not? How does this study help to answer the question of whether multiculturalism is working?

Second-Generation Finnish Canadians: A Disappearing Ethnicity?

What happens to a person's sense of ethnicity when there are no obvious racial or religious differences from the dominant culture? Katrina Jurva and Peruvemba Jaya investigated this question in their study of Finnish Canadian young adults, aged 20 to 30, and living in Ottawa, using semi-structured interviews and came to the following conclusions.

Symbolic Ethnicity

Symbolic ethnicity is ethnic identity based on a feeling of being connected to a real or imagined past rather than on daily experience. Symbolic ethnicity does not involve very much risk or change in behaviour. Most of the participants of this study expressed their ethnicity in a symbolic way, by preparing specific foods for special occasions, seeing a Finnish film, or decorating their house with Finnish styles. One participant in the study described her love of Finnish textiles, noting it was a way to acknowledge and show pride in her Finnish heritage. "I just find it's a way to identify myself too. People always ask [what it is], 'Oh, it's the Marimekko poppies,' [I say]. It's that pattern, it's really distinct. So I walk around [with something that has that pattern], instead of walking around with a flag" (Jurva and Jaya, 2008).

symbolic ethnicity: ethnic identity based on an emotional connection to a real or imagined past rather than daily experience

FIGURE 7-31 The Vancouver Olympics (2010) opening ceremony had every possible Canadian icon they could include (singers, dancers, actors, moose, beavers, Mounties, and hockey). Is this really what Canadian identity means?

Canadian Identity

Symbolic ethnicity is also selective. The participants in the study self-selected as Finnish to participate in the study, but most identified as more Canadian than Finnish. They felt that being Finnish was an intrinsic part of being Canadian because they saw Canadian culture as predominantly multicultural. It was hard for participants to separate what was Canadian and what was Finnish, but they did not see this lack of distinction as a problem since it was easy to be both Finnish and Canadian. Canada's diversity was perceived positively, especially in relation to the more homogenous Finnish culture. A participant concluded that "Canada is very, very diverse and it's better to consider that diversity sort of a strength because everybody sort of brings their weaknesses and strengths to the table, and the more diversity that you have, the sort of more balance of view you have in the overall" (Jurva and Jaya, 2008).

The respondents' ability to feel Canadian was probably also related to their physical appearance. It was easier for them to integrate into a dominantly white society because they also were white. Their ethnicity for them was a personal issue; they were not defined by others because of their racial features. They did not feel any contradiction between being Finnish and being Canadian.

Institutional Completeness and Transnationalism

Jurva and Jaya investigated the issue of institutional completeness. **Institutional completeness** is the ability of individuals to live a full life within their cultural community. Can they shop at cultural stores, converse in their language, make friends, find a mate, find employment, and get assistance within the cultural community? Studies have found that ethnic identity is stronger when there is more institutional completeness.

Ottawa has a low level of institutional completeness. With only two Finnish cultural institutions (a language school for children and an adult leisure group), it is impossible to live in a Finnish enclave. The young adults in the study felt that they did not belong in the adult group since it was composed mostly of older adults of their parents' generation. One girl commented, "I feel like I'm not, in a sense, worthy of going to any of those meetings because I'm not Finnish enough. I feel like I'm not a good representation of a Finn" (Jurva and Jaya, 2008).

Most of the young adults had, however, travelled to Finland as children or adults, and much of their sense of being Finnish came from these visits. Travelling to connect with one's roots is part of the newer trend of **transnationalism**. Prior to globalization, the formation of ethnic enclaves through institutional completeness was the best way to preserve a culture in Canadian society, but today the Internet and increased travel make it possible for people to participate in their culture through global ties. The researchers found that the young Finns were more connected to current Finnish culture than the older generation, who relied more on their peer group in Canada to provide a connection to their ethnicity.

When it is possible to communicate with relatives via video and other digital technologies in remote locations, buy any desired cultural item online, or stay current about "home" events through online news, videos, and other forums, the site of culture becomes online as well as at community centre. Transnational identities, which do not rely on cultural enclaves to create a sense of ethnicity, are changing the face of Canadian multiculturalism.

institutional completeness: the ability of a person to live a full life within his or her own cultural enclave

transnationalism: the maintenance of an ethnic identity by staying connected with relatives in other countries and staying informed of political and other developments in the country of origin, often through digital technology

> ❓ Are these youth able to achieve a bicultural identity? Why or why not? How does this study help to answer the question of whether multiculturalism is working?

Migration Revisited: Canadians in the Interconnected Age

Online communication has changed our methods of communicating both locally and globally, but is it an adequate substitute for local cultural communities? The research is not yet clear, but we have some indications of where we might be headed.

Caribbean migrants have well-established routes of migration through the United States and Canada and often see their travels as temporary aspects to gain education or employment or to earn money to send back home. With relatives established in many urban centres across North America, these people view migration as a way to get ahead, though not necessarily as a permanent move.

Other groups with long-established migration patterns are diplomats, academics, and international government workers. These groups often feel a contradiction between their elite status and their personal sense of loss and dislocation. Ayla, a permanent resident of Canada, born in Turkey but living in Europe because she is pursuing an academic career, prefers to call herself a *global citizen* or *nomad* rather than a *migrant*. She finds a sense of identity through the use of her first language, even though she lived in Turkey for only a few years as a child. "Turkish [is my mother tongue]. Because when I want to swear, express my love, my anger, in a nutshell all my feelings, I still switch to Turkish. I still dream in Turkish." Ayla's home page is a Turkish newspaper, she cooks Turkish food at home, and she is more informed of Turkish politics than Canadian, even though she is nominally a resident of Canada (Fay, 2005).

FIGURE 7-32 Does Toronto's Caribana parade demonstrate multiculturalism or transnationlism?

Yet another type of migrant is the First World transient service worker in the booming south. Canadian, American, and European workers have been moving to Grand Cayman as it has become a banking centre and as they find themselves unemployed or unfulfilled in their home countries. Grand Cayman is seen as a temporary residence, and, indeed, the island actively discourages permanent residency for foreign workers.

Both those who wish to stay and those who are prepared to leave their home country are faced with the uncertainty of employment. Globalization has freed up labour to move across borders to fill specific needs but at a cost to local communities (Vered, 2001).

REFLECT AND RESPOND

1. Is multiculturalism working in Canada? Use evidence from this section to support your point of view.
2. How has global migration and connectedness changed the lives of Canadians?
3. Generate a research question on the topic of digital communication and ethnicity that you could investigate. What method would you use? What sources would you need to consult?

CHAPTER 7 REVIEW

Knowledge and Understanding/Thinking

1. Explain how social customs in Canada are changing because of digital technologies. How are customs different in different social contexts?

2. Explain how restorative justice works in the Kpelle moot in Liberia and in the sentencing circles of Canada.

3. What are the purposes of religion? Explain how one of the examples given in this chapter fulfils the purposes of religion.

4. What are the dangers of racial ideas? Why are humans physically different from one another?

5. What is the difference between race and ethnicity? Give an example to illustrate your answer.

6. Describe the effects that assimilation and multiculturalism have on culture.

7. How is culture an agent of socialization? Give examples.

Thinking/Communicating

8. Are sentencing circles and other restorative practices working? Research recent cases in Canada where sentencing circles have been used, and formulate a thesis.

9. What are the advantages and disadvantages of using sentencing circles and community justice forums? When do you think they would be most useful? Explain.

10. Recent studies have shown that Canadians are less and less religious. Explain how other institutions are or are not fulfilling the purposes of religion.

11. Does race exist? Create a T-chart to list the evidence for both sides.

12. Which theory of ethnic identity formation do you think is most valid? Explain with reference to the case studies presented in this chapter.

13. Choose two statements made by individuals in this chapter, and explain how each speaker's bias influences her or his statements.

Communication/Application

14. Research a First Nations community in your area. What problems do the people face, and what solutions are being generated? How are traditional cultural practices being used to solve problems? Prepare a report based on your research.

15. In Ali's study of teens in Toronto, she asked the teens to create collages and diagrams to express their culture.
    a) What would your cultural collage look like? Draw a diagram or create a collage of your culture/ethnicity, and compare it to those of your classmates. What trends do you see? Are there similarities and differences?
    b) How do the collages and diagrams address ideas of multiculturalism and ethnicity? How is this exercise different from what was done in the study?

16. Is digital technology bringing Canadians closer together or driving us further apart? Devise an observation or interview study to try to answer this question. Write a report of your findings.

17. Choose someone in your community to interview about his or her ethnicity or race. Before your interview, write a research question based on one or more of the theories and studies presented in this chapter.

18. Based on the evidence provided in this section and your own research findings, do you agree with the following statement: Canadian multiculturalism is working. Provide evidence for your argument in a debate, essay, or paragraph response.

19. What connections can be made between assimilation, socialization, residential schools, and the challenges First Nations peoples face today? Organize your response in an organizer or as a visual.

20. Select one of the case studies in this chapter, and explain in a journal entry or using a graphic organizer how the study can help anthropologists understand human behaviour and culture in the present.

CHAPTER 8

Psychology and Us

Humans are naturally social beings. We often seek to be with other people, whether they are our families and friends or others we meet at school, in clubs, or at work. What happens in our brains or to our personalities as we interact with others? In this chapter, you will learn psychological explanations for why we conform to group pressures, how we feel prejudice, and how the groups to which we belong contribute to our sense of identity. You will also learn how environment and the various agents of socialization interact with our personalities, as well as how to prepare oral presentations to share your research.

Chapter Expectations

By the end of this chapter, you will:
- use a psychological perspective to analyze patterns of socialization
- identify and describe the role of socialization in the psychological development of the individual
- explain the ways in which context and the influence of other individuals can affect people's emotional and behavioural responses
- communicate the results of research and inquiry effectively using a format appropriate to the purpose and audience
- demonstrate an understanding of the general research process by reflecting on and evaluating your own research process and results

Key Terms

abstract
amygdala
behavioural shift
bystander effect
chameleon effect
cross-cultural psychology
cultural/ethnic identity
deindividuation
ego identity
ingroup
longitudinal study
national identity
outgroup
psychological acculturation
serotonin
social identity
stigma

Landmark Case Studies

Jane Elliot: Brown Eyes/Blue Eyes

FIGURE 8-1 We interact with people regularly. How does this shape our behaviour

Key Theorists

Gordon Allport
Solomon Asch
John Bargh
John Berry
Tanya Chartrand
Jane Elliot

Erik Erikson
David Hutchison
Irving Janis
A. Jenness
Lawrence Kohlberg

Daniel Levitin
Linda S. Pagani
Lee Ross
Mark Snyder
Philip Zimbardo

Spotlight on Psychology — *Conformity*

> **Before You Read**
> Do you know someone who followed along with others in a group even though they knew the group was wrong? In what situations are teens likely to encounter this type of situation?

People's attitudes, beliefs, and actions are shaped by a number of factors. One such factor is social influence. As demonstrated by Stanley Milgram's Obedience experiment in Chapter 5, people who never thought they would seriously hurt someone chose to shock a person in another room to what they believed to be near death when told to do so by a figure in authority. Similarly, people have a tendency to conform—to adjust their behaviour to match that of a group standard—when it seems as if they may be the odd one out.

Psychologist Solomon Asch wanted to understand the nature of conformity on healthy, intelligent people and conducted a series of experiments in the 1950s on this topic.

In the first of Asch's experiments, groups of six people sat around a table and answered seemingly easy questions. However, only one of them was the actual subject of the experiment. The other five had been carefully trained in how to respond without raising the real subject's suspicions. The group had to make judgments about which line from a set of three matched the standard line shown (see Figure 8-2). The subject of the experiment was always the last to give a response.

At first, everyone in the group gave the correct answer to ensure that the test subject did not become suspicious of the study's true intentions and to increase group unity. Then members of the group all started to give the same wrong answer. For example, if the answer was obviously line 1, the others would each say line 2 was the correct answer. Did the subject go against the group and give the answer he or she knew to be correct?

Asch discovered that people are often influenced by the responses of others. Only 29 percent of the subjects would not give the same answer as the others in the group. The remaining 71 percent gave the same answer even when they knew the group's answer was incorrect. A control group, in which subjects looked at the lines on their own, yielded incorrect answers less than 1 percent of the time, indicating that the wrong answers given by subjects were due to conforming to others' answers. In later versions of the experiment, Asch found that the number of people giving the wrong answer changed the results—if there was another person who agreed with the subject, it was easier for him or her to resist the pressure to conform.

So why did intelligent people who knew the answer to a simple question give a response they knew to be incorrect? How does this apply to other situations? Most people want to have the approval of those around them. While we all have unique personalities, with our own specific likes and dislikes, it is not unusual to say you like a particular band or movie star if he or she is popular among your friends.

QUESTIONS

1. Why did Asch use clearly defined lines as the stimuli in his experiments?
2. Review Milgram's Obedience experiment on page 198 and Zimbardo's Stanford Prison experiment on page 238. How are these experiments related to the Asch experiment in terms of their message about the nature of social influence?

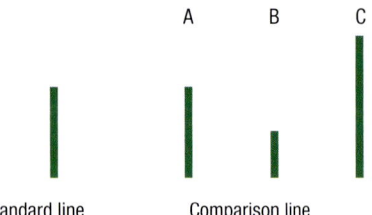

FIGURE 8-2 Sets of lines like these were used in Asch's experiment. The correct answer was meant to be obvious so Asch could study the reaction of the subject when others gave an incorrect answer.

Research and Inquiry Skills

Presenting Research in Psychology

Once their research is completed, psychologists then share their results with their colleagues. This may include writing a report, publishing an article in an academic journal, creating a Web site or Web page, and/or creating a poster presentation. It is important to note that, whatever the format, there are certain elements that remain constant. The research plan elements that you learned about in Chapter 5 must be included: an *introduction* that contains the purpose and hypothesis, a *method* that shows how the research was conducted, the *results* of the research, and a *discussion* that analyzes the results.

Poster Presentations

A poster presentation is a specific method used to convey results to colleagues whereby the research is presented on a poster and described verbally by the study's authors. Often these presentations are delivered as part of a larger conference, where participants have the opportunity to visit the various displays and learn more about the research.

The poster should show all of the important elements of the study as noted above. This can be done in a variety of ways, but we will discuss one popular approach used by psychologists.

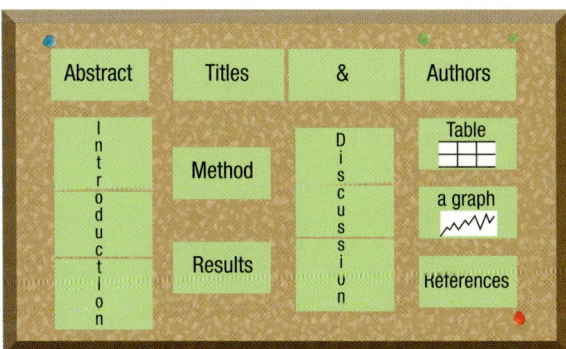

↑ **FIGURE 8-3** This is an example of one way to create an effective poster presentation. What do you notice about the layout of the poster and the way the different sections are organized?

The sections of the poster flow from the top down, rather than across, and are broken down into four invisible columns (see Figure 8-3). The title and list of authors are centred at the top of the poster. The **abstract** appears at the top left next to the title so that others can find out information about the study quickly. Below the abstract is an introduction to the area under study, which includes an explanation of why the research was undertaken. The method and results fit into the second column, with the discussion next to them. In the final column, any tables or graphs appear, with the references at the very bottom.

> **abstract:** a brief summary of the study's methods and findings

Use the following checklist when you want to create an effective poster presentation:

- ☐ Have an attention-grabbing title: use a font that is large and easy to read from a distance.
- ☐ Plan your layout carefully, ensuring that all important elements have been included.
- ☐ Use powerful visuals, such as charts, diagrams, and images (e.g., art, symbols), to reinforce your written words.
- ☐ Edit all written elements of your poster to ensure there are no errors.
- ☐ When you present your poster, try to involve your audience by giving them opportunities to react to, think about, and discuss what you are saying.

Activities

1. Create a poster presentation for the topic you and your partner researched in Chapter 5. Discuss how you would use visuals to display your results. Consider which of the following would best convey your information:
   a) a pie chart   c) a line graph
   b) a bar graph   d) a photo

2. If you do not have access to a computer, what alternative approaches can you use to create an effective poster?

3. Reflect on your poster presentation. Answer the following questions honestly:
   a) Does your poster contain all of the necessary sections and information?
   b) Is your poster clear and visually appealing?
   c) Do your visuals support what you say in your presentation?

Section 8.1 Influence of Others on Self

As you learned in Chapter 3, socialization is the process of learning how to act and interact in groups and situations. From a psychological point of view, socialization is an important aspect of development. Read on to learn more about how social factors affect our behaviours and attitudes.

Psychology and Socialization

Socialization begins as soon as a newborn baby bonds with his or her parents and continues throughout life. According to *social learning theory*, children learn social behaviours by observing and imitating the behaviours of those around them. The behaviours are reinforced by rewards or punishment. As the primary agents of socialization, parents need to teach their child appropriate social skills at each stage of childhood.

Socialization and Emotional Development

For many children, effective socialization is linked to fewer problems throughout their school years and beyond. They develop friendships more easily and have a stronger sense of identity. They also have a greater understanding of their emotions and how to deal with them. Generally, psychologists believe that there are specific social skills that children learn as they age (see chart below).

> **Before You Read**
>
> In what ways have your siblings influenced your behaviour? If you do not have any siblings, predict the influence having a sibling might have had on you.

SOCIAL DEVELOPMENT NEEDS FROM BIRTH TO 12 YEARS	
Age	**Developmental Milestones**
Birth to 6 months	Develop trust • make eye contact and begin to smile at primary caregiver; cuddle up to familiar people
6 to 18 months	Explore self, feelings, and surroundings • crawl away from parents; play with others; communicate needs by pointing
18 to 36 months	Begin to develop perspective • have vocabulary of about 200 words; play with other children; understand that others have different opinions than them
3 to 5 years	Develop a sense of purpose • continue to have curiosity and imagination; play competitive games; develop sense of right and wrong
6 to 12 years	Develop self-confidence • expand social environment; pick up social cues from others; work co-operatively; learn to cope with mistakes

The Importance of Play in Childhood Development

Parents often assume that it is important for their children to spend a lot of time with others their own age in order to socialize them. While some social time with peers, or "play dates," to develop preschool social skills is healthy, early socialization should primarily come from parents or guardians. These adults have a wealth of social and emotional resources that children's peers do not, such as the ability to describe emotions verbally and interpret others' emotions, predict long-term consequences for actions, and use problem-solving skills. Modelling and explaining behaviour is a positive way that parents help their children to develop the necessary social skills.

The Social Skills of Only Children

A child who does not have siblings may develop social skills in a different manner than those children who do have siblings, at least early in life. Indeed, parents often observe that their only child seems to have fewer social skills when he or she enters kindergarten. To investigate whether only children have a social disadvantage later in life, researchers at Ohio State University asked 13 446 teenagers who had participated in an eight-year **longitudinal study** of adolescent health to name five male and five female friends. They discovered that only children were just as likely to be named as a friend as those who had siblings. The researchers concluded that while only children are more likely to have difficulties with social skills in kindergarten, over time they learn the appropriate skills and catch up to the others by adolescence.

Social Isolation and Emotional Development

Some children feel socially isolated, or set apart from others to the point that they have little social interaction. Social isolation can be due to poor social skill development, shyness, or prolonged illness. Isolated children can experience some or all of the following problems:

- academic difficulties: inattentiveness, failure
- behavioural difficulties: delinquency, aggression, substance abuse
- emotional difficulties: peer rejection, isolation, stress
- psychological difficulties: memory loss, anxiety, depression

School Shootings

In recent years, cases of extreme aggression based on social isolation have shocked Canadians into seeking answers. The 1999 shootings at Colorado's Columbine High School and a week later at W.R. Myers High School in Taber, Alberta, made people stop and take notice of the very real effects of isolation. In both cases, the shooters had been teased and bullied relentlessly by their peers. Sadly, school shootings are not new, as demonstrated by the tragic shooting of female students at Quebec's École Polytechnique in 1989. Fortunately, very few isolated individuals respond in this way. What can be done to ensure that incidents like these never occur again?

More to Know...
Look to Chapter 4 for more about socialization in different cultures and Chapter 3 to read about agents of socialization.

longitudinal study: research that follows the same people over a long period of time

Open for Debate
Does playing video games isolate gamers or help them connect with others? Often gamers spend long periods in their rooms or basements, playing games alone. New technology allows players to connect from all over the world as they play against one another. So, what effect do video games have on social skills? What role might age, gender, and ethnicity play?

amygdala:
the part of the brain that regulates emotion

Changes in the Brain

Social isolation can lead to aggression and anxiety, which are caused by the activation of the neurons that lead to the **amygdala**, the part of the brain that regulates emotion. Researchers at the University of Illinois at Chicago College of Medicine discovered that the effects of social isolation may be due to a resulting change to a hormone in the brain. Mice were used to study the effects of isolation since humans and animals react similarly to the stress of isolation. Researchers found that one of the two enzymes needed to produce the hormone that reduces the effects of stress had decreased by 50 percent in the isolated mice. This suggests that aggressive behaviour and anxiety may occur because the amygdala is missing the hormone needed for its regulation. The researchers believe that by identifying the roots of anxiety aggression, drug treatments can be developed for extreme cases of isolation.

Improving Social Skills

Effective programs exist for children identified as having difficulties with social skills. These programs can include social skills training and exposure to different social situations, including those with children their own age. A social skills training program involves weekly sessions in which children learn specific skills such as how to start and maintain conversations, join groups, co-operate with others, solve problems, and greet others. With practice over time, children can improve their social skills.

> ❓ What is the difference between a person who is shy or introverted and someone who is socially isolated? Look back to Chapter 5 before you discuss your answer with a partner.

The Effect of Media on Socialization

Use of electronic media, such as television and cell phones, and digital media, such as video games and social media, are a part of life for many Canadian children and adolescents. In 2009, Americans spent $25.3 billion on video games and equipment; in Canada this number was $1.7 billion. When children are watching television and playing video games, they are not socializing in traditional ways. Research has shown a correlation between watching television and children's attention span: children who watch more than 2 hours of television per day are 1.5 times more likely to develop attention-span difficulties. But does TV viewing affect social skill development? And what other factors might affect this correlation?

Young Children and Television

Research has shown that the best way for children to learn language is by interacting with people. Several studies have shown a correlation between watching television and language development, such that the more time young children spent watching television, the longer it took them to learn speech. Specifically, their speech development suffered if two-way communication was replaced by watching television. Since verbal communication is a key social skill, these findings are significant.

IN THE FIELD

Sport Psychologist Shaunna Taylor

An Olympic athlete faces a lot of pressure when competing at such a prominent international event. He or she has expectations for greatness from thousands of people in the home country, not to mention the pressure he or she has placed on himself or herself. How do these athletes handle all the pressure to compete for their country? How do elite level athletes keep their doubts at bay?

Many athletes turn to sport psychologists for help. Canadian Shaunna Taylor is one such psychologist. She is a member of the Canadian Sport Psychology Association and runs a private practice in Ottawa where she works with local and national athletes. Sports psychologists work with athletes both during their training and during their competition.

Sport psychology is an applied psychology that helps athletes improve their performance in a multitude of ways. These psychologists work with athletes to regulate their emotions and stress; improve their confidence, concentration, and decision-making abilities; and learn techniques that enhance performance. Sport psychologists are also there when athletes face difficult times such as recovering from an injury, and facilitating the process to leave an elite sport.

To become a sport psychologist, Shaunna earned an MA in Sport Performance Counselling and Mental Preparation. She is also a certified counsellor and is a mental preparation consultant. She is currently a doctoral candidate in the health sciences.

FIGURE 8-4 Shaunna Taylor is a Canadian sport psychologist. Why might an athlete seek her services?

QUESTIONS

1. What might attract a psychologist to sport psychology? What personality characteristics would help a sport psychologist do his or her job?

2. In what sport(s) do you think a sports psychologist would be most beneficial? Explain your answer.

Other studies of young children who watch television have shed light on other problems. The Quebec Longitudinal Study of Child Development Main Exposure, run by psychologist Dr. Linda S. Pagani, studied 1314 children from the age of 29 months to 10 years. Parents noted how much television their toddlers watched, and the children's body mass index was recorded at the age of ten. Researchers discovered that when young children watched too much TV, they were more likely to develop problems such as obesity and poorer academic skills as assessed by their teachers. Moreover, they were 10 percent more likely to be victimized by their peers, including being rejected, teased, and assaulted.

Gaming for Good?

According to the 2008 U.S. study, *Teens, Video Games, and Civics*, about 97 percent of teens play video games. This finding means video games have the potential to affect the vast majority of youth.

FIGURE 8-5 These children are watching television together. Is the television helping or hindering them socially? Is TV viewing a social behaviour or an independent behaviour?

FIGURE 8-6 Pac Man was a popular game in the 1980s. How have video games changed since then?

Recent studies that focus on violence and social skills development show short-term aggression following the playing of violent video games; however, there hasn't been a lot of research in this area. But researchers did discover that teens are far more social while playing video games than was previously thought. There are many popular multiplayer games that allow adolescents to play with their friends present in the room or with others via the Internet.

In terms of younger children, significant research hasn't been done since the 1980s—and video games have come a long way since the days of "Pac Man"—so the specific effects on young children are not as clear. Still, a 2008 study determined that 82 percent of two- to five-year-olds play video games, so greater psychological investigation is now necessary. For now, experts such as Dr. David Hutchison, a professor at Brock University who studies video gaming and learning, say parents need to vary their children's activities between video games and other social activities, such as playing sports and playing with their friends. Balance is the key.

? Make a prediction about the impact of electronics use in the future on social skills. What are some possible research questions?

Socialization and Immigration

When a family immigrates to a new country, each member goes through a process of socialization. **Cross-cultural psychology**, a field of psychological research rooted in anthropology, focuses on aspects of culture, such as the psychological differences between the dominant culture and subcultures, cultural ideas about intelligence, and the effect of culture and environment on perception. Research on the socialization process for immigrants is starting to emerge from this field.

cross-cultural psychology: an area of study that looks at the effect of culture on human behaviour

Identity

The concept of identity, and identity crisis, was developed by Erik Erikson based on his own immigrant experience. While he discussed the notion in terms of adolescent development, the concept of identity is important to understanding how newcomers establish their sense of self in a new environment. Actually, an individual can have many identities, some of which overlap, including:

- **ego identity:** a conscious sense of self developed through social interactions, which is constantly changing
- **social identity:** a sense of belonging based on membership in different groups (family, ethnic, occupational, etc.), which changes over one's life
- **national identity:** sense of belonging to a specific country and having shared feelings, regardless of country of origin
- **cultural/ethnic identity:** a connection to a cultural group that helps define who a person is

How do you define yourself? Do any of your self-definitions overlap or influence each other? You can use a mind map or software program to demonstrate this visually.

Connecting Psychology to Anthropology

Cross-cultural psychologists look at both universal behaviours and unique behaviours to identify the ways in which culture impacts our behaviour, family life, education, and social experiences, among other things. Ethnic identity is one area of interest to both anthropologists and cross-cultural psychologists.

More to Know...

Look back to Chapter 2 to learn more about Erikson's concept of identity crisis.

Psychological Acculturation

John Berry, a psychology professor at Queen's University, has researched acculturation, the meeting of two or more cultural groups and the resulting cultural changes to each group. **Psychological acculturation** describes the psychological effects that an individual experiences, such as changes in attitude and behaviour, that result from acculturation. Berry believes that the attitudes of individuals within a dominant and nondominant (or immigrant) cultural group shape how they interact and change one another as a result.

The chart below describes the psychological preconditions of the dominant group that influence the range of possible interactions with the nondominant group. It also describes the attitudes of the nondominant group. Finally, the arrows show that the behaviours of each group are altered due to their interaction. Any behaviour is subject to change. This change is called **behavioural shift**.

> **More to Know...**
> You were introduced to John Berry's acculturation theory in Chapter 7.

psychological acculturation: change in the cultural behaviour and thinking of a person or group of people through contact with another culture

behavioural shift: a change in behaviour resulting from contact with another culture

POTENTIAL ACCULTURATION STRATEGIES

Nondominant Group (Immigrant) Strategies

- **Integration:** Some aspects of the original culture are maintained, but there is participation in the larger culture.
  Example: wearing the *hijab* (Muslim head scarf) with jeans and a T-shirt.
- **Separation:** Individuals choose to keep their cultural heritage and avoid contact with other cultural groups.
  Example: living, working, shopping, communicating, and spending spare time solely within Little Italy.
- **Assimilation:** Individuals want to have daily interaction with other cultural groups and leave behind their own cultural heritage.
  Example: wearing jeans and a T-shirt and no longer wearing the *hijab*.
- **Marginalization:** Individuals may not maintain their cultural heritage and do not have relationships with others.
  Example: feeling pressured to forego your Greek heritage but still feeling isolated from others.

Dominant Group Strategies

- **Multicultural:** Most individuals accept cultural diversity.
  Example: society accepts people from all cultures living in the community.
- **Segregation:** Most individuals demand the separation of newcomers from the dominant group.
  Example: the belief that newcomers from China must live in Chinatown.
- **Melting pot:** Most individuals expect newcomers to adapt to the dominant culture.
  Example: the belief that everyone who lives in Canada should have the same attitudes and practices.
- **Exclusion:** Marginalization is imposed by most of the dominant group.
  Example: forcing others to act as "Canadians."

REFLECT AND RESPOND

1. How does psychological acculturation relate to anthropology and sociology?
2. Compare the chart entitled "Social Development Needs from Birth to 12 Years" on page 364 to Piaget's and Erikson's stages of development. How are they similar? What accounts for their differences?
3. In pairs, list foods from various ethnic groups that you can find in your local grocery store. How can acculturation explain how Canadians connect with immigrants through food?

Conformity

> **Before You Read**
>
> List the situations in your life when you were expected to do what the group was doing.

One topic of interest to social psychologists is when and why people choose to conform to groups. As you learned in Chapter 6, conformity is the inclination to align your attitudes, beliefs, and behaviours with those around you. Examples include what you wear and the music you listen to. What are the pressures that people encounter? Consider the following scenario: You are with a group of friends who are teasing another student. What do you do? Join in? Walk away? Speak up?

While there have been many experiments to understand the nature of conformity, a few stand out as being more influential. Psychologist A. Jenness was the first social psychologist to study conformity. In 1932, he used the ambiguous situation of having participants guess the number of beans in a glass jar. He found that participants' answers changed once they heard what others in the group thought. Jenness's work was expanded on by Muzafer Sherif in 1935 with his Autokinetic Effect experiment, in which participants guessed how far a small speck of light projected onto a screen in a dark room had moved. When put in groups, participants' estimates tended to conform to those of others in the group. Finally, Solomon Asch's series of experiments, which you learned about at the beginning of this chapter, demonstrated the impact that group social pressure can have on individual decision making.

FIGURE 8-7 How many beans do you think there are in this jar? Do you think your answer would change if you learned others had radically different guesses?

Factors That Affect Conformity

Social psychologists have learned that there are various factors that affect whether an individual will conform. The chart below provides a summary of these factors and how they have been demonstrated through research.

FACTORS THAT AFFECT CONFORMITY		
Factor	Source	Influence on Conformity
Group size	Solomon Asch	Large groups tend to have higher rates of conformity; however, that rate doesn't change much after groups reach four or five members.
Group unanimity	Muzafer Sherif Solomon Asch Philip Zimbardo	When everyone in a group appears to agree, participant conformity is high. Even one person voicing disagreement decreases the conformity of participants.
Public vs. private response	Muzafer Sherif Solomon Asch	When participants are able to give answers privately (for example, written rather than spoken), conformity decreases.
Self-esteem	Solomon Asch Philip Zimbardo	Those with lower self-esteem are more likely to conform because they want to belong. Conversely, participants are less likely to conform when they are confident in themselves or their abilities.
Ambiguous situation or difficult task	Muzafer Sherif Solomon Asch	When a task is difficult or ambiguous, participants look to others in the group for cues as to how to react, assuming the others will know what to do. The more difficult the task, the greater the conformity.
Status of members or group	Solomon Asch Stanley Milgram	If a group member is knowledgeable, such as a teacher, or has a high status, such as a workplace superior, other participants are likely to conform to that person's views. There is also higher conformity to a group that has high status.

> Which of the factors that affect conformity have you experienced? Provide examples.

The Effects of Conformity

It turns out that conforming isn't necessarily a bad thing. Rather it's a natural aspect of social interaction. Have you ever noticed that you might act, dress, or speak in a similar manner as your friends do? The **chameleon effect**, which is the mimicking of others' body language, actually happens quite often and helps others like us. For example, in the past, boys emulated Justin Bieber's haircut. In their 1999 study, Tanya Chartrand and John Bargh conducted a series of experiments to test the theory. One experiment included 78 participants who interacted with confederates—people who were part of the research team but acted as subjects in front of the real participants. When the confederates altered their body language to mimic that of the participants, they scored higher in a survey that measured likeability. In other words, we are more apt to like others who act the way we do.

As you learned in Chapter 6, social psychologist Irving Janis first defined *groupthink* in 1972. In psychology, this concept can be used to explain faulty decisions, largely made by policy makers in groups. Groupthink results in ignoring reasonable alternatives in favour of taking irrational actions. Conditions that allow groupthink to exist include an isolated, cohesive group that has a strong or authoritarian leader. For example, engineers of the 1986 Space Shuttle *Challenger* raised concerns about faulty parts prior to its launch, but a group at NASA decided to have the launch as planned to avoid negative press. The space shuttle exploded, and all aboard died.

Janis defined eight symptoms of groupthink:

chameleon effect: the mimicking of the body language of a person with whom we are interacting

> **VOICES**
> When people are free to do as they please, they usually imitate each other.
> Eric Hoffer, writer

EIGHT SYMPTOMS OF GROUPTHINK

1. an **illusion of invulnerability**, shared by most or all the members, which creates excessive optimism and encourages taking extreme risks;
2. **collective efforts to rationalize** in order to discount warnings which might lead the members to reconsider their assumptions…;
3. an unquestioned **belief in the group's inherent morality**, inclining the members to ignore the ethical or moral consequences of their decisions;
4. **stereotyped views of enemy leaders** as too evil to warrant genuine attempts to negotiate, or as too weak and stupid to counter whatever risky attempts are made to defeat their purposes;
5. **direct pressure** on any member who expresses strong arguments against any of the group's stereotypes, illusions, or commitments …;
6. **self-censorship** of deviations from the apparent group consensus, reflecting each member's inclination to minimize to himself [or herself] the importance of his [or her] doubts and counterarguments;
7. a **shared illusion of unanimity** concerning judgments conforming to the majority view (partly resulting from self-censorship of deviations, augmented by the false assumption that silence means consent);
8. the emergence of **self-appointed mindguards**—members who protect the group from adverse information that might shatter their shared complacency about the effectiveness and morality of their decisions.

There are ways to limit the effect of groupthink. For example, inviting experts from outside the group or a "devil's advocate," someone whose job is constructive criticism, can help. Also, the leader of the group should avoid giving his or her opinion so others do what they believe is right, not what they think is expected.

> **?** Think back to the earlier scenario where a group of your friends are teasing another student. How are the factors of conformity playing a role there?

IN FOCUS: The Bystander Effect

If you saw someone in need of help, would you help that person? What if you were in a large crowd? The **bystander effect** is a concept in social psychology used to explain why the larger the number of people in a group, the less likely it is that individuals will stop to help someone in an emergency. Sometimes this concept is called *Genovese syndrome* because it is linked to the terrible murder of Kitty Genovese (see Figure 8-8).

On a New York City night in 1964, Kitty was attacked several times by a stranger while walking to her apartment. The first stabbing was in a stairwell that was clearly visible by neighbouring apartments. A neighbour shouted at the attacker and he fled. She survived the first attack, but her attacker returned ten minutes later, stabbed her repeatedly, and sexually assaulted her. While she screamed for help, 38 of her neighbours opened their windows and turned on their lights, yet did nothing to stop the attack. However, once the attacker left, someone did call the police. Why did no one help Kitty?

FIGURE 8-8 Kitty Genovese's screams for help were heard by her neighbours, yet nobody came to help her as she was being stabbed and sexually assaulted.

If an individual sees another person who needs help, he or she is likely to do so. However, certain criteria must be met. Psychologists John Darley and Bibb Latané (1968) determined that in order to help someone in an emergency, an individual must first notice the incident, then interpret it as an emergency, and finally assume responsibility for helping. An individual is also more likely to help if he or she is the only person who has witnessed an incident.

On the other hand, once other people are present, the following four mechanisms may come into play, leading to the bystander effect:

- **self-awareness:** When an individual feels there is an audience, his or her actions may be inhibited because of the fear of making a fool of himself or herself in front of others.
- **social cues:** People look to others for cues of how to behave. So, if no one acts, it reinforces the notion that no one should act.
- **blocking mechanisms:** In an emergency situation where there are a lot of people around, someone stepping in to act (for example, to help a victim) can actually block others from doing so.
- **diffusion of responsibility:** People assume that someone else will help so they don't have to.

Using Virtual Reality to Understand the Bystander Effect

Although numerous experiments have studied the bystander effect in a controlled environment, it would be unethical to test the theory in a real emergency. However, researchers will soon have an opportunity to study how real people react to extreme situations thanks to "virtual humans" that are being created by Professor Jian Zhang at the National Centre for Computer Animation (NCCA) in England. These virtual humans will be used to measure behavioural, physiological, emotional, and cognitive responses to situations in a virtual world. Increasingly, psychologists are linking up with computer animation specialists to create controlled environments for social psychology experiments.

QUESTIONS

1. Should there be a law stating that bystanders must intervene? Explain why or why not.
2. On Christmas Day, 2010, a U.K. woman announced on her Facebook page that she had taken many pills and would soon be dead. Some of her 1082 "friends" commented on her status, yet none called for help or went to check on her. Her lifeless body was discovered the next day. What does this suggest about the bystander effect in the digital age?

Issues in Youth Conformity

In 2006, the alleged terrorist plot of the "Toronto 18" was discovered. Eighteen people had allegedly been recruited by Al Qaeda to commit acts of terrorism in Canada. There were plots to blow up prominent buildings and to create a large Al Qaeda type cell in Toronto, with the aim to create disorder that would scare Canadians into withdrawing troops from Afghanistan. What's interesting is that the group was composed entirely of young males, most under the age of 25. Based on research on young men, there is some evidence that shows that young men are more likely to join a terrorist group. Why is this so?

University of Toronto psychology professor Jordan Peterson believes the link between **serotonin** and social status is one key. He has discovered in his studies with rhesus monkeys—which tend to travel in all-male groups after puberty—that if their social status decreases, so does the serotonin levels in their brains. This suggests that our need to have status within a group, and thus belong to a group, is biological. Added to this, developmental psychology professor Marc Lewis points out that the brains of teenage males are not fully developed, especially the prefrontal cortex that controls decision making and planning ahead. Finally, psychologist William Pollack believes boys are still socialized according to old values of being brave, strong, and macho. Of course, the percentage of boys who engage in extreme behaviour is low, but the pressure to join a group and conform to its philosophy can sometimes lead young people to make decisions they would otherwise never contemplate.

Nonconformity

There are always those who do not conform to the group or obey authority. For example, not everyone in Asch's experiment conformed to the group. What is different about these people or the way they think?

One reason could be a sense of morality. According to Lawrence Kohlberg's *theory of moral development*, some people will not conform because of their moral beliefs. His stages of development are loosely based on Piaget's stages but move beyond them in scope. In early childhood, morality is related to avoiding punishment or gaining rewards. If they reach the sixth and final stage, individuals no longer base their morality on what is socially acceptable, but on what is moral in principle. These individuals are not likely to conform to a group that is doing something wrong because they are guided by their own ethical principles and are not seeking approval by the group.

serotonin: a chemical messenger in the brain that is associated with feelings of well-being

FIGURE 8-9 Teenage boys tend to hang out together in groups. What does the boys' body language tell you about their social status in this group?

VOICES

Never doubt that a small group of thoughtful, committed citizens can change the world; indeed, it's the only thing that ever has.
Margaret Mead

REFLECT AND RESPOND

1. Which factors of conformity are confirmed by Asch's experiment?
2. How might conformity be experienced in the workplace? How could you research this topic?
3. In 2002, there was speculation that Iraq had weapons of mass destruction and the administration of President George W. Bush created a policy of "pre-emptive use of military force against terrorists and rogue nations." How does the U.S. attack on Iraq fall under the category of groupthink?

Prejudice: A Psychological Perspective

Before You Read
Make a list of the groups to which you belong. How do you define yourself in those groups? Does your self-definition change when you are in different groups?

Think back to Chapter 6. Prejudice is prejudgment or judgement of someone based on stereotypes and biases. How can psychology help us understand the roots of prejudice and how to overcome it?

Prejudice

As you learned in Chapter 6, in 1954 social psychologist Muzafer Sherif and his colleagues conducted the Robbers Cave experiment that studied the roots of prejudice between two groups. They divided twenty-two 11-year-old boys into two groups at a camp. While each group bonded doing regular camp activities and created group names and flags, they were unaware of the other's existence. Then the groups were allowed to find each other and intergroup conflict soon emerged in the form of name calling and singing mean-spirited songs about the group. This simple experiment demonstrated how quickly and easily individuals identify with a group and create conflict with those outside that group.

More to Know...
You learned about Sherif's study in Chapter 6. How do his ideas apply to the psychology of group thinking?

ingroup:
a social group formed when its members identify with one another

outgroup:
a social group toward which an individual feels disrespect or opposition; sometimes treated badly by the ingroup

Ingroups and Outgroups

We can understand the boys' behaviour in Sherif's experiment in terms of **ingroups** (any social group to which an individual feels he or she belongs) and **outgroups** (any individuals who don't belong to the social group in which an individual feels he or she belongs). An ingroup is formed when members identify with one another. For example, when your school competes with another, ingroups and outgroups are clearly defined and obvious on the field or arena. Members of an ingroup do not necessarily behave in a hostile way toward outgroups. It is a sense of belonging that bonds them. In fact, most of us belong to many ingroups. However, sometimes—as in the case of Sherif's campers—hostile behaviour does help reinforce a group's identity and sense of belonging. Understanding the interplay between ingroups and outgroups can help us understand why some groups become hostile toward others.

According to psychologist Gordon Allport, "Hostility toward outgroups helps strengthen our sense of belonging, but it is not required.... The familiar is preferred. What is alien is regarded as somehow inferior, less 'good,' but there is not necessarily hostility against it..." (1954, p. 42). Allport recognized that attachment to one group does not necessarily mean hostility toward another. However, he realized that ingroups require something that differentiates them from other groups that indicates who is "in" and who is "out." This differentiation, by definition, involves defining who is part of "us" and who is not, and ingroups therefore imply outgroups. For example, members of your school's basketball team are an ingroup. By definition, if you're not on the team you're part of the outgroup. This does not mean that the team members view others as inferior; it just means that there are people who are not on the team.

It's simple—you can't have an in-crowd unless you leave somebody out of it—without uncool, there is no cool. So basically, you're nothing without me. HA!

Suzie would later win a Nobel Prize for her Theory of Special Social Relativity.

↑ **FIGURE 8-10** Explain Suzie's reasons for speaking to the group in terms of ingroups and outgroups.

Hate Crimes in Canada

Figure 8-11 shows the prevalence of hate crimes in Canada. Compared to other violent crimes, hate crimes have a greater impact on victims and communities because they target people for core features of their identity. Effects of hate crimes on victims often include psychological distress, such as depression, stress, anger, and post-traumatic stress disorder. The effects on communities are equally significant. The offender sends a message that members of the group are not welcome in a particular neighbourhood, school, or workplace. Thus hate crimes victimize the individual as well as entire communities.

Who commits hate crimes? Researchers have found that aggression and anti-social behaviour is common and perpetrators seem "normal." Many have a family history of violence and abuse. Some researchers suggest that perpetrators of hate crimes use the defence mechanism of projection, whereby they unconsciously direct feelings about themselves onto another person to help cope with their own abuse.

What can be done about hate crimes? Aside from the need for strong legislation to respond to crimes, it is also important to challenge stereotypes, reduce intergroup conflicts, and encourage understanding and appreciation of others' diversities. Individuals have to take a stand.

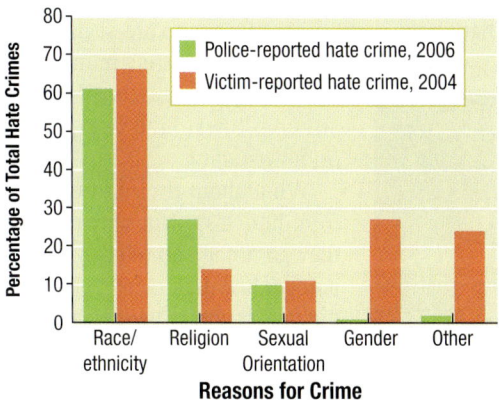

FIGURE 8-11 Look for trends in the graph, and use your understanding of psychological theories to propose reasons for those trends. Also, why might there be a disparity between police-reported and victim-reported hate crimes?

Prejudice and the Brain

Even when we consciously try not to judge people based on their appearance, our brains do so anyway, to a certain extent. Psychology professor Stephen Porter, at the University of British Columbia, says that, according to his 2010 study, our brains take as little as 38 milliseconds to judge trustworthiness in the faces of those we've just met. Our brains are looking for three indications: signs of dominance (associated with violence), strong facial features (associated with anger), and symmetry (associated with attractiveness). However, our unconscious biases are not always trustworthy. In other studies, participants could accurately tell the difference between whether or not someone was lying only about 50 percent of the time. What does this suggest about our first impressions of people?

? What implications do Stephen Porter's findings on prejudice have for judges and juries in our legal system?

More to Know...
Look back to Chapter 2 to read more about the defence mechanism of projection.

Open for Debate
On October 7, 1998, Matthew Shepard was brutally assaulted and murdered because he was gay. While homosexuals and transgendered individuals have equal rights under the law, they continue to be the target of hate crimes. Does the psychology of ingroups and outgroups provide a viable explanation for this behaviour? Explain.

VOICES
The social psychology of this century reveals a major lesson: often it is not so much the kind of person a man [sic] is as the kind of situation in which he finds himself that determines how he will act.
Stanley Milgram
(*Obedience to Authority: An Experimental View*, 1974)

Landmark Case Study

Jane Elliot: Brown Eyes/Blue Eyes

In 1968, elementary school teacher Jane Elliot conducted an experiment in her classroom that would lead her students and others to change the way they thought about racism and prejudice. In response to the assassination of Dr. Martin Luther King, Jr., she devised a scenario that taught her all-white Grade 3 students about the roots of discrimination and racism by having each student experience it firsthand. Her exercise and the student reunion 14 years later have been documented in the film *A Class Divided*.

Elliot had 28 students in her class. She began her lesson by discussing news of the assassination and then moved on to discuss racism and discrimination in general. While her students were familiar with the topics and understood that racism was wrong, she couldn't stop there because of their "sympathetic indifference." None of them, in their all-white community of 898, had experienced racism. Nor did they know very much about people of other races. What they did know tended to be negative, which Elliot presumed was learned from their parents, television, and radio. She asked the children if they thought they knew what it was like to be Black in America and if they'd like to find out. They answered yes.

The Experiment

Elliot began by randomly dividing the class into "blue-eyed" and "brown-eyed" groups. Immediately she established that the "blue-eyed" children were smarter and better than the others. She praised them and gave them privileges such as a longer recess and being first in the lunch line. Meanwhile, the "brown-eyed" children were given collars to wear and were disciplined and ridiculed for the smallest of errors (see Figure 8-12). A few days later, Elliot made the brown-eyed group the superior group and made the blue-eyed group wear the collars.

▲ **FIGURE 8-12** Jane Elliot's Grade 3 class during the experiment. What does the body language suggest about this group of students?

Results

The results were astounding. Elliot remarked, "I watched what had been marvellous, co-operative, wonderful, thoughtful children turn into nasty, vicious, discriminating little third-graders in a space of 15 minutes (*Frontline*—"A Class Divided")." She also discovered that the children who had been told they were smarter actually performed better in testing. Likewise, the children who were wearing the collars performed worse in testing and their behaviour changed. Some became sullen while others behaved worse than ever before. She had not told the students to behave in any particular manner, yet they subconsciously demonstrated discriminatory behaviour.

Influence

Today, Elliot still gets invited to conduct this experiment, albeit in adult workplaces. Her findings with adult workers are no different than with the Grade 3 children over 40 years ago: people still treat those who are seen as inferior in a negative manner. Elliot is now trying to change attitudes toward race, sex, and homosexuality.

What about the children from her class? Not only did they go home and tell their parents how bad racism was, they never forgot their lesson. In follow-up reunions and interviews, they continue to show the positive effects of the experiment, saying that they believe they are more empathic and sensitive people as a result.

QUESTIONS

1. Why did Jane Elliot feel this exercise was the best way to teach her students about prejudice?
2. Do you think Elliot's experiment would meet today's ethical guidelines for psychologists? Explain why or why not.
3. What changes might Elliot use in her adult workplace experiments?

Scapegoating

Have you ever been blamed for something you didn't do? As you learned in Chapter 6, scapegoating refers to pushing the blame and responsibility away from oneself and onto others. For example, in experiments where students were made to experience failure, they subsequently put down another person or a rival school in order to restore their own self-esteem. A person's anger and hostility are projected outward at the scapegoat target, leading to an "us versus them" mentality, which can then lead to serious negative consequences. Individuals, such as those in an outgroup, can be targeted individually or as a whole. This can happen anywhere in society—at school, on a sports team, at home, or at work. For example, when a group of students who dress very differently from most of the others at school are automatically blamed for vandalism, they are scapegoats. Even nations and ethnic groups can be scapegoats as you read in Chapter 6.

Psychologists believe there are several elements at play that explain why scapegoating occurs. Targeting a scapegoat could be a psychological defence mechanism that protects the perpetrator from feeling unacceptable emotions, such as hostility and guilt. Also self-deception could be involved because the accuser denies her or his own feelings of shame and guilt. Since this denial is often done unconsciously, it is difficult for the accuser to stop himself or herself from scapegoating. Make sure when you accuse someone of an offence that you have concrete proof to avoid creating a scapegoat.

Promoting Heroism

Philip Zimbardo, a psychologist whose work has shown how easily evil acts can be encouraged, is now researching heroism. He and his fellow researchers in the Heroic Imagination Project believe that each of us has the potential to be a hero. They hope to demystify how people choose to be heroes—instead of succumbing to issues such as the bystander effect—so that every one of us can feel as if we can make a positive difference in the lives of those around us.

Already Zimbardo has tips for how to encourage what he calls "heroes in waiting" in children. Essentially, we need to foster "heroic imaginations" in children by using the guidelines in the chart at the right.

> **Open for Debate**
>
> Is there such thing as an "altruism instinct"? In a recent study of three-month-olds, the babies often selected puppets that were shown helping other puppets over those that didn't. If we prefer those who help others, then why is the bystander effect so strong?

> **Connecting Psychology to Sociology**
>
> Scapegoating can be an outcome of frustration-aggression theory. Immigrants are often scapegoated during harsh economic times as others blame them for their lack of financial stability. As people become increasingly frustrated at their lack of job opportunities, they blame newcomers for taking their jobs.

> **WAYS TO PROMOTE HEROIC IMAGINATION IN CHILDREN**
>
> 1. Encourage awareness. Heroes have a good sense of when people are in trouble. If we sense that things are a little bit out of place or don't fit, we can avert the danger before it happens, like stopping a bullying classmate.
> 2. Show kids they have the power to resolve conflicts. Teach kids that it's more heroic to resolve conflicts through dialogue than by fighting.
> 3. Foster action instead of inaction. It's easy to be a bystander when we see someone being bullied, but research shows that kids are more likely to do something if their parents and friends expect them to.

REFLECT AND RESPOND

1. How could the Heroic Imagination Project be used to foster positive behaviour/citizenship in younger students?
2. How can psychologists be employed to reduce hate crimes?
3. Zimbardo's Heroic Imagination Project is an example of which psychological school of thought?
4. Prepare an oral presentation about ingroups and outgroups in your community. Be sure to have a hypothesis.

Issues in Mental Illness

Before You Read

How is mental illness portrayed in the media and by society?

Our social attitudes about mental illness have changed dramatically throughout the last century. No longer are relatives with mental illness locked up in "insane asylums" and forgotten. However, problems still exist that affect the lives of Canadians with mental health concerns.

The Stigma of Mental Illness

As we have seen with outgroups, those who are different from us are sometimes seen in a negative manner. This can lead to prejudice and **stigmas**. A stigma is a belief that leads to social disgrace. Many people with mental illness are stigmatized.

stigma: a belief that leads to social disgrace

The consequences of a stigma can be devastating for the recipient. People who are stigmatized can feel fear and face rejection in various areas of their lives. They might have difficulties getting or maintaining a job and a loss of self-esteem. Sometimes they avoid getting the help they need because they feel embarrassed.

VOICES

A nation's greatness is measured by how it treats its weakest members.
Mahatma Ghandi

According to the Centre for Addiction and Mental Health, one in five Canadians will experience mental illness in his or her lifetime. Yet the stigma associated with mental illness does not appear to be going away, according to the Canadian Medical Association. Its 2008 survey measured people's experiences with and attitudes toward the health care system, including mental health. The survey uncovered the following attitudes:

- Almost half of Canadians, 46 percent, think people use the term *mental illness* as an excuse for bad behaviour.
- One in four Canadians are fearful of being around those who suffer from serious mental illness.
- Half of Canadians would tell friends or co-workers that they have a family member with a mental illness, compared to 72 percent for a diagnosis of cancer or 68 percent for diabetes.
- Most Canadians, 61 percent, would be unlikely to go to a family doctor with a mental illness, and 58 percent would shy away from hiring a lawyer, child care worker, or financial adviser with the illness.

Skills Focus

The Canadian Medical Association used a survey to uncover the attitudes of Canadians toward mental illness. Suggest relevant topics related to mental illness within your school for which a survey would be appropriate.

With mental illness affecting so many of us, why is there still a stigma? For one thing, stereotypes of mental illness are shown as negative in popular culture. Horror movies are filled with "psychos" killing innocent people. People also casually throw around terms such as *crazy* in everyday conversation. Finally, mental illness has not been discussed openly and honestly in society. Frank discussions would allow for a more positive viewpoint of mental illness.

Six-time Olympic medallist Clara Hughes is hoping to eliminate the stigma of mental illness (see Figure 8-13). She has joined a national campaign to get people talking about mental illness in an open and honest manner. After her first Olympic games, Hughes suffered from depression and now wants to ensure that others have an opportunity to get the help they need if they face a similar situation.

↑ **FIGURE 8-13** Clara Hughes, who once suffered from depression, smiles as she announces her involvement in a campaign to eliminate the stigma of mental illness.

Facing Stigma

Each of us deserves to be treated with dignity and respect. The Centre for Addiction and Mental Health has seven suggestions to change the prejudice and discrimination faced by those experiencing mental illness:

1. Know the facts: educate yourself about the facts, not the myths.
2. Be aware of your attitudes and behaviour: everyone grows up with some negative attitudes from family, friends, and society, but we can change the way we think and see people as unique human beings and not stereotypes.
3. Choose your words carefully: speak with accurate and sensitive words; for example, say "a person with schizophrenia" instead of saying "a schizophrenic."
4. Educate others: challenge myths and negative attitudes with positive, real information.
5. Focus on the positive: focus on the positive contribution that everyone, including those with mental illness, can make to society.
6. Support people: treat all individuals with dignity and respect, and support their efforts to get well.
7. Include everyone: ensure that everyone has the opportunity to take an equal part in society.

Diagnoses and Medication

Another issue in the area of mental health, sometimes related to stigma, is the overdiagnosis and overuse of medication. Medication is often used to help children diagnosed as having attention deficit hyperactivity disorder (ADHD) or Asperger syndrome (an autism spectrum disorder) far too often and at times incorrectly. The increase in these diagnoses can be attributed to a number of factors, such as increased knowledge of symptoms. However, some psychiatrists argue that these diagnoses are being used as a quick fix for a child who misbehaves. How can we ensure that people are not being wrongly diagnosed?

Seniors often face the opposite problem: they are often underdiagnosed. In one study, only about half of seniors with symptoms of major depression were being treated for it by their doctors. This happens because their symptoms are misread as signs of aging or as part of physical conditions. As well, mental illness symptoms often look different in seniors than in young people, and there are often access issues due to the poor mobility of many seniors. Finally, the stigma of mental illness can stop seniors from seeking the help they need. Conversely, seniors are easily overmedicated. To help them deal with difficult feelings that come with aging, such as sadness, grief, and anxiety, they are prescribed drugs as a quick fix.

REFLECT AND RESPOND

1. In your own words, explain why there is still a stigma around mental illness in Canada.
2. Suggest concrete measures that your school could take to improve attitudes toward mental illness.
3. Research with a partner the mental health supports available in your community. Communicate to your peers orally and/or visually.

Section 8.2 Personality and Environment

From our home to the workplace, influences on our personality abound. So far we've seen how our sense of self can be influenced by socialization. In this section, you will explore the various influences on your personality, including family environment, the media, and the workplace.

Influence of Family Environment

Have you ever visited a friend and noticed that his or her family members speak or behave in a similar way to that of your friend? That's because the family influences many aspects of your personality and behaviour. The way you interact with your parents and siblings can have a great influence on the way you conduct yourself in other situations.

Parental Influence

While there is some debate about exactly how much influence the family has on an individual's personality, most psychologists believe family is instrumental, especially in the early years of development. Generally, there are at least three ways in which parents can influence the emotional and behavioural responses of their children:

1. **Direct interaction:** This involves direct communication between the parent and child. It includes the transfer of knowledge, such as naming an unfamiliar object in a book. Parents' rewarding of desired behaviours and punishment of behaviours that are undesired are also part of this influence.

2. **Emotional identification:** By the age of four or five, children unconsciously believe that some of their parents' attributes, including personality and character, are their own. For example, a child whose father is shy may believe that he or she is also timid. This tendency is stronger among children who have unique physical features that are similar to those of a parent. Children also identify with the family's class and ethnic or religious group. These identifications have a greater influence if parents act on what they say. A child is more likely to value the arts if his or her parents both encourage a love for the arts in their child and demonstrate an interest in them, which often reflects the class of the family.

3. **Family stories:** A more symbolic form of identification occurs through the telling of stories or myths of particularly accomplished family members. For example, a parent may tell the story of Grandma who started her own business or of cousin Johnny who competed in the Olympics. On hearing the recounting of a story, a child feels a sense of pride due to the biological relation he or she has to these successful family members.

FIGURE 8-14 How do our parents shape our personalities?

Before You Read

How would you describe your family's values to someone you just met? Make a list of the words you would use. Then ask a friend to describe your personality. Write down the words your friend uses in a column beside your first list. Is there a connection between your personality and your family?

Skills Focus

As social scientists, psychologists try to gather empirical data to support explanations. Of the three mechanisms of parental influence—direct interaction, emotional identification, and family stories—which one do you think is the easiest for psychologists to measure? Why?

More to Know...

Look back to Chapter 5 to learn more about how your birth order might influence your personality.

Our parents' influence also extends beyond childhood. For example, a child whose parental interactions focused on vocabulary development early on is more likely to master elementary school tasks and, as a result, feel more confident as he or she progresses through school.

How Can Parenting Styles Influence Personality?

How did your parents or guardians react the last time you did something you knew was wrong? The answer might indicate the type of parenting style they use. Developmental psychologists often turn to the parenting style categories developed in the 1960s: authoritative, authoritarian, permissive, or neglectful.

Figure 8-15 describes each of the parenting styles. *Responsiveness* refers to how much parents try to foster their child's individuality and self-regulation by understanding and supporting his or her needs. *Demandingness* indicates the way parents try to get their children involved in the family as a whole, their maturity expectations, and their willingness to confront and discipline a disobedient child.

FIGURE 8-15 Parenting styles are a complex combination of factors. Think of a parent you know, and consider where he or she would fit in this model.

	RESPONSIVENESS	
	High	**Low**
High DEMANDINGNESS	**Authoritative** • set and enforce rules consistently, and explain the reasons	**Authoritarian** • impose rules and expect obedience
Low	**Permissive** • have few rules and use little punishment	**Neglectful** • are uninvolved and expect little

Parenting Style and Personality

Studies have shown that each parenting style is correlated to particular behavioural outcomes (see chart on the upper right). Keep in mind that psychologists can speak only in terms of generalities because there are other genetic and environmental influences on personality.

It is important to note that although there is a correlation between the parents' style of parenting and their child's behaviour, it does not mean that the parenting style is the cause of the child's behaviour. It's possible that the child's behaviour is, in fact, influencing the way in which his or her parents respond. Other factors, such as common genes, may also influence both the parent and the child.

In addition, most parents do not neatly fit into one category. Some researchers argue that these categories should really be viewed as a continuum since most parents tend to show some overlap between two categories.

While most child-rearing experts agree that an authoritative parenting style is the most effective, this may not hold true across cultures. In cultures where obedience is highly valued, an authoritarian style may be viewed as most desired.

FIGURE 8-16 Which parenting style is represented in this photo? How might this style affect the child in psychological terms?

PARENTING STYLES	
Parenting Style	**Children's Behaviour**
Authoritative	Children are well behaved and do well at school, are emotionally healthy, and are socially adept.
Authoritarian	Children are relatively well behaved, their social skills are not as strong, and they are more likely to suffer from anxiety, depression, and poor self-esteem.
Permissive	Children are not as high achievers at school and have good social skills, higher self-esteem, and lower anxiety and depression rates, but they are more likely to show problematic behaviour such as drug use.
Neglectful	Children are likely to have low academic achievement and low self-esteem.

Issues Related to Family Environment

While issues such as eating disorders and criminal behaviour have root causes in both biology and environment, the role of the family environment is of particular interest to researchers.

Eating Disorders

In Canada, 1 to 8 percent of people have an eating disorder called *bulimia nervosa*, in which they binge on high-calorie foods and then make themselves vomit to reduce the guilt for having overeaten. *Anorexia nervosa*, an eating disorder in which a normal-weight person diets and becomes significantly underweight, affects fewer than 1 percent of Canadians. Eating disorders such as anorexia, bulimia, and overeating are illnesses for which there is no one single cause. However, much research has been done to investigate some of the possible causes.

A negative family environment can be a contributing factor, as can social and cultural pressures, hormonal abnormalities, and even genetic factors. Parental views of weight are also a factor. In one American study, 40 percent of 9- and 10-year-old girls who were worried about their weight were urged to lose weight by their mothers. Also, studies show that people suffering from bulimia are more likely to have a family history of emotional disorders, obesity, and addiction. Those with anorexia are more likely to come from a family that is competitive and high achieving.

According to the Canadian Psychological Association, family therapy is an effective approach to treating these disorders, especially for young people. However, it is important for parents to model healthy eating habits for their children from a young age, since this can positively influence their eating habits, which can help prevent eating disorders before they start.

FIGURE 8-17 This teen is being arrested. What factors in his home life might have influenced his behaviour?

Criminal Behaviour

Problems that exist in the family environment can have negative effects on children. For example, psychologists Nadia Garnefski and Sjoukje Okma's study of nearly three thousand 15-and 16-year-old students found a correlation between growing up in a home that has a weak family bond with poor communication skills and developing anti-social, aggressive, or criminal behaviour. Home life is, of course, not the only factor, and because this is just a correlation, we cannot conclude that a negative home life causes criminal behaviour. Other studies indicate that the children of parents who are violent and have been arrested are more likely to be violent and have encounters with the law, and those who grow up in an abusive home or are neglected are 50 percent more likely to commit crimes.

Runaway Teens

Have you ever wondered how people come to live on the streets? While there is no single path to homelessness, perhaps by understanding some of the causes, we can eliminate, or at least reduce, this situation in our cities and towns. Unfortunately for young people, family life is one strong factor related to homelessness.

In 2002 in Canada, 52 390 children ran away from home, 96 percent of whom were between the ages of 12 and 17. While 75 percent of runaways usually return home within a week, that still leaves a lot of children on the streets. Why do teens run away? According to police, 56 percent of teens said they were "thrown out" by their parents, while 47 percent said leaving home was their own decision. Not surprisingly, most children who run away are leaving unhappy homes. One Toronto study indicated that 40 percent of girls and 19 percent of boys leave home because of sexual abuse. Also, physical abuse at home was reported by 59 percent of girls and 39 percent of boys. Other factors for leaving home include parental violence, drug and alcohol abuse, negligence, and poor relationships with parents. Some children feel that their home is not a safe place and believe the only option they have is to leave.

VOICES

Nowhere here
To call my home
No one near
To call my own
All that's left
Is for me to roam
Somebody please
Help me hang on

Lyrics from "Homeless Child" by Ben Harper

Understanding Family Influence

Psychologists who study the influence of family on personality have a tough job. Regardless of how much time children spend with their parents early in life, there are still other influences. There are genetic influences that come into play, as you learned in Chapter 5. Also, other extended family members can have an influence depending on how much time they spend with a child. When we start going to religious institutions, daycare settings, and school, our peers have increasing influence, and the widespread reach of the media is influential as well. Exactly how much influence do parents have, given the other possible influences, and how can psychologists scientifically study that influence?

Although there are significant research challenges inherent in studying family influences, psychologists have been able to develop some strategies:

1. Study observable behavioural characteristics that link to personality traits, including talkativeness, aggression, activity, and rule keeping.
2. Use factor analysis, a statistical technique that lets researchers categorize information, to understand the relationship between personality traits, such as extroversion, and family environment.

Open for Debate

Where do parents learn how to parent? Given the various consequences that can result from poor parenting, should there be some sort of compulsory government-sponsored parenting course? If so, at what age should this course be offered?

More to Know...

Look back to page 208 to learn more about factor analysis and how it is used to understand the influences on personality.

REFLECT AND RESPOND

1. Review the parenting styles diagram on page 381, and describe what each parenting style might look like.
2. What type of parent do you hope to be for your children? Explain your choice using research from this section.
3. Explain why studying family influence is a difficult task for psychologists.
4. Read the lyrics to Ben Harper's song about a homeless child. What does the song suggest about the child's self-esteem level? How might the child's home life have contributed to the belief that he or she is a burden? List the ways the child is being socialized.

Influence of Friends and Group Environments

> **Before You Read**
> Make a list of the different groups (for example, friends, clubs, sports) to which you belong. Now make a list of what you value most (for example, honesty, competition, teamwork, fun). Can you link your values to the groups to which you belong?

Why do you choose to hang out with your friends? Do you have the same interests and attitudes or play on the same sports teams? No matter how we choose our friends and the various groups to which we belong, social scientists have no doubt that our personality and behaviours are influenced by them.

Friends

At different stages of a person's development, friends have varying levels of influence on him or her. Most significantly, friends become increasingly important from school age into adolescence, while the influence of family decreases but is still strong. During adolescence, friendships are safe spaces for adolescents to explore their identities and develop a sense of belonging and acceptance. So how much influence do our friends have on our personalities?

Studying the influence of peers in adolescence is complex. One reason is that friends tend to gather because they have similar interests and academic standing and enjoy doing activities together. So it is difficult to judge where similarity ends and the influence starts. That is, do your friends influence your behaviour or were you similar in these ways to begin with, leading you to become friends? Also, unlike in childhood, teens often have multiple levels of friends (such as best friends and good friends) and belong to groups (such as cliques and crowds). While close friendships are intimate and usually long lasting, teens tend to move between other cliques and crowds that are largely based on demographics (for example, age, gender) and interests. Finally, research shows that even though parents' influence decreases throughout adolescence, it is still greater than that of the peer group.

> **More to Know...**
> Look ahead to Chapter 9 to learn more about friends and groups from a sociological perspective.

How Important Are Friendships in Adolescent Development?

University of Western Ontario psychologist Lynne Zarbatany is researching the role of friendship in early adolescent adjustment. The research is ongoing, but she has found that two basic human motivational forces, communion (the need for connection and closeness) and agency (the need for prominence), account for variation in friendship needs of pre-adolescents and adolescents. They can also predict the emotional consequences of failure to meet friendship needs, such as loneliness. These findings suggest that friendship is not experienced the same way by everyone but rather is shaped by the personalities of the individuals within the friendship. Work relating personality traits to various types of social behaviour (competition and social support) among pre-adolescents, adolescents, and adult friends is ongoing.

↑ **FIGURE 8-18** What brought these teens together?

Conforming to Expectations

Why do TV sitcoms play laugh tracks at the funny parts? Do we change our behaviour because we think we are supposed to? Social psychologist Mark Snyder studied this question in 1977 when he discovered that we instinctually pick up cues from others and conform to their expectations. In his study, men and women met for the first time by having a conversation using microphones and headsets, with no face-to-face interaction. Beforehand, each of the men was given a biography of the woman he would speak to as well as a photo. The men didn't know the women they would meet were not the people in the photos. Half the men were given a picture of a woman who had been judged to be very good-looking, while the other half believed the woman with whom they would be speaking was not very physically attractive.

Snyder found that during the conversation the women instinctively conformed to what the men expected from them. For example, in situations where the men expected to speak with an attractive woman, the women behaved in a way stereotypical of attractive people: they spoke more animatedly and seemed to enjoy the conversation more. So it can be concluded that people instinctively change their behaviour to conform to what is expected by others.

FIGURE 8-19 Suggest some reasons why this woman could be smiling while on the phone.

Self-Monitoring

We don't all conform to the same degree. Through his continuing research, Snyder believes there are "high self-monitors" and "low self-monitors." High self-monitors are people who change their behaviour to suit the situation and use cues to decide how to act. They also like to show off their skills and choose friends who will help them improve these skills. For example, if being good at hockey is important to some self-monitors, they will seek out a top player to teach them how to improve their play. Similarly, if they want others to believe they are upper class, they will choose friends who demonstrate wealth.

On the other hand, low self-monitors are people who act according to their "true self" and do not behave in ways that go against this. They choose their friends based on common interests rather than what their friends can do for them.

While high self-monitors might seem shallow by comparison, this is not necessarily the case. They are far more aware of subtle body-language messages and social nuances and can express their feelings more easily (depending on the situation) than low self-monitors.

> Think about your interactions with your friends and in groups. Do you think you are a high self-monitor or a low self-monitor? How has your method of self-monitoring influenced your behaviour?

False Consensus

Another concept that makes influences of groups difficult to judge is the false consensus effect. Most people believe that others have the same viewpoints as them. For example, if you like a particular band, you are more likely to believe that others do as well. In 1977, social psychologist Lee Ross first studied this concept using a series of experiments. He asked participants to decide which of two ways a conflict could be resolved. Participants also had to predict what others would decide and then describe the type of person who would make the opposite decision to theirs. The results indicated that we tend to think others make decisions in the same way we do, and when they don't, then we think they are unacceptable or defective in some way. We often take the attitude of "how could they think that way?" or that the obvious solution is based on how we think about the situation. For example,

Open for Debate

Some people believe that there is no such thing as "altruism," while a 2010 series of studies indicates that people don't like it when others are too selfless. Are people truly altruistic or does the person gain some form of social benefit as a result?

new parents may believe that giving their baby a soother when she's crying is standard protocol, but may be surprised to find out that other parents don't believe in this practice.

Crowds

Soccer fans in Europe are famous for their boisterous, sometimes violent, behaviour, acting in ways many of them wouldn't dream of outside the crowd environment. Why does being in a crowd change a person's behaviour?

Among the first social scientists to study crowd behaviour was Gustave Le Bon in the late 19th century. He believed that in crowds, people's normal psychological faculties are overridden by instincts and that behaviour is driven by instinct rather than intellect. He suggested that within a crowd, people come to think as one, in a manner that is different from what each person believes individually. He also argued that a crowd is susceptible to suggestibility and a high level of emotionality.

Some of Le Bon's ideas were used by the media to create propaganda and in the Holocaust by Adolf Hitler to get masses of Germans to act on their emotions and fears of people of Jewish descent. Thus we have known for quite some time that people in crowds can be influenced to alter their behaviour.

An Elaborated Social Identity Model of Crowds

Does being part of a crowd affect our personality? The simple answer is no, personality is hardly altered by crowds. We are in crowds only for a specific reason and for a relatively short amount of time. Yet, according to social psychologist Stephen Reicher, crowds do have different identities and intentions, and the individuals who create those crowds therefore take those on as well. Consider the difference between the crowd at a popular hockey game versus the crowd of protestors at a G20 summit. Their reasons for gathering are entirely different and therefore so are their identities. Crowds can influence individual decisions and behaviour. How they influence us depends on the type of crowd and our reasons for being in it.

> **More to Know...**
> Look back to Chapter 2 to learn more about the psychology of crowds in terms of flash mobs.

↑ **FIGURE 8-20** How do the people in this crowd demonstrate their crowd identity?

REFLECT AND RESPOND

1. What makes studying the influence of adolescent peer groups so complex? Identify the factors and explain what makes them complex.
2. Describe a situation in which you altered your behaviour to suit what you thought others expected of you.
3. Look back to the list you made at the beginning of this section on page 384 about your values. Create a collage of images that represent the values you know are from or reinforced by the groups to which you belong.
4. Is an online community a group that can influence someone's personality? Explain your answer.

Influence of Media on Personality

The music we listen to, the books we read, the movies we see—all of these are ways to demonstrate aspects of our personality. According to Cambridge University psychologist Peter Jason Rentfrow, even though our media choices look different, they usually share certain characteristics. He believes there are five "entertainment-preference dimensions":

- *aesthetic* (which includes classical music, art films, and poetry)
- *cerebral* (which includes current events and documentaries)
- *communal* (which includes romantic comedies, pop music, and daytime talk shows)
- *dark* (which includes heavy-metal music and horror movies)
- *thrilling* (which includes action-adventure films, thrillers, and science-fiction).

Keep these dimensions in mind as you read through this section.

The Power of Music

Dr. Daniel Levitin, professor of psychology and neuroscience at McGill University, studies how music relates to cognition. He works with experts in a variety of fields, including anthropologists, to understand how the brain and music co-evolved, as well as music's effects on the brain. For example, listening to music increases important aspects of our biology such as the production of oxytocin, antibodies, serotonin, and key neurotransmitters. As well, there are aspects to how the brain works that go hand in hand with music. For instance, the brain automatically does a "template match," such that if rock music is played using different instruments than usual, such as steel drums, we still recognize it as rock music. Levitin is still working on a question that has eluded psychologists: why do we love some music and dislike other types?

What Is the Link Between Music, Personality, and Behaviour?

You already learned about the relationship of music to the brain, but how does it influence personality and behaviour? On the surface, the relationship between music choice and personality can be quite circular—while your personality probably influences the types of music you choose, the music to which you listen can also influence your behaviour. The difficulty for psychologists is teasing out how much influence music has on behaviour.

Many people, for instance, use music to modify their mood. They select songs or bands depending on how they want to feel. Sometimes the effect can be quite dramatic. In 2003, researchers at universities in Iowa and Texas conducted a series of experiments on 500 university students that explored the relationship between violent music and violent thought and feelings. In the experiments, some students listened to violent songs while others listened to nonviolent songs by the same artists. Also, student personality differences in terms of aggression were controlled in the experiments. Then

> **Before You Read**
>
> In pairs, make a list of all the types of media that you encounter in a typical week. Next, rank the media based on how much you believe each one affects your thoughts and behaviour.

"Your son pays attention in class, but only to his iPod and cell phone."

FIGURE 8-21 Is your use of technology influencing your interactions with those around you? List the positive and negative impacts that social media have had in your life. What are the implications of these impacts? What role does limited time have on your life?

> **Skills Focus**
>
> In the 2003 study in Iowa and Texas, which students were the experiment group and which ones were the control group? Look back to page 57 to remind yourself of their definitions.

> **More to Know...**
> Music therapy is a new form of treatment for a variety of ailments and is actually showing promise in the fight against Alzheimer's disease.

the participants classified words that could be aggressive and nonaggressive, such as *rock* and *stick*. The researchers found that students who listened to violent music—even when the lyrics were humorous—were more likely to interpret words as aggressive. The songs increased their feelings of hostility even in situations that posed no real threat. In the real world, these findings suggest that people's music choices may influence their perceptions of others, their social interactions, and even whether they develop an aggressive personality.

? Do you ever listen to specific songs or bands when you need a pick-me-up or are feeling down? Why do you select that particular music?

Internet Communication

How often do you check your Facebook, Twitter, and/or email accounts? Would you rather look up information in a book or on the Web? The Internet is now a part of daily life for most Canadians. Because the Internet is still relatively new—it was popularized in the 1990s—it's hard to identify any of its long-term effects on personality. However, a number of psychological studies have been conducted to understand how individuals behave because of the Internet.

> **Skills Focus**
> Design an experiment to study how students react when they must function without the Internet or other electronic communication for three days. How will you monitor behaviour and observe reactions? How will you collect answers and what will you do with them? What do the results indicate?

North Americans are addicted to email. According to a 2010 survey by America Online (AOL), 47 percent of people claim to be hooked, 25 percent can't go three days without checking email, 60 percent check their email while on vacation, and 59 percent check email in the bathroom! Email can also cause stress. According to multiple studies, not only do we check email more often than we think we do, but also don't communicate as effectively over email, which causes stress for the sender and receiver, since lack of body language cues makes it difficult to convey emotions such as anger and humour. Sarcasm also doesn't translate well. Finally, businesses now buy smartphones or other communication devices for their employees, which makes people feel they have to answer text messages and calls even during off-work hours.

Why are people addicted to their email? Between unwanted advertisements (spam) and forwards asking us to send the email to 10 others or risk eternal bad luck, legitimate emails from our friends looking to chat are not as common. But these are the emails we hope we'll find when we log in to our inbox, and this type of interval-based reinforcement is what keeps us coming back.

VALERIE THRIVED IN AN INTERNET COMMUNITY THAT HAD NO IDEA THAT SHE WAS A CHICKEN...

↑ **FIGURE 8-22** What happens when someone enjoys his or her Internet identity more than his or her offline self?

Cyber Identity

Do you know someone who has misrepresented himself or herself on the Internet? There are many ways to express identity, and we all have different aspects of our identities that we show depending on the situation. The Internet is another space that allows for such exploration.

The Internet has changed the way we behave in that it reduces our inhibitions. The anonymity and invisibility we have online gives us a sense of disconnect from our "real-world" personality. Psychologists

> **VOICES**
> Make it thy business to know thyself, which is the most difficult lesson in the world.
> Miguel de Cervantes, novelist

refer to this loss of individuality when immersed in a group environment as **deindividuation**. Because people (incorrectly) assume that they can't be easily identified when they're online, they are more likely to post intimate details of themselves to social networks. This assumption also allows them the freedom to express themselves to others in ways they might not be willing or able to do in face-to-face situations.

deindividuation: the loss of a person's sense of individuality and personal responsibility when immersed in a group environment

POINT/COUNTERPOINT

Adolescents' Online Identities

Since social networking online is now an important aspect of communication for adolescents, it is becoming an influence on personality development. Psychologists agree that it is normal behaviour for teens to explore different aspects of their identity during their adolescent years. Now that most Canadian families have Internet access at home, teens have a new venue for such exploration. As you read through the arguments below, consider the risks and benefits to having an alternate online personality.

Trying Out New Identities Online Is Healthy	Different Online Identities Can Lead to Loss of Real Self
• The *looking-glass self* is what social scientists call the process of imitating others and getting feedback on that imitation; this process is a normal part of adolescence that helps to create a sense of self. • There is less emotional risk to trying out new ways of behaving, looking, or sounding online because the lack of face-to-face contact provides non-threatening opportunities to practise social skills. • The various online activities and groups that teens belong to, which can reach around the globe, offer a special chance to focus on specific aspects of their personality that they might not otherwise be able to develop. • Those who feel isolated or have low self-esteem in their real lives can fill a need for friendship online, perhaps with others they would never otherwise have been able to meet.	• Today's teens are the first generation born with the Internet, and it may be too soon to tell the effects it will have on personality. • Gossip, public shaming, bullying, and harassment may be taken to extremes online because of presumed anonymity by the person engaging in these behaviours. However, because these behaviours can be performed on a larger public scale, with many teens having an average of 100 to 150 social networking "friends" looking on, this type of harassment can cause a major blow to self-esteem for the person being bullied. • Problems occur when the teen's online self separates further and further from his or her core self-concept; the teen feels like an imposter, which reduces self-esteem and self-confidence. • Some Internet users become so spellbound by their online life that they spend less and less time in their real life. This online obsession can lead to an addiction that can be damaging to their real life.

QUESTIONS

1. Using the evidence above, make a hypothesis about online identities. Suggest some possible survey or interview questions to test your hypothesis.
2. Predict the impact on an individual of using different online identities in five years. Explain the reasons behind your prediction.

Psychology of Cyberbullying

Bullying behaviour is unfortunately not a new behaviour. As you learned in Chapter 6, thanks to the popularity of the Internet, bullying has expanded into cyberspace. Bullying online can happen at any time and is more difficult to see than traditional forms of bullying that often happen at school. It includes sending or posting threatening, hurtful, or embarrassing messages, getting other people to do so, and excluding someone from an online group. Posting personal or false information and spreading rumours is also a type of cyberbullying. The speedy transmission of these messages to a large number of people and the anonymity of the bullies mean that cyberbullying can be extremely traumatic for victims. A research study of youth released in 2009 indicated that 40 percent were victims of cyberbullying and 16 percent admitted to bullying others.

Psychologists believe that adolescent bullies tend to be highly emotional and have low self-control. They establish dominance and leadership in peer groups by proactively using aggression, and they tend to perceive negative intent where there was none. They are also more likely to come from homes with little parental warmth and involvement. Finally, they don't have much empathy for their peers. Research is now looking into the profile of a cyberbully. A study by Bulent Dilmac in 2009 showed that cyberbullies tend to be aggressive and show a need for attention and superiority. Previous engagement in cyberbullying was also a predictor of future cyberbullying.

Psychological Impact

Cyberbullying is still a relatively new phenomenon, and, as such, a lot of empirical research is still needed to fully understand its psychological impact. Adolescent victims are likely to report depression and lower self-esteem. There is often a decrease in academic achievement, sometimes to the point that students drop out of school. Most tragically, cyberbullying can sometimes lead to suicide. For example, in 2006 Megan Meier, a 13-year-old girl, hanged herself after she received nasty messages via social media.

Solutions?

Tanya Beran, a psychologist at the University of Calgary, studies school bullying and cyberharassment. According to her research, avoiding the Internet is not suggested as an appropriate measure against bullying because this will only cut children off from their peer group. As well, the bullying probably takes place face to face, and thus will not stop just because the victim stops going online. Instead, schools should promote responsible online behaviours for students from an early age and make sure to follow up immediately on any reported bullying. These steps are especially important as computers become more frequently used in the classroom. Other options include application software (apps) that reports breaches of terms of use (such as on Facebook) and that can link children to help lines.

❓ What efforts do you see in your school to combat cyberbullying?

FIGURE 8-23 Rachel Wade of Tampa, Florida, is currently serving a 27-year prison sentence for stabbing Sarah Lundmann to death. The incident occurred after the girls exchanged threats in texts, social networking sites, and voicemail. What insight can psychologists offer to teens, parents, and educators to stop this aggression, especially before it gets to such an extreme level of violence?

Open for Debate

School boards can take action against a student for engaging in acts of cyberbullying at home on his or her personal computer. Is this an invasion of privacy or a necessary method to deal with cyberbullying?

Influence of Social Media

In September, 2010, a 16-year-old girl was gang-raped at a party near Vancouver. The horrors of that evening continued as onlookers took photos and videos and then posted them on the Internet. Two teens were charged with distributing and producing child pornography after the photos appeared on Facebook and one person was charged with sexual assault. Police believe there are more offenders in this case who have yet to be caught. Eventually, the girl quit school because of the abuse she endured. This incident goes beyond cyberbullying to encompass serious legal and social issues. Of course, most of what we post online on social networking sites involves nonhurtful activities and interesting events in our lives. Moreover, social media provide unique opportunities to quickly connect with our friends and family, and for others to connect with us. Social media have become such important means of communication that, as of 2009, four out of five Canadians used them. Therefore, psychologists ask, How are social media affecting us?

Can You Live Without Facebook?

Think back to the experiment you created earlier for the Skills Focus on page 388: what would students do without being able to access the Internet or other electronic communication for three days? In September 2010, students and faculty at Harrisburg University of Science and Technology in Pennsylvania did something similar: they participated in an experiment where they could not go on any social media for a week. The purpose was to see how important social media are in their lives. Both during and after the ban, participants were surveyed and questioned in focus groups. The researchers discovered that 40 percent of students spent 11 to 20 hours per day using social media, and some faculty admitted to spending over 20 hours per day.

On the other hand, there were many benefits of the "media blackout." Participants spent the time they usually spent on Facebook doing other things: 21 percent did homework, 10 percent read online news, and 6 percent did more exercise. Also, 25 percent of students said they had better concentration in classes, 33 percent felt less stressed since there was no expectation to update their status or check that of others, and 10 percent reported enjoying more face-to-face conversations. One student said that the week-long ban felt like a "vacation."

> **VOICES**
> Thank you to everyone who has been there to help me through this terrible ordeal. But to the people who did not support me, who called me names, who spread lies about me—thank you because you made me much stronger than I've ever been before.
> Statement from gang-rape victim, 2011

> **More to Know...**
> Look back to the concept of the bystander effect. Why did the teens use their cell phone to record the event, but no one called 911?

> **Open for Debate**
> Is social media addictive, or are addictive personalities more likely to enjoy social media?

FIGURE 8-24 Thanks to the Internet and Facebook, virtual connections are made between millions of people all over the world. Why might this be of interest to psychologists, sociologists, and anthropologists?

? What are the ways media are a part of your life? Make a list with a friend, and then rank the items in the list in terms of impact. What is making the greatest impact on you?

The Psychology of Rumours and Gossip

Social media is an excellent way to stay in touch with friends. It can also be used to spread rumours and gossip. Gossip is social talk meant to evaluate, provide group solidarity, and give social network information. The gossip around the lunch table about who's dating whom is often accompanied by judgment and decisions about whether the pairing is appropriate, for instance. Rumours, on the other hand, involve the spread of usually inaccurate information to others. For example, after Hurricane Katrina hit New Orleans in 2005, there was a rumour that the U.S. government blew up the levees. People couldn't believe the devastation caused by the hurricane and needed an explanation for why the levees failed, even if it sounded improbable. Both rumours and gossip fulfil psychological needs.

FIGURE 8-25 What is gained by sharing gossip and spreading rumours?

Why Do We Believe Rumours?

Rumours have been around for centuries, and even though they often sound strange, people tend to believe them anyway. Why? One reason is a person's psychological motivation to make sense of an uncertain situation. According to psychologists Nicholas DiFonzo and Prashant Bordia, this motivation includes "fact-finding, relationship-enhancement, and self-enhancement" (2006). We believe rumours much of the time because we don't have the time or interest to research everything we hear, and rumours are often passed off as truth. Since we are, fundamentally, social beings, rumours are a way that we can work together to make sense of our world.

Why Do We Gossip?

Psychologists point to our need to be social to help explain why gossiping is so common, even though it's often hurtful. Sharing stories about mutual acquaintances is also one way to build relationships with others. However, if you're the subject of negative gossip, you're unlikely to see the positive side. Nigel Nicholson, an evolutionary psychologist, explains that there are three functions of gossip, which are used simultaneously: networking, influence, and social alliances. Because we are status conscious, we use networking, including gossip, to keep up to date with what is fashionable and who is at the top of the social hierarchy. Gossip can also influence others to think of us in a certain light, which either improves our status or retains it. We use the information gained from gossip to form social alliances with those we hope can provide us with a suitable place in the social hierarchy.

Interestingly, men and women both gossip, but the content differs. Since men tend to have a competitive drive, they are interested in others' status (thus the common interest in sports statistics). Women tend to tell moralistic tales about social inclusion (who's worthy of praise or criticism).

> **Skills Focus**
>
> Research an issue related to rumours and/or gossip in your school. Create a psychology poster presentation to deliver your findings.

Consumer Psychology: The Psychology of Persuasion

North Americans are inundated with advertising, so we are often on guard against marketing when we watch television or go shopping. Marketing experts know they have only a moment to convince us to keep watching their commercial. Consumer psychology uses psychological theories and approaches to understand consumer behaviour. While there are many techniques used to get you to buy products, we'll discuss a few ways psychology has contributed to getting you to open your wallet.

How Persuasion Works

According to psychologist Kevin Dutton, there is an artful psychology to how persuasion works. Its elements can be summed up by the acronym SPICE:

- **S**implicity: The brain prefers simplicity and equates it with truth, so messages should be simple.
- **P**erceived self-interest: People are interested in things that are beneficial to them, so show them how the thing will benefit them.
- **I**ncongruity: A lack of harmony or appropriateness is the basis of most humour, and making people feel good via humour helps persuade them. Incongruity also acts as a distraction, which disables the brain's neurological security system, so messages should be humorous or distracting in some way.
- **C**onfidence: People must feel sure they are making a good decision, but not pushed into it, so make them believe they are making the decision on their own.
- **E**mpathy: Communicating with someone on his or her wavelength helps the person accept a suggestion, so messages should consider a person's unique characteristics.

Of course, these techniques are not unique to marketing; they can be used by anyone who wishes to persuade someone.

> **Skills Focus**
> Select a marketing campaign or commercial that you find particularly convincing. Analyze it according to the SPICE elements.

Did You See That?

Ryerson University's Melanie Dempsey and University of Toronto's Andrew Mitchell are psychologists who came together to see if they could get participants to choose the obviously inferior of two brands of pens by using positive and negative subconscious messages. The participants viewed hundreds of product advertisements; there were 20 negative images connected to the superior pen ads and 20 positive images connected to the inferior pen ads. In a follow-up experiment, participants were presented with information showing that the superior pens were better. However, when given the choice of which pen was the best, participants tended to choose the inferior pens. Dempsey and Mitchell suggested that these choices were made because participants had been conditioned to think positively about the inferior pen in the first part of the experiment. They suggest that we make consumer decisions based on not only what we know about a product's attributes, but also subconscious information.

Duke University psychologist Gavin Fitzsimons and his team study "short brand exposures," which can include brand logos seen in passing and product placements in TV shows and video games (see Figure 8-26). The typical American sees 3000 to 10 000 brand logos a day. Since many American TV shows are shown here, it is likely that Canadians see a large number of brand logos each day as well. This technique is effective because viewers' defences are down and they aren't looking at the brand logos with a critical eye, since their brains don't even really register that they've been exposed to them. With all that exposure, do we really have any choice in the products we buy?

FIGURE 8-26 New York City's Times Square is surrounded by advertising. Do you think these ads influence passersby to buy a particular product?

REFLECT AND RESPOND

1. How would you know if a friend who enjoys spending time on the Internet was experiencing deindividuation? What would you do if you thought this were the case?
2. How do you determine whether the information you are being told is factual or a rumour? With a partner, create a list of criteria to help you decide.
3. Develop a questionnaire to help you understand the nature of cyberbullying at your school. Present your results with your class and/or the student body at school in a psychology poster presentation.

Influence of Workplace Environments

On average, Canadian adults spend one-third of their waking lives at work, so it's no wonder that psychologists are now studying ways to improve the workplace environment. Using theories and empirical research, psychologists can help improve a variety of workplace issues.

Industrial/Organizational Psychology

Industrial/organizational (I/O) psychology is a branch of applied psychology that is interested in how workers think, feel, and behave at work. Its goals are to help people feel satisfied in their work and to help organizations maximize their human resources. To accomplish these goals, I/O psychologists examine issues such as positive and negative co-worker interactions, prejudice, stress and burnout, and work–life balance. In terms of the work itself, they examine task variety, repetition, and difficulty. These psychologists can work with managers and employees to improve life at work by providing services such as conflict management workshops and leadership development programs, as well as using results of employee surveys to manage change initiatives.

Research has identified factors that contribute to positive and negative work interactions. For example, co-worker support and empowerment lead to positive feelings at the workplace, while hostility and a sense of injustice can lead to a negative perception.

> **Before You Read**
> Using a Venn diagram, compare how you behave at work or in volunteer placements with how you behave with your friends. What accounts for the differences and similarities?

FIGURE 8-27 In 2010, the Toronto Police Service (TPS) won the American Psychological Association's Psychologically Healthy Workplace Award in Ontario. The TPS had improved its health and wellness services for its employees and their families to address physical and psychological health issues.

Engineering Psychology

One specific area of applied psychology in the workplace is engineering psychology. Psychologists working in this field—sometimes called *applied experimental* or *human factors psychologists*—study and improve interactions between humans and machines. The study of these interactions includes examining communication and decision making, computer-information systems, and even energy and transportation systems. In other words, it includes most of our workplace interactions in our increasingly technological world. For example, researchers in this field might look at improving the design of medical equipment to reduce medical errors or improving traffic systems to reduce accidents. These psychologists aim to create safer, more effective, and more reliable systems in our workplaces. To do so, they need to understand the limits to human performance and the job requirements.

Open for Debate

A Facebook page is a personal expression of oneself. Many people use it to post photos, ideas, and their relationship status, and to communicate with friends. It can also be a quick way for others to get to know a person. Should employers be allowed to check social networking sites such as Facebook or MySpace to learn about potential or current employees? Why or why not?

The Right Person for the Job

Part of making a workplace run smoothly is hiring the right people. Potential employees not only need to have the appropriate skills, but also need to fit into the specific culture of the workplace. When employers are hiring, they don't always get the full picture from an interview or resumé, so they are increasingly turning to pre-employment tests. There are a range of tests that examine characteristics such as ethics, motives, personality traits, intelligence, specific aptitudes and skills, ability to work as part of a team, and reliability. Used properly, these assessments can help employers make predictions about who is the best person for the job and who will stay with the company.

While these pre-employment tests are currently not used as widely in Canada as they are in the United States, their use is on the rise. The results of personality tests illustrate their usefulness. In workplaces that use them, employees tend to stay with the company longer, customer satisfaction is increased, and absenteeism is down—all of which are results of a happier workforce.

Social Media in the Workplace

Social media have already changed the Canadian workplace. Today many workplaces accept and expect employees to use social media. Whether for communicating socially and providing some mental downtime or for getting in touch with clients, social media are being used more often because of the ease and instantaneous nature of the communication. Workplaces even educate their employees on how to use the technology and in what ways.

However, managing social media is still a challenge. For example, as of March 2010, there were 10 million Facebook users in Canada, and LinkedIn, a social media site for professionals, was adding 75 000 users each month. These social media are not only popular, but also take up a lot of our time. Email is just as time consuming. According to a 2004 study, email takes up 23 percent of the employees' day because they often use email to communicate and to track tasks. As well, typical office workers open 70 percent of their emails within 6 seconds of arrival at work, and 85 percent view their emails within 2 minutes of arrival. That's a lot of checking!

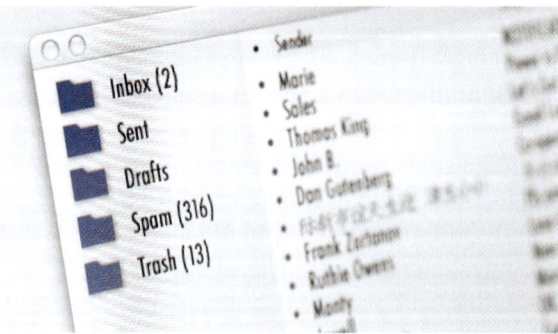

FIGURE 8-28 Email is considered a necessity in many working environments. How do you think businesses conducted their work before email became popular?

❓ Why is it important that interviews be held if a pre-employment test reveals a candidate's qualities?

Workplace Motivation

What would make you want to go to work every day and enjoy what you were doing? Employees work better when they are happy in their jobs. However, workers need different types of motivation depending on their age, according to an empirical study published in 2005. The 100 respondents of the study were followed for 5 years and each year were asked to answer a questionnaire based on motivational theories, such as Maslow's Hierarchy of Needs. Interestingly, the results showed that younger people tended to adjust to their workplace's social climate and rely on that socialization as motivation to excel. Then as workers aged, they looked to achieve self-actualization, the highest stage of Maslow's hierarchy. To do so, they sought higher positions within their profession.

Mental Health in the Workplace

When people think of mental health issues, they often forget how these can affect the workplace. As of 2002, mental health claims (mostly depression) were the fastest growing category of disability in Canada. In addition, mental health issues can lead to other health problems, and also cost the employer lost business and revenue. For example, high levels of job stress can double a person's chance of a heart attack. As employers pay more attention to mental health issues, psychologists are helping them improve workplace conditions.

Stress in the Workplace

In Canada, many researchers are examining aspects of workplace psychology. Workplace stress is one of the key problems in organizations that is being studied by Canadian researchers. According to a 2007 survey by the American Psychological Association, 74 percent of employees list work as a cause of stress. It is estimated that stress costs Canadian companies anywhere from $12 billion to $33 billion annually in lost productivity. Stress can not only decrease job performance, but also cause health problems, such as high blood pressure and cardiovascular and infectious diseases, and affect relationships with family and friends. Recent Canadian studies indicate that 25 percent of workers have high levels of work–family conflict, which increases stress. Healthy workplaces not only reduce stress, but also have better morale and atmosphere, fewer injuries, and lower absenteeism rates.

> **More to Know...**
> Look back to Chapter 2 to learn more about Maslow's Hierarchy of Needs.

FIGURE 8-29 What motivation strategy is being used in this workplace? Based on the reading above, are these workers being socialized or are they at the self-actualization stage?

REFLECT AND RESPOND

1. Use a Venn diagram to explain the similarities and differences between industrial/organizational psychology and engineering psychology.
2. Employers are increasingly using personality tests to select future employees. Using a T-chart, list the advantages and disadvantages of this approach.
3. Why should employers worry about stress in their workplace?
4. Research an employee-friendly workplace. Consider choosing one that has recently won an award for its employee programs. How does it address issues such as motivation and mental health?

IN FOCUS: Chilean Miners

On August 5, 2010, a copper and gold mine in Chile collapsed, trapping 33 Chilean miners in a compartment more than 600 metres underground. Rescuers assumed that no one had survived the collapse, so for the first 17 days, the men were completely cut off from the world and faced dwindling food and water supplies, and had to deal with the psychological effects that come with that type of isolation. Some had considered suicide and cannibalism before the drill reached them on day 17.

Communication was established through a bore hole about the size of a grapefruit. This was the only means of passing the men fresh oxygen and supplies such as hydration gels, water and food, letters from family, bibles, and even soccer videos that were sent down to them until they were rescued. Meanwhile the miners were confined to a rescue chamber about 46 square metres big—around the size of an average home's living room. What happened when they argued? How did they deal with the fear and frustration of being trapped? How would they survive and not suffer psychological consequences?

Close Quarters

It is important to note that the miners were used to working in these conditions, so the psychological effects were not as severe as they would have been if the average person had been trapped. Interestingly, the conditions in the chamber were similar to those experienced by astronauts when they live on the International Space Station. So the Chilean government quickly called NASA psychologists and doctors for advice. They immediately helped the miners establish daytime/nighttime routines that included specific exercises and team-building activities. It was important for the men to keep their spirits up to deal with the psychological ordeal. They also needed to establish roles and ways of dealing with conflict that would maintain the camaraderie they needed to survive. One of the miners took on the role of leader. Although we don't know the whole story, it seems that the men were brought together by their need to survive, rather than torn apart by it.

It's Not Over Yet

The miners were rescued after being trapped for 69 days underground (see Figure 8-30). Yet psychologists' work continued. As men were brought to the surface one by one, psychologists and psychiatrists monitored them for signs of panic but also underlined the importance for them to spend time with family. Psychologists also warned the men that they might experience insomnia, nightmares, and anxiety in the weeks or months following their rescue. However, because they survived an ordeal that few others ever have, psychologists also expected them to experience self-confidence as well as a greater appreciation of family and friends.

The miners also were faced with a new reality: they were famous. While they were trapped, journalists researched and broadcast the miners' lives to the world. Psychologists taught them how to handle their fame but expressed concern about the possible jealousy and competition for book deals and TV interviews. Although the 33 miners made a pact of silence, some have disclosed they are now suffering from PTSD. All but one experienced psychological problems such as nightmares, difficulty focusing, sadness, and depression after their rescue.

FIGURE 8-30 The rescue capsule, the "Phoenix," was just big enough for one person. Each miner was in the capsule for 15–20 minutes as he was pulled to the surface.

QUESTIONS

1. How might the miners' families help their loved ones as they adjust to normal life?
2. Research the psychological effects of the miners being trapped and their experiences after rescue.
3. What might the outcome have been had the miners not all worked together to stay alive? What does this outcome suggest about teamwork in other work environments?

YOUTH PERSPECTIVES

Ginny Elliot

The primary goal of school is to have a positive impact on students' lives. For Ginny Elliot of Fergus, Ontario, that impact came in the form of inspiration to enter the Child and Youth Worker program at the college level (see Figure 8-31).

Q: *What did you like about the Introduction to Sociology, Anthropology, and Psychology course?*

A: I found it really interesting. I enjoyed the projects like researching mental illness and the interview assignment. I got to interview a guy from Afghanistan to find out how he was adjusting to life in Canada. I also liked being introduced to the theories; now that I'm in college I appreciate knowing that I've already been introduced to theorists like Freud and Piaget. Plus we saw really cool videos that showed what we were learning.

Q: *What do you like about the Child and Youth Worker program?*

A: I like that you get a lot of placement time to practise what you're learning. It's a three-year program. Every year in the first semester, you take six or seven classes, and in the second semester, it's all placement. In the year one placement, you work in a public school, in year two, you work in a group home, and then you get to pick your placement in the third year.

Q: *Could you describe what placement is like?*

A: I'm assigned to 15 different students to work with one-on-one, but I also help in a classroom. I also job-shadow the child and youth counsellor in the school. So far, I've mainly worked with students with behavioural issues like ADHD and ADD, but I'm also trained to work with depression or if they reveal abuse I know what to do. I get to see the other side of school—I can go in the staff room and chat and work with the teachers.

FIGURE 8-31 When she's not honing her skills in a classroom environment, Ginny learns to work with children from the CYC office.

Q: *What do you hope to do when you graduate?*

A: I would like to be a child and youth counsellor (CYC) at a high school because I enjoy working more with teens than with younger kids.

Q: *What made you choose that career?*

A: I enjoyed the related courses I took in high school and was interested in psychology, plus I liked the placements available in college. They're interesting and I like working with kids. It also helps that I know someone who is a CYC, so I talked to her about it.

Q: *What advice do you have for students who are trying to figure out what they want to pursue?*

A: Don't just settle for something. Research all the programs available in both college and university to figure out the best option for you.

QUESTIONS

1. What surprised you the most about Ginny's experiences?
2. How does this course prepare you for other possible careers besides being a CYC?

CHAPTER 8 REVIEW

Knowledge and Understanding/Thinking

1. On page 370, you learned about the factors that affect conformity. Which of those factors apply to the behaviour of individuals in the following situations:
   a) being part of a crowd at a hockey game
   b) being at a school pep rally
   c) visiting elderly relatives
   d) watching a fight outside school
   e) being members in a cult
   f) being a cyberbully on Facebook

2. Describe the ingroups and outgroups at your school or in your community. Suggest ways to help these groups interact and get to know one another better.

3. Create a graphic organizer that illustrates the psychological influence of family, friends, groups, school, social media, and the workplace on an individual you know.

4. How might the branches of behavioural, developmental, and applied psychology be used to improve the workplace for employees?

5. What is the difference between being a leaders in a group and controlling a group?

Thinking/Communicating

6. What type of social science research method would be best to find out the effects of bullying in your school? Create a research plan, conduct your research, and present your findings to your peers in a psychology poster presentation. Once you complete your research, answer the following questions:
   a) What are the strengths of your research method? What were areas of concern or problems that you encountered?
   b) What do your findings signify?
   c) What further research could you suggest be done on this topic?
   d) What are the strengths and weaknesses of your research?

7. Plan an approach to deal with bullying in your school or community that includes a plan for bystanders, the bully, and the bullied.

8. Where does your personality end and behaviour begin? In other words, how do you know if something is affecting your behaviour or your personality?

9. Using a Venn diagram, compare how a developmental psychologist and a behavioural psychologist might account for parental influence on personality.

10. Should the Brown Eyes/Blue Eyes classroom experiment be conducted in schools today? Explain your reasoning. Refer to the concepts of bias and unconscious bias in your response.

Communication/Application

11. How do you think people who belong to your various socialization groups would describe you? Make a word web containing each agent of socialization (family, friends, school, media, work, religion and/or other groups). Are you the same or different when you are with each group? Why?

12. For one of the following topics, draft out a poster presentation using ideas from this chapter or other research you have completed:
    a) acculturation
    b) bystander effect
    c) conformity
    d) groupthink
    e) social isolation

13. Select four agents of socialization that have influenced your personality (you could include family, friends, school, media, work, a team, or a club). Plot a graph to show how much you think each agent of socialization influenced you at different ages of your life. Assign the *y*-axis a rating scale of 1 to 10 (10 being the most influential), and plot age 1 to your current age along the *x*-axis. Add visuals to represent each stage. Create a legend that shows each agent of socialization you will plot, along with its assigned colour.

14. Create a Web page, wiki, or model that would provide useful information about adolescents exploring identity online. Include information for those directly affected and for their friends and family. Think of your audience to help you use appropriate language and tone.

15. Suggest strategies that the government of Ontario could use to reduce or eliminate the stigma associated with mental illness in our society.

16. Write a persuasive paragraph about social networking so that someone who has never used it can understand its impact on teens in Canada.

CHAPTER 9

Sociology and Us

In this chapter, you will learn how social identity is formed in different situations by examining the factors that lead to the development of identity, including norms, social attitudes, and social networks. You will examine the key characteristics of subcultures, cults, and deviance. You will study how society is organized and examine theories that help explain social stratification, inequities, and alienation in society. Furthermore, you will study social structures and institutions and practise presenting and reporting on issues in sociology.

Chapter Expectations

By the end of this chapter, you will:
- use a sociological perspective to analyze patterns of socialization
- identify and describe the role of socialization in the psychological development of the individual
- assess how diverse personality traits shape human behaviour and interaction in a variety of environments
- compare the procedures and ethical problems of major psychological experiments in socialization
- communicate the results of research and inquiry effectively using a format appropriate to the purpose and audience
- use terms relating to sociology correctly
- demonstrate an understanding of the general research process by reflecting on and evaluating your own research process and results

Key Terms

ableism
achieved status
ageism
alienation
anomie
ascribed status
collectivist society
counterculture
cult
cultural universals
deviance
glocalization
group-based identity
individualistic society
labelling
meritocracy
personality view of behaviour
postmulticulturalism
role identity
sexual orientation
situation view of behaviour
social change
social cohesion
social fragmentation
social inequality
social institution
social integration
social mobility
social status
social stratification
strain theory of behaviour

FIGURE 9-1 Norway took the gold for women's 4 × 5 km cross-country skiing relay at the Vancouver 2010 Olympic Games. Each athlete competed as part of her team, and each team represented its country. How does this model the ways in which individuals relate to their social groups and to society as a whole?

Landmark Case Studies

Food for Thought: The Influence of Social Networks on Health

Key Theorists

Howard Becker
Peter Burke
Nicholas A. Christakis
Kingsley Davis
Emile Durkheim
Karl Marx
Robert Merton

Walter Mischel
Wilbert Moore
Richard Nisbett
Adrienne Rich
Rosalind Sydie
Melvin Tumin

Spotlight on Sociology

Joshua Bell Plays the Metro

Before You Read

What would make you stop and watch something while you were out in a public place? Why would you stop?

On Friday, January 12, 2007, a violinist performed six classical pieces at L'Enfant Plaza metro stop in Washington, DC. It was the morning rush hour, and very few of the 1097 passengers who walked by noticed the musician. Many were in too much of a rush trying to get to work.

None of the passersby knew it, but the musician was world-renowned violinist Joshua Bell, playing masterpieces of classical music on a violin worth $3.5 million. *The Washington Post* arranged the performance as an experiment. Would ordinary people recognize beautiful music and great talent in an unusual setting?

The results of the study dumbfounded even Bell. In the 45 minutes that Bell played, only seven people briefly stopped to take in the performance (see Figure 9-2). Twenty-seven people gave money, giving Bell a total of $32.17 in donations. The other 1070 people who passed through the metro that morning hurried by Bell without noticing his music. Only one person recognized the musician, and she arrived near the end of his performance.

The researchers concluded that there was no pattern, ethnic or demographic, to the people who stopped to listen to Bell's music or make a donation, with one exception. One demographic group behaved consistently: every child that walked past tried to stop and watch. Every time, a parent hurried the child along.

Reviewing the video of the performance weeks later, Bell noted that one thing surprised him. He understood why people did not stop to listen, since most of them were hurrying to get to work. But, he said, "I'm surprised at the number of people who don't pay attention at all, as if I'm invisible. Because, you know what? I'm makin' a lot of noise!" (Weingarten, 2007). In a different setting, patrons pay hundreds of dollars to hear him play, and he earns thousands of dollars for a single performance. Context and perception do matter.

QUESTIONS

1. Why do you think children consistently wanted to stop and listen while most of the adults did not?

2. Looking at the different stages of development (Erickson or Piaget), what are the developmental differences between a child and an adult?

3. What are the expectations of the people walking to the subway?

FIGURE 9-2 Joshua Bell performing at a Washington metro station. How does context affect your perception of identity?

Research and Inquiry Skills

The Washington Post experiment you read about on the previous page is an excellent example of a sociological inquiry. The researcher's objective is clear: to prove that perception of identity is dependent on context. The quantitative data is meaningful and obtained directly from observations of Bell's metro performance. The analysis and synthesis of the results are very strong. Finally, the researchers are able to draw substantial conclusions. In social science, researchers present their findings more formally, either as written reports or oral presentations. Conclusions must also be based on more than one experiment.

Writing Reports

The final stage of the sociological method of inquiry is to synthesize and present, in written or oral format, conclusive information about the research question. In the formal written report, the sociologist analyzes and interprets information presented in primary and secondary sources and evaluates the results of the data collected (through questionnaires and interviews, for example). The sociologist also synthesizes all sources of data and draws conclusions about the topic.

First, the sociologist analyzes data from primary and secondary sources by evaluating statistics, tabulating questionnaire results, and summarizing interview responses in order to make generalizations and find common themes emerging from the data collected.

Next, the sociologist interprets the results and draws conclusions about how the research compares to other studies on the topic. The sociologist explains how his or her work adds to the overall understanding of the topic and writes a formal report that introduces the topic, clearly states a hypothesis, and highlights key evidence in support of the original assumption (see Figure 9-3). Finally, the report draws conclusions and calls on other researchers to conduct further research into the issue or topic. The final product may also take the form of an oral presentation.

Activities

1. Imagine that you are writing a formal report about the Bell study. Identify the purpose of the study and its hypothesis. Outline a few key topics that would be included in the evidence section.

2. What other hypothesis could the findings of the Bell study support?

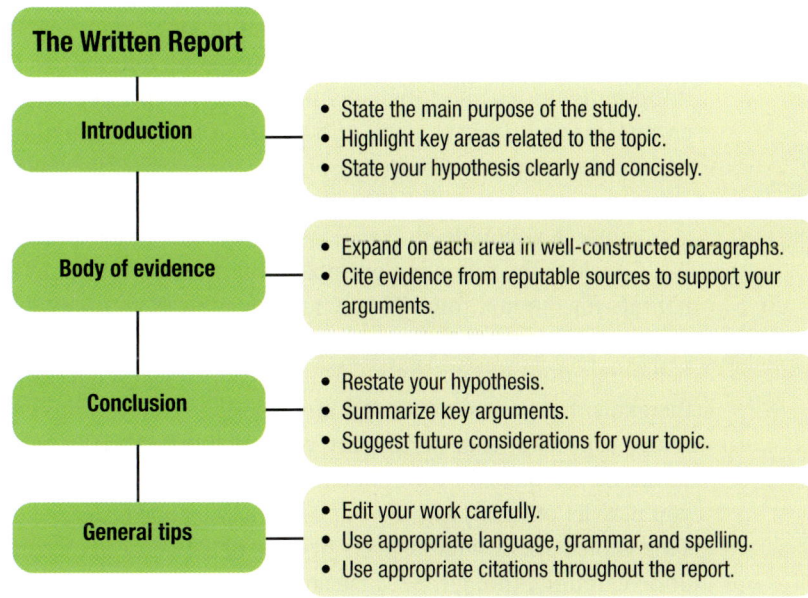

↑ **FIGURE 9-3** The parts of a written report for a sociological inquiry

Section 9.1 Identity in Different Contexts

Understanding different social contexts is one of the greatest challenges of social living. In some ways, the individual needs to be like a chameleon (see Figure 9-4). This small lizard can change its colour to adapt to its environment. The ability to adapt to a multitude of settings is very important for anyone living in the complex environment of modern society. In this section, you will examine how culture, social attitudes, and deviance influence and shape social identity and behaviour.

FIGURE 9-4 A chameleon changes colours to blend in with its environment. How do we adapt our identities to different situations?

What Determines Social Identity?

Before You Read
What do you think *social identity* means?

As you know from previous chapters, the primary agent of socialization is the family. The early learning that occurs in a family influences how an individual develops a social identity later on. As a child grows up, his or her family teaches that child about appropriate and inappropriate social behaviour for specific social gatherings and settings. The child internalizes and applies these important lessons about behaviour. Ideally, when faced with complex social circumstances, he or she will know how to read the situation and apply the appropriate response. These lessons are very culturally specific, however, since they are rooted in the family. The ability to interact in diverse situations is a valuable skill indeed.

Consider the following example. You meet your boyfriend's or girlfriend's parents for the first time. This type of meeting is certainly one of the most anxious moments that young couples experience. The parents scrutinize your behaviour during the meeting. You do your best to impress them using all the skills that your parents and life experiences have taught you. You decide which aspects of your personality you will disclose to the parents. Your identity in this case is guided by the situation or context. In other less stressful situations, you may let other aspects of your personality guide or influence your behaviour. This choice about what aspects of your personality to disclose must be done carefully, though, because sometimes the inability to choose the right response may actually set you apart from the group you want to belong to.

How might your behaviour be different if you travelled to another city to watch your favourite sports team play? What if the rival fans in that city were known to be passionate and at times violent? You could support your team by wearing a jersey and cheering loudly, or you could quietly watch the game, aware that you are surrounded by others who do not share your views. The social context determines how much of your personality you choose to show. Like the chameleon, the individual draws on many resources to function in the countless interactions that make up social life.

There are many ways to explain social identity. For example, symbolic interactionists explain social identity as the individual's perception of himself or herself reflected in other people and social groups (see Figure 9-5). Based on that reflection, the individual evaluates the circumstances and responds appropriately. Society always dictates the modes of behaviour that are most appropriate, but it is up to the individual to respond and proceed accordingly.

Social identity can be based on external factors in an individual's environment. In a given environment, the individual must weigh the costs and benefits of behaving in a certain way. In every situation, the individual decides what version of himself or herself to show. In this way, the individual builds a unique social identity.

There are many theories about the formation of social identity. In 1968, American psychologist Walter Mischel claimed that an individual's behaviour changed from encounter to encounter. This became known as the **situation view of behaviour**. Mischel's ideas conflicted with another popular theory of the period known as the **personality view of behaviour**. The personality view suggests the individual's personality leads to consistent responses that rarely change from one situation to another. American sociologist Peter Burke offers yet another persuasive theory about the formation of social identity. His identity control theory distinguishes between two types of identities an individual may possess. He calls the first **role identity**, in which an individual acts in order to fulfil the expectations of a specific role. The other he calls **group-based identity**, in which an individual is defined by belonging to a group with whom he or she shares similar values and beliefs.

FIGURE 9-5 How is your identity a reflection of society?

situation view of behaviour: the belief that the individual's behaviour changes from encounter to encounter

personality view of behaviour: the belief that the individual shows consistency in behaviour from one situation to another

role identity: the behaviour an individual displays in order to fulfil the expectations of a specific role (for example, a student)

group-based identity: the development of self-concept and identity through membership in a social group with whom the individual shares similar values and beliefs

❓ What is another analogy (other than the chameleon) for how individual behaviour is adapted to a particular social setting? How is *social identity* defined using the symbolic interactionist approach?

Norms and Social Identity

As you learned in earlier chapters, norms are the expectations about proper behaviour for a specific social group. Norms are the ground rules for living harmoniously in society. Based on these "rules" for behaviour and conduct,

Define:
Define a standard of acceptable social behaviour and exchanges between individuals in society.

Control:
Control the type of behaviours and responses individuals may have in any given social interaction or situation.

Prevent:
Prevent negative, disorganized, and offensive behaviours that threaten the established rules of society.

FIGURE 9-6 Norms help to guide social behaviour in three different ways.

Connecting Sociology to Psychology

The experiments by Milgram and Asch and the Stanford Prison experiment all highlight the dangers of following social norms too closely. Psychology is concerned with the behaviour and mental processes of an individual, whereas sociologists are concerned with the impact on the individual's social identity and on society in general when norms are followed or rejected.

---

the group is able to define positive behaviours in society as well as control and prevent negative behaviours among its members. When the individual learns and internalizes the norms of a particular society, he or she is able to develop "normal" responses to specific situations and form a healthy social identity.

Norms also help to regulate social encounters between members of a group or individuals within society. When people follow norms, their behaviour is predictable and easily recognizable to others. Norms also help alleviate any ambiguous behaviour that could lead to inefficient communication among people in society. Figure 9-6 outlines the functions that norms perform in society.

Following or Deviating from Norms

There are many benefits to following society's "code of behaviour." Sometimes, however, following norms too closely can have disadvantages. For example, an individual who tries to shape his or her conduct too closely on social norms may be at a disadvantage if he or she travels to another place where social norms are significantly different.

An individual who deviates from the norms of his or her society and chooses behaviour that opposes the "code" may be marginalized, punished, or shunned by his or her social group. To avoid this social rejection, an individual may accept a common social attitude shared by the social group even though he or she does not agree with it. In this way, social behaviour and identity may be challenged or limited by the norms of a society. Challenging norms can also lead to positive changes in society.

The undesirable consequences of following social norms too closely are highlighted in Milgram's obedience experiment (discussed in Chapter 5), Asch's conformity experiment (discussed in Chapter 8), and the Stanford Prison experiment (discussed in Chapter 5). In each case, the individuals went along with the prominent behaviour of the group even though the consequences to themselves and others were devastating.

> **REFLECT AND RESPOND**
>
> 1. Create a graphic organizer that defines *social identity* and lists elements that contribute to its development.
> 2. What are some examples of social norms in your social group (for example, your school or community)? What functions do they serve?
> 3. Using a theory of identity of your choice, explain how norms influence social identity.
> 4. Is identity the sum of an individual's choices? Or are there other, more primal influences that shape social identity?

Social Attitudes and Identity

The prevalent social attitudes of a society may have a significant influence on the development of social identity in the individual. Many of us have strong opinions about the value of education, work, religion, and family. Our ideas about each are further shaped by messages in the media about what it means to be successful and what family life should look like. Our opinions may align with society's views or stand in direct opposition to them. Depending on where an individual stands on any given issue, that person may be forced to act as others do in society even though he or she may disagree with their beliefs.

For many social issues, the individual must learn to integrate both views, perhaps even resolve the internal conflict and shape his or her response and identity accordingly. This integration is easily done on simple issues, such as recycling. Most people will put plastic bottles in recycling bins even if they do not feel strongly about recycling because social attitudes about caring for the environment have become increasingly prominent. Unfortunately, not all social attitudes are that easy to accommodate. For many, strong beliefs related to religion or cultural ideals, for example, are harder to overcome or change when they conflict with contemporary social attitudes.

> **Before You Read**
> What are social attitudes? How do you think your attitudes on social issues might be different from that of your parents' generation?

Testing Social Attitudes: Sexual Orientation

Sexual orientation may be defined as an emotional and sexual attraction toward another person. Individuals attracted to members of the opposite sex have a heterosexual orientation. In most societies around the world, heterosexual orientation is the norm. Conversely, those who experience an emotional or sexual attraction toward members of the same sex have a homosexual orientation. Although homosexuality has existed in all societies throughout history, it is less common than heterosexuality. In many cultures around the world, homosexuality is often viewed negatively. In some cases, it may even be considered deviant behaviour and be treated as a crime.

Homosexuality remains an important social topic in Canada today and has gained increasing social acceptance in the past decade. For example, in June 2003, same-sex couples were granted the right to legally marry in Ontario, and Gay Pride parades are well attended in large cities such as Toronto (see Figure 9-7).

sexual orientation: an emotional and sexual attraction toward another person

FIGURE 9-7 Many people attend Gay Pride parades as participants and observers. To what extent is this a sign that homosexuality is gaining more social acceptance?

Sexual Orientation and Adolescence

Social acceptance by one's peer group is important to developing a healthy social identity. Unfortunately, social acceptance may be problematic for lesbian, gay, bisexual, transgender, or queer (LGBTQ) people, particularly LGBTQ adolescents. Surveys by several LGBTQ advocacy groups reveal that many teens struggling with their sexuality are often the victims of abuse and bullying by their peers. For example, in their National Climate Survey on Homophobia in Canadian Schools, the LGBTQ advocacy group Egale discovered that 6 out of 10 LGBTQ students reported being verbally harassed about their sexual orientation and about 75 percent reported feeling unsafe in at least one place in the school.

As part of a 2010 initiative called the *It Gets Better Project*, several well-known Canadian personalities spread positive messages about homosexuality and adolescence through videos on YouTube (see Figure 9-8). The campaign began in response to the suicides of several teens after they were bullied for being gay. Aimed at LGBTQ teens, the videos feature a cross-section of celebrities, public figures, athletes, and average people sharing their experiences about coming out to their families and friends, and about how their lives have gotten better since high school. The goal of the campaign was to give hope to adolescents struggling with issues related to bullying, sexual orientation, and social identity that, in time, they will find acceptance in a broader social network. The *It Gets Better Project* carries important sociological implications for social identity. It is an excellent example of how social identity changes depending on the context. In this case, the determinant for social identity is age, specifically adolescence. Adolescents who experience social stigma attached to homosexuality may find that this stigma lessens as they age and pass through other life stages.

> **More to Know...**
> In Section 9.2, you will examine a number of other social groups that struggle to find a place and voice in society.

> **Connecting Sociology to Psychology**
> In psychology, the *social learning theory* states that children observe and imitate the gender-specific behaviours of other people, especially their parents. In sociology, the *gender schema theory* suggests that children also view themselves through a "gender lens." This lens is based on cultural learning of what it means to be male or female.

FIGURE 9-8 Rick Mercer is one of the prominent Canadians featured in this *It Gets Better* video. What effect do you think this project might have on an individual facing social rejection because of his or her sexuality?

REFLECT AND RESPOND

1. List four factors that affect social attitudes.
2. Describe a situation in which your attitude toward an issue was considerably altered to suit a specific social setting or group.
3. In your opinion, what role do the media play in developing social attitudes?
4. Describe the connection between age and social identity.
5. Using sexual orientation as an example, explain how social attitudes may come to define an individual's social identity and interactions.

What Is Culture?

Many social attitudes come from society's cultural beliefs. In any discussion about social identity, we must therefore consider the cultural forces at work on the individual. In sociological terms, culture refers to the ways in which social groups differentiate themselves from other groups. These differences are based on language, modes of dress, tastes in food, social etiquette, attitudes and roles, religious values, and political beliefs (see Figure 9-9). Culture is commonly accepted and learned by members of a society through the process of socialization as one generation passes along its values to the next. In this way, socialization unifies, communicates, and maintains the cultural beliefs of society. Culture is an essential tool that helps to explain behaviour among a specific group as well as toward other groups. It also helps the individual explain his or her behaviour and helps to decode the behaviour of others around him or her.

Culture influences one's perception and self-concept, so its effects are also seen on the development of social identity. Along with the specific beliefs of one's primary culture, an individual is also shaped by a number of beliefs common across all cultures. These are known as **cultural universals**. No matter where people live in the world, they share universal traits such as use of language, division of labour, and classifications based on age and gender.

Culture guides individuals in diverse social situations. We rely on our culture and all its symbols (such as language and social etiquette) to help us make appropriate decisions in a variety of situations. Our cultural beliefs and values are a source of security in circumstances that may be unfamiliar or uncomfortable. Culture can act as a navigational tool through many of life's challenging social interactions.

> What is an example of a cultural universal in your community or family? How does culture affect the development of an individual's social identity?

> **Before You Read**
> How are cultural differences expressed or celebrated in your community?

cultural universals: beliefs common across all cultures

FIGURE 9-9 Powwows are celebrations of Aboriginal culture. They often include music, dancing, costumes, crafts, and food. How is dance an example of a cultural universal?

Deviance

As you know, norms help establish behaviours that are acceptable to society. They also highlight behaviours that are unacceptable to mainstream culture. Social behaviour that does not fit with the established rules of society is typically shunned and, in extreme cases, punished. Some people even consider **deviance** as a personality flaw in individuals. For most sociologists, however, this is not an accurate definition of *deviance*. In sociology, *deviance* refers to a violation of society's norms and accepted standards.

Many generations after they were developed, Durkheim's theories still provide a solid base for defining and studying deviance. Durkheim was the first to write about **anomie** as a basis for deviance. In his definition, *anomie* refers to a state of normlessness and represents an individual's breakdown in the face of social standards and change. In other words, *anomie* means a lack

deviance: a violation of society's norms and accepted standards

anomie: a state of normlessness

IN FOCUS: Richard Nisbett: The Geography of Thought

Richard Nisbett, a researcher at the University of Michigan Institute for Social Research, studies culture and its effect on the individual's perception of the external world. He contends that cultural differences have a direct impact on how the mind works. In his words, "[W]hen you have a diverse group of people from different cultures, you get not just different beliefs about the world, but different ways of perceiving it and reasoning about it, each with its own strengths and weaknesses" (Swanbrow, 2003, para 1).

After conducting many studies, Nisbett and his colleagues from China, Korea, and Japan found that East Asians and Americans (or Westerners) had qualitatively different responses to the same situation. One experiment was designed to test whether East Asians or Westerners are more likely to attend to the whole or to a particular object within the whole. Japanese and American participants viewed an animated underwater scene similar to the image in Figure 9-10. They then reported what they had seen.

Nisbett found that American participants usually referred to a large fish in the foreground, while Japanese participants usually referred to background elements, such as the lake or the pond in which the fish were swimming. Japanese participants made 70 percent more statements about background elements than Americans. Japanese participants also made 100 percent more statements about the relationships between animate and inanimate elements, noting, for example, that "a big fish swam past some gray seaweed" (Swanbrow, 2003, para 6).

In another study, Nisbett and his researchers examined how likely Korean and American

FIGURE 9-10
What do you see in this picture?

participants were to cite situational or personality factors when predicting how people would behave in a given situation. They found that Korean participants were much more likely to base their predictions on situational factors rather than personality characteristics, compared to their American counterparts.

So what happens when Asians live in North America? According to Nisbett, Asians easily adapt to the American perspective in as little as one generation in the United States.

Nisbett did note that it would not be easy to teach one culture's tools to individuals in another culture without total immersion in that culture. To Asians, he argues, the world is complex, understandable in terms of the whole rather than parts. To the Americans, the world is a simpler place, made up of objects that can be understood without reference to context.

QUESTIONS

1. What does Nisbett's work suggest about the relationship between culture and social identity?
2. How would anthropologists respond to Nisbett's findings? What questions would they have? What kind of experiments would they perform to study these phenomena?
3. How might an individual affect the society that he or she joins?

---

of social order and structure. According to Durkheim, *deviance* is the violation of the norms established by a particular society. Deviance can be an extremely attractive alternative to the restrictive rules of society. In some cases, deviance can lead to a life of crime. And even though it is just one subset of deviance, criminal behaviour is largely studied and debated by a number of disciplines, including sociology. For our purposes, we will concentrate on the social implications of deviance and leave the crime to criminologists.

Deviance is useful to help determine how one casts aside the expected roles of society in favour of behaviour that is sometimes seen as destructive and counterproductive to living in harmony with other members of one's society (see Figure 9-11). What kind of social identity could develop as a result of deviance?

Robert Merton and Deviance

Durkheim talked about anomie as a cause for social breakdown and deviance. Similarly, American sociologist Robert Merton studied the extent to which deviance is a product of the social structure in which an individual lives. Merton claimed that deviance was the result of a few fundamental conditions in society. First, each society has a particular set of goals. Second, each society provides the means by which to achieve those goals. When individuals are unable to achieve the goals of their society, they resort to deviant behaviour to achieve them.

FIGURE 9-11 These anti-nuclear activists are demonstrating deviant behaviour. Which social norms are they violating?

In North American culture, for example, great value is placed on the individual attainment of success and wealth. At the same time, the means to achieve that success are unevenly distributed among the members of the society. Merton claimed that for those who are incapable of achieving success, the likelihood of deviant behaviour may be substantially higher. This explanation would also help explain why criminal behaviour is more likely in societies that value success and wealth. Deviance can therefore be described as the behaviours of individuals who knowingly violate the norms, cultural beliefs, and moral standards of their society. These individuals may be marginalized and often do not feel included in the creation of the norms, cultural beliefs, and moral standards of their society. Their actions shape who they are and who they aim to be in society. They purposefully stand on the fringe and accept a social identity that is different from that of their peers.

This theory is more widely known as Merton's **strain theory of behaviour**. This theory states that people are more likely to pursue illegitimate actions in order to achieve society's most valued goals when they cannot access institutionalized or other mainstream paths to the goal. For example, a student may want to be a doctor but does not have the financial resources to attend medical school. Or a person may want to be a singer or actor but is not considered attractive enough. According to the strain theory of behaviour, these individuals would be more likely to pursue their goals through illegitimate means. When society stresses the achievement of cultural goals but does not equally emphasize the means to achieve those goals and when individuals are blocked from reaching the "wealth goals" of society, these individuals may use illegal methods for attaining success. In other words, deviance is created from the very system that means to control it.

strain theory of behaviour: a belief that individuals are more likely to pursue illegitimate actions in order to achieve society's most cherished goals when they are blocked from accessing the institutionalized means to these goals

Deviance is found naturally within society. Merton believed that it was society itself that caused it. Further, Merton believed that when societal norms or socially accepted goals place pressure on the individual to conform, they force the individual to either work within the structure it has produced or become members of a deviant subculture.

> ❓ Why does Durkheim's view of deviance based on anomie still make sense today? How is deviance a form of social identity? Can you think of some popular figures in society who could be considered deviant?

Alienation

alienation:
feeling of separation or isolation

Unequal access to social rewards or privileges can lead to **alienation**. Alienation is the estrangement an individual feels from a community (see Figure 9-12). Consider the following scenario. A number of your classmates are going on a school trip to Europe, but you cannot afford to go. Your friends talk about it for weeks, and you are tired of hearing about it. They return and tell you what a great time they had and how they have all become closer because of their shared experiences. Besides the photos you are forced to look at every day at lunch, you have to hear about the trip again during Art History class when the group makes a presentation about the trip. The final straw is the reunion the group is planning after graduation. This scenario can be applied to any situation in which you were made to feel apart from the group. Although this scenario represents the microview of alienation, it can be extended to society at large.

Social inequalities, cultural differences, and alternative lifestyles have an alienating effect on the individual. When these conditions are present, the alienation takes on a psychological dimension. Social isolation may occur as well. The individual who is alienated and socially isolated comes to see himself or herself as an outsider, not reflected in the political, social, or economic activities of his or her society.

Karl Marx was one of the first theorists to write about the conflict between the different social classes. To Marx, alienation is the inability of humans to be reflected in the means of production that guide the economy. Workers feel alienated from the products they make and the economic process that brings about their production. In contrast, when workers are given some control over the modes of production and see themselves reflected in these modes, the workers feel a part of the system and see their efforts as contributing more than just labour. The workers in this case feel invested in their work because they see themselves reflected in the economic system. We can use this Marxist model to explain alienation from more than just the economic perspective; in social situations, individuals experience alienation because they do not see themselves fully reflected in the processes, structures, and institutions that govern them. Marx argued that private property and capitalism alienated workers from what they created. He broke down the issues into the following: workers do detailed work without seeing the whole; manual and mental labour are separated; they do boring, repeated tasks; and they do labour without creativity.

An individual may feel alienated from society in different ways. He or she may feel alienated from the roles, norms, and values of society. Or the individual may realize that the social institutions in place do not serve him or her effectively. In each instance, the individual feels excluded from certain social privileges and benefits that are enjoyed by others. Many sociologists think that an individual who does not see the possibility of realizing his or her goals and aspirations because of some perceived obstacle in society will withdraw from social activities, possibly becoming alienated. Quite often, the alienated individual will also reject the dominant culture and beliefs of society.

FIGURE 9-12 Alienation is a natural by-product of living in society. Are there different degrees of alienation?

> **More to Know...**
> You learned about Karl Marx and his theories in Chapter 3.

> Why might people feel alienated from society? What examples of alienation have you witnessed in your school or community?

IN FOCUS: Alienation and Mental Health

Individuals affected by mental health issues may experience social alienation. Along with the social exclusion they experience, they also have to contend with the ever-present stigma, the negative attitude or behaviour, around mental health issues in Canadian culture. Those struggling with mental health frequently describe stigma as a burden to carry along with the disorder. The Canadian Centre for Addiction and Mental Health (CAMH) is a beacon of hope for those with mental health and addiction issues. It provides valuable support and insight into the problems of stigma and alienation. CAMH's goal is to eliminate stigma and reduce alienation while providing treatment and care to its patients. It emphasizes that mental health problems are no different than other health problems that do not carry the same stigma, such as heart disease or cancer. According to CAMH:

- One person in five in Canada (over six million people) will have a mental health problem during his or her lifetime.
- One in seven Canadians aged 15 and older (about 3.5 million people) have alcohol-related problems.
- Mental health and substance use problems affect people of all ages, education and income levels, religions, and cultures and with all types of jobs.

CAMH offers advice for people to help them recognize and avoid stigmatizing people with mental health problems. According to CAMH, stigma includes:

- having fixed ideas and judgments—such as thinking that people with substance use and mental health problems are not normal or not like us, that they caused their own problems, or that they can simply get over their problems if they want to
- fearing and avoiding what we don't understand—such as excluding people with substance use and mental health problems from regular parts of life (for example, from having a job or a safe place to live)

Source: Canadian Centre for Addiction and Mental Health, 2010

QUESTIONS

1. How does CAMH define *stigma*?
2. How might reducing stigma surrounding mental illness reduce social alienation of mentally ill people and integrate them into mainstream society?

Subcultures

Mainstream culture is the common point of reference for most individuals living within a society. It represents the general attitude and beliefs of the population. Mainstream culture includes shared ideas and values about gender roles, religious beliefs, forms of government, and certain practices, including rituals, holidays, and dating and marriage practices. Sociologists need to question who defines what the mainstream culture is and what role institutions such as media play in the construction of this idea. There is always a bias in how mainstream culture is defined.

Within mainstream culture, most people are able to fulfil their needs and aspirations without issue. For others, however, mainstream culture does not adequately satisfy or reflect their individual aspirations. These individuals may seek to express themselves outside of mainstream culture in an attempt to fulfil personal and social needs. Their pursuits may lead them to join a subculture.

Connecting Sociology to Anthropology

Anthropologists and sociologists both study subcultures. An anthropologist may study how a subculture spreads to different cultures. A sociologist might investigate the impact on an individual's social identity if the subculture he or she belongs to is absorbed into the mainstream.

A subculture is a small group of people within a larger group who share a common system of values, beliefs, attitudes, behaviours, and lifestyle that are different from those of the dominant culture. Members of a subculture share a common identity and language that are often exaggerated or distorted versions of mainstream culture (Figure 9-13). It is possible to have several subcultures within a larger dominant culture and for them to coexist quite peacefully. Two elements seem to be present in any sociological discussion about subcultures. First, the term *subculture* is often used to describe deviance from the norm. Second, subcultures are prevalent among youth.

FIGURE 9-13 Cybergoth and hip hop are two examples of subcultures. What beliefs or ideas do you think they each value? How do they relate to mainstream culture?

Deviant behaviour is an observable pattern of actions that deviates from the norm. But sociologists must consider who defines this norm. Deviant behaviour often reflects a need by individuals to challenge the power structures of the community.

Many of the well-known theories about subcultures and deviance share a common theme. Time and time again, most theories cite the frustrated, socially and economically limited middle class youth as the predominant figures in subcultures and deviant behaviour. American sociologist Howard Becker used a theoretical approach known as **labelling**, or social reaction theory, to define deviant behaviour. In this approach, the key determinant for deviant behaviour is belonging to a subculture. According to the labelling theory, the individual is more likely to develop deviant behaviour if he or she participates in a subculture. This approach may appear rigid to many since it predisposes members of a subculture to deviant behaviour.

labelling:
a theoretical approach for defining deviant behaviour, in which the key determinant for deviant behaviour is belonging to a subculture

FIGURE 9-14 The vampire subculture has existed for more than a century. Do you think it is still a subculture, or has it been absorbed by the mainstream?

Most subcultures, like the ones described in the chart on the next page, are harmless outlets for creative self-expression (see Figure 9-14). Ironically, given time and exposure, a subculture may become so popular that it is absorbed by mainstream culture and adopted by many who may have originally opposed it. However, subcultures sometimes act as catalysts for more destructive or violent groups such as gangs or cults. In these instances, the members participate fully in the rituals and beliefs of their social group and reject many of society's norms in the process.

SOME WELL-KNOWN SUBCULTURES IN NORTH AMERICA	
Subculture	Origin and Description
Vampire	1890s–present: This group originated in the 1890s with publication of *Dracula* by Bram Stoker. More recently, new groups were inspired by Anne Rice's Vampire Chronicles series and Stephanie Meyer's Twilight series.
Beat generation or beatnik	1950–1960: Anti-conformist youth rejected mainstream lifestyles of the affluent society of the '50s.
Comic books/manga	1960s–present: This group reads books that rely heavily on graphic arts and are often female-centred.
Punk	1970s: Based on the growing popularity of punk rock bands, such as the Sex Pistols, young adults rejected conventional lifestyles in favour of jarring fashions and art.
Hip hop	1970s: Urban New York youth culture based on rap and music sampling developed unique dancing and modes of dress along with graffiti as artistic expression.
Trekkie	1970s: Avid *Star Trek* fans adopted mannerisms and dress of the popular TV show and its spinoffs and held conventions and gatherings to showcase their collections and lifestyle.
Cybergoth	1980s: The term *cybergoth* was coined from the role-playing video game *Dark Future*. Dress includes black clothing with hints of neon colours, as well as platform boots. This subculture derives from the cyberpunk, goth, and raver subcultures.
Extreme/alternative sports	1980s–present: Snowboarding began in the 1980s and became an Olympic sport in 1998.
Grunge	1990s: This subgenre of alternative rock was inspired by punk and heavy metal. Dress is noted for unkempt hair and clothing. Some argue grunge moved from subculture to mass culture with the success of bands such as Nirvana and Pearl Jam.

More to Know...
The heavy metal subculture is discussed in Chapter 1. The Japanese hip-hop subculture is discussed in Chapter 4.

❓ What is the role of subcultures in society? What are some benefits of belonging to a subculture? What other subcultures can you identify?

Countercultures and Cults

More extreme than subcultures are **countercultures** that stand defiantly opposed to the dominant culture of society. Countercultures reject the most prevalent values and most important norms of society and tend to replace these with extreme views on violence, family, and loyalty. Countercultures can provide positive, constructive challenges to the status quo. Examples include suffragettes and civil rights activists. Many went to jail for their beliefs and actions that were opposed to the dominant culture of the time. More recently, LGBTQ activists and anti-globalization movements are working to challenge values and norms.

counterculture: a subculture that rejects the most popular values and most important norms of society and replaces them with extreme views on violence, family, and loyalty

cult:
an extremist religious group with rigid social and moral views that oppose those of mainstream culture, typically guided by a charismatic leader

A **cult** is a type of counterculture. It is an extremist religious group whose social and moral views are rigid and whose rituals and observances are typically guided by a charismatic leader. The group's religious beliefs usually stand outside of the dominant religious beliefs held by mainstream culture. Similar to subcultures, cults seem to attract alienated, urban, male, white, middle-class youth. Most have been members of the Christian or Jewish communities, and they have attended services regularly. These individuals are drawn into the cult by its charismatic leader who identifies with their plight, may offer notions of salvation, and may prey on their vulnerability, demanding unquestioning commitment from members.

Through rituals and practices, cults blatantly shape and influence the behaviour of their followers. The individual in this social context develops a distorted and exaggerated version of his or her previous personality. Participating in the cultic rituals ensures that the individual is resocialized to fit the expectations of the group. A new reality is formed, and, as a result, a new identity is forged for the individual. The highly destructive nature of cultic beliefs sets cults apart from subcultures. Unlike most subcultures, cults may turn to violence as a means of exerting power and control over their members. Some cults may leave a path of destruction and death when they become large and influential enough.

One of the most infamous examples of cult violence occurred at the Peoples Temple Agricultural Project ("Jonestown") in Guyana in 1978. A total of 914 members of the cult, including 276 children, died by drinking a cocktail of cyanide and sedatives mixed with Kool-Aid. Cult leader Jim Jones died of a gunshot wound. In 1993, another spectacle of horror and disbelief took place in Waco, Texas. The Branch Davidian compound was set ablaze with cult leader David Koresh and his followers inside (see Figure 9-15). Koresh set the building on fire after a 51-day standoff with police. At least 70 people died in the fire. In both instances, individual needs and beliefs were surrendered to the belief system of the cult.

> How do cults alter the individual's idea of mainstream culture and society? How do cults establish social identities for their members?

↑ **FIGURE 9-15** What effects do you think cults have on mainstream society?

REFLECT AND RESPOND

1. Examine and explain how subcultures help to establish social identity for their members.
2. Create a scenario about deviance, and role-play it with different endings, depending on the theories you use.
3. Create a list of subcultures other than those mentioned in this chapter that have come into existence during your generation's time. Briefly describe their beliefs.
4. Identify the social group most susceptible to subcultures, gangs, and cults. Provide reasons for why this is the case.

Social Networks

As you learned in Chapter 6, a social network is a structure that includes individuals connected by one or more elements, such as friendship, financial affiliations, and social relationships. Through social networks, individuals exchange cultural information, social values, and knowledge. German sociologist Georg Simmel was among the first in the field to write about social networks. He claimed that society was nothing more than associations between free individuals and that for a view of society one need look no further than the patterns and forms of the associations created by its members. From the simplest of interactions, even between two people, one is able to piece together a picture of society and its values. It is hard to believe that the topic was part of sociological discussions so long ago because the term *social networking* has come to mean something entirely different since the advent of computers and cyberspace. Undoubtedly, Simmel could not have predicted that his social networks would come to reside in virtual communities all over the Internet today. Nonetheless, Simmel's views offer great insight into the various expressions of social interaction in which people engage.

Today, the discussion about social networks refers to the virtual communities that you may remember reading about in earlier chapters. Today, technology is a means of spreading messages, exchanging information, marketing and selling new products, advertising, and communicating with other members of society. The recent phenomena of social networks such as MySpace and Facebook allow an individual to alter his or her reality and identity by constructing, deconstructing, and reconstructing a new profile at will. The individual decides how others view him or her and dictates the breadth and depth of information made available to "friends" online. In real time or cyberspace, the effect of the social network on an individual's identity is undeniable. People tend to choose social networks that seem to reflect their beliefs, cultural traditions, and tastes, as well as lifestyle. Of course, like any other kind of social interaction, belonging to social networks may influence your social identity positively or negatively (see Figure 9-16).

Before You Read
How do social networks such as Facebook allow you to express your social identity? What are some other forms of social networking?

More to Know...
You learned about social networks in Chapter 6.

Open for Debate
The development of technology-based social networks is relatively recent, and more research needs to be done to understand the sociological impact. How do you think social networking affects socialization? What research method would you use to investigate this topic?

FIGURE 9-16 What you post online can have real consequences. How do your social networks today affect your life?

Signs of the social networking times.

Landmark Case Study

Food for Thought: The Influence of Social Networks on Health

In a landmark study, Nicholas A. Christakis of Harvard Medical School studied more than 12 000 people over 32 years and discovered that social networks strongly influence an individual's chances of gaining weight. Christakis's work, which is hailed as innovative and brilliant, shows that there is a causal relationship between one's belonging to social networks in which members are obese and becoming obese oneself. In other words, belonging to social networks in which members are obese causes obesity in an individual. In fact, it is the first study to explore links between social networks and any chronic condition.

Described by Christakis as a "social contagion," obesity spreads from one member of a social network to another, beginning with spouses and making its way to friends. The study suggests that when one person in a social network is obese, it becomes more socially acceptable for other members of the social network to gain weight as well. These new social norms can spread quickly. As Christakis explains:

▲ **FIGURE 9-17** The friends with whom you choose to have dinner can influence more than just the conversation. Do you think your social networks are affecting your health?

> *What spreads is an idea. As people around you gain weight, your attitudes about what constitutes an acceptable body size changes, and you might follow suit and emulate that body size.... It may cross some kind of threshold, and you can see an epidemic take off. Once it starts, it's hard to stop it. It can spread like wildfire.* (Stein, 2007, para 7)

The researchers involved in the study stressed that their results do not suggest that people should end relationships with members of their social networks who are obese or have gained weight, or that they should otherwise stigmatize obese people. The researchers noted that close friendships have many positive health effects. Rather, the results of the study suggest that forming relationships with people who have healthy lifestyles may have a positive effect on an individual's health. See Figure 9-17.

Because, as Christakis explains, people tend to emulate others who resemble them, social networks can influence an individual's physical well-being as well as his or her social identity.

QUESTIONS

1. According to Christakis's study, how are social networks linked to health and lifestyle?
2. How do social networks influence behaviour and establish social identity among members of a group?
3. Do Christakis's findings accurately describe your social network?

REFLECT AND RESPOND

1. Does the acceptance of subcultures lead to greater acceptance of deviant behaviours? What effect does the acceptance of subcultures have on social norms?
2. How are globalization, anomie, and the Internet connected from a sociological perspective?

The Global Identity

If the world were a village of 100 people, there would be:

60 Asians,

14 Africans,

12 Europeans,

8 people from Central and South America, Mexico, and the Caribbean,

5 from the United States and Canada, and

1 person from Australia or New Zealand.

82 would be non-white; 18 white.

(Sustainability Institute, 2005)

> **Before You Read**
>
> Can your social identity be adapted to life in another part of the world?

With the advent of technology and easier travel to remote locations, developments and events that occur outside of an individual's culture are as likely to influence behaviour as local events do. Perhaps the most infamous events to demonstrate the impact of a global culture on the individual would be the terrorist attacks on New York and Washington, DC, on September 11, 2001. These events changed the sociological landscape as drastically as they changed world culture. For example, travel restrictions have made flying more challenging, limiting what can be taken on a flight. For this reason, the powerful effect of globalization must be considered in any discussion about social identity. As you learned in Chapter 4, globalization is the integration of government policies, cultures, social movements, and financial markets on a worldwide scale affecting countries and cultures around the world. Society is not limited by geographic borders.

Globalization has broadened the scope of sociology, and sociology has brought global culture to the individual. Globalization as a framework naturally entails a macro-approach to society and social behaviour. This framework therefore threatens to overshadow the valuable micro-approach.

↑ **FIGURE 9-18** Technology and travel have made world cultures more accessible today. How does this view of the world support or challenge your view of the world?

A new way of viewing the social world, large and small, has developed called **glocalization**. This concept was developed to help alleviate the strain between the macro- and micro-approaches to sociology. Glocalization is simply the practice of addressing global issues by taking local action. For instance, companies and individuals can buy fair-trade coffee or chocolate. The slogan that best represents proponents of glocalization, also known as *glocals*, is "think globally, act locally." Today, glocalization helps to explain a number of different social phenomena across many different cultures.

glocalization: a way of thinking globally about a group's interests but acting locally

> ❓ What other examples of glocalization can you suggest to describe your community or experience?

IN FOCUS

Think Globally, Act Locally: Fair Trade

Globalization has opened up world markets, but some people argue that it allows the farmers and artisans who produce some of the products sold to be exploited, especially those in less industrialized countries. Fair Trade is a trade model that benefits these marginalized producers. It also benefits consumers by helping them make informed choices about the products they buy.

You may have seen the Fair Trade logo on products such as coffee, chocolate, sugar, or clothing (see Figure 9-19). Products that carry these logos have been certified by Fairtrade Canada.

FIGURE 9-19 Have you seen this Fair Trade logo on products? Did you know what it meant?

The certification process ensures that producers of goods and the companies that buy and distribute those goods meet minimum social, environmental, and economic standards. These standards encourage social and economic development and help make the producers sustainable, both environmentally and economically.

For example, Fair Trade certification ensures that producers are paid a fair price for their goods. Coffee is one product that many Canadians buy. Canadians drink about 40 million cups of coffee each day! In the traditional economic model, out of every dollar that Canadians spend on coffee, producers are paid just $0.11. Under the Fair Trade model, producers are paid $0.28 (see Figure 9-20). Workers must also be paid a fair wage. They must work in safe environments and be able to join trade unions. Child labour and forced labour are not permitted.

Along with the Fair Trade price, producers also receive a premium, which is an amount of money that goes into a fund shared by producers and workers. Decisions about how the fund is used must be made democratically. It is often used for local development, such as building wells that provide clean water or expanding farms to create more jobs.

Although Fair Trade has many social implications, it is also an important environmental initiative. Producers must limit their use of agricultural chemicals and manage their water and energy use. They must reduce, reuse, recycle, and compost waste and manage the soil properly.

FIGURE 9-20 A worker picking coffee cherries on a Fair Trade certified farm in Nicaragua. The farm is part of a cooperative that has used the Fair Trade premium to improve local roads and build a new school.

QUESTIONS

1. Explain why Fair Trade is a good example of glocalization.
2. How do you think the environmental standards of the Fair Trade program support social sustainability? Economic sustainability?
3. Describe another consumer decision that could have global impact.

REFLECT AND RESPOND

1. Describe how technology has contributed to globalization. Use examples.
2. What do you think all cultures have in common?

Canadian Social Structures and Institutions

Section 9.2

Imagine standing on the top floor of a tall building in a busy city. What would you see if you looked out the window at the bustling cityscape below? You would likely see pedestrians coming and going and traffic. Sociologists looking at the city from the same vantage point would see an entirely different view. They would see emerging patterns of social activity in the streets. Now imagine standing in the lobby of the same building. From this perspective, you would likely see people hurrying to one place or another. Sociologists might make observations about the people's distinct patterns of behaviour. Finally, stepping onto the sidewalk, you would find yourself immersed in busy urban life. Sociologists would recognize examples of social inequities that keep some of the people from achieving their full potential in society. Viewing individuals from the homeless person to the well-dressed executive, sociologists would be able to distinguish the roles and expectations placed on each by society and would see society's structure and institutions in action. In this section, you too will examine the forces at work in society from its institutions, its stratification of groups, and the cultural currents.

Social Structures and Organization

When sociologists study how a particular society is organized, they seriously consider the influence of cultural beliefs. As you discovered in Section 9.1, culture is an important factor influencing how members of a group interact. Sociologists also consider cultural factors as they map out how roles and various resources are made available to society's members. Think about Canadian society for a moment. How easy is it to get a promotion or to move from one role to another in social groups? The ease with which an individual moves from one role to the next depends largely on the beliefs held by the society, as well as the institutions in place to facilitate the move (see Figure 9-21). In society, as in most groups, you will take on different roles and achieve different statuses. Your status determines what rights and responsibilities you will enjoy. Not every society creates the most favourable conditions for its members to advance. Societies are often defined by their economic activity and their political beliefs. These classifications are useful to the sociologist as well.

Before You Read
What does social status mean to you?

"Actually, Lou, I think it was more than just my being in the right place at the right time. I think it was my being the right race, the right religion, the right sex, the right socioeconomic group, having the right accent, the right clothes, going to the right schools..."

FIGURE 9-21 What does this cartoon suggest about the structure and organization of society?

Collectivist and Individualistic Societies

collectivist society: a community in which the group is more important than its individual members, so individual needs are secondary to collective thought and action

individualistic society: a community based on the belief that individual rights and the freedom of the individual to pursue his or her own happiness are more important than the interests of the group

Collectivist and **individualistic societies** have several defining features. Less industrialized countries tend to be collectivist societies, whereas more industrialized countries tend to be individualistic societies.

In collectivist societies, the individual commonly interacts with specific members of a religious or ethnic group for social and economic reasons. Since social structures tend to be more segregated in this type of society, individuals have fewer interactions with people from different groups. All the time spent together in communal tasks allows individuals to feel more involved and attached to members of their group (see Figure 9-22).

In individualistic societies, the individual has various social and economic interactions with a wide range of groups. The social structure in this society is integrated, which means individuals are likely to meet and deal with a number of widely diverging groups. Individuals find it easy to shift frequently from one group to another and can feel loyalty to a variety of groups. What follows is a brief look at the fundamental differences between the two social models.

Figure 9-23 summarizes the characteristics of collectivist and individualistic societies. As you can see, each society views and values relationships differently. The more collectivist a particular culture is, the more social relationships matter. In an individualistic society, on the other hand, relationships are important but do not represent a primary concern for an individual in that society. For our purposes, assume that Western Europe and North America are individualistic societies while Asian countries, such as Japan and China, are collectivist in nature.

FIGURE 9-22 Japan is an example of an industrialized country that is a collectivist society. How might the school these students attend be different from yours?

FIGURE 9-23 Collectivist and individualistic societies have distinct features.

Collective Society	Individualistic Society
Members are interdependent on one another.	Members are guided by a personal definition of self. Individual characteristics are valued and expressed among the group.
Values include belonging, modesty, conformity, uniformity, harmony, and cooperation.	Values include autonomy, competition, independence, freedom, and assertiveness.
Social behaviour is guided by norms, obligations, and duties.	Social behaviour is guided by personal attitudes, needs, and rights.
The individual's personal and communal goals are very similar.	The individual's personal and communal goals are not neccesarily the same.

REFLECT AND RESPOND

1. Identify some of the underlying beliefs of collectivist societies and individualistic societies.

2. Look at Figure 9-23 and examine the role played by the individual in each society. List some benefits of living in such a system.

Multiculturalism

Canada is an individualistic society, but we have long opened our door to immigrants from collectivist societies. As a result, most Canadians have learned to accept a number of different values from both social models and have managed to live in relative harmony. The reason for this success lies in our policy of multiculturalism.

Multiculturalism is the political and social belief that ethnic and cultural diversity is the ideal (see Figure 9-24). As you learned in Chapter 7, the fundamental beliefs underlying multiculturalism are equality and mutual respect for all of society's ethnic or cultural groups. In Canada, multiculturalism has been a federal policy since 1971. The *Canadian Multiculturalism Act* (1985) sets forth the government's policy to recognize all Canadians as full and equal participants in Canadian society. As such, we are asked to practise tolerance and acceptance toward newly arriving immigrants to Canada.

In sociological terms, the policy of multiculturalism is at the heart of an interesting debate about social equality and what it means to be totally inclusive. To many who study society, policies such as multiculturalism tend to foster more **social cohesion**, a way of integrating economic and social policies in order to allow citizens to easily interact with one another. Social cohesion is an ongoing process in Canada. The goal is to eliminate inequality and social challenges that some groups experience in society. Too many challenges and inequalities lead to **social fragmentation**, the failure of society to fully integrate minority groups into the mainstream culture. Fragmentation forces some groups to see themselves as separate entities within society who are not meant to enjoy the same privileges as others do. This view will no doubt lead to the disintegration of norms that govern social behaviour and relationships.

While social cohesion remains the ideal, at least from the point of view of mainstream culture, societies such as Canada are happy to bring about **social integration** for their most vulnerable groups. Social integration refers to the process by which minority groups are brought into the mainstream culture and are able to enjoy the same rights, opportunities, and services available to the majority. However, some minority groups are not able to experience social integration or social cohesion.

? What are some examples of social cohesion and social fragmentation? How does multiculturalism lead to social integration? Should tolerance and acceptance be concepts included in multiculturalism?

FIGURE 9-24 What does a multicultural society look like to you?

Before You Read
What does it mean to live in a multicultural society?

More to Know...
Multiculturalism in Canada was discussed from an anthropological perspective in Chapter 7.

social cohesion: a way of integrating economic and social policies in order to allow citizens to easily interact with one another

social fragmentation: the failure of society to fully integrate minority groups into the mainstream culture

social integration: the process by which minority groups are brought into the mainstream culture and are able to enjoy the same rights, opportunities, and services available to the majority

Postmulticulturalism

Over the past several decades, Canadian and foreign sociologists have been supportive of the cultural and ethnic diversity that Canada boasts and have praised the official multiculturalism policy. Support for multiculturalism among Canadians increased over six years: 85 percent of Canadians agreed that multiculturalism is important to Canadian identity in 2003 compared to 74 percent in 1997 (Kymlicka, 2010).

Most Canadians would say that multiculturalism in Canada is working well. However, there are some, and their numbers are growing, who would argue that multiculturalism is no longer feasible given the events of the last decade. Certainly the events of September 11, 2001, have had a huge impact. Many social scientists have studied these events and the resulting new modes of social behaviour.

The emerging belief among a number of sociologists is that multiculturalism actually leads to greater fragmentation than cohesion in society. This view states that in multicultural nations, such as Canada, ethnic minorities are made to feel marginalized. They come to occupy some of the lowest positions in Canadian society since the unequal distribution of power here makes their social advancement impossible (see Figure 9-25). From 1980 to 2005, the income of the bottom 20 percent of income earners decreased 20.6 percent, and the income of the top 20 percent of income earners increased 16.4 percent. Put another way, the rich got richer and the poor got poorer. The argument against multiculturalism also states that multiculturalism emphasizes differences instead of eliminating them. Instead of giving ethnic minorities the tools to integrate into society, multiculturalism turns a spotlight on their differences.

In the post–9/11 world, some sociologists, such as Lloyd Wong, have come to accept that we are in a postmulticultural world. **Postmulticulturalism** suggests that multicultural policies are only segregating, rather than integrating, diverse racial, ethnic, and religious groups. According to this view, governments and societies should be developing different methods for integrating immigrants into our society, using new models that will bring about social cohesion, promote assimilation, and encourage a common identity.

postmulticulturalism: the view that new models are needed to bring about social cohesion

FIGURE 9-25 Social fragmentation leads to a society where not all people have equal access to all positions or jobs. What examples of social fragmentation can you identify in your community?

Our Home and Native Land

The Canadian way of life is complex. Consider the ethnic diversity and the challenges that might occur when trying to accommodate so many different religious expressions, political beliefs, and family structures into one unified identity for our nation. It would seem that we have our work cut out for us, and yet we manage, for the most part, to get along surprisingly well (see Figure 9-26). In spite of all of the challenges, some sociologists believe that multiculturalism reflects an optimistic view of society. Where else can you find neighbourhoods in which Christmas and Eid are celebrated equally? Or a community in which one can find a mosque down the block from a temple or church?

FIGURE 9-26 These volunteers from the Islamic Foundation of Toronto worked with the Darchei Noam synagogue to support a local homeless youth shelter. To what extent does this illustrate social cohesion?

> ❓ How does Canada's policy of multiculturalism benefit all Canadians? What are its limitations?

The Case of Hérouxville, Quebec

The small town of Hérouxville northeast of Montreal, with few immigrants, drew national and international attention when it created a declaration of social norms for all its inhabitants and new immigrants to follow. The town's officials and mayor have been very vocal about their policy and have come under fire by a number of ethnic groups. Nonetheless, they see the declaration as a positive step in preserving their community's long-held traditions.

According to the official Hérouxville blog, the policy was created to help new residents integrate into Hérouxville more easily. The social norms are based on the traditions of long-time residents. The blog advises new residents that "the lifestyle that they left behind in their birth country cannot be brought here with them and they ... have to adapt to their new social identity" (Municipalité Hérouxville, 2010). For example, the official policy is that schools should be a place where religious influences are not present, except for Christmas decorations or Christmas carols, if desired.

Open for Debate

Issues related to multiculturalism make headlines in Canada regularly. For example, in Montreal, men were banned from prenatal classes at one community centre to accommodate Muslim, Sikh, and Hindu women. And in Alberta, a court case ensued after a decision to allow the Hutterite group the right to obtain photo-free driver's licences.

REFLECT AND RESPOND

1. Describe how multiculturalism might lead to social fragmentation instead of social cohesion.
2. Imagine that you have been asked to address a group of newly arrived immigrants to Canada. What might you say about the policy of multiculturalism in this country? What would you say about living in an individualistic society?
3. Choose one of the news stories from the Open for Debate box above, and explain how it might be considered postmulticultural.

Skills Focus

Draft an outline for a formal report about the advantages and disadvantages of being schooled in Hérouxville as an immigrant. Be sure to describe evidence that supports your thesis.

Social Stratification

Before You Read
Another word for *strata* is *layer*, so *stratification* can also mean *layering*. How might the term *stratification* apply to society?

Some social relationships are based on privileges held by one group and denied to another. One way to explain the inequitable relationships is through the analogy of a social event in which a buffet dinner is served. All the guests have been invited to participate, but some are given an earlier time on the invitation and are therefore able to choose from a variety of dishes. Those arriving later to the dinner may, in fact, have fewer choices than the people from the first group even though they are attending the same event and seated next to one another. In the same way, each society is the primary stakeholder of all of its resources. It acts much like the hosts of the buffet mentioned above. Society decides what resources are offered and to whom. It is clear from this example that not everyone has access to the same resources, and unfortunately the resources are not always equally distributed.

Historically, in North American society, only the most privileged individuals actually enjoyed all the available power and prestige. Although there has been change, there is still a fair amount of **social stratification** in the United States and Canada. The richest Canadians are the Thomson family with over $23 billion. The richest 1 percent make over $405 000 a year, while a single person on welfare received just over $16 000 in Ontario, well below the poverty line. Social stratification refers to the institutional and social processes that define certain types of occupations and goods as socially desirable. These social elements are given great value and are governed by strict rules for how they are distributed across various individuals and groups. So, in such a system, inequality is sure to develop. In other words, a distinct class, or strata, of people holds the fundamental means by which to attain power and prestige in society. The remainder of individuals struggle to access the resources their society has to offer. Social stratification has been widely analyzed and discussed by all sociological schools of thought, including the conflict approach. You may remember Marx's view about this very issue in Chapter 3. Figure 9-27 summarizes how the three sociological schools of thought explain social stratification and inequality.

social stratification: the institutional and social processes that define certain types of occupations and goods as socially desirable

VOICES
The repossession by women of our bodies will bring far more essential change to human society than the seizing of the means of production by workers.
Adrienne Rich, Sociologist and poet

Functionalism:
Stratification matches the most qualified people to the most important positions in society and it assures that those individuals are rewarded (i.e., financially). Inequality enters into the discussion because some jobs are more valued than others in society.

Conflict Theory:
Inequality exists because some people are willing to exploit others for their personal gain. According to Marx, stratification uses force rather than voluntary participation to achieve its goal. Marx also claimed that inequality occurs when the less powerful class adopts the ideas of the dominant class.

Symbolic Interactionism:
Children are socialized to believe that a person's social class is the result of talent and effort. Personal attributes are assigned to the hard-working individual who has achieved success and to the unmotivated individual who does not get ahead in life. Judgments are also made about an individual's self-esteem (higher classes have positive self-esteem while lower classes may be suffering from low self-esteem).

↑ **FIGURE 9-27** The theory of social stratification explained by sociological schools of thought

Social Status

Regardless of the social structure, an individual will try to achieve goals believed to be possible given his or her talents, education, and skills. Sometimes, however, those attributes are not enough. As you learned earlier, society defines which skills and talents are more important than others. For example, some skills are prized because they are uncommon. In this way, society stratifies its members. You also know that there are many different types of stratification, such as those based on occupation and education. Another way to distinguish between members of a society is to classify them based on their **social status**. Social status refers to the importance of the position a person holds in society. Individuals can occupy a position of high social status, one of low social status, or somewhere in between. There are two types of social status: achieved and ascribed.

Achieved and Ascribed Status

As Canadians, we live in a society that relies on social status as a means of measuring a person's personal and social success. Think of all the things that seem to matter in a person's life, such as education, occupation, and marital status. These are all examples of **achieved status**. What happens when someone does not attain the highest level of education available or chooses not to marry? How will that affect his or her social status? More important, what would be the result of a system that bases its notions of success on **ascribed status** only, the traits we inherit at birth, such as race, sex, ethnicity, and wealth? For many sociologists, this system would be problematic because it would suggest that a person's future status is determined at birth. In other words, unless you were born into a wealthy family with direct links to certain educational and occupational prospects, you would not succeed in society. To some extent, Canadian social status does depend on ascribed status, even though we often like to assume it is based on achieved status. Sociologists study the ways in which a given society determines social status and determine the likelihood and nature of stratification that will occur as a result. They also study the ability and success rate for an individual to move from one level of social status to another (see Figure 9-28).

social status:
the importance of the position a person holds in society

achieved status:
the position that an individual holds in society based on his or her accomplishment of a particular task or role

ascribed status:
the position that an individual holds in society that is determined at birth and over which he or she has no control

Acheived
refers to a status that the individual earns, based on his or her ability to accomplish a particular task or role he or she can perform well (e.g., profession, education).

Ascribed
refers to a status that is determined at birth and over which the individual has no control (e.g., gender, race).

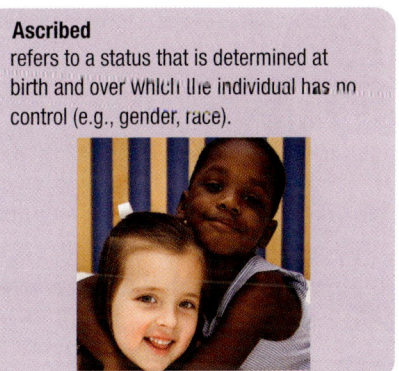

↑ **FIGURE 9-28** To what extent does an individual's social status in Canada depend on ascribed status or on achieved status?

Social Mobility

social mobility: the process by which people change their status in a community

Social stratification seems to present a pessimistic view of society, in which our life course is set out at birth. In such a system, is it even possible to change the circumstances and be motivated enough to try to achieve and attain a different social status? Despite the inequality that social stratification presents, the desire to achieve a higher status is a strong force among individuals of any society. The process undertaken by individuals, families, and other social groups in order to move up or down the social ladder is called **social mobility** (see Figure 9-29). Some sociologists would argue that social mobility is possible. It is more likely in individualistic societies than collectivist societies and is a driving force behind human motivation in any social group.

A 1945 study by two American sociologists, Kingsley Davis and Wilbert Moore, remains an important commentary on social stratification. The study argued that all societies aim to match the most capable people to the important jobs. This model identified two criteria that determine the status of a position: functional importance and scarcity of talent or skill. For example, the positions of Supreme Court judge and prime minister are associated with privilege and prestige. The individuals who can perform the tasks required for these positions have demonstrated abilities that the general population cannot easily attain. The candidates for these positions must have been part of a privileged and prestigious group. They would have attended the best schools and come from prosperous families. As a result, these jobs draw from a small pool of individuals. Under this system, there is unequal access to positions of high authority and prestige. Davis and Moore concluded that societies use social stratification to ensure that important positions are filled by the most qualified individuals.

There are many criticisms of Davis and Moore's approach to social stratification. For example, sociologist Melvin Tumin disagreed that the importance of a job could always be measured by how much money or prestige it involved. Tumin argued that if Davis and Moore were right, all societies would be **meritocracies**. In a meritocracy, ability alone would determine who went to university and what jobs people had. Tumin's research, however, concluded that gender and family income were more important predictors of people's jobs than ability. He also identified other motivations for work other than money or prestige, such as joy and pride in artisanship.

FIGURE 9-29 Oprah Winfrey was born into poverty but is now one of the richest people in the world. She gives away millions of dollars each year, some to this school in South Africa. What are some possible reasons for her generosity?

meritocracy: a social system in which positions are given to people according to individual ability or worth

REFLECT AND RESPOND

1. What does it mean for a social system to be based on achieved status? On ascribed status? Use examples of each to explain.
2. Summarize the functionalist, symbolic interactionist, and conflict theory views of social stratification. Which do you find most convincing? Why?
3. Is social mobility possible in Canada? What factors make social mobility easier? More difficult?
4. Why might Davis and Moore's theory of social stratification be considered controversial or elitist?

Social Inequality

One way sociologists account for the differences in a society's population is to study the inequality that exists. At the most basic level, and in most cultures around the world, individuals are likely to experience inequitable conditions at some point in their lives. Sociologists define **social inequality** as the inability of some people and the success of others to attain access to the privileges, rewards, or assets of society. Social inequality exists for circumstances of ethnicity, race, gender, ability, age, and income (see Figure 9-30). In Section 9.1, you read about sexual orientation and the discrimination that some teens face as a result of their sexuality. That type of discrimination, too, is a form of social inequality if it means that an LGBTQ person is refused work or denied certain privileges enjoyed by the mainstream heterosexual community.

As is the case in other complex societies, in Canada we cannot distinguish a single source of inequality. It seems as though the more sophisticated the culture is, the more ways its members are divided and classified. There are many ways in which a person may come to experience inequality from his or her peers. The chart below describes some conditions that create social inequality.

> **Before You Read**
> Have you ever felt as though you were being treated unfairly or denied a certain privilege because of your age, gender, race, or religion?

social inequality: the inability of some people and the success of others to attain access to the privileges, rewards, or assets of society

FIGURE 9-30
Homelessness is a challenge in large urban centres and represents a real social inequality in Canadian society. What other examples of social inequality exist in your community?

> **VOICES**
> A novel theoretical development in recent years is the analysis of the consequences of stereotyped reasoning or statistical discrimination.... This analysis suggests that the *beliefs* of employers, teachers, and other influential groups that minority members are less productive *can* be self-fulfilling, for these beliefs may cause minorities to underinvest in education, training, and work skills, such as punctuality. The underinvestment does make them less productive.
> Gary Becker, Nobel Prize–winning economist

CONDITIONS FOR SOCIAL INEQUALITY	
Characteristic	Explanation
wealth	an individual's family assets and material possessions that result in social respect and power in society
occupation	the level of prestige that is attached to a profession or job and the possibility of social mobility that the job facilitates
personal credentials	belonging to influential groups or organizations that create positive social opportunities and lead to increased social status
postsecondary education	the ability to complete a degree that will lead to elite roles and prestige in areas of business or academics

The "isms" in Sociology

To place value and distinguish groups based on the characteristics of ability, age, gender, race, and social class also create social distinctions known as **ableism**, **ageism**, sexism, racism, and classism. The chart below defines and gives examples of each.

ableism: discrimination based on assumptions about a person's ability or disability

ageism: discrimination against individuals or groups because of their age

Open for Debate

A young woman fired from her job at Citibank claimed she was fired because employers said she was too attractive and wore clothing that was too distracting to her co-workers. Citibank cites incompetence as the reason for her dismissal. The case is going to trial. Based on this information, do you think this woman's dismissal may be an example of sexism? Give reasons to support your answer.

CHARACTERISTICS OF THE "ISMS" IN SOCIOLOGY

Condition	Definition	Examples
Ableism	Discrimination or social prejudice based on assumptions about people with physical disabilities; the assumption that able-bodied is the norm	• A building has stairs but no wheelchair ramp for access. • Transit systems do not have access for wheelchairs. • A visually impaired student cannot access text resources on a field trip.
Ageism	Discrimination against individuals or groups based on their age. It affects all life stages, from young to old, but tends to affect the young and elderly more than the middle-aged.	• An elderly person is talked down to and assumed to know nothing about new technology. • A teenager is subjected to a body search for suspected shoplifting even though he was nowhere near the store.
Sexism	Individual or institutionalized discrimination based on gender	• A woman earns less than a man for doing the same job. • A man is looked down upon because he stays home and cares for his children. • An older, more experienced woman is passed up for a promotion. A young man gets the position instead.
Racism	An attribution of inferiority to a particular racial group and the use of the principle to propagate and justify the unequal treatment of this group (individual direct, subconscious indirect, and institutional)	• Viola Desmond, a 32-year-old, black, middle-class woman was wrongly convicted and fined for sitting in the white section of a segregated theatre in Nova Scotia in 1946. • Police do not respond to reports of a missing Aboriginal woman in British Columbia.
Classism	Discrimination based on social class; attitudes and policies that tend to benefit the upper class and exclude lower classes	• A school expects students to pay in order to participate in a field trip. • A student from a wealthy family is rejected by his peers, who assume he is selfish and greedy. • A family is seated toward the back of a restaurant because they do not fit in with the upscale patrons of the restaurant.

THE LANGUAGE OF SOCIAL SCIENCES

The Gini Coefficient

Italian statistician Corrado Gini created the *Gini coefficient*, the most commonly used measure of income inequality. It calculates the extent to which the distribution of income among individuals within a country deviates from a perfectly equal distribution. A Gini coefficient of 0 represents perfect equality; that is, every person in the society has the same amount of income. A Gini coefficient of 1 represents perfect inequality; that is, one person has all the income and the rest of the society has none.

In the mid-2000s, Canada's Gini coefficient was 0.317, higher than it was in the mid-1990s.

In the mid-2000s, Denmark ranked first out of 17 peer countries with a Gini coefficient of 0.232. Sweden, Austria, Finland, France, Belgium, the Netherlands, Switzerland, Norway, Germany, and Australia also ranked higher than Canada. Japan, Ireland, the United Kingdom, Italy, and the United States ranked lower than Canada. The United States had the highest Gini coefficient: 0.381.

QUESTIONS

1. What impact does income inequality have on social stratification?

IN FOCUS — Feminist Theory

Women were basically invisible in sociology until the advent of second-wave feminism in the 1960s. Feminist criticisms of classical sociology included the following points:

- Women are ignored in classical sociology.
- Definitions and models of sociology exclude women's actions.
- Marx's analysis of class and class struggle has little to do with women's experiences.
- The biological differences between men and women are ignored.
- Class analysis is part of the early study of difference, but gender, race, and ethnic inequalities are disregarded.

Canadian sociologist Rosalind Sydie noted that women were traditionally viewed as being associated with nature or biology, while men were considered to be more rational. Many sociological models were based on social explanations of society, culture, economy, and politics, but biology was used to explain women's roles in the household, family, marriage, and society.

The United Nations Decade of Women began in 1976, and the idea of a global "sisterhood" was challenged because many white, privileged, Western women were considered to benefit from the advantages of their male counterparts.

As the second-wave feminists continued to challenge assumptions of gender and sexuality, Adrienne Rich (1980) claimed that heterosexuality, like motherhood, should be recognized and studied as a political institution.

REFLECT AND RESPOND

1. Define *social inequality*. What conditions make social inequality possible in Canada?
2. Describe examples of ableism, ageism, sexism, racism, and classism other than those in this section.
3. Describe a feminist perspective of social inequality and alienation.

Social Institutions

Before You Read
What does the term *institution* mean to you?

When most people hear the word *institution*, they think about a building, such as a school, hospital, or prison. In sociology, however, the term *institution* means something more specific and complex. To sociologists, a **social institution** is an organization or social framework whose function is to meet the basic needs of its members by providing direction and operating principles for society.

For example, a prison is both a physical institution and part of the social institution known as government, which is responsible for maintaining public order. Similarly, a university or college is a public institution and part of the institution of education. The underlying goal of all social institutions is to satisfy individual needs and provide an orderly structure for the benefit of all society. Social institutions also provide a way for different agents of socialization to transmit important beliefs and attitudes to the population.

Although distinct in their roles and overall purpose, social institutions all perform the basic function of promoting social cohesion outlined in Figure 9-31.

social institution: an organization or social framework whose function is to meet the basic needs of its members by providing direction and operating principles for society

Sociologists Take Sides: Theoretical Perspectives of Social Institutions

Conflict theorists such as Marx would agree that the purpose of social institutions is to meet the needs of their members. Their greatest criticism of social institutions is the fact that these institutions may have strayed from their original purpose to serve the individual. Over time, social institutions have come to represent the interests of a small, wealthy, and privileged minority. According to the conflict theorists, marginalized groups in society may not be fully recognized by social institutions because social power is in the hands of the wealthy few, who allow only minimal access to the social resources that were meant to serve all of society. Conflict theorists have come to see institutions as roadblocks, hindering the general population from gaining equal access to social resources.

Structural functionalists such as Max Weber would say that social institutions perform an integral function in modern life and that their core purpose is the welfare of the individual. To functional theorists, the institutions themselves are an undisputable necessity for social living. They model social norms and provide positive reinforcement for appropriate behaviour.

Functions of Social Institutions

Satisfy the basic needs of society's members (e.g., health care)

Demonstrate dominant values and beliefs (e.g., Charter of Rights and Freedoms)

Establish enduring patterns of social behaviour (e.g., caring for children)

Define roles for individuals to emulate (e.g., husband and wife)

↑ **FIGURE 9-31** Society is complex, and so are its institutions. How do social institutions support Canadian identity?

REFLECT AND RESPOND

1. What are some examples of social institutions other than those mentioned in this section? Which ones do you belong to?
2. Use a graphic organizer to outline the key beliefs about social institutions according to conflict theory and structural functionalism.

Social Institutions and Their Primary Goals

Each social institution contains a set of social norms, roles, and behaviour expected of its members. Among the many important institutions that guide public life, there are five that sociologists have discovered that repeatedly appear in all cultures around the world. These are the family, religion, education, government, and economy (see the chart below).

> **Before You Read**
> How have your family and your education influenced your identity?

SOCIAL INSTITUTIONS AND THEIR PRIMARY GOALS

Institution and Core Beliefs	Representatives of Institution	Individual Needs Served
Family • fidelity • respect • nurturance • knowledge • support • loyalty	• individual members (father, mother, daughter, son, etc.) • nuclear family • extended family • adoptive parents • same-sex parents • relatives	• socializes children • is responsible for reproduction • perpetuates marriage • establishes positive self-concept and self-esteem • provides emotional nurturance
Religion • worshipping • faith • charity • tolerance • ethics • morals	• worshipper • religious leaders of churches, mosques, synagogues, and temples • spiritual leaders and healers	• satisfies spiritual needs of individuals • provides solace for life's crises and tragedies • models altruistic behaviour • promotes tolerance of other groups
Education • obedience • punctuality • knowledge • practical skills • respect	• students • teachers and administrators • college and university professors	• transmits knowledge and skills from one generation to the next • continues the socialization process begun at home with the family • prepares students for the workforce
Government • obedience • loyalty • pride • justice • patriotism • respect • equality	• political leaders • political parties • elected officials • judges • police officers • civil servants	• demonstrates the legitimate use of power by governing members • models respect for the nation and its symbols • instills a sense of belonging and pride of country • enforces social order (law and law enforcement) • administers to the well-being of the population • attempts to unify society
Economy • ethics • efficiency • competition • honesty • integrity	• banks • small businesses • corporations	• regulates the distribution of goods and services • establishes an appropriate work ethic • teaches the value of honesty and hard work as a way to get ahead • teaches the laws of supply and demand

Family

> **Skills Focus**
>
> Analyzing data is an important part of sociological research. Review the data from the Vanier Institute below, then analyze it. What trends do you notice? What conclusions can you draw?

As you know, the family is the primary agent of socialization and the most important institution in Canadian society. Like all institutions, it is continuously adapting to an ever-changing population. The nuclear family was considered the ideal for many generations. Today, Canadians are challenging the notion that nuclear families are the only avenue through which children can be properly socialized. As a result of changing attitudes toward parenting and marriage, the family as an institution has grown to include lone-parent families, same-sex families, and common-law and blended families. More than any other institution, the family has demonstrated that diversity and tolerance are possible in a society as complex as Canada. Even with such remarkable changes, the institution of the family remains a dominant force directing Canadian society. This is true for most cultures around the world, too. The family's influence is hard to dispute.

In all cultures, the institution of the family is responsible for promoting universal functions, such as regulating reproduction and sexual behaviour. It is also responsible for socializing and teaching the youngest members social norms. From day to day, the family helps develop lifelong lessons, such as the importance of respect and obedience. These skills are further explored as children enter school. In this way, the family can be seen as a blueprint for social norms and beliefs. In addition to all its social and practical functions, the family is responsible for the economic maintenance and recreation of its members.

According to the Vanier Institute of the Family, the changing face of Canadian families has left an indelible mark on whom we are as a nation. It also says something about our social values. We have fashioned a dynamic new identity based on a new definition of family. In its analysis of the 2006 Census, the Vanier Institute tracked the changes to the family for over two decades (see the chart below). The nuclear family is clearly not the only option for Canadians today.

VANIER INSTITUTE OF THE FAMILY AND FAMILY TYPES						
Percentage Distribution of Census Families by Type (1981–2006)						
	1981	1986	1991	1996	2001	2006
Families without children* at home						
Married couples	28.2%	28.2%	29.2%	28.6%	29.0%	29.9%
Common-law couples	3.7	4.5	5.8	6.2	7.5	8.5
Families with children* at home						
Married couples	55.0	51.9	48.1	45.1	41.4	38.7
Common-law couples	1.9	2.7	4.0	5.5	6.3	6.9
Lone-parent families	11.3	12.7	13.0	14.5	15.7	15.9
Same-sex couples as % of all couples	0.6%	0.2%	0.4%	0.6%	0.4%	0.8%

* Children of any age who live in the home

Source: Statistics Canada, 2006 Census of Population

The family is the only institution to use nurturance and emotional support as a basis for all its relationships. Other institutions such as religion do so in a limited manner, but the family's ability to nurture self-esteem, creativity, and self-confidence sets it apart. In many ways, the family is the foundation on which well-adjusted young adults emerge ready and capable of fully participating in other institutions and society itself (see Figure 9-32).

↑ **FIGURE 9-32** There are many types of Canadian families. How do you define *family*?

❓ How does the family act as a blueprint for membership in society? What do the Vanier Institute's findings suggest about changes to the Canadian family?

Religion

On a personal level, religion can serve a number of purposes. It can provide an individual with a sense of serenity and calm, help celebrate important rituals of life, and provide support in times of grief and personal tragedy. On an intellectual and philosophical level, it can help explain the origins of the world, the universal order that governs it, and the presence of good and evil.

For many individuals, religious beliefs are developed in the family starting at a very young age through initiation rites, such as a Catholic baptism, a Hindu ear-piercing ceremony (Karnavedha), or a Jewish bris. Although different, these ceremonies serve to teach the young faithful about the rituals and beliefs of their religion. Throughout the course of his or her life, a worshipper will attend prayer services, observe important rites, and learn sacred scripture. In this way, religion helps the worshipper explain natural phenomena, such as birth and death.

> **Connecting Sociology to Anthropology**
>
> From an anthropological perspective, religion helps people to understand ultimate questions, such as why are we here? What is death? Why does evil happen to some people and not to others? How does this compare to the sociological perspective of religion?

In the social arena, religion helps individuals to develop charity, compassion, and altruism. Most of the world's well-known religions are based on these elements. For many cultures around the world, religion is a deeply integrated part of the fabric of society. As such, it exerts a great deal of influence on other institutions as well. In one way or another, organized religions such as Buddhism, Christianity, Hinduism, Islam, and Judaism have been known to create social cohesion as well as social conflict among their believers and their society.

As social institutions, religious organizations serve a social purpose. Many host charity events and community meals and perform public service. The basis for these activities is charity and goodwill. As such, they are not restricted to members of that specific religious organization but are extended to the community as a whole. For many, these gatherings help alleviate the stress and alienation that secular life may bring. In this sense, religion is a constructive force in society. It is also quite common for religious groups to come together to promote peaceful resolution to global issues and, closer to home, work in conjunction with government agencies to alleviate social inequality and injustice locally.

Before 1971, less than 1 percent of Canadians ticked the "no religion" box on national surveys. Two generations later, nearly a quarter of the population, or 23 percent, say they aren't religious. A look at the youngest Canadians suggests the transformation is gathering speed. In 2002, 34 percent of 15 to 29 year olds said religion was highly important to them. Data from Statistics Canada's 2009 General Social Survey show that number tumbled to 22 percent. This demographic shift raises profound questions about our social values, the fate of our cultural heritage, the institutions that once formed the bedrock of our communities, and access to political power. See the chart below.

RELIGIOUS AFFILIATION AND ATTENDANCE AMONG CANADIANS AGED 15 AND OLDER						
	1985	1990	1995	2000	2004	Percentage Point Change 1985–2004
Population aged 15 and over	100	100	100	100	100	...
No religious affiliation	12	12	15	20	19	7
Frequency of attendance						
Not in the last 12 months	19	23	27	21	25	5
Infrequently[1]	28	28	24	28	25	–3
At least monthly	41	37	33	31	32	–9

[1] Attended religious services, but only a few times a year or less frequently.
Source: Statistics Canada, General Social Survey

> How does religion promote social cohesion? What patterns do you notice in the chart? Do you think the data in the chart above holds true for all religions?

Education

On the surface, it would appear that the purpose of going to school is to get good grades by completing your homework and other assignments. That is the most basic purpose of school, but if you consider education an institution that extends beyond the four walls of your classroom, you will realize that it is an institution steeped in traditions, rituals, and rites of passage for many youth all over the world. Of course, not all systems are the same and not all countries value the same set of skills or body of knowledge. Wherever you are a student, the purpose of education is to transmit knowledge, skills, and social values from one generation to the next. The knowledge and skills you learn in school are building blocks for the next phase of your life: entry into the workforce. For some students, that part of education may not be that apparent, while others are more aware of the connection. Moreover, education provides a number of social and life management skills that are meant to lead to students' independence.

> **Skills Focus**
> Use the evidence in the table on this page or the previous page to write a thesis statement and a paragraph that could be used as part of a report. Be sure to cite the evidence in your paragraph using APA conventions.

Education's Other Functions

Consider the following scenario. Evan and Emmanuel are two students in the same Ontario high school. They share all of the same classes and participate in many of the same extracurricular activities the school offers. Although the goal of education is to instill knowledge and skills that are upheld in society at large, Evan's and Emmanuel's experiences may differ widely. Perhaps Evan is part of a different social class and Emmanuel is part of a visible minority. Both boys bring their individual and cultural differences to the school community, and, as a result, the educational system must respond to those needs equitably. Education must offer both boys access to the same resources and serve them equally as they head out into the workforce. At all levels, education must represent all groups fairly and equitably. Toward that end, important features are entrenched in the institution of education. So, on any given day, both Evan and Emmanuel, and other students like them, are exposed to the same important features. See the chart below for an explanation of the features.

FEATURES OF EDUCATION	
Defining Feature of Education	**Explanation**
Socialization and roles	• Students learn about punctuality and respect for authority and others.
Discipline and obedience	• Students come to accept and respect the authority of teachers and rules of the school. • Students learn to use self-control in their dealings with peers and others. • Students learn to take responsibility for their own actions, including actions taken against others.
Knowledge and skills	• Students study and complete assignments. • Students meet all the expectations outlined in the curriculum and interact with the material critically.
Competition and collaboration	• Students are encouraged to participate in extracurricular activities to develop healthy competition. • Students must contribute to classroom activities such as debates to help foster collaboration and teamwork.

The Future of Education

During the 1950s when the television became a household fixture in North America, it was widely believed that television would revolutionize many aspects of life, including education. Many social commentators saw "old-fashioned" schools becoming a thing of the past as the television craze took hold. More than 60 years later, the "old-fashioned" schools are still with us.

FIGURE 9-33 How will technology affect the future of education? What should stay the same? What should change?

Today the same concerns over technology are surfacing again. This time it is computer technology that stands to threaten the "old-fashioned" system. Many people believe that this is one battle education may actually lose unless educational experts and academics find a way to marry the two traditions. The key is to reconcile the current state of education with the huge potential of technology. As you learned in Chapter 7, some schools are cracking down on cell phone use, but some experts are trying to find more ways to incorporate the technology that has come to define the twenty-first-century learner (see Figure 9-33). This example shows that the structure of our educational system may not adequately reflect the rapid technological changes occurring today. Perhaps the future of education involves integrating computer technology as a means of building the knowledge and skills that will lead to career paths yet to be developed. Not surprisingly, many experts tell us that we need to continue to honour the oral tradition and communal nature of schools as they have always existed. In other words, there is room for both the old and the new in our classrooms. The concept of socio-economic equity comes into play here as we consider who has access to this technology and who does not, and whether this unequal accessibility suggests different outcomes for children. For example, students who are less familiar with the technology used to present material may be at a disadvantage, and not all students have equal access to this technology at home. Even if there is a computer, it may have to be shared by more than one sibling.

> What are the key features of the Canadian educational system? How does technology help you learn? What are some other challenges to using technology in the classroom?

Government

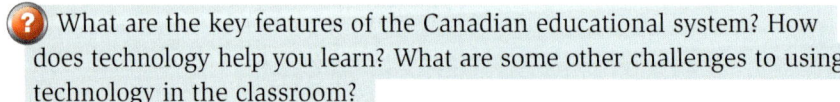

FIGURE 9-34 Laws maintain social order, and those who break them are punished. But what if the social order is oppressive to one or more groups?

Every human society is based on a guiding principle that is upheld by authority figures—religious or secular—and by the general population. The guiding principle for most countries is a political idea. For example, the fundamental principle around which Canada was built is democracy. In China or Cuba, the guiding principle is Communism.

Aside from the political idea, society is also defined by distinct roles and obligations that help advance the fundamental beliefs of its members. Laws may be written to facilitate appropriate social conduct for the people (see Figure 9-34). This process is often referred to as the *institutionalization of norms*. Laws give the government ultimate authority to govern people's social interaction and to intervene when individuals violate the norm. To some people, this power may appear constrictive, but without laws, society would certainly degenerate into chaos. Our elected officials are given the power to make decisions for society, and we, the citizens, grant them that authority by means of our political vote. As you learned in Chapter 6, the Charter of Rights and Freedoms provides the standard for which many cases are determined. The role of government in society is multifaceted, and law enforcement represents only a small portion.

Government institutions must provide for the social and economic welfare of their people. With its many social programs and policies, the Canadian government tries to ensure that the most vulnerable and needy receive the support they need. Through these incentives and based on appropriate policies, the government hopes to alleviate social inequalities. However, social inequalities in Canada are on the rise among certain groups, including Aboriginal populations and other marginalized groups. The government also oversees other institutions, such as family and religion.

Skills Focus

Draft an outline of a formal report representing the teens' side of the tanning-salon issue, which you might deliver to the Minister of Health. Include a strong introduction and thesis, followed by solid arguments supported by evidence. Draw valid conclusions about government involvement in the issue.

POINT/COUNTERPOINT

Use of Tanning Salons by Minors

In some cases, the government, through its ministries, suggests proper modes of behaviour and restricts access of certain social groups to certain privileges.

Should the Government Ban Tanning Salons for People Under 18?

Government Needs to Protect Individuals	Individuals Can Make Their Own Decisions
• Not all parents can make informed decisions for minors about the consequences. For example, some parents don't know that tanning salons increase the risk of melanoma by 75 percent for people under 30. • We have laws prohibiting minors from buying cigarettes and consuming alcohol. • New Brunswick, some U.S. states, and some other countries already have laws that restrict the use of tanning salons. • New research is not always communicated to the public.	• Parents can make decisions for minors for health care or tanning salons. • Minors can go to a beach or pool and stay in the sun as long as they or their parents permit without any legislation. • If parents and teens know the risk, they can make informed choices on their own. • Tanning salons are legal.

Source: *The Globe and Mail*, July 18, 2010.

QUESTIONS

1. Create a mind map of social institutions and explain how they relate personally to yourself. Add a third layer that demonstrates a possible scenario if the institution did not exist.
2. How and why does government oversee the family and religion? Debate the need for more or less government involvement in these social institutions.

Open for Debate

Politicians need votes to be elected. In order to vote, however, you need an address. This makes voting difficult for homeless individuals, so they are less able to vote for politicians who will best represent their interests. Is this system fair?

Medicine and the Military

While all social institutions work to satisfy the needs of their members, there are some with specific mandates to keep society safe, whether from pandemics or from the threat of violence from an internal or external force. The health care system and the military both serve a safety function in Canadian society (see Figure 9-35). Think about the recent outbreak of the H1N1 flu virus and the Ministry of Health's response shortly thereafter. A massive effort was undertaken to get the vaccine to as many Canadians as possible. Community centres suspended activities so that local residents could receive the vaccine in makeshift clinics.

Canada's health care system consists of 13 provincial and territorial programs. The federal, provincial, and territorial governments work together to manage and deliver health care to Canadians. It is considered universal health care because the system is based on need, rather than the ability to pay, and is available to all residents of Canada.

Similarly, the Canadian military exists to preserve our way of life and to keep our nation safe from external threats. In our peacekeeping capacity, we extend our valued notion of peace and safety to countries around the world in their greatest moments of crisis. Canadian peacekeepers provide humanitarian relief after natural disasters, protect civilians during conflicts, help organize elections, and perform many other functions.

Medicine
- Provides health care to all members and prevents disease among population
- Preserves life
- Provides proactive solutions to extend life and ensure a high standard of living for the elderly

Military
- Protects a nation from internal and external threats
- Assists in relief efforts around the world and maintains peace
- Promotes honour, patriotism, and nationalism among the population
- Teaches obedience and discipline to soldiers
- Members act as ambassadors around the world for our way of life and beliefs
- Provides domestic protection (e.g., in response to natural disasters)

FIGURE 9-35 The military and medical communities keep society safe. Which of these has the most impact on your life?

❓ Do we need more or less government involvement in society? Who gains and who loses in each of these choices?

Economy

A country's economic institution is closely related to the nation's government. The economy serves a number of important functions, such as the production of goods and the organization of the labour force. The economy and its related institutions, such as small businesses and large corporations, are concerned with the supply and demand of goods and efficient methods to produce profit. In many countries, banks are the most powerful economic institutions. They are the keepers of the nation's currency. The strength of a nation's currency is an important indicator of how a country's economy is performing.

On a more human level, economic institutions provide society with appropriate examples of leadership styles and teach the importance of honesty and a strong work ethic among its employees and workers. They also highlight the importance of ownership and personal financial success in society.

In sociological terms, there are two distinct views about the role of workers in the modern-day economy. The first is somewhat pessimistic and sees the workers as insignificant mechanisms in the larger, more important machine. This view dehumanizes the efforts of the individual. The second, more optimistic view contends that the workers are an integral part of the success of any company and, with encouragement and praise, will produce outstanding results (see Figure 9-36).

> **Skills Focus**
> Stating your hypothesis clearly is important when you write reports. Develop a hypothesis about the role of workers in Canadian society. What kind of study could you conduct to test your hypothesis?

FIGURE 9-36 Workers in a Chinese chicken factory and at the Googleplex headquarters in Australia. What message does each workplace send to its workers?

? What should an employer provide for its employees? What does an employer provide that social institutions do not?

IN FOCUS: Googleplex

Google's headquarters, or Googleplex, is located in Mountain View, California. It has become a model for many companies for how to increase employee satisfaction. It has demonstrated to numerous economic institutions that changes are necessary to the current system and that accommodations for a different kind of worker are needed. The *Googlers*, as they are called, test the notion that economic efficiency can occur only when workers are confined to individual tasks, roles, or locations. At Googleplex, employees are encouraged to travel around the headquarters on bicycles or scooters and bring their pets to work. There are employee groups for meditation, film appreciation, wine tasting, and salsa dancing. Employees at all levels are encouraged to contribute. For example, any employee is free to pose a question to one of the company's founders at one of Google's weekly meetings. Individual achievements are celebrated as well as team accomplishments.

QUESTIONS

1. How does Googleplex reflect the needs of the generation of workers that is now entering the workforce?
2. In what industries might the Google model work effectively? Ineffectively?
3. How might Google's model result in greater productivity?
4. What key element is present for the workers at Googleplex that is missing for the alienated workers Marx described? How does this link to anomie?

REFLECT AND RESPOND

1. Select a social institution, and create a Venn diagram to organize ideas about how it affects you and society. Label one circle "Me" and the other "Society."
2. Rank the social institutions discussed according to how important you think they are. Select criteria such as who benefits and loses, social justice, and others you determine relevant.
3. What social institutions are not discussed in this section? What functions do they serve for society?
4. What important components of education would be lost if there were no more traditional classrooms?
5. If religion is on the decline in Canada, what other institution or institutions might take its place?

Social Change

In Section 9.1, you read about social identity and a person's ability to adapt to variable situations. Now consider a similar chameleon, this one representing an entire society (see Figure 9-37). You learned that, at the microlevel, the individual is capable of change. Here you will read about the capacity for change at the macrolevel as society adapts to reflect the values and beliefs of its people. **Social change** is a society's attempt to incorporate different values and beliefs into its existing structure. It also involves modifying public institutions to create social and cultural progress.

For better or worse, society and its institutions do their best to keep up with the fast-paced and ever-changing face of their members, but they often find themselves lagging behind. Think of the example used earlier about technology in schools and the proposal to incorporate cell phones in Ontario classrooms. In this scenario, students are leading the charge. They are more capable of incorporating and using technology than the institution that is meant to prepare them for the workforce. As a result of these changing student values and needs, education has already moved toward integrating technology into the classroom and will continue to progress in this field in the future.

You also read about the changing structure of the family. Here, too, the general population has moved away from the nuclear family that was once considered the only acceptable family type. The trend toward cohabitation, the increasing divorce rates, and the emergence of same-sex families have changed the face of family life forever. Canadians are letting their government know that modifications are necessary in this important social institution. As a result, the government has instituted new marriage laws and the definition of family has been broadened to include formerly marginalized groups. Acknowledging changes such as those occurring in education and the family will ensure that social structures and institutions remain current and capable of progressing with their population.

Before You Read

Is society capable of changing as rapidly as an individual living in it?

social change: a society's attempt to incorporate different values and beliefs into its existing structure and to modify public institutions to instigate social and cultural progress

FIGURE 9-37 Just as the individual changes, so does society. How do you shape the social groups you belong to?

REFLECT AND RESPOND

1. Select one social institution, and ask a person who is at least 20 years older than you to explain how changes to this institution have affected him or her.
2. How has social change affected your family or school? Consider technology, family, entertainment, etc., and explain how one sociologist would explain this change.
3. What happens when one institution changes, but others do not, or do not accept the change? Discuss a specific example.

CHAPTER 9 REVIEW

Knowledge and Understanding/Thinking

1. How might you alter your social identity in each of the following scenarios:
   a) meeting your childhood idol many years later as an adult
   b) meeting an important expert in a field you are currently studying
   c) meeting relatives from another part of the world you've never seen before
   d) being introduced to your ex-boyfriend's/girlfriend's new partner

2. Using Canadian culture as an example, evaluate how difficult/easy it might be for a new immigrant to experience social integration. Think about such national symbols as hockey when you compose your answer.

3. Describe society's attitude toward sexual orientation in Canada. How is this attitude changing?

4. Examine the differences among the conflict, structural functional, and symbolic interactionist explanations for social stratification. Which one do you think is most useful for sociological inquiry? Explain why.

5. Identify reasons why social change may be necessary in each of the following institutions. Are they meeting the needs of those they serve?
   a) education
   b) medicine
   c) family

Thinking/Communicating

6. Suggest and plan possible ways your school community might combat negative attitudes toward LGBTQ adolescents and reduce the bullying that occurs as a result of sexual orientation.

7. Create a cartoon that demonstrates how "isms" impact career choices or social behaviour.

8. Using the case study "Food for Thought: The Influence of Social Networks on Health" (see page 420), create your own case study about behaviour that may be contagious among the members of the group.

9. Dramatize, role-play, or blog (or use another method of your choice) to show how events such as those that occurred on September 11, 2001, have a profound effect on cultures around the world and how individuals from remote corners of the world are influenced. Choose a recent event as an example. Examine the role of the media and technology in your answer. Also consider what freedoms you are willing to give up in the name of security.

10. Consult the chart entitled "Conditions for Social Inequality" (see page 431). Add a column entitled "In Action," and provide a few examples of the inequality that may occur for each characteristic.

11. Provide reasons for how and why an individual may become alienated from the following groups. Include in your answer a description of the social expectations of the group.
    a) family
    b) friends
    c) co-workers
    d) a religious group

Communication/Application

12. If you wanted to veer from social norms and create a subculture, what would the subculture look like? Give your subculture a name, and describe its norms, beliefs, manner of dress, and any other particulars you think might be appropriate to know about your group.

13. Create three scenarios that clearly define an achieved status.

14. Write a draft of an oral presentation or formal report, which you would consider delivering to the premier, your school principal, or school council, that expresses your views about the use of cell phones in the classroom.

15. Using the information included below about education from Section 9.2, write a report card for how well your high school performs in each of the categories using the model of strengths, weaknesses, and next steps.

Defining Feature of Education	Explanation
Socialization and roles	• Students learn about punctuality and respect for authority and others.
Discipline and obedience	• Students come to accept and respect the authority of teachers and rules of the school. • Students learn to use self-control in their dealings with peers and others. • Students learn to take responsibility for their own actions, including actions taken against others.
Knowledge and skills	• Students study and complete assignments. • Students meet all the expectations outlined in the curriculum and interact with the material critically.
Competition and collaboration	• Students are encouraged to participate in extracurricular activities to develop healthy competition. • Students must contribute to classroom activities such as debates to help foster collaboration and teamwork.

16. Refer to the In Focus: Alienation and Mental Health feature in Section 9.1 (see page 415), and extend the discussion to another alienated group in society. Produce a simple fact sheet, similar to the CAMH example in the text, for any group you believe experiences alienation in modern Canadian society (for example, the elderly, teen moms, homeless people).

APPENDICES

APPENDIX 1: Research and Inquiry Skills

The following is an alphabetical list of research and inquiry skills used in this text, along with an introduction, chapter and page references.

Analyzing and Interpreting Research Information (Chapter 5, p. 199)

One job of social scientists is to analyze and interpret the research data that they have gathered. For survey data, you can create graphs to compare the data. For interviews or observations, you will have to sort the data into different categories.

Assessing and Recording Sources (Chapter 3, p. 95)

When using secondary sources, it is important to be certain that they are reputable. Reputable sources can include textbooks; journal, magazine, and newspaper articles; and research reports. It's also important to review what the leading experts have written about the subject you are researching. Finding reputable sources is especially important when researching online. You should select Web sites that come from trustworthy organizations, such as universities and governments. After you've selected your sources, it is important to cite your sources. In the social sciences, it is common to use the style of the American Psychological Association (APA) style.

Creating a Central Research Question (Chapter 1, p. 17)

The first step is coming up with a central research question on a topic that interests you. A research question must be testable and as unbiased as possible. We all have biases. They can come from our culture, our point of view, and our interests. Social scientists have established research methods and practices to try to reduce these biases.

Creating a Research Plan (Chapter 4, p. 135)

All research is driven by a purpose; it begins with an interest that leads to a question. Research questions are often vague at the beginning and become more specific. Research can also change direction as the researcher collects and analyzes data and information. It's important to analyze your information as objectively as possible and avoid making judgments or drawing conclusions before the research is complete.

Creating a Research Plan in Psychology (Chapter 5, p. 199)

Conducting research in psychology includes common expectations and procedures. These processes are likely more similar to research you have done in Science than in History or Geography. It is important to follow the steps completely so that you get an understanding of how a psychologist conducts his or her research.

Evaluating Sources (Chapter 7, p. 319)

Do you believe everything you read or hear? Why are some sources more reliable than others? As an anthropologist or any other kind of researcher, you always need to evaluate your sources. When evaluating a source, a social scientist asks: Who wrote this? When? Why? Can I trust the person? What is his or her bias, worldview, and goals?

Gathering and Processing Information (Chapter 6, p. 259)

Sociologists consult several sources of information when conducting their research. A sociologist begins with a review of literature, which is a search for and examination of credible, reputable studies conducted by others in the discipline. The literature may include journals, books, and statistical records. The review of literature reveals whether a topic is worthy of research. Typically, after a review of literature, the sociologist may refine the original research question and formulate a hypothesis.

Presenting Research in Psychology (Chapter 8, p. 363)

Once their research is completed, psychologists then share their results with their colleagues. This may include writing a report, publishing an article in an academic journal, creating a Web site or Web page, and/or creating a poster presentation. It is important to note that, whatever the format, there are certain elements that remain constant.

Quantitative and Qualitative Research (Chapter 2, p. 57)

Generally, the various ways in which social scientists conduct their research can be categorized into quantitative and qualitative methods.

Recording Data and Analyzing Information (Chapter 1, p. 17)

When you are doing research, you will need to collect data (small factual pieces of information) and information to test your hypothesis. Data becomes information when it is interpreted by someone. Record how you collected your data and where you found your information. Summarize the information and think about how it answers your research question.

Sources in Social Science (Chapter 2, p. 57)

When you conduct research in the social sciences, you must select from a variety of primary and secondary sources. *Primary sources* (for example, interviews, observations, surveys) are obtained from field research, while *secondary sources* (for example, research reports, newspaper articles, journal or magazine articles) summarize what other people have to say about a topic.

Surveys (Chapter 3, p. 95)

Once social scientists develop their central research question (see Chapter 1), they follow specific steps to make sure their research is completed scientifically and systematically. Surveys are important tools to help social scientists collect empirical evidence.

Variables and Control Groups in Social Science (Chapter 2, p. 57)

When social scientists have an issue or a topic they wish to research, they first must develop a central research question. This question becomes the focus of an experiment, where a researcher looks at the effects of one factor on another. These factors are called variables. You need to avoid making a conclusion until you finish your research. Look at the following example of a good central research question to learn more about experiments: Does using a cell phone at school affect students' grades?

Writing Reports (Chapter 9, p. 405)

The final stage of the sociological method of inquiry is to synthesize and present, in written or oral format, conclusive information about the research question. In the formal written report, the sociologist analyzes and interprets information presented in primary and secondary sources and evaluates the results of the data collected (through questionnaires and interviews, for example). The sociologist also synthesizes all sources of data and draws conclusions about the topic.

APPENDIX 2: Landmark Case Studies

The following is a list, organized by discipline, of the landmark case studies, along with an introduction, chapter and page references.

Anthropology

Death Without Weeping: Poverty and Family Roles (Chapter 4, pp. 176–177)

"Why do the church bells ring so often?" Nancy Scheper-Hughes asked her host Nailza de Arruda after she moved into a corner of her hut in Alto do Cruzeiro, a slum in Northeast Brazil in the summer of 1965. Nailza replied "It's nothing, just another little angel gone to heaven" (Scheper-Hughes, 1989).

James Gibbs: The Kpelle Moot (Chapter 7, pp. 326–327)

Anthropologist James Gibbs studied the Kpelle people of central Liberia. He observed the proceedings in a moot or informal court. The Kpelle also have a formal court system that is coercive and arbitrary in its use of justice. The formal system is useful for dealing with assaults, possession of illegal charms, and thefts by unrelated individuals. It is not helpful in dealing with domestic issues such as marriage, inheritance, and divorce, where the relationship must continue after the case. The coercive and arbitrary nature of the court generally drives disputants apart.

Richard Lee and the Dobe Ju/'hoansi (Chapter 1, pp. 26–27)

Richard Lee, one of Canada's most distinguished ethnographers, has lived and worked with the Dobe Ju/'hoansi (pronounced *zhut-wasi*), a group of San people of Southern Africa for almost 40 years, starting back in the 1960s. (In the past, this group has also been referred to as the !Kung.) In that time the Dobe Ju/'hoansi have changed from a relatively isolated hunter-gatherer society, who foraged for food, to an integrated herding and farming society.

Shakespeare in the Bush (Chapter 4, p. 180)

An excerpt from anthropologist Laura Bohannan's article "Shakespeare in the Bush" was originally published in 1966. She was living among the Tiv in West Africa and discovered, to her disappointment, that none of the religious rituals that she had hoped to observe would be performed during the rainy season. To pass the time, the villagers drank homemade beer and told stories. When Bohannan was asked to tell a story from her culture, she decided to retell Hamlet in hopes of proving to a colleague back home that Shakespeare is universal.

Steel Axes Among the Yir Yoront (Chapter 4, p. 155)

The Yir Yoront are an Aboriginal people of Australia. For centuries, they had made and used stone axes, necessary for just about all of their daily activities, including chopping firewood, building shelters, making tools, gathering plants, fishing, and hunting. Axes always belonged to men. If a woman needed to use an axe, an event that occurred several times a day, she had to borrow one from a man, usually her husband, whomever refused. Children and younger men also had to borrow axes from their fathers or older brothers. So the axes reinforced kin relationships, social status, and hierarchy for the Yir Yoront.

Psychology

Jane Elliot: Brown Eyes/Blue Eyes (Chapter 8, p. 376)

In 1968, elementary school teacher Jane Elliot conducted an experiment in her classroom that would lead her students and others to change the way they thought about racism and prejudice. In response to the assassination of Dr. Martin Luther King, Jr., she devised a scenario that taught her all-White third-grade students about the roots of discrimination and racism by having each student experience it first-hand. Her exercise and the student reunion 14 years later have been documented in the film *A Class Divided*.

Genie: The Story of an Isolate Child (Chapter 5, p. 206)

The story of "Genie" is of particular importance to understanding the influence environment has on an individual's development. Genie is an example of a child who suffered acute social deprivation, otherwise known as an isolate. She grew up without any significant human contact and had minimal language acquisition.

Mary Ainsworth (1913–1999): Infant–Mother Attachment (Chapter 2, pp. 80–81)

Noted North American psychologist Mary Ainsworth's study of child development has become the groundwork for our understanding of mother–infant separation and how it influences interactions later in life. As demonstrated by Harlow's work with rhesus monkeys, attachment to a caregiver happens early on in life and is necessary for survival. Infants usually become attached to those who are familiar and responsive to their needs. They use this attachment as a secure base from which to explore their environment. Mary Ainsworth was interested in learning more about the ways in which infants were attached to their parents.

Philip Zimbardo (1933–): Stanford Prison Experiment (Chapter 5, pp. 238–239)

In 1971, psychologist Philip Zimbardo conducted his famous experiment where prison life was re-created in the basement of Stanford University's Psychology Department building. He and his team were curious to understand the psychological effects of acting as a prisoner or prison guard.

Sociology

The Clark Doll Experiment (1939) (Chapter 6, p. 298)

Starting in 1939, Dr. Kenneth Clark and his wife, Dr. Mamie Clark, conducted a study about the racial biases among children in the United States. The Clark Doll experiment, as it became known, tested young African-American children to determine how race related to their self-image. The experiment consisted of showing each child a white doll and a black doll and giving instructions to the child in a particular order.

Food for Thought: The Influence of Social Networks on Health (Chapter 9, p. 420)

In a landmark study, Nicholas A. Christakis of Harvard Medical School studied more than 12 000 people over 32 years and discovered that social networks strongly influence an individual's chances of gaining weight. Christakis's work, which is hailed as innovative and brilliant, shows that there is a causal relationship between one's belonging to social networks in which members are obese and becoming obese oneself. That is, belonging to social networks in which members are obese causes obesity in an individual. In fact, it is the first study to explore links between social networks and any chronic condition.

CNN Doll Experiment (2010) (Chapter 6, p. 299)

Seventy years after the original Clark Doll experiment was administered by the Clarks, CNN and Anderson Cooper repeated the experiment on a new generation. In an attempt to discover whether much had changed in the last 70 years, CNN hired child psychologist Margaret Beale Spencer from the University of Chicago, along with two testers and one statistician, to design an updated experiment.

Henri Tajfel: The Social Identity Theory (Chapter 6, pp. 262–263)

Sociologists have long known that humans are a social species. We seek interaction with others whenever possible and use those experiences to shape our future responses and behaviours. From the daily interactions with others, we learn about important social roles and values. The study of group behaviour is an integral part of sociology. Observing group behaviour and interactions between members of a group can reveal important information about individual motivation and social values.

Stanley Milgram: Subway Experiments (Chapter 6, p. 289)

During the 1970s in New York, a famous breaching experiment was led by Dr. Stanley Milgram. He got the idea from his mother-in-law, who complained that passengers would not give up their seat for her on the subway. Etiquette in Western society specifies that people are supposed to give up their seats on public transit for the elderly, people with disabilities, people who are infirm, and pregnant women, but otherwise the seating is first come, first served. Milgram used his students as researchers. At first, they resisted participating since they knew giving up a seat for people who appeared to be able to stand was not done in New York.

William Foote Whyte and the Street Corner Society (Chapter 3, p. 106)

William Foote Whyte (1914–2000) was an economist who, through a study of a poor Boston neighbourhood in the 1930s, created the model for urban ethnography and set the standard for this methodology in sociology, becoming a pioneer in participant observation. His book, *Street Corner Society: The Social Structure of an Italian Slum*, remains one of the best-selling works to be produced for urban sociology and is a classic reference for all sociologists.

APPENDIX 3: Key Theorists

To aid in further research, the following is a list, organized by discipline, of the key theorists referred to in this text.

Anthropology

Mehrunnisa Ahmad Ali
Ruth Benedict
Franz Boas
Laura Bohannan
Rachel Burr
Amber Case
Napoleon Chagnon
Noam Chomsky
Raymond Dart
Charles Darwin
E.E. Evans-Pritchard
Gary Fine
Dian Fossey
Ruth Freed
Stanley Freed
Slavenka Drakulić
Biruté Galdikas
George Gmelch
Jane Goodall
Neeti Gupta
Keith N. Hampton
Marvin Harris
Peruvemba Jaya
Diamond Jenness
Donald Johanson
Katrina Jurva
Mikel J. Koven
Louis Leakey
Mary Leakey
Richard Leakey
Stephen Leavitt
Richard Lee
Bronislaw Malinowski
Margaret Mead
Gerald Murray
Nancy Netting
Rebecca Popenoe
Ken Pryce
Edward Sapir
Sue Savage-Rumbaugh
Nancy Scheper-Hughes
Lauriston Sharp
Pavna Sodhi
Claire Sterk
Evangelia Tastsoglou
Tricia Wang

Psychology

Alfred Adler
Gordon Allport
Solomon Asch
Albert Bandura
John Bargh
John Berry
Thomas J. Bouchard
Tanya Chartrand
Noam Chomsky
Carlo DiClemente
Paul Ekman
Jane Elliot
Erik Erikson
Hans Eysenck
Viktor Frankl
Sigmund Freud
Howard Gardner
Fritz Heider
Karen Horney
David Hutchison
Irving Janis
A. Jenness
Carl Jung
Daniel Levitin
Elizabeth Loftus
Abraham Maslow
Stanley Milgram
Walter Mischel
Linda S. Pagani
Ivan Pavlov
Jean Piaget
James O. Prochaska
Carl Rogers
Lee Ross
B.F. Skinner
Marc Snyder
Leta Stetter Hollingworth
John Watson
Philip Zimbardo

Sociology

Albert Bandura
Howard Becker
Peter Burke
Nicholas A. Christakis
Kenneth Clark
Mamie Clark
Auguste Comte
Charles Cooley
Kingsley Davis
Robin Dunbar
Emile Durkheim
Erving Goffman
Mark Granovetta
Charles Hofling
Irving Janis
Karl Marx
George Herbert Mead
Robert Merton
Walter Mischel
Wilbert Moore
Richard Nisbett
Talcott Parsons
Adrienne Rich
Muzafer Sherif
Rosalind Sydie
Dorothy Smith
Henri Tajfel
Melvin Tumin
Max Weber
Scot Wortley
C. Wright-Mills

GLOSSARY

A

ableism:
discrimination based on assumptions about a person's ability or disability

abstract:
a brief summary of the study's methods and findings

acculturation:
the meeting of two or more cultural groups and the resulting cultural changes to each group

achieved status:
the position that an individual holds in society based on his or her accomplishment of a particular task or role

acting crowd:
a group of people fuelled by a single purpose or goal

ageism:
discrimination against individuals or groups because of their age

agents of socialization:
people and institutions that shape an individual's social development

alienation:
feeling of separation or isolation

altruism:
the principle of unselfish regard for the needs and interests of others

amygdala:
the part of the brain that regulates emotion

analytical psychology:
a branch of psychology founded by Carl Jung, based on the idea that balancing a person's psyche would allow the person to reach his or her full potential

anomie:
a state of normlessness

anticipatory socialization:
the process of learning how to plan the way to behave in new situations

archetypes:
universal symbols that tend to reappear over time; includes models of people, behaviours, and personalities

ascribed status:
the position that an individual holds in society that is determined at birth and over which he or she has no control

attention deficit/hyperactivity disorder (ADHD):
a type of developmental disorder characterized by inattention, impulsiveness, and overactivity

attribution theory:
the belief that a person's behaviour is the result of his or her disposition or an external situation

B

behavioural shift:
a change in behaviour resulting from contact with another culture

bicultural identity:
a sense of oneself as being strongly rooted in two cultures

bilineal:
a kinship system in which people trace their ancestry through both their mothers and fathers

bipedalism:
the trait of habitually walking on two legs

bridewealth:
a cultural system where the groom (or the groom's family) must pay a father in order to marry his daughter

bureaucracy:
a large administration that pursues a wide variety of goals

bystander effect:
a concept in social psychology used to explain why the larger the number of people in a group, the less likely it is that individuals will stop to help someone in an emergency. Sometimes this concept is called *Genovese syndrome* because it is linked to the terrible murder of Kitty Genovese.

C

cargo beliefs:
religious convictions in Papua New Guinea that ancestors will reward the living with goods as a token of their love and approval

casual crowd:
a group of people in the same place at the same time but who do not have a common goal

census:
an official periodic count of a population including such information as sex, age, education, and occupation

cerebrum:
the largest and most developed portion of the brain, which is responsible for controlling memory, understanding, and logic

chameleon effect:
the mimicking of the body language of a person with whom we are interacting

chaperone:
an older or married woman who accompanies or supervises a young unmarried woman on social occasions

circumcision:
the surgical removal of the foreskin of the penis; often performed as part of a ceremony at birth or during adolescence

clan:
a group of several lineages in a patrilineal or matrilineal society in which people are related but cannot always trace exact relationships

classical conditioning:
a type of learning where a once neutral stimulus comes to produce a particular response after pairings with a conditioned stimulus

classism:
systemic or personal actions that discriminate against persons according to their socio-economic level, which leads to human needs being unmet

client-centred therapy:
a humanistic therapy developed by Carl Rogers in which the client plays an active role

cognition:
the mental processes in the brain associated with thinking, knowing, and remembering

cognitive dissonance:
the theory that people are motivated to reduce the discomfort they feel when their behaviour doesn't match their attitude

collective unconscious:
the shared, inherited pool of memories from our ancestors

collectivist society:
a community in which the group is more important than its individual members, so individual needs are secondary to collective thought and action

compliance:
social behaviour by an individual that may be contrary to his or her beliefs but is exhibited nonetheless in order to achieve rewards and avoid punishments

conditioned response:
the learned response to a previously neutral stimulus

conditioned stimulus:
an originally neutral stimulus that comes to trigger a conditioned response after being paired with an unconditional stimulus

conformity:
the process by which one changes one's thoughts, feelings, and behaviour to meet the expectations of a group or authority figure

conscious:
information that we are always aware of; our conscious mind performs the thinking when we take in new information

conventional crowd:
a large group of people gathered for a clear purpose who behave according to expectations

correlation:
a measure that indicates a relationship between two factors but does not indicate causation; in a positive correlation, one variable goes up precisely as the other goes up; in a negative correlation, one variable goes up precisely as the other goes down

counterculture:
a subculture that rejects the most popular values and most important norms of society and replaces them with extreme views on violence, family, and loyalty

cross-cultural psychology:
an area of study that looks at the effect of culture on human behaviour

cult:
an extremist religious group with rigid social and moral views that oppose those of mainstream culture, typically guided by a charismatic leader

cultural/ethnic identity:
a connection to a cultural group that helps define who a person is

cultural universals:
beliefs common across all cultures

culturally constructed:
created or shaped by a culture

culture:
the total system of ideas, values, behaviours, and attitudes of a society commonly shared by most members of a society

cyberpsychology:
a new field of psychology that studies the influences of technology on people and the ways it can be used to treat mental illness

D

defence mechanism:
the ego's way of distorting reality to deal with anxiety

dehumanize:
to deprive people of their human qualities; to degrade or deny the humanity of another person

deindividuation:
the loss of a person's sense of individuality and personal responsibility when immersed in a group environment

demography:
the study of the structure and development of human population

denial:
a defence mechanism whereby a person refuses to recognize or acknowledge something that is painful

deviance:
a violation of society's norms and accepted standards

differential association:
the theory that individuals learn the values, attitudes, techniques, and motives for criminal behaviour through interaction with others

discrimination:
the act of treating groups or individuals unfairly based on their race, gender, or other common characteristic; can be overt or systemic

displacement:
the shift of an emotion from its original focus to another object, person, or situation

DNA:
Deoxyribonucleic acid; the molecule that carries genetic information in all living systems and provides the most basic explanation of the laws of genetics

drive-reduction theory:
the idea that our physiological needs create drives that need to be reduced, which motivates us to satisfy this need

dyad:
a group consisting of two members

E

ego:
Freud's term for the rational part of the mind, which operates on the reality principle

ego identity:
a conscious sense of self developed through social interactions, which is constantly changing

emic perspective:
the point of view of an insider of a culture

empirical:
based on facts, statistics, and data

ethnocentric:
believing that one's own culture is superior to all others

ethnography:
the written account of a culture

ethnology:
the study of the origins and cultures of different races and peoples

etic perspective:
the point of view of an outsider to a culture

euphemism:
a word or set of words used to indirectly describe an uncomfortable or inappropriate concept or idea in a socially acceptable way

explicit cultural knowledge:
information about a culture that is easily explained and described

expressive crowd:
a large number of people at an event who display emotion and excitement

extinction:
in operant conditioning, the diminishing of a conditioned response due to a lack of reinforcement

extrinsic motivation:
desire to perform a task due to external factors, such as a reward or the threat of punishment

extroversion:
directing one's interests outward, especially toward social contacts

F

factor analysis:
a statistical technique that identifies patterns of related test items (factors)

feral:
unwanted child deserted at a young age and raised by animals

fetish:
a specific object believed to have magical powers

fixation:
the continued focus on an earlier stage of psychosocial development due to an unresolved conflict at the oral, anal, or phallic stage

fossil:
preserved remains of biological matter

frame of reference:
a person's total life experience, including cultural beliefs and learning

free association:
a method used in psychoanalysis where a patient relaxes and says whatever comes to mind

functional differentiation:
divisions that are created to help deal with a complex environment; these divisions operate independently but are connected to one another

fundamental attribution error:
the tendency to overestimate the impact of personal disposition and underestimate the impact of social influences when analyzing the behaviours of others

G

gender identity:
an individual's sense of being male or female

globalization:
the process by which economies, societies, and cultures become integrated through a worldwide network

glocalization:
to think globally about a group's interests but act locally

group-based identity:
the development of self-concept and identity through membership in a social group with whom the individual shares similar values and beliefs

groupthink:
the effects of collective pressure on the decision-making abilities of individual members of a group

H

heredity:
physical characteristics and aspects of personality and behaviour that are passed down genetically from your relatives

hominin:
a human or human ancestor

homophily:
the tendency to associate with those who are similar to us

horticultural:
a form of semi-nomadic agriculture

hypodescent:
a system of racial classification where children of mixed-race couples are identified as members of the ethnic group who is less privileged in society

hypothesis:
a tentative assumption made from known facts as the basis for investigation

I

id:
Freud's term for the instinctual part of the mind, which operates on the pleasure principle

identity crisis:
a time in a teenager's life filled with extreme self-consciousness as he or she attempts to test and integrate various roles

identity moratorium:
a status in which the adolescent is in crisis and unable to accomplish tasks necessary to becoming an adult, and explores other youth subcultures

individualistic society:
a community based on the belief that individual rights and the freedom of the individual to pursue his or her own happiness are more important than the interests of the group

informal group:
a less intimate gathering of people in which member interaction is not governed by explicit rules

informal justice system:
a system of social pressure to control behaviour, used most often in nomadic or non-hierarchical societies

informant:
a reliable and knowledgeable person who provides specific information to an anthropologist studying his or her community

ingroup:
a social group formed when its members identify with one another

instinct theory:
the theory that involuntary and unlearned processes direct our behaviours

institutional completeness:
the ability of a person to live a full life within his or her own cultural enclave

intelligence:
a person's ability to solve problems and reason effectively; a social construct used to explain why some people are better than others at cognitive tasks

interculturalism:
a proposed policy in Quebec emphasizing cultural and economic integration of immigrants and French-language learning

intrinsic motivation:
desire to perform a task for its own sake

introversion:
directing one's interests inward

Islamophobia:
prejudice against and fear of Islamic beliefs and Muslims

isolate:
child raised in near isolation within a human household

K

kinship:
the relationship between two or more people that is based on common ancestry, marriage, or adoption

L

labelling:
a theoretical approach for defining deviant behaviour, in which the key determinant for deviant behaviour is belonging to a subculture

liminal stage:
the second stage in a rite of passage, when the initiate is in a state of transition between the old and the new

lineage:
all the male relatives in a family that can be traced back to one common direct ancestor

logotherapy:
a form of psychotherapy that tries to help the patient find the aim and meaning of his or her own life as a human being without accessing the medical aspect of mental health

longitudinal study:
research that follows the same people over a long period of time

M

macrosociology:
an approach of sociology that analyzes social systems on a large scale

mass hysteria:
the widespread irrational reaction to a perceived danger

matrilineal:
a kinship system in which people trace their ancestry through their mothers

meritocracy:
a social system in which positions are given to people according to individual ability or worth

meta-analysis:
a study combining the results of many other studies

microsociology:
the study of small groups and individuals within a society

mob:
a disorderly crowd of people

monogamy:
a relationship where an individual has one partner. Serial monogamy refers to monogamous relationships that occur one after another.

multiculturalism:
an ideology that states that all cultures are of equal value and should be promoted equally within the same nation. In Canada, multiculturalism is a policy that protects ethnic, racial, linguistic, and religious diversity

N

naive realism:
the belief that everyone else defines the world in the same way you do

national identity:
sense of belonging to a specific country and having shared feelings, regardless of country of origin

negativity bias:
the tendency to recall and react to unpleasant events more easily than positive ones

neo-Freudians:
psychologists who modified Freud's psychoanalytic theory to include social and cultural aspects

neuroscientist:
a scientist who specializes in the study of the human brain

neurotic disorder:
a mental disorder involving anxiety and fear

norms:
expectations about how people should behave

O

obedience:
the act or habit of doing what one is told or submitting to authority

objective:
type of conclusions based on facts and data and uninfluenced by personal perspectives, prejudices, or emotions

operant conditioning:
a type of learning that uses rewards and punishment to achieve a desired behaviour

outgroup:
a social group toward which an individual feels disrespect or opposition; sometimes treated badly by the ingroup

P

panic:
a highly emotional and irrational response on the part of an individual or a group to a dangerous or harmful social event

participant observation:
the careful watching of a group, in some cases living with its members and participating in their culture

patrilineal:
a kinship system in which people trace their ancestry through their fathers

perception:
the process of how an individual takes in information visually and with the other senses

personality:
an individual's characteristic pattern of thinking, feeling, and acting

personality view of behaviour:
the belief that the individual shows consistency in behaviour from one situation to another

phobia:
anxiety about a specific object, activity, or situation

placemakers:
people who access the Internet in public to create social interactions

polyandry:
a form of marriage with one wife and multiple husbands

polygamy:
a form of marriage that involves multiple partners

polygny:
a form a marriage between one husband and multiple wives

positivism:
the application of the scientific method to obtain quantifiable data in order to understand society

post-traumatic stress disorder (PTSD):
a type of anxiety disorder characterized by the reliving of a traumatic event through flashbacks and nightmares

postmulticulturalism:
the view that new models are needed to bring about social cohesion

potlatch:
a sacred ceremony of First Nations peoples on the Northwest coast of North America in which property is given away to enhance status

prejudice:
an individual judgment about or active hostility toward another social group

primary group:
a set of people with whom an individual has strong emotional and personal connections

primary socialization:
the process of learning the basic skills needed to survive in society

projection:
a defence mechanism whereby a person attributes their own threatening impulses onto someone else

prosocial behaviour:
a form of altruism in which individuals or groups demonstrate empathy toward and care for the welfare of others without benefit to themselves

psychoanalytic theory:
Sigmund Freud's theory that all human behaviour is influenced by early childhood and that childhood experiences influence the unconscious mind throughout life

psychodynamic theory:
an approach to therapy that focuses on resolving a patient's conflicted conscious and unconscious feelings

psychological acculturation:
change in the cultural behaviour and thinking of a person or group of people through contact with another culture

psychotic disorder:
a broad term that indicates severe mental disorder characterized by a break from reality

R

racism:
erroneous judgment, assumptions, opinions, or actions toward a person or group, based on the belief that one race is superior to another

radiometric dating:
a process that is used to determine the age of an object, based on measuring the amount of radioactive material it has

rationalization:
social actions motivated by efficiency or benefit, not custom or emotion

reciprocity:
an economic system of formal and informal sharing among members of a society to distribute resources fairly

redistribution:
an economic system of collecting resources centrally and handing them out them among members of a society

reflexivity:
the practice of reflecting on your own world view, biases, and impact on the culture you are studying

repression:
a process in which unacceptable desires or impulses are excluded from consciousness and left to operate in the unconscious

resocialization:
the process by which negative behaviour is transformed into socially acceptable behaviour

restorative justice:
an approach to justice that focuses on restoring harmony and balance to the community by focusing on the needs of both the victim and the offender instead of punishment

review of literature:
a search for and examination of credible, reputable studies conducted by others

riot:
civil disorder stemming from a social grievance, caused by a disorganized crowd exhibiting aggression, who may turn to acts of violence, vandalism, and destruction of property

rite of passage:
a ceremony, ritual, or event that marks an individual's passage from one stage of life to another

ritual:
prescribed behaviour in which there is no real connection between the action and the desired outcome

role:
the expected behaviour of a person in a particular social position

role identity:
the behaviour an individual displays in order to fulfil the expectations of a specific role (for example, a student)

S

sanction:
informal or formal penalty or reward to ensure conformity within a group

sapienization:
the process of learning uniquely human social customs centred on marriage, the family, and the household

scapegoat:
a specific person or group of people who become the target of hatred or blame for the hardships of others

secondary group:
a large, impersonal gathering of people in which members' roles are measured by their contributions to a common goal or purpose

secondary socialization:
the process of learning how to behave appropriately in group situations

self-actualization:
reaching one's full potential; occurs only after basic physical and psychological needs are met

self-enhancement:
the belief that you are more competent and generally better than your actions and behaviour indicate

serotonin:
a chemical messenger in the brain that is associated with feelings of well-being

sexism:
attitudes or behaviours based on predetermined ideas of sexual roles that discriminate against others because of their sex

sexual orientation:
an emotional and sexual attraction toward another person

situation view of behaviour:
the belief that the individual's behaviour changes from encounter to encounter

smart mob:
a large group of strangers who use electronic media to organize and stage surprise public gatherings

social change:
a society's attempt to incorporate different values and beliefs into its existing structure and to modify public institutions to instigate social and cultural progress

social cohesion:
a way of integrating economic and social policies in order to allow citizens to easily interact with one another

social customs:
expected and ideal behaviours of a society

social fragmentation:
the failure of society to fully integrate minority groups into the mainstream culture

social identity:
(psychology) a sense of belonging based on membership in different groups (family, ethnic, occupational, etc.), which changes over one's life

social identity:
(sociology) the way you define yourself to the world and to yourself

social inequality:
the inability of some people and the success of others to attain access to the privileges, rewards, or assets of society

social influence:
the effect of other people on a person's thoughts and actions

social institution:
an organization or social framework whose function is to meet the basic needs of its members by providing direction and operating principles for society

social integration:
the process by which minority groups are brought into the mainstream culture and are able to enjoy the same rights, opportunities, and services available to the majority

social mobility:
the process by which people change their status in a community

social role:
expectations attached to particular social positions

social shield:
a device or object used to avoid interactions with other people

social status:
the importance of the position a person holds in society

social stratification:
the institutional and social processes that define certain types of occupations and goods as socially desirable

socialization:
the continuing process where an individual learns the appropriate behavioural patterns, skills, and values for his or her social world

solidarity:
the ties that unite members of a group

stereotype:
an exaggerated view or judgment made about a group or class of people

stigma:
a belief that leads to social disgrace

strain theory of behaviour:
a belief that individuals are more likely to pursue illegitimate actions in order to achieve society's most cherished goals when they are blocked from accessing the institutionalized means to these goals

subculture:
a small group within a larger group who shares a common system of values, beliefs, attitudes, behaviours, and lifestyle distinct from those of the larger group

subjective:
type of conclusions shaped by a person's cultural and personal perspective, feelings, and beliefs

superego:
Freud's term for the moral centre of the mind

supernatural:
all of the things that are outside known laws of nature

survey:
a set of questions used on a sample of the population study about opinions, values, or actions

symbolic ethnicity:
ethnic identity based on an emotional connection to a real or imagined past rather than daily experience

T

taboo:
a restriction on behaviour to help ensure a good outcome

tacit cultural knowledge:
information about a culture that the people within the culture or organization know but have difficulty explaining

technological diffusion:
the adoption by one culture of a technology invented by another culture

threshold:
a level or point at which something would or would not happen; a tipping point

transnationalism:
the maintenance of an ethnic identity by staying connected with relatives in other countries and staying informed of political and other developments in the country of origin, often through digital technology

true mobiles:
people who access the Internet in public to specifically avoid social interactions

U

unconditioned response:
the natural response to an unconditioned stimulus

unconditioned stimulus:
a stimulus that naturally triggers a response

unconscious:
information processing in our mind that we are not aware of; according to Freud, it holds our unacceptable thoughts, feelings, and memories; according to Jung, it includes patterns of memories, instincts, and experiences common to all

upstander:
a person who takes action, particularly when the easiest or most acceptable course is to do nothing, when they believe something is right

V

values:
shared ideas and standards that are considered acceptable and binding

virtual community:
a group of individuals who communicate online

W

wage labour:
work for which wages are paid

REFERENCES

Chapter 1

American Anthropological Association. (1998). *American Anthropological Association Statement on "Race"*

Bernard, H. R. (2006). *Research Methods in Anthropology: Qualitative and Quantitative Approaches*. Lanham MD: Alta Mira Press.

Bronislaw Malinowski. (2008). *New World Encyclopedia*.

Canadian Society of Forensic Science. (2007). *All You Ever Wanted to Know About Forensic Science in Canada But Didn't Know Who To Ask*.

CBC. (2008). *Scientists find 17 living relatives of 'iceman' discovered in B.C. glacier*.

Collishaw, N. (2009). *History of Tobacco Control in Canada*. Physicians for a Smoke Free Canada.

Diamond, Jared. (1994, November 1). Race without color. *Discover*.

Dunn, S., [director] & McFadyen, S. [director]. (2008). *Global Metal*. [documentary]. Canada: Seville Pictures Warner Home Video.

Edgar, B. (2007, November/December). Lucy Up Close. *Archaeology Magazine*, 60 (6).

Ember, C.R., & Ember, M. (1999). *Anthropology*. Upper Saddle City, New Jersey: Prentice-Hall.

Friedl, E. (1978) Society and Sex Roles. *Human Nature*, 1(4), 68–75.

Goodall Jane. (2007, June), TED Talks: Jane Goodall helps humans and animals live together [Video]

Government of British Columbia Ministry of Natural Resource Operations. (2008). *Kwaday Dan Ts'inshi*.

Grambo, Rebecca. (2006). *Digging Canadian History*. Walrus Books: Vancouver.

Jablonski, Nina. (2007). *Race: Only Skin Deep*. American Anthropological Association.

Laidlaw, S. (2007, April 2). Creationism Debate Continues to Evolve . *The Toronto Star*.

Lavenda, Robert H and Emily A. Schultz. (2010). *Core Concepts in Cultural Anthropology*. McGraw-Hill Higher Education, New York.

Lee, Richard. (1993). *The Dobe Ju/'hoansi, 2nd edition*. Orlando, Florida. Harcourt Brace.

Lewin, Roger. (1998). *Principles of Human Evolution: A Core Textbook*. Malden, MA: Blackwell Science.

Malinowski, B. (1961). *Argonauts of the Western Pacific: An Account of Native Enterprise and Adventure in the Archipelagoes of Melanesian New Guinea*. New York, NY: E. P. Dutton & Co.

Margolis, M. E. (1984). *Mothers and Such: Views of American Women and Why They Changed* (Unabridged. ed.). Berkeley, CA: University of California Press.

Matras, Yaron. (2002). *Romani: A Linguistic Introduction*. Cambridge, UK: Cambridge University Press.

Myers, V. (2010, June 23). Argentine Woman to Identify Dead with Skills Learned at Mercyhurst College. *Erie Times-News*.

Natural Resources Canada (2010). *Trailblazer: Diamond Jenness: 1886–1969*.

O'Neill, D. (2010, January 2). *Modern Human Variation: Distribution of Blood Types*.

Peoples, J., & Bailey, G.. (2003). *Humanity: An Introduction to Cultural Anthropology* (6th ed.). Boston, MA: Thomson Wadsworth.

Raffaele, P. (2006, November 1). Speaking Bonobo. *Smithsonian Magazine*.

Rumbaugh, D., Savage-Rumbaugh, S., & Fields, B. (2010.). Additional Studies Into Ape Language and Primate Intelligence. *Great Ape Trust*.

Schwimmer, B. (2007). *Anth1220 A04 Cultural Anthropology A04*. University of Manitoba.

Sheremata, D. (1996, May 13). Knee-deep in the Killing Fields of Rwanda: An Edmonton Anthropology Student Unearths Genocide Victims. *Alberta Report*.

The Leakey Family. (2010). *The Leakey Foundation*.

Thomas, P. (2003). Forensic Anthropology: *The Growing Science of Talking Bones*. New York, NY: Facts on File.

Chapter 2

Bartholomew, K., & Horowitz, L. M. (1991). Attachment styles among young adults:

A test of a four-category model. *Journal of Personality and Social Psychology, 61*, 226–244.

Epstein, R. The myth of the teen brain. *Scientific American Mind*, April/May 2007, pp. 57–63.

Gage, N., & Berliner, D. (1991). *Educational psychology* (5th ed.). Boston, MA: Houghton Mifflin.

Hollingworth, H. L. (1943/1990). *Leta Stetter Hollingworth: A Biography*. Bolton, MA: Anker Publishing Company. (Reprint of 1943 edition published by University of Nebraska Press.)

Jung, C. (1964). Approaching the unconscious. In C. Jung, (Ed.), *Man and his Symbols*. New York, NY: Dell Publishing.

Loftus, E. F., & Pickrell, J. (1995). The formation of false memories. *Psychiatric Anals*, 25, 720–725.

Maslow, A. (1943). A theory of human motivation. *Psychological Review, 50*, 370–396.

Sternberg, R. J. (1982). *Handbook of Human Intelligence*. Cambridge, UK: Cambridge University Press.

Chapter 3

Barron, C., & Lacombe, D. (2005, February) Moral Panic and the Nasty Girl. *Canadian Review of Sociology and Anthropology*.

Bearak, B. (1999). M.N. Srinivas is Dead at 83; Studied India's Caste System. The *New York Times*.

CBC News. (2008). *Energy Drinks Linked to College Students' Risky Behaviour*.

CBC News. (2008). *Court Orders 4th trial for Ellard in Murder of Victoria Teen Reena Virk*.

CBC News. (2009). *The Murder of Reena Virk and Trials of Kelly Ellard*.

Feij, J. A. (1998). Work socialization of young people. In P. I. D. Drenth, H. Thierry, & C. J. deWolf (Eds.), *Handbook of work and organizational psychology* (Vol. 3, pp. 207–256). Hove, England: Psychology Press/Lawrence Erlbaum Associates, Inc.

McGinn, D. (2010). Chill, Dad: He just loves Beyonce. *The Globe and Mail*.

Smith, Dorothy. (1987). *The Everyday World As Problematic: A Feminist Sociology*. Boston, MA: Northeastern University Press.

Statistics Canada. 2000. *Crime statistics*. The Daily. 18 July.

Steinberg, C.D. (2009). Reena Virk Story: Senseless Teen Violence—Senseless Waste. *York Region Anti-Bullying Coalition*

University of Buffalo (2008, July 24) *Energy Drinks Linked to Risk-Taking Behaviors Among College Students*.

Valkenburg, P. M. (2004). *Children's Responses to the Screen: A Media Psychological Approach*. Hillsdale, NJ: Lawrence Erlbaum Associates, Inc.

Chapter 4

Altieri, L. (Producer), & Omori, E., (Director). (2003). *Skin Stories*. United States: PBS.

Bahnsen, C. (2007). Real Men Don't Eat Turtle Eggs. *E-The Environmental Magazine*, 18(3), 14–16.

Beckham, S. B. (1988). The American Front Porch: Women's Liminal Space. In *Investigating Culture: An Experiential Introduction to Anthropology*. Delaney, C (2004). Boston, MA: Blackwell Publishing Ltd.

Boas, F. (2005). Scientists as Spies. *Anthropology Today*, Vol. 21, No. 3, p. 27.

Bohannan, L. (1966) Shakespeare in the Bush. In *Investigating Culture: An Experiential Introduction to Anthropology*. Delaney, C. (2004) Boston, MA: Blackwell Publishing Ltd.

Brennan, D. (2002) Men's Pleasure, Women's Labor: Tourism for Sex. *Conformity and Conflict: Readings in Cultural Anthropology*. McCurdy, D, Spradley, J. (2008). Boston: Pearson (2008).

Brown, M. (2011). Google Maps Mashup Documents Libyan Protests. *Wired U.K.*

Burr, R. (2002). Shaming of the Anthropologist: Ethical Issues During and in the Aftermath of the Fieldwork Process. *Anthropology Matters*, 4(1).

Case, Amber. Ted Talks: We Are All Cyborgs Now. [Video]

CBC News. (2007). *Bullied Student Tickled Pink by Schoolmates' T-shirt Campaign*.

CBC The Fifth Estate. (2007). *Timeline: History of Polygamy*.

Condry, I. (2004). B-Boys and B-Girls: Rap Fandom and Consumer Culture in Japan. In *Fanning the Flames: Consumer Culture and Fandom in Japan*, ed. William Kelly, pp. 17–39. Albany NY: SUNY Press.

Ellis, J. (2008). *Tattooing the World*. New York, NY: Columbia University Press.

Ember, C.R., & Ember, M. (2009). *Cross-Cultural Research Methods*. Landham, MD: Altamira Press.

Ervin, A.M. (2001). *Canadian Perspectives in Cultural Anthropology*. Scarborough, ON: Nelson Thomson Learning.

Fish, Jeffrey. (1995). Mixed Blood. *Conformity and Conflict: Readings to Accompany Miller, Cultural Anthropology*. McCurdy, D, Spradley, J. (2008). Boston, MA: Pearson Education.

Fong, P. (2009, September 24). Polygamy Charges Tossed Out; B.C. Judge Backs Two Leaders in Bountiful Who Say Province Went Prosecutor Shopping. *The Toronto Star*, A.10.

Gardner, A. (2000). At Home in South Sinai. *Nomadic Peoples*, 4(2), 48+.

Geertz, C. (2001). Life Without Fathers or Husbands. *Conformity and Conflict: Readings in Cultural Anthropology*. McCurdy, D, Spradley, J. (2008). Boston, MA: Pearson Education.

Gmelch, G. (2006). *Inside Pitch: Life in Professional Baseball* (New Ed ed.). Toronto, ON: Bison Books.

Gray, C.H. (1995). *The Cyborg Handbook*. New York, NY: Routledge.

Heine, S.J., & Hamamura, T. (2007). In search of East Asian Self-Enhancement. *Personality and Social Psychology Review*, 11, 1–24

Hrdy, Sarah Blaffer. (1992). The Myth of Mother Love.(Book Review Desk). *The New York Times Book Review*.

Irwin, A. (2008). Redeployment as a Rite of Passage. *Canadian Defense and Foreign Affairs Institute*.

Kilbride, Philip L. (1996). African Polygyny: Family Values and Contemporary Changes. In *Applying Cultural Anthropology: An Introductory Reader*. 4th ed. Aaron Podolefsky and Peter J. Brown, eds. 1999. Mountain View, CA: Mayfield Publishing Company.

Kuwahara, Makiko. (2005). *Tattoo: An Anthology*. New York, NY: Berg, Oxford International Publishers Ltd.

Lee, Richard. (1993). *The Dobe Ju/'hoansi*, 2nd edition. Orlando, Florida. Harcourt Brace.

Maginnis, T. (1995). How's Your Personal Distance? *F&P Friends and Partners : Welcome*.

Malinowski, B. (1929). Practical Anthropology. *Africa: Journal of the International African Institute*. Vol. 2, No. 1, pp. 22–38.

McCurdy, D. (1997). Family and Kinship in Village India. In *Conformity and Conflict: Readings in Cultural Anthropology*. McCurdy, D, Spradley, J. (2008). Boston, MA: Pearson Education.

McCurdy, D., and J. Spradley (2008). *Conformity and Conflict. Readings in Cultural Anthropology*. Boston, MA: Pearson Education.

McFate, M. (2005). Anthropology and Counterinsurgency: The Strange Story of their Curious Relationship. *Military Review*, 85(2), 24.

Netting, Nancy S. Two-lives, one partner: Indo-Canadian youth between love and arranged marriages. *Journal of Comparative Family Studies* 37.1 (2006): 129+. Student Edition.

O'Brien, J. (2009). *Encyclopedia of Gender and Society*, Vol 2. Thousand Oaks CA: Sage Publications Inc.

Patten, S. (2006). Medical Anthropology: Improving Nutrition in Malawi. In *Conformity and Conflict: Readings in Cultural Anthropology.* McCurdy, D, Spradley, J. (2008). Boston, MA: Pearson Education.

Peoples, J., & Bailey, G.. (2003). *Humanity: An Introduction to Cultural Anthropology* (6th ed.). Boston, MA: Thomson Wadsworth.

Popenoe, R. (2005). Ideal. In *Fat: The Anthropology of an Obsession*. Kulick, D., Meneley, A. eds. (pp. 9–28). New York, NY: Tarcher.

Profanter, A., & Cate, S. R. (2009). Deal Justly with Them…(In)Justice in Polygyny: The Male Perspective. *The Journal of Social Psychology*, June (149.3), 223 (19).

Schafft, G.E. (2007). *From Racism to Genocide: Anthropology in the Third Reich*. Champaign, IL: University of Illinois Press.

Scheper-Hughes, N. (1989) Death Without Weeping. In *Classic Readings in Cultural Anthropology* (3 ed.). Ferraro, G. ed. (2009). Belmont, CA: Wadsworth Publishing.

Scheper-Hughes, N. (1989) Death Without Weeping: Has Poverty Ravaged Mother Love in the Shantytowns of Brazil?. *Natural History*, pp. 8–16

Seth, R. (2008). *First Comes Marriage: Modern Advice from the Wisdom of Arranged Marriages*. New York, NY: Simon & Shuster.

Sharpe, L. (1952). Steel Axes for Stone-Age Australians. In *Conformity and Conflict: Readings in Cultural Anthropology.* McCurdy, D, Spradley, J. (2008). Boston MA: Pearson Education.

Sheppard, M. (1996). Proxemics. *UNM Computer Science*.

Starkweather, K.E. (2010). *Exploration into Human Polyandry: An Evolutionary Examination of the Non-Classical Cases.* (Master's thesis).

Statistics Canada. (2009). *Father's Day By the Numbers*.

Statistics Canada. (2010). *Deaths.* The Daily.

Turner, T., Txukarramãe, M., & Carlos, L. (2006, April 4). Kayapó set to fight massive dam Project. *Survival International—The Movement for Tribal Peoples*.

Whitmore, R. (2008). The Maori—Tattoo—New Zealand in History. *New Zealand in History*

Chapter 5

Demers, S., & Bennett, C. (2007). Single-sex classrooms. *What works? Research into Practice*. Ontario: Literacy and Numeracy Secretariat.

Heyman, G. (2009). *Addiction: A disorder of choice.* Cambridge, MA: Harvard University Press.

Josephson Institute. (2008). *Report Card on the Ethics of American Youth*.

Kinsey, A. (1948). *Sexual behavior in the human male.* Philadelphia, PA: Saunders.

Krantz, J. H., & Dalal, R. (2000). Validity of web-based psychological research. In M. H. Birnbaum (Ed.), *Psychological experiments on the internet* (7–11). San Diego: Academic Press.

Kraut, R. E., Olson, J., Manaji, M., Bruckman, A., Cohen, J., & Couper, M. (2003). Psychological research online: Opportunities and challenges. *American Psychologist, 59*(2), 105–117.

Martino, W. (2008). Boys' underachievement: Which boys are we talking about? *What Works? Research Into Practice*.

McDevitt, D. M., & Ormrod, J.E. (2007). *Child development and education.* Upper Saddle River, NJ: Pearson Education/Merrill.

Milgram, S. (1979). Quoted in Neiman, S. *Moral Clarity: A guide for grown-up idealists.* FL: Houghton Mifflin.

Sax, L. (2005). The Promise and Peril of Single-Sex Public Education.

Sax, L. (2008, March). Teaching Boys and Girls Separately. *The New York Times*.

Siegel, S. (2004). Intra-administration associations and withdrawal symptoms: Morphine-elicited morphine withdrawal. *Experimental and Clinical Psychopharmacology, 12*(2), 3–11.

Statistics Canada. (2003). Alcohol and illicit drug dependence. *Supplement to Health Reports*, Volume 15, 2004.

Statistics Canada. (2006). CANSIM: Table: Television viewing, by age and sex, by province.

Statistics Canada. (2007). Recycling in Canada. *EnviroStats*, Volume 1(1).

Canadian Council of Learning. (2006). *Liars, fraudsters and cheats: Dealing with the growth of academic dishonesty.*

Schor, J.B. (2004). *Born to Buy: The Commercialized Child and the New Consumer Culture.* New York, NY: Scribner.

Chapter 6

ABC News. (2001, November 29). *Travelers Stranded Sept. 11 Get Warm Welcome.*

CBC News. (2004). *David Reimer: The Boy Who Lived as a Girl.*

CNN. (2010). Study: *White and Black Children Biased Toward Lighter Skin.*

Coloroso, B. (2008). *The Bully, the Bullied, and the Bystander.* New York, NY: HarperCollins.

Cotroneo, C. (2007, May 18). A Victim of Racial Profiling. *The Toronto Star*.

Craig, W. M., & Pepler, D. J. (2007). Understanding Bullying: From Research to Policy. *Canadian Psychology*, 48, 86–93.

Derby, P. (2009). Views From Behind The Camera's Lens. In *A Report on Camera Surveillance in Canada Part*

Two. pp. 37–50. Surveillance Camera Awareness Network (SCAN).

Diebel, L. (2007, July 21). "Ghetto Dude" Email Sent by Mistake: Province. *The Toronto Star*.

Harris, D. A. (2003). *Profiles in Injustice: Why Racial Profiling Cannot Work*. New York, NY: The New Press.

Hudson, B. (1993). Racism and Criminology: Concepts and Controversies. In B. Hudson and D. Cook (eds.), *Racism and Criminology*. London UK: Sage.

Koskela, H. (2004). Webcams, TV Shows and Mobile Phones: Empowering Exhibitionism. *Surveillance and Society*, 2:2/3, 199–215.

Luo, M. (2004) Excuse Me. May I have your seat?. *The New York Times*.

Rheingold, H. (2002). *Smart Mobs: The Next Social Revolution. Transforming Cultures and Communities in the Age of Instant Access*. Cambridge, MA: Perseus Books Group.

Seals, A. (2009), Are Gangs a Substitute for Legitimate Employment? Investigating the Impact of Labor Market Effects on Gang Affiliation. *Kyklos*, 62: 407–425.

Chapter 7

Ali, M. A. (2008, Summer). Second-Generation Youth's Belief in the Myth of Canadian Multiculturalism. *Canadian Ethnic Studies Journal*, 40(2), 89 (19).

Amarasingam, A. (2008). Religion and Ethnicity Among Sri Lankan Tamil Youth in Ontario. *Canadian ethnic studies journal*, 40(2), 149–170.

Angus Reid. (2010). *Canadians Truly Proud of Flag, Hockey, Armed Forces and Health Care System*.

Bazemore, G., & Umbreit, M. (2001). Circle Sentencing. *Juvenile Justice Bulletin*, 4.

Benthall, J. (1991). Invisible Wounds: Corporal Punishment in British Schools as a Form of Ritual. *Child Abuse & Neglect*. Vol. 15 (4) pp. 377–388).

Berry, J. W., Kim, U., Power, S., Young, M., & Bukaji, M. (1989). Acculturation attitudes in plural societies. *Applied Psychology, 38*, 185–206.

Bodley, J. (2000). *Cultural Anthropology: Tribes, States, and the Global System*. Mountainview CA: Mayfield Pub.

Bouchard, G., & Taylor, C. (2008). *Fonder l'avenir: Le temps de la conciliation* [Building the future: A time for reconciliation].

Byers, M., & Tastsoglou, E. (2008). Negotiating Ethno-Cultural Identity: The Experience of Greek and Jewish Youth in Halifax. *Canadian ethnic studies journal, 40*(2), 5–34.

Cazabon. A. [writer/director] (2010). *3rd World Canada*. [Documentary]. Canada.

CBC News. (2009, May 4). *Cole Harbour High School Closed Following Brawl*.

Corbeil, J.P., & Houle, R. (2010). *Statistical Portrait of the French-Speaking Immigrant Population Outside Quebec (1991 to 2006)*. (Catalogue Number No. 89-641-XWE).

Dallaire, C., & Denis, C. (2005, Spring). Asymmetrical Hybridities: Youths at Francophone Games in Canada. *Canadian Journal of Sociology, 30*(2), 143–169.

Department of Justice Canada. (2004, January 30). Newsroom. In *Section 43 of the Criminal Code (Corporal Punishment)*. [Fact Sheet]

Diamond, Jared. (1994, November 1). Race without color. *Discover*.

Dib, K., Donaldson, I., & Turcotte, B. (2008). Integration and Identity in Canada: The Importance of Multicultural Common Spaces. *Canadian Ethnic Studies Journal, 40*(1), 161–188.

Drakulic, S. (2001). On bad teeth. In S. Hirschberg & T. Hirschberg (Eds.), *One World, Many Cultures* (4th ed., pp. 475–482). Needham Heights MA: Allyn and Bacon.

Ember, C.R., & Ember, M. (1999). *Anthropology*. Upper Saddle City, New Jersey: Prentice-Hall.

Encyclopedia of Canada's Peoples. (2008). *The Aboriginal Peoples*.

Encyclopedia of Canada's Peoples. (2008). *The Dual Colonial Legacy*.

Fay, M. (2005). Refracting Mother Tongues: Considering Mobility Through Language. *Journal of International Women's Studies, 6*(3), 18–31.

Freed, R.S., & Freed, S.A. (1985). The Psychomedical Case History of a Low-Caste Woman of North India. *Anthrological Papers of American Museum of Natural History*, vol 60, part 2, pp. 101–228.

Gibbs, J. (1963, January). The Kpelle Moot: Therapeutic Model for the Informal Settlement of Disputes. *Africa, 33*(1), 1–11.

Hampton, K. N., & Gupta, N. (2008). Community and Social Interaction in the Wireless City: Wi-Fi Use in Public and Semi-Public Spaces. *New Media and Society, 10*(6), 831–850.

Hassan, G., Lashley, M., Measham, T., & Rousseau, C. (2008). Caribbean and Filipino Adolescents' and Parents' Perceptions of Parental Authority, Physical Punishment, and Cultural Values and Their Relation to Migratory Characteristics. *Canadian Ethnic Studies Journal, 40*(2), 171–187.

Ibrahim, A. (2003). Marking the Unmarked: Hip-Hop, the Gaze & the African Body in North America. *Critical Arts, 17.1*(2), 52–71.

Jurva, K., & Jaya, P. S. (2008). Ethnic Identity Among Second-Generation Finnish Immigrant Youth in Canada: Some Voices and Perspectives. *Canadian Ethnic Studies Journal, 40*(2), 109–129.

Khan, A. (2011, February 4). You Are What You Tweet—And Where You Tweet It, Study Finds. *Los Angeles Times*.

Koven, M. J. (2009). "You Don't Have to be Filmish": The Toronto Jewish Film Festival. *Ethnologies, 21*(1), 115–132.

Leavitt, S. C. (2000). The Apotheosis of White Men?: A Reexamination of Beliefs about Europeans as Ancestral Spirits. *Oceania, 70*(4), 304–316.

Lilles, H. (2002). *Circle Sentencing: Part of the Restorative Justice Continuum* [Plenary speaker]. International Institute for Restorative Practices.

Madibbo, A.I. (2006). *Minority Within a Minority: Black Francophone Immigrants and the Dynamics of Power and Resistance.* New York, NY: Routledge.

McCurdy, D., and J. Spradley (2008). *Conformity and Conflict. Readings in Cultural Anthropology.* Boston, MA: Pearson Education.

Ottawa Citizen. (2007, October 3). *ole Harbour Rebirth.*

Phinney, J. (1993). A Three Stage Model of Ethnic Identity Formation in Adolescence. In, *Ethnic Identity: Formation and Transmission Among Hispanics and Other Minorities.* M. E. Bernal & G. P. Knight (Eds.). pp. 61–80.

Quinion, M. (1999, November 13). Rule of Thumb. [blog post]

RCMP. (2010, November 15). Contract and Aboriginal Policing. In *Restorative Justice: Recommitting to peace and safety* (Royal Canadian Mounted Police).

Reilly, E. (2008, February 16). School Staff Facing Assault Charges. *The Toronto Star.*

Saul, J. R. (2008). *A Fair Country: Telling Truths About Canada.* Toronto: Viking Canada.

Siebold, S. (2010, October 17). Merkel says German Multiculturalism has Failed. *Reuters.*

Sodhi, P. (2008). Bicultural Identity Formation of Second-Generation Indo-Canadians. *Canadian Ethnic Studies Journal, 40(2),* 187(13).

Wang, T. (2009, November 5). Flash Ethnography: Observations of a Doctor's Use of Mobile Tech with a Patient. [Blog post].

Chapter 8

Allport, G. W. (1954). *The Nature of Prejudice.* Cambridge, MA: Addison-Wesley.

America Online (AOL). (2010). Email Addiction Results. *Email's Dark Side: 10 Psychology Studies.*

American Psychological Association. (October, 2007). *Stress in America.*

Anderson, C. A., & Carnagey, N. L. (2003). Exposure to violent media: The effects of songs with violent Lyrics on aggressive thoughts and feelings. *Journal of Personality and Social Psychology, 84(5),* 960–975.

Canadian Medical Association. (August, 2008) *National Report Card on Health Care in Canada.*

Chartrand, T. L., & Bargh, J. A. (1999). The chameleon effect: The perception–behavior link and social interaction. *Journal of Personality and Social Psychology, 76(6),* 893–910.

Darley, J. M., Latané, B. (1968). When Will People Help in a Crisis? *Psychology Today,* pp. 54–57, 70–71.

Dawkins, S. (2010). The psychology of personality: Self-Monitoring by Mark Snyder.

DiFonzo, N. (2008, October). Around the Watercooler: Exploring the Psychology of Rumors. *Psychology Today.*

Dilmac, B. (2009). Psychological needs as a predictor of cyber bullying: A preliminary report on college students. *Educational Sciences: Theory and Practice, 9(3),* 1307–1325.

Experiment Resources (2010). Ross' false consensus effect experiments.

Lenhart, A., Kahne, J., Middaugh, E., Rankin McGill, A., Evans, C., & Vitak, J. (2008). Teens, video games, and Civics. PEW Internet & American Life Project.

Peters. W. [Director/Producer] (1985). A Class Divided. [Documentary] United States: PBS.

Porter, S., Brinke, L., & Gustaw, C. (2010). Dangerous Decisions: The Impact of First Impressions of Trustworthiness on the Evaluation of Legal Evidence and Defendant Culpability. *Psychology, Crime & Law, 16 (6),* 477–491.

Chapter 9

Becker, G. (1993). *Human Capital: A Theoretical and Empirical Analysis, with Special Reference to Education.* Chicago IL: University of Chicago Press.

Kymlicka, W. (2010), The Rise and Fall of Multiculturalism? New Debates on Inclusion and Accommodation in Diverse Societies. *International Social Science Journal,* 61: 97–112.

Municipalité Hérouxville. (2010) *Hérouxville Town Charter.*

Rich, Adrienne. (1994). Compulsory Heterosexuality and Lesbian Existence. In *Blood, Bread, and Poetry.* New York, NY: Norton Paperback.

Stein, R. (2007, July 26). Obesity Spreads in Social Circles as Trends Do, Study Indicates. *The Washington Post.*

Swanbrow, D. (2003). *The Geography of Thought: How Culture Colors the Way the Mind Works.* Institute for Social Research University of Michigan.

Weingarten, G. (2007, April 8). Pearls Before Breakfast. *The Washington Post.*

INDEX

A

ableism, 432, 432t
abnormal socialization, 121–123
Aboriginal people
  Australian Aborigines, 63, 341
  Canadian Aboriginal peoples. *See* First Nations
  human remains, return of, 181
abstract, 363
Abu Ghraib, 182, 239
academic dishonesty, 240
acculturation, 343, 369
accuracy, 319
achieved status, 429
achievement motivation, 218–219
acting crowd, 283
acupuncture, 304f, 305
addiction, 231
Adler, Alfred, 212, 219
adolescence
  the brain, 89
  cyberbullying, 390
  developmental tasks, 144
  extended adolescence, 144–145
  friends, 384
  identity crisis, 76
  online identities, 389
  peer influences, 126, 384
  puberty, 144
  runaway teens, 382–383
  Samoan adolescents, 24–25, 24f, 121
  sexual orientation, 410
  tanning salons, 441
  video games, 367–368
advertisements for children, 249–250, 249f
Afghanistan, 215, 229, 253
Africa, 172, 339
ageism, 432, 432t
agents of socialization, 78, 124–127, 166–168, 271
aggression, 72, 72f, 274, 292–294
aging, 302
agricultural societies, 160
the Agta, 149
Ainsworth, Mary, 80–81
air conditioning, 154
Alberta Sexual Sterilization Act, 104
Albrechtslund, Anders, 310
Ali, Mehrunnissa Ahmad, 344–345
alienation, 414, 415
Allport, Gordon, 374
alternate-gender identity, 150–151
Alto do Cruzeiro, Brazil, 176–177
altruism, 281, 377, 385
Alzheimer's disease, 86, 232
American Anthropological Association, 49, 179, 189, 337
American Psychological Association, 231, 250, 397
American Sociological Association, 295
American True Colors systems, 62
Amish cultures, 139
amygdala, 83f, 85, 366
anal stage, 74t
the Anasazi, 152–153
animal care committees, 67
animal experiments, 67, 188
animal hoarding, 233
animal rights groups, 67
anomie, 411–412
anorexia nervosa, 148, 382
L'Anse aux Meadows, 35
anthropology
  applied anthropology, 190–193
  attitudes of anthropology, 178–179
  and behaviour, 152–177
  cultural anthropology. *See* cultural anthropology
  cyborg anthropology, 134
  described, 14
  ecological anthropology, 192
  ethical issues, 178–193
  ethical transformations, 181–189
  fields of anthropology, 14–15f
  forensic anthropology, 44–45
  medical anthropology, 190–191
  and the military, 181–182
  physical anthropology, 37–51
  and psychology, 30, 66, 148, 188, 213
  and sociology, 20, 114, 137, 297, 320
  understanding cultures, 320–336
anticipatory socialization, 119
APA style, 95
apartheid, 49
applied anthropology, 190–193
applied experimental psychologists, 395
Archaeological Services Inc., 34
archaeology, 18f, 34–36, 181
archetypes, 61
"Ardi," 40f, 41
Ardipithecus ramidus, 40f, 41, 41f
Argentina, 45
arranged marriage, 170, 171, 266
artifacts, 23, 181, 181f
Asch, Solomon, 362, 362f, 370, 370t, 373, 408
ascribed status, 429
Asperger syndrome, 379
assimilation, 369t
Astrolabe, 348
attachment, 80–81, 81f
attention deficit/hyperactivity disorder (ADHD), 230, 232, 379
attitude, 220–223, 409–410
attitude-change theories, 222, 222f
attribution theory, 224
Auschwitz, 69
Australia, 353
Australian Aborigines, 63, 341
Australopithecus afarensis, 38, 40f
Australopithecus africanus, 39
authoritarian parenting style, 381f, 381t
authoritative parenting style, 381f, 381t
Autokinetic Effect experiment, 370
autonomy *vs.* shame and doubt, 76t
Avanzini, Marco, 15f
Aversion Project, 237t
avoidant attachment, 81, 81f
Ayres, A. Jean, 232

B

babbling, 88
Balmès, Thomas, 99
Bamber, Dean, 44
Bandura, Albert, 55f, 72, 292
Barbeau, Marius, 181
Bargh, John, 225, 371
baseball, 183
basic needs, 68f
the Bassa, 156
Bates, Elizabeth, 88
Beale, Margaret, 299
Becker, Gary, 431
Becker, Howard, 416
the Bedouin, 153
Behavioral Analysis Unit (BAU), 224, 225
Behavioral Sciences Unit (BSU), 225
behaviour
  aggression, 292–294
  and anthropology, 152–177
  and attitude, 220–223
  changing our behaviour, 227, 227f
  collective behaviour, 280–282, 283, 285
  conformity, 286–291
  criminal behaviour, 382
  crowd behaviour, 56, 283–285, 386
  energy drinks, and risky behaviour, 94
  gender behaviours, 265
  groupthink, 290
  and mental health, 228–231
  and motivation, 216–219
  obedience, 290–291
  and psychology, 216–233, 216f
  social behaviour, 113–118
  social belonging and groups, 276–279
  social thinking, 224–227
  and sociology, 276–294
behavioural genetics, 205
behavioural profiling, 224–225
behavioural psychology, 64–66
behavioural shift, 369
behaviourism. *See* behavioural psychology
Bell, Joshua, 404
belongingness needs, 68f
Benedict, Ruth, 15f, 25, 181
Beran, Tanya, 390
Berlin wall, fall of, 99

Bernstein, Paula, 201*f*
Berry, John, 343, 369
the Bhil, 167, 170*f*
Bhutan, 149, 174
bias, 78, 319
bicultural ethnicity, 342
bicultural identity, 351–352, 351*f*
Big Five factors (personality), 208, 208*t*
BigItUp International, 117
bilineal, 166, 168
Binet, Alfred, 202, 243
Binet IQ test, 75
Bingham, Mindy, 77
biological explanations, 213, 217
bipedalism, 40, 41
birth order, 212, 212*f*
black people, 339–340
Blackmore, Winston, 173
Blackwood, Egerton, 117, 117*f*
Blaffer-Hrdy, Sarah, 177
Blair, Heather, 247
Bleiweiss, Ira, 269*f*
blended family, 125*t*
blocking mechanisms, 372
blood type, 50, 50*f*
Boas, Franz, 15*f*, 28, 325
Bobo Doll experiment, 72, 72*f*
body build, 341
body dysmorphic disorder, 148
body image, 147–148
body language, 33, 158
body modification and body art, 142
The Body Shop, 67
Bohannan, Laura, 180
Bones, 44, 44*f*
bonobo communication, 48
books, citation of, 95
Bordia, Prashant, 392
Borneo, 46, 47
Boroditsky, Leta, 88
Boston Strangler, 225
Bouchard, Thomas J., 201
Bouchard-Taylor Commission, 347, 348
Bountiful, British Columbia, 173
Bowlby, John, 80
the brain, 82–89
  amygdala, 83*f*, 85, 366
  cerebral cortex, 83*f*
  cerebral hemispheres, 83, 83*f*
  cerebrum, 83
  controlling the ever-changing brain, 85–86
  corpus callosum, 83*f*
  fMRI image, 83*f*
  frontal lobe, 83*f*
  hippocampus, 83, 83*f*
  how the brain works, 83
  imaging technology, 82
  and Internet use, 87
  language development, 88
  and motivation, 217
  neurons, 83
  neuroscientists, 82
  perception, 84
  prejudice, 375
  social isolation, 366
  the teen brain, 89
  temporal lobe, 83*f*
brain damage, 85
branches, 19
branding, 142
Brazilian *tipos*, 338–339, 339*t*
breaching experiments, 288, 288*f*, 289
bridewealth, 172
Briggs, Katharine, 62, 207
Bristol, England, 185
Broadcast Code for Advertising to Children, 250
Brown, Roger, 33
brown eyes/blue eyes experiment, 376
Brown v. Board of Education, 298
Brussel, James A., 224–225
bulimia nervosa, 148, 382
bullying, 292–293, 293*f*
bureaucracy, 109–110
Burke, Peter J., 265
Burr, Rachel, 187
Butler, Jean, 206, 245
Byers, Michele, 354
bystander effect, 372

C

Cambridge, Nova Scotia, 151
Canada
  applied policy, 193
  black people, 340
  Canadian culture, 23, 137, 144–145, 66, 316*f*, 322–324, 337–357
  Canadian identity, 137, 355–356
  corporal punishment laws, 353
  distribution types, 161
  English Canada, 346
  Finnish Canadians, 355–356
  First Nations communities, 349–350
  French-Canadian culture, 346–349
  Greek and Jewish youth in Halifax, 354
  hate crimes, 375, 375*f*
  multicultural society, and identity, 351–357
  multiculturalism, 337, 344–350, 425–427
  polygamous community in, 173
  postindustrial economy, 160
  race, 339–340
  social structures and organization, 423–424
Canadian Centre for Addiction and Mental Health (CAMH), 246, 415
Canadian Charter of Rights and Freedoms, 173, 268, 346
Canadian civil service, 110
Canadian Council on Learning, 240
Canadian Medical Association, 378
Canadian Mental Health Association (CMHA), 252
Canadian Multiculturalism Act, 137, 347, 425
Canadian Personality Dimensions, 62, 62*f*
Canadian Psychological Association, 234, 382
Canadian Society of Forensic Sciences, 45
Canadian Sociological Association (CSA), 295, 303
capital punishment, 325
Carr, Nicholas, 87
Carrotmob, 56
Carter, Kevin, 297
Case, Amber, 134, 134*f*
case studies
  brown eyes/blue eyes, 376
  child death in Northeast Brazil, 176–177
  Clark Doll experiment, 298–299
  Genie, the story of an isolate child, 206
  Henri Tajfel, and social identity theory, 262–263
  James Gibbs, and the Kpelle moot, 326–327
  Mary Ainsworth and infant-mother attachment, 80–81
  Philip Zimbardo and Stanford Prison Experiment, 238–239
  Richard Lee and the Dobe Ju/'hoansi, 26–27
  "Shakespeare in the Bush" (Bohannan), 180
  social networks, and health, 420
  Stanley Milgram, and subway experiments, 289
  steel axes among the Yir Yoront, 155
  William Foote Whyte and the Street Corner Society, 106
casual crowd, 283
Cazabon, Andrée, 349–350
cell phones as ATMs, 165, 165*f*
census, 302–303
central research question, 17
Centre for Addiction and Mental Health, 378
cerebral cortex, 83*f*
cerebral hemispheres, 83, 83*f*
Chagnon, Napoleon, 15*f*, 16, 16*f*
chameleon effect, 371
Champagne and Aishihik First Nations (CAFN), 36
chaperones, 265
Chartrand, Tanya, 371
cheating, 240
Chicago school, 110–111
child abuse, 122, 185
child death in Northeast Brazil, 176–177
child labour, 96
childcare, 148
children
  abnormal socialization, 121–123
  advertisements for children, 249–250, 249*f*
  attention deficit/hyperactivity disorder (ADHD), 230, 232, 379
  bullying, 292–293
  child abuse, 122, 185
  core knowledge, 75

early childhood
  experiences, 59
 feral, 122–123
 gender identity, 265
 gender-specific toys, 121
 gifted children, 78
 infant-mother
  attachment, 80–81, 81f
 isolates, 123, 206
 language development,
  32–33, 88
 memories, and influence
  of others, 73
 nature-deficit disorder,
  232
 and parents' antisocial
  beliefs, 275
 perfectionism, 211
 play, 365
 social isolation, 365–366
 social skills, 365, 366
 socialization. *See*
  socialization
 and television, 366–367
 video games, 368
Chilean miners, 398
chimpanzees, 46, 47, 47f
China, 424
Chipchase, Jan, 165
chisel tattooing, 143
choleric, 62
Chomsky, Noam, 15f,
  32–33, 55f, 66, 88
choppers, 43
Choy, Wayson, 137
Christakis, Nicholas A., 420
*The Chrysanthemum and
  the Sword* (Benedict),
  25, 181
circumcision, 140
citation, 95
Citibank, 432
clans, 167
Clark, Kenneth, 298–299
Clark, Mamie, 298–299
Clark Doll experiment,
  298–299, 342
class, 300–303
A Class Divided, 376
classical conditioning, 64,
  65f, 66
classism, 268, 432t
Clement, Tony, 303
client-centred therapy, 70
climate, 152–153, 341
closure, 84, 84f
cobbles, 43
cognition, 72
cognitive development
 stages, 75, 75t

cognitive dissonance, 220
cognitive explanations,
  217–218
cognitive psychology, 72–73
cognitive revolution, 72
Colapinto, John, 267
cold climate adaptation, 152
Cole Harbour High, 340
collaborative workplace, 71
collective behaviour, 208,
  280–282, 283, 285
collective solidarity, 282
collective unconscious, 61
collectivist cultures, 287–288
collectivist society, 424
colonialism, 104
Coloroso, Barbara, 293
colour perception, 156
Columbine High School, 365
communication, and human
  relationships, 111
communication technology,
  309–311
Community Justice Forums
  (CJF), 329
competition theory, 271
complex tools, 165
compliance, 287
compulsive hoarding, 233
Comte, Auguste, 92f, 97
concrete operational stage,
  75t
conditioned response, 64
conditioned stimulus, 64
Condry, Ian, 184
conflict theory, 105
conformity, 262, 286–291,
  362, 370–373, 408
conscious, 59
consistency theories, 222f
consumer psychology,
  393–394
control groups, 57
conventional crowd, 283
convergence theory, 280
Cooley, Charles, 93f, 111
Coombe, Rosemary E., 31
core knowledge, 75
Cornerville, 106
corporal punishment laws,
  353
corpus callosum, 83f
correlation, 89, 89f
countercultures, 417–418
counting populations, 21
Couric, Katie, 273
courtship, 265–266
CPA Code of Ethics for
  Psychologists, 234, 234t,
  240, 241, 242

Crayola, 269
criminal behaviour, 382
Criminal Minds, 224
Cro-Magnons, 42
Croatia, 321
cross-cultural psychology,
  368–369
crowd behaviour, 56,
  283–285, 386
crowds, 283–285, 386
CSI, 44
cults, 417–418
cultural anthropology
 see also anthropology
 archaeology, 18f, 34–36
 cultural materialism, 29,
  29f
 cultural relativism, 28
 described, 18, 18f
 ethnology, 18f, 22–25
 feminist anthropology, 30
 fields of cultural
  anthropology, 18f
 and forensic
  anthropology, 44
 functional theory, 28
 informants, 20
 interviews, 20–21
 linguistic anthropology,
  18f, 32–33
 moral dilemmas, 185–187
 participant observation,
  24–25
 physical anthropology,
  37–51
 postmodernism, 31
 race, 338–340
 research tools, 20–21
 schools of thought, 28–31
cultural diffusion, 184
cultural/ethnic identity. *See*
 ethnic identity
cultural expressions, 98
cultural materialism, 29, 29f
cultural relativism, 28
cultural universals, 411
culturally constructed, 30
culture
 as agent of socialization,
  166–168
 and body language, 33
 Canadian culture, 23,
  137, 144–145, 166,
  316f, 322–324, 337–357
 collectivist cultures,
  287–288
 countercultures, 417–418
 cultural materialism, 29,
  29f
 defined, 18

digital technology, effect
 of, 324
disappearing cultures, 23
and economic systems,
 159–161
ethnology, 22–23
and family roles, 175–177
female identity and
 culture, 146–148
and gender, 146–151
geography of thought,
 412
globalization, impact of,
 162–165
and greetings, 116, 116t,
 158
and identity, 136–151,
 411–418
individualistic cultures,
 287
Japanese culture, 25f
and language, 156–158
and legal systems,
 325–329
male identity and culture,
 148–150
marriage, 169–174
multiculturalism, 337,
 344–350, 425–427
North American culture,
 25f
physical discipline,
 352–353
and physical
 environment, 152–153
religion and ritual,
 330–336
social customs, 320–324
as social influence, 115
subculture, 31, 415–416
and technology, 154–155
understanding cultures,
 320–336
world view, 22
cut marks on bones, 43
cyber identity, 388–389
cyberbullying, 293–294, 390
cyberpsychology, 233
cyborg anthropology, 134

D

Da Costa, Mathieu, 340
Danielle, 123
Darego, Abgani, 147f
Darley, John, 372
Dart, Raymond, 14f, 39
Darwin, Charles, 15f, 39,
 49, 104
data, recording, 17

dating, 265–266
Davidson, Richard, 85, 86
Davis, Kingsley, 430
Davis, Kiri, 299
Day of Pink, 151
de Arruda, Nailza, 176
de Cervantes, Miguel, 388
de Chardin, Pierre Teilhard, 293
"Dear Boy," 39, 40f
decorative scarring, 142
defence mechanisms, 60
Defense of Animals, 67
dehumanize, 292
deindividuation, 389
demandingness, 381
dementia, 232
demography, 301–302
Dempsey, Melanie, 393
denial, 60
dependent variable, 57
DeSalvo, Albert, 225
The Descent of Man (Darwin), 39
Desmond, Viola, 340
developmental psychologists, 59, 74–79
developmental tasks, 260–261
deviance, 306, 411–413, 416
Dhillon, Baltej, 115
diagnoses, 379
Diagnostic and Statistical Manual of Mental Disorders (DSM), 228, 229
diagrams, 17
DiClemente, Carlo, 227
dictatorships, 164
differential association, 292
diffusion of responsibility, 372
DiFonzo, Nicholas, 392
digital technology, 154, 324
Dilmac, Bulent, 390
disappearing cultures, 23
disciplines, 19
discrimination
 causes, 271–274
 defined, 268
 forms of, 269f
 and identity, 268–271
displacement, 60
division of labour, by gender, 30t
DNA, 42, 42f, 200
Dobe Ju/'hoansi, 21, 21f, 26–27, 168, 325
doctors, and netbooks, 323–324
Dodge, Kenneth, 353

Doidge, Norman, 85
Drakulic, Slavenka, 321
dreams, 63
"Dreamtime," 63
drive-reduction theory, 217
Dunbar, Robin, 278
Dunbar number, 278
Dunn, John, 211
Dunn, Sam, 31
Durkheim, Emile, 92f, 101–103, 101f, 282, 412, 413
Dutton, Kevin, 393
dyad, 276

E

early childhood experiences, 59
East Asian culture, 175–176, 412
East Berlin, 99
eating disorders, 148, 382
Echterhoff, Gerald, 73
École Polytechnique, 365
ecological anthropology, 192
economic systems, 159–161
economy, 443
Edith experiment, 200
education, 71, 439–440, 439t
ego, 59, 59f
ego identity, 368
Eisenstein, Jacob, 323
Ekman, Paul, 226
electroencephalogram (EEG), 82, 82f
electronic sources, 95
Ellard, Kelly, 120
Elliot, Ginny, 399
Elliot, Jane, 376
email, 388, 395
emic perspective, 179
emotional development, 364, 365–366
emotional intelligence (EQ), 245
empirical, 95, 235
empowering exhibitionism, 310
energy drinks, and risky behaviour, 94
engineering psychology, 395
English Canada, 346
English language, 157
enrichment curriculum, 78
environment, 200–205
Epstein, Robert, 85, 89
equality, 98
Erikson, Erik, 55f, 76–77, 76t, 144, 261, 368

Ervin, Alexander, 193
esteem needs, 68f
ethics
 animal research, 67, 188
 in anthropology, 178–193
 CPA Code of Ethics for Psychologists, 234, 234t, 240, 241, 242
 decisions based on psychological beliefs, 248–251
 ethical guidelines, 179
 and experimentation, 235–242
 informed consent, 135
 intelligence tests, 243–244
 ISA Code of Ethics, 295–296
 Little Albert experiment, 65
 and mental illness, 252–253
 neuroethics, 251
 psychology, 188
 in psychology, 234–253, 234t
 racial profiling, 306–308
 in research, 135
 research dilemmas, 185–189
 research subjects, 296–297
 in sociology, 295–311
 studying the unstudiable, 245
 surveys at school, 246
 unethical experiments, 236–237, 236–237t
ethnic identity, 342–343, 351, 354, 368
ethnicity, 342–343
ethnocentric, 28
ethnocentrism, 274
ethnology, 22–25
 culture, study of, 22–23
 defined, 18f, 22
 kinship, 22
 participant observation, 22, 22f
 participant observation, challenges of, 24–25
etic perspective, 178–179
the Etoro, 151
eugenics, 104
Eugenics Board, 104
euphemisms, 157, 157t
evaluation of information, 17
evolution
 see also physical anthropology

 natural selection, 39, 49, 50, 104
 origins of humans, 39
 and religion, 39
 social evolution, 103
 survival of the fittest, 104
 timeline of human evolution, 41f
"Evolution of Common Things," 78
excellence, 210
exclusion, 369t
expectations, 384–385
experimentation, and ethics, 235–242
explicit attitudes, 220
explicit cultural knowledge, 178
expressive crowd, 283, 284
extended family, 125t
extinction, 66
extrinsic motivation, 217–218
extroversion, 207
Eysenck, Hans, 207

F

Facebook, 266, 294, 310, 391, 395
Facial Action Coding System (FACS), 226
facial expressions, 226, 226f
Facial Expressions experiment, 236t
facial patterns, 208
factor analysis, 208
Fair Trade, 422
false consensus, 385–386
false memories, 72–73
family, 113f, 114, 124–125, 125t, 277, 277f, 304, 380–383, 436–437, 436t
family roles, 175–177
Fantz, Robert, 75
Farrer, Claire, 141
FBI (Federal Bureau of Investigation), 225
fear, and collective behaviour, 285
feeling, 62
female identity and culture, 146–148
female rites of passage, 141
feminine psychology, 30, 60–61
feminist anthropology, 30
feminist sociology, 107–108
feminist theory, 433
feral, 122–123

Festinger, Leon, 220
fetishes, 183
field notes, 22
fields, 19
fieldwork, 178–179, 183–184
Fine, Cordelia, 214
Fine, Gary, 185
fingerprints, 341, 341*f*
Finnish Canadians, 355–356
First Nations
   artifacts of, 23
   body language, 33
   communities in Canada, 349–350
   dancing, 149
   dream interpretation, 63
   languages, 32
   potlatch, 159, 161
   residential schools, 318
   sentencing circles, 327–329
   two-spirited, 150
Fitzsimons, Gavin, 394
fixation, 74
flash mobs, 56, 285
flow charts, 17
Flynn effect, 203, 203*f*
focusing therapies, 86
foraging societies, 21, 30, 159, 163
"The Forbidden Experiment," 245, 245*f*
Ford, Marguerite, 33
forensic anthropology, 44–45
formal justice systems, 325
formal operational stage, 75*t*
Fort Erie, Ontario, 34
Fossey, Dian, 14*f*, 46, 46*f*, 188
fossils, 38, 39
founding nations, 137
fourth gender, 114, 150
frame of reference, 319
francophone communities, 346–349
Frankl, Viktor, 55*f*, 69, 69*f*, 226
free association, 60
Freeman, Derek, 24–25
French-Canadian culture, 346–349
Freud, Sigmund, 55*f*, 59–60, 63, 63*f*, 74, 74*t*, 217, 261
Freudian slip, 59
Friedl, Ernestine, 30
friends, 384
front porch, 154
frontal lobe, 83*f*
frustration-aggression theory, 274

functional differentiation, 102
functional magnetic resonance imaging (fMRI), 82, 83*f*
functional theory, 28, 222*f*
Functional Types, 62
Fundamentalist Church of Jesus Christ of Latter-Day Saints (FLDS), 173

G

G20 Summit, 283
Gage, Phineas, 82, 82*f*
Galapagos Islands, 39
Galdikas, Biruté, 14*f*, 46, 47, 188
Galton, Francis, 202
"Game of Death," 198
gamma-aminobutyric (GABA), 86
gamma waves, 85
gangs, 279, 286
garbage, 35
Gardner, Howard, 244
Garfinkel, Harold, 288
Garnefski, Nadia, 382
gender
   and agents of socialization, 78
   and the classroom, 247
   and culture, 146–151
   female identity and culture, 146–148
   fourth gender, 114, 150
   intersex, 114, 150
   male identity and culture, 148–150
   meaning of term, 114
   vs. sex, 114
   as social influence, 114
   socialization, 264
   and socialization, 121
   and standardized testing, 78
   third gender, 114, 150, 150*f*
gender behaviours, 265
gender differences, 77, 213–215
gender identity, 214, 264–265
gender inequality, 107–108
gender roles, 148, 213, 215, 264–265
gender schema theory, 214, 410
General Social Survey, 438
generativity *vs.* stagnation, 76*t*
genetic influences, 203

Genie, 88, 123, 206, 245
genital stage, 74*t*
genocide, 44, 274
Genovese, Kitty, 372
geography of thought, 412
Germany, and multiculturalism, 344
Gibbs, James, 326–327
gifted children, 78
Gini, Corrado, 433
Gini coefficient, 433
global identity, 421–422
global perspective
   division of labour and gender, 30*t*
   Fair Trade, 422
   greetings, 116, 116*t*
   suicide rates, 102*f*
globalization, 160, 162–165, 184, 357, 421, 422
glocalization, 421
Glowatski, Warren, 120
Gmelch, George, 183
goals, 219
Goddard, Henry, 243
Goffman, Erving, 264
Goodall, Jane, 14*f*, 37*f*, 46, 47, 188
Googleplex, 444
gorillas, 46
gossip, 392
Gould, Stephen Jay, 243
government, 440–442
government campaigns, 223
Graham, Robert K., 203
grammar, 33
Granovetter, Mark, 281
Gray, Chris Hables, 134
Gray, John, 213
Greek communities in Halifax, 354
Greene, David, 218
greetings, 116, 116*t*, 158
group-based identity, 407
group conflict, 258
group influence, 262–263, 279
groups, 276–279
groupthink, 290, 290*f*, 371
Gupta, Neeti, 322

H

Haiti, 192
Halifax, 354
Hall, G. Stanley, 89
Hampton, Keith N., 322
the Hanumbo, 156
Harlow, Harry, 79, 123, 237*t*
Harper, Ben, 383

Harris, Marvin, 15*f*, 29
hate crimes, 375, 375*f*
headbangers, 31
health, 304–305, 420
Health Canada, 94
health care system, 442
Hearn, Shawn, 253
heavy metal music and fans, 31, 31*f*
Heider, Fritz, 224
heredity, 200–205, 205*f*
Heroic Imagination Project, 377, 377*t*
heroism, 377
Hérouxville, Quebec, 427
Heyman, Gene, 231
hidden curriculum, 125
Hierarchy of Needs, 68, 68*f*, 119, 219, 397
Highly Sensitive People (HSP), 209
Hinduism, 29
hip hop, 184
hippocampus, 83, 83*f*
historical linguistics, 32
history, and archaeology, 35
Hitler, Adolf, 104, 224, 386
HMS *Beagle*, 39
H1N1 flu pandemic, 285
hoarding disorder, 233
Hofling, Charles, 291
Hollingworth, Leta Stetter, 55*f*, 78
Holocaust, 104, 274, 386
homelessness, 431*f*
hominins, 38
Homo erectus, 39, 40*f*
Homo habilis, 39
Homo sapiens, 42
homophily, 266
homosexuality, 150, 151, 248–249, 294, 409–410
Honour House, 253, 254*f*
Hopi language, 157
Horney, Karen, 55*f*, 60–61
horticultural, 159
hot climate adaptation, 153
Hovland, Carl, 222
"(How) Does the Sexual Orientation of Parents Matter?" (Stacey), 108
Hua, Cai, 169
Hughes, Clara, 378, 378*f*
human factors psychologists, 395
Human Genome Project, 200
human rights, and racial profiling, 308
human variation, 37*f*, 49–51, 188–189

humanism. *See* humanist psychology
humanist psychology, 68–71
humanistic education, 71
humans
  blood type, 50, 50*f*
  evolution. *See* evolution
  and other primates, 47–48
  skin colour variations, 51
  subgroups, 49
humors, 62
hunter-gatherers. *See* foraging societies
Hussein, Saddam, 224
Hutchison, David, 368
hypodescent, 338, 339
hypothesis, 17, 259

I

Ibrahim, Awad, 339
id, 59
identity
  alternate-gender identity, 150–151
  bicultural identity, 351–352, 351*f*
  Canadian identity, 137, 355–356
  and culture, 136–151, 411–418
  and discrimination, 268–271
  ego identity, 368
  ethnic identity, 342–343, 351, 354, 368
  female identity and culture, 146–148
  gender identity, 264–265
  global identity, 421–422
  group-based identity, 407
  male identity and culture, 148–150
  and multicultural society, 351–357
  national identity, 368
  rites of passage, 138–145
  role identity, 407
  role theory, 264–267
  and social attitudes, 409–410
  social identity, 260–263, 368, 406–408
  and sociology, 260–274
identity crisis, 76
identity moratorium, 144
identity *vs.* role confusion, 76*t*
ignorance theory, 274
imagination, 61

immigrant services, 193
immigrants, 348–349
immigration, 368–369
immune function, 86
imperialism, 346
implicit attitudes, 220
in-text citation, 95
incorporation, 139
independent variable, 57
India, 29, 108, 167, 174, 266
indigenous peoples, 164
individualistic cultures, 287
individualistic society, 424
Indo-Canadians, 170, 171, 351–352
industrial/organizational (I/O) psychology, 395
Industrial Revolution, 96, 96*f*, 102, 160
industrial societies, 160
industry *vs.* inferiority, 76*t*
infant-mother attachment, 80–81, 81*f*
informal groups, 276
informal justice systems, 325
informants, 20
information analysis, 17
informed consent, 135
infrastructure, 29*f*
ingroups, 374
initiative *vs.* guilt, 76*t*
Innuinait (Copper Inuit), 22
inquiry. *See* research and inquiry skills
Inspector of the Feeble-Minded, 104
instinct theory, 217
institutional completeness, 356
institutionalization of norms, 440
institutions, 101
"insulting the meat," 26–27
integration, 369*t*
integrity *vs.* despair, 76*t*
intelligence, 202
intelligence quotients (IQs), 203–204
intelligence testing, 202–204, 243–244
interculturalism, 347, 347*t*
International Sociological Association (ISA), 295
International Visual Sociology Association (IVSA), 311
Internet
  and the brain, 87
  communication, 388–389
  cyber identity, 388–389

  cyberbullying, 293–294, 390
  dating and courtship, 266
  ethical experiments, 242
  protestors and, 164
  social influence, 115
  social media, 391, 395
  social networking, 310, 419
  virtual community, 277
  Wi-Fi, and social interactions, 322–323
intersex, 114, 150
intervention, 187
interviews, 20–21, 135, 178
intrinsic motivation, 217, 218
introversion, 209
Introversion/Extroversion scale, 62
intuition, 62
Inuit, 116*t*, 144–145, 152, 159, 325
invasion-succession model, 301
Iran, 149, 164*f*
Iraq, 182, 229–230, 239
Iroquois, 63
ISA Code of Ethics, 295–296
Islamophobia, 270, 272
isolates, 123, 206
It Gets Better Project, 294, 410

J

Jamaica, 353
James, William, 223
Janis, Irving, 290, 371
Japan, 25, 25*f*, 33, 149, 184, 287–288, 424, 424*f*
Jaya, Peruvemba, 355
Jenness, A., 370
Jenness, Diamond, 15*f*, 22, 23, 181
Jensen, J. Eric, 86
Jewish communities in Halifax, 354
"Jim Twins," 201
Johanson, Donald, 14*f*, 37*f*, 38
John Hopkins Center for Alternatives to Animal Testing, 67
Johnson, Wendell, 236*t*
Jones, Jim, 418
Jones, Terry, 270
Jonestown, Guyana, 418
Josephson Institute, 240
journals, citation of, 95
Jung, Carl, 55*f*, 61–62, 63
Jurva, Katrina, 355

K

Kalahari People's Fund, 27
Kanzi, 48, 48*f*
Karsh, Yousuf, 137
Kaufmann, Jean Claude, 198
the Kayapó, 163–164, 163*f*
Kelly, Kevin, 155
Kent, James, 206, 245
Khaldun, Ibn, 96
Khalsa, Dharma Singh, 86
Kinsey, Alfred, 248–249
kinship, 22
kinship systems, 166–168
Kirtan Kriya meditation, 86
Kitchenuhmaykoosib Inninuwug (KI), 349–350
K'naan, 137
Knight, David, 294
Kogawa, Joy, 137
Kohlberg, Lawrence, 373
Koresh, David, 418
Koskela, Hille, 310
Koven, Mikel J., 336
the Kpelle, 326–327
Krogh, Kathryn, 289
Ku Klux Klan, 49, 340
Kula Ring, 28
Kuo, Frances, 232
Kwaday Dän Ts'inchi, 36, 181

L

labelling, 416
lactose intolerance, 342
Laetoli footprints, 40, 40*f*
Lake Turkana, Kenya, 39
landfills, 35
Landis, Carney, 236*t*
landmark case studies. *See* case studies
language
  Aboriginal people, 32
  body language, 33, 158
  and culture, 156–158
  development, 32–33, 88
  English language, 157
  and human relationships, 111
  linguistic anthropology, 32–33
  Sapir-Whorf hypothesis, 88, 156
  and thought, 88
L'Anse aux Meadows, 35
Lansford, Jennifer, 353
Latané, Bibb, 372
latency stage, 74*t*
Le Bon, Gustave, 386

Leakey, Louis, 14f, 39, 39f, 40, 46
Leakey, Mary, 14f, 39, 39f
Leakey, Richard, 39, 40
learned helplessness, 236t
learned theory, 271
learning theories, 222f
Leavitt, Stephen, 334
Lee, Richard, 15f, 21, 21f, 26–27
left-handedness, 248
legal systems, 325–329
Lehne, Gregory, 121
Lehrer, Jonah, 217
Leman, Kevin, 212
Lepper, Mark R., 218
Lerner, Gerda, 107
Levin, Aubrey, 237t
Levitin, Daniel, 387
Lewis, Marc, 373
LGBTQ (lesbian, gay, bisexual, transgender or queer), 410
Liberia, 156
Lie to Me, 226
life cycle, 260–261
Life in a Day, 311
life stages, 260–261, 261t
liminal stage, 139
lineages, 167
linguistic anthropology, 18f, 32–33
LinkedIn, 395
literature, 137
Little Albert experiment, 65, 236t
Little Mosque on the Prairie, 272–273
Loftus, Elizabeth, 55f, 72–73
logotherapy, 69
lone-parent family, 125t
longitudinal study, 365
looking-glass self, 111, 123, 389
love needs, 68f
"Lucy," 37f, 38, 38f, 40f
Lundmann, Sarah, 390f

M

Maasai circumcision, 140
MacMurchy, Helen, 104
macrosociology, 100
"Mad Bomber," 224–225
magnetic resonance imaging (MRI), 67
Maier, Steve, 236t
Malawi, 190–191
Malaya, Oxana, 122–123
Malaysia, 353
male identity and culture, 148–150
male rites of passage, 140
Malinowski, Bronislaw, 15f, 22, 28, 181, 183
Malthus, Thomas, 29
manners, 320–324
Manners, Jordan, 117
the Maori, 143
mapping, 21
marginalization, 369t
Margolis, Maxine, 29
marketing, 223
Marlow, Cameron, 278
marriage, 169–174
Marshmallow Experiment, 221
Marx, Karl, 29, 93f, 97, 101, 105, 109, 110, 414, 434
masculinity, 149–150
Maslow, Abraham, 55f, 68–69, 119, 219, 397
mass hysteria, 285
mass public grief, 282
Massai greetings, 116t
matrilineal, 166
Mayawati, 108f
McCurdy, David, 167
McDonald, Robert V., 231
McDougall, William, 217
Mead, George Herbert, 93f, 111
Mead, Margaret, 15f, 24–25, 24f, 121, 181
meaning in life, 226
Mecca, 44, 100f
media
    as agent of socialization, 127
    and children, 366–368
    moral panic, 120
    and personality, 387–394
    as social influence, 115
    television, 366–367
medical anthropology, 190–191
medication, 379
meditation, 85, 86
Mehta, Deepa, 137
Meier, Megan, 390
melancholic, 62
Melnyk, Laura, 73
melting pot, 369t
memory, 86
memory alteration, 250–251
Memory and Aging Research Center, 87
men
    childcare, 148
    identity and culture, 148–150
    rites of passage, 140
    and skirts, 149
mental health
    alienation, 415
    and behaviour, 228–231
    diagnoses and medication, 379
    and ethics, 252–253
    new research in, 232–233
    stigma, 378–379, 415
    in the workplace, 397
Mercer, Rick, 410f
meritocracies, 430
Merkel, Angela, 344
Merton, Robert, 413
Mescalero Apache puberty rites, 141, 141f
meta-analysis, 175
Metesky, George, 225
Mexico, 149–150
microexpressions, 226
microsociology, 100
migration, 357
Milgram, Stanley, 198, 234, 237t, 289, 362, 408
the military, 181–182, 249, 442
Miller, Kathleen E., 94
Mills, C. Wright, 93f, 112
the Minangs, 166f
mind mapping, 17
mindfulness meditation, 86
Minnesota Multiphasic Personality Inventory (MMPI), 62, 224
Mischel, Walter, 221, 407
Mishna, Faye, 293
the Mistassini Cree, 159
Mitchell, Andrew, 393
mixed-race couples, 338–339
mobs, 283
Mohanty, Chandra Talpade, 107
Money, John, 236t, 267
monkey drug trials, 237t
monogamy, 172
Monster Study, 236t
Mont-Saint-Grégoire sugarhouse, 348
Moore, Wilbert, 430
moral development theory, 373
moral dilemmas, 185–189
moral illiteracy, 240
moral panic, 120
Morris, Donny (Chief), 349
Moses, Philip, 327
motivation, 216–219, 397
mourning rituals, 138
MUGs (men's unbifurcated garments), 149
multicultural society, and identity, 351–357
multiculturalism, 337, 344–350, 369t, 425–427
multiple intelligences, 244, 244t
Murray, Gerald, 192
Museum of Civilization, Ottawa, 23, 181f
music, 387–388
Muslim culture, 44, 172, 348
Myers, Isabel Briggs, 62, 207
Myers-Briggs Type Indicator (MBTI), 62, 207

N

the Na, 169–170, 170f, 175
naive realism, 179
Napoli Square, Boston, 106f
Nassiah, Jacqueline, 308, 308f
National Council of Women, 104
national identity, 368
National Sex Offender Registry, 225
national symbols, 98f
natural selection, 39, 49, 50, 104
nature-deficit disorder, 232
Nawaz, Zarqa, 273, 273f
Nazi Germany, 49, 69, 188–189, 274, 280, 386
Neander Valley, Germany, 42
Neanderthals, 42, 42f
Neda, 164f
negative correlation, 89f
negative eugenics, 104
negativity bias, 218
neglectful parenting style, 381f, 381t
neighbourhoodism, 300
neo-Freudians, 60, 76
Nepal, 174
Netting, Nancy, 170, 171
neuroethics, 251
neurons, 83
neuroplasticity, 85
neuroscientists, 82, 213
neurosexism, 214
neurotic disorder, 61
neurotic disorders, 228
New York Times, 289
Niagara River, 34
Niger, 147–148

Ninger, Alexander, 207
Nisbett, Richard, 412
nonconformity, 373
nonhuman primates, 46–48
norms, 98, 279, 288, 407–408
North American culture, 25f, 33, 412, 413, 417t, 424
nuclear family, 125t

O

Obama, Barack, 270
obedience, 198, 213, 237t, 290–291, 408
obesity, 270, 420
objective, 24
objectivity, 98
O'Connell, James, 142
O'Connor, Kieron, 233
Odawa, 63
Okma, Sjoukje, 382
Olduvai Gorge, Kenya, 39
Oler, James, 173
On the Origin of Species (Darwin), 39, 49
Ondaatje, Michael, 137
Ontario Human Rights Code, 308
Ontario's cultural history, 34
open education, 71
operant conditioning, 65–66
Operational Stress Injury Social Support, 253
oral stage, 74t
orangutans, 46, 47
Ottawa-Carleton District School Board, 246
Ötzi, 142
outgroups, 374

P

Pacom, Diane, 142
Pagani, Linda S., 367
paleoanthropology, 38–43
 ancient bones, study of, 38
 bipedalism, 40, 41
 defined, 37f, 38
 map of African finds, 40f
 origins of humans, 39
 stone tools, 43, 43f
Palmer, Debbie, 173
panic, 280
Paranthropus boisei, 40f
parental influence, 380–381
parental leave, 148
parenting styles, 381, 381f, 381t
parents, and antisocial beliefs, 275
Parsons, Talcott, 92f, 103, 112

participant observation, 22, 22f, 24–25, 110–111, 135, 187
participatory surveillance, 310
patrilineal, 166, 167
Patten, Sonia, 190
Pavlov, Ivan, 54f, 64, 67
Payakan, 163–164
peer groups, 126
People for the Ethical Treatment of Animals (PETA), 67
perception, 84, 156
perceptual constancy, 84
perceptual sets, 84
perfectionism, 210–211, 210f
periodicals, citation of, 95
permissive parenting style, 381f, 381t
Persian culture, 149
personal belief dilemmas, 185
personal unconscious, 61
personality, 207–212, 380–389
 Big Five factors, 208, 208t
 birth order, 212, 212f
 categorizing personality, 207
 defined, 62
 facial patterns, 208
 family environment, 380–383
 friends and group environments, 384–386
 introversion, 209
 media influences, 387–394
 and music, 387–388
 and parenting style, 381
 perfectionism, 210–211, 210f
 predicting personality, 208
Personality Dimensions, 62, 62f
personality view of behaviour, 407
persuasion, 393–394
Peters, Russell, 351f
Peterson, Jordan, 373
phallic stage, 74t
Philpots, Michelle, 250
Phinney, J.S., 342, 342f
phlegmatic, 62
phobia, 228
photographs, 21
physical anthropology, 37–51
 and ethics, 181
 fields of physical anthropology, 37f

human variation, 37f, 49–51
 moral dilemmas, 188–189
 paleoanthropology, 37f, 38–43
 primatology, 37f, 46–48
 race, 341–342
physical discipline, 352–353
physical environment, 152–153
Physicians for Human Rights, 44
physiological needs, 68f
Piaget, Jean, 55f, 75, 75t
Pickrell, Jacqueline E., 73
piercings, 142, 142f
Pink Shirt Day, 151
placemakers, 322–323
plagiarism, 95, 234, 240
play, 365
pleasure principle, 59
Pohnpei, Caroline Islands, 142
point/counterpoint
 anthropologists, and the military, 182
 Internet, and the brain, 87
 skin colour variations, 51
point-form notes, 17
Pollack, William, 373
pollen analysis, 42
Pollution Watch, 305
polyandry, 172, 174
polygamy, 172–174
polygyny, 172
Polynesian greetings, 116t
Polynesian tattoos, 143
Popenoe, Rebecca, 147, 185
population density, 302
Porter, Stephen, 375
Portuguese students, 345
positive attraction, 226
positive correlation, 89f
positive eugenics, 104
positivism, 97
post-traumatic stress disorder, 85, 229, 253
poster presentations, 363
postindustrial societies, 160
postmodernism, 31
postmulticulturalism, 426–427
potlatch, 159, 161
poverty, and family roles, 176–177
"Practical Anthropology" (Malinowski), 181
pre-employment tests, 395
pre-operational stage, 75t
prehistoric archaeology, 35

prejudice, 268, 271–274, 374–377
PREVNet, 293
Price, Jill, 250
Price, Travis, 151
primary group, 111, 276–277
primary socialization, 119
primary sources, 57, 259, 319
primatology, 37f, 46–48, 188
prison, and mental illness, 252
Pro-Test, 67
Prochaska, James O., 227
procrastination, 210
product adaptation, 165
profiling, 224–225, 306–308
Progressive Matrices test, 243–244
projection, 60
prosocial behaviour, 281–282
prostitution, 186
Pryce, Ken, 185
psychoanalytic theory, 59
psychodynamic theories, 59–63
psychological acculturation, 369
psychological disorders, 205, 205f
psychological needs, 68f
psychology
 and anthropology, 30, 66, 148, 188, 213
 approaches to understanding behaviour, 74–89
 and behaviour, 216–233, 216f
 behavioural psychology, 64–66
 the brain, 82–89
 cognitive psychology, 72–73
 conformity, 370–373
 consumer psychology, 393–394
 cross-cultural psychology, 368–369
 of cyberbullying, 390
 development of self, 200–215
 developmental psychologists, 59, 74–79
 dreams, 63
 engineering psychology, 395
 ethical issues, 234–253, 234t

feminine psychology, 30, 60–61
humanist psychology, 68–71
industrial/organizational (I/O) psychology, 395
motivation, 216–219
personality, 207–212, 380–389
of persuasion, 393–394
prejudice, 374–377
psychodynamic theories, 59–63
research plan, 199
rumours and gossip, 392
schools of thought, 54–55f, 58–73
sex and gender differences, 213–215
and socialization, 364–369
and sociology, 78, 123, 208, 261
sport psychology, 367
psychosexual stages of development, 74, 74t
psychosocial stage model theory, 76t, 144
psychotic disorders, 228
puberty, 144
punishments, 217–218

Q

qualitative research, 57, 68, 111, 118
quantitative research, 57, 68, 118
Quebec, 346–349
Quebec Longitudinal Study of Child Development, 367
questionnaires, 199

R

race, 49–50, 337–343
racial beliefs, 49
racial profiling, 306–308
racism, 268, 339, 342, 346, 432t
radiometric dating, 39
Rafaat, Mehran, 215
rain, 152–153
Rainforest Foundation, 164
rapid eye movement (REM), 63
Rathje, William, 35
rational decision theory, 281
rationalization, 109
Ratiu, 82f
RCMP, 115, 173, 225, 249

reality principle, 59
reciprocity, 159, 161
redistribution, 159
reduction, 67
refinement, 67
reflexivity, 24
Reicher, Stephen, 56, 386
Reichs, Kathy, 44f
Reid, Evon, 300
Reimer, David, 236t, 267
reintegration, 139
relevance, 319
reliability, 319
religion, 39, 127, 330–336, 348, 437–438, 438t
religious freedom, 115, 173
Remembrance Day, 282
Rentfrow, Peter Jason, 387
replacement, 67
Report Card on the Ethics of American Youth, 240
reports, 405
repressed memories, 72–73
repression, 60
research
  see also research and inquiry skills
  cultural anthropology, 20–21
  empirical research, benefits of, 235
  ethics. See ethics
  informants, 20
  interviews, 20–21, 135
  limits of, 259
  methods, 135
  participant observation, 22, 22f, 24–25, 110–111, 135
research and inquiry skills
  see also research
  analysis of information, 17, 199
  central research question, 17
  citation, 95
  control groups, 57
  evaluation of sources, 319
  gathering and processing information, 259
  hypothesis, 17
  interpretation of information, 199
  interviews, 178
  qualitative research, 57, 68, 111, 118
  quantitative research, 57, 68, 118
  recording data, 17
  reports, 405

  research plan, 135, 199
  results, presentation of, 363
  sources, 17, 57, 95
  surveys, 95, 199
  variables, 57
research dilemmas, 185–189
research plan, 135
research subjects, 296–297
residential schools, 318
resistant attachment, 81, 81f
resocialization, 119
responsiveness, 381
restorative justice, 326–329
review of literature, 259
rewards, 217–218
Rheingold, Howard, 285
rhesus monkeys, 79
Rhymester, 184f
Rich, Adrienne, 428, 433
Richard, Matthieu, 85, 85f
Ridley, Matt, 165
Rigler, David and Marilyn, 206, 245
riots, 280
risky behaviour, and energy drinks, 94
rites of passage, 138–145
  body modification and body art, 142
  coming of age in contemporary Canadian culture, 144–145
  defined, 138
  female rites of passage, 141
  male rites of passage, 140
  three-stage process, 139, 139f
ritual, 136, 183, 330–336
road signs, 32f
Robbers Cave experiment, 258, 374
Rogers, Carl, 55f, 70, 70f
role, 98, 279
role identity, 407
role theory, 264–267
Romani people, 32
Romania, 204, 204f
Ross, Lee, 385
Royes, Dameion, 117
rule of thumb, 352
rumours, 392
runaway teens, 382–383
Rwanda, 44, 46, 325f
Rymer, Russ, 206f

S

sacred cow, 29f
safety needs, 68f

Saitoti, Tepilit Ole, 140, 140f
same-sex family, 125t
same-sex marriage, 169
Samoa, 24–25, 24f, 121, 143
San people, 26–27, 159
sanctions, 279
sanguine, 62
sapienization, 320
Sapir, Edward, 15f, 32, 181
Sapir-Whorf hypothesis, 88, 156
SARS-Stock, 284
Saskatoon Open Door Society, 193
Savage-Rumbaugh, Sue, 14f, 48, 48f
Savea, Tupuola, 143
scapegoats, 274, 377
Schafft, Gretchen, 189
Schein, Elyse, 201f
schemas, 214
Scheper-Hughes, Nancy, 176–177
schizophrenia, 228
school shootings, 365
schools, 125, 247
schools of thought
  cultural anthropology, 28–31
  meaning of, 19
  psychology, 54–55f, 58–73
  sociology, 96–112, 100t
Schuster, C.R., 237t
Scott, Ridley, 311
sea turtle eggs, 149–150
secondary group, 277
secondary socialization, 119
secondary sources, 57, 135, 319
secure attachment, 81, 81f
segregation, 139, 369t
"Selam," 38, 40f
selective breeding, 104
self-actualization, 68, 68f, 219
self-awareness, 372
self-concept, 175–176
self-discipline, 221
self-enhancement, 175
self-fulfillment needs, 68f
self-monitoring, 385
Seligman, Mark, 236t
semi-structured interviews, 20–21, 135, 178
seniors, 379
sensation, 62
sensorimotor stage, 75t
sensory processing disorder (SPD), 232

Index NEL 475

sentencing circles, 327–329
separation, 369t
serotonin, 373
sex, 114
sex differences, 213–215
sex workers, 162
sexism, 268, 432t
sexual orientation, 409–410
Shah, A.M., 108
Shaikh, Zaib, 273
"Shakespeare in the Bush" (Bohannan), 180
Shanidar Cave, Iraq, 42
Shankman, Paul, 25
Sharp, Lauriston, 155
Shelburne, Nova Scotia, 340
Shepard, Matthew, 375
Shepherd, David, 151
Sherif, Muzafer, 258, 370, 370t, 374
the Shona, 156
Shoot With This program, 117
shyness, 209
sibling differences, 204–205
sick neighbourhood, 305
sickle cell anemia, 341
Siegel, Shepard, 231
Simmel, Georg, 419
situation view of behaviour, 407
the Siwan, 151
skin colour variations, 51
Skinner, B.F., 54f, 65–66, 67, 88
Skinner box, 66, 66f
slavery, 104, 340
slum, 106
Small, Gary, 87
smart mobs, 285, 285f
Smith, Ashley, 252
Smith, Dorothy, 93f, 107
Snake Hill Cemetery, 34, 34f
Snyder, Mark, 384–385
social attitudes, 409–410
social behaviour, 113–118
social belonging, 276–279
social change, 445
social cohesion, 425
social controls, 306
social cues, 372
social curriculum of schools, 126
social customs, 320–324
social Darwinism, 103, 104
social determinants of health, 305
social development, 364, 364t
social evolution, 103
social facts, 102

social fragmentation, 425
social identity, 260–263, 368, 406–408
  see also identity
social inequality, 414, 431–433
social influence, 113–115
social institutions, 434–443, 434f, 435t
social integration, 425
social isolation, 365–366
social judgment theories, 222f
social learning theory, 214, 410
social media, 391, 395
social mobility, 430
social networking, 310, 389, 419
social networks, 118, 278, 419–420
social reaction theory, 416
social roles, 264–265
social sciences
  see also specific social sciences
  animal experiments, 67
  Gini coefficient, 433
  language of social sciences, 19
  research and inquiry skills. See research and inquiry skills
  sex and gender, 114
social shields, 322
social skills, 365, 366
social status, 373, 429–430
social stratification, 428–430
social structures and organization, 423–424
social thinking, 224–227
social work, 117
socialization, 119–123
  abnormal socialization, 121–123
  and adolescence, 89
  agents of socialization, 78, 124–127, 166–168, 271
  anticipatory socialization, 119
  categories of socialization, 119–121
  defined, 111
  described, 113, 119
  and emotional development, 364
  and family structure, 124–125, 125t
  and gender, 121

gender socialization, 264
and immigration, 368–369
primary socialization, 119
and psychology, 364–369
resocialization, 119
secondary socialization, 119
sociological perspective, 320
ultimate goal of, 119
society, and humanism, 70–71
socio-emotional development for girls, 77t
sociolinguistics, 33
sociological imagination, 112
sociology
  and anthropology, 20, 114, 137, 297, 320
  and behaviour, 276–294
  Berlin wall, fall of, 99
  class, 300–303
  and communication technology, 309–311
  conflict theory, 105
  cultural expressions, 98
  defining sociology, 97
  demography, 301–302
  described, 92
  ethical issues, 295–311
  feminist sociology, 107–108
  "field view," 108
  functions of sociologists, 97–99
  and health, 304–305
  and identity, 260–274
  inclusive nature of, 297
  "isms" in sociology, 432, 432t
  macrosociology, 100
  microsociology, 100
  objectivity, 98
  and psychology, 78, 123, 208, 261
  roots of sociology, 96
  schools of thought, 96–112, 100t
  structural functionalism, 101–104
  study of sociology, 92–93f
  symbolic interactionism, 109–112
  universality, 98
  value judgments, 304–305
  visual sociology, 311
Sodhi, Pavna, 351
solidarity, 276
Sosua, Dominican Republic, 162

sources
  assessment and recording, 17, 95
  citation, 95
  electronic sources, 95
  evaluation of, 319
  primary sources, 57, 259, 319
  secondary sources, 57, 135, 319
  in social science, 57
South Africa, 49, 237t
SPD Foundation, 232
Spelke, Elizabeth, 75
Spencer, Herbert, 104
Speyer School, 78
SPICE, 393
sport psychology, 367
Sri Lanka, 174
Srinivas, Mysore Narasimhachar (M.N.), 108
Stacey, Judith, 108
stage-model theories of ethnicity, 342–343, 342f
stage theories
  Erikson's stages of psychosocial development, 76t
  Freud's psychosexual stages of development, 74, 74t
  Piaget's stages of cognitive development, 75, 75t
  socio-emotional development for girls, 77t
standardized testing, 78
Stanford-Binet IQ test, 78, 202, 203, 243
Stanford Prison Experiment, 237t, 238–239, 408
Starkweather, Katherine, 174
statistical analysis, 103, 297
steel axes, 155
stereotypes, 225, 268
sterilization, forced, 104
Sterk, Claire, 186
Stern, Aaron, 200
stigma, 378–379, 415
stone tools, 43, 43f
strain theory of behaviour, 413
Strange Situation experiment, 80–81, 80f
stress, 397
striving for perfection, 219
structural functionalism, 101–104

structural linguistics, 32–33
structure, 29f
structured interviews, 21
Stryker, Sandy, 77
Stuart, Barry, 327
student-centred education, 71
student surveys, 246
subculture, 31, 415–416, 417t
subjective, 24
subway experiments, 289
suicide, 102–103, 102f
Suicide (Durkheim), 102–103
summary of information, 17
superego, 59
superstructure, 29f
Surrogate Mother experiment, 79, 123, 237t
Surveillance Camera Awareness Network (SCAN), 309
surveys, 95, 97, 113, 199, 246
survival of the fittest, 104
Sutherland, Edwin, 292
Sydie, Rosalind, 433
symbolic ethnicity, 355
symbolic interactionism, 109–112
symbols, 61, 98f, 111

T

taboos, 183
tacit cultural knowledge, 178
Tagliamonte, Sali, 323
Tajfel, Henri, 262–263
Takooshian, Harold, 289
Talos, Ion-Florin, 82f
Tamil community, 354
tanning salons, 441
Tanzania, 46
Tastsoglou, Evangelia, 354
Tatshenshini-Alsek Park, British Columbia, 36
tattoos, 142, 142f, 143
Taung, South Africa, 39
Taung's child, 40f
Taylor, Jill Bolte, 85
Taylor, Shaunna, 367
Taylor-Helmick, Tracy, 251
technological diffusion, 154
technology
  and Canadian culture, 322–324
  communication technology, 309–311
  and culture, 154–155
  dating and courtship, 265–266

digital technology, 154, 324
smart mobs, 285
teenagers. *See* adolescence
Teens, Video Games, and Civics, 367
teeth, 321
television, 366–367
temporal lobe, 83f
Terman, Lewis, 202, 243
Thailand, 353
thinking, 62
third gender, 114, 150, 150f
Third World Canada (Cazabon), 349
"Third World Woman," 107
Thomas, William, 109
Thompson, T., 237t
thought, and language, 88
threshold, 281
Tibet, 116f, 116t, 174
Tierney, Patrick, 16
the Tiv, 180, 180f
tobacco, 35
Toronto, and multiculturalism, 344–345
"Toronto 18," 373
Toronto District School Board, 246
Toronto Jewish Film Festival, 336
traffic jams, 101f
Tragically Hip, 233
transference, 60
transgendered, 150
transition, 139
transnationalism, 356
Transtheoretical Model of Change, 227
Trobriand Islanders, South Pacific, 22, 28, 183
true mobiles, 322
trust *vs.* mistrust, 76t
Tully, Judy, 265
Tumin, Melvin, 430
twin studies, 201
Twitter, 294, 323
two spirited, 150

U

"Ukrainian Dog Girl," 122–123
unconditioned response, 64
unconditioned stimulus, 64
unconscious, 59, 60, 63
"Under Western Eyes: Feminist Scholarship and Colonial Discourses" (Mohanty), 107–108

Understanding Animal Research, 67
unethical experiments, 236–237, 236–237t
unions, 160
United States, 338–339, 353
universality, 98
University of California-Los Angeles (UCLA), 67
unstructured interviews, 20
upstanders, 269
urban concentration, 302
urban sociology, 300, 301

V

value judgments, 304–305
values, 98, 320–324
van Gennep, Charles-Arnold, 139
Vanier Institute of the Family, 125, 436, 436t
variables, 57
veterans, 253
Victor (feral child), 245, 245f
video games, 365, 367–368
video surveillance, 309–310
violence, 120, 280
Violent Crime Linkage Analysis System (ViCLAS), 225
Virk, Reena, 120
virtual community, 277
Virtual Iraq, 229–230, 233
virtual reality, 372
virtual therapy, 229–230, 229f, 233
visual sociology, 311
vivisection, 67
Volkswagen, 223

W

Waco, Texas, 418
Wade, Rachel, 390f
wage labour, 160
Wake, Robert, 249
"walking marriage," 170f
Walsh, David, 221
Wang, Tricia, 323
War of the Worlds (Wells), 280
Washington Post, 404
Watson, John, 54f, 65, 236t
Weber, Max, 93f, 101, 109–110, 434
Welles, Orson, 280
West Berlin, 99
Western Europe, 116t, 424
Western families, 175–176

Whyte, William Foote, 106
Wi-Fi, and social interactions, 322–323
Winfrey, Oprah, 430f
Wolff, Ivana, 45
women
  cultural ideals, 29, 29f
  division of labour, by gender, 30t
  female violence, 120
  feminine psychology, 30, 60–61
  feminist anthropology, 30
  feminist sociology, 107–108
  feminist theory, 433
  gender differences, 77
  identity and culture, 146–148
  rites of passage, 141
Wong, Lloyd, 426
workplace, 71, 126, 395–397
World Health Organization, 102f, 284, 285
World Trade Center attacks, 270, 282, 421, 426
world view, 22
worldwide perspective. *See* global perspective
Wortley, Scot, 307
W.R. Myers High School, 365

X

X-ray techniques, 67

Y

Yanomamö, 16
Yir Yoront, 155
yoga, 86
Youth Criminal Justice Act, 328
youth sports, 211
YouTube, 310, 311

Z

Zarbatany, Lynne, 384
Zhang, Jian, 372
Zimbardo, Philip, 237t, 238–239, 370t, 377
Znaniecki, Florian, 109
Zukerman, Helen, 336

CREDITS

t = top, c = center, b = bottom, l = left, m = middle, r = right, bkgd = background

Text/Figure Credits

Chapter 1
21 (t), 26–27 From Lee. THE DOBE JU/ 'HOANSI, 2E. © 1994 Wadsworth, a part of Cengage Learning, Inc. Reproduced by permission. www.cengage.com/permissions; **30** EMBER, CAROL R.; EMBER, MELVIN R., ANTRHOPOLOGY, 9th Edition, © 1999, p. 295. Adapted by permission of Pearson Education, Inc., Upper Saddle River, NJ.; **50** DISTRIBUTION OF HUMAN BLOOD GROUPS 2ND EDITION by Mourant et al (1976) Maps between pp.1016–1017. By Oxford University Press

Chapter 2
62 Personality Dimensions is a registered trademark of Career/LifeSkills Resources Inc.; **87 (l)** All rights reserved. Republication or redistribution of Thomson Reuters content, including by framing or similar means, is expressly prohibited without the prior written consent of Thomson Reuters. Thomson Reuters and its logo are registered trademarks or trademarks of the Thomson Reuters group of companies around the world. © Thomson Reuters 2008. Thomson Reuters journalists are subject to an Editorial Handbook which requires fair presentation and disclosure of relevant interests.; **(r)** Adapted from 'The Shallows': This is Your Brain, June 2, 2010. © NPR. http://www.npr.org/templates/story/story.php?storyId = 127370598

Chapter 3
102 © Copyright 2003 World Health Organization; **125** Vanier Institute of the Family

Chapter 4
180 From Natural History, vol.75, no.8 (August 1966): 28; copyright © Natural History Magazine, Inc. 1966

Chapter 5
210 Fritz Ridenour, Untying Your Knots (Old Tappan, N.J.: Revell, a division of Baker Publishing Group © 1988), pg. 112. Used by permission.; **234** Copyright 2000, Canadian Psychological Association. Permission granted for use of material.; **236–237** http://listverse.com/2008/09/07/top-10-unethical-psychological-experiments/

Chapter 6
293 Craig, W.M., Pepler, D.J., Jiang, D., & Connolly, J. (in preparation). Victimization in Children and Adolescents: A developmental and relational perspective.; **295–296, 303** Canadian Sociological Association

Chapter 7
326 From James L. Gibbs, "The Kpelle Moot," Africa, vol. 33, No.1, 1963; **328–329** From A Comparison of Four Restorative Conferencing Models by Gordon Bazemore and Mark Umbreit, February 2001, Juvenile Justict Bulletin, OJJDP; **347–348** Excerpts from Building the Future: A Time for Reconciliation, Bouchard, G., & Taylor, C. (2008), © Government of Quebec

Chapter 8
371 From Janis, Irving L.. Victims of Groupthink, 1E. © 1972 Wadsworth, a part of Cengage Learning, Inc. Reproduced by permission. www.cengage.com/permissions; **375** "Police-reported and victim-reported hate crimes, by type of motivation", adapted from Statistics Canada publication Hate Crime in Canada, 2006, no. 17, Issue 2008017, http://www.statcan.gc.ca/pub/85f0033m/2008017/c-g/5200136-eng.htm; **383** Homeless Child, music and lyrics by Ben Harper.

Photo Credits

Introduction
2–3 AP Photo/The Yomiuri Shimbun, Hiroaki Ohno; **4** Simon Roberts/Getty Images; **5** Sparky/Getty Images; **6** Photo by Martin Schoeller/AUGUST; **7 (t)** David Wei/GetStock.com; **(bl)** James Balog/Getty Images ; **(br)** © Lawrence Weslowski Jr | Dreamstime.com; **8 (t)** Science Photo, **(b)** Getty Images; **9 (t)** www.CartoonStock.com, **(b)** ScienceCartoonsPlus.com

Unit Opener 1
12–13 Absodels/Getty Images; **12 (l)** MAURO FERMARIELLO/SCIENCE PHOTO LIBRARY, **(m)** Tish1 /Shutterstock, **(b)** © Linda Bair | Dreamstime.com

Chapter 1
14–15 MAURO FERMARIELLO/SCIENCE PHOTO LIBRARY; **14 (b)** Science Source/Photo Researchers, Inc.; **15 (bl)** AFP/Getty Images , **(br)** iStock © Auke Holwerda; **16** Photograph by Napoleon A. Chagnon; **19 (tl)** © Rene Drouyer | Dreamstime.com, **(tr)** © Monkey Business Images/Shutterstock **(bl)** Terry Vine/Blend Images/Getty Images, **(br)** © Robert van der Hilst/CORBIS, **(bkgd)** Maugli/Shutterstock; **21 (b)** Irven Devore/Anthro-Photo File; **22** Crawford/Anthro-Photo File; **23** Dave Reede/Getty Images; **24** Margaret Mead Papers, Manuscript Division, LOC.; **25 (t)** Tibor Bognar/Alamy, **(b)** © Velvet/Corbis; **27** Stan Washburn/Anthro-Photo File; **29 (t)** © H. Armstrong Roberts/ClassicStock/Corbis, **(b)** Barbara Freeman/Getty Images; **31** RONALD WITTEK/dpa /Landov; **32** ANDY CLARK/Reuters /Landov; **33** E. Dygas/Getty Images; **34** Courtesy of Archaelogical Services Inc.; **35** John Sylvester Photography/Firstlight; **36** © Fred Hirschmann/Science Faction/Corbis; **37 (l)** © Morton Beebe/CORBIS, **(r)** © Karl Ammann/CORBIS; **38** JOHN READER/SCIENCE PHOTO LIBRARY; **39** JOHN READER/SCIENCE PHOTO LIBRARY; **41** © HO/Reuters/Corbis; **42 (t)** © Federico Gambarini/dpa/Corbis, **(b)** www.CartoonStock.com; **44** AF archive/Alamy; **45 (l)** TOMAS BRAVO/Reuters /Landov, **(r)** D. ROBERTS/SCIENCE PHOTO LIBRARY; **46** The Dian Fossey Gorilla Fund International; **47** © Gallo Images/CORBIS; **48** Great Ape Trust; **49** © Raynald Bélanger | Dreamstime.com

Chapter 2
54–55 Tish1/Shutterstock; **54 (b)** RIA NOVOSTI/SCIENCE PHOTO LIBRARY; **55 (b)** Bill Anderson/Photo Researchers, Inc.; **56** © Frank Gaglione Photography; **58** Allen Donikowski

/Getty Images; **63** Rue des Archives/The Granger Collection, NYC; **67** © Dr. Heinz Linke/iStock; **69** Hulton Archive/Getty Images; **70** © Roger Ressmeyer/CORBIS; **71** © Monkey Business Images | Dreamstime.com; **72** Bandura, A., Ross, D. & Ross, S.A. (1961) Transmission of aggression through imitation of aggressive models. Journal of Abnormal and Social Psychology, 63, 575–82; **77** Indeed /Getty Images; **78** www.CartoonStock.com; **79** Photo Researchers, Inc.; **80** University of Virginia Visual History Collection (RG-30/1/10.011). Special Collections, University of Virginia Library.; **82 (t)** Southern Illinois University/Photo Researchers, Inc., **(b)** JACOPIN/SCIENCE PHOTO LIBRARY; **83 (r)** SOVEREIGN, ISM/SCIENCE PHOTO LIBRARY; **85** Photo courtesy Waisman Brain Imaging Lab, University of Wisconsin-Madison; **86** James Lauritz /Getty Images; **90 (tl)** © Michael Blackburn/iStock, **(tr)** Ziggy © 2007 Ziggy & Friends. Used by permission of Universal Uclick. All rights reserved., **(bl)** Lynne Harty Photography /Getty Images; **(br)** Galushko Sergey/Shutterstock

Chapter 3

92–93 © Linda Bair | Dreamstime.com; **93 (b)** Courtesy of Dorothy E. Smith; **94** Burke/Triolo Productions/Getty Images; **96** © North Wind Picture Archives. All Rights Reserved; **97** www.CartoonStock.com; **98 (lt)** Vladimir Chernyanskiy/Shutterstock, **(lb)** © Marco Kopp | Dreamstime.com, **(bl)** © Birute Vijeikiene | Dreamstime.com, **(br)** © Marilyn Nieves/iStock; **99** AP Photo/John Gaps III; **100 (t)** © Aidar Ayazbayev | Dreamstime.com, **(b)** © Aldo Murillo/iStock; **101 (l)** Michael Klinec/Alamy, **(r)** The Art Gallery Collection/Alamy; **103** Crispin Rodwell/GetStock.com; **104** American Philosophical Society; **105** nlc008648/Library and Archives Canada; **106** Courtesy of The Estate of Jules Aarons and Gallery Kayafas; **107** www.CartoonStock.com; **108** TANUSHREE PUNWANI/Reuters /Landov; **110 (t)** John Foxx/Stockbyte/Getty Images, **(b)** Getty Images; **113** Stockbyte/Getty Images; **114** © R. Gino Santa Maria | Dreamstime.com; **115** © NADEEM KHAWER/epa/Corbis; **116** © Dave Bartruff/CORBIS; **117** Photo by Dameion Royes; **118** Purestock/Getty Images; **119** © david bronson glover/iStock; **120** CP PHOTO/Chuck Stoody; **121** Jack Jones/GetStock.com; **122** Trinity Mirror/Mirrorpix/Alamy; **123** Melissa Lyttle/St. Petersburg Times; **124** © Tracy Whiteside | Dreamstime.com; **125** Blend Images/Getty Images; **126** Denkou Friends/GetStock.com; **127** Onoky/Getty Images

Unit Opener 2

130–131 © jim kruger/iStock; **130 (t)** CP Photo/Richard Lam, **(c)** Clarissa Leahy/Getty Images, **(b)** © Ashley Gilbertson/VII Network/Corbis

Chapter 4

132 (t) CP Photo/ Richard Lam; **132–133** AFP/Getty Images; **133 (tl)** Chris Arend/Getty Images, **(tr)** AR2008-Z136-03 http://www.combatcamera.forces.gc.ca/netpub/server.np?original=9877&site=combatcamera&catalog=photos National Defence. Reproduced with the permission of the Minister of Public Works and Government Services, 2011., **(br)** jochem wijnands/GetStock.com; **134** Photo by Kris Krüg, www.staticphotography.com; **136** © Hugh Sitton/Corbis; **138** © Charles & Josette Lenars/CORBIS; **140** © Carol Beckwith/photokunst; **141** Martin Etter/Anthro-Photo; **142** © Ron Chapple Studios | Dreamstime.com; **143** Getty Images; **145** AlaskaStock/Masterfile; **146 (t)** Glenbow, na-5535-3, **(b)** © Hulton-Deutsch Collection/CORBIS; **147 (t)** Rebecca Popeno, **(b)** AFP/Getty Images; **149 (t)** Ian Thraves/GetStock.com, **(b)** Michelle Gilders/GetStock.com; **150** AFP/Getty Images; **151** Photograph by: NICK BRANCACCIO, The Windsor Star; **152** © Wolfgang Kaehler/CORBIS; **153** National Geographic/Getty Images; **154** Time & Life Pictures/Getty Images; **155** © The Print Collector/Heritage-Images/Imagestate; **156** © Chris Nolan | Dreamstime.com; **158** © Louise Gubb/CORBIS SABA; **160** MICHAEL DUNLEA/GetStock.com; **162** © Reinhard Eisele/CORBIS; **163** © Ricardo Azoury/CORBIS; **164** David McNew/Getty Images; **166** © Agnes Dherbeys/VII Mentor Program/Corbis; **168** Richard Katz/Anthro-Photo; **169 (t)** Stephen Coburn/Shutterstock, **(b)** Michael Stuparyk/GetStock.com; **170 (t)** © Christopher Pillitz/In Pictures/Corbis, **(b)** Piers Helsen; **171** © Amruta Bangad | Dreamstime.com; **172** © Earl & Nazima Kowall/CORBIS; **173** THE CANADIAN PRESS/Jonathan Hayward; **174** Getty Images; **175** Monkey Business Images/Shutterstock; **177** © Paul Almasy/CORBIS; **180** Glenn Davis Stone; **181** © Canadian Museum of Civilization, S95-933 (Artifact IV-D-606, figure of a loon carved from antler); **182** Photo by Staff Sgt. Sean A. Foley. Photo Courtesy of U.S. Army; **184** © Everett Kennedy Brown/epa/Corbis; **188** www.CartoonStock.com; **191** © africa - Fotolia.com; **192** Joanna Gleason/Landov

Chapter 5

196–197 Clarissa Leahy/Getty Images; **201** BRUCE GILBERT/MCT /Landov; **202** www.CartoonStock.com; **204 (t)** Getty Images, **(b)** Christopher Robbins/Getty Images; **206** Perry, B.D. Childhood experience and the expression of genetic potential: what childhood neglect tells us about nature and nurture Brain and Mind 3: 79–100, 2002; **209** © Shelly Perry/iStock; **211** www.CartoonStock.com; **214** PhotoAlto/Laurence Mouton/Getty Images; **215** © Saul Schwarz/Corbis; **216** Condor 36/Shutterstock; **217** THE CANADIAN PRESS/Frank Gunn; **220 (t)** Rick Madonik/GetStock.com, **(b)** © 2008 Tristan Savatier/Getty Images; **221** Ulrich Matuschowitz/GetStock.com; **223** Photo by KJ Vogelius; **224** CBS-TV/THE KOBAL COLLECTION/ZINK, VIVIAN; **225** © Purestock/Getty Images; **226** Paul Ekman, Ph.D./Paul Ekman Group, LLC; **228** © Stockbyte/PunchStock; **229** Getty Images; **232** SW Productions/Getty Images; **233** ALEX GARCIA/MCT/Landov; **238–239** © Philip G. Zimbardo, Ph.D., Professor Emeritus, Stanford University; **240** Andersen Ross/Getty Images; **242** DAJ/Getty Images; **245** The Granger Collection, New York; **246** © Zurijeta | Dreamstime.com; **248** Ron Levine/Getty Images; **249** © Zuura/iStock; **251** Getty Images; **252** THE CANADIAN PRESS/Tom Hanson; **253** THE CANADIAN PRESS/Darryl Dyck

Chapter 6

256–257 © Ashley Gilbertson/VII Network/Corbis; **258** © Randy Faris/Corbis; **260 (t)** © Anton Seleznev/iStock,